Investments

Investments

10TH EDITION

HERBERT E. DOUGALL

C. O. G. Miller Professor of Finance, Emeritus
Stanford University

FRANCIS J. CORRIGAN

Professor of Business Administration
University of Santa Clara

PRENTICE-HALL, INC., Englewood Cliffs, New Jersey   07632

Library of Congress Cataloging in Publication Data

Dougall, Herbert Edward.
    Investments.

    Includes bibliographies and index.
    1. Investments.   I. Corrigan, Francis J., joint
author. II. Title.
HG4521.D65 1978   332.6'78   78-453
ISBN 0-13-504597-5

© 1978 by Prentice-Hall, Inc., Englewood Cliffs, New Jersey 07632

LC No. 78–453

0–13–504597–5

Printed in the United States of America

10 9 8 7 6 5 4 3 2 1

PRENTICE-HALL INTERNATIONAL, INC., *London*
PRENTICE-HALL OF AUSTRALIA PTY. LIMITED, *Sydney*
PRENTICE-HALL OF CANADA, LTD., *Toronto*
PRENTICE-HALL OF INDIA PRIVATE LIMITED, *New Delhi*
PRENTICE-HALL OF JAPAN, INC., *Tokyo*
PRENTICE-HALL OF SOUTHEAST ASIA PTE. LTD., *Singapore*
WHITEHALL BOOKS LIMITED, *Wellington, New Zealand*

Contents

II INVESTMENT MEDIA 45

Preface

Remarkable developments in the field of investments in very recent years have required a thorough rewriting of this book. In addition, substantial changes in the organization of its subject-matter have been made in order to broaden the scope of the book and to coordinate the material in an orderly and systematic fashion.

Since publication of the ninth edition in 1973, the whole investment scene has changed dramatically. The most spectacular development was the stock market collapse in 1973–1974—the sharpest decline since the 1930s. The chief contributor to this shock was the decline in price-earnings multiples that reflected the persistence of high long-term interest rates and inflation. The so-called glamour-growth stocks were hit the hardest; the "two-tier" market was badly deflated. Since 1974 many "growth" and "blue-chip" stocks have failed (1977) to return to the levels of 1966–67, but lesser stocks recovered remarkably in 1976–77. In general, however, common stocks lost their reputed attraction as an inflation hedge. Bond prices fell in 1973–75 as long-term interest rates reached a very high level. This level has been maintained. But short-term rates, also extremely high in the earlier 1970s, fell more than 50% by mid-1977, then rose again. Very substantial changes in investment policy and strategy became necessary to cope with these basic shifts in the market scene.

Special victims of the market weakness, to which their own unwholesome policies contributed substantially, were the real estate investment trusts which had attracted so much attention and money in the early and mid-1970s.

The interest of individuals in stock ownership continued to decline, while institutions, especially retirement plans, achieved a dominate role in ownership and trading in equities. The loss of faith in stocks by individuals was also reflected in the continuing net redemptions of conventional mutual funds. This industry was aided greatly, however, by the appearance and substantial growth of new "money-market," income, and tax-exempt funds. Bonds continued to attract increasing attention from the "small investor."

The concept of "total value," which includes the expectation of continued price appreciation, suffered a rude shock. With general stock market averages lower in 1977 than at their peak in 1967, the 10-year total return consisted of dividend yields of 3 to 4%.

A development that has heartened the student and practitioner of "conservative" investment policy has been the return of attention to value and income in stock investments.

The period saw great changes in the whole machinery of market trading and price reporting; the trend towards a national securities market persisted. Great interest in options trading led to new organized markets for these instruments, which attracted much of the previous trading volume from stocks.

In the government field, the financial collapse of New York City shook the pattern of yields on municipal securities and undermined the faith of investors in municipal bond ratings. But yields on "tax-free" bonds subsequently declined more than those on high-grade corporate issues.

Very important new legislation affected institutional investment policy by its complexity and uncertainty. The most comprehensive was the Employee Retirement Income Security Act ("ERISA") which, among many other features, included the concept of personal liability of those persons and groups classed as "fiduciaries," and, together with market uncertainty, fostered the trend towards conservatism in investment portfolios. Tax legislation changed the rates and burden in a succession of Acts of Congress. Especially drastic was the rewriting of the Federal inheritance tax code.

The period saw important changes in accounting and corporate financial reporting and regulation, bringing desirable improvement in the matter of disclosure of important investment information.

Professional money managers and individuals gave increased attention to all types of risk and to their measurement and control.

The development of computer techniques made possible the use of more sophisticated theories and mathematical models in investment policy and portfolio management.

In addition to recognizing these and other developments, important organizational changes have been made in this new edition of *Investments*.

A new chapter (Chapter 3) recognizes the importance of the money markets and their interrelations with the capital or long-term markets.

The burgeoning importance of Federal agencies requires an extensive discussion of their role in public and private finance (Chapter 6).

The discussion of convertible securities and warrants is now related to that of common stocks (Chapter 9).

The former chapter on foreign securities is deleted, and multinational companies are discussed in Chapter 9.

A new chapter is added in Part III to mark a growing interest in short-term investments by individual and institutional investors (Chapter 10).

The previous separate chapter on mathematics of investment has been deleted, and that material is now located throughout the book where pertinent, especially in Chapters 8 and 9.

The topic of real estate home ownership has been deleted so as to permit more attention to real estate securities and real estate investment trusts (Chapter 12).

There is now only one chapter on general sources of investment information (Chapter 13). Special sources of current data concerning various types of governments and industries are now listed in appropriate chapters.

In line with the general plan of the book to follow the logical steps in the investment process, a new chapter on measuring investment results is included in Part IV (Chapter 23).

The discussion of railroad securities has been condensed somewhat to permit attention to the analysis of airlines and motor carriers (Chapter 28).

Analysis of shares in savings and loan associations is added to that of bank securities (Chapter 29).

All factual information and the discussion of regulation, taxation, and economic factors affecting investments have been updated through the period 1976–1977.

Charts have been added to aid in the interpretation of statistical data.

We are indebted to many individuals and organizations for ideas and information. Advance data were provided by the Federal Deposit Insurance Corporation, the United States League of Savings Associations, the American Council of Life Insurance, the National Association of Mutual Savings Banks, the staff of the *Federal Reserve Bulletin*, Fireman's Fund Insurance Company, and by a number of banks, corporations, publishers, and investment advisory service firms whose permission to cite their material is gratefully acknowledged. Special thanks are due Donaldson, Lufkin and Jenrette Securities Corporation and MacKay-Shields Financial Corporation, both of New York, for the charts that appear throughout the book.

HERBERT E. DOUGALL

FRANCIS J. CORRIGAN

The Economics
of Investment

Part

I

The Nature of Investment and Investment Media

SCOPE: This chapter discusses the concept of investment and outlines the major types of investment media that are available to individuals and institutions. The order of discussion is: (1) the financial and economic meaning of investment, (2) investment versus speculation, (3) classification of investment media, and (4) scope of this edition.

Financial and Economic Meaning of Investment

From the point of view of investors or suppliers of capital, investment is the commitment of present funds in order to derive future income in the form of interest, dividends, rent, or retirement benefits, or of appreciation in the value of the principal.

From this financial standpoint whether the money saved and invested is devoted to a "productive" use in the economic sense is not important. A government bond whose proceeds are used for destructive missiles is just as much an investment as a new share of stock sold by a corporation to finance plant expansion.

Nor from the financial standpoint does it matter whether the investor is purchasing a security from someone else, or whether the funds are to be used for new assets. The purchase in the open market of a "secondhand" instrument, such as a bond, a share of stock, or a mortgage, is just as much an investment as the purchase of a security issued for new capital. In fact, most investments, in the popular sense, are transfers of financial assets from one person to another.

These ideas on the nature of investment in the financial or popular sense should be contrasted with its meaning in the economic sense. In this latter context the term implies the formation of *new* and *productive* capital in the form of new construction, new producers' durable equipment, or additional inventories. The Gross National Product is the value of all goods and services produced in a given period, or its equivalent, the total expenditures for goods and services, which fall into four main categories: (1) personal consumption expenditures, (2) gross private domestic *investment*, or business expenditures for plant, equipment, and increased inventories, (3) net foreign *investment*, or the difference between the spending by foreigners for American exports and the spending by America on its imports, and (4) government purchases of goods and services.

However, the financial and economic meanings of the term are related. Part of the savings of individuals, which flow into the capital market either directly or through institutions, are devoted to new permanent capital financing. Investors as suppliers and investors as users of long-term funds thus find a meeting place in the market. The interrelations between supply and demand for investment funds are developed further in Chapters 2 and 3. In most of the discussion in this book, however, the term *investment* will be used in its financial sense, and investments will include those media or instruments into which savings are placed.

Investment versus Speculation

Discussions of the process of investment often seek to sharpen its meaning by contrasting it with speculation. But the line of demarcation is difficult to draw. Traditionally, investment involves limited risk and is, therefore, confined to media whose future income is relatively certain and whose principal is "safe," whereas speculation involves taking possibly high risk. This concept of investment is frequently used in the financial services where one may find lists of recommended securities classed as "investment grade" whereas others are labelled "speculative."

One difficulty with this distinction is that, owing to the uncertainties of the future, all commitments for future income and return of principal involve some risk. Risk is a matter of degree, and the line between low risk and high risk is often purely arbitrary. If all securities were ranked in order of risk, from a short-term Federal obligation to the weakest common stock, where would the line between investment and speculation be drawn?

Another difficulty is that the degree of uncertainty must be measured differently for different types of media. For many bonds and mortgages the probability of receiving the future stream of interest payments, and the principal at maturity, may be appraised accurately and an appropriate yield may be offered that will reward for risk. But in the case of equities, principal is ordinarily recoverable only in the marketplace, and income is a distribution of profit at the discretion of the issuer. How does one measure the "safety" of a stock? Only by estimating the future course of market value and dividends. Furthermore, the reward for risk-taking, in the form of a "reasonable" rate of return must, in the case of many stocks, include future appreciation; even Treasury bonds produce higher yields than many widely held stocks.

The distinction between investment and speculation on the basis of risk is faulty for other reasons. A marketable Federal bond—a riskless investment insofar as payment of interest and principal at maturity is concerned—involves risk of two other types: (1) the purchasing-power risk, or possibility of decline in the real value of the interest and principal, and (2) the money-rate risk, or risk of decline in market value when interest rates rise. When one buys a fixed-dollar obligation, is he not "speculating" on the future value of money and on the future market value of his security?

Another distinction was formerly made between investment and speculation, namely, that an investment must be represented by a contract by a responsible debtor to repay the original money outlay at a definite date with a definite return in the meantime. Certainly the record of stocks as a class, with respect to dollar loss, is not as strong as that of bonds; yet some high-risk bonds are virtually worthless and many stocks have an eminently respectable record. One cannot logically dignify a poorly secured bond as an investment and ignore a strongly entrenched stock merely because it represents ownership and hence has possibilities of loss (and of profit).

Another distinction is still frequently drawn on the basis of the holding period for which the commitment is made. The speculator is said to be interested in trading for the quick turn, the investor in long-run holding. There is an element of validity in this position. But many corporations and individuals make short-term commitments that afford a high degree of protection, and many "speculators" hope for very material gains over a period of years.

Another distinction is found in the *motive* of the supplier of funds. The investor is said to be interested in income; the speculator, in capital appreciation. The difficulty with this concept is that it would exclude from investment common stocks which yield little or no current return but which offer steady growth through reinvestment of earnings, an increase in principal value, and eventual payment of substantial dividends. It would include in investment stocks and bonds of very high risk which are currently yielding a very high income that may disappear tomorrow.

To deal with this problem, the concept of "income" is expanded by some to include relatively long-term price appreciation so as to justify low- or even no-dividend stocks in an investment program. This makes sense to the investor in higher income tax brackets who avoids dividend income and prefers the reinvestment of corporate earnings. When he needs cash, he can sell off some of his shares and pay the lower long-term capital gains tax.

A final distinction is found in the role of analysis. The investor's appraisal aids him to make a rational choice and even a precise valuation of the security; the speculator is interested in market action apart from its validity. The investor asks, what is the security worth? The speculator asks, how will the price move? But even the "speculator" may investigate a situation thoroughly; to do otherwise would be to gamble. And no analysis will remove all of the uncertainties.

Analysis of these distinctions between the two concepts reveals that an exact line of demarcation is difficult, if not impossible, to draw, although they are not without value. Thinking about them requires the investor to identify his financial objectives, to decide how much risk he is willing to assume, and to plan his course of action for both the near and the longer term. Some investors can take little or no risk and must be content with a modest return; others can assume considerable risk and can base their plans on the possibility of a high return. Some investors must concentrate on high-grade bonds and other relatively safe commitments in order to assure the income that their plans require; others can logically acquire equities, provided that the selection, timing, pricing, and diversification are adequately handled. Some investors can reasonably acquire short-term holdings at little or possibly large risk, while others must frame a long-range program that emphasizes income, relates risk with reward, and relies on little or considerable capital appreciation.

An old saying holds that a good investment is a successful speculation. Such a concept is useful if it suggests that risk is a matter of degree and that some risk is inevitable. The concept is dangerous in that it suggests that intelligent planning and selection may not be worthwhile. There is a very wide range of securities and other media to fit a wide range of investment goals. The problem of investment is to relate media and goals intelligently.

Investment Media

Many types of investment media are available, and no investment program can properly be constructed unless the investor has familiarized himself with the various alternatives. Some investment media are simple and direct; others present complex problems of analysis and investigation. Some are familiar, some are relatively strange. Some are more appropriate for one type of investor than for another.

The major investment media are described in Part II of this book, and their use in the investment programs of individuals and institutions is described in Part IV. Part V provides an approach to analysis of corporate securities, the category that presents the greatest problems of selection and valuation. At this point, we shall examine briefly the various forms in which investment media are classified.

Classification of investment media

    A. Classification by general form
        1. Insurance and retirement group
           (a) Life insurance
           (b) Annuities: fixed and variable
           (c) Government retirement plans; Social Security
           (d) Private pension plans; insured and trusteed
        2. Deposit group
           (a) Savings and time deposits in commercial banks
           (b) Deposits in mutual savings banks
           (c) Accounts in savings and loan associations
           (d) Shares in credit unions
        3. Short-term investments group
           (a) Business commercial paper and acceptances
           (b) Short-term government debt
           (c) Negotiable bank certificates of deposit

    4. Securities group
      (a) Bonds, notes, and stocks of business or commercial corporations
        (1) Industrial companies
        (2) Public utility companies
        (3) Transportation companies
      (b) Securities of financial companies
        (1) Investment companies; bonds and shares
        (2) Commercial bank debentures and stocks
        (3) Shares in savings and loan associations
        (4) Insurance company stocks
        (5) Securities of finance and loan companies and other special types
      (c) Government and government-sponsored securities
        (1) U.S. Government obligations: marketable and nonmarketable
        (2) Bonds of federal agencies
        (3) State and municipal bonds
        (4) Securities of foreign governments
    5. Real estate group
      (a) Real estate
        (1) For occupancy
        (2) For income and/or gain
      (b) Shares in real estate companies and syndicates
      (c) Obligations secured by real estate
        (1) Mortgages
        (2) Mortgage-backed securities
        (3) Shares in real estate investment trusts
    6. Business group; direct investment in business property
  B. Other classifications
    1. By investor status
    2. By security
    3. By maturity features
    4. By degree of marketability
    5. By tax status
    6. By degree of management required
    7. By degree of risk
    8. By degree of protection against price changes

Insurance and retirement group   Life insurance should have priority in most financial plans. Insurance is the only means by which most investors can provide a substantial estate for dependents. And most types of contracts contain a savings or investment element that is available during the life of the insured. These aspects of insurance, and the means by which provision for retirement may be made through annuities, Social Security, and pension plans, are discussed in Chapter 4.

Deposit group   This group includes the banking-type investments held primarily for liquidity but producing some income. Four investment media belong in this group: savings and time deposits in commercial banks, deposits in mutual savings banks, accounts in savings and loan associations, and shares in credit unions. These claims on institutions provide liquidity, modest income, and (under ideal circumstances) little or no risk of dollars of principal. They are discussed in Chapter 5.

For millions of investors, United States Savings bonds are real rivals of banks and other depositories for liquid savings, and they offer almost the same liquidity, and certainly equal or even greater safety than deposits offer; therefore, a discussion of their characteristics is included in Chapter 5.

Short-term instruments group   Highly liquid high-grade short-term instruments have always played a leading role in bank and corporation investment portfolios. During periods of very high yields, such as the middle 1970s, they became increasingly significant in individuals' plans. They are discussed in Chapter 10.

Securities group   The following classification is based on type of issuer, without attempting at this point to discuss the investment qualifications of the securities.

Securities of Business Corporations   These are of two general types: bonds and stocks (preferred and common). A widely used classification involves a threefold division: (1) industrials, including manufacturing, merchandising, extractive, and service concerns; (2) public utilities, including companies in electric light and power, gas, gas transmission, telephone, telegraph, water, and local transit; and (3) transportation, including railroad, trucking, airline, and bus companies. Each of these main groups can be further subdivided.

Other useful methods of classifying business corporation securities are (1) by legal status of owner: bonds (and corporate notes) and stocks; (2) by type of pledge or lien, if any: secured bonds and mortgages, and unsecured instruments, debenture bonds and stocks; (3) by purpose of issue—whether issued for specific purposes or used to finance general working capital and capital expansion needs; (4) by degree of participation in earnings—whether they bear a fixed or an uncertain income. Most bonds and preferred stocks bear a fixed rate of return, while common stock has no fixed rate, receiving the net income distributed as dividends at the discretion of directors; (5) by maturity and redemption features. Preferred and common have no maturity date, since they involve no promise to pay principal. However, the call feature in preferred stock, and to a certain extent its fixed liquidating value, limit the amount of any payment of capital to its holders under certain conditions. Bonds, with very few exceptions, have a definite maturity date and usually include provisions for redemption before maturity at the option of the corporation.

The above classifications are suggestive of many that may be used in studying and comparing corporate securities. Chapters 8 and 9 describe the characteristics of bonds and stocks, and offer general conclusions concerning their investment merits. A general approach to the analysis of corporate securities is set forth in Chapter 24, while Chapter 25 deals with the difficult problem of their valuation. The analysis of individual industrial, utility, and transportation securities is the content of Chapters 26–28.

SECURITIES OF FINANCIAL COMPANIES   The securities issued by six main types of private financial institutions play an important part in many investment programs: debentures, preferred stock, and common shares of investment companies; debentures and shares of commercial banks and bank holding companies; shares in savings and loan associations and parent companies; shares in insurance companies, including nonmutual life, property, and liability companies; and bonds and shares of finance companies. Through these institutions the investor can make an indirect commitment in a portfolio of securities and other instruments. Investment companies are discussed in Chapter 11, and real estate investment trusts in Chapter 12. The analysis of bank, savings and loan, and insurance stocks is included in Part V (Chapters 29 and 30) so as to utilize the general approaches to analysis developed earlier in that section of the book. Securities of finance and loan companies are not discussed, as being too specialized for this book, as are those of brokerage and investment management firms.

GOVERNMENT SECURITIES   From the standpoint of volume, government securities take first place in the investment scene. Their importance to individual and institutional investors can scarcely be overemphasized. In addition to all banks, all insurance companies, many thousands of trust estates, endowment funds, business corporations, government agencies, and investing concerns, millions of individuals own government securities.

Three classes of government obligations are discussed in this volume: (1) direct and guaranteed debt of the United States (Chapter 5); (2) bonds of states and municipalities (Chapter 6); and (3) bonds of Federal agencies. The first group can be subdivided by maturity, by tax status, by ownership, by marketability, by purpose of issue, and by other characteristics. State and municipal bonds are likewise divisible into various categories. In the third category, the unguaranteed bonds of sponsored Federal agencies are included because they have the moral, if not the actual, backing of the Federal government. They are discussed in Chapters 6 and 12.

Real estate group   The most important real estate investment is the ownership of domestic property for occupancy. The most significant single investment that most families make is in a home. Investment aspects of home ownership and of real estate for income and/or capital gain are omitted from this book, which is devoted to securities. Shares in real estate companies and syndicates and real estate investment trusts are discussed in Chapter 12.

Obligations secured by real estate hold an impressive place in many investment portfolios, especially those of institutions. Mortgages and other instruments are discussed in Chapter 12.

Business group   The savings of a great many individuals are directed toward the purchase or expansion of business ventures, especially in smaller concerns. But discussion of this type of investment would involve a discussion of business operation and management itself. Furthermore, funds invested by proprietors are not subject to rapid recovery in the marketplace. For these reasons no attempt is made in this volume to discuss this type of investment.

Other classifications   Other groupings of investments are very useful:

By INVESTOR STATUS   The investor is a creditor when he holds corporate and government bonds, has a savings account in a bank or other institution, owns a mortgage, or has a life insurance or annuity contract. For the most part these might be called "fixed-income obligations." The investor is an owner of "equities" when he owns preferred and common stocks or real estate or has a share in a business. (Preferred stock belongs in the ownership category, but most investors in this type of security place it in the fixed-income category because of its usually limited return and fixed liquidating value.)

By SECURITY   All equities are unsecured. Some debt instruments, such as debenture bonds of corporations and all direct obligations of Federal, state, and local governments, have no lien on specific assets, but represent general promises to pay and so are secured only by general assets and earnings. Lack of specific security does not necessarily represent a weakness. The strongest unsecured corporate obligations, together with government bonds, receive the highest rating. Bank deposits, and claims against insurance companies, are likewise "unsecured." Mortgage bonds and mortgages have a claim to specific assets pledged for their support, in addition to a general claim.

By MATURITY FEATURES   Equities lack a maturity date because they do not represent promises to pay. As noted previously, however, preferred stocks have features that give them a semblance of maturity, especially the call feature by which they mature at the option of the corporation. Shares in investment companies of the open-end (mutual) type represent equity, but are redeemable on demand. This gives them maturity of a sort but not a fixed value. Perhaps we might better say that they enjoy *liquidity* rather than a definite maturity. With rare exceptions debt instruments mature at a specified time or at optional dates, as in the case of Treasury bonds. Most life insurance contracts and annuities mature at death or retirement age.

By DEGREE OF MARKETABILITY   Marketability means access to ready purchase and sale without substantial loss owing to imperfections of the market itself. (It does not imply liquidity in the sense of little risk of loss.) In the case of securities, it is measured roughly by volume of trading. Investments differ considerably with respect to marketability. Listed securities and those traded actively over-the-counter enjoy superior marketability. But many bonds and stocks have no ready market or must be traded in large amounts. One disadvantage of mortgages is a relative lack of marketability. The benefits of insurance, annuity, and pension contracts are transferable only under limited conditions, although the cash-surrender value of an insurance policy is available on demand.

The need of marketability varies greatly among investors. It is often most essential, and income may have to be sacrificed to obtain it.

BY TAX STATUS   The tax status of investments becomes more important as the rates of income and estate taxes increase and as the investor gets into higher tax brackets. The search for total or partial exemption plays an important part in the planning of many investors and has a significant effect on the prices and yields of certain securities. The tax status of securities is discussed in Chapter 17, with emphasis on income taxation.

BY DEGREE OF MANAGEMENT REQUIRED   Investors differ in the degree to which they are willing and able to assume the responsibility of managing their investments. The appeal of different types of investments is, therefore, affected by their relative freedom from care. The time and effort spent on selecting and managing investments depends upon (1) their relative safety; (2) the extent to which the investor chooses media such as mutual funds or common trust funds through which the problems of management are turned over to professionals; and (3) whether the security is specialized in nature. United States Savings bonds are carefree because they are simple and straightforward. An annuity is carefree because of its relative safety and because the insurance company assumes the problems of portfolio management. Real estate mortgages lack this carefree quality because they need constant attention and require special training and experience if held in large amounts.

BY DEGREE OF RISK   With the exception of U.S. Savings bonds, risk of loss of dollars of income or principal is found in all investments. Even Treasury bonds rise and fall in market value as interest rates change. Deposits in insured banks and savings and loan associations may approach being riskless insofar as principal is concerned, but the income derived from deposited savings varies with the times. Life insurance companies "guarantee" a rate at which their reserves are built up, and the strong companies have a remarkable record. Corporate securities run the whole gamut from very high-grade short-term obligations to worthless stocks. Bonds as a group have a stronger record than stocks as a group. Yet each group contains a wide range of quality.

BY DEGREE OF PROTECTION AGAINST PRICE CHANGES   All investments that promise to pay income, principal, or both, in a fixed number of dollars, are vulnerable to the changes in the purchasing power of the dollar. Only equities (common stocks and real estate) and debt securities that are low grade or that have participation or convertible clauses offer protection against a rise in the price level, and these only imperfectly or in varying degrees and over a considerable period of time. One of the tragedies of savings and investment is that the greater the need for a "hedge against inflation," the less able the investor is to afford such a hedge. The assurance of dollars of income and principal is so important to the investor of limited means that the risk involved in holding most equities is an expensive luxury.

Common stocks, shares of investing institutions such as fire insurance companies and investment trusts that hold portfolios of common stocks, and weak and speculative bonds and preferred stocks or those selling at a substantial discount, offer possibilities of appreciation and of increased income as prices rise, and thus may protect the buying value of the investor's funds and income to a certain extent. This factor is very important whenever the investment fund is designed to provide an income for living purposes. It constitutes a strong appeal for including securities of these types, along with fixed-income obligations, in many investment portfolios.

Scope of the Book

This chapter has introduced our subject by defining the nature of investment and investment media. Chapters 2 and 3 will develop further some of the economic aspects of the subject, emphasizing the flow of funds into and out of the capital and money markets, the interrelation among the different segments of those markets, and the basic influences that determine the rates of return on investments.

Intelligent planning of an investment program requires a considerable background, including knowledge of the alternative types of investment media that are classified earlier in this chapter. Chapters 4 through 12 (Part II) describe and evaluate these media. A general description of corporate securities is included here, but the more detailed approach to their analysis is reserved for later chapters.

Additional background information is provided in Part III (Chapters 13 through 17). As aids to investment planning and management, the investor should be acquainted with the sources of investment information and with the types of advice that are available. These are discussed in Chapter 13.

The procedures by which investments—particularly corporate securities—originate, and the operations of the securities markets, are important segments of investment knowledge without which the investor cannot act intelligently. These matters are described in Chapters 14 and 15, while Chapter 16 is designed to acquaint the reader with the procedures through which his actual securities orders are effected.

To an increasing extent tax considerations are entering into investment planning and selection, and this situation promises to persist for many years to come. Tax matters have been singled out for special attention in Chapter 17 and are also referred to elsewhere wherever important.

We are now ready (Part IV) to consider the planning and executing of an investment program. The first step is to determine the goals toward which savings will be directed and to analyze the various types of risks that confront the investor and the means of minimizing or avoiding them (Chapters 18 and 20). The principles that govern the investment policy and portfolio management of individuals and institutions form the subject matter of

Chapters 20 through 22. In Chapter 23, methods of reviewing performance and providing the basis of change are outlined.

After goals and general media have been determined, specific investments are selected, and changed with changing conditions. The major media of investments, including corporate securities, are described in Part II. Because of their greater complexity and lack of homogeneity, a special section on the analysis of corporate securities comprises Part V of this edition.

REFERENCES

AMLING, FREDERICK, *Investments: An Introduction to Analysis and Management*, 4th ed., Chapter 1. Englewood Cliffs, N.J.: Prentice-Hall, Inc., 1978.

BADGER, R. E., H. W. TORGERSON, and H. G. GUTHMANN, *Investment Principles and Practices*, 6th ed., Chapter 1. Englewood Clifis, N.J.: Prentice-Hall, Inc., 1969.

GRAHAM, BENJAMIN, *The Intelligent Investor*, 4th. rev. ed., Chapter 1. New York: Harper & Row, Publishers, 1973.

GRAHAM, BENJAMIN, D. L. DODD, and SIDNEY COTTLE, *Security Analysis*, 4th ed., Chapters 4, 8. New York: McGraw-Hill, Inc., 1962.

The Capital and Money Markets: Nature and Scope

SCOPE: This chapter and Chapter 3 describe the forces at work in the investment market and its major subdivisions, and provide the economic background for an understanding of the movement of prices and the returns available on the more important types of investment media. More detailed discussion of these forces is reserved for later chapters. We should note at this point that in addition to the factors associated with the particular security, mortgage, or other investment—such as its quality and marketability—general economic factors play an important part in determining its value and income. These factors include those which affect the flow of funds into and out of the financial markets as a whole, and those which influence particular segments. The order of discussion in Chapter 2 is: (1) definition and distinctions among the capital, money, and investment markets; (2) limitations of the discussion; (3) the capital market—characteristics and instruments; (4) scope of the capital market; (5) the money market—characteristics and instruments; (6) scope of the money market, (7) the role of institutions in the investment markets.

The Capital, Money, and Investment Markets

The markets distinguished In the economic sense, capital formation is the change in the stock of the capital goods represented by producers' durable equipment, new construction (including residential nonfarm construction), and business inventories. In 1976 gross private domestic capital formation was $240 billion. After capital consumption allowances, such as for depreciation and depletion, the net figure was $127 billion, or 7.5% of Gross National Product of $1692 billion.

In a modern capitalistic economy, capital formation would be impossible without a market or group of markets for the transfer of savings (mainly through a variety of institutions) to those seeking funds for investment in economic goods and services. To effect such a transfer, a variety of instruments representing money and claims to money are employed. Savers provide the funds and expect to receive interest, dividends, or rent. Users—investors in the economic sense—offer the hope of income, price appreciation, or both.

In the financial sense, the *capital market* is the market for the instruments that represent longer-term funds. It consists of a sprawling complex of

14

institutions and mechanisms whereby intermediate-term funds (represented by loans, say, up to ten-year maturity) and long-term funds (represented by longer-maturity loans and corporate stocks) are pooled and made available to business, government, and individuals, and where outstanding instruments are transferred.

In contrast with the capital market, the *money market* focuses on debt instruments only, with maturities ranging from one day to one year. It too involves a complex of institutions, dominated by the Federal Reserve and commercial banks. It emphasizes the purchase and sale of new instruments rather than trading in outstanding claims.

In the economic sense, investment means the commitment of funds to capital assets. In this sense, investors are the *users* of funds—their own or those acquired in the market. In the sense in which we shall use the term, however, investors are on the other side of the transaction. They supply the funds by acquiring debt and equity instruments with their savings, and they also transfer these instruments among each other. In financial terminology, the *investment market* includes the market(s) for funds, both short and long term. To many this term involves only the organized securities exchanges.

We shall use the term in the broad sense. Our discussion includes both the long- and short-term segments of the investment market, including the primary sale and purchase of, and secondary transactions in, the instruments classified in the previous chapter.

Any firm distinction between the money and capital markets is somewhat arbitrary. Suppliers of funds may direct them to one or to both markets, and users of funds may draw funds from either market. Furthermore, funds flow back and forth between the two. And some institutions serve both markets. Rates in the two are interrelated with changes in the general demand for and supply of funds.

Perhaps the chief characteristic distinguishing the two markets is the liquidity and quality of the instruments that are issued and transferred. Federal funds are real money. Short-term government and commercial paper are "near-money" instruments, subject to very slight price risk. The longer-term instruments issued in or traded in the capital market, especially corporate stocks, show considerable price variation.

Limitations of the discussion In this chapter and in Chapter 3 the discussion has three major limitations. First, it is limited to the flows of funds and yields that are associated with the generally marketable *instruments* ordinarily included in discussions of investments, rather than open-account transactions between suppliers and users of funds. These instruments may be involved in both *negotiated* transactions, that is, directly between supplier and user, and in *open-market* transactions, where supply and demand meet on an impersonal basis. For example, long-term credit extended by commercial banks through the purchase of bonds (instruments) is included in the discussion, but the extension of credit in the form of term loans (open account) is not, save for brief mention. Using another example, the purchase of shares of stock directly from a corporation and in the open market are both included because both involve the use of instruments, but investment in the net worth of an unincorporated business is not considered. As a final example, short-term paper placed by finance companies both directly with investors and sold through dealers is discussed, but negotiated loans from commercial banks are not.

A second and allied limitation in the discussion in this and the following chapter is that certain whole segments of long- and short-term financial transactions are excluded, including consumer credit, trade credit (with the exception of the use of banker's acceptances), agricultural credit, credit used in securities transactions (including call loans), highly specialized real estate credit, and transactions in real estate by individuals and households for occupancy or for income. Few traditional investment instruments are employed, in these areas, in either negotiated or open-market supply-demand transactions, so they are customarily excluded from investment discussions.

The third limitation in Chapters 2 and 3 is that we confine the analysis mainly to the primary long- and short-term markets, where new instruments are issued and acquired, and do not expand into the *secondary* markets such as stock exchanges where outstanding instruments are traded. These latter are described in Chapter 15 and their impact on investment returns and on investment programming is considered where pertinent.

The Capital Market: Nature and Instruments

The characteristics of the capital market and its components may be classified and measured in various ways. In so doing, it is apparent that there are a number of submarkets, each of which has distinguishing features and in which there are partially independent rates of yield. Similarly, data on the magnitude of the market(s) is measured somewhat arbitrarily, because, as we have noted, for our purposes certain important components are omitted.

Characteristics   The capital markets, as we discuss them, involve certain major characteristics:

1. The instruments involved are intermediate- or long-term in maturity, involving both debt and equity.

2. The demand for funds represented by these instruments comes from five general categories of users: individuals and households, business and financial corporations, the Federal government, state and local governments, and foreign borrowers.

3. The supply of new funds comes from the same sectors, but is mainly funnelled within the markets through financial institutions. These institutions include (1) financial intermediaries, which receive funds from savers and then lend to borrowers, and (2) borrowing intermediaries, which then lend to fund users. (See below.)

4. The scope of the markets is very wide—wherever intermediate- or long-term debt and equities are produced or transferred. Although geographical barriers are breaking down somewhat, much stratification still remains, especially in the mortgage submarket.

5. Both negotiated and open markets are used heavily. The latter, in which we are mainly interested, are more concentrated and competitive, and transactions in them influence the prices and yields of longer-term instruments almost immediately.

6. Most transactions involving long-term instruments in the open markets represent transfers among investors in over-the-counter and organized exchange markets rather than the raising of new funds in the "primary" markets. Nevertheless, the prices and yields at which existing instruments are transferred largely determine those of new issues.

Capital market instruments   The major investment media in the intermediate- and long-term markets are:

1. U.S. Government securities due in more than one year. We emphasize those that are marketable and whose yields vary with changing credit and capital market conditions.

2. Longer-term debt of Federal agencies, both those which are a part of Federal departments and/or are Federally owned, and those that are privately owned but are Federally sponsored.

3. Long-term debts of states and local governments and the securities of their authorities and sponsored enterprises.

4. The long-term debt of corporations represented mainly by corporate bonds but including other instruments, such as corporate mortgage debt.

5. Corporate stock, preferred and common, both newly issued, and traded over-the-counter or on organized exchanges, when outstanding.

6. Mortgages, including residential, commercial, and industrial liens, with emphasis on those whose volume and yields reflect more than local influences.

Scope of the Capital Market

The financial importance in 1955–1976 of the long-term or capital market is indicated by the data in Table 2-1 on the size of the major components that compete for funds.

Bonds   At the end of 1976, the direct Federal government debt (including guaranteed obligations of the Federal Housing Administration) stood at $654 billion, a record-high figure. And this total was expected to increase substantially in 1977. Excluding U.S. Savings bonds and other nontransferable obligations, the marketable debt was $421 billion. Of this amount, $308 billion was held by "the public"—commercial banks, other institutions, and individuals. Longer-term debt moves steadily into the short-term category. And all maturities are so closely interrelated with respect to both supply and demand that attention to only the long-term portion is somewhat arbitrary. But it is interesting to note that at the end of 1976 only $210 billion or 50% of the marketable debt had a maturity of over one year, that is, belonged in our "capital market" category. The reasons for the emphasis on shorter-term financing are discussed in Chapter 6.

TABLE 2-1   Selected Media in the Capital Market, 1955–1976
(at year-end, in billions of dollars)

	1955	1960	1965	1970	1973	1976
U.S. Govt. gross debt[a]						
Total	$281	$290	$321	$389	$470	$654
Marketable	163	189	215	248	270	421
Due in over 1 year	97	115	121	130	129	210
Federal agency debt						
Budget agencies	—	—	—	2	11	22
Sponsored credit agencies	3	8	14	39	59	81
State and local govt. debt						
Total	48	75	106	156	205	257
Long-term securities	44	67	95	131	175	225
Corporate long-term debt						
Net long-term	90	139	209	360	493	626
Bonds outstanding (domestic)	58	85	113	187	240	329
Domestic corporate stock						
(net, at market value)[b]						
Total	283	395	709	859	857	945
Listed	239	335	573	681	764	899
Over-the-counter[c]	37[d]	53[d]	120	138	136	172
Mortgage debt						
Total	130	207	326	452	635	889
Residential (1–4 family)	88	141	213	280	385	558

[a]Including noninterest-bearing debt.
[b]Excluding intercorporate holdings, shares in closed corporations, and investment company shares.
[c]Excluding investment company shares.
[d]Estimated.

Sources: *Federal Reserve Bulletin* (including flow-of-funds tables) ; *Survey of Current Business;* Securities and Exchange Commission, *Annual Reports* and *Statistical Bulletin; Treasury Bulletin;* U.S. Department of Commerce, Bureau of the Census, *Summary of Government Finances* (Annual).

The unguaranteed debt of Federal credit agencies represents obligations of high quality whose yields are only slightly above those of Federal securities of equal maturity. (See Chapter 6.)

State and local government debt has expanded greatly in the last 30 years. Of the total of $257 billion at the end of 1976, $225 billion of long-term securities were outstanding.

Net corporate long-term debt of $626 billion at the end of 1976 includes debt over one year to maturity, including bonds, mortgages, term loans, and net long-term trade credit, but excludes intercorporate debt. The figure of $329 billion of bonds (domestic corporations) is the most important for our purposes. Listed domestic corporate bond issues, with a total par value of approximately $146 billion constituted about 44% of total corporate bonds outstanding. But in terms of number of issues, most publicly held corporate bond issues are traded over-the-counter.

Corporate stocks   The estimated value of all domestic corporate stocks outstanding was $933 billion at the end of 1976. There are about 1 1/2 million active business corporations in the United States, but most of these are relatively small. Stocks of the major corporations are listed on the organized exchanges or traded on the over-the-counter market. At the end of 1976 listed corporate stocks, both preferred and common, had a market value of $889 billion. Unlisted stocks were worth about $119 billion, exclusive of shares of investment companies and foreign companies.[1]

Real estate mortgages Real estate mortgages outstanding at the end of 1976 totalled $889 billion. Of this, $58 billion was farm debt; the balance represented the financing of one- to four-family residential properties ($558 billion), multifamily residences ($101 billion), and industrial and commercial properties ($172 billion).

The above are the major components of the long-term investment market. Long-term funds also flow into and out of unincorporated businesses, real estate ownership, and of foreign governments and businesses.

The Money Market: Nature and Instruments

It would be incorrect to suggest that there is only one "money market" for high-grade short-term debt instruments. There are, in fact, thousands of locations where direct transactions take place between borrower and lender, as well as regional submarkets that are linked together and with the New York market in an efficient system to handle any amount and volume of transactions at any time. All of these are engaged in helping major economic units adjust their cash or liquidity positions.

Characteristics The central "open" money market is mainly that complex of facilities in New York where idle funds, drawn from all over the country, are transferred through intermediaries, chiefly the Federal Reserve Banks, large commercial "money-market banks" via the city correspondent system, and dealers in government securities and other "near-money" instruments. There are also perhaps 25 regional open markets dominated by local metropolitan banks. The central and regional open money markets create a national market in short-term (mainly bank) credit, and in so doing also create a national short-term interest rate structure.

Although the large institutions in the central open money market deal directly with each other, transferring funds largely on a wholesale basis, special middlemen form an integral part of the system. About 20 dealers specialize in making an over-the-counter market for Federal government and agency securities. These dealers are the link between the Federal Reserve and the money market. Their best customers are commercial banks and large corporations seeking liquid funds or providing such funds by purchasing short-term instruments. Other important users of this market are investment bankers and stock exchange commission brokers. Other dealers specialize in commercial paper and bankers' acceptances. Money brokers specialize in bringing together money-market borrowers and lenders. A few of these make a market in "Federal funds."

---

[1]Source: Securities and Exchange Commission, *Statistical Bulletin*. The total of $884 billion is net after intercorporate holdings, but includes closely held (untraded) stock ($198 billion).

The whole role of Federal Reserve banks and commercial banks in the money market is complex and central to an understanding of the monetary and credit system of the country. The reader is directed to the references at the end of Chapter 3 for authoritative sources. Our interest here lies in the specific instruments originated and traded in the open markets and in the investment policies that are involved in their use. To repeat, the major participants are the Federal Reserve banks and the commercial banks. The former look at the money market to maintain an adequate money supply through its open-market operations and the operations of its 12 discount windows.[2] The supply of "Federal funds" or excess commercial bank reserves at the Federal Reserve banks, and rates charged on 24-hour loans of these reserved funds, are also functions of Federal Reserve policy. In addition, the Federal Reserve banks act as fiscal agent of the United States Treasury Department in issuing and redeeming debt. The commercial banking system holds the funds traded on the market and transfers them on a national basis. This produces a remarkable national uniformity in interest rates on each of the several instruments.

Money-market Instruments   Chapter 10 is devoted to short-term investments so these will be defined here only briefly. This list is limited to the major types of instruments.

FEDERAL FUNDS   The legal reserves that member banks are required to keep against deposits are mainly in the form of account balances at the several regional Federal Reserve banks. Banks that need to improve their reserve positions may borrow ("purchase") other banks' excess reserves through the bank correspondent system. Such loans are known as Federal funds. The typical loan is for one day. The interest rate is usually close to the discount rate the Federal Reserve banks charge member banks when they borrow directly; the rate is higher when excess reserves are scarce or when the Federal Reserve wishes to discourage credit expansion. Federal funds rate is viewed as a bell-wether rate and is watched carefully as an indication of Federal Reserve open-market operations and of possible changes in the money supply. (See page 40.) Practically all transactions in Federal funds are direct or primary between member banks, but there is something of a secondary market through dealers in Treasury securities.

Although Federal funds are a very important money-market instrument, they are not classed as an "investment" because they are not available to individuals and non-banking institutions as a source of, or outlet for, funds. They are omitted therefore from our discussion of short-term investments in Chapter 10.

---

[2]See works on Federal Reserve operations for discussion of open-market operations through which the Federal Reserve (through its open-market committee) seeks to increase (or decrease) commercial bank reserves through purchase (or sale) of government securities, and also of discount operations where commercial banks replenish their reserves (at the Federal Reserve discount rate) by borrowing on Government securities.

U.S. GOVERNMENT SECURITIES DUE WITHIN A YEAR   The chief component is the Treasury bill, issued with original maturities of up to one year. Three-month bills predominate. Denominations usually range from $10,000 to $1,000,000. Bills are sold competitively in amounts of $500,000 and more at a discount from face value. Chapters 6 and 10 discuss these further.

FEDERAL AGENCY SECURITIES DUE WITHIN A YEAR   The Federal agencies, especially those that are government sponsored but privately owned, are heavy borrowers in the capital market. Their bonds enter the money market as they move towards maturity. But some obligations originate as short-term. Agency obligations have an active market at yields slightly above those on direct Federal debt. They are described in Chapters 6 and 12.

BANKERS' ACCEPTANCES   Bankers' acceptances are time drafts (up to six months) drawn on and "accepted" (guaranteed) by a bank which has agreed to do so for an importer or a holder of merchandise, thus substituting bank credit for commercial credit. Denominations may range as high as $1,000,000. The issuing commercial firm (or exporter) sells the draft in the secondary market on a discount basis. Such instruments are widely used in foreign trade. "Prime" acceptances bear the guarantee of the strongest commercial banks and so are very high quality paper.

COMMERCIAL PAPER   These are short-term, negotiable, unsecured promissory notes, with maturities of 90 to 180 days usually. Two main types are: (1) paper that is placed directly by finance companies on a discount basis with lenders and investors, and (2) paper sold by finance companies, commercial and industrial corporations, and affiliates of commercial banks, through dealers. The first may have maturities of as long as 7 months. The second are usually available in maturities between 30 and 180 days; both types enjoy a limited secondary market. Because this paper is unsecured, only the obligations of the strongest corporate issuers are considered "prime." (See Chapter 10.)

NEGOTIABLE "CDs"   Negotiable time certificates of deposit in denominations of $100,000 or more, issued by commercial banks, have become an important money-market instrument. Their original maximum interest rates are set by "Regulation Q," but their open-market rates are determined in a growing secondary market. (Chapters 5 and 10 discuss these further.)

OTHER INSTRUMENTS   Additional money-market instruments which, because of their specialized nature and market, are not discussed here, include: (1) short-term tax anticipation and housing loans of local municipal governments or their authorities (Chapter 7); (2) brokers' loans representing stock market credit (Chapter 16); (3) repurchase agreements made by commercial banks to Federal Reserve banks, and between commercial and industrial firms and dealers, under which the seller of securities agrees to buy them bank at a fixed date, say, 15 days; and (4) Eurodollar claims representing bank deposits in a currency other than that of the host country.

Scope of the Money Market

The financial importance of the money markets from 1955–1976 is indicated in Table 2-2. Only the major *instruments* outlined above are included. Direct and negotiated short-term credits are excluded.

TABLE 2-2 Selected Media Outstanding in the Money Markets, 1955–1976 (at year-end, in billions of dollars)

	1955	1960	1965	1970	1973	1976
Federal funds[a]	c	$ 1	$ 2	$ 9	$ 26	$47
U.S. Govt. marketable debt due in less than 1 year	$66	74	94	124	142	211
Treasury bills		39	60	88	108	164
Federal agency debt due in less than 1 year	c	c	8	22	28	37[d]
Short-term municipal debt	2	3	6	13	15	20[d]
Bankers' acceptances (dollar)	c	2	3	7	9	23
Commercial paper						
Total	2	4	9	33	41	52
Financial companies (thru dealers)[b]	1	1	1	6	6	7
Financial companies (direct)[b]	1	3	7	20	27	32
Other (corporations etc.)	—	—	1	7	8	13
Large negotiable CDs	c	c	16	26	65	64

[a]Includes securities sold under repurchase agreements.
[b]Includes finance companies and bank-affiliated companies.
[c]Not available.
[d]Estimated.
Source: Federal Reserve Bulletin.

The dollar magnitude of instruments outstanding in the money market is only a small proportion of the values in the capital market, but the short-term market is much more sensitive and volatile. Shifts in yields on short-term funds are soon reflected in changes in long-term rates as funds move back and forth.

The volume of all money-market instruments increased substantially in the 1970s. The increase in Federal funds reflected the expansion of the money supply. Short-term Federal and agency debt grew with the Federal fiscal program (including deficits) and with the avoidance of longer-term, less flexible financing. Acceptances and commercial paper outstanding kept pace with the growth of the economy. The biggest increase occurred in the expansion of large negotiable bank certificates of deposit, reflecting two (related) main influences: (1) the tightness of money and the banks' need to borrow to take care of customers; (2) the record high rates of interest paid to investors. (See p. 205.) Chapter 10 is devoted to investment interest in, and policy with respect to, short-term instruments.

Institutions in the Capital and Money Markets

Flows of funds into, out of, and within the capital and money markets are both direct and indirect. Direct flow involves suppliers and users without any intermediate organization, as when a corporation sells securities directly to investors or when one investor lends on a mortgage directly to the borrower. But most primary market funds flow through institutions that gather money from savers and supply it to individuals, government, and business by acquiring financial instruments issued by these users. In the secondary markets, a different set of institutions, dealers, brokers, and organized exchanges, bring buyers and sellers of outstanding instruments together.

Classification of financial institutions in the primary markets
All financial institutions have one thing in common, that is, their assets consist primarily of financial instruments: various types of bonds, stocks, mortgages, and short-term money-market loans, in portfolios that contain one major type, or a combination of types. Beyond this, institutions can be classified in a number of ways. The following classification is by type of service rendered:

Deposit institutions:
    Commercial banks
    Mutual savings banks
    Savings and loan associations
    Credit unions
Special lending institutions:
    Finance companies (consumer and other)
    Federal credit agencies
Insurance and pension institutions:
    Life insurance companies
    Property and liability insurance companies
    Noninsured private pension funds
    State and local government retirement funds
    Federal retirement and insurance funds
Investment institutions:
    Investment companies
    Real estate investment trusts

This classification is rather arbitrary because some institutions belong in more than one category. For example, commercial banks are both general lending institutions and deposit-type institutions. Credit unions are similar to finance companies in that they lend to consumers. Investment companies make some private placements, that is, buy securities directly from issuers. Thus, they serve as intermediaries, although they are mainly engaged in holding portfolios that represent transfers to them of bonds, notes, and stocks from other owners. The same is true of real estate investment trusts, which acquire assets directly from borrowers, but also enter the secondary markets. Certain institutions are omitted because they function primarily in the secondary market; but they may, because of their inventories, be more than marketing concerns. For example, dealers in stocks, bonds, and commercial paper all carry portfolios of instruments awaiting resale.

Another method of classification is based on the intermediation role of the institution. In the strict economic sense, financial "intermediaries" gather surplus funds from savers—households, business, foreign investors, and to a limited extent, governments—and issue securities or record claims in favor of these suppliers, paying interest on same. Then they channel these funds to users—households, business, agriculture, government—and receive income (at higher rates) on their advances. The deposit institutions and the insurance and pension institutions (except property and liability insurance companies) clearly belong in the "intermediaries" group, and the flow of funds into their control (intermediation) and out of their control (disintermediation) has a powerful influence on interest rates and yields.

Still another classification is based on whether an institution is operating in the long-term or capital market, or in the short-term or money markets. Most of the listed institutions operate in both. For example, commercial banks are mainly concerned with short-term credit, but acquire bonds and mortgages and accept deposits for more than a year. Mutual savings banks and savings and loan associations operate in the long-term market mainly because their assets consist primarily of mortgages. But both own some short-term paper for liquidity purposes, and their deposits, although not classified as demand deposits, are subject to withdrawal.

The supply and demand for both long-term and short-term funds in the investment markets, the influence of banking and other intermediaries and of the Federal Reserve system, and the resulting interest rates and yields, form the subject matter of the next chapter.

Marketing and trading institutions   In secondary markets, the marketing institutions play a prominent role by serving as middlemen. Investment bankers and mortgage companies merchandise new debt and equity instruments. Dealers and brokers in securities, mortgages, and money instruments, together with securities exchanges, are involved in the transfer of already outstanding instruments. Some firms operate in both the primary and secondary markets. For example, many securities firms engage in both investment banking and securities brokerage.

The institutions in the secondary markets not only aid in preserving the liquidity of the financial system; they also play an important role in the determination of interest rates and yields in the open markets, and these rates, in turn, largely determine the rates and yields on new instruments in the primary markets.

REFERENCES

See end of Chapter 3.

Capital and Money Markets: Flow of Funds and Yields

SCOPE: In the previous chapter the characteristics, the financial scope, and the institutions serving the capital and money markets were discussed briefly. Emphasis was on primary rather than secondary markets, and on the use of securities and other investment instruments rather than on direct financing. Segments of the markets, such as trade, general agricultural, and consumer credit, were somewhat arbitrarily ignored.

In this chapter the discussion of the markets continues with attention to the factors of supply and demand for long- and short-term funds represented by investment instruments and the resulting returns on those instruments. The order of discussion is: (1) interrelations of the money and capital markets, (2) suppliers of investment funds (demand for investments), (3) demanders of investment funds (supply of investments) (4) return on major investment instruments, and (5) shifts or changes in actual investment yields in recent years.

Interrelations of Capital and Money Markets

In the previous chapter it was noted that no firm distinction can be made between the long-term (capital) and the short-term (money) markets. From the standpoint of flow of funds, it is worth repeating that some suppliers place funds in both markets (that is, buy instruments), directly and through institutions, and some users derive funds (that is, sell instruments) in both markets. Some suppliers are also users in one or the other markets, that is, are simultaneously both borrowers and lenders, again both directly and through institutions. It follows that interest rates and yields in the two major markets are interrelated. Divergencies between long- and short-term rates constantly appear, but the general course—upward or downward—is common to both. Within each major market submarkets are found where rates and yields differ, but again the general directions of change are the same.

In the following discussion of the supply of and the demand for investment funds, both long- and short-term, the role of institutions should be kept in mind. These gather funds from investors seeking securities and other instruments (suppliers of funds) and place them with the various issuers of instruments (demanders or users of funds). In most discussions of sources and uses of funds the institutions are listed as the major sources. They are in fact only vehicles through which the *original* sources—savings, credit, tax money, etc.—are channeled. The following discussion stresses the original sources and eventual users, with due attention to the financial intermediaries through which most funds flow. The concentration of money under institutional control makes these the most powerful influence in the markets; their policies go far to shaping the prices and rates of return of investment instruments.

Suppliers of Investment Funds: Demand for Investments

Funds for investment in investment instruments are derived from five main sources: (1) individual (or household) savings and liquidation of other assets; (2) savings and transfers by nonfinancial corporations; (3) governments and their agencies; (4) banks and finance companies; and (5) foreign sources. With the exception of the last, the investment policies of these groups are discussed in appropriate chapters throughout this book.

Individual savings Individuals and households use savings as the major source of funds for acquiring investments. They also liquidate other assets and re-invest in securities and mortgages. Individuals put their savings mainly into long-term instruments (securities and mortgages) either directly or, more importantly, through a variety of institutions, including most of those listed in the previous chapter, which in turn invest in a variety of instruments. In recent years the interest of individuals in corporate bonds and in short-term money market paper has substantially increased however. (See Chapters 8 and 10.) Most bonds and stocks purchased do not represent the investment of new capital, but are acquisitions of securities that are already outstanding.

The most familiar measure of personal savings is the U.S. Department of Commerce figure of disposable personal income, less personal outlays, shown in Table 3-1.

TABLE 3-1   Trends in "Personal Saving," 1960–1976 (in billions of dollars)[a]

Item	1960	1965	1970	1972	1974	1976
Personal income	$400	$537	$801	$943	$1,153	$1,375
Less personal tax and nontax payments	51	65	115	141	170	193
Disposable personal income	349	472	686	801	983	1,182
Less personal outlays[b]	332	442	635	752	911	1,105
Equals personal saving	17	30	51	49	72	77
Personal saving as a percentage of disposable income	4.9%	6.2%	7.4%	6.2%	7.3%	6.5%

[a]Statistical discrepancies are the result of rounding.
[b]Personal consumption expenditures, consumer interest payments, and transfer payments to foreigners.
Source: U.S. Department of Commerce, *Survey of Current Business.*

The ratio of personal saving to disposable personal income has varied from year to year. During World War II it climbed to more than 20%. largely because people were unable to buy many types of consumer goods. It ran between 5 and 6% in the early 1960s, increased greatly in 1967–1970, and reached 8.1% in 1973. This reflected individuals' reluctance to spend during periods of economic stagnation or uncertainty. The year 1976 showed a more normal rate of 6.5%.

The fact that individuals "saved" a certain total amount, according to U.S. Department of Commerce figures, does not mean that they added only that much to their holdings of cash assets, securities, insurance, and pension reserves. These assets can be increased by funds diverted from other uses. Table 3-2 shows the annual net increase in financial assets, the net invest-

TABLE 3-2 "Individual Savings," 1960–1976 (in billions of dollars)

Item	1960	1965	1970	1972	1974	1976
Currency and demand deposits	$ 1.0	$ 7.5	$ 8.9	$ 14.8	$ 5.1	$ 11.3
Savings accounts	12.1	28.0	43.6	71.0	57.9	105.7
Securities						
U.S. Savings bonds	−.3	.6	−3.4	1.3	3.0	4.7
Other U.S. Govt. and agency	—	1.5	−12.8	3.3	4.2	−4.6
State and local govt. obligations	3.6	1.8	−.8	2.2	11.2	6.4
Corporate and foreign bonds	.7	.5	9.5	4.2	5.3	5.9
Investment company shares	1.4	3.3	2.8	−.5	−.5	.3
Other corporate equities	−2.0	−5.4	−3.5	−4.0	−.7	−2.4
Commercial paper	—	—	−3.2	—	7.9	−.9
	3.5	2.3	−3.4	1.3	30.2	9.5
Misc. financial assets	3.7	3.6	5.2	11.4	8.4	15.3
Private insurance and pension reserves	8.4	12.2	15.5	17.7	23.5	34.8
Govt. insurance and pension reserves	3.2	4.7	8.9	11.6	12.5	17.0
Gross increase in financial assets	31.9	58.4	78.7	127.6	137.7	193.6
Increase in debt						
Home mortgage debt	11.6	17.1	14.7	41.5	35.3	62.2
Other mortgage debt	2.6	6.5	7.4	15.9	12.4	10.6
Consumer credit	4.6	9.6	5.9	18.6	9.8	20.5
Other debt	3.0	6.9	5.1	14.3	2.6	17.4
	21.8	40.2	33.0	90.3	60.0	110.7
Net financial saving	10.1	19.6	45.7	37.3	77.7	82.9
Net investment in tangible assets	20.6	36.8	29.1	64.7	37.6	47.5
Individual savings	$30.7	$55.0	$74.8	$102.0	$115.3	$130.4

Sources: 1960: Securities and Exchange Commission, *Statistical Bulletin;* 1965–1976: *Federal Reserve Bulletin.* (flow of funds). Data may not add due to rounding.

ment in tangible assets, and total individuals' savings. These figures rose sharply in 1965–1970 as funds were poured into deposit-type investments and reserves. Securities investments declined substantially in 1969 and the early 1970s as individuals avoided the stock and bond markets. Some revival in bonds appeared in 1974–1976, but a net decline in equities continued as institutions took over the flow of funds into stocks. It is interesting to note the increase in short-term commercial paper (and "money-market funds") in 1973–1974 as individual investors turned for the first time to these instruments to take advantage of the high short-term interest rates then prevailing.

In 1973–76, gross financial savings grew from $49 to $194 billion, but a large amount of debt was paid off. The figure of $130 billion for "individual savings" in 1976 contrasts with that of $77 billion of "personal saving" in Table 3-1.[1]

As indicated in the table, a large part of the savings of individuals does not flow directly into securities and mortgages, but is invested by financial institutions serving as intermediaries between the savers and the money and capital markets. The growth of savings institutions is discussed in Chapters 4 and 21.

The table reveals the direct acquisitions of investment media. Corporate bonds are bought when yields are high (as in 1973–1975) and stocks are not in favor. Each year showed a net reduction in stockholdings, as the drift towards institutional investment of equities continued. Short-term paper came into favor in 1973–1974 when interest rates were very high. Thus, the individual investor supplies the capital market directly and through savings institutions, and the money market via commercial banks and by direct purchase (through dealers).

Nonfinancial (business) corporations   Our chief interest in nonfinancial or business corporations as suppliers of funds in the financial markets lies in their use of savings and other resources, directly and through institutions, to acquire investment instruments rather than plant and equipment, inventories, and business and consumer receivables. They purchase corporate securities directly for control rather than for investment. They acquire some short-term tax-exempt bonds. To the extent that their accounts in banks represent cash deposits, they indirectly, through the banks, supply finds to the financial markets, mainly short term. Their chief direct acquisitions are in the money market where they acquire open-market paper as a temporary investment of emergency cash or of funds raised in the long-term market and awaiting investment in business assets. This was a particularly attractive location for idle cash in the middle 1970s when very high short-term interest rates prevailed on Treasury bills and other "money" instruments. However, business corporations are by far net borrowers rather than net lenders in both the capital and money markets. They issue many times the amount of securities that they purchase.

---

[1]The latter figure excludes the increase in government and pension fund reserves, net investment in consumer durable goods, and net savings by farm corporations.

Estimates of acquisitions of investment instruments by business (nonfinancial) corporations in the period 1960–1976 are:[2]

	1960	1965	1970	1972	1974	1976
U.S. Govt. and agency securities	−$5.4	−$1.7	$2.2	−$2.4	$3.5	$8.3
State and local securities	− .2	.7	− .6	1.0	.6	−1.1
Open-market paper	.7	.8	1.2	1.4	− .6	4.2

Governments and agencies Governments draw from the financial markets many times the volume of funds that they supply. That is, they are very much net debtors.

Aside from temporary investments in refunded issues, the Federal government directly supplies very little funds to the open capital and money markets. The very substantial investments of Federal retirement and insurance plans are mainly in special nonmarketable issues. (See Chapter 4.) Federal budget agencies, however, do invest in home, multifamily, and farm mortgages; but the bulk of supply comes from sponsored Federal agencies whose acquisitions are mainly home and farm mortgages. State and local governments purchase (and sell off) substantial amounts of Treasury, agency, and municipal securities, and mortgages. State and local government retirement plans are very important suppliers of funds to the financial markets through acquisition of various types of government bonds, mortgages, and corporate bonds and stocks. (See page 445.)

The following schedule shows the combined acquisition of investment instruments by the above government suppliers of funds, for the period 1960–1976. Virtually the entire amount went into the long-term capital market as shown by the following schedule.[3]

	1960	1965	1970	1972	1974	1976
U.S. Govt. and agency securities	$1.0	$3.3	$ .6	$7.0	$10.4	$14.8
Municipal securities	.2	−.3	−.2	−.1	−.3	3.2
Corporate bonds	1.1	2.3	4.5	4.5	6.4	5.6
Corporate stocks	.1	.3	2.1	3.7	2.6	2.6
Mortgages	1.6	1.9	6.5	3.2	14.7	11.6

Commercial banks It is somewhat arbitrary to single out the flow of commercial bank funds into financial market instruments because the bulk of their funds, representing individual and corporate savings plus the credit they extend, is used in direct over-the-counter transactions. For it is the *total* supply of bank funds, along with the total demand, that largely determines the yields on short-term instruments and has a major influence on the yields of certain long-term instruments such as Government bonds, municipal bonds, and mortgages.

---

[2]Bankers Trust Company, *Credit and Capital Markets* (annual); *Federal Reserve Bulletin*.
[3]*Ibid.*

As depository intermediaries, banks channel into the capital market funds represented by savings deposits, mainly individuals' savings. A portion of primary demand deposits (representing actual cash) must be kept in required primary reserves (chiefly at the Federal Reserve banks), and a substantial amount is invested in secondary reserves consisting of high-grade money-market instruments. Although bank credit is represented mainly by short-term open-account business and personal loans, it also takes the form of purchases of commercial paper. Long-term bank credit is extended mainly through purchases of long-term Federal and municipal government securities and mortgages.

Thus, banks not only channel into productive use the individual and business savings left with them, they also supply additional credit that increases the supply of capital and makes possible increased total spending by individuals, business, and government.

The limits to bank credit expansion affect the supply of long-term as well as short-term funds. These limits are set by the reserve position of the banking system. This in turn is affected by the banks' own liquidity and, more importantly, by Federal Reserve policy. Thus, the "tight money" policy of the Federal Reserve in 1955–1959, 1965–1966, and 1969–1970 restricted the flow of bank funds into investments and was one of the two main causes of increasing interest rates. The other was the pressure of demand for investment funds in all segments of the capital and money markets that was not matched by the flow of savings. The whole pattern of prices and yields on securities, mortgages, bonds, and, to a certain extent, stocks, is influenced by the money supply and its regulation. Insofar as bond prices and yields are concerned, the open-market operations of the Federal Reserve Open-market Committee and, to a lesser extent, the discount rate are the most effective weapons of bank credit control.[4]

Commercial banks' (and their holding companies') acquisitions of capital- and money-market instruments in the period 1965–1976 are shown in the following schedule.[5] Direct loans, unsecured loans, and consumer financing are omitted.

	1960	1965	1970	1972	1974	1976
U.S. Govt. & agency securities	$2.1	−$2.8	$10.8	$6.5	$1.0	$19.6
Municipal bonds	.6	5.1	10.7	7.2	5.5	2.9
Corporate bonds	−.2	−.1	.8	1.7	1.1	−.6
Mortgages	.7	5.7	2.1	16.8	12.8	13.6
Open-market paper	−.3	−.3	1.5	−.2	2.2	3.7

[4]Changes in the discount rate are one of three major "indirect" methods by which the Federal Reserve influences the supply of bank credit. The others are (1) open-market operations, the purchase or sale of Treasury bonds by the Federal Reserve banks so as to increase or diminish the member banks' reserve account positions; and (2) changes in the member-bank legal reserve account (deposit at the central bank) ratio, expressed as a percentage of bank deposits. Reductions in the reserve ratio mean that bank loans and deposits can be increased with no increase in the dollar amount of legal reserves.

[5]Bankers Trust Company, *Credit and Capital Markets* (annual); *Federal Reserve Bulletin*. Total long-term and short-term funds supplied both directly and indirectly, are also cited in these sources.

The influence of banks in the submarkets for Treasury securities, state and local bonds, and mortgages is apparent, as are the substantial shifts between these important investments. (See page 415.)

Federal Reserve banks The role of the Federal Reserve banks and of Federal Reserve policy is a complex subject and will not be attempted here. The supply of funds into the capital and money markets is roughly represented, however, by the net acquisition of U.S. government securities, including those acquired in "open-market operations" for purposes of credit control.

The following data show the net changes in ownership of direct Federal and agency marketable debt in the period 1960–1976.[6]

	1960	1965	1970	1972	1974	1976
U.S. obligations						
Due in less than one year	$-3.2	$-.2	$ .3	$1.4	$2.8	$ 4.8
Other	4.0	4.0	4.7	-1.7	-.8	4.3
	$ .8	$3.8	$5.0	$-0.3	$2.0	$ 9.1
Obligations of Federal agencies	—	—	—	0.7	3.2	.9
	$ .8	$3.8	$5.0	$ 0.4	$5.2	$10.0

The 1972 decline reflected a sell-off of obligations in an effort to tighten money. This policy was reversed in 1974–1976 to encourage cyclical recovery.

Foreign suppliers Foreign investors in American financial instruments vary their acquisitions greatly from year to year. The following data show their purchases of *domestic* marketable American securities in the period 1960–1976.[7] Purchases of government securities are influenced mainly by interest rates in the United States, as in 1970, 1974, and 1975 when rates were very attractive. The year 1975 saw a record purchase of $4.5 billion of American stocks, reflecting faith in the growth of the American economy. Buying continued in 1976 at a lower rate.

	1960	1965	1970	1974	1976	1976 (est.)
U.S. Govt. & agency marketable securities	.5	-.7	$7.3	$4.5	$6.9	10.8
Corporate bonds	.1	—	.3	-.1	.5	—
Corporate stocks	.2	-.4	.6	2.2	.5	2.5
Open-market paper	.6	-.1	.5	-1.1	6.6	2.5

Demanders of Investment Funds
(Supply of Investments)

The demand for investment funds (that is, supply of investment instruments) comes from the same main groups that supply the funds, but in much different proportions and in different degrees in the two major markets.

[6]Source: *Federal Reserve Bulletin.*
[7]Bankers Trust Company, *Credit and Capital Markets* (annual).

Individuals and households   Individuals seek funds in the capital market chiefly for the financing of residential real estate and for farm financing. The bulk of the mortgages on which they borrow are originated or acquired by savings institutions, banks, life insurance companies, Federal credit agencies, and, to a certain degree in recent years, real estate investment trusts. Their demand for funds, and hence the supply of mortgages, is directly related to housing starts. The significance of this demand since 1960 is indicated by Table 3-3. The data do not include farm mortgages.

TABLE 3-3   Residential Real Estate Financing, 1960–1976
(dollar figures in billions)

	1960	1965	1970	1972	1974	1976
Private housing starts (000s)	1,252	1,473	1,434	2,357	1,338	1,540
Mobile home shipments (000s)	103	216	401	576	329	250
Annual increase in mortgages outstanding						
1–4 family	$10.4	$15.4	$13.4	$43.7	$31.4	$67.7
Multifamily	2.1	3.6	6.9	12.7	7.0	1.5

Sources: Federal Reserve Bulletin; Bankers Trust Company, *Credit and Capital Markets.*

The "credit crunch" in 1969–1970 depressed mortgage financing and drove mortgage yields to the then highest levels in modern times. Very substantial revival in net mortgage growth took place, beginning in 1972. Volume was retarded by the repetition of high interest rates in 1974, but recovered in 1975, then burst to a new high of more than $67 billion in 1976. In contrast to residential financing, multifamily financing fell off sharply in 1975–1976 as a result of previous overbuilding.

Individuals' demand for short-term funds is evidenced mainly in bank loans by unincorporated businesses, not in the issuance of investment instruments in the money markets.

Business and financial corporations   *Business* demand for investment funds is reflected mainly in the increase in corporate security offerings when internal sources are not sufficient to finance expansion. As shown by Table 3-4, total new corporate security offerings have steadily increased as a means of financing increased inventory and plant requirements. Bonds played an increasing role until 1968–1969, when the volume of this financing fell off somewhat with the growing credit strain that culminated in the "credit crunch" of 1969–1970. The immense increases in bond financing in 1970 and 1975 are, at first sight, somewhat surprising in view of the high interest rates that then prevailed. The fact that bond interest (unlike dividends on stock) reduces taxable corporate income was an important factor. Even with yields on high-grade corporate bonds at 8 to 9%, the after-tax cost of borrowed capital was still substantially lower than that of common stock, for most companies.

The rise in volume of bond financing was maintained through 1971–1972, reflecting the need on the part of many companies to bolster their cash

TABLE 3-4   New Corporate Securities Offered for Cash, 1960–1976
(in millions of dollars)

| | | Bonds | | | | Total |
	Total	Publicly Offered	Privately Offered	Preferred Stock	Common Stock	Gross Proceeds
1960	$ 8,081	$ 4,806	$ 3,275	$ 409	$1,664	$10,154
1965	13,720	5,570	8,150	725	1,547	15,992
1970	30,315	25,384	4,931	1,390	7,240	38,945
1971	31,999	24,790	7,209	3,679	9,236	44,914
1972	27,727	18,347	9,378	3,373	7,750	40,787
1973	21,049	13,244	7,802	3,337	7,642	32,025
1974	32,066	25,903	6,160	2,253	3,994	38,313
1975	42,756	32,583	10,172	3,458	7,405	53,619
1976	42,262	26,453	15,308	2,789	8,305	53,356

Sources: Securities and Exchange Commission, *Annual Reports* and *Statistical Bulletin*; *Federal Reserve Bulletin.*

positions after the "liquidity crisis" of 1970, but high interest rates in 1973–1974 discouraged new debt financing. The big spurt in 1975–1976 reflected economic recovery and some slight decline in interest cost. It is interesting to note that privately placed (unregistered) bond issues have declined in volume in recent years. Their chief buyers, the life insurance companies, have turned in part to less traditional types of investments. (See Chapter 22.)

The small volume of preferred stock offerings until 1965 reflects the relative disadvantage of this type of financing from the standpoint of an issuer's tax position as compared to long-term debt, and its waning appeal to investors who increasingly prefer either the safety of debt instruments or the appreciation possibilities of common stock. The substantial amount of preferred stock financing in 1971–1976 is accounted for primarily by a large volume of convertible issues whose main appeal lies in the holders' option to exchange for common, and by the need of public utility companies for equity financing that offered some advantages of fixed cost of capital.

The volume of common stock financing varies with the changing need for new capital, the economic outlook, the pattern of interest rates, and the general level of stock prices. The low volume in 1960 reflected a recession in that year, and the great decline in 1962 resulted from the break in stock prices in that year which discouraged new stock flotations. Large increases in 1970–1972 reflected the use of conservative financing to retire short-term debt, improve financial structures, and help finance continued investment in new capital assets. The recession and the great drop in prices in 1973–1974 cut common stock financing, but economic and market revival brought a new impetus to junior financing. Debt continued to have appeal, and internal sources of funds (retained profits and depreciation) provided ample funds for economic growth.

Because some new securities are issued for refinancing purposes, the proceeds of securities sold for "new money" are substantially less than the gross volume of financing. Nevertheless, when a company sells a refunding bond issue this affects the market because it must compete for funds with other issues.

Business demand for long-term funds is also reflected in the annual volume of multifamily (apartment) and commercial mortgage financing, which reached an all-time high of $25 billion in 1972 and 1973, or 36% of total mortgage financing, falling off to $13 1/2 billion in 1976.

Demand for short-term funds by business and financial corporations is centered primarily in bank loans, but open-market business and finance company commercial paper has bulked large in recent years. (See Table 2-2.) The volume issued rose from $900 million in 1965 to $14 billion in 1974, in spite of record high interest rates in 1974 that reflected in part the scramble for liquid funds by corporations. Volume fell off sharply in 1975–1976 as other funds became available.

Governments and agencies   Government demand for funds is indicated by the offering of new Federal, state, and local securities and by bond issues sold by federal agencies. (See Table 3-5.)

TABLE 3-5   New Issues of Public Securities Sold for Cash, 1960–1976
Gross Proceeds (in millions of dollars)

Issue	1960	1965	1970	1972	1974	1976[c]
U.S. Govt.	$ 7,906	$ 9,348	$14,831	$17,080	$12,968	$35,000
Federal agencies[a]	1,672	2,731	16,181	12,825	21,641	20,000
State and local govt.	7,230	11,148	17,762	23,070	24,315	35,313
Other[b]	579	889	949	1,589	2,000[c]	2,200
Total	$17,387	$24,116	$49,723	$54,564	$60,924	$92,513

[a]Nonguaranteed issues.
[b]Includes foreign government and World Bank bonds.
[c]Estimated.
Sources: Securities and Exchange Commission, *Statistical Bulletin; Federal Reserve Bulletin.*

Large parts of public securities are issued to retire existing debt. Nevertheless, they compete for funds in the capital market and thus have a significant effect on the general pattern of interest rates.

The large volume of Federal government and agency financing in years like 1970 and 1971 is explained in Chapter 6. When this has been accompanied by high municipal government and corporate bond sales, the great total demand for borrowed funds helps to explain the record high bond yields that have prevailed in recent years. (See p. 40.) New public financing continued very high in 1972 through 1976 as a result of Federal deficits. The general rise in interest rates through 1973–1975 was shared by Federal obligations whose yields reached new peaks in the fall of 1975, then declined substantially with the easing of money. (See Chapter 6.)

The very substantial rise in the debt offerings of federally sponsored agencies in the 1970s is revealed in Table 3-5. These securities add to the competition for very high-grade funds. Although the data in Table 3-5 represent gross proceeds of new offerings rather than net increase in debt after refunding, they indicate the competing demand for funds in both the long- and short-term markets.

We should note in passing the increasing significance of financing by state and local governments, which in recent years has accounted for a growing percentage of total government and corporate securities issued.

But newly issued mortgages and securities make up only a small part of the total supply of long-term investments. They only add to the existing securities already outstanding—the "secondhand" securities that are also available.

The data in Table 3-5 do not distinguish between the use of the capital and money markets by public borrowers. The Federal government has placed chief reliance on short-term securities. Treasury bills have comprised 52% of net Federal marketable issues outstanding in the period 1970–1975. In 1976, 1–5-year notes were emphasized.

Banks Commercial banks go to the financial markets with new securities and other instruments, but this source of funds is negligible compared to other inflows. During 1970–1972 banks increased their debentures and stock outstanding by about $2.5 billion a year. Since then, equity financing has produced $1 billion a year. Time and savings deposits are far more important. Our interest lies in the negotiable certificates of deposit which, as noted in Chapter 2, form a very significant portion of money-market instruments. Annual increases in the period 1960–1976 were (in billions of dollars) :[8]

1960	1965	1970	1972	1974	1976
$1.1	$3.7	$15.2	$9.8	$28.5	$−17.5

The substantial variations in certificates outstanding (as in 1970 and 1974) reflect the banks' need to attract funds from individual and institutional investors by offering competitive yields that in those years were very high. In 1975–1976 recession and lower interest rates brought this type of financing to a substantial net liquidation.

Foreign borrowers Foreigners obtain funds in the American financial markets in amounts that in some years make them net borrowers, depending on the comparative interest rates in the United States and abroad. The chief instruments sold are foreign bonds and stocks, and bankers' acceptances. Data for these placements in the period 1960–1976 follow:[9]

	1960	1965	1970	1972	1974	1976 (est.)
Foreign bonds	$ .6	$1.2	$1.0	$1.0	$2.2	$8.5
Foreign stocks	.1	− .3	—	− .4	− .2	.3
Bankers' acceptances	.6	− .1	.8	−1.0	7.1	1.0

[8]*Federal Reserve Bulletin.*
[9]Bankers Trust Company, *Credit and Capital Markets* (annual).

Foreign stocks play a very small role. The biggest variations are found in acceptances. Except for unusual years, such as 1974 and 1975 when increased imports from the U.S. required large financing, foreigners are net suppliers to the American markets for funds represented by investment instruments.

Return on Investment Instruments

Rates of return in the various segments of the capital and money markets tend to rise and fall together, reflecting the conditions of supply and demand prevailing in the whole market. In addition, investment funds are frequently shifted from one segment of the markets to another; each segment thus competes to a certain extent with each of the other segments. However, special influences, both of supply and demand, and of regulation and control, make each main type of investment somewhat independent, and thus the available returns are seldom if ever uniform. This is especially true within the capital market. Much more uniformity is found in the money market.

Later we shall discuss the special influences that determine the yields available on each of the major types of investments. At this point only some of the major factors will be outlined. These influences are over and above the ebb and flow of supply and demand for investment funds in general.

U. S. Government securities The chief special influences on this group are the monetary policy of the Federal Reserve system and the fiscal and debt management policy of the Treasury. (See Chapter 6.) Federal Reserve policy influences the prices and yields on Government securities directly through the changing holdings of securities by the Federal Reserve Banks. More indirectly, policy influences the relative appeal of Government securities as commercial bank assets, compared to loans. Fiscal and debt management by the Treasury is influential through the amount and maturities of Government securities offered or retired. Yields on marketable Federal obligations would be "pure interest" rates if it were not for the impact of these special influences. In addition, the rates of return on U.S. Savings bonds and other nonmarketable types of Federal debt are fixed by legislation, and may or may not match the going rates on marketable bonds.

State and local government bonds Prices and yields in this group reflect supply and demand conditions in the bond market as a whole, as well as three special factors: (1) the volume and timing of new offerings, (2) the exemption of interest from income taxation (Federal and that of the issuing jurisdiction), and (3) the vacillating demand by commercial banks. (See Chapter 7.) The outpouring of state and municipal bonds in the postwar period would have lifted the yields on these bonds to a *relatively* high level except for their tax appeal and the increasing bank demand. Yields did reach record highs in 1970 and 1974–1975 in line with the high level of bond yields as a whole, but in 1976 they were somewhat lower.

Corporate bonds The course of prices and yields of high-grade corporate bonds is discussed in Chapter 8. These movements are influenced chiefly by the "bellwether" Government bond yields, and by the volume of new financing and the supply of funds in this segment of the market. The spread between yields on Government bonds and high-grade corporate bonds reflects the fact that the latter are private obligations and, in many cases, have much poorer marketability. A special influence on this category of investments is the institutional market. Life insurance companies, banks, corporate trustees, pension funds, and other institutional buyers are the major market for high-grade corporate bonds, and the ebb and flow of savings into and out of these institutions has an important impact on the whole bond market. Also, these institutions may shift their funds from one category of investments to another within the limits set by governing regulations.

A powerful special influence on bond yields—inflation—appeared in the 1970s. Bond investors demanded compensation for the declining purchasing power of interest and principal, in addition to a return on capital. This factor, along with others, is discussed in Chapters 8, 9, and 19.

Prices and yields of second-grade corporate bonds are also influenced by the trend of long-term interest rates; but since the payment of their interest and principal is less certain, they are also affected by the outlook for corporate profits. Within the whole category of corporate bonds, the quality of the individual issues, their marketability, maturity, and special features cause their prices and yields to differ at any one moment of time.

Corporate stocks While bonds and stocks in general appeal to different types of investors, all have the privilege of choosing between the two. And many users of capital also have a choice between borrowing and selling stock. Thus, some relationship should exist between the yields on "bond money" and "stock money," and this is true insofar as preferred stocks are concerned. Dividends on common stock can also be regarded as a return on capital. As bond prices and yields rise and fall, so theoretically should common stock prices and yields rise and fall, to the extent that stock prices are influenced by general forces of supply and demand for long-term capital. And one would expect a rather consistent spread between the yields on the two types of securities.

For over three decades, from the early 1930s to the mid-1960s, this relationship failed to appear. Except in occasional years the two series went their separate ways. The dividend yield on the Standard & Poor's Industrial Stock Series declined from nearly 300% of the yield on the same service's high-grade bond series in 1950 to 40% in late 1972 and to 45% in mid-1976. In the "credit crunch" years of 1966, 1969–1970, and 1973–1974, however, bond and stock prices both declined, and yields on both types of securities increased. A major cause of weakness in stock prices was the high level of interest rates that made bonds attractive to both individuals and institutions. In 1971–1972 and 1976, improved stock prices and declining bond yields still left stock yields far below those on fixed-income securities.

The prices and yields of stock are swayed by factors that are even more potent than the supply of, or demand for, investment funds in general, notably the outlook for the economy as a whole and for corporate profits in particular. These forces will be discussed in greater detail in Chapters 9 and 20.

As we shall see, preferred stocks represent investments that, like bonds, usually provide a fixed return. However, because they represent ownership, preferred stocks should command a higher return than high-grade bonds with similar earnings protection. But their special income tax advantage to corporate owners depresses their yields below those of bonds of equal quality. (See p. 171.) Changes in prices and yields through time are caused chiefly by (1) the general factors affecting bonds and (2) the earnings prospects of their issuers. Very high-grade preferred stocks move in the market like bonds; the lower the quality of the preferred stock, the more its price and yield movements resemble those of common stocks.

Mortgages   This category is more specialized than any of the others. The rise and wane of savings, the special institutional demand for mortgages, and the fluctuating demand for funds needed for real estate financing are the important influences. Government restrictions also affect the available yields of certain types of mortgages such as FHA-insured and VA-guaranteed mortgage loans. (See Chapter 11.) Yields on all mortgages are consistently higher than those on high-grade bonds because of their specialized character, poorer marketability, and awkward denominations. Mortgage interest rates also reflect substantial regional differences, although widespread institutional demand has tended to reduce the local differentials somewhat.

Short-term investments   Interest returns on various money-market instruments reflect the factors of supply and demand for investments as a whole, plus the special pressures on, and supplies of, short-term funds. Federal Reserve policy and bank credit conditions are the most powerful influences. "Credit crunch" conditions show up first in this sensitive market and push short-term yields above the long term. Forces affecting rates on "money" instruments are discussed in Chapter 10.

The Course of Investment Yields

The general discussion above of the factors at work in the investment market has been confined to the broad categories of investments without taking into account the substantial differences that exist in almost all of the major categories with respect to quality and individual features. Methods of analyzing individual securities from the standpoint of quality, as well as more detailed attention to their special characteristics, are reserved for later chapters.

But the impact of the general factors discussed above can be seen at work in data that show the changing pattern of investment returns. Table 3-6 shows representative interest rates and yields in various segments of the

TABLE 3-6 Variations in Selected Interest Rates and
Securities Yields, 1961–1976

Investment Medium	Sept. 1966	May 1967	Jan. 1970	May 1972	Aug. 1974	Dec. 1976	July 1977
Short-term credit							
Federal funds	5.4%	3.9%	9.0%	4.2%	12.0%	4.6%	5.4%
U.S. Govt., 3-month bills	5.3	3.6	7.9	3.7	8.7	4.3	5.2
U.S. Govt., 9-to 12-month issues	5.8	3.9	7.5	4.5	8.9	5.8	5.6
Prime commercial paper, 4–6 months	5.9	4.6	8.8	4.5	11.7	4.6	5.4
Prime bankers' acceptances, 90-day	5.7	4.4	8.6	4.3	12.0	4.6	5.4
Bank prime rate	6.0	5.5	8.5	5.0	12.0	6.3	6.8
Federal Reserve discount rate	4.5	4.0	6.0	4.5	8.0	5.3	5.3
Medium-term credit							
U.S. Govt., 3- to 5-year issues	5.6	4.7	8.1	5.7	8.6	5.9	6.6
Municipal bonds, high-grade, 5 years	3.8	3.5	5.8	4.0	6.1	4.1	4.3
Corporate bonds, high-grade, 5 years	6.3	5.3	8.8	6.7	8.8	7.0	7.1
Long-term credit							
U.S. Govt., Treasury bonds	4.8	4.7	6.8	5.6	7.3	6.4	7.2
Municipal bonds, long-term (Moody's Aaa)	3.9	3.7	6.4	5.1	6.4	5.1	5.3
Corporate bonds, long-term (Moody's Aaa)	5.5	5.2	7.9	7.3	9.0	8.0	7.9
Corporate bonds, long-term (Moody's Baa)	6.1	6.0	8.8	8.2	9.8	9.1	9.0
Mortgage loans, residential, conventional	6.6	6.4	8.3	7.4	9.1	9.0	9.0
Savings institutions							
Commercial bank passbook accounts	4.0	4.0	4.5	4.7	5.0	5.0	5.0
Mutual savings bank accounts	4.5	4.7	5.0	5.2	5.2	5.2	5.2
Savings and loan assoc. passbook accounts	4.7	4.7	5.0	5.2	5.2	5.2	5.2
U.S. Savings bonds, Series E, to maturity	4.1	4.1	5.0	5.5	6.0	6.0	6.0
Stocks							
Preferred (Standard & Poor's)	5.2	5.2	7.0	6.9	8.6	7.7	7.8
Common (Standard & Poor's)	3.7	3.2	3.5	2.9	4.8	4.0	4.5

financial markets in the 1961–1976 period. The dates selected are those at which yields in general were at the extreme highs and lows. Although we are concerned mainly with the course of yields on long-term and short-term instruments, intermediate-term rates are included, along with returns available at savings institutions. The bank "prime rate" and the Federal Reserve rediscount rate are included in the short-term category.

In mid-1961 relatively easy credit conditions prevailed. The economic expansion into 1965 brought a modest increase in rates, which culminated in "tight money" conditions and the "credit crunch" of 1966. By the autumn of that year, most short- and long-term rates reached their highest postwar peaks. Nonmarket rates such as the Federal Reserve discount rate, the nominal (contractual) yield on FHA-insured mortgages, and yields on savings had also been adjusted upward.

With the lessening of the credit crisis, yields declined in early 1967. Then renewed economic expansion and enormous demands for credit and capital funds, and a severe shortage of both long- and short-term money, drove most yields to their highest levels in history by the beginning of 1970, in the second postwar "crunch." Severe liquidity problems of corporations aggravated conditions in the financial markets and helped to produce an almost panic condition, of which the "prime" rate of 8 1/2% was ample evidence.

The subsequent decline in some yields, especially the short-term, in the first quarter of 1971 was steeper than in any equivalent period in history. More bank credit was available. Federal Reserve policy was one of easing credit, and savings available for long-term investment were greatly expanded; but, as discussed later, all yields did not change in like degree. Continued large demands for long-term funds, depressing political and social developments, and continued concern about corporate liquidity (especially after the bankruptcy of the Penn Central Company in June) produced wide differentials among the rates on different types of financial instruments. During the remainder of 1971 most market yields vacillated around a lower average. Short-term rates were eased by continual expansion of the money supply. That the "credit crunch" was over was well evidenced by a decline in the prime rate to 4 1/2% in early 1972. Rates paid on savings deposits also began to weaken at that time. Yields on long-term bonds and mortgages held fairly steady.

Table 3-6 and Chart 3-1 reveal the variations in the general rate structure of the total money and capital markets from time to time. They also show that ordinarily, regardless of the height or depth of the general pattern of interest rates, shorter maturities bear lower yields than longer-maturity obligations of the same type. The table also shows, however, that as interest rates rise, the influence of the difference in maturity declines. Indeed, in periods of very "tight money" conditions, such as in 1966, 1970, and 1974, short-term rates push above long-term rates. More normal relationships between short- and long-term rates prevailed until late 1965–mid-1966, although, as a result of the Administration policy of keeping short-term rates high to prevent gold outflow and long-term rates low to encourage expansion, the spread between maturities was smaller than in previous "normal" periods. By the middle of 1966, the "yield curve" again showed higher short-term than long-term yields, and very little difference between intermediate- and long-term yields; that is, the curve was flat after an early hump. Although all yields declined in early 1967, the hump persisted.

The "crunches" of 1970 and 1974 show that during and after periods of severe credit and capital crisis, although all yields change dramatically, the greatest variation takes place in the short-term group. (See Chapter 8.) For example, yield on 91-day Treasury bills rose from about 3.7% in May 1972 to almost 8% in August 1974, then fell to 4.3% in December 1976. Normally, over any extended period, long-term instruments bear higher yields than short-term paper of equal quality, but panic conditions reverse this relationship. The 12% rate on Federal funds in the summer of 1974 is a dramatic example. The decline in rates is almost as precipitous. In early 1977 the Federal funds rate was 4.5%, reflecting a reversal in money supply. In general, short- and long-term rates stiffened in the first half of 1977.

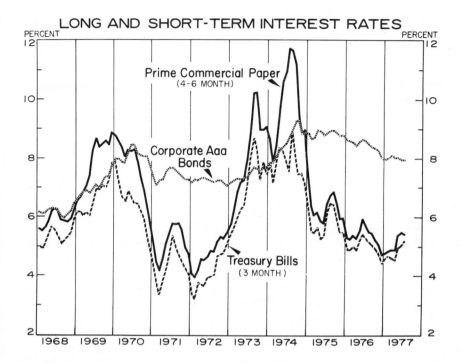

LONG AND SHORT-TERM INTEREST RATES

Prime Commercial Paper (4-6 MONTH)

Corporate Aaa Bonds

Treasury Bills (3 MONTH)

1968 1969 1970 1971 1972 1973 1974 1975 1976 1977

Source: MacKay-Shields Financial Corporation, New York. Reprinted with permission.

Chart 3-1 shows the course of yields for three types of Federal securities in recent years.

Differences in the quality of investments have an obvious influence on the returns that will satisfy investors. Other things being equal, the higher the risk, the higher the rate. As the table shows, U.S. Government obligations, with their "riskless" characteristics, bear the lowest rates (with the exception of municipal bonds) in any particular maturity group and at any time, regardless of the general level of rates. High-grade bonds yield lower rates of return than medium-grade bonds. Bankers' acceptances (drafts honored by banks) and prime commercial paper (short-term unsecured notes of large firms with high credit standing) bear lower rates than prime direct short-term business loans. Marketable good-grade and high-grade bonds usually bear lower rates than real estate mortgages except under unusual circumstances. (See Chapter 12.) In relating quality to yields, however, two special factors should be mentioned. The lower yields of municipal bonds, as compared to Treasury obligations, are attributable to the exclusion of municipal bond interest payments from income subject to Federal income taxes. Yields on high-grade preferred stocks are similarly depressed by their tax advantage: Taxed *corporate* investors enjoy an 85% deduction on preferred dividend income. The normally higher yields on mortgages than on bonds reflect in part the poorer market for mortgages as compared to securities.

As mentioned previously, although a very considerable flow of funds occurs between the various segments of the whole investment market, certain barriers or special factors tend to "departmentalize" the market to some extent and prevent uniformity of returns even when maturity and quality are similar. The rates paid by savings institutions tend to change at much less frequent intervals than open-market rates. The yields on Savings bonds are fixed by the government and not by the market, so that the influence of competition shows up only in occasional revisions of these yields some time after rates on other media have changed. And the mortgage market is influenced by regulations and restrictions on institutional investors, by geographical differences in the flow and demand of investment funds, and to a certain extent by legislation, as in the case of the nominal rates on FHA and VA mortgages.

The influence on interest rates of the credit control policies of the Federal Reserve, while very real, is not too apparent in Table 3-6. The rise in the discount rate (the rate at which member banks can borrow at the central bank and thus increase their legal reserves) accompanies the rise in interest rates in the period shown. In other years, not shown on the table, several adjustments were made in the discount rate, both upward and downward. Usually this rate is changed after money-market conditions have changed; at other times, the change is designed to influence the course of rates, and it does so to varying degrees.

As suggested previously, the yields on preferred stocks change with those of bonds, since both are fixed-income types of securities. The yields on the high-grade preferred stock series rose to a peak in early 1970 and declined thereafter when interest rates declined. (The relatively low yield on preferred stocks, as compared to bond yields, is explained by their tax advantage to corporate owners and by their short supply.)

The relation between bond yields and common stock yields is not as direct, however. Dividends on common stocks are a distribution of profits, and hence depend not only on net earnings, but also on dividend policy. Yields are the net result of a number of variables on both the income and the price sides. Stock yields can rise when interest rates are declining, and contrariwise. Nevertheless, a very sharp change in interest rates is also reflected to a certain extent in a change in dividend yields, since the latter are a return on capital. However, this influence may be entirely overcome by others of much greater importance. Stock yields are more volatile, rising and falling as prices reflect changing estimates of corporate earnings and dividends and the valuation of these basic factors. But in very recent years bond and stock prices, and hence their yields, have often trended together. Prices of both types of securities rose during most of 1970, declined together in the spring of 1971, then rose dramatically with President Nixon's announcement of controlled wages, prices, and imports in August. Yields of both types followed a contrary course. However, in the autumn of 1971 the relationship between bond and stock prices and yields reverted to a more traditional pattern as bond prices rose with declining yields, while stock prices fell. Stock and bond prices fell precipitously in 1973–1974. Stock prices rallied strongly in 1975–1976, almost to previous peaks. Bond prices rose mildly as interest rates softened somewhat from their previous record levels.

In general, yields on common stocks have been much lower than bond yields, and the spread between the two widened to record proportions in 1970–1972 and 1976. The explanation is that stock prices reflect the outlook for earnings and their reinvestment more than their dividend payout. The preference of most investors for appreciation over current income from stocks is strikingly evident. There was almost an inverse relationship between the valuation of earnings (as measured by the price-earnings ratio) and the share of earnings distributed in dividends. The high-ratio high-priced "glamor stocks" offered little or no yield.

After the great decline in stock prices ended in 1974, and through the general maket recovery in 1975–1976, stock yields rose as corporations turned to higher dividend payouts. The yields on the previous top-tier growth stocks rose very substantially to reflect both increased dividends and lower prices. But because bond yields remained high, the substantial spread between bond and stock yields persisted. See Chart 9-2 and Table 9-4.

This very general account of the play of forces in the investment market provides only a broad explanation of a complicated subject. In later chapters the influences affecting returns from particular types of investments will be discussed more specifically.

REFERENCES

BADGER, R. E., H. W. TORGERSON, and H. G. GUTHMANN, *Investment Principles and Practices*, 6th ed., Chapter 1. Englewood Cliffs, N.J.: Prentice-Hall, Inc., 1969.

BANKERS TRUST COMPANY, *Credit and Capital Markets*. New York: Bankers Trust Company, annual.

BOARD OF GOVERNORS OF THE FEDERAL RESERVE SYSTEM, *Flow of Funds Accounts*, 1945–68, 1965–73. Washington, D.C.: The Board, 1970, 1974.

DE PRANO, MICHAEL, et al., eds., *Money, Financial Markets, and the Economy*. Belmont, California: Dickenson Publishing Company, Inc., 1970.

DOUGALL, H. E., and J. E. GAUMNITZ, *Capital Markets and Institutions*, 3rd ed. Englewood Cliffs, N.J.: Prentice-Hall, Inc., 1975.

GOLDSMITH, R. W., *A Study of Saving in the United States*, Three volumes. Princeton, N.J.: Princeton University Press, 1955.

———, *The Flow of Capital Funds in the Postwar Economy*. New York: Columbia University Press, 1965.

———, *Financial Institutions*. New York: Random House, Inc., 1968.

HEMPEL, G. H., and J. B. YAWITZ, *Financial Management of Financial Institutions*. Englewood Cliffs, N.J.: Prentice-Hall, Inc. 1977.

HENNING, C. N., et al., *Financial Markets and the Economy*. Englewood Cliffs, N.J.: Prentice-Hall, Inc., 1974.

HOMER, SYDNEY, *A History of Interest Rates*. New Brunswick, N.J.: Rutgers University Press, 1963.

Institutional Study Report of the Securities and Exchange Commission, Supplementary Volume No. I, Chapter 4. 92nd Congress, 1st Session, House Document No. 94–64, 1971.

KESSELL, R. A., *The Cyclical Behavior of the Term Structure of Interest Rates*. New York: Columbia University Press, 1965.

KROOS, H. E., and M. R. BLYN, *A History of Financial Intermediaries*. New York: Random House, 1971.

KUZNETS, SIMON, *Capital in the American Economy: Its Formation and Financing*. Princeton, N.J.: Princeton University Press, 1961.

LINDOW, WESLEY, *Inside the Money Market*. New York: Random House, 1972.

MEISELMAN, DAVID, *The Term Structure of Interest Rates*. Englewood Cliffs, N.J.: Prentice-Hall, Inc., 1962.

Money Market Instruments: The Risk and the Return, rev. ed. New York: Morgan Guaranty Trust Co., 1970.

POLAKOFF, M. E., et al., *Financial Institutions and Markets*, Chapters 1, 4, 19, 20. Boston: Houghton Mifflin Company, 1970.

ROBINSON, R. I., and DWAYNE WRIGHTSMAN, *Financial Markets: The Accumulation and Allocation of Wealth*. New York: McGraw-Hill, Inc., 1974.

SMITH, P. F., *Economics of Financial Institutions and Markets*. Homewood, Ill.: Richard D. Irwin, Inc., 1971.

VAN FENSLEMAKER, J., ed., *Readings in Financial Markets and Institutions*. Englewood Cliffs, N.J.: Prentice-Hall, Inc., 1969.

VAN HORNE, J.C., *Function and Analysis of Capital Market Rates*. Englewood Cliffs, N.J.: Prentice-Hall, Inc., 1970.

WOODWORTH, G. W., *The Money Market and Monetary Management*, 2nd ed. New York: Harper and Row, Publishers, 1972.

Part

Investment
Media

Life Insurance, Annuities, and Retirement Plans as Investments

SCOPE: The purpose of this chapter is to discuss the investment aspects of life insurance and of various arrangements for retirement income that are usually based on formal contracts with institutions. The order of discussion is: (1) investment aspects of life insurance, (2) types of policies, (3) investment merits, (4) fixed-dollar annuities, (5) variable annuities, (6) private pension funds, (7) individual tax-free pension plans, (8) Pension Reform Act of 1974, (9) state and local government retirement funds, and (10) Federal retirement plans and Social Security.

Discussion of life insurance in a work on investments is appropriate for several reasons: (1) The reserve liabilities of life insurance companies represent the largest single collection of individuals' savings in any one type of institution; (2) these savings are invested in securities and mortgages so that insurance company investments are a large share of institutional investments in general; (3) millions of individuals invest through insurance companies and are, therefore, greatly concerned with insurance company investment policy.

Provision for retirement is an important investment objective, and a substantial volume of savings is devoted to acquiring income from institutions that contract to make fixed or semifixed payments after an agreed time has elapsed. In addition to the premiums on annuities sold by life insurance companies, the annual contributions to uninsured private pension funds, Social Security, and Federal and state retirement plans total approximately $120 billion per year.

We are concerned in this chapter with what these institutions do for the investor. The investment policies of the institutions themselves are discussed in later chapters.

Life Insurance as an Investment

Life insurance companies provide one of the most important forms of savings. At the beginning of 1977 their assets totalled $322 billion, and their policy reserves $259 billion. In 1976 their annual income exceeded $88 billion, of which nearly 75% was derived from premium payments. (Additional data on the industry are given in Chapters 22 and 30.)

The investment aspects of life insurance Life insurance enters into investment planning in three major respects: (1) Insurance is the only feasible method by which most investors can provide an adequate immediate estate for dependents; (2) most insurance contracts have a policy reserve that represents savings and that is available in the form of cash values or policy loans;(3) the insured may create a retirement fund for himself after the need of protection for dependents has declined or disappeared.

The premium paid for insurance is usually a level premium that is the same each year even though the risk of death increases with age. It is fixed at the time the policy is issued and is based on the age of the insured. It consists of three elements: a sum contributed toward the company's operating expenses—the "office premium" or "load," an amount necessary to reimburse the insurance company for carrying the risk of premature death of the insured, and an amount added to reserves and invested at a "guaranteed" rate to cover future death loss at the more advanced age. Disregarding the first item, we see that part of the premium goes for current *protection* and part into the policy reserve or *investment* element.

This latter element constitutes the cash value that is available (after a stated period, often the first two or three years) through cancellation of the contract or in the form of a policy loan. The reserve may also be used to extend the term of the insurance or to purchase a paid-up policy for a reduced amount of insurance if the insured wishes to stop paying premiums on the original policy. Or it may be used to provide an annuity at retirement.

The premium is calculated on the basis of the probability of death by age as indicated by a mortality table; an assumed rate of earnings on invested reserves (as low as 3 to 4%); expected selling expense, office expenses, and taxes of the company; and the type of policy issued. Savings on the first three of these may be substantial. In the case of mutual companies (and participating policies of stock companies) they may be returned to the policyholder in the form of "dividends," be left with the company at interest, or be used to reduce the annual premium or to purchase additional paid-up insurance. The "dividend" is not a true profit, but simply a return of excess premium paid by the policyholder.

Major types of policies   In comparing the cost of similar policies issued by different companies, one should make sure that their provisions and benefits are identical and then compare the *net* cost over a period of years, that is, premiums less any dividends. Another and perhaps preferable method of determining the net cost is to compare the total premiums paid in, less "dividends," less the cash-surrender value at the end of a given period. The cost may be zero, or even a negative amount. Dividends are not paid in regular amounts and are not assured, but depend on the company's experience with respect to costs and investment income.

The following annual gross premiums at age 25 for various types of policies and the cash-surrender values at age 65 were representative in 1977 on contracts of $10,000 or more. Premiums on participating policies were somewhat higher:

	Premium per Thousand	Cash Value Age 65
Five-year term[a]	$ 5.05	—
Straight life	13.62	$ 578
Family income (20 years)	17.21	590
Twenty-payment life	21.91	690
Retirement income at 65	25.91	1,628
Twenty-year endowment	43.36	[b]

[a]Renewable and convertible.
[b]Paid off at $1,000 at age 45.

Since the year-to-year cost of protection for each $1,000 of insurance is the same for each age of issue, the difference in gross premiums on various policies (at the same age) depends on the investment element (reserve) in the policy. A *term* policy is renewed annually at an increasing premium, or issued at an annual level premium for a certain term such as five years, ten years, "term to sixty-five," and so forth. The face value is paid only if death occurs within the stipulated period. It has no recovery value at the end of the term. Since nothing is paid for survival, the insurance company need not accumulate a reserve for that purpose. Longer-term contracts, say, for fifteen to twenty years, have a small reserve element that increases during the earlier years, but declines to zero at the expiration of the period. To the investor desiring the greatest temporary protection at the least outlay, the term policy is the best choice. As shown by the schedule of rates, at age 25 an annual premium of $100 would buy $19,800 of protection for five years through a five-year term policy (renewable and convertible into permanent protection), $7,340 in straight-life protection, $5,810 through a twenty-year "family-income" policy, $4,560 in twenty-year paid-up life insurance, $3,860 in a retirement-at-65 income policy, and $2,300 in twenty-year endowment insurance. (Deducting the "dividends" or rebates, the actual cost of each type might, of course, be considerably reduced.)

Arguments for term insurance include: it provides maximum protection per dollar of premium outlay when needs are greatest (for example, when children are young and the insured's income is modest); the difference between the premium on term insurance and a higher-premium form may be invested at a higher rate than would be earned by the insurance company; it may be converted into a permanent form of insurance without medical examination within a certain period of time before the expiration of the term policy if permanent protection is needed; there may be an option to renew the contract for a further period without medical examination; it may be used to insure the payment of debt in case the borrower dies before the debt matures. The nonrenewable and declining term insurance associated with mortgage financing is a frequent example.

Arguments against term insurance are the inability of many people to save systematically unless compelled to save in order to keep insurance in force; the lack of a cash reserve that would be available in emergencies and that

49

would keep the policy in force if the insured were unable to meet his premiums; the high cost or even impossibility of renewal at the expiration of the period; the natural lethargy that leads to failure to convert or renew and hence to expiration of the protection. Perhaps the best plan for the young man is to take out convertible term insurance to the full amount of his need and change to permanent insurance as soon as he can afford to do so. To offset the practical difficulties that this plan involves, the family-income policy is recommended.[1] This combines ordinary life with decreasing term insurance and pays a monthly income upon the death of the insured until the expiration of a specified date (say, ten or twenty years from date of issuance) and the face of the policy as of that date. The annual premium is somewhat greater than that for term insurance and less than that for whole-life insurance.

Whole-life policies provide permanent protection. The *straight-life* policy requires premiums until the insured dies or reaches age ninety. Advantages of this form are: the insured is never without protection; the savings or investment element is substantial; the premium remains constant; at retirement, or when the insured no longer has dependents, the reserve value may be taken in cash or used for an annuity; if at a later age continuing the premiums becomes difficult or if the need for protection declines, the paid-up values may be used to extend the insurance for a term or to buy a reduced amount of protection for life. The chief disadvantage is that the maximum amount of temporary protection is not obtained, say, during the establishment of a family by a younger man; to keep the full amount of insurance in force, payments must be continued long after the earning years have ceased.

Preferred-risk straight-life policies are issued at lower than regular rates to persons willing to buy a minimum of $5,000 or $10,000 at one time and who have excellent medical histories and are not engaged in hazardous occupations. The premiums are usually lower and the cash values higher than for the corresponding straight-life policies.

Limited-payment life policies are also whole-life policies, but premiums are paid at a higher rate for a period (say, for twenty or thirty years), after which the policy continues in force for life without further payments. Advantages of this form are: protection is obtained for life; premiums are paid when the policyholder is most capable of earning; a substantial investment element or cash value is accumulated in the twenty or thirty years that will protect against death loss after premium payments are no longer required. The major disadvantage is that the insured has substantially less protection per dollar of premium than is afforded by term or straight-life insurance when the protection may be most needed (in other words, the possible overemphasis on savings and underemphasis on protection).

Endowment policies offer protection for a specified period of time (say,

---

[1]Not to be confused with the "family-maintenance" policy under which all members (and prospective members) of a family are covered by one contract, with varying amounts of protection per member.

twenty or thirty years), at the end of which the policy matures and the amount of the policy is paid to the insured himself. The endowment policy combines an increasing savings fund protected by decreasing term insurance. If the insured dies during the period, the beneficiaries are paid the face amount; if he lives, he collects it himself. Advantages of endowment insurance are: where the need for protection is small and the need for savings is predominant, the insured is forced to save to keep his policy in force; the goals of insurance may be met whether the insured lives or dies; the very substantial cash value provides a cash fund or fund for conversion into retirement protection. The main limitations are: protection expires when the policy matures; low current protection is afforded per dollar of premium; the difference between the premium on "cheaper" insurance and on endowment insurance of the same amount could be invested safely and, in the event of the insured's death before the policy expired, would also increase the estate for dependents.

The *retirement-income* policy combines whole-life insurance with a life income payable in units (say, $10 per month for each $1,000 to $1,500 of insurance) at the selected retirement age. These are "expensive" policies because they build up savings even faster than endowment policies maturing at the same age. (In the previous table the retirement-income policy assumes retirement at age 65, whereas the endowment policy matures at age 45; an endowment policy maturing at age 65 would require a much lower annual premium.) This type of policy is really a retirement annuity with death benefits added. The cash value can be substantial.

Investment merits Life insurance offers, in various degrees, a valuable combination of protection and investment. However, many feel that the two should not be combined in one contract. The rate of return on that part of the premium which represents an investment commitment is substantially below that which an individual can get on sound securities. However, the lower rate of return assumed by the insurance company is *compounded*—something the individual investor may not accomplish. In addition, that portion of the investment income that goes to build up the reserve is tax-free. The compulsory savings requirement, the encouragement to systematic thrift, safety of the funds, and the convenience and freedom from managerial care on the part of the insured are strong arguments for substantial investment values in life insurance contracts for many, perhaps the majority of investors.

A major disadvantage of life insurance is that its fixed-dollar benefits lose purchasing power during periods of inflation. Protection can be obtained by the purchase of additional coverage, but only at higher premiums as age increases and if medical requirements can be met. The insurance industry has been investigating the possibilities of variable life insurance, in which the beneficiary would receive at least the policy's face value, and possibly a higher benefit from the appreciation of equity investments held as reserves. Such policies are already permitted in several states, including New York.

Annuities as Investments

Fixed-dollar annuities   The traditional *annuity* provides a fixed return with safety at or prior to retirement age. A series of equal annual dollar installments are received at once or after an agreed age, usually ao long as the annuitant lives, in return for a lump-sum payment or regular annual premiums. The longer the annuitant lives in comparison with the average, the more he receives in relation to what he has paid. If he is short-lived, he may receive back much less than he has invested. The life annuity is simply a means of assuring a certain income which cannot be outlived. Since a part of the principal, in addition to the interest earned, is returned each year, the return to the annuitant is larger than that which would be produced by interest income alone. The penalty of this higher income is the complete liquidation of principal at the death of the annuitant, at least in the straight-life annuity described below. The more important types of annuities can be described very briefly. A *single-premium* annuity is purchased by the payment of one lump sum, the payments to begin at a stipulated age for the life of the annuitant. *Installment-payment* annuities call for premiums periodically over a period of years to the date of retirement, after which the annuitant receives an income for life. A *life insurance* annuity is purchased by the proceeds of a life insurance policy which are distributed as an annuity in lieu of a lump sum. Most life insurance policies provide for this type of settlement option.

From the standpoint of benefits, annuities can be classified as *immediate*, which pay a given sum periodically for life following purchase, or *deferred*, in which income does not begin until some time in the future, usually at the estimated end of the annuitant's income-producing period. Possibly the most common type is the installment-payment type whose income will be deferred until retirement age. Death benefits and possibly cash-surrender values are available prior to, but not after, retirement. *Joint and last-survivorship* annuities pay an income to two or more persons, such as husband or wife, as long as either survives.

A *straight-life* annuity provides income to the annuitant for his lifetime only. In case of early death, he may have received only a fraction of what has been paid in. Consequently, straight-life annuities are not so common today as annuities with special features attached, such as the *life-annuity with installments certain*, which pays an income for life, but guarantees to make a minimum number of payments, such as for ten or twenty years irrespective of the time of death of the annuitant. An *installment-refund* life annuity pays an income for life, but provides for a continuation of installments to beneficiaries or estate until the payments total the premiums paid, should the annuitant die before that time. A *cash-refund* life annuity is similar, but provides for the payment in cash of the balance of the premiums paid. Such annuities often contain substantial cash values. The advantage of the refund type is that income or principal is available for dependents in the event the annuitant should die before the dependents have economic independence. The *retirement-income* (insurance-plus-income) *policy* was described above.

The cost of annuities and the income received from them depend on the age and life expectancy of the annuitant, the rate earned by the insurance company, and the form of the policy. The following rates show the amount of a monthly straight-life *nonparticipating* annuity that could be purchased from a prominent company with an immediate lump-sum payment of $1,000, based on rates quoted in 1976, assuming an interest rate of 3%.

| | Annuity per Month | |
Age at Purchase	Male	Female
50	$6.08	$5.57
55	6.67	6.04
60	7.42	6.70
65	8.42	7.60
70	9.68	9.00

The annuity payment increases as the age at time of purchase increases and the life expectancy decreases. When interest rates are low, the above payments would be attractive. At age 65, for example, a male annuitant would receive about three times the interest income from an investment at 3% that produced $2.50 a month. This was because the return consisted of both principal and interest. But in recent years such annuity payments have been unsatisfactory. In 1977, $1,000 invested in a high-grade bond produced interest income of 8% or $6.67 a month, and the principal remained intact. Under such conditions only those fixed annuities whose benefits are increased through participation in "dividends" would have much appeal, save to the very aged.

Ordinary annuities have the advantages of certainty of a fixed income for life, convenience, freedom from care, and compulsion to save. For the investor of limited means, a definite income for retirement is assured. For the man of wealth, fixed-dollar annuities will provide a fixed income (using part of capital) and leave a larger portion of his total fund free for other investments. But in addition to their loss of appeal during periods of high interest rates, fixed annuities suffer, as do all fixed-income investments, from the reduced purchasing power resulting from inflation. The interest rate at which the reserves are compounded is low, and premium rates have been increasing in recent years to reflect the increase in the average life-span. Fixed annuities lack the appeal of common stock investments that has been reflected in the growth of corporate pension funds, mutual investment funds, and other vehicles for sharing in an expanding economy. The number of *individual* annuities in force dropped from its previous peak of 1,279,000 in 1952 to 1,140,000 in 1965, but rose to 3,279,000 1976. The annual income rose to $3.6 billion in 1976,[2] due in large part to the demand for individual retirement accounts (IRAs).

[2]American Council of Life Insurance, *Life Insurance Fact Book 1976*, New York: The Council, 1977.

Variable annuities Under the variable annuity the annuitant's premiums are invested in a diversified list of common stocks, as are the dividends on the stocks. Each annuitant acquires, as his share in the accumulated reserve, an increasing number of "accumulation units" or "premium units" that vary in value with the value of the total portfolio. Upon retirement, the accumulation units are transferred to the annuity fund, all of which is still invested in common stocks. The annuitant thereafter receives periodically either the dollar value of the number of "annuity units" attributable to him or a combination of fixed and variable income.Such units are calculated on the basis of assumed and actual mortality experience, income, and expense. In the event of death prior to retirement, the total value of the accumulation units is paid to the beneficiary.[3]

The purposes of the variable annuity are to provide a protection hedge against expected long-term inflation, to increase annuity income by sharing in the rising values and dividends of common stocks, and to provide a steady increase in living standards. The company engages in dollar-cost averaging in common stocks that are expected to rise in value, over the long run, more than the cost of living—in short, to preserve and increase *real* retirement income. The first such annuity was offered in 1952 by College Retirement Equities Fund, an affiliate of Teachers Insurance and Annuity Association, and is available only to personnel of college, university, foundation, and research organizations. Table 4-1 shows, for July 1952–December 1976, the average annual value of CREF accumulation units and the value of annuity units (calculated annually), compared to the average monthly value of Standard & Poor's 500 Stock Index and the annual average of the Bureau of Labor Statistics Consumer Price Index. Until 1973 at least, the rise in the value of the CREF units, and of stocks in general, greatly exceeded the increase in the cost of living.

The growth of the variable annuity was slowed by problems of jurisdiction as well as by resistance on the part of some large life insurance companies. In 1959 the U.S. Supreme Court ruled that such contracts were securities and thus were subject to the Federal securities laws—especially the Securities Act of 1933, which imposes registration and prospectus requirements, and the Investment Company Act of 1940, under which the contracts would be regulated as mutual investment funds.[4] They were also subject to supervision by state insurance departments. Eventually, however, the Securities and Exchange Commission set up stipulations whereby life insurance companies could sell variable annuities if the assets in which the reserves were invested were segregated in special accounts. A number of companies now offer these contracts either directly or through subsidiaries, sometimes in connection with the sale of mutual funds.[5] An important legal provision in most states is

---

[3]For formulas used in calculating the value of accumulation and annuity units, see R. I. Mehr, *Life Insurance: Theory and Practice*, 4th ed., Chapter 6. Austin, Texas: Business Publications, Inc., 1970.

[4]*S.E.C. v. Variable Annuity Life Insurance Co.* (Valic), 359 U.S. 65 (1959).

[5]For a summary of the legal history of the variable annuity as sold by life insurance companies see *Institutional Investor Study Report of the Securities and Exchange Commission*, Chapter VI. 92nd Cong., 1st Sess., House Document No. 92–64, 1971.

TABLE 4-1   C.R.E.F. Unit Values v. Stock and Consumer Prices

	C.R.E.F. Values Accumulation Unit	Annuity Unit	Standard & Poor's 500 Stocks (1941–43 = 10)	B.L.S. Consumer Price Index (1967 = 100)
	(average of monthly values)	(annual)[a]	(average of monthly values)	(monthly average)
1952	$10.06[b]	$10.00[c]	$ 25.06[b]	$ 79.5
1953	9.87	9.46	24.73	80.1
1954	12.59	10.74	29.69	80.5
1955	16.44	14.11	40.49	80.2
1956	19.09	18.51	46.62	81.4
1957	18.83	16.88	44.38	84.3
1958	20.40	16.71	46.24	86.6
1959	25.72	22.03	57.38	87.3
1960	25.85	22.18	55.85	88.7
1961	30.71	26.25	66.27	89.6
1962	26.38	26.13	62.38	90.6
1963	28.93	22.68	69.87	91.7
1964	32.98	26.48	81.37	92.9
1965	36.69	28.21	88.17	94.5
1966	36.96	30.43	85.26	97.2
1967	41.64	31.92	91.93	100.0
1968	43.44	29.90	98.70	104.2
1969	42.89	32.50	97.84	109.8
1970	35.98	28.91	83.22	116.3
1971	43.18	30.64	98.29	121.3
1972	51.52	35.74	102.90	125.3
1973	44.79	31.58	107.43	133.1
1974	33.49	26.21	82.85	147.7
1975	35.68	21.84	85.17	162.1
1976	40.80	26.24	102.01	170.5

[a] As of May 1.
[b] Six months, July-December.
[c] As of July 1.
Sources: Annual Reports, T.I.A.A.-C.R.E.F., *Survey of Current Business.*

that once annuity payments begin, they must be fixed-dollar annuities. At the end of 1976, 2 million persons were covered by group and individual variable contracts. Income paid in 1976 was $183 million. Reserves totalled $9.3 billion.[6]

Variable annuity plans sold to individuals must be registered under all major Federal securities acts. They are also subject to state "blue-sky" regulations and to the control of insurance commissioners. They are still prohibited in some states; in others, some companies specialize in writing

[6] American Council of Life Insurance, *op cit.*

this form of contract. Life insurance companies offer individual contracts, but their chief interest is in group annuities for pension plans.

This new type of annuity has much to commend it. If over the long run the course of the market value of the common stocks (and reinvested dividends) coincides with or exceeds the cost of living, a hedge against inflation is obtained both while the premiums are being paid and after retirement. In the meantime, by dollar-cost averaging, advantage is taken of the variations in the market price of stocks, and much of the risk of fluctuations is minimized. In addition, the investor enjoys a tax-free accumulation of dividend income and capital gains until retirement payments begin; at retirement age his income presumably falls in a lower tax bracket. The investor must understand, however, that shorter-run fluctuations in the value of the fund can take place (as in 1962, 1966, 1970 and 1973–1974), causing sharp variations in the value of his accumulation units before retirement, and of his dollar income after retirement. The whole assumption is that the *long-run* increase in the cost of living will be more than matched by the *long-run* increase in common stock values.

Arguments raised against the variable annuity, especially against its sale by life insurance companies, are: common stocks inevitably involve risk, and no insurance company should engage in the sale of retirement benefits that are not guaranteed and that pass the risk along to the investor; there have been and will likely continue to be periods of substantial length during which common stocks have declined very sharply in value, whereas the cost of living has increased or remained relatively stable, or declined in much lesser degree (for example, September 1929–July 1932; March 1937–March 1938; October 1939–April 1942; May 1946–February 1948;April 1956–October 1957; December 1961–June 1962; February–October 1966; May 1969–June 1970; January 1973–September 1974); during a real recession period many investors will be unwilling to continue to pay premiums in the face of shrinking income and declining stock prices, thus losing the benefit of averaging.

Many investors have been attracted by the advantages of the variable annuity. In the case of individuals, the best arrangement would be the purchase of a *combination* of fixed- and variable-annuity benefits, from a company which has demonstrated its superior ability to manage a growth fund, and without the freedom to "cash out" the accumulated values prior to retirement, or at least for a waiting period of several years. Investors must be prepared to see the value of their units rise and fall with the course of the stock market, and to continue to pay their premiums through faith in the dollar-averaging process and the long-run rise in stock values.

Many investors participate in variable annuities on a group pension plan basis. The sale of variable annuities received a sharp blow in the great decline in stock prices in 1973–1974. Their continued acceptances will depend on the course of equity markets and the skill with which their portfolios are managed, together with the growth of Keogh, IRA, and tax-free annuities for the self-employed which are described later in this chapter.

Retirement Funds as Investments

Private pension funds A large and growing number of companies and nonprofit organizations now provide pension and retirement benefits to employees in both executive and rank-and-file levels. Most of these plans are voluntary; others have arisen as features of union bargaining. At the beginning of 1977 some 43 million employees were covered by over 200,000 private retirement plans. The more important reasons for the great growth of private pension plans are: growth in employment; increase in the number of persons over 65; use of such plans to increase productivity and attract and hold employees; a company sense of social responsibility; union bargaining for pensions as fringe benefits; concern over inflation (and hence the growth of investment of pension funds in common stocks); the tax structure, which permits tax-deductible contributions by employers, under qualified plans, tax-exemption of the income and capital gains of the funds, and tax-deferment of employee benefits.

Most corporate pension plans can be classified as insured (administered by insurance companies), or self-administered (or trusteed). Insured plans involve the purchase by the company of annuity contracts; the investments of the fund are managed by insurance companies. Self-administered funds are usually placed in the hands of a bank as trustee who may act as a mere custodian, or may make the investment decisions. Some trusteed plans are "actuarial" in the sense that the retirement benefits are known in advance; monthly payments are based on previous career average pay or on final year's pay. Others are "final-account-balance" funds; that is, the employee's balance is not known until his retirement. This is especially the case for plans which are based in whole or in part on profit-sharing contributions; on retirement, the balance to the employee's credit is invested in an annuity or distributed according to some other system of payment.

Pension plans vary widely with respect to the type of employees covered, the service and age requirements for eligibility to participate, the retirement age involved, the proportion of employees' versus employer's contributions, and the type of benefits received. Plans also differ as to whether the employer's contributions include a varying profit-sharing element. Wide variations also exist with respect to the number of years of credited service at which the employee is fully "vested," that is, can leave the company's service without forfeiting any of the company's contribution; his benefits would still be in effect only on retirement. Where a severed employee has contributed to the fund, the plan usually provides for repayment of his own contribution, with interest, on early retirement or severance.

The importance and growth of private pension funds in the years 1955–1975 are indicated in Table 4-2. The data include multi-employer and union-administered plans and plans of nonprofit organizations, but are dominated by those of corporate employers.

Insured plans are administered and their benefits paid by life insurance

TABLE 4-2   Private Pension Funds, 1955–1976

	1955	1960	1965	1970	1975	1976
Persons covered[a] (in millions of persons)						
Insured plans	3,800	4,900	6,200	9,300	14,980	$ 16,985
Noninsured plans	11,600	16,300	19,100	20,400	25,000	26,000[b]
	15,400	21,200	25,300	$ 29,700	39,980	$ 42,985
Contributions (in millions of dollars)						
Insured plans	$ 1,380	$ 1,490	$ 2,100	$ 3,150	$ 10,250	$ 14,715
Noninsured plans	2,460	4,040	6,270	10,790	21,430	24,000[b]
	$ 3,840	$ 5,530	$ 8,370	$ 13,940	$ 31,680	$ 38,715
Benefit payments						
Insured plans	$ 180	$ 390	$ 720	$ 1,330	$ 2,520	$ 2,735
Noninsured plans	670	1,360	2,650	6,030	12,330	13,500[b]
	$ 850	$ 1,750	$ 3,370	$ 7,360	$ 14,850	$ 16,285
Reserves or assets (book value)						
Insured plans	$11,300	$18,800	$27,300	$ 41,200	$ 71,700	$ 88,400
Noninsured plans	16,100	33,100	59,200	97,000	145,200	160,400
	$27,400	$51,900	$86,500	$138,200	$216,900	$248,800

[a]Exclusive of annuitants receiving benefits.
[b]Estimated.
Sources: U.S. Department of Health, Education and Welfare, Social Security Administration, *Social Security Bulletin;* Securities and Exchange Commission, *Statistical Bulletin;* American Council of Life Insurance, *Life Insurance Fact Book.*

companies to which funds are remitted regularly for the purchase of annuities. During his employment, the employee's claim is adjusted to changes in pay and in the company's contribution. Two main types of insured plans are administered on a group basis for each contracting employer. Under the "group deferred annuity" arrangement, the contracting employer buys a paid up annuity or contributes a specific amount for its purchase in each year for each employee. Under the "group deposit administration" plan, contributions are not made according to a predetermined fixed schedule, but are adjusted according to the plan's experience, and benefits can be flexibly determined.

A number of smaller insured plans are operated on an individual pension trust basis; that is, separate policies are maintained for each employee. Life insurance companies also administer "tax-sheltered" plans under the Keogh Act and other special arrangements for the self-employed and for small businesses. (See below.)

The size of the pension fund reserves of the various insured types was as follows at the end of 1976:[7]

[7]American Council of Life Insurance, *Life Insurance Fact Book* 1977.

Group annuities	$67.3 billion
Individual policy pension trusts	6.0
Keogh plans and tax-sheltered annuities	5.9
Other	9.2
	$88.4 billion

The data in Table 4-2 show that until recently insured private plans lagged steadily behind trusteed or uninsured plans because it was difficult to tailor the plans to suit the needs of different employers and because the type of plan in vogue—deferred annuities—did not allow flexible timing or size of contributions nor shifts in reserves among different types of investments. Insured plans showed a low rate of return compared to that produced by trusteed plans because their reserves were mingled with general insurance company assets and were subject to the restrictions on investment policy. Investment earnings of qualified insured pension plans were subject to federal income taxes until the formula for calculating insurance company taxes was changed in 1959.

In recent years insured plans have regained much lost ground. There has been a considerable shift to the more flexible deposit administration type of plan. This has been accelerated by the authorization of separate accounts for different employer's reserves rather than merging these reserves with general assets and liabilities. Separate accounts were legalized in Connecticut and New Jersey in 1959 and in New York in 1962, and are now authorized in all but a few states. They have also been made exempt from the Investment Company Act and are no longer regulated as mutual funds.[8] Separate accounts grew from $100 million in 1964 to $15.4 billion in 1976.[9]

The separate account has made possible the investment of life insurance company pension reserves in common stocks and has made insured plans much more competitive with the uninsured. Group and individual variable annuities have also given the insurance companies a more attractive package of pension wares.[10]

Uninsured (trusteed) pension and profit-sharing portfolios are managed by company committees, professional investment advisors, or the banks that serve as trustees. Frequently two or more managers are engaged to manage portions of a fund on a competitive basis. Most portfolios are free from legal restrictions with respect to the types of investments permitted. Some funds are conservatively invested and must meet strict actuarial requirements. Others are invested at considerable risk. Generally speaking, the employer's pension or retirement committee determines the general nature of the portfolio and the goals to be achieved. Investment principles and policies of uninsured funds are discussed in Chapter 23.

[8]*Institutional Investor Study Report of the* S.E.C., *op. cit.*, Chapter VI. This source contains detailed information on insured pension plans and especially on the history, organization, characteristics, and management of separate pension accounts.

[9]S.E.C. *Statistical Bulletin*, April 1977.

[10]At the beginning of 1977, there were 38,450 group variable plans covering 1,337,000 persons. American Council of Life Insurance, *op. cit.*

At the end of 1976 the assets of uninsured private pension funds reached $160 billion at book value and $174 billion at market value. Insured fund reserves totalled $88 billion at book value.[11] Total private pension fund assets are expected to reach $300 billion by 1980 and cover possibly two-thirds of the private work force.

Individual "tax-free" pension plans   The tax-exempt feature of corporate pension plans has been extended to self-employed individuals under the Keogh Act. Owners of businesses (proprietors or partners holding more than a 10% interest) may establish plans for themselves (and must include all full-time employees who have three or more years of service) whereby a part of the owner's contributions to his own plan and all of his contributions for employees may be deducted from taxable income. Earnings from this plan accumulate tax-free until withdrawn, and participants are not taxed on their benefits until distributions are actually made. Under the pension fund reform law described below, the maximum annual tax-deductible contribution was raised from $2,500 to the lesser of 15% of earned income or $7,500, to be placed in a tax-free long-term retirement account. Contributions for covered employees are a percentage of their compensation at the same rate.

Funds withheld under the Keogh plan may be invested in special U.S. Retirement Bonds which yield 3 3/4 to 5%, bank and savings and loan trust accounts, life insurance company annuities, and shares in qualified mutual investment companies. In 1976 1.2 million persons were covered by plans with reserves of $4.3 billion.[12]

Another individual investment retirement arrangement is the investment annuity. Recent amendments to the income tax code permit an individual to fund a future annuity by turning over to a financial institution some of his existing assets such as certificates of deposit, savings accounts, and even stocks and bonds. The policyholder controls the investment, and can switch it from a savings account to a CD or vice versa, or even in and out of stocks. Like the IRA plan described below, the investment annuity is funded with after-tax dollars. The policyholder is not liable for any income taxes until the annuity begins to pay off, presumably when he is in a lower tax bracket. The following example shows the accumulation (compounded semi-annually) over a 10-year period for an individual in the 30% tax bracket with funds earning 7 3/4%.

Annual Contribution	Without Investment Annuity. Net of 30% Tax	With Investment Annuity with Tax Deferred	Increase in Income
$1,000	$17,312	$21.710	$ 4,398 or 38%
$4,000	$69,252	$86,838	$17,586 or 38%

[11]S.E.C. *Statistical Bulletin.* April 1977. The total assets of all private and public pension funds, including insured and noninsured private funds, state and local government retirement funds, and Federal retirement funds including Social Security reserves, was $409 billion. *Ibid.*

[12]American Council of Life Insurance, *Pension Facts*, 1976.

Another arrangement for individual retirement accounts was provided in the Pension Reform Act of 1974 described below. This applies to employees who are either ineligible for company-sponsored plans or working for firms that have no pension plan. An individual can set up his own plan by contributing 15% of his compensation, or of his earned income if self-employed, up to a maximum of $1,500 a year. Contributions to an "IRA" account are deductible from gross income for Federal income tax purposes. Income earned is free of income tax until it is paid out. Assets in an IRA account may be kept in a trusteed or custodial account with a bank or other financial institution, in an annuity contract, or in a qualified retirement bond. (See Chapter 6.) The money set aside may also be put into certain life insurance endowment contracts.

The aphorism that a "penny saved is a penny earned" is especially true when one considers the compounding effect of contributions either to a Keogh or an IRA plan. If, for example, $7,500 were placed annually for 10 years under the Keogh plan with a savings and loan association with a passbook rate of 5 1/4% per annum, compounded daily, the accumulation would be worth $101,247.39 in 10 years. In 20 years, it would have grown to $272,399.77. A contribution of $1,500 per year would be worth $20,249.49 in 10 years and $54,479.57 in 20 years. If funds were employed at higher interest rates, the growth would be even more dramatic. Consistent saving is, of course, a prerequisite of such results. At the end of March 1976, 1.4 million persons had IRAs with reserves of $81.9 billion.[13]

Pension reform act of 1974   On Labor Day, 1974, the Employee Retirement Income Security Act of 1974 (ERISA) was signed into law. This comprehensive legislation was designed to safeguard the retirement benefits of American workers while preserving the private pension system. Basic areas covered in the Act include:

1. Enrollment of all full-time employees by age 25 after one year's service.

2. Graduated vesting rights rising to 100% vesting by 15 years of employment, thus giving workers a "claim" on their pension rights in the event of job termination.

3. Protection to surviving spouses.

4. The application of rigid funding standards to employers.

5. Easier portability of pensions for those who change jobs.

6. A mandated employer contribution to a federally operated insurance fund (The Pension Benefit Guaranty Corporation) to guarantee payment of vested benefits for defined benefit plans which are not sufficiently funded.

7. Provisions for more generous individual pension plans. (See above.)

8. Strict fiduciary responsibility applied to plan administrators (and their advisors) and trustees.

9. Reports on operations and financial condition to be submitted to participants and to the Department of Labor.

---

[13]*Ibid.*

The investment implications of this law, especially of the last point above, are indicated in Chapter 22.

State and local government retirement funds   A great increase in retirement coverage of state and local government personnel has accompanied the growth of government functions at the non-Federal level. At the end of 1976 about 10 million persons were covered by over 2,300 separate plans. One cannot generalize about the size and adequacy of the benefits received by individual members, because of the variety of plans and types of employees covered. The assets of these plans totaled $117 billion at the end of 1976. Government securities and corporate bonds predominate as investments, although a growing number of plans are now introducing some common stocks into their portfolios to provide growth and protection from inflation. The emphasis, however, remains on long-run safety of principal and assurance of income. The assets of these funds grow much more rapidly than their payout requirements. Thus in fiscal 1976 total receipts amounted to $18.8 billion while only $8.4 billion were paid out in benefits.[14] Like corporate pension funds they need little immediate recovery of principal, and what is needed is amply provided by the type of assets held. (See Chapter 22.)

The widely publicized strained finances of New York City have focused attention on the fiscal condition of other state and local government retirement plans. Major cities must fund hundreds of millions of dollars to meet future liabilities, and better disclosure of their situation is bound to be required.

Federal retirement systems   Not including Social Security, there are over a dozen retirement systems for civilian employees of the Federal government, covering over 4 million persons and holding assets (at book value) of $44 billion at the end of 1976.[15] The largest of these is the U.S. Civil Service Retirement System with over 39 million active workers on its roll. The Federal government also administers the Railroad Retirement System covering 1 million workers and holding assets of $3.1 billion (1976). The reserves of all of these plans are mainly invested in U.S. Government obligations (see p. 446).

Summary of pension plans   The growth of all pension plans (excluding Social Security) is summarized in Table 4-3. Over 55 million persons participated in these plans in 1976, and assets (at book value) totalled $428 billion—an increase of 350% since 1960.

Social Security   At the end of 1976, over 150 million persons including self-employed, had Old Age, Survivors, and Disability Insurance (OASDHI) wage credits under the Federal Social Security Act. In addition to retirement income, the legislation provides for disability insurance and other family

[14]U.S. Department of Commerce, Bureau of the Census, Finances of Employee-Retirement Systems of State and Local Governments. Washington, 1977.

[15]American Council of Life Insurance, *Life Insurance Fact Book* 1977; S.E.C. *Statistical Bulletin*, April 1977.

TABLE 4-3 Private and Public Pension Funds, 1960–1975
(numbers in millions; dollars in billions)

	Persons Covered		Assets (book value)	
	1960	1975	1960	1976
Private[a]				
Insured funds	4.9	15.0	$18.8	$ 88.4
Noninsured funds	16.3	25.0 (est)	33.1	160.4
	21.2	40.0 (est)	$51.9	$248.8
Public				
State and local	5.1	10.8	19.6	117.2
Federal[b]	2.6	6.6	16.4	62.3
	7.7	17.4	$36.0	$179.5
Total	28.9	57.4	$87.9	$428.3

[a]Includes funds of corporations, multiemployer and union funds, and those of nonprofit organizations.
[b]Includes Civil Service Retirement program (various) and Railroad Retirement funds. Excludes Old Age, Survivors, and Disability Insurance.
Sources: American Council of Life Insurance, *Life Insurance Fact Book;* Securities and Exchange Commission, *Statistical Bulletin.*

benefits before retirement, survivors' life insurance, and hospital-medical benefits. During working years employees and their employers, and self-employed persons, pay Social Security contributions which are placed in special funds. Monthly cash benefits are paid when the worker retires, dies, or becomes disabled. Thirty-two million persons received $64.7 billion in benefits in 1975.[16] At the end of 1976, OASDHI reserves totalled $35 billion.

For persons who meet the eligibility requirements (the required number of "quarters" of covered earnings), the maximum monthly retirement benefits at age 65, based on average annual earnings after 1950 (to a maximum of $16,500), were $474 a month (as of 1977).[17] The maximum monthly income to survivors (widow with two or more minor children) was $830. Workers who have become disabled are entitled to disability benefits that are functions of age and years of credited work. The system also provides a lump-sum death benefit of three times the monthly retirement payment with a maximum of $255.[18]

In 1965 hospitalization ("Medicare A") was added to the Social Security program. With few exceptions, persons aged 65 or over become automatically eligible for hospital insurance. Additional medical (doctor bill) insurance ("Medicare B") is obtained (as of 1977) with a premium of $7.70 a month which is matched by the Federal government.[19]

[16]American Council of Life Insurance, *op. cit.*

[17]Benefits at this level are not payable until later, because it will take some time for average earnings to reach $16,500 and the maximum creditable earnings for earlier years are at lower levels.

[18]For details on qualifications for coverage, benefits, conditions producing full or partial benefits after retirement, definition of "self-employed," and other provisions, see U.S. Department of Health, Education and Welfare, *Social Security Handbook on Old-Age, Survivors, and Disability Insurance.* Washington, D.C.: Government Printing Office, 1969. All changes through 1974 are explained in Commerce Clearing House, Inc., *Social Security and Medicare Explained.* New York, 1974.

[19]For details, see U.S. Department of Health, Education and Welfare, Social Security Administration, *Your Medicare Handbook*, available at Social Security offices.

The cost of Federal Social Security, including hospitalization, is financed by an employment tax that, in early 1977, was 5.85% paid by both employer and employee on the first $16,500 of income. Self-employed persons are eligible for benefits and pay 1 1/2 times the employee tax. "Medicare B" premiums were an additional $7.70 a month in 1977.

Social Security benefits form the foundation on which the investor can expand his provision for insurance and retirement income. Many private retirement plans have been adjusted to make Social Security the first portion of a larger plan, since for many investors the benefits are more generous than they would be if based on actuarial calculations.

REFERENCES

BAILARD, T. E., et al., *Personal Money Management*. Chicago: Science Research Associates, 1973.

BANKERS TRUST COMPANY, *Study of Corporate Pension Plans*. New York: Bankers Trust Company, 1975.

BELTH, J. M., *Life Insurance: A Consumer's Handbook*. Bloomington, Ind.: Indiana University Press, 1975.

BOGEN, J. I., ed., *Financial Handbook*, 4th rev. ed., Sec. 19. New York: The Ronald Press Company, 1968.

BOOTH, PHILIP, *Social Security in America*. Ann Arbor: University of Michigan-Wayne State University, 1973.

CAMPBELL, P. A., *The Variable Annuity*. Hartford, Conn.: Connecticut General Life Insurance Company, 1969.

CASEY, W. J., *Life Insurance Planning*. New York: Institute for Business Planning, Inc., 1975 (Loose leaf).

COHEN, J. B., and A. W. HANSON, *Personal Finance: Principles and Case Problems*, 6th ed. Homewood, Ill.: Richard D. Irwin, Inc., 1972.

COMMERCE CLEARING HOUSE, *Social Security and Medicare Explained*. Chicago: Commerce Clearing House, Inc., 1974.

———, *Pension Plans Guide*, rev. ed. New York: Commerce Clearing House, Inc., 1975.

———, *Pension Reform Act of 1974*. Chicago: Commerce Clearing House, Inc., 1974.

COSTELLO, MARY, *Social Security Financing*. Washington, D.C.: Editorial Research Reports, 1972.

DONALDSON, E. F., and J. K. PFAHL, *Personal Finance*, 5th ed. New York: The Ronald Press Company, 1971.

Employee Pensions in State and Local Governments. New York: The Tax Foundation, Inc., 1976.

GREENOUGH, W. C., *A New Approach to Retirement Income*. New York: Teachers Insurance and Annuity Association, 1964.

———, and F. P. KING, *Pension Plans and Public Policy*. New York: Columbia University Press, 1976.

Handbook On Pension Reform Law; Employee Retirement Income Security Act of 1974. Englewood Cliffs, N.J.: Prentice-Hall, Inc., 1974.

HASTINGS, PAUL, and NORBERT MIETUS, *Personal Finance.* New York: Holt, Rinehart & Winston, 1972.

HOFFMAN, G. V., and J. S. ROSENBLOOM, *Personal Financial Planning.* New York: McGraw-Hill Book Co., 1975.

HUEBNER, S. S., and KENNETH BLACK, JR., *Life Insurance,* 9th ed. New York: Appleton-Century-Crofts, 1976.

Institutional Investor Study Report of the Securities and Exchange Commission, Chapter VI, and Supplementary Volume I, Chapters 2 and 5. 92nd Congress, 1st Session, House Document No. 92–64, 1971.

JACOBS, DONALD, et al., *Financial Institutions,* 5th ed. Homewood, Ill.: Richard D. Irwin, Inc., 1972.

JOHNSON, G. E., *Variable Annuities.* Washington, D.C.: The Reprint Company, 1970.

McGILL, D. M., *Preservation of Pension Benefit Rights.* Homewood, Ill.: Richard D. Irwin, Inc., 1972.

MACHINERY and ALLIED PRODUCTS INSTITUTE, *Social Security and Private Pension Plans.* Washington, D.C.: The Institute, 1972.

MACKIN, J. P., *Protecting Purchasing Power in Retirement: A Study of Public Employment Retirement Systems.* New York: Fleet Academic Editions, Inc., 1971.

MATTESON, W. J., *Life Insurance and Annuities from the Buyer's Point of View.* Gt. Barrington, Mass.: American Institute for Economic Research, 1969.

MEHR, R. I., *Life Insurance: Theory and Practice,* 4th ed. Austin, Texas: Business Publications, Inc., 1970.

MELONE, J. J., and E. T. ALLEN, *Pension Planning: Pension, Profit-Sharing and Other Deferred Compensation Plans,* rev. ed. Homewood, Ill.: Richard D. Irwin, Inc., 1972.

MURRAY, R. F., *Economic Aspects of Pensions: A Summary Report.* New York: National Bureau of Economic Research, 1968.

Pension Facts. New York: American Council of Life Insurance, annual.

Pensions and Pension Plans: Selected References 1971–1974. Washington, D.C.: U.S. Department of Labor, 1974.

POLAKOFF, M. E. et al., *Financial Institutions and Markets,* Chapters 7, 8. Boston, Mass.: Houghton Mifflin Co., 1970.

PORTER, SYLVIA, *Sylvia Porter's Money Book.* Garden City, N.Y.: Doubleday & Co., Inc., 1975.

Private and Public Pension Plans: The New Legislation and Future Prospects. Washington: Machinery and Allied Products Institute, 1975.

SCHOTTLAND, C. I., *The Social Security Program in the United States,* 2nd ed. New York: Appleton-Century-Crofts, 1970.

SCHULZ, JAMES, *Pension Reform in the U.S. and Abroad.* Hanover, N.H.: University Press of New England, 1974.

SHORE, WARREN, *Social Security: The Fraud in Your Future.* New York: Macmillan Publishing Co., Inc., 1975.

STILLMAN, R. J., *Guide to Personal Finance.* Englewood Cliffs, N.J.: Prentice-Hall, Inc., 1975.

STOEBER, EDWARD A., *Pension Reform Act Explained: New Guidelines for Corporate, Keogh and Individual Retirement Plans.* Cincinnati, Ohio: The National Underwriter Company, 1974.

UNGER, M. A., and H. A. WOLF, *Personal Finance*, 3rd ed. Boston: Allyn and Bacon, 1972.

————, *Employee Retirement Systems of State and Local Governments*, 1967 Census of Governments. Topical Volume 6, Studies No. 2, Washington, D.C., 1968.

U.S. DEPARTMENT OF COMMERCE, BUREAU OF THE CENSUS, *Finances of Employee Retirement Systems of State and Local Governments.* Washington, D.C.: The Bureau, annual.

U.S. SENATE, 94th Congress Committee on Finance, *The Social Security Act (as amended through January 4, 1975) and Related Laws.* Washington, D.C.: U.S. Government Printing Office, 1975.

U.S. SOCIAL SECURITY ADMINISTRATION, *Social Security Handbook; Your Social Security; and Your Medicare Handbook.* Washington, D.C.: revised periodically.

WIDICUS, W. W., and E. T. STITZEL, *Personal Investing.* Homewood, Ill.: Richard D. Irwin, Inc., 1976.

Deposit-type Investments: United States Savings Bonds

SCOPE: This chapter discusses the investment aspects of claims against institutions that hold the liquid savings of individuals, pay a modest return on those savings, and stand ready to provide cash on demand or on short notice. Following the presentation of data on total savings, the order of discussion is: (1) savings and time deposits in commercial banks, (2) deposits in mutual savings banks, (3) accounts in savings and loan associations, (4) shares in credit unions, (5) the "Financial Institutions Act," and (6) U. S. Savings bonds.

United States Savings bonds differ from deposits in form, and are the obligations of the U. S. Government. But they have many characteristics of deposit-type investments and the general motives behind their purchase are similar to those pertaining to the deposit group; hence, they are included here.

Other major "savings" media—life insurance, annuities, private pension plans, and government retirement funds—were discussed in the previous chapter.

Growth of Institutional Savings

The liquid portion of the great and growing accumulation of personal savings is represented in large part by the increase over the years in the accounts of the institutions that receive such savings and, in turn, make them available to the investment market. The year-end figures given in Table 5-1 are indicative of the trend. Table 5-1 reveals the enormous accumulation of financial savings in deposit-type and other major financial intermediaries, and in U.S. Savings bonds. Intermediaries are institutions that pool savings and funnel them into the money and capital markets. The deposit-type or "thrift" institutions appeal chiefly to the smaller investors who seek safety and liquidity, but who have difficulty gaining access to markets directly, or prefer not to invest directly. Such investors also value the deposit insurance feature. The exception is the appeal of large-denomination bank certificates of deposit to large investors. Insurance-type institutions serve all types of investors. Savings bonds appeal chiefly to the small investor for safety of principal and other features.

Savings and loan accounts and the various pension and retirement fund reserves show the greatest relative increase in the 21 years covered in Table

TABLE 5-1 Institutional Savings, 1955–1976
(in billions of dollars)

	1955	1960	1965	1970	1976
Deposit-type					
Commercial bank savings and time deposits	$48.4	$71.6	$146.7	$231.1	$501.5
Mutual savings bank deposits	28.1	36.3	52.4	71.6	122.8
Savings and loan association accounts	32.1	62.1	110.4	146.4	336.0
Credit union shares and deposits	2.4	5.0	9.2	15.4	39.3
Postal Savings deposits	1.9	0.8	0.3[a]	—	—
U.S. Savings bonds (redemption value)	57.9	47.2	50.3	52.5	72.3
Insurance-type					
Life insurance company reserves[b]	74.8	97.7	126.2	164.0	259.2
Uninsured private pension fund reserves (book value)	16.1	33.1	59.2	97.0	160.4
State and local govt. retirement fund reserves	10.7	19.6	33.1	58.1	117.2
Federal insurance and retirement fund reserves[c]	15.8	17.4	21.4	33.1	62.3

[a]The Postal Savings System was discontinued in March 1966.
[b]Includes insurance, annuity, and pension fund reserves.
[c]Excludes Social Security Fund.

Sources: Federal Reserve Bulletin; National Association of Mutual Savings Banks, *National Fact Book;* United States Savings and Loan League, *Savings and Loan Fact Book;* Credit Union National Association, *Credit Union Yearbook;* American Council of Life Insurance, *Life Insurance Fact Book;* Securities and Exchange Commission, *Statistical Bulletin; Treasury Bulletin.*

5-1. As indicated in Chapter 3, the role in the capital and money markets of the institutions holding these savings, along with other financial intermediaries, cannot be overemphasized.

In this chapter, as in Chapter 4, we are concerned with the investment aspects of placing money with intermediaries. In Chapters 21 and 22 we shall see what the intermediaries do with the money.

Interest-Bearing Deposits in Commercial Banks

Most of the 46,000 banking offices in the United States operated by the 14,400 commercial banks furnish savings facilities. About half of the interest-bearing deposits consist of ordinary savings accounts which have no specific maturity, are not subject to check, are available only to individuals, and on which the bank has the legal right (rarely exercised) to require 30 days' notice of intention of withdrawal.

In addition to ordinary savings accounts, two other major types of interest-bearing accounts are available: (1) nonnegotiable time deposits in various denominations and maturities (including multiple-maturities), and (2) negotiable certificates of deposit (CDs) in large denominations (generally $100,000 and over).

The interest rates paid on savings and time deposits by member banks are subject to Regulation Q of the Board of Governors of the Federal Reserve System. Interest may not exceed the maximum rate payable by state banks on like deposits under the laws of the state in which the bank is located. In recent years the competition for funds among banks has been working to the advantage of the saver, for interest rates on savings and time accounts have shown a substantial increase. Because they must maintain greater liquidity, commercial banks neither earn nor pay as much on their thrift accounts as do savings and loan associations.

The following schedule shows the maximum interest rates that member banks were permitted to pay on various savings accounts, as of July 1977.

	Annual Rate	Effective Annual Rate If Compounded Daily
Regular savings	5.0%	5.13%
90-day time deposit open accounts	5.50%	5.65%
Other (less than $100,000)		
90 days to 1 year	5.50%	5.65%
1 to 2 1/2 years	6.0%	6.18%
2 1/2 years or more	6.50%	6.72%
4 to 6 years (minimum $1000)	7.25%	7.52%
6 years or more (minimum $1000)	7.50%	7.79%
$100,000 or more	no limit	no limit

All national and most state banks are members of the Federal Deposit Insurance Corporation (FDIC), which insures individual accounts up to $40,000. For this reason most depositors in insured banks need not be concerned about the ultimate safety of their funds. They have liquid assets drawing a modest rate of return. At the end of 1976, 98% of all commercial banks were insured. These banks held 99% of all commercial bank deposits. The proportion of insured to total deposits in insured banks was 67%.[1]

The savings account offers safety, immediate recovery of principal, convenience, and modest income. No tax advantages are enjoyed, as interest on accounts is fully taxable. Such accounts, together with time accounts, are mainly useful as a cash reserve and for accumulating funds to be invested later in other types of investment media. Negotiable certificates of deposit bear higher yields and are more comparable to short-term securities as an investment medium. (See Chapter 10.)

How commercial banks invest the funds placed with them in savings and time deposits is discussed in Chapter 21.

Growth of negotiable CDs During 1973–1975 the volume of large denomination bank certificates of deposit reached record heights, rising to $93 billion in January 1975. This growth reflected the appeal of unusually

[1] *Annual Report of the Federal Deposit Insurance Corporation*, 1977.

high interest rates, which reached 13 1/2 per cent in mid-1974, and attracted funds from investors disillusioned with the stock market, and from individuals and companies who drew surplus funds from checking accounts and (in the case of individuals) from regular savings accounts. Corporations and other organizations, using sophisticated methods of forecasting cash flows, switched idle cash into CDs and other money-market instruments. (See Chapter 10.) The volume of CDs has remained substantial although declining to $59 billion in May 1977 when interest rates had declined to 5 1/4 per cent, increasing to $65 billion in October 1977.

New developments In November 1975, commercial banks were permitted to open regular savings accounts for corporations in amounts up to $150,000. And the Federal Reserve authorized member banks to offer transfer service by telephone, between savings and checking accounts, which has encouraged more efficient cash management.

Deposits in Mutual Savings Banks

Importance of the group The 473 mutual savings banks (with 2,080 branches) are chartered in eighteen states, primarily in the New England and Middle Atlantic States. Nearly three-quarters of the banks are located in New York, Massachusetts, and Connecticut, and over 78 per cent of savings deposits are located in these three states. There are only 8 such banks in the Middle West and 11 on the Pacific Coast (Washington, Oregon, and Alaska). Such institutions appeal especially to the small investor who requires a maximum of safety. As explained in Chapter 21, savings banks are permitted to invest their deposits solely in those securities and mortgages that are approved by law.

Although mutual savings banks comprised only 10 per cent of all banks in the United States at the end of 1976, they held 19 per cent of the nation's savings and time deposits. Table 5-2 shows their combined assets and liabilities in summarized form.

Of interest here is that the ratio of capital funds to deposits was 7.3%; cash and U.S. Government and agency obligations covered deposits by 9.1%.

Character of deposits Mutual savings banks are organized without capital stock, and net earnings are distributed to depositors as interest. Earnings above established interest rates are carried to the general reserve (surplus) account, which belongs to the depositors. Each depositor has an equitable share in the surplus, irrespective of the period of his deposit. The mutuals operate under the direction of self-perpetuating boards of trustees and are chartered and supervised by state banking authorities.

About 61% of deposits are ordinary passbook accounts. The remainder are "special" deposits, including time or term accounts with specific maturities. No deposits are payable on demand. In the case of passbook accounts, a rarely exercised right is reserved to require notice of intention of withdrawal, varying from 10 days to 90 days in the various states. Over

TABLE 5-2   Condensed Statement, Mutual Savings Banks
December 31, 1976 (in millions of dollars)

		Amount	Percentage of Total
	Assets		
Cash and balances with banks		$ 2,355	1.7%
U.S. Govt. and agency obligations		9,109	6.7
Municipal bonds		2,417	1.8
Corporate and other bonds		26,143	19.4
Corporate stocks		4,381	3.2
Mortgage loans (net)		81,630	60.6
Other loans		5,183	3.8
Real estate and other assets		3,594	2.7
Total		$134,812	100.0%
	Liabilities		
Deposits[a]		$122,877	91.2
Other liabilities		2,884	2.1
General reserve accounts		9,051	6.7
Total		$134,812	100.0%

[a]Virtually all deposits are time deposits.

Sources: National Association of Mutual Savings Banks, *National Fact Book* (New York: The Association, 1977) ; *Federal Reserve Bulletin.*

their long history, mutual savings banks have maintained an excellent safety record. While only a portion of the mutuals have chosen to join the Federal Deposit Insurance Corporation,[2] their enviable record, financial strength, insurance of deposits (in some cases), and strict state regulation provide the same safety and liquidity that can be enjoyed through commercial bank savings accounts. Only a few mutuals have chosen to join the Federal Reserve System. In New York State the banks have, however, subscribed to stock in two central organizations of their own, both formed in 1933—the Savings Banks Trust Company, which advances funds to members on the security of bond investments, and the Institutional Securities Corporation, formed to purchase mortgages from member banks.

The amount of deposits that can be accepted from one person by any one bank is limited, for example, to $15,000 (exclusive of accrued interest) in New York and to $25,000 in New Jersey. This discourages large "investment" accounts that might be withdrawn in full on short notice. The rate of interest paid on deposits varies with changes in money- and capital-market conditions. Competition for funds was especially severe from the period of the "credit crunch" of 1966 through the next "crunch" in the spring of 1970, and again in 1973–1974. Ceiling or maximum rates are set by the individual states and range (1977) from 5 1/4% on ordinary passbook deposits to as high as 7 3/4% on time deposits of one year or more to maturity, depending on size. Rates

[2]As of December 31, 1976, 331 mutual banks were insured by the FDIC, while all others were insured by state funds. [National Association of Mutual Savings Banks, *National Fact Book* (New York: The Association, 1977).] Balances in mutual savings banks in Massachusetts are insured by the Mutual Savings Central Fund and in Connecticut by the Savings Banks Deposit Guarantee Fund.

usually exceed those paid on commercial bank time and savings accounts and are about equal to those paid by most savings and loan associations on accounts of similar size and maturites.

Summary and recent developments The mutual savings bank provides a safe place for small savings, legal protection, modest income, and a convenient means of accumulating a reserve fund. Although the savings departments of commercial banks provide substantially the same service, they often pay a lower rate of interest.

A growing development in the savings bank field has been the sale of life insurance policies by savings banks in Massachusetts (since 1907), New York (since 1938), and Connecticut (since 1941). Such policies have the advantages of lower premiums (owing to lack of sales commissions and a lower rate of lapse) and a higher initial cash-surrender value. At the beginning of 1977, $9 billion of such protection was in force.[3]

Like savings deposits in commercial banks, mutual savings bank deposits are safe, liquid, convenient, and produce modest income. The income is fully taxable. How the deposits are invested by the banks is discussed in Chapter 21.

Accounts in Savings and Loan Associations

General characteristics Savings and loan associations are devoted almost entirely to the accumulation of funds in savers' accounts and the investment of these funds in urban mortgage loans. There were approximately 4,860 savings and loan associations with combined assets, at the end of 1976, of $392 billion. They are currently the source of 47% of the dollar amount of all home loans. The old building and loan associations, chartered only by states, were organized primarily for the purpose of cooperative home financing. Since the early 1930s, however, the depository function has grown in importance, and today the savings and loan associations are actively competing with banks and insurance companies for the thrift funds of individuals. Their rapid growth is indicated by the data on savings in Table 5-1.

Federal associations are chartered under legislation passed in 1932 which set up the Home Loan Bank Board. They are mutual in type, that is, owned by depositors who elect the directors. They are examined and supervised by the Federal Home Loan Bank Board, and must have their accounts insured by the Federal Savings and Loan Insurance Corporation (FSLIC). At the end of 1976, 2019 associations, or 42% of all associations, were operating with federal charters. They controlled 57% of the total assets of the industry.

State-chartered associations (2,839, or 58% of the total) now control 43% of industry assets. They are supervised and examined by their respective banking or savings and loan departments or commissioners. 2107 state

---

[3]National Association of Mutual Savings Banks, *National Fact Book*, 1977.

associations are mutuals; the other are organized in some twenty states, notably California, Illinois, Ohio, and Texas, whose statutes permit "permanent stock associations," owned and managed by shareholders. This type had $87 billion of assets at the end of 1976.

Status of the accounts Originally, savings and loan associations were not depositories. Savers placed funds in associations, invested in "shares." Depositors in banks received interest; accountholders in savings and loan associations received dividends, after provision for operating expenses and reserves. In the course of time, state-chartered associations developed the passbook account. And in many states court decisions confirmed that accounts in savings associations and in banks were identical in that the holder is a creditor. Under the Housing and Urban Development Act of 1968, federally chartered associations are permitted to describe accounts as "deposits" and to refer to earnings on accounts as "interest." In short, associations are real depository institutions.

Associations are permitted to offer a variety of accounts. Regular passbook accounts comprise about 40% of deposits. (Some associations issue variable rate accounts bearing higher rates than those paid on ordinary accounts and which must be maintained for at least a year.) The certificate account is the other major type of savings instrument. Certificates are issued in fixed maximum amounts with fixed maturities.

Interest rate ceilings, set by the Federal Home Loan Bank Board and/or state authorities, are presently (1977) 5 1/4% on regular passbook accounts, 5 3/4% on certificates of from 90 days to 1 year in maturity (with various minimum denominations), and 6 1/2 to 7 3/4% on maturities of 2 to 6 years or more. Yields on all of these are higher if held to maturity with interest compounded daily. Actual rates paid vary from state to state to reflect different competitive conditions. The great flow of savings funds into savings and loan associations in 1971–1972, together with the decline in interest rates earned on mortgages, put downward pressure on interest rates paid on deposits. But with the very sharp rise in yields on money-market instruments and bonds in 1973–1975, disintermediation took place and was not reversed until the second quarter of 1975.

The savings and loan account is not a demand account; checks cannot be written against it. From 70 to 80% of the assets of the typical association consist of mortgage loans on owner-occupied homes which the borrower pays back in regular monthly installments. The liquidity provided by a commercial bank is not to be expected under these conditions. Associations are prepared to meet ordinary withdrawals (retirements of shares) on demand; some require 30 days' notice for withdrawals, except in cases of real emergency. When unable to meet withdrawals, the Federal- and most state-chartered associations require the holders of accounts to file written applications for withdrawal. The institution must then either pay the amount of withdrawal requested within 30 days or apply at least one-third and in some states as much as two-thirds of cash receipts to the holders of accounts in the order of filing; holders of an account in Federal associations applying for more than $1,000 receive that amount and their applications are renumbered and placed at the end of the list. The right is also given to the board of directors to repurchase not more than $200 of any one account in any month without regard to other provisions.

In recent years almost all associations have been meeting requests for funds in full on demand or on relatively short notice. Cash reserves, availability of loans from the Federal Home Loan Banks (FHLB), and the large holdings of government securities provided sufficient liquidity, save for a few failures in 1973–1975. Mergers have strengthened many situations. However, the generally less liquid character of the assets should not be overlooked. Since September 1950 the manner of insurance settlement in case of default has been virtually identical for insured banks and insured savings and loan associations. The FDIC (or the FSLIC) pays insured deposits (or accounts) either by cash or by making available to each insured depositor (or accountholder) a transferred balance in a new insured institution in the same community or in another insured institution. All Federal savings and loan associations and 2,025 state associations carry and pay for insurance (up to $40,000 per account) with the FSLIC, established in 1934. Together such associations carry about 98% of the entire savings and loan resources of the country and thus represent the industry.

As of 1976 the FSLIC had assets of $4.5 billion, of which nearly 95% consisted of cash and U.S. Government obligations. It insured accounts of 4404 institutions with combined assets of $383 billion. The savings in these institutions totalled about $375 billion, of which 98% was fully insured.[4]

The well-managed savings and loan association provides a safe place for savings. The investor cannot expect to receive the higher returns paid by associations as a result of their earnings on mortgages (in comparison with rates paid on bank savings accounts) and be assured of the same liquidity.

Statement of condition　　The statement (Table 5-3) for all savings and loan associations and cooperative banks at the end of 1976 indicates the character of their work and the protection afforded accountholders. Cash and government bonds were 10.6% of accounts. The showing of individual associations in this respect would cover a wide range. The investor should obtain a recent statement of his local association and inquire carefully into its conditions and management. Of special importance is the proportion of reserves and undivided profits to share capital, the liquidity position, and the quality of the mortgage portfolio.[5] Associations whose accounts are insured by the FSLIC are required to allocate to reserves each year an amount that will meet minimum "benchmark" and other requirements.[6] In addition, the Federal Home Loan Bank Board is authorized to

---

[4]United States League of Savings Associations, _Savings and Loan Fact Book_, 1977.

[5]The investment policy and restrictions on investments of savings and loan associations are discussed in Chapter 21.

[6]These are determined by the ratio of net worth to specified assets (balance due on conventional mortgage loans plus 20% of the balance due on VA and FHA loans). By the end of the thirtieth year, and for each year thereafter, accumulated reserves must equal at least 7% of total savings accounts. In addition, an association must maintain a net worth equal to its benchmark reserves plus 20% of "scheduled items" (loans delinquent 90 days or more).

TABLE 5-3 Combined Statement of Condition of All Savings and Loan Associations, December 31, 1976 (in millions of dollars)

	Amount	Percentage of Total
Assets		
Cash on hand and in banks / Investment securities	$ 35,660	9.1%
Mortgage loans	323,130	82.4
F.H.L.B. stock	2,800	0.7
Real estate owned	1,900	0.5
All other assets	28,509	7.3
Total	$391,999	100.0%
Liabilities and Reserves		
Savings balances	$336,030	85.7%
Borrowed money	19,087	4.9
Loans in process	6,836	1.7
All other liabilities	8,015	2.1
Net worth	22,031	5.6
Total	$391,999	100.0%

Source: Prepared by the United States League of Savings Associations from reports of the Federal Home Loan Bank Board and state supervisory authorities.

establish "liquidity requirements" (cash and U.S. securities) within a range of 4 to 10% of total savings and borrowings payable. This rate has varied with the times and was 7% in 1977 [7]

Federal Home Loan Banks The Federal Home Loan Bank Board supervises Federal savings and loan associations, the FSLIC, and the eleven regional Federal Home Loan Banks. All Federal associations are required to hold stock in the Federal Home Loan Banks; other stockholders consist of state associations electing membership, and a few savings banks and insurance companies. The required member institution stockholdings are now 1 % of outstanding mortgage assets, plus 1/12 of the debt to the regional Bank (if debt equals or exceeds 12 % of total loans). The chief source of funds of the Federal Home Loan Banks has been the issuance of consolidated notes and debentures, of which $16.8 billion were outstanding at the end of 1976. (See p. 92.) This represented a substantial decline from the peak figure of $21.9 billion at the end of 1974. The reduction reflects the influx of new funds into the associations in 1975, part of which was used to reduce borrowings.

An important function of the Federal Home Loan Banks is to make loans to members against home mortgages, government bonds, or stock in the Banks assigned as security. The charter of a Federal association permits it to borrow up to one-half of its capital (savings accounts plus earnings credited

[7]In addition, short-term Government securities must equal 3% of savings and borrowings payable on demand or due in 1 year or less.

thereto). The amount that may be borrowed from sources other than a Federal Home Loan Bank is limited to one-tenth of such capital. However, with prior approval of the Federal Home Loan Bank Board, the association may borrow an unlimited amount from its Federal Home Loan Bank, upon such terms as may be required by the Bank. This gives the Banks considerable control over the supply of mortgage credit.

The Federal Home Loan Bank Board sets limits on the rates paid by associations on savings accounts, by withholding bank loans for those that do not abide by its maximum requirements, and, as we have seen, establishes reserve and liquidity requirements.

Negotiable Order of Withdrawal (NOW) accounts Federal regulations affect the kinds of deposits that banks and savings institutions may accept. Banks are not permitted to pay interest on checking accounts, and savings institutions are barred from offering checking accounts. As a result of an underlying dissatisfaction with these regulations, negotiable order of withdrawal (NOW) accounts were permitted by the Federal Government to be introduced on a trial basis in Massachusetts and New Hampshire. Subsequently, they have spread to other states in New England.[8] NOW accounts allow transfers of funds from no-passbook savings accounts to other parties. They thus combine the convenience of a checking account with the income of savings bank interest. Investors must weigh the interest received against the charge for check-writing privileges. In some cases the annual charge for writing checks may exceed the benefits received.

Financial Institutions Act

The brief experience with NOW accounts suggests that the traditional service identities of banks and other institutions are becoming blurred. Savings and loan institutions, chafing under traditional regulations, have sought freedom to expand their operations by offering a comprehensive package of services. Dissatisfaction with the *status quo* was expressed in the Hunt Report of 1971 (The Report of the President's Commission on Financial Structure and Regulation) which sought to liberalize the activities of depositary institutions.

No Congressional action was taken on the Hunt Report. In August 1973 "The President's Recommendations for Changes in the U.S. Financial System" were submitted to Congress. In 1973 and 1975, proposed legislation entitled the "Financial Institutions Act" (FIA) was sent to Congress. A House subcommittee was appointed to undertake a study of "Financial Institutions and the Nation's Economy" (FINE).

The FIA and the FINE recommendations would grant new powers to thrift institutions to improve their ability to compete for savings. Ceilings on interest rate would be eliminated 5 1/2 years from the enactment of the FIA.

[8]By court decision, NOW accounts were phased out May 31, 1976, in New York State.

The proposed legislation would also provide broader new lending and investing powers:

1. Thrift institutions would be permitted to engage in trust activities.
2. Lending powers to consumers would be expanded.
3. Thrift institutions could invest in commercial paper, brokers' acceptances, and corporate debt.
4. Thrift institutions could make construction loans not necessarily tied to permanent financing.
5. Savings and loan associations would be permitted to offer checking accounts where state-chartered associations are permitted to do so.
6. Commercial banks, along with savings institutions, would receive mortgage interest tax credits; the credit would be limited to mortgages on properties for low- and moderate-income owners and renters.
7. Federally chartered commercial banks could offer negotiable orders of withdrawal (NOW) accounts to both individuals and corporations.

No legislative action has been taken (as of 1977) on these proposals for transforming savings banks and associations into "full service" operations, but continued study may very well lead to much more competition among financial institutions, despite opposition by the commercial banks.

Shares in Credit Unions

Credit unions are nonprofit Federal- or state-chartered thrift organizations formed to serve the members of a particular group such as the employees of a business firm or government office, or members of a church, trade union, or fraternal organization. The credit union is managed by officers and directors elected by the members, and its activities and accounting are subject to strict governmental regulation. The savings of the members are pooled and made available to members through loans. Savings are represented by shares in the union, on which annual dividends of up to 7 % are now (1977) paid. Installment loans are made for a variety of consumer purposes, and any earnings remaining after expenses and legal reserves are returned in the form of dividends.

Although legally a sixty-day notice of withdrawal may be required, most credit unions make a practice of repurchasing shares on demand, so that the shares are considered savings accounts by most members. The investor should check the management of the union, its cash and government bond holdings, and the adequacy of its reserves. (Federal credit unions are required to add 20 % of annual net earnings each year until they are built up to a total of 10 % of shares outstanding.)

In October 1970, by Federal statute, federally chartered unions were required, and state-chartered unions could elect, to apply for share account insurance of $40,000 per account through the National Credit Union Administration. This places the shares of insured unions on the same protected basis as the deposits of banks and savings and loan associations. By 1976, all Federal unions had qualified for insurance, and 40 % of state-chartered organizations had joined. In some states, state insurance systems have been set up.

The National Credit Union Administration replaces the former Bureau of Federal Credit Unions under the U.S. Department of Health, Education, and Welfare. The Administration, through six regional offices, examines and supervises all aspects of federally chartered unions' operations.

As of December 1976, there were 23,000 credit unions operating in the United States and Territories, with total assets of $44.8 billion Total savings (shares and deposits) amounted to $39 billion. These provided funds for loans to 34 million members.[9]

A number of credit unions have managed to move into third-party payments by offering "share-drafts" which are, in effect, checks. Interest is not paid on that portion of a member's account that covers his draft.[10]

U.S. Savings Bonds

Although Savings bonds could logically be considered in Chapter 6 on Federal obligations, it seems more appropriate to discuss them in the section devoted to savings types of investments because Savings bonds "compete" with the deposit types of investments for the liquid savings of millions of investors.

Amount outstanding   United States Savings bonds were first issued in 1935 to furnish a medium of investment for the savings of individuals and to help meet Federal deficits. During World War II, great emphasis was placed on the accumulation of these bonds, and in the post-World War II and post-Korean War periods the Treasury Department has persisted in maintaining the interest of investors in these securities. New forms have been developed, and the terms of the older bonds have been changed to make them more attractive.

The growth in importance of this medium of saving is indicated by Table 5-4 showing the amounts outstanding (at redemption value) and the character of ownership at the end of selected years.

Following the large issuance during the war, the outstanding amount of Savings bonds, particularly Series E bonds, continued to increase until 1951, when new sales and the current accrual of redemption values began to fall behind redemptions, reaching the low point in 1960. Since then a modest annual excess of new sales over redemptions has resulted in a moderate increase in the outstanding total.

---

[9]*Credit Union*, March 1977; *Federal Reserve Bulletin.*

[10]In spring 1977 Federal credit unions were authorized to make 30-year mortgage loans, unsecured loans of up to 15 years, and loans on mobile homes.

TABLE 5-4 Savings Bonds Outstanding
(in billions of dollars)

| Year | Held by | | Total |
(December 31)	Individuals	Others	Outstanding
1940	$ 2.8	$0.4	$ 3.2
1945	42.9	5.3	48.2
1950	49.6	8.4	58.0
1955	50.2	7.7	57.9
1960	45.7	1.5	47.2
1965	49.7	0.6	50.3
1970	52.1	0.4	52.5
1971	54.4	0.5	54.9
1972	57.7	0.4	58.1
1973	60.3	0.5	60.8
1974	63.4	0.4	63.8
1975	67.3	0.6	67.9
1976	72.0	0.3	72.3

Sources: *Treasury Bulletin; Federal Reserve Bulletin.*

Types Savings bonds are now issued in two series: E and H.

Series E Bonds The distinctive features of the Series E bonds are:

These bonds are issued in denominations ranging from $25 to $10,000 maturity value.

The bonds do not bear any stated rate of interest, but are sold at 75 % of face value. The 25 % accumulation when the bond is due represents its interest to maturity. Bonds issued to May 1, 1952, had a maturity of ten years and produced 2.9 % at maturity. The maturity period was reduced and the yield to maturity was increased six times in order to make the bonds more attractive in competition with yields available elsewhere. In December, 1973, the maturity was reduced to 5 years, providing a rate of interest of 6 % compounded semiannually and if held to maturity.

The bonds are redeemable at the option of the holder at any time after two months from the date of issue at a fixed price schedule under which the redemption price gradually increases from the purchase price to the face value at the end of the last year. Under this plan, the investor is protected against any depreciation in the dollar value of his investment during the entire period. If the bonds are redeemed well before maturity, the rate of income return as indicated by the established redemption prices will be substantially less than that obtainable if the bonds are held until the maturity date. Moreover, if the bonds are redeemed, the rate of yield voluntarily surrendered on the unexpired period of the bonds will be higher than the maturity rate. As shown in Table 5-5 (which applies to bonds issued December 1, 1973 and after), if a bond is redeemed after four years, the redemption price of $91.88 (per $100 of face value) would afford a yield of 5.14 % for the four-year period; however, a yield of 9.48 % would be required from an alternative investment to equal that which would have

TABLE 5-5 United States Savings Bonds (Series E)
Redemption Values and Income Yields

Period after Issue (beginning June 1, 1970)	Redemption Value	Yield Gained (if held)	Yield Lost (if redeemed)
First 1/2 year	75.00%	0.00%	6.00%
1/2 year to 1 year	76.40	3.73	6.25
1 to 1 1/2 years	78.44	4.54	6.37
1 1/2 to 2 years	80.40	4.69	6.57
2 to 2 1/2 years	82.40	4.76	6.83
2 1/2 to 3 years	84.56	4.86	7.15
3 to 3 1/2 years	86.84	4.45	7.59
3 1/2 to 4 years	89.24	5.03	8.29
4 to 4 1/2 years	91.88	5.14	9.48
4 1/2 to 5 years	94.08	5.25	12.93
5 years (maturity)	100.80	6.00	—

been obtainable through holding the bond to just under 4 1/2 years. The remarkable rate of 12.93% (annual rate) would be lost if the bond were redeemed just before maturity date.

To discourage redemption of previous issues, their redemption values and yields have been increased whenever new issues have been offered on a more attractive basis. There is now a bewildering variety of redemption price schedules which should be carefully checked by holders of the bonds. For example, bonds that were issued (for $75) in June 1943 had a redemption value of $270 on June 1, 1977 (after three ten-year extensions).

Owners of bonds have the option of retaining matured bonds for one or more extension periods of 10 years. No savings bond ever issued has reached final maturity, if the owner has chosen to hold it.

The bonds are nontransferable (except to heirs) and are redeemable only by the registered owners, thus protecting the holders against loss from theft, forgery, fire, and similar causes.

The bonds may be purchased by any investor other than a commercial bank. They may be registered in the name of one individual or of two individuals as co-owners (either of whom may redeem the bond), or as owner and beneficiary.

The maximum purchase permitted any individual investor is now $10,000 (issue price) for each calendar year of issue. Of course, several times the limit could be bought in the same family through the use of joint ownership.

The bonds may be purchased at commercial, savings, Federal Reserve banks, and savings and loan associations, or directly from the Bureau of Public Debt, Washington, D.C.

SERIES H (CURRENT INCOME)BONDS These bonds were first issued June 1, 1952, and are available in denominations ranging from $500 to $10,000. Unlike the E's, they are sold at 100% of face value and pay interest semiannually by check for their maturity of ten years. They are redeemable at par six months from the issue date, at one month's notice. Their average yield to maturity is now (1977) 6% compounded semiannually. If redeemed before maturity, the yield is reduced because the semiannual interest checks are lower in the first year than in the later years. Like the E bonds, they are issued to all investors except commercial banks. Investors' purchases are limited to $10,000 maturity value each calendar year. The transfer provisions are the same as those of the E bonds. Interest is subject to Federal, but not to state income taxes.

Investment characteristics   The advantages of Savings bonds may be summarized as follows:

They are as safe as any investment can be, and they do not suffer from market-price fluctuations. Their exact redemption value is known at all times. They provide complete recovery of principal (after the initial waiting period).

They are redeemable at the option of the holder. This enables the investor to switch to higher-yielding investments when interest rates rise.

Interest is automatically compounded semiannually. To achieve this with corporate bonds requires the immediate reinvestment of the interest at the yield rate.

Two income tax advantages are enjoyed: (1) interest is free from state and municipal levies, and (2) on Series E bonds, the interest may be reported as income currently as it accrues or all at once when the bond is redeemed. Under the latter option, interest is tax-free until redemption, and the redemption date may be chosen so as to place the income in a lower tax bracket, say, after the investor has retired, or in a year in which other income is lower. (However, if substantial amounts of bonds mature or are redeemed in one year, especially if the taxpayer's other income in that year is high, the interest may be taxed at a higher rate.)

Owners of outstanding E bonds may exchange $500 or more at current redemption values, for H bonds which pay interest by check. The appreciation of the older bonds is not taxed until the H bonds are cashed in or mature.

Automatic transfer to co-owners, heirs, and beneficiaries is permitted.

Registration permits ease of replacement in the event the securities are lost or destroyed.

Bonds are easily purchased and redeemed without any commission charge.

Many businesses cooperate with the Treasury Department by withholding, on request, wage or salary increments for the regular purchase of Savings bonds.

Occasionally, yields on Savings bonds have been competitively attractive.

Chief disadvantages are:

Savings bonds are not transferable (except to estates) and so may not be used as collateral.

The fixed returns on Savings bonds have often lagged behind those of alternative investments, and even when increased to induce more new sales and fewer redemptions, improvement has sometimes been too late. Thus in November 1973, interest rates on deposit-type investments ran from 4 1/2% on bank passbook accounts to as high as 5 3/4% on smaller time deposits with two-year maturities, and marketable Treasury bonds were yielding over

6%. But the yield on Savings bonds ran only 3% to 5.5%, depending on issue date and maturity. The increase in yield to 6% in December 1973 made them more competitive, but only after the substantial decline in market yields, beginning in July 1974. In 1975–1976 they enjoyed the biggest annual increases in net sale on record.

Some investors object to the fact that Series E bonds do not provide current income. The objection is probably not serious in most cases, because H bonds are available by new purchase or through exchange.

Yield is sacrificed if the bonds are redeemed before maturity.

These bonds have the same disadvantage as all fixed-principal and fixed-income investments, namely, that their real value in terms of purchasing power declines with the rise in the price level.

REFERENCES

AMERICAN INSTITUTE OF BANKING, *Savings and Time Deposit Banking*. New York: The Institute, 1968.

COX, A. H., JR., *Regulation of Interest Rates on Bank Deposits*. Ann Arbor, Mich.: Bureau of Business Research, Graduate School of Business Administration, University of Michigan, 1966.

DOUGALL, H. E., and J. E. GAUMNITZ, *Capital Markets and Institutions*, 3rd ed., Chapters 3 and 4. Englewood Cliffs, N.J.: Prentice-Hall, Inc., 1975.

DUBLIN, JACK, *Credit Unions: Theory and Practice*. Detroit: Wayne State University Press, 1971.

FEDERAL HOME LOAN BANK BOARD, *Study of the Savings and Loan Industry*. Washington, D.C.: U.S. Government Printing Office, 1970 (4 volumes).

Federal Savings Institutions. House Committee on Banking and Currency, Report No. 1643, 90th Congress, 1st Session. Washington, D.C.: U.S. Government Printing Office, 1967.

Financial Institutions and the Nation's Economy (FINE); compendium of papers prepared for the FINE study, June 1976. 94th Congress, 2d session. Washington, D.C.: U.S. Government Printing Office, 1976.

The Financial Reform Act of 1976; hearings before the Subcommittee on Financial Institutions Supervision, Regulation and Insurance. 94th Congress, 2d session, 1976. Washington, D.C.: U.S. Government Printing Office, 1976.

FRIEND, IRWIN, *Study of the Savings and Loan Industry*. Submitted to the Federal Home Loan Board (Washington, 1969).

GOLDSMITH, R. W., *Financial Institutions*. New York: Random House, Inc., 1968.

GREBLER, LEO, *The Future of Thrift Institutions*. Danville, Ill.: Joint Savings and Loan and Mutual Savings Banks Exchange Groups, 1969.

JACOBS, DONALD, et al., *Financial Institutions*, 5th ed. Homewood, Ill.: Richard D. Irwin, Inc., 1972.

KENDALL, L. T., *The Savings and Loan Business: Its Purposes, Functions, and Economic Justification*, a monograph prepared for the Commission on Money and Credit. Englewood Cliffs, N.J.: Prentice-Hall, Inc., 1962.

MEYER, M. J., and J. M. McDANIEL, *Don't Bank on It*. Lynbrook, N.Y.: Farnsworth Publishing, 1970.

MOODY, J. C., and G. C. FITE, *The Credit Union Movement*. Lincoln, Nebraska: University of Nebraska Press, 1971.

NATIONAL ASSOCIATION OF MUTUAL SAVINGS, *Mutual Savings Banks: Basic Characteristics and Role in the National Economy*, a monograph prepared for the Commission on Money and Credit. Englewood Cliffs, N.J.: Prentice-Hall, Inc., 1962.

PORTER, SYLVIA, *Sylvia Porter's Money Book*, Chapters 2, 22. Garden City, N.Y.: Doubleday & Co., Inc., 1975.

PRATHER, W. C., *Savings Accounts*, 5th ed. Chicago: American Savings and Loan Institute Press, 1974.

REPORT OF THE PRESIDENT'S COMMISSION ON *Financial Structure and Regulation*. Washington, D.C.: U.S. Government Printing Office, 1971.

ROBINSON, R. I., and D. WRIGHTSMAN, *Financial Markets: The Accumulation and Allocation of Wealth*. New York: McGraw-Hill Book Co., 1974.

THE FIRST BOSTON CORPORATION, *Securities of the United States Government*. New York: The Corporation, *biennial*.

WELFLING, WELDON, *Mutual Savings Banks: The Evolution of a Financial Intermediary*. Cleveland: Press of Case Western University, 1968.

(See also References, Chapter 21.)

U. S. Government and Agency Securities

SCOPE: This chapter discusses the investment characteristics of the obligations of the Federal government and its agencies and explains the predominant position they have attained in the investment field. The order of discussion is: (1) short history of Federal debt, (2) types of Federal debt, (3) Federal agencies, (4) bonds of international institutions, (5) territorial bonds, (6) investment tests—ability to pay and willingness to pay, (7) other criteria, (8) tax position, (9) yields on Federal bonds, (10) ownership, (11) market for government bonds, and information on U. S. Government securities.

The importance of Federal debt is indicated by its size—the amount outstanding at the end of 1976 totalled $653 billion—and by the fact that this amount represented about 72% of the total public debt (Federal, state, and local) at that time. Federal obligations support the liquidity and solvency of the financial institutions that are its chief owners. Individuals, who own over $100 billion or over 15% of the Federal debt, also have a very substantial stake in this medium of investment. The impact of the monetary and fiscal management of the Federal debt on the market prices and yields of securities affects all types of investors and all segments of the capital market.

Short History of the Federal Debt

At the beginning of the present century, the total debt of the Federal government amounted to slightly over $1 billion ($16 per capita) with an annual interest charge of $33.5 million. As of December 1976, the comparable figures (not including agency debt) were $653 billion ($3,020 per capita) with annual interest of nearly $41 billion. How did the Federal debt grow to such astronomical size, and what types of issues appeared during the 7 1/2 decades?

During the first decade of the century, total debt was reduced to $913 million. In addition to general financing, Panama Canal bonds were issued as direct obligations for the purpose of financing the construction of the interocean waterway.

During the second decade, war financing increased Federal interest-bearing debt to a peak of $25.2 billion in 1919, with annual interest of $1.1 billion. The main components of the debt by 1920 were the Liberty and Victory Loan bonds, which have now been retired, and the shorter-term

Treasury notes and *certificates*. In addition, two new types appeared: (1) the *Postal Savings* bonds, which are no longer sold but which were used to enable depositors in the Postal Savings System to invest more than the maximum of $2,500 permitted in a savings account; (2) *Federal Land Bank* and *Joint Stock Land Bank* bonds, which were issued under the Farm Loan Act of 1916 as *instrumentalities* rather than obligations of the Government.

TABLE 6-1 Public Debt of the United States, December
31, 1976 (in millions of dollars)

Public issues	
Marketable issues	
Treasury bills	$163,992
Certificates of indebtedness	—
Treasury notes	216,669
Treasury bonds	40,615
Total marketable	$421,276
Nonmarketable issues	
U.S. Savings bonds	71,853
(at current redemption value)	
Treasury bonds, Savings and investment series	2,262
Foreign series securities and other	27,322
Government account series	129,744
Total nonmarketable	$231,181
Total interest-bearing public debt	652,457
Matured debt on which interest has ceased	
Debt bearing no interest	1,086
Total public debt	$653,543

Source: Treasury Bulletin, March 1977.

During the prosperous 1920s, almost $10 billion were pared from the Federal debt, which totalled $15.9 billion in 1930 with annual interest charges of $660 million. *Treasury bonds*, issued primarily for the purpose of refunding higher-interest war loan bonds, were prominent in this period.

The 1930s produced a great increase in Federal debt resulting from the deficits of that period. In 1940 interest-bearing debt reached the unprecedented figure of $42.4 billion, an amount regarded by many at the time as about the maximum that could be supported (the legal debt limit was set by Congress at $45 billion in 1941). However, interest rates were maintained at a low level, so that the annual interest charges in 1940 amounted to only $1 billion, the same as on the $24 billion debt of 1920. Decline in the demand for funds on the part of business, the sale of Federal obligations to banks, and emphasis on short maturities were the chief explanations for the phenomena of increasing debt and decreasing interest rates.

During the 1930s, a variety of issues of Federal agencies and instrumentalities appeared. The *Federal Home Loan Banks* were created in 1931 with authority to issue so-called instrumentalities. In 1932, the *Home Owners' Loan Corporation* was created with authority to issue bonds guaranteed by the Federal government in exchange for home mortgages in default. In the same year, the *Federal Farm Mortgage Corporation* was established with similar authority to issue guaranteed bonds in exchange for farm mortgages in default. The *Reconstruction Finance Corporation* (since liquidated) was also established in 1932 with power to issue obligations backed by Federal guarantee for the purpose of making loans to business organizations in need of financial assistance. Subsequently, the *Commodity Credit Corporation*, the *Federal Housing Administration*, and the *U.S. Housing Authority* were created with power to make loans bearing Federal guarantees. These are described below. In 1935, U.S. Savings bonds were authorized to be sold directly to investors. In addition to these new issues sold to the public, several special types were created for internal fiscal purposes.

World War II produced an astronomical increase in debt resulting from the Federal deficits of the war and immediate postwar periods. The then peak of $278 billion in interest-bearing debt (including guaranteed obligations) was reached in February 1946 with annual interest charges of $5.4 billion. This tremendous total was composed of all types of obligations— marketable Treasury bonds, notes, certificates of indebtedness, and bills; nonmarketable issues including Savings bonds and Savings notes; and a variety of special issues for special fiscal funds. Again the generally low rates of interest in the capital market, the sale of nonmarketable issues to banks and individuals, and emphasis on short maturities, together with fiscal control of money rates, kept interest charges low in relation to principal.

The fiscal year ending June 30, 1947, saw the first Federal surplus after 16 consecutive years of deficits. By June 1948, interest-bearing debt had been reduced to $250 billion. In the whole 1948–1977 period, however, surpluses appeared in only six fiscal years—1951, 1955, 1956, 1957, 1960, and 1969. During that period the debt increased to $653 billion by the end of 1976.[1] Even during the booming 1960s, deficits were the order of the day, and the recession years of 1968 and 1970–1971 made necessary an unusual volume of Federal financing. The very large deficit in fiscal 1971–1972 reflected the Government's attempt to stimulate the economy and the extraordinary cost of the Vietnam war. After a year of near-balance in fiscal 1973–1974, enormous deficits in fiscal 1975 and 1976 reflecting recession, great expansion of Federal services, and the reduction in Federal income taxes (for 1975), sent the public debt to over $650 billion. This increase in debt plus the unprecedented rise in interest rates through 1975 caused the annual interest burden to pass the $40 billion mark in fiscal 1976.

Changes in debt reflect not only budget surpluses and deficits but also changes in the Treasury's cash balances and the effect of certain trust fund transactions and transfers.

A number of new Federal "agencies" of various types were created in the 30 years following World War II. These are described below. Agency debt burgeoned to over $103 billion at the end of 1976.

---

[1]To legalize the great growth in debt, Congress has raised the debt limit periodically from $45 billion in 1940 to $752 billion in 1977.

Types of Debt

Treasury bills   Treasury bills are sold at auction through the Federal Reserve Banks at rates that reflect the condition of the short-term money market at the time of offering. They are issued on a discount basis, with a maturity of between 13 weeks and one year. They are payable to the bearer in denominations ranging from $1,000 to $1,000,000. Federal Reserve and commercial banks are the chief market, but individuals, and especially corporations, find in them a liquid investment for short-term funds that on occasion has yielded very high rates of interest. In August 1974, yields on representative three-month bills were 8.96%—the highest in history. They declined to 4.35% in December 1976 and rose to over 6 3/4% in autumn 1977. For further discussion see Chapter 10.

Certificates of indebtedness   Certificates of indebtedness are bearer instruments issued with a maturity of one year or less and carry one coupon providing for payment of interest and principal at maturity. Denominations range from $1,000 to $1,000,000. Banks, individuals, and corporations find in them a liquid investment. At the end of 1976, none were outstanding.

Treasury notes   Treasury notes are coupon instruments issued with maturities of from one to 10 years. They are owned chiefly by the Federal Reserve and commercial banks. Denominations now (1977) range from $5,000 to $500 million. A $1,000 denomination was offered for the first and only time in the latter part of 1974 and was largely oversubscribed by individual investors. The yields to maturity on representative three- to five-year maturities reached 8.6% in 1974—the highest on record—but declined to 5.96% in December 1976. In autumn 1977 the rate was 6.6%.

Treasury bonds   Treasury bonds are now issued with maturities of over 10 years. They fall into two main classes: fully marketable issues eligible for purchase by all investors, including banks, and nonmarketable "Investment Series" bonds. The latter bear interest at 2 3/4% and are issued in denominations ranging from $1,000 to $10,000,000. They are convertible at the owner's option into five-year 1 1/2% marketable Treasury notes. They are designed primarily for large institutional investors, but those in a deceased individual owner's estate can be applied to the payment of Federal estate taxes. Other minor types of nonmarketable issues are held by foreign governments and their monetary authorities.

Marketable Treasury bonds are available in denominations ranging from $1,000 to $1,000,000 in a wide range of maturities. Until 1971 the statutory limit of 4 1/4% for coupons prevented the issuance of such bonds when market yields exceeded that rate. In the spring of 1971, Congress removed the limitation from $10 billion of bonds. This was increased to $12 billion in March 1976. Yields on outstanding Treasury bonds have varied widely through the years, reflecting the rise and fall of long-term interest rates. In

August 1974, the yield on representative issues reached an all-time high of 7.3%, but declined to 6.4% in December 1976, and rose to 7.3% in autumn 1977. Different maturities bear different yields. (See p. 101.) The lowest yields are available on "deep discount" bonds bearing low coupons, reflecting their advantage from the standpoint of capital gains taxes, especially on certain issues (known as "flower bonds") that are acceptable at par in payment of Federal estate taxes.

U. S. Savings bonds   These bonds are nontransferable and hence nonmarketable. Their redemption prices are so arranged as to provide yields at lower rates than are obtainable if held to maturity. In December 1976, $72.3 billion were outstanding (at current redemption value). Two different classes are available to investors (other classes are still outstanding, but are no longer issued):

Series E Savings bonds issued beginning December 1, 1973 have a maturity of five years. Each purchaser is limited to amounts of not more than $10,000 face (maturity) value within a calendar year. These bonds are sold on a discount basis at 75% of maturity value, and yield 6% compounded semiannually if held to maturity. They are redeemable at any time (after the first 60 days of issue) at values stated on the bonds, and may be exchanged at any time for Series H bonds.

Series H Savings bonds are issued at par and are redeemable at par. Interest is payable semiannually by check. On bonds bought beginning December 1, 1973, the yield is 5.6% compounded semiannually for the first five years, and 6.5% for the remaining five years to maturity.

Further details concerning these issues and their investment characteristics are found in Chapter 5.

Miscellaneous types   Other nonmarketable obligations include: (1) *Retirement-plan bonds* are available for purchase only in connection with bond-purchase plans and pension and profit-sharing plans under the Self-Employed Individuals Retirement Act of 1962 [Keogh Act (see p. 60)]. They bear denominations of from $50 to $1,000. Values increase each six months according to a special table. Interest (reaching 6% to maturity on bonds issued after January 1, 1974) is paid only on redemption. (2) *Depository bonds* (2%) are issued to banks in compensation for the cost of servicing government payrolls. They are acceptable as collateral for deposits of Federal funds. (3) *Individual retirement bonds* have been issued since January 1975 as an internal investment by persons not covered by a retirement plan and who wish to set up an Individual Retirement Account arrangement (see p. 60). (4) *State and local government series* bonds are bought by municipal governments wishing to reinvest the proceeds of "advance refunding" of their tax-exempt debt. (5) *Foreign series bonds* are issued to foreign governments and monetary authorities. (6) Government account series bonds are special issues sold to a variety of Treasury trust funds.

Directly guaranteed debt   In recent years, the Federal Housing Administration and the District of Columbia Armory Board have been the only Federal "agencies" to borrow funds that are fully, directly, and unconditionally guaranteed as to principal and interest by the U.S. Government and to enjoy an investment status equal to that of U.S. obligations. Bonds of a number of other agencies are indirectly guaranteed, however, as indicated in the next section.

Federal "Agency" Bonds

The term Federal "agency" bonds is used rather loosely to denote the debt of privately owned corporations sponsored by the Federal government, government-owned corporations, and government departments which borrow money for a variety of public purposes on the Federal level. As Table 6-2 shows, there are four categories of such "agencies." The table shows the type of ownership, debt financing employed, extent (if any) of Federal guarantee of principal and interest, and income tax status of the various obligations.

Federally sponsored agencies or enterprises The first category consists of credit agencies (or, strictly speaking, enterprises) that are now privately owned, but which were originally owned and/or sponsored by Federal authority. The bonds of these "agencies" or enterprises are not guaranteed by the Government, but its strong moral obligation gives them an investment standing that is second only to that of direct Federal debt. Yields are slightly higher than those on Federal obligations with similar maturities. Interest on bonds is fully taxable by the Federal government, but is exempt from state and municipal income taxation. Bonds outstanding at the end of 1976 are shown in Table 6-3.

The Farm Credit Act of 1933 provided for the formation of a District Bank for Cooperatives in each of the 12 Farm Credit Districts. These banks, under the supervision of the Farm Credit Administration, make loans to eligible farmers' cooperative associations that own their stock. *Consolidated bonds* of all 12 banks, or bonds in which a Central Bank for Cooperatives participates, are sold to provide funds for loans.

The Federal Land Banks were created under the Farm Loan Act of 1916 for the purpose of supplying long-term credit to farm owners. An eligible loan must represent a first mortgage on unencumbered farm property in an amount not exceeding 65% of the appraised normal value, repayable in installments over a period of between five and 40 years. These loans become the collateral security for bonds issued by the banks.

Loans handled by the Federal Land Banks are made principally through local Land Bank Associations, which own the banks' shares. The borrowers must buy stock in their local associations to the extent of 5% of the loan. The associations, in turn, guarantee each loan, which they pass on to the Federal Land Bank in which they share ownership. The present practice is to issue *consolidated bonds* representing the joint obligation of the entire group. Commercial banks and individuals hold the bulk of Land Bank bonds.

TABLE 6-2 Federal "Agencies"

Agency	Owned by	Types of Debt Financing	Federal Guarantee	Income Tax Federal	Income Tax State
I. Federally Sponsored Enterprises					
Banks for Cooperatives	Cooperative Associations	Secured bonds	None	Taxed	Exempt
Federal Land Banks	Land Bank Associations	Secured bonds	None	Taxed	Exempt
Federal Intermediate Credit Banks	Production Credit Associations	Consolidated debentures	None	Taxed	Exempt
Federal Home Loan Banks	Members of System	Consolidated bonds and notes	None	Taxed	Exempt
Federal Home Loan Mortgage Corp.	Federal Home Loan Banks	Guaranteed and participating certificates	GNMA	Taxed	Exempt
Federal National Mortgage Association (FNMA)	Private		GNMA	Taxed	Exempt
		Discount notes	None	Taxed	Taxed
		Mortgage-backed bonds	GNMA	Taxed	Taxed
Student Loan Marketing Association	Participating institutions	Loans from Federal Financing Bank	Indirect	Taxed	Taxed
II. Federally Owned					
Federal Financing Bank (FFB)	U. S. Treasury	Notes and Treasury loans	Underwritten	Taxed	Exempt
Govt. National Mtge. Association (GNMA)[a]	U. S. Treasury	Participating certificates	Indirect	Taxed	Taxed
Export-Import Bank (Eximbank)	U. S. Treasury	Notes, debentures, and participating certificates	Indirect Indirect	Taxed	Taxed
Tennessee Valley Authority (TVA)	U. S. Treasury	Loans from FFB	None	Taxed	Exempt

[a]Also guarantees "pass-through" securities backed by mortgages.

TABLE 6-2 Federal "Agencies" (cont'd.)

Agency	Owned by	Types of Debt Financing	Federal Guarantee	Income Tax Federal	Income Tax State
III. *Executive Departments*					
Housing & Urban Development (HUD)		New communities debentures	Secretary of Treasury	Taxed	Exempt
Federal Housing Administration (FHA)		Debentures	Fully and unconditionally	Taxed	Exempt
Farmers Home Administration (FMHA)		Insured notes; certificates of beneficial interest	Fully and unconditionally	Taxed	Taxed
General Services Administration (GSA)		Public Building Trust participating certificates	Underwritten	Taxed	Exempt
Maritime Administration		Merchant Marine bonds and notes	Underwritten	Taxed	Exempt
Small Business Administration (SBA)		Guaranteed debentures	Underlying collateral by USA	Taxed	Exempt
U. S. Postal Service		Bonds and notes; loans from FFB	Indirect Indirect	Taxed	Exempt
IV. *District of Columbia*					
Washington Metro. Area Transit Authority		Bonds	Indirect	Taxed	Exempt[a]
District of Columbia Armory Board		Guaranteed stadium notes	Fully and unconditionally	Taxed	Exempt

TABLE 6-3 Debt of Federally Sponsored Credit Enterprises, December 31, 1976. (in millions of dollars)

Banks for Cooperatives	$ 4,330
Federal Land Banks	17,127
Federal Intermediate Credit Banks	10,494
Federal Home Loan Banks	16,811
Federal Home Loan Mortgage Corporation	1,150
Federal National Mortgage Association	30,565
Student Loan Marketing Association	410
Total:	$80,887

Sources: Treasury Bulletin; Federal Reserve Bulletin.

The 12 Federal Intermediate Credit Banks were created in 1923 to rediscount paper of and make loans to production credit and cooperative associations. Noncallable *consolidated* bonds are issued as the joint and several obligations of the 12 banks, which (since 1968) own the banks' stock. Their chief market is financial institutions. Bonds usually have a maturity of nine months.

In addition to the securities just mentioned, consolidated system-wise discount notes are also issued jointly on behalf of the three farm credit systems.

The Federal Home Loan Banks were described in Chapter 4. They issue bonds secured by the mortgages offered as collateral by borrowing members aggregating 190% (in unpaid principal) of the bank bonds. Although these bonds may be issued by separate banks, in which event the other banks are jointly liable, the present practice is to issue *consolidated bonds* as the joint liability of all 11 banks. Discount notes are also issued.

The Federal Home Loan Mortgage Corporation ("Freddie Mac") was created in 1970 to strengthen the existing secondary market in FHA and VA mortgage loans and to develop a new secondary market for conventional mortgages. It buys mortgages from the Federal Home Loan Banks and their member banks, and from other institutions whose deposits are insured by agencies of the Federal government. Its capital stock is held by the Federal Home Loan Banks. The corporation issues certificates backed by pools of mortgages.

The Federal National Mortgage Association ("Fannie Mae") was first organized in 1938 to purchase and sell FHA-insured and VA-guaranteed mortgages. Fannic Mae is entirely privately owned (since 1968), but it is subject to regulation by the Secretary of Housing and Urban Development. Its purpose is to provide a secondary market for mortgages insured by the FHA or guaranteed by the administrator of Veterans Affairs. Fannie Mae originally bought or sold mortgages to supply or soak up funds, depending on the supply of and demand for mortgage credit. It now deals in commitments rather than in mortgages, by holding weekly auctions of forward commitment funds with the prices and yields determined by the bidders. It is still the only substantial secondary market for Federally supported mortgages. Fannie Mae finances its operations by selling debentures and short-term discount notes, mainly to institutions, and its shares are traded on the New York Stock Exchange.[2]

The Student Loan Marketing Association ("Sallie Mae") was created in 1972 to provide a secondary market for insured student loans made under the Guaranteed Student Loan Program. Its common stock is owned by financial and educational institutions that are qualified as insured lenders under the program. To date it has borrowed exclusively from the Federal Financing Bank. (See below.) Its obligations are backed by the full faith and credit of the United States.

Agencies owned by the U. S. Government   Separate agencies owned by the U.S. Treasury and which perform a variety of services are included in Table 6-4. As of the end of 1976, their outstanding debt was $17.6 billion.

TABLE 6-4   Public Debt of Government-Owned Agencies, 1976 (in millions of dollars)[a]

Government National Mortgage Assn. (GNMA)	$ 4,120
Export-Import Bank	8,574
Tennessee Valley Authority	4,935
Total	$17,629

[a]Includes debt of the Federal Financing Bank incurred to finance these agencies.

Source: Treasury Bulletin.

The Federal Financing Bank was created in 1974 to consolidate the financing of a number of agencies under one umbrella. The Bank is able to raise funds at a more attractive rate than can the individual agencies, thus reducing interest costs and the number of borrowers entering the capital market. Several agencies which borrowed in the public market in the past are now financed through the Bank.

The Government National Mortgage Association ("Ginny Mae") was formed in 1968 as a corporate entity within the U.S. Department of Health, Education and Welfare to take over the special-assistance programs and liquidating functions formerly performed by the Federal National Mortgage Association. It buys mortgages that meet institutional standards but for which market funds are not freely available. It is also engaged in liquidating the original Fannie Mae portfolio. An activity that has become very important in financing home building is its guarantee of securities issued by mortgage bankers and other qualified investors. These "pass-through" certificates are secured by pools of FHA, VA, and Farmers Home Administration mortgages. Ginny Mae raises its own funds by selling participation certificates on its mortgage portfolio, using the proceeds to repay advances by the Federal government. The typical pool of mortgages is formed by a mortgage bank. If the pool is approved, GNMA issues its own securities

[2]See Chapter 12 for further discussion.

against the pool. Principal and interest are paid by the repayments passed through from the underlying pool after deduction of servicing and guaranty fees. The minimum denomination is $25,000. "Timely payment" of interest and principal is guaranteed by GNMA, and so indirectly by the full faith and credit of the United States.[3]

The Export-Import Bank (Eximbank) assists in foreign trade financing by extending loans, guarantees, and credit insurance. It is financed by discount notes, debentures, and participating certificates in its loan portfolio. Its obligations are considered to be backed by the full faith and credit of the United States.

The Tennessee Valley Authority was established in 1933 to develop power and the economy in the Tennessee River and adjacent areas. It is authorized to issue bonds and notes that are a fixed charge against net power proceeds (ahead of interest and depreciation). Discount notes of four-month maturity are sold at auction. Power bonds are offered at competitive bidding, similar to the practice in public utility financing. Since 1974 it has been financed by loans from the Federal Financing Bank. Its obligations have no Federal guarantee, direct or indirect.

Executive departments   A number of Federal executive departments or agencies under departmental auspices have issued securities.

The Department of Housing and Urban Development (HUD) administers a program of financial assistance to housing, including the issuance of "new communities debentures." These are supported by the Secretary of the Treasury's obligation to lend money to guarantee repayment. The department also supports (with Treasury funds) the payment of notes issued by local housing and urban renewal agencies. (See Chapter 7.)

The Federal Housing Administration (FHA) is now administered by HUD. As indicated in Chapter 12, it insures FHA mortgage loans and issues debentures in payment of insurance commitments. The debentures ($575 million at the end of 1976) are fully and unconditionally guaranteed by the United States.

The Farmers Home Administration (FmHA) in the Department of Agriculture extends loans in rural areas for farms, homes, and community facilities. Sale of certificates of beneficial interest financed its activities until April 1974. These are secured by the full faith and credit of the Government. Programs are currently financed through the Federal Financing Bank.

The General Services Administration (GSA) is an agency in the executive branch of the Federal Government, which among other functions, finances federal construction projects by issuing participating certificates. These are not directly guaranteed, but are considered "obligations of the United States."

The Maritime Administration is a division of the Department of Commerce. Merchant Marine bonds and notes are issued in series (one for each ship) to finance private construction and are guaranteed by the full faith and credit of the Government.

[3]For additional discussion, see Chapter 12.

The Small Business Administration (SBA) provides financial and management assistance to Small Business Investment Companies (SBICs), by purchasing their debentures and issuing its own obligations secured by pooled collateral. SBA debentures are backed by the full faith and credit of the United States. Currently they are being sold to the Federal Financing Bank rather than to the public.

In 1971 the United States Postal Service began operations as an independent establishment in the executive branch of the U.S. Government, succeeding to the business of the Post Office Department. It issues bonds and notes and borrows from the Federal Financing Bank to finance land and buildings for postal use. The Secretary of the Treasury stands by to purchase its obligations, and so these are indirectly guaranteed by the Government.

District of Columbia agencies   A small agency, the District of Columbia Armory Board, has issued $20 millions in bonds to construct and maintain a stadium; these bonds are directly guaranteed by the United States.

The Washington Metropolitan Area Transit Authority finances mass transit facilities in the greater Washington, D.C., metropolitan area. It issues bonds which must of necessity be purchased by the Secretary of Transportation, and so these are considered guaranteed by the United States.

Summary   As indicated in Table 6-2 and the ensuing discussion, Federal "agency" bonds include a wide variety of sources and types. They also differ with respect to Federal guarantee of principal and interest. Only three are "fully and unconditionally guaranteed." Others are indirectly guaranteed through the provisions of various Federal legislative acts. Others have no guarantee at all, but have Federal sponsorship and enjoy its moral support.

Yields on agency bonds are only slightly higher than those of direct U.S. Treasury obligations.

Bonds of International Institutions

Three international institutions, of which the United States is a member, have issued bonds in the United States and abroad. They are not "agencies of the Federal government." Their obligations are fully subject to Federal and state income taxes. A large number of states have approved their purchase by financial institutions.

"World Bank" bonds   The International Bank for Reconstruction and Development was established in 1945 under the Bretton Woods Agreement Act to assist in the reconstruction and development of the production facilities and resources of the nations belonging to the Agreement. Of the capital stock of $30.9 billion subscribed by the member nations as of September 30, 1976, $27.8 billion has been paid in. In addition to bonds in other currencies, World Bank dollar bonds were outstanding in the amount of $7.9 million as of June 30, 1976. Until the amount of bonds outstanding reaches $6.35 billion, they are backed in full by the commitment of the U.S. Government, because that is the portion of the subscribed capital for which the United States is subject to call. Interest on these bonds is fully taxable.

Asian Development Bank bonds   This international organization has 41 governments as members. Its purpose is to foster economic growth and cooperation in Asia and the Pacific. Of the Bank's capital stock of $3.676 billion, the United States has subscribed $362 million or one-third of its committment. In addition to borrowing in other countries, the Bank had sold $275 million in dollar bonds as of June 30, 1976. They have the highest quality rating. Their interest is fully taxable.

Inter-American Development Bank   The purpose of this international institution is to further the economic and social development of its 24 American members. On June 30, 1976, the capital subscription of the United States was $362 million with $2,047 million subject to call. The Bank's outstanding funded debt includes bonds sold in a number of countries, including the United States.

Territorial Bonds

The only bonds of this class are those of the Commonwealth of Puerto Rico, of which $1,061 million were outstanding as of June 30, 1975. Their interest and principal are solely the responsibility of the Commonwealth. They are, however, exempt from all U.S. Federal and state income taxes. Since December 1961, debt service in any fiscal year may not exceed 15% of average annual revenues of the Commonwealth's treasury during the two preceding fiscal years.

Investment Tests of Federal Obligations

The safety of the bonds of the United States depends entirely upon the ability and willingness of the American people to carry the debt, that is, to provide, through taxation, funds sufficient to assure the payment of principal and income when due. Other desirable investment qualifications include ready marketability, collateral value, and *relative* stability of price and, hence, of yield compared to other types of securities. But actual stability has been notably absent in recent years.

Ability to pay   The burden of public debt, while enormous in terms of its dollar amount, is best measured by its relation to national wealth and income, and to the likelihood of its continued increase or its reduction. Certain data that help to point up these comparisons are given in Table 6-5.

The enormous Federal debt reached its immediate postwar peak in 1946 in terms of amount outstanding and per capita, and interest as a per cent

TABLE 6-5 Data on Federal Finances and Direct Debt[a]

Fiscal Year ended June 30[c]	Budget Receipts[b] (millions)	Budget Outlays[b] (millions)	Surplus or Deficit (millions)	Public Debt[a] (millions)	Public Debt per Capita ($)	Computed Annual Interest on Public Debt (millions)	Public Debt as a Percentage of National Income	Computed Interest as a Percentage of National Income	Computed Interest Rate on Public Debt
1940	$ 5,144	$ 9,062	$− 3,918	$ 42,968	$ 326	$ 1,095	52.9%	1.3%	2.58%
1945	44,475	98,416	−53,941	258,682	1,849	4,964	142.5	2.7	1.94
1950	36,495	39,617	− 3,122	257,357	1,702	5,613	109.0	2.3	2.20
1955	65,469	68,509	− 3,041	274,374	1,670	6,387	83.7	1.9	2.35
1960	92,492	92,223	+ 269	286,331	1,591	9,316	69.5	2.3	3.30
1961	94,389	97,795	− 3,406	288,971	1,579	8,761	68.1	2.1	3.07
1962	99,676	106,813	− 7,137	298,201	1,604	9,519	65.2	2.1	3.24
1963	106,560	111,311	− 4,751	305,860	1,621	10,119	63.4	2.1	3.36
1964	112,662	118,584	− 5,992	311,713	1,629	10,900	60.0	2.0	3.56
1965	116,833	118,430	− 1,596	313,819	1,622	11,467	55.4	2.0	3.68
1966	130,856	134,652	− 3,796	316,097	1,616	12,516	50.8	2.0	3.99
1967	149,552	158,254	− 8,702	322,893	1,635	12,953	49.2	2.0	4.04
1968	153,671	178,833	−25,161	345,367	1,732	15,404	48.3	2.2	4.50
1969	187,784	184,548	+ 3,236	352,895	1,752	17,087	46.0	2.2	4.89
1970	193,743	196,588	− 2,845	370,094	1,819	20,339	47.5	2.5	5.56
1971	188,392	211,425	−23,033	397,305	1,927	20,254	46.3	2.4	5.14
1972	208,649	231,876	−23,227	426,435	2,048	21,545	44.8	2.3	5.09
1973	232,225	246,526	−14,301	457,317	2,179	26,591	43.0	2.5	5.87
1974	264,932	268,392	− 3,460	474,235	2,243	30,741	41.8	2.7	6.56
1975	280,997	324,601	−43,604	533,188	2,503	33,509	44.2	2.8	6.35
1976	300,005	365,610	−65,605	620,432	2,890	39,494	46.4	3.0	6.44

[a]Public debt excludes guaranteed securities.
[b]1940–1945: Administrative budget; 1955–1977: Unified budget.
[c]Beginning October 1976, the Federal fiscal year runs from October 1 to September 30. There was a transition quarter July 1 to September 30, 1976.

Sources: Treasury Bulletin; Federal Reserve Bulletin.

of national income. A general reduction of debt from 1947 through 1951 was accompanied by a decline of principal per capita and as a per cent of national income, and of interest in relation to national income. Except for a pause, 1956–1957, debt rose steadily to its all-time peak in 1976. On a per capita basis, however, it declined to less than $1,600 by 1957 and levelled off at about that figure until the increases in 1968–1976. In June 1976, the per capita figure stood at nearly $2900. Its relative decline in terms of national income continued steadily to a new low figure in 1974. But as a percentage of national income, the interest burden remained around 2% until 1968, rising to 2.8% in 1976. In terms of the burden on the economy, the interest expense is more significant than the principal. The real test of ability to pay lies not so much in the dollar amount of debt and annual interest, but in the size of these items in relation to wealth and income, and in the ability of the American people to carry an annual Federal budget of over $350 billion. Of greatest concern is that, reflecting increased borrowing and higher interest rates, the annual interest bill now approaches 9% of Federal budget outlays.

Analysis of the annual Federal budget reveals that three-quarters of the expenditures are associated with wars—past conflicts, present outlays resulting therefrom, and preparedness for and prevention of future wars. The elimination of fear of war would be the greatest single aid to the debt situation. But some additional steps can be taken to place the debt in a manageable position, including economical management of government expenditures, retirement of some debt in times of peak prosperity, and wider distribution of debt outside the banking system to reduce its inflationary influence. There is no danger of debt repudiation in terms of dollars. In terms of what the dollar will buy, each dollar of debt and interest has become steadily less valuable with successive increases in the price level.

Willingness to pay   An axiom of the investment business is that the "will to pay" must be present in every good loan. Even though unwilling debtors can at times be forced to pay, no investor voluntarily buys into a law suit. Bonds of national governments, moreover, are issued by sovereign powers, which are usually immune from suits by creditors. Thus, the only real basis for national government loans is confidence in the good faith of the borrowing nation. The best test of good faith is found in the simple record of past transactions.

In a relative sense, the debt record of the Federal government of the United States has been excellent. At no time in the history of the nation has there been a dollar default in the payment of interest or principal on a Federal bond. The record, however, is not perfect. A blemish was the cancellation in 1933 of the gold payment clauses in Government bonds. These clauses had been placed in the bonds as a method of guaranteeing buyers against loss from the decline of purchasing power of their money in the event that the nation should either reduce the gold content of the dollar or abandon the gold standard entirely. In fairness, we should state that when the gold clauses were cancelled, holders of bonds which were not then due were permitted to have their bonds redeemed immediately at face value. Holders were thus permitted to employ their money in any alternative commitment which might seem preferable in the light of possible monetary inflation.

The virtual abandonment of gold in August 1971, when the value of the dollar was allowed to "float" in terms of foreign currencies, and the subsequent revaluation in 1972 from $35 to $38 an ounce, did not represent a default situation. Dollar obligations, both foreign and domestic, are paid in dollars. What the dollar is worth, however, is another matter.

Other investment criteria Federal securities meet the highest standards of recovery of principal (at maturity), assurance of income, and collateral value (with the exception of Savings bonds). The marketable issues are free from care with respect to ultimate payment, but not from price risk. While there is an immediate and active market, prices can and do move sharply in reflection of interest rate changes. Savings bonds provide absolute recovery of principal at a schedule known in advance.

Tax Position of Government and Agency Bonds

As explained in Chapter 17, direct Federal obligations do not enjoy any special advantages insofar as Federal income taxes are concerned. They are on a par with the obligations of states and municipalities in being exempt from state income taxation, but lack the exemption from Federal income taxes enjoyed by the latter. The fact that income from certain Federal bonds is fully taxable, whereas that from municipal bonds is nontaxable explains why the latter, if high-grade, produce a lower yield on equivalent maturities.

The income tax position of Federal agency bonds is indicated in Table 6-2. Like Federal bonds, the interest on agency bonds is subject to Federal income taxes. Their status with respect to state income taxes varies, as seen in Table 6-2.

The principal of all Federal and agency bonds is subject to Federal and state estate and inheritance taxes.

Yields on Federal Bonds

Special influences All direct obligations of the United States are equal in quality. Differences in yield are functions of differences in maturity and tax-saving appeal. Inspection of quotations on government securities on any one day, such as found in the leading metropolitan papers, show the influence of maturity noted in Chapter 8. On October 3, 1977, yields ranged from a low of 5.88% for the 7 1/2s due in December 1977 to a high of 7.68% for the 8 1/4s due in May 2000–2005. Bid prices ranged from 77 30/32 to 105 20/32.

Bonds issued during periods of low interest rates, and bearing low coupons, sell at substantial discounts. This gives them a capital gains advantage and drives the price up and their yield down below that of other bonds of like maturity. Most of these discount bonds are "flower bonds," or those accept-able at face value in payment of Federal estate taxes. An example is found in the 3s of February 1995, selling on October 3, 1977, to yield 4.8%, while the 7s of May 1993–1998 sold on the same day to yield 7.33%.

Price and yield record Through time, the yield (and, hence, the price) of marketable Government securities varies with the rise or fall of the interest rates on short- and long-term money. Because Federal securities are the closest of all obligations to being riskless, their yields represent the nearest thing to "pure interest" known to the money and capital markets. They would represent pure interest if they were not subject to special government influence. Such influence takes two forms: (1) Treasury Department debt management, including the use of nonmarketable issues, variation of maturities, and purchase and sale of securities by Treasury investment accounts; and (2) Federal Reserve System policies, which influence the prices and yields of bonds through open-market operations, and more indirectly through discount-rate policy and "moral suasion."

Yields on Government bonds have varied through time to reflect the changes in money rates, and their prices have changed accordingly. Table 6-6 shows the course of average annual yields and prices of Treasury bonds

TABLE 6-6   Yields on Treasury and High-Grade Corporate Bonds

	Long-Term Treasury Bonds		High-Grade Corporate Bonds—Average
	Average Price	Average Yield	Yield (Moody's Series)
1940	107.2	2.21	2.84
1945	102.0	2.37	2.62
1950	102.5	2.32	2.62
1955 (old series)	93.9	2.84	3.06
1960 (new series)	86.2	4.01	4.41
1961	87.6	3.90	4.35
1962	86.9	3.95	4.33
1963	86.3	4.00	4.26
1964	84.5	4.15	4.40
1965	83.8	4.21	4.49
1966	78.6	4.66	5.13
1967	76.6	4.85	5.51
1968	72.3	5.25	6.18
1969	64.5	6.10	7.03
1970	60.5	6.59	8.04
1971	67.7	5.74	7.39
1972	68.7	5.63	7.21
1973	62.8	6.30	7.44
1974	57.5	6.99	8.57
1975	57.4	6.98	8.83
1976	58.6	6.78	8.43

Sources: Treasury bonds: *Federal Reserve Bulletin;* Corporate bonds: *Moody's Bond Survey.*

in selected years. To provide a comparison, the average yield on high-grade corporate bonds (Moody's series) is also shown.

The prices and yields of long-term Government bonds have been by no means stable. From the peak of 111.0 in 1941, the average price declined to 93.0 in 1956, the lowest level in over two decades. This decline reflected the substantial stiffening of interest rates in a "tight money" situation that brought them, by 1957, to the highest level in over two decades. Toward the end of 1957 the rates turned downward, and the prices of "money bonds" turned up.

Yields dropped slightly in the depression year of 1958, but rose to a new peak in the tight money period of late 1959, and prices reached the then historical low. After a decline in 1961, yields again took an upward, and prices a downward, course, so that in 1970 the former reached their highest level and the latter their lowest level on record, only to rise to still higher (and lower) record levels in 1974.

Historically, at any one time the yields on different marketable issues have differed primarily as a result of different maturities—the longer the maturity, the higher the yield. But the sharp rise in long-term interest rates that was especially acute in 1955–1957, 1958, 1966, 1969–1970, and 1973–1974 was accompanied by an even greater rise in short-term and intermediate-term rates. The usual spread reflecting differences in maturities was greatly diminished and at times disappeared altogether, so that investors had little incentive to purchase the long-maturity issues with their greater price risk. A sharp break in interest rates in 1970 and early 1971 sent short-term yields well below the long-term, and the more normal pattern of yields–maturities was resumed. The next "credit crunch" in 1973–1974 shot all yields to new record highs, and short-term rates pushed to very large spreads over the long-term. (See Chart 6-1.) The normal pattern was resumed later. Table 6-7 shows the changing relationships in yields at interest rate peaks and lows in recent years and Chart 6-1 shows yields on an *inverted* scale for the postwar period for three types of Federal securities.

TABLE 6-7 Yields on U.S. Government Securities, Selected Dates

	May 1961	Sept. 1966	June 1967	Jan. 1970	Mar. 1971	Aug. 1974	Dec. 1976	Oct. 1977
Three-month bills	2.29%	5.36%	3.53%	7.87%	3.38%	8.7%	4.3%	6.1%
Six-month bills	2.44	5.79	3.88	7.78	3.50	8.9	4.5	6.3
Nine- to twelve-month issues	2.72	5.80	4.40	8.82	3.66	8.9	5.8	6.5
Three- to five-year issues	3.28	5.62	4.96	8.14	4.74	8.6	5.9	7.0
Long-term issues	3.73	4.79	4.86	6.86	5.71	7.3	7.2	7.2

Source: Federal Reserve Bulletin.

Ownership of Government Bonds

With $650–700 billion in direct and unconditionally guaranteed bonds outstanding, U.S. Government issues have a dominant position in the current American investment market. They comprise a very important earning asset of the banks of the country, second only to total loans, and

YIELDS OF U.S. GOVERNMENT SECURITIES

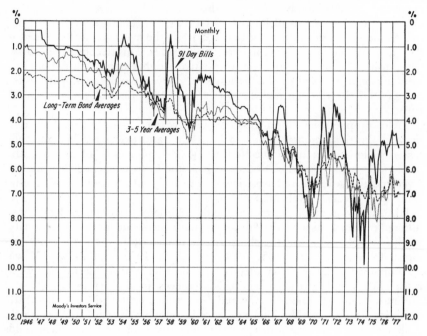

Source: Moody's Bond Record. Reprinted with permission.

are the chief asset of the Federal Reserve Banks. They also form a very substantial proportion of the portfolios of the leading financial institutions and are also popular with individuals desiring maximum safety and liquidity.

The ownership of outstanding Federal direct and guaranteed debt at the end of 1960, 1970, and 1976 is seen in Table 6-8.

Commercial banks are big holders of Treasury notes and intermediate-term bonds; they also have a substantial investment in Treasury bills. The Federal Reserve Banks are interested primarily in the short-term bills. Individuals hold the bulk of the savings bonds and are important holders of long-term marketable bonds. Insurance companies and mutual savings banks concentrate their holdings in Treasury bonds, particularly in the medium- and longer-term maturities. United States Government agencies and trust funds own special issues and long-term marketables. Business corporations concentrate on short maturities.

The bulk of Federal agency bonds is owned by institutional investors.

Primary and Secondary Markets

The Federal Reserve Banks serve as agents of the Treasury in issuing and redeeming government securities. Banks and a relatively small number of dealers form the chief primary market.

TABLE 6-8   Ownership of Federal Securities (dollars in billions)

	Dec. 31, 1960		Dec. 31, 1970		Dec. 31, 1976	
	Amount	%	Amount[a]	%	Amount[a]	%
Total outstanding	$290.4	100.0%	$389.2	100.0%	$653.5	100.0%
Held by:						
Commercial banks	62.6	21.6	62.7	16.1	102.5	15.7
Federal Reserve Banks	27.4	9.4	62.1	16.0	97.0	14.8
Total banks	$ 90.0	31.0%	$124.8	32.1%	$199.5	30.5%
Individuals	66.3	22.8	81.2	20.9	100.8	15.4
Insurance companies	11.9	4.0	7.4	1.9	12.3	1.9
Mutual savings banks	6.3	2.2	3.1	0.8	5.5	5.8
Other corporations	19.7	6.8	7.3	1.9	25.5	3.9
State and local governments	17.0	5.9	27.8	7.1	41.6	6.4
U.S. Government agencies						
and trust funds	55.0	18.9	97.1	24.9	147.1	22.5
Other investors[b]	24.2	8.3	40.5	10.3	121.2	18.6
Total nonbank investors	$200.4	69.0%	$264.4	67.9%	$454.0	69.5%

[a]Excludes guaranteed debt.
[b]Includes savings and loan associations, dealers and brokers, nonprofit institutions, corporate pension funds, foreign investors, and miscellaneous.

Source: Treasury Bulletin.

Trading in marketable U.S. Government and agency securities takes place primarily in the over-the-counter market, through dealer specialists, and banks. So active is the market that the trading range on any day is very narrow. No securities are more marketable or more liquid in the sense of immediate recovery of principal. To the institutions mentioned above, and to individuals seeking liquidity, they have a prime appeal. Also of interest is that trading in Government and agency securities is exempt from Government regulation, including exemption from the standard margin requirements of the Board of Governors of the Federal Reserve System.

Information on Government Securities

Primary sources of information on U.S. securities are the official reports of the Treasury Department:

    1. Circular giving specific information on each issue prepared at the time of issue.

    2. Daily and monthly statement of the Treasury showing revenue and disbursements for year to date and amount of the Federal debt.

    3. *Treasury Bulletin* (monthly) showing the composition and ownership of the Federal debt, market quotations and yields, and financial and fiscal data.

    4. Annual report of the Secretary of the Treasury, with statistical appendix, giving a comprehensive picture of Federal fiscal operations during the year.

    5. Annual reports of the various government corporations and credit agencies, such as the Farm Credit Administration (Farm Mortgage Corporation, Federal Land Banks, Federal Intermediate Credit Banks), Commodity Credit Corporation, and the Federal National Mortgage Association.

Secondary sources of information on U.S. Government securities include:

1. *Federal Reserve Bulletin* and *Federal Reserve Chart Book*.
2. *Governmental Finances*, published by the U.S. Department of Commerce, Bureau of the Census (annually).
3. *Moody's Manual of Investments, Municipal and Government; Moody's Bond Survey*.
4. *Securities of the United States Government and Federal Agencies*, published by the First Boston Corporation, New York (biennially).
5. Standard & Poor's *The Fixed Income Investor*.

REFERENCES

BOARD OF GOVERNORS OF THE FEDERAL RESERVE SYSTEM, *Treasury-Federal Reserve Study of the Government Securities Market*. Washington, D.C.: U.S. Government Printing Office, 1960.

BREAK, G. F., et al., *Federal Credit Agencies*, research studies prepared for the Commission on Money and Credit. Englewood Cliffs, N.J.: Prentice-Hall, Inc., 1963.

DOUGALL, H. E., and J. E. GAUMNITZ, *Capital Markets and Institutions*, 3rd ed., Chapter 7. Englewood Cliffs, N.J.: Prentice-Hall, Inc., 1975.

FEDERAL NATIONAL MORTGAGE ASSOCIATION, *Background and History of FNMA*. Washington, D.C.: The Association, 1969.

FIRST BOSTON CORPORATION, *Securities of the United States Government and Federal Agencies*, 27th ed. New York: The First Boston Corporation, 1976.

GAINES, T. C., *Techniques in Treasury Debt Management*. New York: Free Press, Inc., 1962.

HAWK, W. A., *The United States Government Securities Market*. Chicago: Harris Trust and Savings Bank, 1973.

LEVINE, S. N., ed., *Financial Analyst's Handbook*, Volume II, Chapter 11. Homewood, Ill.: Dow Jones-Irwin, Inc., 1975.

LEVY, M. E., *Cycles in Government Securities. I. Federal Debt and its Ownership*, Studies in Business Economics No. 78. New York: National Industrial Conference Board, 1963.

MELTZER, A. H., and GERT VON DER LINDE. A *Study of the Dealer Market for Federal Securities*. Materials prepared for the Joint Economic Committee, 86th Congress, 2nd Session. Washington, D.C.: U.S. Government Printing Office, 1960.

POLAKOFF, M. E., et al., *Financial Institutions and Markets*, Chapter 17. Boston: Houghton Mifflin Co., 1970.

ROBINSON, R. I., and D. WRIGHTSMAN, *Financial Markets: The Accumulation and Allocation of Wealth*, Chapter 14. New York: McGraw-Hill, Inc., 1974.

SCOTT, I. O., JR., *The Government Securities Market*. New York: McGraw-Hill, Inc., 1965.

WOODWORTH, G. W., *The Money Market and Monetary Management*. New York: Harper and Row, Publishers, 1972.

(See also References, Chapter 10, for special works on short-term Government securities.)

Bonds of State and Local Governments

SCOPE: This chapter discusses the investment position and methods of analyzing the bonds of the states and their political subdivisions. The order of discussion is: (1) amount and growth of debt, (2) classification of borrowing units, (3) sources and uses of revenues, (4) types of debt: general, special assessment, revenue, warrants, (5) difficulties of analysis, (6) tests of ability to pay, (7) willingness to pay, (8) legality, (9) bond ratings, (10) form of bonds, (11) tax status, (12) yields, (13) municipals market, and (14) investment position.

Amount and Growth of Debt

As of June 30,1976, gross state debt was $81 billion and local government debt $167 billion, or a total of $248 billion.[1] Table 7-1 shows relative growth of the three main types of public debt—Federal, state, and local—for selected fiscal years (as of June 30).

In comparison with the Federal debt, the volume of state and local debt does not appear alarming, but in the last 32 years it has grown much faster than the Federal debt, both in amount and on a per capita basis. Prior to World War I, state debt was very small, and municipal debt was substantial in amount. The expansion of state and municipal services caused both types to increase severalfold by 1940. During World War II retirements exceeded new issues. Since 1945 the great expansion of debt has reflected the growth of state and local public services, the increase in population and its steady urbanization, and the rising operating and capital costs of government.

Classification of Borrowing Units

Including special tax districts, United States has over 78,300 state and local governmental units.[2] Of these, possibly 30,000 have issued bonds from time to time. State and local governments may be classified as follows:

[1]Estimated.

[2]U.S. Department of Commerce, Bureau of the Census, 1972 *Census of Governments*, Vol. 8: *Guide to the 1972 Census of Governments*, p. 8, 1975.

TABLE 7-1   Gross Public Debt (June 30)

	Federal[a]		State[b]		Local[b]	
	Amount (millions)	Per Capita	Amount (millions)	Per Capita	Amount (millions)	Per Capita
1940	$ 42,968	$ 326	$ 3,590	$ 27	$ 16,693	$127
1945	258,682	1,849	2,425	17	14,164	101
1950	257,357	1,702	5,285	35	18,830	125
1955	274,374	1,670	11,198	68	33,069	201
1960	286,331	1,591	18,543	103	51,412	286
1965	313,819	1,622	27,034	139	72,478	374
1966	316,097	1,616	29,564	151	77,487	395
1967	322,893	1,635	32,472	164	81,185	410
1968	345,367	1,732	35,663	178	85,492	478
1969	352,895	1,748	39,553	196	93,995	466
1970	370,094	1,819	42,008	206	101,563	496
1971	397,305	1,927	47,800	232	111,034	538
1972	426,435	2,048	54,453	261	120,029	576
1973	457,317	2,179	59,375	283	129,110	615
1974	474,235	2,243	65,296	310	141,300	671
1975	533,198	2,503	72,127	338	149,096	700
1976	620,432	2,890	81,000[c]	380[c]	167,000[c]	780[c]

[a]Exclusive of guaranteed debt.
[b]1960–1975 data include Alaska and Hawaii.
[c]Estimated.

Sources: U.S. Department of Commerce, Bureau of the Census, *Historical Summary of Governmental Finances; Governmental Finances, annual.*

A. Regular governmental units
   1. States
   2. Counties and parishes
   3. Cities, towns, and boroughs
   4. Townships
B. Special tax districts
   1. School districts
   2. Water districts and sanitary (sewer) districts
   3. Road districts and street improvement districts
   4. Park districts and the like
   5. Drainage, irrigation, and levee districts
C. Statutory authorities
   1. Bridge authorities or commissions
   2. Port authorities
   3. Toll road commissions or authorities
   4. Miscellaneous (hospital, college dormitory, parkway, etc.)
D. Municipal utilities departments (electric, water, etc.)
E. Special housing authorities

Bonds of the first two categories above are classified as *general obligations* supported by the power to tax. Those of the third and fourth groups are ordinarily called *revenue* or *nonguaranteed* bonds. Housing authority issues are a special type of revenue bond, although they are further supported by state or Federal guarantee.

Bonds issued by the states are the obligations of sovereign powers. With the exception of New York, where the state constitution specifically grants such permission, state governments may not be sued by individuals or corporations, although one state may sue another state. Investors must, therefore, rely principally upon the good faith of the states. That most state bonds are accorded high investment rating is a testimonial to the importance of intangible factors in contrast to tangible property and legal protection.

The political subdivisions include not only counties and cities, but also towns, villages, and numerous varieties of districts, many of which overlap. Municipalities have certain powers that have been delegated by state authority so they may act as agencies for local administration. They are incorporated under a general state law or receive special charters under separate legislative acts. The powers usually delegated are: (1) police power for the maintenance of law and order; (2) taxing power, from which necessary revenues are secured; and (3) eminent domain, which confers the right to take private property, at fair compensation, for public use.

Regular governmental units possess broad general powers. Their activities produce little revenue, and taxes are their principal source of income. They ordinarily issue bonds by pledging their general credit; but they may also pledge specific revenues or may create a special district or an authority to issue revenue bonds. Districts also have the power to tax, but they are organized to promote a specific activity. Statutory authorities and municipal utilities or departments are public corporations without the power to tax. They are organized for the purpose of operating revenue-producing projects.

Sources of Revenue

The revenues from which state governments meet their general obligations include Federal aid and the various taxes levied by the respective state legislatures. (See Table 7-2.) A share of the general property tax collected by local authorities was once an important source of state revenue, but in most states this has been replaced by revenue from special taxes imposed for state purposes. Retailer' occupational taxes (sales taxes) have sprung into prominence, along with individual and corporate income taxes, and the very important gasoline taxes and automobile licenses. Other sources include cigarette taxes, inheritance and estate taxes, special taxes on public utilities, and a variety of miscellaneous types. The relative importance of these sources differs in the various states. Federal aid to states has taken a sharp increase since World War II. The grants have been mainly for highways and public welfare.

The types of taxes levied to pay state expenses and to service its debt are of considerable importance to the investor. Generally, the absence of any predominant source provides a diversification that tends to promote stability of income.

The most important single source of revenue for local governments is the

TABLE 7-2 Revenues and Expenditures of State and Local Governments, 1975 (year ended June 30; dollars in millions)

Revenues	States Amt.	%	Local Govts. Amt.	%
Intergovernmental revenue (net)	$ 37,827	24.5%	$ 61,975	38.8%
Taxes				
Property	1,451	0.9	50,040	31.3
General sales	24,780	16.0	4,322	2.7
Selective sales and gross receipts[a]	18,566	12.0	2,147	1.3
Individual income	18,819	12.2	2,635	1.6
Corporate income	6,642	4.3	—	—
Motor vehicle and operators' licenses	3,941	2.5	302	0.2
All other taxes	5,956	3.8	1,864	1.3
Total taxes	$ 80,155	51.7%	$ 61,310	38.4%
Current charges and misc. revenue	16,629	10.8	23,047	14.4
Utility revenue	—	—	10,867	6.8
Liquor stores revenue	2,129	1.4	338	0.3
Insurance trust revenue	17,892	11.6	2,194	1.4
Total revenue	$154,632	100.0%	$159,731	100.0%

Expenditures[b]	States Amt.	%	Local Govts. Amt.	%
Education	$ 54,012	39.0%	$ 64,956	45.4%
Highways	17,483	12.6	8,270	5.8
Public welfare	25,559	18.5	9,733	6.8
Health and hospitals	10,158	7.3	9,878	6.9
Public safety and correction	3,414	2.5	8,348	5.8
Natural resources	3 554	2.6	855	0.6
Housing and urban renewal	632	0.4	3,050	2.1
Sanitation	—	—	7,387	5.2
Interest on general debt	3,272	2.4	5,511	3.8
Other expenditures	20,220	14.7	25,160	17.6
Total expenditures	$138,304	100.0%	$143,148	100.0%

[a]Chiefly motor fuel, alcoholic beverages, tobacco products, and public utility taxes.
[b]Includes capital outlays: state, $17.3 billion; local, $27.5 billion.
Source: U.S. Department of Commerce, Bureau of the Census, *Governmental Finances in 1974–1975.*

general property tax, but to an increasing degree special taxes and aid from state and Federal governments are relied upon for income.[3] The relative importance of these sources varies from place to place. As of June 1975, local governments obtained their general revenues (aside from general borrowings) from the sources noted in Table 7-2.

Uses of Revenue

The uses or expenditures to which state revenues are applied are also indicated in Table 7-2. Of the total, the most important single type is aid to local governments. Interest and debt retirement make only a modest drain on

[3]In the fiscal year ended June 30, 1975, states contributed $51.1 billion to local governments, mainly for education and public welfare.

revenues. Ideally, the annual revenues of the state should more than cover each year's operating expenses and, in addition, provide adequately for debt service. Debt service includes the annual interest charge and the provision for repayment of principal, either by redemption of serial issues or by sinking fund.

The revenues of municipalities are used for the purposes indicated in Table 7-2. Public safety, public welfare, highways, and education predominate. General revenues are insufficient to take care of substantial capital expenditures as the need arises. Hence, the municipalities must issue debt instruments whose carrying costs and retirement are spread over the years and charged to current receipts.

Purposes of Bond Issues

States have traditionally borrowed principally to finance the construction of long-term improvements, although important exceptions to this pattern appeared in the extensive borrowing to provide funds for emergency relief in the 1930s and in the heavy bond emissions for veterans' bonuses after World War II. More modern debt has been incurred for educational facilities, highway construction, park development, state institutions, grade-crossing elimination, social service and health programs, veterans' bonuses, and housing (guarantee of local housing authority notes and bonds), and to meet special types of operating expenses. The relative importance of the financing by state governments of the major types of durable improvements and other functions is shown in Table 7-3.[4]

TABLE 7-3   Purposes of Long-Term State Debt
             Outstanding June 30, 1975
             (dollars in millions)

	Amt.	%
Education	$17.0	25.2%
Highways	16.3	24.2
Hospitals	2.3	3.4
Water transportation	0.5	0.7
Veterans' Administration bonuses	0.6	0.9
Other and unallocable	30.8	45.6
Total	$67.5	100.0%

Source: U.S. Department of Commerce, Bureau of the Census, State Government Finances in 1975, p. 41.

Municipalities constantly face extraordinary expenditures that cannot conveniently be met from current revenues, and so loans are arranged to spread the cost over a period of years. The variety of purposes for which bonds are issued by municipalities is suggested by the following list:

[4]Federal Reserve Bulletin reports the purposes of issues for new capital on an annual basis.

Bridges	Libraries
Buildings	Parking facilities
Emergencies and catastrophies	Police facilities
Fire equipment	Public utilities
Funding of floating debt	Public welfare
Grade crossings	Recreation and parks
Harbor improvements	Schools
Highways	Sanitation and sewage disposal
Hospitals	Street improvements
Housing	Urban renewal

Education facilities and municipal utilities still comprise the most important purposes for local municipal loans. Streets, sanitation, housing, and urban renewal are also important. Special types of operating expenses are also funded, and considerable refunding takes place annually. Although no exact relationship exists between the amount of debt financing and capital expenditures, most debt is incurred to anticipate, then to fund, part of the cost of new fixed assets. The balance of capital cost is currently financed from special taxes and Federal grants.[5]

Types of Debt

Bonds of states and local political subdivisions can be classified into principal groups.

General obligations The interest and principal of *general obligations* or "full faith and credit bonds" are supported by the full taxing power of the governing unit. Investors prefer the unlimited tax obligations of states that pledge their "full faith and credit" and whose constitutions provide for unlimited taxation for debt service. The New York State Constitution provides that the legislature shall annually provide by appropriation for the interest and maturing principal of state debts as they fall due; failing such an appropriation, the Comptroller must set aside from the first revenues thereafter received a sum sufficient to meet such payments.

Other full faith and credit bonds are payable primarily from certain special pledged sources of revenue; but, in addition, the unit agrees unconditionally to cover any deficit that may later develop in the special fund. Thus, a water bond might be issued by a municipality with the pledge of its full faith and credit, but with the expectation that the bond would be serviced from the earnings of the water department. If these earnings are insufficient, the issuing unit must levy taxes to make up the deficit. Similarly, bonds payable initially from a specific tax, but which rest ultimately on the power to levy taxes, belong in this category.

[5]In fiscal 1975 the capital outlay by states and local governments totalled $44.5 billion. But the net long-term debt issued in that year (after retirements) totalled only $10.0 billion. U.S. Department of Commerce, Bureau of the Census, *Government Finances in 1974-1975.*

As of June 30, 1975, of the total long-term state debt of $67.5 billion, $33.7 billion or 50% were full faith and credit obligations. Of gross long-term local debt totalling $133.9 billion, $81.8 billions or 61% fell in this category. The pledge to levy taxes may or may not be limited as to rate or amount. The power of taxation may be limited by either a constitutional or a statutory provision to, say, a certain number of dollars per thousand of property valuation.(For example, Alabama has a constitutional limitation on *state* property taxes of $6.50 per $1,000 of property assessed at 30% of market value.) The issuer is obliged only to exercise its powers of taxation up to this limit for the payment of the obligation or to make good any deficiency in a special fund primarily pledged for its payment. Such bonds are known as *limited tax bonds*.

Because most states have tax-limit legislation in effect, most bonds of local governments deserve the *limited tax* title. In many states, however, the tax limit does not apply to debt service, for which payment unlimited taxes may be levied.

The term *general obligation* applies to any obligation for the service of which the issuing governmental unit has pledged its entire tax revenues, whether raised by a general property tax or by a tax from a special source, or from a limited area of property. Thus, *tax district* bonds belong in the category of general obligations although the district may be established for the promotion of only one activity and only the property within the district may be subject to levy. Some special districts have been formed for the purpose of avoiding the tax limits that prevail for the municipality. School districts have been established to serve communities beyond existing incorporated areas. They have issued bonds for the purpose of erecting school buildings, payable out of taxes levied on all property in the areas served, irrespective of whatever towns might be included therein. The bonds are general lien obligations of the entire district. But the generally favorable experience with school district obligations has not always extended to other types such as irrigation and road district bonds. The quality of tax district bonds is far from uniform.

The restriction of a low debt limit tends to encourage financing by district bonds which are not part of the legal debt of an included municipality. Even in New York State, where the debt limits of 5 to 10% of the five-year average full value of taxable realty are usually adequate for local municipal credit, the legislature faces continual requests for the establishment of new tax districts.[6] In Illinois, where the local debt limit is set at 5% and where appraisal values are much lower than in New York, the inducement to establish tax districts is almost irresistible. At one time in Cook County, more than 400 units of government had power to levy general property taxes. This extreme overlapping contributed greatly to the financial difficulties of the Chicago area during the 1930s. California permits tax districts to be formed for such purposes as: airport, boulevard, cemetery, fire protection, sanitation, water, garbage disposal, highway lighting, irrigation, library, health,

---

[6]Different limits apply to different classes of municipalities, for example: 10% for Nassau County, 7% for other counties; 10% for New York City, 7 to 9% for other cities; 5% for school districts.

memorial, mosquito control, parks, museum, utility, recreation, and transportation.

The investment position of tax district bonds depends upon the purpose for which the district was created, as well as the wealth, income, and *total* debt burden of the included area. The existence of overlapping tax districts greatly complicates the problem of financial analysis. In 1975, Albany, N.Y., reported a bonded debt of $21.1 million. This amount did not include Albany's share (87.89%) of the debt of the Albany Port District ($7,500,000), but did include the school debt of $13.1 million. At the end of 1975, the net bonded debt (general obligations) of Chicago was reported at $267,750,000, but did not include $93,735,000 in park bonds, $240,555,000 in school district bonds, or $179,550,000 in sanitary district bonds, all general obligations. Investors in tax district bonds should realize that published financial statements do not include the debts of underlying municipalities. Buyers of regular municipal bonds should understand, in turn, that the financial statements of cities do not include the proportionate debts of overlapping tax districts, which, as shown previously, may exceed the internal debt.[7] The short prospectuses issued by municipal bond dealers sometimes include, sometimes exclude, data on overlapping debt.

Special assessment bonds   When loans are made to improve facilities in certain parts of the city, such as street pavements and the extension of water and sewer lines, the cost is often placed on those property owners who are directly benefited through assessments which are usually spread over a series of years. Assessment or "improvement" bonds are issued with interest and amortized principal payable, not from the general tax levy, but from these assessments. Thus, a claim against some of the property in a city is less secure than a claim against all the property. Accordingly, assessment bonds are regarded as inferior to general-lien local bonds, and bear higher yields. As a practical matter, however, city credit is at stake in the payment of assessment bonds, and cities usually supply funds from other sources for the payment of charges on these bonds when assessment collections prove temporarily inadequate. Such bonds are known as *general-specials*.

Unless specifically backed by the credit of the community, the special assessment bond is suitable only for local investment funds. It has the advantage, along with other local debt, of exemption of interest from Federal income taxes and from state income taxes in the state of issue.

Revenue bonds   Revenue bonds are usually payable solely from revenues derived from the operation of a public facility or from some special source of revenue (such as motor fuel taxes), rather than from general tax

---

[7]The effect of overlapping districts upon comparative tax rates was clearly illustrated by the contrast of the two leading California cities in 1975. The tax rate in San Francisco (city and county) was $66.85 per $1,000 of assessed valuation, plus $42.97 for the unified school district with the same area limits, and $5.18 for the rapid-transit district, or a total of $115.00. However, no separate school district bonds were outstanding—all bonds for school purposes were the general obligations of the city and county. The city rate in Los Angeles was $30.91 per $1,000, but the total rate was $142.85 after including five overlapping districts. Each city used an assessment basis of 25% of true value.

collections. The use of revenue bonds to finance the construction or acquisition of public works has become popular in all parts of the country for projects as varied as toll bridges, toll highways, electric light and power plants, gas plants, water works, sewer systems, swimming pools, parking areas, state university dormitories, and, in at least one instance, a crematorium. Between 1950 and 1976 the outstanding revenue obligations and other nonguaranteed long-term debt increased more than twentyfold, and by mid-1976 accounted for about 45% of total state and local long-term debt. Revenue bonds reflect the attitude that the users of a public facility should support it. More important, they offer a means of financing public projects or services without tax increases and without violating the debt limits that apply to "full faith and credit" debt.

Most revenue bonds are issued by special authorities, departments, or commissions rather than by regular governmental units. Their major purpose is to keep down the direct debt and the tax rate. Other reasons are: (1) to make the project self-supporting, (2) to avoid having to refer an increase in debt to the electorate, (3) in some cases to obtain a lower interest rate where the general credit of the municipality is not strong, (4) to avoid setting up a special district in which all taxpayers would not receive equal benefits from the facility, and (5) to finance the construction of industrial facilities to be leased to private enterprise.

Because the position of these bonds depends solely upon the earning power of the project or on special taxes, they should be regarded as distinctly different from ordinary municipal bonds payable from general tax collections. However, revenue bonds may be in a stronger position and bear lower yields than those of privately owned public utility companies for four important reasons. First, the rates charged for the use of the facility can be raised, in most states, without securing the approval of the public utility commission. Second, the enterprise is usually tax-free, and thus avoids the burden of corporation taxes, which take as much as 20% of the gross revenues of private utility companies. Third, income from revenue bonds is exempt from Federal income taxes. Fourth, the enterprise is in little, if any, danger from competition or expiration of a franchise privilege.

Some argue that revenue bonds are entitled to as good rating as general-lien bonds because the projects are self-supporting, self-liquidating, and independent of tax collections. In certain cases, interest on revenue bonds has been maintained by cities in default on their bonds payable from taxes. During periods of recession, however, the argument loses much of its validity when declining revenues impair interest payments.

Under recent practice, revenue bonds are frequently issued under a corporate title differing from the name of the municipality or area wherein the project is located. Examples are the Triborough Bridge and Tunnel Authority (New York City) and the Calumet Skyway (Chicago).

Many projects financed by revenue bonds operate beyond the limits of one municipality, for example, the San Francisco-Oakland Bay Bridge (California Toll Bridge Authority) and the Port of New York and New Jersey Authority (various bridges, tunnels, airports, and terminals within a 25-mile radius). The most prominent of these to appeal to the national market in recent years have been the toll-road bonds issued by a number of express roads linking cities in the East, the Middle West, and the South. Some examples are the New York State Thruway Authority, the Ohio Turnpike Commission, the Illinois State Toll Highway Commission, and the Maine Turnpike Authority.

Revenue bonds have become an important part of public finance. When issued in connection with soundly conceived and well-managed projects, they are entitled to a good investment rating. However, not all projects offer equally attractive investment opportunities. The list of projects regarded as suitable for revenue bond financing includes, in addition to the traditional gas and electric utility, water, and sewer purposes, such enterprises as airports, urban transportation, hospitals, parking, public markets, college dormitories, and various types of recreational facilities.[8]

Of note is the New York City practice of issuing bonds for many revenue-producing purposes, such as rapid transit, docks, and water supply, and designating such bonds as general obligations payable from general revenues, including tax collections. However, these bonds issued by the city are issued through "authorities," rather than by the city directly. In 1976 they all bore the low rating of Caa. Ratings were later suspended.

In the 1960s a new type of revenue bond appeared, issued to finance facilities built by municipalities to be leased to private corporations. The purpose, was, of course, to attract industry. For example, in September 1976, an issue of industrial revenue bonds due 1986 was sold by the Parish of East Baton Rouge, La., to finance the acquisition of pollution control facilities at a wood pulp manufacturing plant leased and operated by Georgia Pacific Corporation. Although the rental payments are believed to be sufficient to service the debt, Georgia Pacific has also unconditionally guaranteed the principal and interest of the obligation.

Industrial revenue bond issues totalling more than $1,000,000 are not exempt from Federal income taxes unless the proceeds are used for a "public purpose" as in the illustration above.

The strength of the revenue bond depends mainly on the coverage of interest and maturing principal afforded by earnings, with a sufficient margin of safety allowed for contingencies. The ratio of the investment in plant to the outstanding net debt is an indicator of asset protection, and in a few states revenue bonds may be specifically secured by a mortgage lien on the property. The revenues from the project go into a revenue fund, from which the following are provided, in order, for: (1) operating expenses, (2) depreciation fund, (3) debt service, and (4) special reserves. Any surplus revenues after these items may revert to the city or be used for additions or for special bond retirements. An unusual arrangement is found in the case of the bonds of the California Toll Bridge Authority; the Highway Department of the State of California pays the maintenance expenses of the San Francisco-Oakland Bay Bridge and other bridges operated by the Authority so that the *gross* revenues are available for other operating expenses and debt service.

---

[8]For a convenient summary of types and provisions of revenue bonds, see Moody's *Municipal and Government Manual*.

Occasionally a revenue bond may be backed by both taxing power and derived revenues, but this arrangement is exceptional and defeats the usual objective of providing a capital improvement without adding to the general tax load.

The quality of revenue bonds ranges from first rate to mediocre or worse. Some are strong enough to sell at yields that are as low as those of the general bonds of the jurisdiction that set up the authority. Some of the toll-road or turnpike bonds issued since World War II have remained high grade. Others, such as the Calumet Skyway Bridge (Chicago), rated Caa in 1977, have fallen in investment status because of sadly discouraging revenues.

The range in quality of revenue bonds is indicated by the spread between their yields and those of high-grade general obligations. In September 1977 the yield on Moody's series of long-term Aaa general municipals was 5.25%, and Baa municipals yielded 5.8%. At the same time, however, a sampling of long-term revenue bonds of general investment interest disclosed yields ranging from 5.4% to 7.75%. Nevertheless, some revenue bonds show such adequate coverage of interest and debt retirement as to make then eligible for purchase by banks and other institutional investors under the regulations of a limited number of states.[9]

Tax-anticipation warrants   Tax-anticipation warrants or notes represent current debt issued in anticipation of a tax levy to meet the financial needs of the state or municipality until the taxes are collected. They are ordinarily a first claim against incoming tax revenues. Their investment quality depends on the credit of the issuing municipality and its tax-collection status. They are sometimes without fixed maturity, with payment date depending on tax receipts.

Special types   Hybrids or combinations of the first three types described above represent *special types* of revenue bonds that are difficult to classify. These include bonds issued by cities or districts with pledge of special utility revenues or receipts from special taxes in addition to the pledge of general credit; revenue bonds further supported by assessments; bonds on which payment is pledged only from specified taxes without unconditional promise to pay; and bonds supported by both project net revenues and the guarantee of the state or municipality.

The obligations of public housing authorities have special characteristics that make them different from ordinary revenue bonds. Of particular importance are the bonds now being issued in very large volume by local public housing authorities created under the laws of the states and authorized to cooperate with the Federal government in carrying out the expressed policy of providing safe and sanitary low-rent housing. Under the U.S. Housing Act of 1937, as amended, the faith of the United States is pledged to the payment of annual contributions to the local housing agency sufficient, with other funds of the local agency, to pay the principal and interest of the bonds

---

[9]States in which qualified revenue bonds are "legals" include California, Connecticut, Florida, Illinois, Maryland, Massachusetts, Michigan, New Jersey, New York, Ohio, Pennsylvania, and Texas.

when due. The bonds are also secured by a pledge of the net revenues of the housing projects. The interest is exempt from Federal taxation; with a few exceptions, the bonds are also exempt from property and income taxes of the states where issued.

Analysis of Municipal Obligations

Special problems The analysis of state and local government securities presents a number of problems. Among these are: (1) the selection of pertinent material from the mass of economic and political information available; (2) the lack of absolute standards for measuring risk, and the consequent reliance on the *comparative* merit of an issue in the light of similar situations; (3) the difficulty of keeping in touch with the changing and complex field of municipal operations and finance; (4) the unsatisfactory and incomplete character of specific credit information; and (5) the complex legal considerations that are often involved. Nevertheless, in spite of these complications, a survey of the most important factors will at least serve to determine whether a bond is high grade, borderline, or low grade. The advice of dealers and services specializing in tax-free bonds is necessary to enable the investor to determine a more exact rating and the appropriateness of a particular bond in his own portfolio.

Ability to pay The three general tests of the investment position of a municipal bond are the ability to pay,[10] willingness to pay, and legality.

Because the sovereign position of a state, in contrast to a political subdivision, places it in a position to pay or default on its debt as it sees fit, willingness to pay might be seen to be the most important test. The fact is that willingness is largely dependent on ability to levy and collect the necessary taxes to meet expenses and debt service.

The analysis of the capacity of a state or of a local municipality to meet its obligations involves an examination of its fiscal condition as shown in its financial statement, together with budgetary material and economic and industrial information. The financial statements are quite different from those of business enterprises, and cover primarily such factors as assessed valuation of taxable property, debt outstanding, tax collections, and debt in relation to property and population.

Financial statements of local municipalities sometimes provide more detail. In any case, the first major item is the assessed value of the taxable property located in the jurisdiction. In the 1976 New York State statement (Table 7-4), this item is listed at $75.5 billion and on the local municipal statement in Table 7-5 at $180.0 million. The use of this figure has limited direct significance in states such as California, where neither real nor personal property is taxed for state purposes. In addition, assessment methods

[10]Detailed schedules of the factors to be considered in analyzing general and revenue bonds have been compiled by the Securities Industry Association. They are reprinted in S. N. Levine, ed., *Financial Analyst's Handbook*, Volume I, Chapter 12, Appendices A and B. Homewood, Ill.: Dow Jones-Irwin, Inc., 1975.

**TABLE 7-4   State of New York Financial Statement,
March 31, 1975**

Assessed valuation of taxable real property (41.86% of full value)		$75,465,000,000
Net bonded debt	$3,109,068,000	
Temporary debt	1,664,385,000	
Total debt*a*		$ 4,773,453,000
Population (1976)	18,075,500	
Debt as a percentage of assessed valuation	6.3%	
Debt per capita	$264	

*a*In addition, the state guaranteed $357,500,000 of bonds of New York State Thruway Authority.

**TABLE 7-5   Local Municipal Financial Statement
Specimen Figures—December 31, 1976**

Assessed valuation (90% basis) of taxable property		
Real property		$180,000,000
Franchise values		4,500,000
Personal property		27,000,000
Total		$211,500,000
Gross bonded debt		$ 16,750,000
Water bonds	$2,125,000	
Sinking fund	375,000	2,500,000
Net bonded debt		$ 14,250,000
Population (1970 census)	121,600	
Tax rate per $1,000 of assessed valuation	$21.20	
Ratio of net debt to assessed value	6.74%	

	Tax Collections	
	% Uncollected at *End of Year*	*% Uncollected on* *Dec. 31, 1976*
1973	15.8%	3.1%
1974	11.6	3.6
1975	10.2	4.6
1976	6.3	6.3

vary greatly throughout the country, so that comparison of states is difficult. Nevertheless, property is a measure of wealth, and property produces income that is taxable.

The value of property has more significance in the case of local municipalities, since their chief source of general revenue is property taxes. In our local municipal financial statement, the *total* property value of $211,500,000 does not include exempt private property or nontaxable city property. Franchise valuations are the values of that part of the property of public utility companies located on public property. Of the three classes of property listed, the value of real property (and buildings) is of outstanding importance. In most communities, tax officials find the problem of appraising personal property extremely difficult, so that payment is readily evaded. Real estate is, therefore, generally relied upon to provide the bulk of tax revenue. The basis upon which property is assessed for tax purposes varies widely. Some jurisdictions use a basis of 100% of "true" value, others use a basis as low as 25%.[11]

With such variations in practice, debt percentages, as well as tax rates, for different municipalities are comparable only after adjustment for differences in assessment methods. A debt ratio (per cent of net debt to property value) of 6% and a tax rate of 2.40% in a city employing a 100% assessment basis are equivalent to a debt ratio of 9% and a tax rate of 3.60% in a city using a 66 2/3% assessment basis.

Although property taxes provide the main source of local income, an increasing share of the total city revenue comes from rents for the use of city properties, fees for various services, and shares in state revenues from special taxes, such as mortgage, bank, and corporation taxes. Such revenues, however, are regarded as being primarily available for operating expenses of the city rather than for debt service.

The tax power of local jurisdictions is limited by economics as well as by law. An unlimited legal power to tax might result in excessively high rates beyond the economic capacity of the taxpayers. Tax power does not guarantee safety to investors. In most states, however, a maximum annual tax rate, restricting the charge to a reasonable limit, is imposed by law upon municipalities. Because of the general rule that operating expenses take precedence over debt service, this tax limit seriously impairs the position of municipal bonds in the states which have imposed tax limits without excluding the cost of debt service on bonds.

The gross debt, as stated, may or may not include temporary obligations to be paid out of tax revenue receivable in the near future. In the illustrative local statement in Table 7-5, the gross debt figure of $16,750,000 did not include $1,160,000 in tax-anticipation warrants.

More specific tests of ability to pay, some of which are indicated by the illustrative statements, follow: (these apply to general obligation rather than to revenue bonds).

RATIO OF NET DEBT TO ASSESSED VALUE.   To arrive at net debt, deduct from gross debt the bonds of self-sustaining enterprises and the sinking fund assets, so that the net debt represents the tax-supported liability within the jurisdiction. Where the same property supports debt of other jurisdictions, such as school districts, this overlapping debt is added on to obtain the real debt burden.

The debt of a state should bear a reasonable relation to its taxable property, even though the state itself may not levy a tax on property. A suggested conservative maximum debt ratio is 5% of true (not necessarily the appraised) value. As shown in the New York State statement (Table 7-4), the net debt amounted to 5% of the assessed value of the real property in the state. As the assessed value averaged about 51% of the full value, the true debt percentage was about half of the figure shown. However, the State debt shown here does

---

[11]Actual market values may be considerably higher than "true" values; an assessment ratio of 50% of "true" value may be, in fact, only 30 to 40% of market value in a growing, desirable community.

not comprise the entire public debt against the property, which also supports local municipal debt.

The ratio of net tax-supported debt to the assessed value of the taxable property of a local municipality (shown by Table 7-5 as 6.74%) is a useful indicator of municipal credit. However, in comparing cities, the ratio of net *overall* (including overlapping) debt to estimated true value (adjusted for the appraisal basis) is mandatory. Because of the increased stability of revenue that comes from diversified properties, large cities have been thought to be better credit risks than small cities. (The New York City experience may upset this notion.) Although 5% may be regarded as a fair standard for a medium-sized city, 4% would not be an unreasonably low limit for a small city, and 6% would not be excessive for a large city.

The population figure shown in Table 7-5 is 121,600, reflecting an increase of nearly 11% in the past decade. As the average increase for the nation over the decade was considerably greater, evidently this city has not made favorable progress in this respect. Although rapid growth is a favorable sign, it is not without its disadvantages. City expenditures must keep pace with this increase in population, with the result that bond issues are almost continuous, and new issues often come on the market before the previous ones have been absorbed. A condition of financial indigestion tends to harm the position of all bonds of the city.

NET DEBT PER CAPITA. This is another widely used "short-cut" indicator of debt burden and, hence, of ability to pay. This figure has serious limitations unless viewed along with statistics on government finance and on the wealth and income of the area. But when accompanied by figures on per capita assessed values and per capita tax receipts, it suggests whether a large debt can be amply supported.

For all fifty states in 1975, the long-term state debt outstanding amounted to $315 per capita, $160 of which was represented by general credit obligations.[12] A maximum of $150 of general debt per capita is often suggested as a criterion. Many of the states are well below this figure; but in others, such as Massachusetts and Delaware, the figure is much higher and suggests a situation of weakness that might have serious repercussions in a period of economic distress.

In analyzing local municipalities, the combined (including overlapping) per capita net debt should be used, especially when comparing different cities.

The per capita debt shown in the illustrative municipal statement (Table 7-5) is $117. While consideration must be given to the relative wealth and income of the community in the use of this item for comparative purposes, a per capita debt of $400 is too high for convenient repayment by any municipality, and $300 is a reasonable maximum.

DEBT SERVICE REQUIREMENTS. The relationship of annual debt service requirements (interest plus principal to be retired) to total annual revenues

---

[12]U.S. Department of Commerce, Bureau of the Census, *Government Finances in 1974–1975*, p. 26.

indicates the ability of the state or municipality to cover its fixed charges. The debt service charge for New York State in 1975 amounted to $328 million, or approximately 3.4% of general state revenues. A maximum of 5% is suggested as a useful criterion for a state. For a municipality, the ratio should not exceed 15% of the annual budget. It was 27% for New York City in 1975.

TREND OF DEBT; DEBT RETIREMENT POLICY.   The trend of the debt of a state or municipality furnishes a good indication of the fiscal policy of the unit. The debt may not have reached unusual proportions up to the present, but if it has been increasing steadily for a number of years, the result may be a decline in its value and rating.

Policies and requirements concerning debt retirement should be examined carefully. Retirement of about 25% of the outstanding debt within the ensuing five years and 50% in 10 years, is highly desirable. Where debt can be retired at this rate within a debt service ratio of 15% of the annual budget, sound financial administration is evident. The use of serial bonds contributes greatly to regular retirement and a balanced debt structure.

LIMITATIONS OF DEBT AND TAX RATE.   As we have seen, statutory debt limits, in terms of assessed value of taxable property, are imposed on local municipalities in most states. These would seem to impose restrictions that would keep the debt within conservative limits. But in some cases the legal limits have been set so high that they provide little restraint upon the issue of debt. And even when the limits are reasonable, evasion is often relatively easy. Assessments can be raised, special districts can be created (unless the state has set an overall debt limit), or revenue bonds may be issued by the unit itself or by an authority created especially for this purpose. Nevertheless, a net debt limitation of 10% of assessed valuation is desirable, for it precludes unlimited borrowing.

Of more importance are the limitations on taxing power, expressed as a per cent of valuation or in dollars per $1,000 of valuation, that are imposed on municipalities in many states, either in the constitution or by special statute or by municipal ordinance. The purpose is to keep the tax rate down and to hold the borrowing of the municipality within reasonable bounds. But the result may impair its credit. If the municipality has reached the limit, it must either increase the assessment or turn to other forms of taxation, or to borrowing.

In appraising the tax limitations, one should note whether they apply to taxation for all purposes, including payment of debt, or whether debt service is excluded. Nevada prescribes a limit of 5 cents per dollar of assessed valuation for all purposes; but New York exempts the debt service from the limitation of a total tax rate of 2% ($20 per $1,000).

From the standpoint of the investor, *unlimited*-tax bonds, which permit the municipality to draw adequately on its resources, are, of course, to be desired, provided that total debt-incurring power is restricted and that the affairs of the unit are managed efficiently.

THE ACTUAL TAX RATE.   The legal limit on the amount of tax levied for operating purposes may create embarrassment if expenses increase or assessed values decline. But even if there is no limit, a high or increasing rate may indicate trouble. If the rate is at an all-time high, there may be resistance on the part of taxpayers, with a resultant lowering of the rate of tax collection, and of the investment quality of the bonds.

The nominal tax rate must, of course, be adjusted for the bases on which property is assessed. The tax rate of $21.20 per $1,000 shown in Table 7-5 is based upon an assessment rate of 90% of full value and is, therefore, equal to a tax rate of $19.10 at full value. Comparisons of rates are misleading unless proper adjustment is made for different bases. An overall tax rate of $30 per $1,000 of true valuation is suggested as a maximum.

THE TAX-COLLECTION RECORD.   It is one thing to levy taxes and another to collect them. The investor should examine both the amount and the trend of the deficiency in tax collections. The data in the specimen local statement indicate that collections have been improving throughout the four-year period. The city collected in 1972 about 84% of the taxes levied during that year, about 88% in 1973, about 90% in 1974, and over 93% in 1975. By the end of 1976, the city had collected 97% of the 1973 levy, 96% of 1974 taxes, and 95% of 1975 taxes. A tax collection record of 90% during the year of levy is regarded as favorable. The older the delinquencies become, the harder they are to collect. A large volume of taxes over a year old may indicate faulty collection machinery, unaggressive collection policy, insufficient income in relation to government expenditures, or the presence of unproductive real estate.

GENERAL ECONOMIC FACTORS.   The general economic condition, resources, and growth of the state or municipality, as indicated by income, wealth, types and diversification of industries, payrolls, population, and other factors, should be examined. Information on such matters in the typical prospectus describing an offering of municipal bonds is very sketchy indeed. The investment manuals often provide considerable detail, but it is difficult to relate to the appraisal of a particular bond at a particular yield. Here again, the investor is likely to rely on the investigation of the issue that has been made by the offering house, and on the bond's rating.

THE CHARACTER OF PUBLIC ADMINISTRATION.   The standing of the public officials, their training, experience, and record, the completeness and frankness of their financial reports, and the stability of local administration are important factors in municipal analysis.

Willingness to pay   The second major test of the quality of municipal bonds is *willingness to pay*, as measured by past record and present conditions. This test is particularly important in the case of state debt, for a state may not be sued without its consent.

Since the Civil War period, the record of state bonds has been free of actual default. The State of Arkansas, in 1933, attempted to force holders of 4 1/4, 4 1/2, 4 3/4, and 5% bonds of that state to exchange them for 3% bonds at par by refusing to continue interest payments on the former issues.

This difficulty, however, was adjusted through a refunding program adopted in 1934, which provided for eventual payment of interest in full. But the action was a severe blow to the credit of the state and suggests that repudiation is not without possibility. The best protection is the restriction of debt to modest proportions relative to wealth and income. In 1975 New York City was willing to pay, but perilously close to inability to pay.

Valid local government bonds are enforceable obligations. Creditors holding bonds in default can sue in a court of jurisdiction and obtain judgment. If no property is available for attachment, a writ of mandamus can be obtained, requiring city authorities to levy and collect additional taxes to cover the claim.

Willingness is a matter of convenience and good faith. Convenience is largely a matter of capacity, whereas good faith is a matter of character. Capacity may best be judged from the financial condition of the city and character from its financial history. A strong financial statement and an excellent debt record are, therefore, the best indication of willingness to pay. This is well illustrated by experience with defaults by numerous Florida cities after the collapse of the land boom in 1926. Chicago was brought to the brink of receivership in 1932 because of delays in tax collections between 1928 and 1931. New York City's crisis in 1975 is well known.

Inability to pay because of inadequate revenues arising out of tax-limit legislation could just as properly be termed unwillingness to pay. As was previously indicated, investors should prefer the bonds of those communities that are obligated to pay their bonds with no limitation as to taxes for such purpose. In fairness, it should be pointed out that many cities have maintained the integrity of their credit ratings through a drastic reduction in operating expenses, and, at the same time actually lowered the tax burden upon property owners. In many instances even grave disasters such as fires, floods, and earthquakes did not prevent the full payment of maturing obligations. Good faith is an excellent municipal asset.

Unlike ability to pay, specific indicators of willingness to pay are difficult to pinpoint. The debt record, the tax-collection record, the fiscal policies of the municipality's administration in the face of adversity are suggestive, however. Cities like Detroit, Mobile, and Atlantic City were forced to default in the early 1930s, but subsequently put through refunding programs, and their credit has been redeemed. Since World War II relatively small losses have been suffered by owners of direct municipal debt, although holders of New York City bonds came close. Defaults of revenue bonds have been much more serious.

The wide publicity stemming from the crisis in New York City's finances created apprehension about the credit worthiness of other communities. Prospective and existing municipal bond buyers began asking: "Can it happen here?" To avoid the prospect of default, the municipal bond buyer must investigate more carefully than ever before the issuer's credit quality.

The 1975 Amendments to the Federal Securities Act set up a new Municipal Securities Rulemaking Board. The Board's function is to find a way around the exemption of municipalities from the standards of full disclosure that are required of corporations when issuing securities. Until this double standard is eliminated, investors will have to continue to search for information concerning the credit standing of municipalities.

Investors seeking the ultimate protection against financial collapse of a municipality should inquire about default insurance. One insurance carrier provides protection against specific defaults of principal and/or interest while the bonds are held in a particular account. The individual investor pays the premium and retains the protection if the bonds are not sold. In a different approach, several large insurance companies have joined together in "The Municipal Bond Insurance Association." Here the issuer pays a single lump-sum premium, and protection remains with the bonds until repaid.

Legality of issue   The third test of the investment position of state and local bonds is *legality of issue*. Practically all states now limit their debt-creating capacity through voluntary restrictions written into the state constitution. These restrictions vary in the different states; in general, they are: (1) no state credit for private benefit, (2) bonds essentially for long-term improvements, and (3) referendum approval on large issues.

A number of states also require that all state bonds must be issued in serial form, that each bond issue mature within the estimated life of the improvement, and that the proceeds of each issue be segregated into a special fund to be used only for the designated purpose and not combined with the general funds of the state.

In the case of bonds of local jurisdictions, legality is of prime importance; first, because creditors are allowed to sue municipalities to compel payment, and, second, because a municipal bond that has been illegally issued is invalid and noncollectible. Instances may be found where courts, to protect innocent investors who have acted in good faith, have held some municipal bonds with minor technical defects to be valid obligations. But the general rule is that buyers of local bonds do so at their own risk and may not plead ignorance if illegality should later be established. All negotiations involving the issuance of municipal bonds are open to public inspection, and the laws regarding such issues are matters of record, so that a plea of ignorance of any defect would not be an acceptable basis in a suit for collection.

Cases involving illegality of issue of local government bonds may be divided into four groups. The *authority of issue* may be inadequate under the powers granted to the city. The *purpose of issue* may be outside the legitimate purposes for which bonds may be issued. The *process of issue* may have violated any one of a score of minute details required by law. The *restriction of issue* may have been ignored in the issuance of bonds to an aggregate amount beyond the legal debt limit of the city. Since the investor is rarely in a position to pass upon such questions, he must rely upon the advice of qualified attorneys.

Investors should be assured that outside counsel has carefully checked and approved the legality of issue, and also that the particular counsel has a recognized reputation in municipal finance. Experienced investors in municipal bonds buy only those issues that have been approved by one of the fewer than 100 law firms in the entire United States that have gained a national reputation in this field.

Municipal Bond Ratings

Two financial services—Moody's Investors Service and Standard & Poor's Corporation—provide a valuable service to investors by publishing quality ratings on a large number of state and local general obligations and revenue bonds.[13]

The small investor may be content to rely on bond ratings for his appraisal of quality. When substantial sums are involved, however, the investor should make his own analysis as a check against the ratings, which are not infallible and are subject to change. Table 7-6 shows selected examples of ratings, by types of issuer.

Examinations of rating lists reveals many bonds of smaller cities, counties, school districts, and local utility revenue bonds, running from Aaa to ratings

TABLE 7-6   Selected Municipal Bond Ratings February, 1977

	Ratings	
	Moody's	Standard & Poor's
States (general obligations)		
Missouri	Aaa	AAA
Georgia	Aaa	AAA
California	Aaa	AAA
Hawaii	Aa	AA
Rhode Island	Aa	AA
Alabama	Aa	AA
Alaska	A-1	A
New York	A	AA
Large cities (general obligations)		
Milwaukee	Aaa	AAA
San Francisco	Aaa	AAA
Cincinnati	Aa	AA
Dallas	Aa	AA
Fort Worth	Aa	AA
Baltimore	Aa	A
Miami	A-1	A
St. Louis	A	AA
Culver City, Ca.	A	A
Jersey City	Baa	BBB+
Philadelphia	Baa	A
Yonkers	Baa	BBB+
Detroit	Baa	BBB
New York City	Caa	—

[13]Moody's ratings are found in *Moody's Bond Survey*; the symbols used are Aaa, Aa, A-1, A, Baa-1, Baa, Ba, B, Caa, Ca, and C. Ratings below B are rare. Many small issues are unrated.

Standard and Poor's uses the symbols AAA, AA, A, BBB, BB, B, CCC, CC, C (reserved for income bonds) and DDD-D (bonds in default). Ratings are found in Standard & Poor's *Bond Guide* (monthly). Ratings below B are rare.

Most revenue bonds are unrated. Very few have the top rating, unless they are guaranteed or are supported by special taxes such as motor fuel taxes.

TABLE 7-6   (Continued)

	Ratings	
	Moody's	Standard & Poor's
Nonguaranteed revenue bonds		
New Haven Coliseum Authority	Aa	AA
Rhode Island Turnpike and Bridge Authority	Aa	—
Port of New York Authority	Aa, A	AA
New York State Thruway Authority	A-1	—
Ohio Turnpike Commission	A	—
Mackinac Bridge Authority	A	—
Chesapeake Bay Bridge Authority	Baa	—
Indiana Toll Road Commission	Ba	BBB
So. California Rapid Transit	Baa	BBB
Dade County, Florida, Water & Sewer	Baa	BBB
Chicago-Calumet Skyway	Caa	—
West Virginia Turnpike Commission	Caa	—
Bellevue Bridge Commission, Nebraska	Ca	—
Dunbar Bridge, West Virginia	Ca	—

Source: Moody's ratings from *Moody's Bond Record;* Standard & Poor's from *Bond Guide.*

of C or lower. Size and rating are not well correlated. With few exceptions, ratings of general obligations of local governments seldom exceed those of the state in which the jurisdiction is located, but they are often as high.

The influence of the ratings by the two agencies is enormous. A drop in a rating brings an immediate drop in price; a rise has a very salutary effect and is immediately exploited in new financing.

Form of Municipal Bonds

The leading features of state and local government bonds are usually prescribed by statute. They are issued in both coupon and registered forms; in some cases, the denominations of the latter type run as high as $1,000,000. Most bond issues mature serially, especially where the proceeds are used to finance depreciating assets. Sinking fund bonds are seen only infrequently. It is, of course, in the interest of the investor that the sinking fund appropriations be used principally to retire the precise bond issues for which the funds are established.

Many municipal bonds include the call feature, making possible redemption before maturity for general or sinking fund purposes, as well as advanced refunding.[14]

---

[14]The purpose of refunding in advance of maturity is to take advantage of a decline in interest rates. A refunding issue may even be sold some weeks or months before outstanding bonds are called. The proceeds are invested in short-term Federal obligations.

Tax Position of Municipal Bonds

Income from all classes of municipal bonds, whether general lien, assessment, or revenue obligations, issued by states, municipalities, special districts, or authorities is exempt from all Federal income taxes. This feature is of particular value to investors whose incomes are subject to heavy tax rates. (See Chapter 18.) Repeated efforts have been made to remove this exemption feature from such issues, but with no success.

In recent years proposals have been made in Congress to allow states and local units to issue taxable bonds on which the Federal government would pay the issuer a subsidy of 25% to 50% of the interest cost. The purpose is to attract investors in the lower brackets to whom tax exemption is not now a benefit. None has as yet (1977) been adopted.

The position of municipals with respect to state personal property or intangible taxes, and state personal and corporate income taxes, is not uniform. Although there are some exceptions, a state obligation or the income therefrom is not usually taxed in the state of issue, nor are the obligations of subdivisions in that state. Interest on obligations of other states and subdivisions thereof is sometimes taxed in other states, sometimes exempt. Exemption from local taxes is particularly valuable in Pennsylvania, Massachusetts, New York, and Virginia where taxes upon holders of out-of-state issues are relatively severe. There is no exemption from capital gains or from Federal or state estate and inheritance taxes.[15]

Because any profit on resale of a municipal bond is taxable at the capital gains rate applying to the investor, buyers of municipal bonds should prefer those bearing coupon rates that approximate the yield to maturity—in other words, bonds priced around par. Income from these bonds is tax-exempt, and such income constitutes most or all of the yield of the bond. If bonds are bought at a substantial discount, any subsequent rise in value is taxable on resale.

Yields

Table 7-7 shows the *average* annual yields on Moody's Aaa and Baa state and local government bond series as compared with the "riskless" yield on U.S. Treasury long-term bond series, for the years 1960–1976. The last two columns show the spread between yields on the highest grade and good-grade municipals.

Yields on state and local government bonds as a group are the result of five main influences:

---

[15]For the tax status within each state of issue, see Moody's Investors Service, *Municipal and Government Manual*, blue section.

TABLE 7-7　Average Annual Yields

	Long-term Treasury	State and Local Government		Spread	Spread
	(1)	(2) Aaa	(3) Baa	(1) over (2)	(3) over (2)
1960	4.01%	3.26%	4.22%	0.75	0.96
1965	4.21	3.16	3.57	1.05	0.41
1966	4.66	3.67	4.21	0.99	0.54
1967	4.85	3.74	4.30	1.11	0.56
1968	5.25	4.20	4.88	1.05	0.68
1969	6.10	5.45	6.07	0.65	0.62
1970	6.59	6.12	6.75	0.47	0.63
1971	5.74	5.22	5.89	0.52	0.67
1972	5.63	5.04	5.60	0.59	0.56
1973	6.30	4.99	5.49	1.31	0.50
1974	6.99	5.89	6.53	1.10	0.64
1975	6.98	6.42	7.62	0.56	1.20
1976	6.78	5.66	7.49	1.10	1.83

Source: Federal Reserve Bulletin.

AVERAGE YIELDS OF LONG-TERM TREASURY, CORPORATE, AND MUNICIPAL BONDS

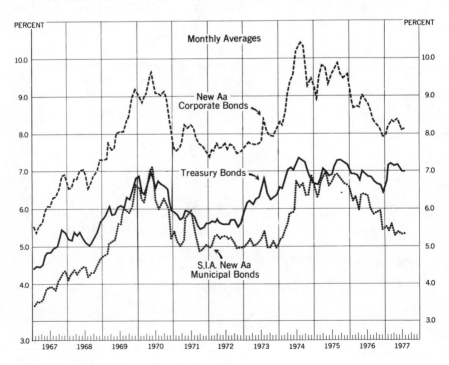

Source: Treasury Bulletin.

128

INTEREST RATES IN GENERAL.   Previous data show that rises and declines in yields on Treasury bonds are accompanied by changes in the same direction for municipals. By midsummer 1970, both reached record levels. Long-term Federal bonds yielded 7.25%, and Aaa municipals 6.95%. These astronomical rates were dramatic evidence of the "credit crunch" that had begun in 1969. Yields on these two categories declined with easier money conditions. A new "crunch" was first felt in the U.S. Government bond market in 1973, and spread to the whole range in 1974–1975. Municipal bonds were under special pressure and produced record yields in 1975, especially for less-than-high-grade bonds, which offered tax-free income of 7 to 8%. Possibly this reflected the New York experience as a special influence. High-grade yields fell sharply in 1976 and early 1977, then levelled off.

The spread between yields on new corporate bonds and the Securities Industry Association new Aa municipal bond series shows the premium paid for bonds of not quite the highest quality. See Chart 7-1.

THE SUPPLY OF NEW SECURITIES OF THIS TYPE.   The net annual increase in long-term municipal public debt (after refinancing) for the years 1965–1976 was (in billions of dollars):[16]

1965	1966	1967	1968	1969	1970	1971	1972	1973	1974	1975	1976
$6.7	$5.1	$5.9	$9.4	$7.2	$8.9	$15.0	$14.8	$14.2	$15.4	$16.7	$17.9

The relation between net new debt and yields, although crude, is apparent. The first "credit crunch" period of tight money that culminated in high yields in 1966 was accentuated insofar as municipal bonds were concerned by the large new financing that had been building up since the early 1960s. Then in 1967–1968 and again in 1970, the huge volume of municipal offerings, accompanying tight money in general, was partly responsible for the record-breaking yields that peaked in mid-1970. Municipal financing continued at a high level in 1971–1972, but easier money conditions more than offset this influence and yields declined substantially. The highest-grade issues yielded 4.95% in early 1973. But then the outpouring of new debt in 1971–1975 helped to force yields to new record highs.

THE SUPPLY OF FUNDS AVAILABLE FOR PURCHASE OF TAX-FREE BONDS.   New issues are absorbed primarily by taxed institutions, especially commercial banks and insurance companies, and by individuals. Bank acquisitions have shown the greatest variations. Demand fell off in 1965–1966 as bank funds were diverted to loans, and yields rose. Again in 1966 commercial bank acquisitions of municipal securities dropped to $1.9 billion from $5.1 billion in 1965, as banks diverted funds to ease the tight short-term loan situation.

[16]Securities Association, *Statistical Bulletin*; Bankers Trust Company, *Credit and Capital Markets*, annual; *Federal Reserve Bulletin*.

Banks were back in the municipals market in 1967 and 1968, and their supply of funds helped to ease the yield level. But in 1969, they again deserted the tax-exempt market in the face of the credit strains of that year. Heavy buying began later in 1970, after the main crisis had passed, and reached $12.6 billion in 1971. Subsequent decline in bank buying brought the figure to $1.7 billion in 1975, and $3.8 billion in 1976, and along with increasing supply, was a major influence in forcing yields to new highs. The high yields did give a substantial impetus to purchases by households and nonlife insurance companies, however. Household orders rose from a negative $0.2 billion in 1971 to $11.2 billion in 1974, dropping to $8.7 billion in 1975 and $6.2 billion in 1976.

THE VALUE OF THE TAX-FREE PRIVILEGE.   This factor is a major influence, as revealed by the spread between Treasury and Aaa municipal yields in Table 7-7. The changes in the spread reflect the forces that pushed Treasury yields to a peak in 1969. After declines in 1970–1972, Treasury bond yields reached peaks in 1973 and 1974, and the spread increased, only to decline in 1975 as municipal bond yields rose to new heights. The forces of supply and demand indicated previously were accompanied by the collapse of New York City credit in 1975 and its discouraging effect on all municipal obligations. It is difficult to measure the possible influence of the decline in income tax rates in 1970 and 1975, but available data on individual and institutional buying suggest that the appeal of the tax-exempt feature remained very potent.

INDIVIDUAL CHARACTERISTICS.   Yields on individual issues are affected by their investment quality or rating, their marketability (largely a function of size), and their state income tax status. The increasing spread between yields on good-grade and high-grade municipals reflects the influence of quality as well as the value of the tax-free privilege. Although more and more individuals seek this benefit as average income rises, loss of faith in lesser-grade municipal bonds has more than offset their tax appeal.

The difference in quality among state bonds is narrow, so that bonds of different states, of equal maturities, sell in a close yield range. Bonds of local municipalities present a wide range of quality and, therefore, present a wide range of yields; this is especially true in the case of revenue bonds. The average investor should confine his purchases to the general-lien bonds of states and of the larger and stronger cities. The lower grades should be bought only by investors skilled in municipal bond analysis or especially familiar with the issuing unit, and able to assume more risk.

The Market for Municipal Bonds

New issues of general obligations are sold by competitive bidding to the some 60 investment houses that specialize in such obligations and to commercial banks which are permitted to act as principals (underwriters) in the purchase of general obligation bonds. Revenue bonds are frequently sold on a negotiated basis. The dealers and "dealer banks" then retail the bonds to investors and maintain an over-the-counter market in them.

After the details of an issue, including its denomination, maturities, and other aspects of its form, have been determined by the administrative officials of the issuing unit, an official notice is published that offers the issue for sealed competitive bidding. The *Daily Bond Buyer* is widely used in this connection to reach the bond trade. Unless the offer is accompanied by a legal opinion that the bonds are legally and regularly issued, bidders generally bid subject to subsequent approval of legality. Usually the bid of the house or joint account (syndicate) that shows the lowest net interest cost to the issuer is accepted.

The successful bidder then reoffers the bonds at a slight markup. The offering circular provides a bare minimum of information, including the financial statement of the municipality and possibly some data on the industry and the general economic condition of the area. The brevity of municipal bond circulars is in sharp contrast to the completeness required in new corporate security offerings under the Securities Act of 1933.

Municipal bonds are usually offered (and later traded) on a *yield basis*; that is, the price is indicated as a yield to maturity rather than in dollars. When short-term interest rates are lower than long-term, the early maturities sell at lower yields than the later ones.

Trading in outstanding state and municipal bonds is carried on over-the-counter through dealer houses specializing in these securities and through municipal bond brokers who serve as contacts between dealers. For trading purposes, the daily *Blue List of Current Municipal Offerings* is of great value in that it lists the current offerings of most municipal houses; between 2,000 and 3,000 issues may be available. The minimum round-lot unit of trading is $5,000 par value.

Although they are never listed on any exchange, municipal bonds of good quality enjoy a ready market. They are much in demand on the part of individuals seeking income tax exemption. Their other major market is among institutions such as commercial banks, insurance companies, and trustees. State bonds may be used by banks in lieu of surety bonds to guarantee the safety of deposit of state funds and by insurance companies under state laws requiring guarantees. The reader is cautioned, however, that at times bids on small lots of municipal bonds may not be readily available. Table 7-8 shows estimates of the ownership of interest-bearing state and local government bonds as of December 31, 1976.

Investment Position of Municipal Bonds

In general, bonds of states enjoy an investment position second only to that of Federal obligations. The spread in yield between the strongest and the weakest bonds is small. Yet the market does make a distinction between the bonds of states with a good past record, a sound economic trend, and stable

TABLE 7-8 Ownership of Long-Term Municipal Debt, 1976 (in billions of dollars)

Ownership	Amount	%
Commercial banks	$104.7	46.4%
Households personal trusts	51.4	22.8
Nonlife insurance companies	35.9	15.9
Life insurance companies	5.6	2.5
State and local governments	6.1	2.7
State and local retirement funds	4.4	2.0
Mutual savings banks	2.4	1.0
Others	15.0	6.7
Total	$225.5	100.0%

Source: Citations in Chapters 5, 21, 22, 29, 30; *Federal Reserve Bulletin,* flow-of-funds tables.

political management, and those of inferior record, poor economic development, and unreliable leadership. As we have seen, bonds of local municipalities, and revenue bonds, range in quality from poor to excellent.

The investor in the lower income brackets should ordinarily avoid municipal obligations. He would be paying for a feature he does not need. But a growing number of investors, even those in moderate income brackets, should calculate the comparative after-tax yields of taxable and tax-exempt bonds. (See Chapter 18.) The higher the taxable income, the greater the value of the exemption and the lower the acceptable yield. Investors who wish to avoid making their own selection of bonds may purchase the shares of funds whose portfolios consist of tax-free bonds and whose income is tax-free. Two types are available: (1) unit trusts with fixed portfolios, whose shares sell for asset value plus a sales charge; (2) open-end funds that first appeared in 1976. (See Chapter 11.)

Information on State and Local Governments

The primary sources of information on state and local governments and their securities are the annual reports prepared by the financial offices of the units. These vary from a brief financial statement to a comprehensive booklet such as that issued by the Comptroller of New York State.

The secondary sources include:

Annual publications of the U.S. Department of Commerce, Bureau of the Census: *State Government Finances; Summary of State Government Finances; City Government Finances; Governmental Finances; Summary of Governmental Finances; State Tax Collections;* and *Local Government Finances in Selected Metropolitan Areas.*

The Blue List of Current Municipal Offerings, a daily compilation of offerings of the larger municipal bond houses.

The Money Manager (New York) devoted mainly to news concerning municipal securities (weekly); *Municipal Bond Sales* (annually).

Dun & Bradstreet's *Municipal Credit Surveys*, on obligors having a substantial
amount of debt outstanding.

Securities Industry Association, *Statistical Bulletin* (quarterly).

Moody's Bond Record and *Moody's Manual of Investments, Municipal and Government.*

Prospectuses and special releases of investment banking houses interested in state
and municipal securities.

Standard & Poor's *The Fixed Income Investor.*

The Tax Foundation, Inc. (New York) *Facts and Figures on Government Finance*
(biennially). (Also includes data on Federal finance.)

The Bond Buyer's Municipal Finance Statistics. New York, annually.

REFERENCES

CALVERT, G. L., ed., *Fundamentals of Municipal Bonds*, 9th ed. Washington, D.C.:
Securities Industry Association, 1972.

CURVIN, W. S., *A Manual on Municipal Bonds*, rev. ed. New York: Smith, Barney &
Co., 1964.

DARST, D. N., *The Complete Bond Book: A Guide to All Types of Fixed-Income Securities.*
New York: McGraw-Hill Book Co., 1975.

DOUGALL, H. E., and J, E. GAUMNITZ, *Capital Markets and Institutions*, 3rd ed., Chapter
8. Englewood Cliffs, N.J.: Prentice-Hall, Inc., 1975.

HEMPEL, G. H., *The Postwar Quality of State and Local Debt.* New York: National Bureau
of Economic Research (distributed by Columbia University Press), 1971.

————, *Measures of Municipal Bond Quality.* Ann Arbor, Mich.: Bureau of Business
Administration, University of Michigan, 1967.

JANTSCHER, G. R., *The Effects of Changes in Credit Rating on Municipal Borrowing Costs.*
Washington, D.C.: Investment Bankers Association of America, 1970.

LEVINE, S. N., ed. *Financial Analyst's Handbook*, Volume I, Chapters 12, 13. Homewood,
Ill.: Dow Jones-Irwin, Inc., 1975.

LOLL, L. M., and J. G. BUCKLEY, *The Over-the-Counter Securities Markets*, 2nd ed.
Englewood Cliffs, N.J.: Prentice-Hall, Inc., 1967.

LUDEMAN, D. H., *The Investment Merits of Big City Bonds.* Boston, Mass.: Financial
Publishing Co., 1973.

MOAK, L. L., *Administration of Local Government Debt.* Chicago, Ill.: Municipal Officers
Association of the United States and Canada, 1970.

OTT D. J., and A. H. MELTZER, *Federal Tax Treatment of State and Local Securities.*
Washington, D.C.: The Brookings Institution, 1963.

RABINOWITZ, ALAN, *Municipal Bond Finance and Administration.* New York: John Wiley
& Sons, Inc. (Interscience Division), 1969.

REILLY, J. F., *Too Good for the Rich Alone: The Complete Guide to Tax-Exempt Bonds for
the Middle-Income Investor.* Englewood Cliffs, N.J.: Prentice-Hall, Inc., 1975.

ROBINSON, R. I., *The Postwar Market for State and Local Government Securities.* Princeton, N.J.: Princeton University Press, 1960.

————, and D. WRIGHTSMAN, *Financial Markets: The Accumulation and Allocation of Wealth.*, Chapter 15. New York: McGraw-Hill Book Co., 1974.

Characteristics of Corporate Bonds

SCOPE: This chapter discusses the general characteristics of corporate bonds from the viewpoint of the investor. The order of discussion is: (1) general characteristics, (2) reasons for use, (3) importance of bond financing, (4) bond indentures, (5) the bond instrument, (6) classification of bonds, (7) concepts of return on bonds, (8) calculation of net yield, (9) other bond yields, (10) ownership of corporate bonds, and (11) investment position of bonds.

General Characteristics

Bonds represent long-term debt, as contrasted with stocks which represent ownership. Claims of all bondholders have priority over the interest of stockholders, both preferred and common. Particular bond issues enjoy preferred claims over other issues when the nature of the preference is definitely stated in the instrument, as in the case of a first mortgage issue. Bonds usually contain a promise to pay a fixed rate of interest, and their principal is payable on a definite date. The bondholder is ordinarily entitled to the fixed income and principal, but to no more.

Bonds normally give the holder no voice in management. Failure to meet the terms of the issue gives the trustee named in the indenture the right to take legal action—either to foreclose on any pledged property or to sue for breach of contract. In a majority of cases, however, default leads to financial reorganization rather than to liquidation.

The position of the bondholder contrasts sharply with that of the stockholder. The bondholder takes risk, but *relatively* less risk than the stockholder in the same corporation. He has made a loan, he expects a fixed rate of income, and he anticipates return of the full face value of the bond at a definite future date. The quality of his bond, as reflected in price and yield, depends on the degree to which the debtor is expected to fulfill these promises.

Reasons for Issuing Bonds

When governments are unable to meet their expenses from current tax income, they have no choice but to borrow. Corporations, on the other hand, have a wider choice of methods with which to finance their operations. Among other ways, they may sell stocks or grow from retained earnings and other "internal" sources. Why do they incur the risk of borrowing? Five main reasons explain the use of bonds:

To lower the cost of funds. Investors are usually satisfied with a lower return from the bonds than from preferred stock of the same company.[1] Bond financing is also often cheaper than common stock financing, as measured by the relation between earnings and market price.[2] The corporation is willing to incur the risk of borrowing in order to save on the cost of part of its capital.

To gain the benefit of leverage. In financial parlance *leverage* means the use of funds bearing a fixed cost in the hope of earning a higher rate than that cost. Thus, if a company can borrow at 8% and put the funds to work to earn 15%, the earnings on the owners' investment are increased. The leverage effect of borrowing, however, results in loss to the owners when the borrowed capital earns less than the fixed charge for its use.

To widen the source of funds. Funds can be attracted from individual investors and especially from investing institutions that are unwilling or are not permitted to purchase stock.

To preserve control. Since bonds ordinarily carry no voting rights, an increase in debt does not disturb the voting power of present owners, at least as long as the bonds are not in default.

To effect tax savings. The interest on bonds is deductible in figuring corporate income for tax purposes, whereas dividends on stock are not.

Borrowing also has definite limitations that the wise corporate management feels obliged to follow. When these limitations are disregarded, the investment position of the bonds suffers, and the cost of borrowed money increases; very substantial overborrowing may lead to default and bankruptcy. In the later sections of this book attention will be given to the tests of sound debt policy from the investor's standpoint.

Importance of Bond Financing

The data in Table 3-4 show the use of bond financing by corporations in the last 17 years. Bonds have far exceeded stocks as means of raising new money by the issuance of securities. However, when retained earnings are

---

[1]An exception is found in the case of high-grade preferred stocks which, because only 15% of their dividends are subject to Federal corporate income taxes, have a special appeal to taxed institutional investors, and so often produce market yields below those on high-grade bonds, even of the same issuer.

[2]The whole subject of the relative costs of debt and equity capital is discussed in works dealing with corporate financial policy; see references at the end of this chapter.

added to new stock issues, equity capital financing has exceeded the use of long-term bonds by a large margin. Large use has, however, been made of other types of long-term debt, such as mortgage notes and term loans.

Bond Indentures

In bond financing the basic document is the *indenture* or trust agreement. This is the contract between the borrowing company and the trustee (usually a bank) or trustees representing the bondholders. It contains all the provisions of the borrowing, and hence, especially in the case of mortgage bonds, is often a long and formidable document. It also includes the duties of the trustee and his relation to the issuer and the bondholders. The trustee's chief duties are to authenticate the bonds, to represent the bondholders by enforcing the terms of the indenture, especially in the event of default, and to handle the details of sinking fund payments, interest payments, and bond redemption.

The Trust Indenture Act of 1939 requires corporations to file trust indentures with the Securities and Exchange Commission in the case of debt securities registered under the Securities Act of 1933. It sets forth the qualifications of the trustee and outlines the material concerning the trustee's actions that must be included in the indenture.

The Bond Instrument

The bond certificate issued to the investor contains only a summary of the main provisions of the borrowing. It is in effect a long-term promissory note. Its title usually indicates the name of the issuer, the rate of interest, the date of maturity, and some suggestion of the nature of any pledged property. The face amount or denomination of each bond is customarily $500 or $1,000, and represents part of a large issue that has been divided into small units for convenience in distribution. A fixed annual interest rate is stated on each bond; interest payments are usually made semiannually. Interest is collected by the owner through the presentation of coupons detached from the bond or of a check from the issuer. Practically all bonds bear definite maturity dates; few American corporations have issued perpetual debt.

Bonds may be *secured*, that is, enjoy a lien on specific pledged assets; or *unsecured*, that is, have a claim on assets in general and junior to any secured issues. Some of the highest-grade bonds are unsecured.

Although all bonds are essentially similar in that they all represent long-term debt, many variations are found in practice. The chief difference lies in the nature of the claim. The issue with a prior claim on valuable assets naturally represents the safer security, taking precedence over any other bonds issued by the same debtor. The title of the bond is usually taken from the nature of the security, such as *first mortgage, collateral,* or *debenture*; or from the purpose of issue, such as *adjustment, refunding,* or *consolidated*; or from some special feature, such as *sinking fund,* or *convertible.* In numerous cases, a combination title is used, such as *first consolidated, adjustment income,* or *first and refunding.* The title, however, serves to describe the issue more than to reflect its investment position. Some first mortgage bonds are inferior to unsecured issues of other companies.

A single company may have several bond issues outstanding. It may also be directly or indirectly responsible for the payment of bonds issued by affiliated companies. In 1976 the Penn Central Transportation System had outstanding 30 bond issues or series, in addition to its equipment obligations. Each of these fits into a definite sequence of claim upon earnings. Industrial companies usually have relatively few issues, and these are less complex. Unsecured debenture issues predominate.

Classification of Bonds

Security The customary bond title indicates the nature of the security behind the obligation (or lack of it), the promised rate of interest, and the maturity date, such as First Mortgage 7s, 1980; Collateral Trust 6s, 1994; Subordinated Debenture 8s, 2001. However, some issues avoid reflecting a junior claim in their titles; or where they are little better than an unsecured claim, some harmless title such as *refunding* 8s or *sinking fund* 7 1/2s may be adopted.

Mortgage bonds are the most common form of secured issues. A mortgage bond is secured by a lien on specific fixed assets described in the indenture, and the extra protection afforded by the mortgage depends on the priority of the lien and the value of the property pledged. This may be the entire fixed property or only a certain section of it, as in the case of railroad divisional bonds. If the mortgage is *closed*, no more bonds may be secured by the same lien. However, corporations have found that such issues may make future financing difficult. The *open-end* mortgage is designed to meet this situation. Under this arrangement, more bonds secured by the same lien may be issued, but certain protective provisions are required to prevent the dilution of the original security: (1) that additional bonds be limited to a proportion (often 75%) of new property added, and (2) that additional bonds be issued only when aggregate interest charges on new and old bonds are adequately earned (say, twice). The effects of expansion of debt (usually in successive series) are also limited if the open-end mortgage contains an *after-acquired-property clause,* which provides that all fixed property "hereinafter acquired" be included in the property pledged.

A further covenant of importance is the penalty clause for failure to meet the various covenants in the indenture. Default in any specified promise renders the entire principal immediately due and payable.

Mortgage bonds may be classified as *senior* and *junior liens,* according to priority of claim. The senior liens, which hold the first claim upon both earnings and (designated) assets, comprise first mortgages. The Duquesne Light Company (Pittsburgh) First Mortgage bonds illustrate such an issue. At times the senior issues are called *prior liens,* illustrated in the Missouri-Kansas-Texas Railroad Company Prior Lien bonds which are senior with respect to part of the property, but which constitute a second lien on other parts of the main line. The senior group also includes a number of nominally junior issues, which are, in many cases, a combination of a large senior claim and a small junior position, or which are preceded by a small amount of prior bonds, or which have gradually advanced in rank with the retirement of earlier claims. The former Pennsylvania Railroad Company General Mortgage bonds are now a senior issue.

Secured junior bonds have a secondary claim upon the designated property. Corporations, however, are reluctant to disclose openly the position of junior issues; they prefer less significant and, in some cases, misleading titles, such as *general*, or *unified*, or *consolidated*, or *first refunding*.

Bonds secured by the deposit of other bonds and stocks are generally termed *collateral* or *collateral trust bonds*. In the event of default the collateral can be seized and sold. The most frequent users are holding or parent companies which have as their main assets securities of other companies. Industrial and public service companies sometimes issue collateral bonds when all of their fixed property is pledged, or they may issue bonds secured by both a mortgage and the deposit of securities.

Three main factors determine the investment standing of collateral trust bonds: (1) the nature and value of the securities pledged, (2) the general credit of the issuer, and (3) the specific protective provisions of the indenture. There should be an ample spread between the value of the collateral and the amount of the debt, and the issuer should be required to maintain this differential. If the value of the collateral is doubtful, the investor must rely chiefly on the general earning power of the company, for if the specific security is worthless, the bonds become in effect a general claim along with unsecured debt. Any clause in the indenture that permits substitution of collateral should be given special scrutiny. The investor should be particularly wary of collateral trust bonds that are secured by common stocks of companies that themselves have bonds and preferred stocks outstanding, and so are in reality junior securities.

A third group consists of those secured by the promise to pay of a company other than the issuer, and includes *guaranteed*, *assumed*, and *joint* bonds. The guarantee may be direct, covering interest, or interest and principal, or it may arise through a lease contract whereby the lessee agrees to pay to the lessor a sum sufficient to cover the interest and/or sinking fund on the bonds. *Assumed* bonds are issues of a company that has been acquired by another by merger or as a result of the reorganization of the original issuer. In taking over the property of the original issuer, the debt of the issuer has been assumed by the successor company. *Joint* bonds are the direct joint obligation of two or more concerns or, more likely, obligations of a company that operates property used by both, such as a terminal, and whose bonds are jointly guaranteed by the users.

Assumed, guaranteed, and joint bonds depend for their quality on: (1) the property and earnings of the original issuer, and (2) the value of the additional promise to pay of the guaranteeing or successor concern. If both elements are very strong, the issue will command high investment respect. The best examples are found in the railway field, where the issues of small corporations that have long since ceased to operate their own properties have been guaranteed or assumed by a large company. If the property is important to the system, such issues rank with the senior issues of the system.

Although these types of bonds have been discussed under the heading of secured issues, they may be either mortgage bonds or unsecured bonds. The factor that gives them special interest is the addition of the credit of a second corporation, or possibly of several other corporations, as in the case of Cincinnati Union Terminal Company First Mortgage bonds, which have a first lien on the terminal property and, in addition, are jointly and severally guaranteed by seven railroad companies.

A fourth group comprises the *debenture* issues, which are not secured by a lien or any specific assets, but rank with the general debt of the issuer. A common provision of modern debenture bonds is that, if the company should issue any mortgage debt, the debentures will be similarly secured. Thus, a debenture issue may move up into the secured category and still be designated by the original title.

Debentures are issued by companies with credit standing ranging from very strong to weak. The debenture issues of the American Telephone and Telegraph Company are considered high grade. The strongest industrial corporation bonds are debentures. The fact that bonds are unsecured does not weaken their investment status if they are the only long-term debt of the issuer and if the general assets and earning power of the issuer provide ample protection. The main strength of any bond issue, secured or unsecured, lies in the earning power of the borrower. But because debentures lack a specific lien on assets, their position may deteriorate if excessive equal or prior debt is issued, or if their backing by general assets, and working capital in particular, is weakened by subsequent developments. The investor should check carefully the *protective provisions* in the debentures that are designed to protect their status. Common provisions include: (1) the equal-coverage clause mentioned above, providing for securing the debentures equally with any new mortgage debt; (2) provision against the payment of dividends that would reduce net assets below a certain figure; (3) requirement that a certain ratio of current assets to current liabilities be maintained before dividends may be paid; and (4) limitation of the *total* funded debt, including the debentures, to a certain proportion of the total assets or of the capital stock or, more frequently, to an amount on which the interest is earned a certain number of times.

Debentures frequently include a sinking fund to provide for regular reduction of principal and, to give them a speculative touch, are often made convertible into common stock.

Debentures are used most frequently by industrial and financial corporations. Railroads and public utilities customarily issue mortgage bonds. Except in unusual cases, the debenture bond of a railroad is preceded by layers of secured debt and is, therefore, a junior security of secondary quality.

A relative newcomer to the family of bonds is the *subordinated debenture*. This is payable after other designated unsecured debt and is the "low man on the totem pole" of bonds. It is widely used by finance companies as a means of increasing the junior capital base so as to support a higher amount of short-term bank debt, while still gaining the interest and income tax advantages that bonds provide. A number of industrial companies have used this type of issue in recent years, for example, Crane Company Subordinated Sinking Fund Debenture Series B 7s, 1994, and (J. C.) Penney Company Subordinated Debenture 4 1/4s, 1994. To add to their appeal, subordinated debentures often include the convertible feature.

Purpose of issue Investors should be very interested in the use to which their funds are put as an important test of safety.

Adjustment bonds are issued in the reorganization of companies in financial difficulties. In practically all cases, interest is payable only if earnings permit. They are a leading type of *income* bond. (See below.) Although these bonds are usually issued under clouded conditions, the eventual success of the company, as shown in the case of the Atchison, Topeka, & Santa Fe Railway Adjustment Mortgage 4's of 1995 (issued in 1895) may place the bonds in the investment category. The Adjustment Income 5's of the Hudson and Manhattan (issued in 1913) fared less auspiciously. They were defaulted in 1955 and the company was placed in bankruptcy. Adjustment bonds are usually protected by a junior mortgage.

Consolidated mortgage bonds are issued to consolidate several separate bond issues into one. They are ordinarily the result of refunding operations and often involve a first mortgage on one part and second or other mortgages upon other parts of the company's property.

Divisional bonds are railway mortgage bonds secured by a first lien on a section of the system. Since they precede other mortgage issues with respect to a claim on a certain division, they are also classified as *underlying* bonds.

Equipment obligations are issued to finance the purchase of equipment—notably railway rolling stock—on the partial-payment plan. Funds for the payment of such purchases are obtained by paying an advance rental or down payment of from 20 to 25% and securing the balance through the sale of serial obligations, payable over a period usually of 15 years. For example, in August 1971 Seaboard Coast Line Railroad Company bought 42 3,600-h.p. locomotives and 10 locomotive units at a total cost of $13,388,000. The company made a cash payment of about 20% and issued $10,650,000 of 8% equipment trust certificates maturing at the rate of $710,000 annually for 15 years.

Equipment obligations have traditionally been regarded as excellent investments and bear relatively low yields, owing to: (1) the essential nature of the equipment; (2) the mobility that would facilitate repossession and ready sale or rent of standardized equipment to another road; (3) the gradual increase in the value of the equity owing to the liquidation of the debt on a scale faster than the wearing-out of the equipment, which normally lasts well beyond 15 years; (4) the adequacy of the cash "throw-off" from depreciation charges, especially if accelerated, to meet the installments; (5) the fact that receivers and trustees in charge of companies in insolvency usually continue to pay interest charges on equipment obligations even though they may allow the mortgage bonds of the company to remain in default; and (6) the excellent investment record of these securities. In only one instance in modern railroad history, that of the Florida East Coast Railway, was the lease disaffirmed and the equipment sold (1936). In this case payments totalling $593.54 per $1,000 certificate were distributed. In three other cases in the 1930s, maturities were extended, and two roads exchanged their certificates for other obligations bearing a lower rate of interest.

The decline in railroad earnings has reduced the investment status of equipment trust obligations considerably, and many of them sold to yield as high as 8 or 9% in the 1970s. Such rates also reflected the generally high level of bond yields. Ratings of the obligations of weak railroads fell to Baa or B, and those of some normally strong companies to as low as A (from Aaa). A substantial improvement in earnings will be necessary to restore equipment debt to its previous high investment position.

Formal equipment obligations are occasionally used by other types of carriers. In September 1976, Flying Tiger Lines issued 15-year equipment trust certificates in the amount of $60,000,000. These funds were used to finance the purchase and modification of three used Boeing 747-100 passenger planes into cargo configurations.

Receivers' certificates are the obligations of a company being operated by a receiver in equity. With proper court approval, they enjoy priority over other obligations, although technically they are not secured by any lien. They are issued to improve the property and the working capital position of the failed company, pending a reorganization. Receivership in equity has largely given way to reorganization under bankruptcy proceedings, and *trustees' certificates* are the modern type of issue.

Refunding bonds are issued for the purpose of getting new capital on a favorable basis. Just as the conversion of a short-term into a long-term debt is known as a *funding* operation, the payment of debt at or before maturity with the proceeds of a new loan is called *refunding*. The main reason for refunding before maturity is to save on interest when interest rates have fallen or when the credit of the issuer has improved. Refunding at maturity is necessary when the company has made no provision for redemption. The investor must examine a refunding issue to determine whether that name is used to disguise a junior issue. Senior issues are usually labelled "First and Refunding."

Terminal bonds are issued for the purpose of financing the construction of terminal facilities in large cities to be used by one or more railroad companies. These companies, either separately (severally) or collectively (jointly), usually assume proportionate responsibility for the debt of the terminal company, either by direct obligation or by guarantee. The 15 companies which own the Terminal Railroad Association of St Louis and guarantee its bonds include several of the most important systems in the country.

Form of issue   Bonds are issued in either *coupon* or *registered* form. Some are interchangeable for a small service fee. *Coupon* bonds are payable to bearer and carry detachable interest coupons. *Registered* bonds are payable only to the registered owner, to whom interest checks are mailed, except in the case of bonds registered as to principal only. The coupon bond may be more conveniently transferred and, hence, may command a price slightly higher than that of the registered bond.

Interim bonds are temporary certificates issued pending the preparation of the *definitive* bonds. Some months are required for the preparation, engraving, and printing of the regular bonds. Meanwhile, the interim certificate evidences ownership and may be readily transferred.

Redemption   Bonds have important features with respect to redemption. *Perpetual* bonds represent permanent obligations and might more properly be termed *perpetual interest-bearing certificates*, as in the case of the Canadian Pacific Railway Perpetual 4% Consolidated Debenture Stock.[3] Some long-term domestic issues, such as the West Shore Railroad 4s of 2361 and the Elmira and Williamsport Railroad Company Income 5s of 2862, might readily be classed as annuity bonds for all practical purposes.

Redeemable bonds, also known as *callable*, may be paid at the option of the issuer during a specified period prior to maturity. Most modern bonds contain the call feature. The price at which the bonds may be repaid is usually computed on a sliding scale, providing for a premium of as much as $4 to $8 per $100 of principal in the event of early redemption, and declining to zero just before maturity. From the investor's viewpoint, the life of callable bonds is uncertain and they are most likely to be called when interest rates are low. The holder may be forced to accept less income if interest rates fall, but may not be able to obtain more income if interest rates rise. Since most bonds are callable, the investor has little choice in the matter. And the call price acts as an upper peg or platform through which the price of the bond is not likely to break except in a very strong bond market and when the chances of call are unlikely.

When money is "tight," as in 1966, 1969–1970, and 1973–1974, corporations must offer investors special inducements to attract their funds. In addition to attractive interest rates, the call privilege is deferred so as to induce purchase without the threat of reduction in interest income. Deferments for five years in the case of utility bonds, and for as long as 10 years in industrials, were common practice. An example is the P. R. Mallory and Company, Inc. 8 7/8's due September 15, 1996, which are not callable by the company until 1986. In the Transamerica Financial Corporation 8 1/2% notes due 2001, beginning in 1984, each note holder may elect to request redemption. This unusual variable-maturity feature offers the investor a hedge against the wider price fluctuations associated with longer-term issues. For the influence of the call feature on bond yields, see p. 154.

Serial bonds are those on which the maturities are spread over a succession of years rather than in a single year. The Southern Railway Equipment 9's were issued in 1970 in the total amount of $9,465,000 repayable at the rate of $631,000 semiannually from 1971 to 1985. Most municipal bonds are retired serially, but corporate examples are unusual.

Series bonds are issued in sequential series under an open-end mortgage.

[3]Debenture stock is a British term for unsecured long-term debt.

Although all bonds thus issued have the same security, each series has distinctive features such as interest rate, maturity date, and call price. This type of financing gives the corporation a maximum degree of flexibility and allows each new issue to meet the prevailing conditions in the market. In 1977, the Pacific Gas and Electric Company had 43 series of open-end mortgage bonds outstanding, designated "A" to "ZZ" with different coupon rates (from 2 3/4 to 9.85%) and maturities (1977 to 2006).

Sinking fund bonds require a fund to be built up during the life of the issue to sink, or liquidate, the debt. Such bonds are more prevalent in industrial issues than in railroads or public utilities, although there is a growing tendency, through the force of regulation, to insert sinking fund requirements in these last types. The amounts annually appropriated for the sinking fund may be: (1) fixed annual amounts—either a certain amount in dollars or a percentage of the bonds issued; or (2) varying annual amounts, increasing or decreasing each year; or (3) an amount varying with earnings; or (4), in the case of extractive industries, an amount proportionate to physical output. The sinking fund may be used to redeem, either by purchase in the open market or by call, outstanding bonds of the same issue; or to invest in other securities. From the investor's viewpoint, the first method stated in each case is preferable. The expression "subject to call for sinking fund only" applies to bonds which are otherwise nonredeemable.

Bonds which are called for sinking fund purposes are drawn by lot and must be surrendered if loss of interest is to be avoided. Corporations keep no record of the owners of unregistered bonds, so there is no notification of redemption other than by newspaper advertising. Such notices are often missed by bondholders, although they can protect themselves by using bank or broker safekeeping service. In partial compensation for the loss of interest and the trouble of reinvestment, the bonds are called at a premium, although such premiums are usually lower than those paid for ordinary refunding.

Sinking fund requirements are particularly important in the issues of corporations with uncertain earnings or whose property is depleted or depreciated through time, such as extractive and real estate companies. Many debenture bonds include the words "Sinking Fund" in their titles to indicate that, although lacking specific security, they must be retired on a regular schedule.

Sinking funds should not be confused with so-called "capital improvement" funds whereby a public utility is permitted to substitute increased investment in property for definite retirement of debt.

Types of participation   Interest payments on some bonds are directly or indirectly contingent upon the earnings of the issuer. As a general rule, these bonds are unsecured debts, although they are occasionally secured by a junior lien. Such *income bonds* are generally issued as part of a financial reorganization under which bond interest charges are "scaled down" to an amount within the reasonable capacity of the enterprise. Income bonds have been used to a large extent in connection with railroad and real estate reorganization. The payment of interest is contingent upon and proportionate to earnings available, up to a maximum rate. The interest is often cumulative; that is, if not earned and paid in one year, it must be paid later before any dividends may be declared. But if the interest is earned, it must be paid, in contrast to preferred stock dividends, which are contingent on earnings *and declaration.* One difficulty is the possible difference of opinion that may prevail as to whether the interest has been earned, in spite of the definition of earnings contained in the indenture. The real earnings of a company, after allowance for maintenance, depreciation, and other items, can be a matter of controversy.

The reputation which income bonds have gained by being associated with failure, together with their inherently weak characteristics, has prevented their frequent use for raising new capital. Their real nature is difficult to explain to investors, and they lack the straightforward features of ordinary bonds or preferred stock. Even the tax advantage enjoyed by the corporation arising from the fact that their interest, unlike preferred dividends, is deductible for tax purposes has not often led to their wide use for ordinary financing. There have, however, been a few exceptions. A review of the use of income bonds, other than in reorganization, reveals that most have been issued to refinance preferred stock. Those sold for new capital have, in the main, been placed privately rather than offered to the general public.

Participating bonds are those that are entitled to share in the net earnings of the company in addition to receiving interest. A participating bond is an anomaly, since it seems to combine stock income with bond safety. Very few such bonds are now outstanding. The modern method of bond participation is through the indirect procedure of conversion or stock-purchase warrants.

Convertible bonds may be exchanged for common stock at the option of the holder at a ratio and during the period stated in the indenture. Because this "equity" feature is so important, this type of bond, with examples, is discussed in Chapter 9.

Bonds *with warrants* bear common stock-purchase warrants, giving the holder the privilege of buying a certain number of shares of stock at a fixed price. The warrants may be valid for a limited or an unlimited period. When detachable, they are often actively traded and have their own market. This type of warrant, with examples, is discussed in Chapter 9.

An investor should realize that in convertible and in warrant bonds, the speculative feature (the option to exchange for or to purchase common stock) has usually been added to enhance the attractiveness of issues that may lack solid investment quality.

Concepts of Return on Bonds

Definitions The calculation of bond prices and yields involves a number of concepts.

Coupon rate is the annual percentage of face value specified in the bond— *viz.*, 5%, 8%—that will be paid until maturity or until the bond is called. The coupon rate is sometimes described as the "nominal yield." The actual per cent return to the investor will be higher or lower than nominal yield if the cost price is less or more than the face value.

Maturity is the number of years (or fractions thereof) that a bond has still to run. A 30-year bond issued in 1970 has a maturity of 22 years as of 1978, 12 years as of 1988 if still outstanding.

Discount is the difference between face value and purchase price when a bond is bought below face value. *Premium* is the amount paid in excess of face value. Treasury bills are always issued at a "discount." (See Chapter 6.) So are United States Savings bonds. (See Chapter 5.) The term "discount" is also used to indicate the difference between the market price and subscription price where common stocks are purchased under "privileged subscription." (See Chapter 9.)

Accumulation is the appreciation in the value of a bond bought at a discount, between the purchase date and the maturity date when it is payable at face value, or the call date when it is payable at the call price.

Amortization is the depreciation in the value of a bond bought at a premium, between the purchase date and the maturity date when it is payable at face value, or the call date when it is payable at the call price.

Accrued interest is the amount of interest that has accumulated on a bond since the last preceding semiannual payment date. In the case of new issues, the date at which interest begins to accrue is stated in the announcement.

The prices of most bonds are quoted on an "and-interest" basis. In addition to the agreed price, the buyer pays the seller the amount of interest accrued since the preceding interest date because interest for the full six months will be paid to the buyer on the next interest date.

Accrued interest on bonds is calculated on the 360-day-year basis, except in the case of certain U.S. Government bonds on which the 365-day-year basis is used. Under the 360-day basis, each month is considered to have 30 days, irrespective of the calender. The seller is entitled to interest up to, but not including, the day of delivery. Thus, if a 5% bond with interest payment dates on January 1 and July 1 (J-J) is sold on Monday, October 12, for regular four-day delivery on Friday, October 16, the seller is entitled to interest for three months (July, August, and September) and fifteen days (up to, but not including, October 16) at 5%, or $14.31. If a 6% bond with interest payment dates on March 1 and September 1 (M-S) is sold on Thursday, October 17, for delivery on Thursday, October 24, the seller is entitled to interest for one month (September) and 21 days (up to, but not including, October 22) at 6%, or $8.50.

Some bonds are sold "flat"; that is, the quoted price includes accrued interest, if any. Such bonds are likely to be either in default, or bonds whose income is uncertain, as in the case of "income bonds."

Net yield. Mathematically, the net yield (*to maturity*) is the per cent return on a bond held to maturity and is a function of: (1) price, (2) coupon rate, and (3) years (or months) to maturity. (A 7% bond bought at 105, due in 20 years, provides a net yield of 6.50% per annum.) Actually, however, the yield determines the price, given the other two factors. Some obligations, such as U. S. Treasury certificates and bills, municipal securities, and equipment trust certificates, are quoted in terms of yield rather than price because of the various maturities that are available.

Current yield is the annual income rate divided by the cost price without regard to accumulation or amortization. (A 7% bond bought at 105, and due in 20 years, provides a current yield of 6.67% per annum.)

Calculation of Net Yield on Bonds

The annual rate of income on bonds is customarily calculated on the basis of net yield to maturity. This involves the use of present values and compound interest.

Present value concept Money has a time value. Those with funds to lend or invest expect a return on their funds. At any rate of interest, a sum of money is worth more at the end of a period than at the beginning. And at any rate of interest, money promised in the future is worth less at the beginning than at the end. Thus, $100 placed in a savings account at 5% is worth $105 ($100 × 1.05) at the end of a year. At the same rate of interest, $105 a year hence is worth only $100 (105 ÷ 1.05) at the beginning.

If interest is withdrawn or not re-invested, at *simple interest* the $100 in our illustration above grows to $105 each year. If the interest is not withdrawn or is re-invested at the same rate, the basis for calculating the next year's interest is $105, so that at the end of the second year the principal has grown to $110.25 ($105 × 1.05). This illustrates the concept of *compound interest*. The concept can be applied to the calculation of present value. The value of $100 to be received one year hence, at 5%, is $95.20 ($100 ÷ 1.05); the value to be received at the end of two years is $90.70 ($95.20 ÷ 1.05). Another way of expressing the concept would be to say that at the rate of 5%, the *discounted present value* of $100 to be received two years from now is $90.70.

Compound interest formula The formula for determining the future value of money invested at compound interest is:

$$(1 + N)^n$$

in which N is the interest rate per year and n is the number of years.

Assume that $1.00 is invested at compound interest credited annually for 20 years at 7%. By consulting a compound interest table (Table 8-1) the value of $(1 + .07)^{20}$ is found to be 3.869.

The indicated value of $1.00 would, therefore, be $3.869, and that of $1,000 would be $3,869.

Present worth formulas The formula for determining the value of a principal sum of money payable at a future time, compound-discounted to the present time, is the reciprocal of the compound interest formula:

$$\frac{1}{(1 + N)^n}$$

TABLE 8-1 Amount of $1 at Compound Interest

Years	5%	5 1/2%	6%	7%	8%	9%
1	1.050	1.056	1.060	1.070	1.080	1.090
2	1.103	1.115	1.124	1.145	1.166	1.188
3	1.158	1.178	1.191	1.225	1.260	1.295
4	1.216	1.244	1.262	1.311	1.360	1.411
5	1.276	1.314	1.338	1.402	1.469	1.539
6	1.340	1.388	1.419	1.501	1.587	1.677
7	1.407	1.466	1.504	1.606	1.714	1.828
8	1.477	1.548	1.593	1.718	1.851	1.992
9	1.551	1.635	1.689	1.838	1.999	2.172
10	1.629	1.727	1.791	1.967	2.159	2.367
11	1.710	1.824	1.898	2.105	2.332	2.580
12	1.796	1.926	2.012	2.252	2.518	2.812
13	1.886	2.034	2.133	2.410	2.720	3.066
14	1.980	2.148	2.261	2.578	2.937	3.346
15	2.079	2.269	2.397	2.759	3.172	3.642
16	2.183	2.396	2.540	2.952	3.426	3.970
17	2.292	2.531	2.693	3.159	3.700	4.328
18	2.407	2.673	2.854	3.380	3.996	4.717
19	2.527	2.823	3.026	3.616	4.316	5.142
20	2.653	2.982	3.207	3.869	4.661	5.604
25	3.386	3.918	4.292	5.427	6.848	8.623
30	4.322	5.149	5.743	7.612	10.063	13.268
40	7.040	8.891	10.286	14.974	21.724	31.409
50	11.467	15.352	18.420	29.457	46.902	74.357

in which N is the discount rate per year and n is the number of years. (See Table 8-2.)

Assume that $1.00 payable in 20 years is to be compound-discounted at 7%:

$$\frac{1}{(1+N)^n} = \frac{1}{(1+1.07)^{20}} = \frac{1}{3.869} = \$0.258$$

The indicated present value of $1.00 is 25.8 cents. The present worth of the principal of a $1,000 bond payable in 20 years, compound-discounted at 7% per annum, is $258.

The formula for determining the value of the total annual interest payments on a bond payable over a period of years, compound-discounted to the present time, is:

$$\frac{C}{1+N} + \frac{C}{(1+N)^2} + \frac{C}{(1+N)^3} \cdots \frac{C}{(1+N)^n} = \frac{C}{N}\left[1 - \frac{1}{(1+N)^n}\right]$$

in which C is the coupon interest rate, N is the net interest rate of yield, and n is the number of years.[4] (See Table 8-3.)

[4]Using the summation symbol, the formula is

$$\sum_{t=1}^{n} \frac{C}{(1+N)^n}$$

148

TABLE 8-2 Values of $1

Years	5%	5 1/2%	6%	7%	8%	9%
1	.952	.948	.943	.935	.926	.917
2	.907	.898	.890	.873	.857	.842
3	.864	.852	.840	.816	.794	.772
4	.823	.807	.792	.763	.735	.708
5	.783	.765	.747	.713	.681	.650
6	.746	.725	.705	.666	.630	.596
7	.711	.687	.665	.623	.583	.547
8	.677	.651	.627	.582	.540	.502
9	.645	.618	.592	.544	.500	.460
10	.614	.585	.558	.508	.463	.422
11	.585	.555	.527	.475	.429	.387
12	.557	.526	.497	.444	.397	.355
13	.530	.498	.469	.415	.368	.326
14	.505	.472	.442	.388	.340	.299
15	.481	.448	.417	.362	.315	.274
16	.458	.424	.394	.339	.292	.252
17	.436	.402	.371	.316	.270	.231
18	.415	.381	.350	.296	.250	.212
19	.396	.361	.331	.276	.232	.194
20	.377	.343	.312	.258	.215	.178
25	.295	.262	.233	.184	.146	.116
30	.231	.200	.174	.131	.099	.075
40	.142	.117	.079	.067	.046	.032
50	.087	.069	.054	.034	.021	.013

TABLE 8-3 Present Value of $1 Each Year

Years	5%	5 1/2%	6%	7%	8%	9%
1	0.952	0.948	0.943	0.935	0.926	0.917
2	1.859	1.846	1.833	1.808	1.783	1.759
3	2.723	2.698	2.673	2.624	2.577	2.531
4	3.546	3.505	3.465	3.387	3.312	3.240
5	4.329	4.270	4.212	4.100	3.993	3.890
6	5.076	4.996	4.917	4.767	4.623	4.486
7	5.786	5.683	5.582	5.389	5.206	5.033
8	6.463	6.335	6.210	5.971	5.747	5.535
9	7.108	6.952	6.802	6.515	6.247	5.985
10	7.722	7.538	7.360	7.024	6.710	6.418
11	8.306	8.093	7.887	7.499	7.139	6.805
12	8.863	8 619	8.384	7.943	7.536	7.161
13	9.394	9.117	8.853	8.358	7.904	7.487
14	9.899	9.590	9.295	8.745	8.244	7.786
15	10.380	10.038	9.712	9.108	8.560	8.061
16	10.838	10.462	10.106	9.447	8.851	8.313
17	11.274	10.865	10.477	9.763	9.122	8.544
18	11.690	11.246	10.828	10.059	9.372	8.756
19	12.085	11.608	11.158	10.336	9.604	8.950
20	12.462	11.950	11.470	10.594	9.818	9.129
25	14.094	13.414	12.783	11.654	10.675	9.823
30	15.392	14.534	13.765	12.409	11.258	10.274
40	17.159	16.046	15.046	13.332	11.925	10.757
50	18.256	16.932	15.762	13.801	12.233	10.962

Assume that a $1,000 bond payable in 20 years carries an 8% coupon rate, and that the interest payments are to be compound-discounted at 7%:

$$\frac{.08}{.07}(\$1,000 - \$258) = \frac{8}{7}(\$742) = \$848$$

The total present worth of both principal and coupons on a $1,000 bond bearing an 8% interest rate payable in 20 years is, therefore, the sum of $258 (the present worth of the principal) plus $848 (the present worth of the coupons), or $1,106. (Note that the investor who pays $1,106 for this bond is paying much more for the future interest payments than for the principal at maturity.)

BOND VALUE FORMULA   The formula for determining the present worth of a bond payable at a future date is obtained by combining the respective formulas for present worth of principal and present worth of coupons as follows:[5]

$$\frac{1}{(1 + N)^n} + \frac{C}{N}\left[1 - \frac{1}{(1 + N)^n}\right]$$

This formula may be reduced and expressed more simply as

$$\frac{N + C(1 + N)^n - C}{N(1 + N)^n}$$

The preceding case of the 8%, $1,000 bond payable in 20 years may now be applied to the simplified combined formula in order to determine the present value of the bond on a 7% yield basis:

$$\frac{.07 + .08(1 + .07)^{20} - .08}{.07(1 + .07)^{20}} = \frac{.07 + .08(3.869) - .08}{.07(3.869)}$$

$$= \frac{.07 + .30952 - .08}{.27083} = \frac{.29952}{.27083} = 1.106 = \$1,106$$

The total value of the bond in question would, therefore, be $1,106, which confirms the separate values of $258 by the principal formula and of $848 by the interest formula.

In the preceding cases, the problem was to determine the price of a bond when the yield is given. In other cases, the problem may be to determine the yield when the price is given.

Assume that a 7% bond due in 50 years is purchased at 105. The net yield would thus be determined by solving the combined formula:

$$1.05 = \frac{N + .07(1 + N)^{50} - .07}{N(1 + N)^{50}}$$

$$1.05N(1 + N)^{50} = .07(1 + N)^{50} + N - .07$$

As a net yield (N) of .0665 brings the two sides of the equation in almost

[5]Using summation, the formula is

$$\sum_{t=1}^{n} \frac{C}{(1 + N)^n} + \frac{1}{(1 + N)^n}$$

exact balance, the bond in question has been bought at a price which affords
a yield of 6.65% per annum.

Bond tables   The mathematical problems that arise most frequently
in connection with bond investment are, first, to determine the net yield of
a bond when price, redemption value, and maturity are known; and second,
to find the price at which a bond of known redemption value and maturity
must be purchased to yield a certain desired return. In either case, the solution is simplified through the use of bond table books.

Bond tables are not complete. Complete tables would show the net yield
on every amount invested at every possible rate of yield for every possible
maturity. Such a compilation is, of course, out of the question. A large assort-
ment of tables is available, with a wide range in coupon rates, maturities,
and prices. The more modern tables reflect the use of low and fractional
coupon rates and provide means by which prices and yields for maturities
involving monthly periods can be determined with a minimum of interpolation.

The *Expanded Bond Values Tables*[6] show the value, to the nearest cent,
of a $100 bond with coupon rates from 1 to 12% at intervals of 1/4% from
1 to 3%, intervals of 1/8% from 3 1/8 to 10%, and intervals of 1/4% from
10 1/4 to 12%. Maturities are shown monthly to five years, quarterly to ten
years, semiannually to forty years, and also at 45, 50, 55, and 60 years.

A specimen page from the *Expanded Bond Values Tables* is shown in Table
8-4. The coupon rate, 7%, appears at the top of the page. Assuming that
a bond maturing in 21 years and bearing 7% interest is purchased at 94 3/4
($947.50), find the net yield. Since the top horizontal row shows the maturi-
ties, reference is made to the column headed 21 years. In this column, 94.75
appears opposite 7.50% in the first vertical column, which shows the net
yield. The required net yield is, therefore, 7.50%.

The second assumption is that the bond has the same maturity, 21 years,
and bears 7% interest; find the purchase price to yield 7.80%. Reference is
made to the column headed 21 years, and directly opposite 7.80%, the
desired net yield, appears 91.80 which shows the required purchase price
to be $918.00 for a $1,000 bond.

Rarely do bond tables give the exact desired information directly, because
either the exact cost of the bond or the desired net yield, as the case may be,
does not appear therein. Interpolation becomes necessary. Interpolation is
a matter of proportion, as it is based upon the assumption that the changes
in the bond table values are proportionate. This assumption is not absolutely
correct, but the degree of variance is too small to be serious.

Assume that a 7% bond is to run 20 years and is purchased at 94.50; find
the net yield. Using the table, the nearest prices that appear are 94.86 and
93.88, which give net yields of 7.50% and 7.60%, respectively. The required
net yield is, therefore, between 7.50% and 7.60%. The difference between
the prices that bracket the solution sought is 0.98 (94.86–93.88); the difference
in yield is 0.10%. The given price 94.50, being 0.36 less than 94.86, will there-

[6]*Expanded Bond Values Tables* (Boston: Financial Publishing Company, 1970).

TABLE 8-4 Bond Values Table, 7%

7%

Yield	18–6	19–0	19–6	20–0	20–6	21–0	21–6	22–0
4.00	138.95	139.66	140.35	141.03	141.70	142.35	142.99	143.62
4.20	135.77	136.40	137.02	137.63	138.23	138.82	139.39	139.95
4.40	132.68	133.25	133.80	134.35	134.88	135.40	135.91	136.41
4.60	129.68	130.19	130.68	131.16	131.64	132.10	132.55	132.99
4.80	126.78	127.22	127.66	128.08	128.50	128.91	129.30	129.69
5.00	123.96	124.35	124.73	125.10	125.47	125.82	126.17	126.50
5.20	121.22	121.56	121.89	122.22	122.53	122.84	123.14	123.43
5.40	118.57	118.86	119.15	119.42	119.69	119.95	120.21	120.45
5.60	116.00	116.25	116.48	116.72	116.94	117.16	117.38	117.58
5.80	113.51	113.71	113.90	114.10	114.28	114.46	114.64	114.81
6.00	111.08	111.25	111.40	111.56	111.71	111.85	111.99	112.13
6.10	109.90	110.04	110.18	110.32	110.45	110.58	110.70	110.82
6.20	108.73	108.86	108.98	109.10	109.21	109.32	109.43	109.54
6.30	107.58	107.69	107.80	107.90	108.00	108.09	108.18	108.27
6.40	106.45	106.54	106.63	106.72	106.80	106.88	106.96	107.03
6.50	105.34	105.41	105.48	105.55	105.62	105.68	105.75	105.81
6.60	104.24	104.30	104.35	104.41	104.46	104.51	104.56	104.61
6.70	103.15	103.20	103.24	103.28	103.32	103.36	103.39	103.43
6.80	102.09	102.12	102.14	102.17	102.19	102.22	102.24	102.27
6.90	101.04	101.05	101.06	101.08	101.09	101.10	101.11	101.12
7.00	100.00	100.00	100.00	100.00	100.00	100.00	100.00	100.00
7.10	98.98	98.97	98.95	98.94	98.93	98.92	98.91	98.90
7.20	97.97	97.95	97.92	97.90	97.87	97.85	97.83	97.81
7.30	96.98	96.94	96.91	96.87	96.84	96.80	96.77	96.74
7.40	96.00	95.95	95.91	95.86	95.81	95.77	95.73	95.69
7.50	95.04	94.98	94.92	94.86	94.81	94.75	94.70	94.65
7.60	94.09	94.02	93.95	93.88	93.82	93.75	93.69	93.64
7.70	93.16	93.07	92.99	92.92	92.84	92.77	92.70	92.63
7.80	92.23	92.14	92.05	91.96	91.88	91.80	91.72	91.65
7.90	91.32	91.22	91.12	91.03	90.93	90.85	90.76	90.68
8.00	90.43	90.32	90.21	90.10	90.00	89.91	89.81	89.73
8.10	89.55	89.42	89.31	89.19	89.09	88.98	88.88	88.79
8.20	88.67	88.54	88.42	88.30	88.18	88.07	87.97	87.86
8.30	87.82	87.68	87.54	87.42	87.29	87.18	87.06	86.95
8.40	86.97	86.82	86.68	86.55	86.42	86.29	86.17	86.06
8.50	86.14	85.98	85.83	85.69	85.56	85.43	85.30	85.18
8.60	85.31	85.15	85.00	84.85	84.71	84.57	84.44	84.31
8.70	84.50	84.33	84.17	84.02	83.87	83.73	83.59	83.46
8.80	83.70	83.53	83.36	83.20	83.05	82.90	82.76	82.62
8.90	82.92	82.73	82.56	82.39	82.23	82.08	81.93	81.80
9.00	81.14	81.95	81.77	81.60	81.43	81.28	81.13	80.98
9.10	81.37	81.18	80.99	80.82	80.65	80.48	80.33	80.18
9.20	80.62	80.42	80.23	80.04	79.87	79.70	79.54	79.39
9.30	79.87	79.67	79.47	79.28	79.11	78.93	78.77	78.62
9.40	79.14	78.93	78.73	78.53	78.35	78.18	78.01	77.85
9.50	78.41	78.20	77.99	77.80	77.61	77.43	77.26	77.10
9.60	77.70	77.48	77.27	77.07	76.88	76.70	76.52	76.36
9.70	76.99	76.77	76.55	76.35	76.16	75.97	75.80	75.63
9.80	76.30	76.07	75.85	75.64	75.45	75.26	75.08	74.91
9.90	75.61	75.38	75.16	74.95	74.75	74.56	74.38	74.20
10.00	74.93	74.70	74.47	74.26	74.06	73.87	73.68	73.51
10.20	73.61	73.37	73.14	72.92	72.71	72.51	72.32	72.14
10.40	72.32	72.07	71.83	71.61	71.40	71.20	71.00	70.82
10.60	71.06	70.81	70.57	70.34	70.13	69.92	69.72	69.54
10.80	69.84	69.58	69.34	69.11	68.89	68.68	68.48	68.29
11.00	68.65	68.39	68.14	67.91	67.69	67.47	67.27	67.08
11.20	67.49	67.23	66.98	66.74	66.52	66.30	66.10	65.91
11.40	66.37	66.10	65.85	65.61	65.38	65.17	64.96	64.77
11.60	65.27	65.00	64.74	64.50	64.27	64.06	63.86	63.66
11.80	64.20	63.93	63.67	63.43	63.20	62.98	62.78	62.59
12.00	63.16	62.88	62.63	62.38	62.15	61.94	61.73	61.54

Source: Reproduced from *Expanded Bond Values Tables,* publication #83, p. 736, copyright 1970, with permission of Financial Publishing Company, Boston, MA.

fore yield 36/98 of 0.10% more than 7.50%, or 62/98 of 0.10% less than 7.60%, making the net yield 7.5367%.

Next, assume that a 7% bond is to run 20 years; at what price should it be purchased to yield 6.75%? The nearest net yields that appear in the table are 6.70% and 6.80%, which require a cost of 103.28 and 102.17, respectively. The difference of 0.10 in rate represents a difference of 1.11 in price. The difference of 0.05% between 6.70% and 6.75% must, therefore, cover a difference of 0.55 in price, making the required price 103.28 — 0.55, or 102.73.

Approximating the net yield   Net yield can be determined approximately by dividing the annual income (interest plus annual accumulation or minus annual amortization) by the average value to maturity (as adjusted by accumulation credits or amortization charges). A 7% bond, due in 25 years, purchased at 80 would afford an approximate net yield (to maturity) of 8.66%, as thus calculated:

Annual interest	$70 (7% of $1,000)
plus	
Annual accumulation......	$8 ($1,000 — $800 = $200 ÷ 25 yrs)
equals	
Annual income	$78
divided by	
Average value	$900 ($800 + $1,000 = $1,800 ÷ 2)
equals	
Net yield (to maturity)	0.0866

An 8% bond due in 20 years purchased at 110 would afford an approximate net yield (to maturity) of 7.14%, calculated as follows:

Annual interest	$80 (8% of $1,000)
minus	
Annual amorization	$5 ($1,100 — $1,000 = $100 ÷ 20 yrs)
equals	
Annual income	$75
divided by	
Average value	$1,050 ($1,100 + $1,000 = $2,100 ÷ 2)
equals	
Net yield (to maturity)	0.0714

The net yield to maturity as calculated in the two preceding examples is an approximate, rather than an exact, figure.[7] The method is accurate

[7]The formula for the approximate yield is:

Discount Bond	*Premium Bond*
$\dfrac{CM + (M - P)/n}{(M + P)/2}$	$\dfrac{CM - (P - M)/n}{(M + P)/2}$

where
C = annual coupon rate (%)
M = maturity value
P = current market price
n = number of years to maturity

enough for many purposes, especially for short- and medium-term bonds selling close to face value. But from a strictly mathematical viewpoint, the annual amortization or accumulation is not a uniform amount, and the actual value would be somewhat higher or lower than the figures here shown discounted to the present. As we have seen, tables are available which permit the ready determination of accurate yields when prices are known, or of exact prices when yields are given.

Other Bond Yields

Yields on callable, sinking fund, and convertible bonds   As noted previously, most modern bonds contain a provision whereby they may be redeemed by the issuer prior to maturity at a premium over offering price. The initial call premium is usually equal to one year's interest and declines toward maturity. The option is with the issuer, and redemption will be made only when it is to the issuer's advantage and, conversely, probably to the holder's disadvantage, as when a higher-interest issue is called and replaced by a lower-interest issue. This presents a problem in yield calculation. The holder of a redeemable bond should always take the most conservative position; that is, use the least favorable maturity option when calculating its yield. If the bond is bought at a discount, and is redeemable either at par or above, he should assume principal payment at the final date of maturity. If the bond is bought at par but is redeemable at a premium, or if it has been bought above par but is redeemable at no less a premium, the same assumption should be made. If the bond is bought above par but is redeemable at par, the yield is calculated on the basis of the nearest call date. If the bond is bought above par but is redeemable at an even greater premium, the net yield should be computed at both optional maturity dates, and the least favorable yield should be selected.

Even if the above procedures are followed, there is still uncertainty as to what the actual yield will be. Suppose a 20-year, 8% bond, callable at 106, with the call price declining to par at the end of 15 years, sells at par to yield 8%. If and when interest rates decline, the issue will likely be called if, including the required premium, the company can refinance at a lower net cost. But if the bond is called, the owner will receive a lower return on the new investment. Therefore, he may now wish to estimate the odds of call, at what price (terminal value) and under what market rates of interest, so as to estimate his real possible yield over the years. The terminal or "maturity" value would be over 100, and special bond yield tables would be used.[8]

Long-term U. S. Treasury bonds are not callable before maturity in the ordinary sense, but have optional maturities, for example, the 4 1/4s of 1987–1992. In choosing the maturity date that will provide the lowest yield, the above rules are followed. In the case of the example just given, the yield on October 3, 1977, at 83 12/32, was 6.00% computed to the last callable date.

---

[8]*Financial Bond Yields: Based on Premium Redemption.* Boston: Financial Publishing Co., 1968.

Bonds and preferred stocks with deferred call dates present a special problem. The deferment provides protection against retirement in a period of declining interest rates. The investor will usually accept a slightly lower yield (say, 1/4%) if he feels there is a good chance that market rates will decline during the deferment period.

The investor can avoid the risk of call by purchasing low-coupon bonds selling at substantial discounts. In doing so he pays, in the form of a lower yield, for the tax advantage that stems from the capital gains prospects of the bond as it moves towards maturity or as interest rates decline.

As indicated in Chapter 9, the conversion feature also affects the yield on convertible bonds and preferred stocks. This is true whenever the market price is above their straight investment value. The premium paid for the conversion privilege may be so high as to depress the yield to a very low, even negative figure. Mathematically, investors must calculate the probable value of the common stock upon conversion of the senior security, as well as the time of conversion. An additional refinement is the probability of forced conversion if the bond is called when its conversion value is above the call price. Thus, a different terminal value is estimated.

Bonds that are callable for sinking fund purposes present a problem, depending on the proportion of the total issue held by the investor. Call for sinking fund purposes is by lot. The investor's particular bonds might be called during a period of lower interest rates. If he holds a large share of the issue, he must again assess the probabilities of call and of changing rates in the bond market.

Current yield on bonds   The "current yield" on bonds is determined by dividing the annual interest payment by the cost price. An 8 1/2% bond purchased at 90 would afford a current yield of 9.44%.

Where the principal of a bond is in default or undergoing readjustment, or where the income is very uncertain, the current rather than net yield is used to indicate the rate of return. This practice should also apply to bonds on which the continuation of interest payments or the payment of principal at maturity is so much in doubt that they sell at very substantial discounts.

Where bonds are bought for trading purposes rather than to hold, the current yield is usually figured.

The yield on convertible bonds is often calculated on a current basis, to reflect the fact that they may someday be converted into common stock and not held to maturity. In addition, their current yield can be compared to the yield on the stock into which they are convertible. This, among other facts, enables the investor to decide whether he prefers to own the convertible bond or the common stock itself.

Total return on bonds   The concept of total return, consisting of cash income plus (or minus) price appreciation (or decline), has become widely used in investment circles. (See Chapters 9, 23.) Although mainly applied to common stocks, it can also show the performance of a bond or a bond portfolio. In years such as 1973–1974, price loss more than offset current interest income. In a recovery year such as 1976, total returns of over 20% were enjoyed even on high-grade bonds.

Market Yield on Bonds

Determinants of market yield on corporate bonds   The mathematical concepts of yield and price discussed previously in this chapter explain how the net yield of a bond is calculated if the price is given, or the price if the yield is given. The yield is the rate of discount applied to the future stream of interest and principal to produce their present value. But what determines that rate of discount or yield that is satisfactory to investors? A large part of this book is devoted to this question, and the valuation of bonds, as discussed in Chapter 24, involves using the acceptable rate, based on analysis of risk and other factors.

A summary of the major factors that determine market yields on corporate bonds follows. Each factor is discussed in appropriate sections of the book.

1. *Determinants of risk-free yield.* (See Chapter 19.)
   (a) Maturity of the obligation (time value of money) (See below.)
   (b) Structure of the interest rate pattern (See below.)
   (c) Premium for purchasing-power risk (inflation)
2. *Additional yield to compensate for risk of default* (See Chapter 20.)
   (a) Rank or priority-of the security
   (b) Analysis (or ratings) of ability to pay; coverage by assets and earnings
3. *Special covenants of the security* (See above and Chapter 20.)
   (a) Restrictions on additional debt or on dividends
   (b) Call provision
   (c) Convertible provision
   (d) Sinking fund provision
4. *Tax status*
   (a) Capital gains advantage of discount bonds (See Chapter 18.)
5. *Market status*
   (a) Marketability and seasoning (See Chapters 6, 7, 9, 12.)
   (b) Institutional market (See Chapters 21, 22.)

Maturity and the yield curve   Bonds and other obligations that have different maturities, but which are alike in other respects, bear different yields. Historically, debts with short maturities have borne lower yields than those with longer maturities. Deviations from this pattern are indicated several times in this book.

The influence of maturity is best indicated by reference to marketable Federal obligations which are uniformly free from the risk of default, but which differ in length of term. "Yield curves" indicate the "term structure of interest rates" at different times. Charts 8–1 and 8–2, where yields are plotted against maturities, are revealing. In 1972, the typical pattern pre-

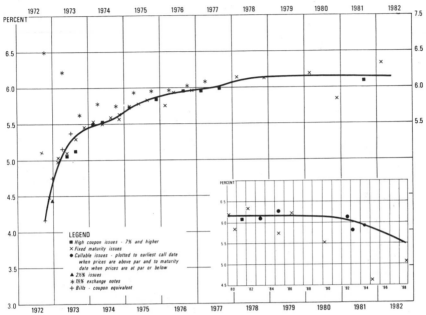

YIELDS OF TREASURY SECURITIES, JUNE 30, 1972
Based on Closing Bid Quotations

LEGEND
■ High coupon issues - 7% and higher
✕ Fixed maturity issues
● Callable issues - plotted to earliest call date
   when prices are above par and to maturity
   date when prices are at par or below
▲ 2½% issues
✱ 1½% exchange notes
+ Bills - coupon equivalent

Note: The smooth curve is fitted by eye. Market yields on coupon issues due in less than 3 months are excluded.

Source: Treasury Bulletin.

vailed—yields rose with maturity, then flattened out after about seven years. In 1974, in a period of tight money and generally high interest rates, the shorter the maturity, the higher the yield.

Actual course of yields Bond yields are one type of long-term interest rates, and they change with the general pattern of interest rates. The spread between yields on high-grade straight corporate bonds and Treasury bonds, and between corporate bonds with different ratings, represents the margin for greater risk and poorer marketability. (Most corporate bonds are unlisted.) As Table 8-5 shows, the premium for risk and poorer liquidity tends to rise as yields in general rise. But this relationship has been by no means uniform.

Yields on high-grade corporate bonds, together with other long-term interest rates, reached record levels in 1970, reflecting the tight situation then prevailing in the capital market. This situation was the result of a tremendous demand for funds, on the part of both governments and corporations, and the inadequate supply of savings available for long-term investment. Bond yields also reflected the tightness of credit in the money market. As more funds became available, bond yields declined substantially

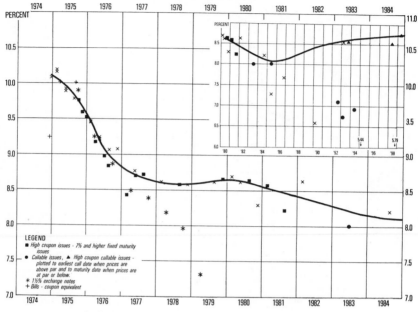

YIELDS OF TREASURY SECURITIES, AUGUST 30, 1974
Based on Closing Bid Quotations

LEGEND
- High coupon issues - 7% and higher fixed maturity issues
- Callable issues, ▲ High coupon callable issues - plotted to earliest call date when prices are above par and to maturity date when prices are at par or below.
- 1½% exchange notes
- + Bills - coupon equivalent

Note: The smooth curve is fitted by eye. Market yields on coupon issues due in less than 3 months are excluded.

Source: Treasury Bulletin.

TABLE 8-5 Bond Yields and Risk Premiums

	Corporate			U.S. Treasury	
	Baa	Aaa	Spread	Long-Term	Spread
	(1)	*(2)*	*(1)* over *(2)*	*(3)*	*(2)* over *(3)*
1960	5.19%	4.41%	0.78	4.01%	0.40
1961	5.08	4.35	0.73	3.90	0.45
1962	5.02	4.33	0.69	3.95	0.38
1963	4.86	4.26	0.60	4.00	0.26
1964	4.83	4.40	0.43	4.15	0.25
1965	4.87	4.49	0.38	4.21	0.28
1966	5.67	5.13	0.54	4.66	0.47
1967	6.23	5.51	0.72	4.85	0.66
1968	6.94	6.18	0.76	5.25	0.93
1969	7.81	7.83	0.78	6.10	0.93
1970	9.11	8.04	1.07	6.59	1.45
1971	8.56	7.39	1.17	5.74	1.65
1972	8.16	7.21	0.95	5.63	1.58
1973	8.24	7.44	0.80	6.30	1.14
1974	9.50	8.57	0.93	6.99	1.58
1975	10.61	8.83	1.78	6.98	1.85
1976	9.75	8.43	1.32	6.78	1.65

Sources: Corporate bond yields: *Moody's Bond Survey;* U.S. Government series: *Federal Reserve Bulletin.*

158

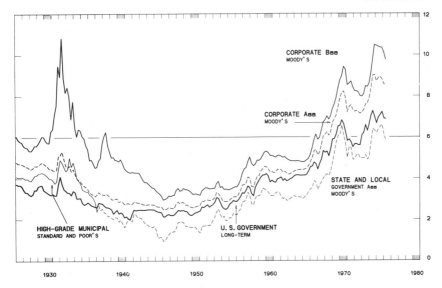

CORPORATE Baa
MOODY'S

CORPORATE Aaa
MOODY'S

STATE AND LOCAL
GOVERNMENT Aaa
MOODY'S

HIGH-GRADE MUNICIPAL
STANDARD AND POOR'S

U. S. GOVERNMENT
LONG-TERM

1930   1940   1950   1960   1970   1980

Source: Federal Reserve Historical Chart Book.

in 1971 and levelled off in early 1972, only to rise to new record heights in 1975. (See Chapter 3.) They declined in 1976 and 1977. Chart 8-3 shows the course of yields on selected long-term bonds since 1950.

In the 1970s, a new and potent force came to dominate the yield on bonds —the factor of inflation. Lenders demanded a premium for the loss of purchasing power. This factor will continue as the chief influence as long as the rate of inflation remains substantial. (See Chapter 19.)

Ownership of Corporate Bonds

At the end of 1976, an estimated $329 billion of domestic corporate bonds were outstanding,[9] in contrast to the $85 billion outstanding at the end of 1960. The average annual net increase (after refunding) of $14 billion per year in the 1960s and through the mid-1970s reflects the economic growth of this period and the advantages of long-term debt financing indicated early in this chapter. A much higher annual volume appeared in 1966–1967 and 1970–1971. In 1970 the increase was over $22 billion, and in 1971 it was $25 billion. The great demand for corporate funds contributed substantially to the record interest rates that prevailed in 1966–1971 and 1974–1975. A special factor in the 1970–1971 period was the need by corporations to improve their cash position after the "liquidity crisis" in 1969 and early 1970.

---

[9]*Federal Reserve Bulletin, flow-of-funds tables.*

This influence was not felt in the later 1970s. But the forces of demand continued, with a net annual increase of $29 to $30 billion in 1975 and 1976 as corporations financed a new post-recession expansion.

Corporate bonds, especially the high grade, have not been attractive to most individual investors until very recent years because their yields were seldom higher than, and were often lower than, the rates paid by savings institutions. And the latter offer no price risk. To wealthier investors, tax-free municipal bonds provide higher after-tax yields. Thus, the main buyers have traditionally been financial institutions. But the weakness of the stock market in 1969–1971 and 1973–1974, accompanied by record-breaking yields on bonds (Table 8-5), turned many individuals towards bonds. The net purchases of households, personal trusts, and nonprofit organizations rose to a peak of $10 billion in 1970. Individuals' demand fell off in 1971–1974, levelled out in 1975, then in 1976 achieved a new peak of $10.5 billion, or 40% of the net increase in corporate bonds outstanding.[10] Table 8-6 shows the ownership of *domestic* corporate bonds at the end of 1976.

TABLE 8-6   Ownership of Domestic Corporate Bonds, 1976
(in billions of dollars)

	Amount	%
Life insurance companies	$113.5	34.5
Uninsured private pension funds	37.9	11.5
State and local government retirement funds	67.6	20.5
Mutual investment companies	7.0	2.1
Mutual savings banks	26.4	8.0
Nonlife insurance companies	13.5	4.1
Commercial banks	7.2	2.2
Individuals, trustees, and minor institutions	56.1	17.1
	$329.2	100.0

Sources: Federal Reserve Bulletin, flow-of-funds tables. See also sources cited in institutional balance sheets, Chapters 3, 4, 21, 22.

Life insurance company ownership is still first in importance. These companies acquire the bulk of their higher-grade industrial bond investments by direct placement. Pension plans and other institutional owners likewise seek to secure a higher long-term yield than that available on Federal obligations. Ownership by individuals rose very substantially with the higher yields in 1969–1972, and again in 1973–1976.

The Investment Position of Bonds

Bonds have traditionally been regarded as the most conservative form of corporate security investment. To the investor who has complete freedom in the choice of his commitments, they provide a combination of dollar safety and convenience surpassing that available in any alternative form of security. To the investing institution which, for reasons of fiduciary safety, is restricted

[10]*Ibid.*

in the choice of securities, bonds provide a satisfactory medium of investment, as evidenced in the billions of dollars carried by these institutions in bondholdings.

Yet no investor can afford to assume that just because a security is a bond, it has inherent strength. Corporate bonds vary greatly in investment quality, from worthless to almost riskless. The investor must examine each security on its own merits, regardless of its legal form. Generalizations concerning any large class of securities are usually dangerous. That some common stock yields are lower than bond yields is not evidence of their superior safety of income and principal, but of the regard in which they are held by investors seeking price appreciation rather than current income. Nor can an investor expect stability in bond prices. As yields on outstanding bonds increase, their prices decline. The average value of AAA corporate bonds was 97.0 in March 1961. In July 1970 it reached 59.0, a decline of 39%, but stood at 66.1 in December 1972. Then the next great rise in interest rates drove the average price down to 55.8 in August 1975.[11] Note that these are prices of long-term bonds; shorter maturities suffered a smaller variation.

Another aspect of bond price action should be noted. As yields in general increase, the prices of low-coupon bonds decline the most, and in periods of high yields reach very low levels. But they have the greatest potential for appreciation in the event of a market turnaround that reflects declining yields. The investor also enjoys a locked-in yield because the chances of call by the corporation are virtually nil. A further advantage is that any subsequent gain on resale is taxable at capital gains rates.

As to whether bonds are "better investments" than stocks, the answer is that most bonds are *safer* insofar as dollars of interest and principal are concerned. Like all debt instruments, their fixed-dollar character provides no protection against the declining purchasing power of their interest and principal. Whether corporate bonds in general, or a certain bond in particular, should be purchased depends on the bond, on the needs and purposes of the investor, and on conditions in the bond market. General principles of bond valuation are set forth in Chapter 25, and much of the material on corporate security analysis in Part V is applicable to the task of determining the investment strength of corporate bond issues.

REFERENCES

BOGEN, J. I., ed., *Financial Handbook*, 4th rev. ed., Sections 14 and 27. New York: The Ronald Press Company, 1968.

CHILDS, J. F., *Encyclopedia of Long-Term Financing and Capital Management*, Chapter 4. Englewood Cliffs, N.J.: Prentice-Hall, Inc., 1976.

CISSELL, ROBERT, and HELEN CISSELL, *Mathematics of Finance*, 4th ed., Chapter 6. Boston: Houghton-Mifflin Company, 1973.

DARST, D. M., *The Complete Bond Book: A Guide to all Types of Fixed-Income Securities*. New York: McGraw-Hill Book Co., 1975.

[11]*Federal Reserve Bulletin.*

DEWING, A. S., *Financial Policy of Corporations*, 5th ed., Book I, Chapters 7–9. New York: The Ronald Press Company, 1953.

DOUGALL, H. E., and J. E. GAUMNITZ, *Capital Markets and Institutions*, 3rd ed., Chapter 9. Englewood Cliffs, N.J.: Prentice-Hall, Inc., 1975.

GRAHAM, BENJAMIN, D. L. DODD, and SIDNEY COTTLE, *Security Analysis*, 4th ed., Chapters 22–26, 29. New York: McGraw-Hill Book Co., Inc., 1962.

GUTHMANN, H. G., and H. E. DOUGALL, *Corporate Financial Policy*, 4th ed., Chapters 10–12. Englewood Cliffs, N.J.: Prentice-Hall, Inc., 1962.

HART, W. L. *Mathematics of Investment*, 5th ed. Lexington, Mass.: D.C. Heath & Co., 1975.

HESS, A. P., and W. J. WINN, *The Value of the Call Privilege*. Philadelphia: University of Pennsylvania, 1962.

HICKMAN, W. B., *Corporate Bond Quality and Investment Experience*. Princeton, N.J.: Princeton University Press, 1958.

HOMER, SYDNEY, and M. L. LIEBOWITZ, *Inside the Yield Book*. New York: Institute of Finance and Prentice-Hall, Inc., 1972.

HUMMEL, P. M., and C. L. SEEBECK, *Mathematics of Finance*. New York: McGraw-Hill Book Co., 1971.

HUSBAND, W. H., and J. C. DOCKERAY, *Modern Corporation Finance*, 7th ed., Chapters 6–10. Homewood, Ill.: Richard D. Irwin, Inc., 1972.

KENT, R. P., *Corporate Financial Management*, 3rd ed., Part IX. Homewood, Ill.: Richard D. Irwin, Inc., 1969.

LEVINE, S. N., ed., *Financial Analyst's Handbook*, Vol. I, Chapters 6, 7, 9, 10, 17. Homewood, Ill: Dow Jones-Irwin, Inc., 1975.

ROSEN, L. R., *The Dow Jones-Irwin Guide to Interest*. Homewood, Ill.: Dow Jones-Irwin, Inc., 1974.

SHAO, S. P., *Mathematics of Management and Finance*, 3rd ed. Cincinnati, Ohio: South-Western Publishing Co., 1974.

SHERWOOD, H. C., *How to Invest in Bonds*. New York: Walker & Co., 1974.

Standard Securities Calculation Methods. New York: Securities Industry Association, 1973.

THOMPSON, F. C., and R. L. NORGAARD, *Sinking Funds: Their Use and Value*. New York: Financial Executives Research Foundation, 1967.

VAN ARSDELL, P. M., *Corporation Finance*, Chapters 14, 15. New York: The Ronald Press Company, 1968.

WESTON, J. F., and E. F. BRIGHAM, *Managerial Finance*, 3rd ed., Chapter 19. New York: Holt, Rinehart & Winston, 1969.

WIDICUS, W. W., and T. E. STITZEL, *Personal Investing*, 2nd ed., Chapter 8. Homewood, Ill.: Richard D. Irwin, Inc., 1976.

WILLIAMSON, J. P. *Investments: New Analytic Techniques*, Chapters 8, 9. New York: Praeger Publishers, Inc., 1971.

Characteristics of Stocks, Convertible Securities, and Warrants

SCOPE: This chapter discusses the general nature of corporate stocks, convertible securities, and warrants from the viewpoint of the investor. Investment policy involving stocks is reserved for later attention. The order of discussion is: (1) general characteristics of stocks, including the legal position of the stockholder and stock terminology, (2) return on stocks, (3) preferred stock—general nature, (4) preferred stocks as investments, (5) classified common stock, (6) guaranteed stocks, (7) common stocks and dividend policies, (8) subscription rights, (9) common stocks as investments, (10) convertible securities, (11) stock purchase-option warrants, (12) special sources of current information on convertible securities and warrants.

The form and title of a security do not determine its investment quality. Many common stocks have had very superior records, and many preferred stocks have become worthless. Nevertheless, the basic distinctions are important, and some general conclusions concerning the relative attractiveness of the two classes of stocks are valid. However, in the case of an individual security, it is the price, earnings and dividend record, prospects, and amount and character of the assets that support the stock, and the securities convertible into stock, that determine their investment quality.

General Characteristics of Stocks

Basic features Stock, whether preferred or common, involves no promises. The owner of a share of stock is part owner of the corporation. His stock gives him the right to share in the *net* assets of the business (if any), the *net* income (if any), and management.

The capital stock is divided into units, called *shares*. As of January 1, 1977, the outstanding stock of J.C. Penney Company comprised 64,500,000 shares, each of which represented 1/64,500,000 share of the net assets or *net worth* of the company. The evidence of ownership of shares is the *stock certificate*. The name of the owner appears on the face of the certificate, together with the number and kind of shares represented by the certificate. The certificate is always a registered instrument; the owner's name is registered on the books of the company. Only the registered owner can assign the stock by signing the blank form on the back of the certificate. The registered owner is the one who receives the dividends, has the right to vote, and otherwise enjoys the privileges of ownership.

Stock certificates are written evidences of ownership of shares of stock and are transferable if properly endorsed and delivered. When stocks are sold, the usual practice is for the owner to endorse them in blank. They may pass through many hands before being registered on the corporation's books in the name of the new owner. The actual registration and transfer is usually handled by a transfer agent appointed by the company.

Corporation stock may have a *par value* of from a few cents to several hundred dollars per share, or *no par* value. The par value is a purely nominal amount which is supposed to show the original investment per share. When the par value has been paid into the corporation, the stock certificate is designated "full-paid and nonassessable." Today the trend is toward low par value stock, or stock without par value, which is full-paid when the original consideration set for each share has been received by the company.

To the investor, no-par stock has a real advantage in that each share simply represents a certain fractional ownership in the corporation without any confusion as to nominal value. A stock with a par value of $50 (Reading Company) may sell, as it did in 1976, as low as $7/8 per share. Probably few of its owners knew that the company had at one time received the equivalent of $50 per share in cash or other assets for this stock. Neither the market value nor the *book value* (dollars of net assets per share of stock) is influenced by the nominal par value after the company has been in operation for some time.

Table 9-1 shows the par value (if any), the book or net asset value at the end of 1976, and the range in market value of selected common stocks for the year 1976. The selection reveals that the market value, based primarily on the prospects for earnings and dividends, is usually considerably different from nominal and book values.

Legal position of the stockholder   As the owners of corporations, stockholders have certain well-defined rights and obligations. Although state laws differ widely with respect to powers of corporations, the position of the stockholder is fairly uniform.

The stockholder has a right to receive dividends when earned and if declared by the directors. The income claim of a stockholder is contingent, differing fundamentally from that of the bondholder, who has a fixed claim and who can take action in the event of default. The stockholder shares in the fortunes of the business, large or small. In the case of common stocks, there is no theoretical upper limit, while most preferred stocks can receive only a maximum stated dividend. Even when earnings are large, stockholders rarely compel dividend payments if the management decides to reinvest the profits in the business. This is true even of preferred stock, except that the preferred has a right to dividends before the common.

TABLE 9-1   Selected Common Stock Values

Company	Par Value, Dec. 31, 1976	Book Value Dec. 31, 1976	Price Range 1976
Suave Shoe Corp.	$ .01	$ 6.06	3 3/8–6 1/2
Merck & Co., Inc.	.02 7/8	14.55	62 5/8–81 1/8
Digicon Inc.	.10	4.08	3 1/8–8 3/8
Chock Full o' Nuts Corp.	.25	1.88^b	2 –4 3/8
Sperry Rand Corp.	.50	33.75^a	38 7/8–51 3/4
Hewlett-Packard Co.	1.00	24.09	80 –117 3/4
Chicago Milwaukee Corp.	1.00	141.47	4 1/4–9 1/4
General Motors Corp.	1.6667	48.94	57 3/4–78 7/8
Signal Companies, Inc.	2.00	40.88	15 3/8–27
Superior Oil Co.	2.50	146.09	148 –241 1/2
El Paso Co.	3.00	14.59	11 3/4–15 3/4
International Business Machines Corp.	5.00	84.60	223 3/8–288 1/2
Southern Calif. Edison Co.	8.33	32.11	18 1/8–23 5/8
Union Pacific Corp.	10.00	84.56	38 –51 1/4
Southern New England Tel. Co.	25.00	44.12	32 7/8–39 1/4
Reading Co.	50.00	76.93	7/8–2 1/2
Raychem Corp.	No par	72.94^c	86 –231
Procter & Gamble Co.	No par	28.14^c	81 7/8–100 1/8
RCA Corp.	No par	15.29	18 7/8–30 1/8
IC Industries, Inc.	No par	73.30^d	16 1/8–22 3/8

[a]March 31, 1976.
[b]July 31, 1976.
[c]June 30, 1976.
[d]December 31, 1975

The stockholder has the right to share in the net assets of the corporation in the event of dissolution. This right has no practical value in the case of failed concerns, even in the case of preferred stocks, which ordinarily have a set liquidating value that must be paid before anything goes to the common. But where there is nothing to distribute, such priority is meaningless.

Unless denied him by the charter of the company, the stockholder usually has the *preemptive* right to subscribe to new issues of common stock in proportion to his existing holdings, so as to preserve his relative share of the assets, earnings, and voting power that might be diluted if the shares were sold to new investors. Because convertible bonds and preferred stock may eventually be exchanged for common and thus increase the common stock outstanding, the stockholder is usually given preemptive rights to subscribe to new convertible securities. Since the subscription price is below market price, the rights to subscribe may have considerable value. The method of calculating the value of rights is given later in this chapter.

The stockholder has a right to inspect the corporate books. This right applies to the general books, such as the minutes of stockholders' meetings and the list of stockholders, rather than to the ledgers and the books of financial record, and is restricted by requirements that make it of little value to an investor unless he wishes to stage a proxy battle with management.

The stockholder has a right to vote in the selection of the board of directors and on all matters affecting the corporate property as a whole, such as sale, merger, or liquidation of the business.[1] The voting right is exercised at the annual or special meetings of stockholders in person or by the use of proxies which delegate voting rights to designated parties. When a stockholders' meeting is called, the management accompanies the notice with a proxy form, which the stockholder may sign and thus convey his votes to the committee acting for management.

Other fundamental rights of a stockholder include the right to receive a certificate representing his shares, to transfer his shares, and to take action against wrongful acts of the management and the majority of stockholders.

The stockholder is liable for the debts of the corporation only to the amount of unpaid subscriptions to the capital stock, and to the difference between subscription price and par value, in the event the former is lower. This limited liability feature is one of the great advantages afforded by the corporate form of organization.

The stockholder is also generally liable for wages of employees for limited periods. This provision applies to employees in subordinate positions, for periods not exceeding three months, under somewhat technical conditions.

Stock terminology   The *authorized* stock is the maximum number of shares of each type that may be issued, as specified in the certificate of incorporation. To change this number, or the provisions of any class of stock, requires the formal approval of stockholders. *Issued* stock is the amount of shares that have been issued for cash, property, or services. Stock reacquired by the company by purchase or donation and not reissued or cancelled is called *treasury* stock. Treasury stock is ordinarily deducted on the balance sheet from the issued stock to show the amount of *outstanding* stock. *Full-paid stock* is, as we have seen, stock for which the corporation has received full payment up to par value, or up to the amount established as the selling price of no-par shares. *Part-paid* stock is stock that has been issued for less than par value or the agreed subscription price. Under the laws of most states, stock cannot be issued unless fully paid.

Return on Stocks

Dividends—declaration and payment   The value of any dividend which may be paid on corporate stock is included in the quoted price of the stock. No calculation of dividend accrual is involved. (An exception is found in the case of new issues of preferred being offered to the public at a certain price "plus accrued dividends from the date of issue.") Dividend payments involve declaration dates (say, March 1), record dates (say, March 20), and payment dates (say, April 15). Persons buying the stock on or before the record date are entitled to receive the forthcoming dividend. Because buyers after the record date (March 20) are not entitled to the next dividend (on April 15), the market price is said to be "ex-dividend" and usually declines

---

[1]The ordinary voting right, that is, to vote for directors, is sometimes denied the holders of preferred stock. (See section below on preferred stock voting rights.)

by the amount of the quarterly payment around the record date, unless other influences offset the effect of the dividend.[2]

Dividend yield The rate of return or yield on corporate stocks, both preferred and common, is determined by dividing the annual cash dividend payment (in dollars) by the market price. A common stock priced at $50 per share and paying an annual dividend of $2 per share has a yield of 4%. Subsequent changes in the market price do not affect the rate of return to holders who paid $50, but do change the yield to new buyers. Subsequent changes in the dividend rate (on common stock) may affect the rate of return to all holders. Dividends on preferred stock are usually a fixed dollar amount.

During the year, the investor may not know the final amount of the annual dividend on common stock. He calculates the yield either by estimating the current 12-month dividend or by using the previous year's dividend.

When dividends are paid in shares of stock rather than in cash, the yield is usually indicated as a percentage increase. Thus, a "2% stock dividend" means that the holder of 100 shares receives two new shares. The investor may calculate the market value if he wishes to do so. Fractional stock dividends are often paid in cash at their market value.

"Earnings yield" Another yield concept in the case of common stocks is the "earnings yield," or relation between earnings per share and market price. Most investors reverse the relationship and think in terms of the price-earnings ratio or multiple. A common stock selling at 60 that is earning $3 per share and pays a cash dividend of $2.40 has an earnings yield of 5% (3 ÷ 60), a price-earning ratio of 20 (60 ÷ 3), and a dividend yield of 4% (2.40 ÷ 60). The concept of "earnings yield" will be used in a number of discussions in this book, especially in Chapter 25.

The significance of yield Dividend rates on most preferred stocks are fixed in time and amount and, therefore, provide a more dependable basis for the calculation of an estimated future rate of income return. Dividend payments on common stocks are more irregular. In many cases the yield on common stock is virtually meaningless; in others, where the dividends are regular and appear dependable, the yield is a significant factor to investors. Whereas in the case of preferred stocks and bonds, the yield reflects the general quality of the security, it may not do so for common stocks where both price and yield may reflect appreciation possibilities and anticipated increases in dividends. The significance of yield in the valuation of common stocks is discussed in Chapter 25.

The concept of "total return" As indicated in Chapter 8, in recent years the concept of "total return" has come into prominence and is being increasingly used to measure the performance of both bonds and stocks. It includes the actual or estimated change in market value in addition to the

---

[2]The rule on stocks listed on the New York Exchange is that transactions shall be ex-dividend on the fourth full business day preceding the record date, or on the day the stock transfer books are closed. Otherwise, shares are ex-dividend on the date of record.

current or expected cash income. Its calculation, usefulness, and limitations are discussed in Chapter 23, and other references to the concept appear throughout this book.

Preferred Stock—General Nature

Types   The capital stock of a company is often divided into two classes, *preferred* and *common*. The provisions of the preferred stock are set forth in the corporate charter. It has priority over the common stock with respect to dividends; that is, no dividends may be paid on the common stock in any year in which the full preferred dividend has not been paid. The amount of the annual preferred dividend, which is limited, is stated either in dollars per share or as a percentage of par value. Preferred dividends are not fixed charges. Like common dividends, they are contingent upon the discretion of the management as represented by the board of directors. However, where the preferred dividend is earned, it is usually paid so as to keep the record clean and to clear the road for common dividends.

Cumulative preferred stock dividends omitted at any time accumulate in the form of arrearages. These arrearages, although not corporate liabilities, must be paid in full before any dividend may be paid on the common stock. *Noncumulative* preferred stock has no prior claim on dividends, except on those for the current year. Past dividends are lost forever.

The advantage of the cumulative feature is not so great as it might seem. A prolonged period of poor earnings may result in an accumulation of dividend arrearages beyond the capacity of the company to pay, so that even a solvent company is almost permanently enjoined from paying any dividends to the common stockholders. Even when the amount of arrearage is not discouragingly large, the holders of cumulative preferred stock are usually persuaded to accept other securities or part cash in lieu of cash in full.

Companies that regularly use preferred stock financing often issue two or more series that share the same rank of priority over the common. But their dividend rates, call prices, and even sinking fund provisions may differ because the several series were sold at different times and under different market conditions. Pacific Gas and Electric Company has (1977) 17 classes of preferred stock, all ranking equally in priority but having dividend rates ranging from 4.36 to 10.46% (on $25 par). Flintcote Company has three classes, one of which, carrying a rate of $4, is known as Preferred and has dividend priority over the second, of which there are two series, known as Convertible Second Preferred. The term *prior preferred* is sometimes used to designate the issue of preferred stock which has priority, although the term *first preferred* is more generally used for this purpose. In such cases, the senior issue is entitled to its full dividend rate before any payment can be made on the junior issue. An example of issues of preferred stock with different priorities is found in Commonwealth Edison Company (Chicago), which has (1977) two "layers" of preferred ahead of the common: $1.45 Convertible Preferred, no par value; and six series of Cumulative Preference, no par value, bearing different dividend rates.

Preferred stock usually has priority also in the distribution of net assets in the event of dissolution. The amount of the preference is stated in dollars per share and generally approximates the original value of the stock, plus any accumulated dividends. This "preference as to assets" rarely has any practical value. Failure usually leaves little or nothing for the stockholders.

Redeemable or callable preferred stock may be retired by the issuing company upon the payment of a definite price stated in the instrument. Although the "call price" provides for the payment of a premium, which may range from $2 to as much as $10 above the face value of the stock, the provision is more advantageous to the corporation than to the investor. When money rates decline, the corporation is likely to call in its preferred stock and refinance it at a lower dividend rate. When money rates rise, the value of the preferred declines so as to produce higher yield. The call price acts as an upper peg or plateau through which the price will break only in a very strong market.

Noncallable preferred stocks and bonds are issued in periods of high interest rates such as 1966, 1971, and 1973–1974. (See Chapter 8.) The issuer is barred from redeeming them later in the event of generally falling yields, or for a certain period, so the investor has important protection against declining income. Pacific Gas and Electric Company's 9.28% preferred, issued in 1970, is noncallable until 1980.

Convertible preferred stock may be exchanged into common stock at the option of the holder. (See p. 184.) Preferred stocks which carry this privilege are likely to be deficient in quality, because ordinarily it is unnecessary to add this feature to a stock that is strong in its own right. However, in periods when common stocks are in demand and rising in value, even strong companies may add the convertible feature to attract investors who would not be enthusiastic about ordinary preferred stock.

As explained later, the exchange ratio is stated in the instrument and is often on a sliding scale whereby the conversion price increases during the conversion period. The longer the investor waits, the less common stock he will receive upon conversion.

Stock purchase-option *warrants* give the owner of the preferred stock the right to purchase common stock from the company at a stipulated price during a specified period. Preferred stock with warrants offers a speculative feature similar to the conversion feature, with the purpose of bolstering the attractiveness of a stock which lacks real strength on its own merits. Their use is also discussed later in this chapter.

Protective provisions and voting rights   In addition to the two basic features of preferred stock noted previously—preference (over the common stock) as to dividends and as to assets—other features may give it investment strength. These are especially important in the case of preferred stock that lacks ordinary voting rights. They include: (1) a repurchase or sinking fund that requires the steady reduction in the amount of preferred outstanding, (2) required approval by the preferred stockholders of the issuance of any funded debt or of additional preferred, and (3) restriction on the payment of common dividends unless a certain working capital position is maintained.

Although the right to vote for the board of directors and thus to participate in management is a fundamental right adhering to all stock, it is often withheld from preferred stock. No great harm is done so long as the company's earnings, dividends, and general financial strength are well maintained. The investor in preferred stock, although a part owner of the corporation, regards himself as an "outside" investor. However, if dividends are not paid, and if he has no voice in management, he needs some protection. Therefore, the preferred usually has the right to vote under certain conditions, even if normal voting power is lacking. It could be given one vote per share after a certain number of quarterly dividends (often four or six) have been omitted. Or, as a class, it may have the right to elect a certain number of directors, or, in some cases, to elect a majority or even all of the directors. Such contingent voting power is a strong inducement to management to earn and pay the preferred dividends and avoid an accumulation. In addition, the preferred usually has the right to vote on certain questions that affect its status considerably, such as the dissolution of the company, the mortgaging or sale of its property, and merger with another concern.

Preferred Stocks as Investments

Variety of grades   In general, preferred stock occupies an intermediate investment position, offering more income but less safety than bonds, and less income or appreciation but more safety than common stocks.

Some preferred stocks resemble bonds in their investment position, but other issues might more properly be placed in the category of common stocks as far as investment quality is concerned. Until recent years many well-known companies had no long-term debt outstanding, so that their preferred stocks had claims on earnings which were not subordinate to or lessened by bond interest payments. So long as this condition continued, these preferred stocks were the senior securities of the enterprise, and this position is reflected in their low yields. There are few important companies in this category today.

Other preferred stocks belong, in terms of safety, in the bond category because of the prosperity of the issuing companies. Certain railroad companies, such as Union Pacific and Santa Fe, certain public utility companies, such as Cleveland Electric, Pacific Telephone, and many small public utility operating companies, and certain industrial companies, such as General Motors, du Pont, and Standard Brands, have established impressive records of earnings over long periods of years, and their preferred stocks enjoy a strong investment position.

Many other preferred stocks, however, especially of industrial companies, belong in the common stock category because of inadequate earnings protection. Investors who bought preferred stocks upon the assumption that the payment of dividends was as certain as the payment of bond interest have found that dividends may be passed and that in liquidation or in reorganization the preferred stockholders are in a very weak bargaining position.

It is not the *form* of a security that gives it value and stability, but the earnings and assets that support it. Nevertheless, because preferred stock lacks the legal claim of the bondholder and the profit and appreciation possibilities of a common stockholder (because of the customary fixed dividend rate, stated liquidating value, and call feature), it has a questionable investment status that is clearly revealed when hard times appear. Were it not for their tax appeal to corporate investors, even the highest-grade preferred issues, well protected by assets and earning power, would yield no more than high-grade bonds of long maturity.

Yields and prices   The price and yield action of a preferred stock is determined by four fundamental factors: (1) the general level of long-term interest rates (the preferred dividend being a fixed annual amount), (2) the earnings and asset strength of the issuer, (3) the special appeal of preferred stocks to the taxed *corporate* investor, and (4) the shortage of high-grade preferred issues. The influence of the first two factors is discussed elsewhere in this volume, as are the methods of appraising them and applying them to specific securities.

The third or tax factor deserves some mention here and helps to explain the data on yields given below. Only 15% of the dividends on preferred stock owned by taxed corporations are subject to Federal corporate income tax. This feature gives preferred dividend income an advantage over bond interest income, and largely explains why yields on very high-grade preferred stocks, held mainly by institutional owners, have been as low as, and even lower than, the yields in bonds of the same companies, since 1960. Another tax influence applies to dividends not covered by the 85% tax-exclusion. The dividends on these preferred stocks, notably public utility issues, are not taxable in part or sometimes not at all because they represent a return of capital. This situation arises when a company that charges accelerated depreciation for tax, but not for "book" purposes, reports little or no taxable income, so that part or all of its dividends are unearned.

The data in Table 3-4 reveal the relative unimportance of preferred stock financing until recent years. The small flow of new issues, accompanied by the demand for preferred stocks on the part of taxed institutional investors, has contributed to the special price and yield pattern found in the preferred stock market in very recent years. The increase in preferred stock financing in 1967, and especially in 1971–1975, is explained by three factors: (1) the appeal of convertible preferred, especially as issued for mergers, (2) the need by public utility companies to balance their capital structures after very heavy debt financing, and (3) occasional very large issues such as those of American Telephone.

The data in Table 9-2 show the course of average annual high-grade and good-grade preferred stock yields, 1960–1976, compared to those of bonds of the same rating, using Moody's industrial series. Both preferred and bond yields rise and fall with general long-term interest rates. The yields on high-grade preferreds would be higher than on high-grade bonds were it not for their tax appeal to institutions. The spread between the yields on high-grade and good-grade preferred stocks has widened during periods of high yields.

The price action of preferred stock is, of course, the opposite of the change

TABLE 9-2   Preferred Stock Yields

	High-Grade Industrials		Good-Grade Industrials		Spread	
	Aaa Bonds	Low-Dividend Preferreds	Baa Bonds	Medium-Grade Preferreds	(2) over (1)	(4) over (2)
	(1)	(2)	(3)	(4)	(1)	(2)
1960	4.28%	4.48%	5.11%	4.80%	.20	.32
1965	4.45	4.07	4.92	4.38	−.38	.31
1966	5.12	4.67	5.68	4.95	−.45	.28
1967	5.49	5.13	6.21	5.39	−.36	.26
1968	6.12	5.62	6.90	5.83	−.50	.21
1969	6.93	6.15	7.76	6.38	−.78	.23
1970	7.77	7.03	9.00	7.25	−.74	.22
1971	7.05	6.55	8.37	6.84	−.50	.29
1972	6.97	6.56	7.99	6.85	−.41	.29
1973	7.28	6.65	8.07	7.01	−.63	.36
1974	8.42	7.48	9.14	8.14	−.94	.66
1975	8.61	7.83	10.26	8.18	−.78	.35
1976	8.23	7.37	9.67	7.81	−.86	.44

Source: Moody's Industrials Manual.

in yield. The prices of even the highest-grade preferreds are, like bond prices, subject to substantial variations as interest rates change. For example, W.T. Grant Company 3 3/4% preferred sold as high as 112 in 1937, but as low as 48 in 1970 when extremely high interest rates prevailed, although the dividend was covered over 100 times. Changes in quality have, of course, always affected yields. Other factors that affect yields are those that have been indicated for bonds. (See Chapter 8.)

Until recent years industrial preferred stocks, including the high-grade, were not attractive to individuals. Their yields were relatively low compared to those on savings types of investments, utility preferred stocks, and corporate and municipal bonds (after taxes). Most of them are traded over-the-counter and have lacked good marketability. Even the remarkable levels of yields on all fixed-income instruments reached in 1974–1976 left industrial preferred stocks still too richly priced for individuals, and their market continued to be the institutional buyers. Utility preferred stocks, however, offered substantially higher yields and found a new market in individuals' portfolios. Yields on Moody's high-grade utility series reached over 10% in 1974 and have remained high.

Classified Common Stock

In the 1920s, a hybrid type of security was developed by the issuance of more than one type of "common" stock, and today the balance sheets of some corporations still show "Class A" and "Class B" common, or "Class A common" and "Common." In some cases the only difference between the two classes of common is that one is devoid of voting rights. Control of the corporation is thus concentrated in one issue.[3] In recent years the trend has been away from nonvoting common. It may not be listed on the New York Stock Exchange, and it is frowned upon by the Securities and Exchange Commission insofar as gas and electric companies are concerned.

Other issues of so-called classified common stock are, in fact, merely weak preferred stocks, with preference as to assets and dividends, but without the other protective provisions ordinarily found in true preferred. A description of such provisions is readily obtained in the investment manuals.

Guaranteed Stocks

Guaranteed stocks are those upon which dividend payments are guaranteed by some company other than the issuer. The guarantee usually arises out of a consolidation of properties under a lease. Such stocks, confined almost entirely to railroads, may be preferred or common. They are more like bonds, however, since dividend payments are fixed, rather than contingent, charges. The amount of the guaranteed dividend is either the regular rate stated on the preferred certificate or a contractual rate on the common stock.

The investment position of guaranteed stock depends upon the nature of the guarantee, the value of the underlying property to the guaranteeing company, and the financial responsibility of the guaranteeing company, but most especially the latter. Stocks guaranteed by the Penn Central and New York Central railroads have suffered from the financial failure of their lessees. Those guaranteed by solvent lines continue to enjoy investment respect.

Common Stocks

General nature   Common stock represents the basic ownership of the company. The claim of the common stockholders to income and assets is subordinate to all other claims, except in the few instances where preferred stock is not preferred as to assets. Ordinary common stock always has voting rights. Common stocks are often called residual *equities*, since they represent that part of the total capitalization contributed by the owners, in contrast to the remainder supplied by creditors and preferred stockholders.

After a corporate reorganization, the shares of the new company are often placed in trust with a small group of trustees for from five to 10 years. *Voting trust certificates* are issued to the stockholders. These securities have all of the characteristics of the common stock itself except voting rights.

Income is paid to stockholders in the form of dividends, which, as the term implies, represent a division of profits. Dividend payments are usually

---

[3]An interesting example of classified common stock is Ford Motor Company's Common (voting), Class A (nonvoting—held by the Ford Foundation), and Class B (voting), with $2.50 par value. These were issued in 1956 as a result of the recapitalization when Ford stock was first made available to the public (by the Foundation).

made quarterly and in cash.[4] The payments may be semiannual or annual. In some instances, dividends are declared in the form of short-term promissory notes, called *scrip*. In rare cases, certain of the corporate assets are distributed as property dividends.

Dividends in the form of stock are in reality a division of the ownership into a larger number of units, and, therefore, not a true distribution of earnings. The result would not be different if the disbursement were made in cash and the money reinvested in new stock. "Stock dividends" are the external evidence of reinvestment of profits in the business. Stockholders who do not wish to increase their investment in the company may sell their stock dividends. In doing so, of course, they are parting with a portion of their equity.

Dividends in the form of stock have a strong appeal to many investors. Where the company is earning a high rate of profits, the stockholder may prefer to have his earnings reinvested. The tax advantages of stock dividends are also appealing to many investors. No income tax is paid when the stock dividend is received, and only a capital gains tax if the dividend shares are ultimately sold at a profit.

Dividend policies   Some common stocks are bought primarily for income, others primarily for price appreciation. In the former case, the stockholder wants some assurance that the current or future return on his common stock will be sufficiently higher than the return on bonds and preferred stock to compensate for the additional risks of common stock ownership. In the latter case, he wants assurance that the retained earnings are employed at a rate that will lead to growth in capital value.

Dividend policies may be divided somewhat arbitrarily in this fashion:

REGULAR DIVIDEND IRRESPECTIVE OF CURRENT EARNINGS   This policy, as followed by the American Telephone & Telegraph Company for many years, is regarded as the investment ideal by many. The disadvantage is that the dividend rate may be maintained too long after earning power has declined. The Penn Central Transportation Company had large losses in 1967–1969 and went into bankruptcy in 1970. But it had paid dividends of $2.40, $2.40, and $1.80 in the three years prior to bankruptcy.

REGULAR DIVIDEND PROPORTIONATE TO CURRENT EARNINGS   The policy of distributing a high proportion of earnings is followed by most operating utility companies so as to attract funds from established investors and lay a basis for future equity financing. And such companies can rely heavily on senior financing, rather than retained earnings, for growth. Few industrials can follow this policy.

---

[4]The American Telephone & Telegraph Company pays a cash dividend on the 10th of January, April, July, and October to all stockholders who were listed on the corporate books on the tenth of the preceding month. The interval between the *record date* and the *dividend date* is provided in order to allow the checks to be prepared for mailing. The magnitude of this task is indicated by the fact that more than 3 million separate stockholders receive checks quarterly from this one company. A mailing schedule is prepared under which all stockholders throughout the country receive their checks at the same time, irrespective of place of residence.

REGULAR DIVIDEND AT MINIMUM RATE   This policy permits companies to pay a small but dependable dividend at all times and to reinvest most of current earnings for expansion purposes. It is characteristic of International Paper and other companies in the paper industry, and of the stronger steel companies, and forms the basis for occasional extra distributions, sometimes in the form of stock.

REGULAR DIVIDEND PAYABLE IN STOCK   This rather unusual policy enables companies to make a distribution to stockholders which they may convert into cash if they desire, but which allows the retention of cash in the business. Current industrial examples are found in Litton Industries, General Instruments, and Marriott Corporation. Many savings and loan associations and their holding companies follow this practice.

REGULAR DIVIDEND PAYABLE PARTLY IN CASH AND PARTLY IN STOCK   This policy, which represents a combination of two methods, is used by a few companies. The cash payments are made quarterly, but the stock payments are made either semiannually or annually to avoid the effect of rapid compounding. Walt Disney Productions, Air Products, Castle & Cooke, and Norton Simon are current examples.

VERY SMALL, ERRATIC, OR NO DIVIDENDS AT ALL   This category includes a wide range of companies, from new, small, and untried concerns which cannot pay dividends, through established firms like Hewlett-Packard whose small payment is only a gesture to outside investors but provides the major shareholders with income, to very rapidly growing concerns like McDonald's whose policy of stock splits has attracted a large investment following.

It is difficult to generalize concerning dividend policy. After great breaks in stock market prices, such as experienced in 1973–1974, investors became much more interested in dividends. This is in contrast to the 1960s and early 1970s when retained earnings were deemed much more valuable, as evidenced by the high price-earnings multipliers applied to the "growth stocks." High interest rates, inflation, and economic recession in 1973–1975, however, deflated these multipliers very substantially and brought a demise to the so-called "two-tier" market.

Table 9-3 shows the earnings and dividends per share on Standard & Poor's 425 Industrial Stock Index for the period 1960–1976. The data indicate the tendency for industrial corporations as a group to retain an increasing portion of earnings. Great variations are, of course, found among individual companies.

The chief reason for the conservative dividend policy of many companies has been that of raising funds for expansion. In addition to short-term borrowing for working capital purposes, three major sources of long-term funds have been available: (1) long-term loans, as represented by bond issues and term loans; (2) the sale of stock; and (3) internal sources, as represented by depreciation reserves and reinvested profits.

The use of the second of these sources is greatly influenced by the level of prices in the common stock market in relation to the company's earnings

**TABLE 9-3   Earnings and Dividends per Share on Standard &
Poor's Industrial Stock Index, 1960–1976**

	Earnings	Dividends	Dividends as a Percentage of Earnings
1960	$3.39	$2.00	59%
1961	3.37	2.08	62
1962	3.87	2.20	57
1963	4.24	2.38	56
1964	4.83	2.60	54
1965	5.50	2.85	52
1966	5.89	2.98	51
1967	5.66	3.01	53
1968	6.15	3.18	52
1969	6.17	3.27	52
1970	5.36	3.28	61
1971	5.96	3.18	53
1972	6.83	3.22	47
1973	8.86	3.48	39
1974	9.69	3.72	38
1975	8.44	3.78	45
1976	10.65	4.25	40

Source: Standard & Poor's *Trade and Securities Statistics,*

and assets. When stock prices are low, to sell stock at less than book value may result in a considerable dilution of the existing stockholders' equity. But even when prices are high in relation to earnings, many corporations prefer to avoid public financing with stock in favor of the easier route of reinvestment. Internal sources and debt financing may provide all of the funds needed for expansion. And management may not wish to increase the number of outstanding shares for fear of dilution.[5]

Many corporations, especially industrials, have, therefore, turned to retention of profits as a major source of funds, and their dividend payments have suffered as a result. Such a policy makes for a more conservative capital structure (unless offset by increased debt), but it may have a corresponding disadvantage to the stockholder in that the value of the retained earnings, as represented by a growing retained earnings account, may not be reflected in an equal growth in market price. If, however, market price does grow in relation to a high current or expected rate of earnings, many stockholders should approve a modest dividend payout because the corporation can invest funds at a higher rate than can the owners, who also avoid income taxes on current dividend income.

With the general rise of common stock prices (as measured by the averages) to their then all-time peak in 1961, and their 1962–1966 recovery from the 1962 decline, some companies again turned to the sale of common stock for new money. Nevertheless, retained earnings and funds representing depreciation continued to be even more important sources. With the subsequent stock price decline in 1966, internal sources became even more

[5]The meaning and importance of dilution is discussed in Chapter 25.

important, in spite of substantial price recovery in 1967. Corporations turned to common stock financing to an unusual extent in 1969 and in 1970, although stocks had suffered the worst bear market in a generation. (See p. 33.) Stocks as well as bonds were sold to reduce current liabilities and improve liquidity. In 1971–1972 utility and communications companies continued to rely on common stock financing of large new plant requirements.

The recession experience in 1973–1975, accompanied by the extremely sharp drop in prices of common stocks, led to a substantial decline in common stock financing and to a concomitant reliance on retention of earnings by industrial companies. Table 9-3 reveals the extraordinary decline in the percentage of earnings distributed in dividends in those years. Payouts increased considerably in 1976 as investors demanded higher yields.

Direct reinvestment of dividends More than 500 New York and American Stock Exchange firms now permit their cash dividends, and in some cases optional cash payments, to be directly reinvested in common stock. Pacific Gas and Electric Company, for example, will reinvest both the cash dividends and optional cash payments of $25 to $1,000 per month in the firm's common stock. The proceeds from these stock sales are used, along with other funds, for plant additions and debt retirement.

Large stock dividends and stock splits When a company declares a dividend in the form of stock, additional shares with the same par or nominal value are issued without any change in the total net worth. A 100% stock dividend doubles the number of shares outstanding, and each share should decline 50% in price since the assets and earnings are divided among twice as many shares. A two-for-one split-up, which doubles the number of shares by reducing their nominal value 50%, should have the same result.

Actually a large stock dividend or a split-up may make the stock more attractive, and cause a rise in price when the event is rumored or announced, for these reasons: (1) A larger number of shares outstanding and a lower trading range per share may improve the marketability and distribution of the stock; (2) the cash dividend rate may not be reduced proportionally, resulting in a larger cash income per old share (as in the case of American Telephone whose old stock paying $9.00 was split in 1959 into three shares each paying $3.30, and again in 1964 into two shares each paying $2.00); (3) attention is dramatically called to the high price per share and to the growth and prospects of the company. Large stock dividends and split-ups are a feature of bull markets.

Subscription Rights

When new stock is issued by a corporation, the shares are customarily offered to existing stockholders at a price below the prevailing market price for the old shares. Rights to subscribe are issued to stockholders in the form of negotiable warrants which must be exercised on or before a specified expiration date. A stockholder owning 100 shares of old stock would receive a transferable warrant representing 100 *rights*, and if the rate of increase is 25%, four rights would be required to purchase one new share at the subscription price.

The issuance of these rights is usually announced in advance of a certain record date. All stockholders of record on that date are entitled to participate in the new issue. The market price of the "old" stock includes the right to participate in the new offering until the record date and is, therefore, said to be *cum-rights*. Because the market price of the old stock after the record date does not include the right to participate in the new offering, it has proportionately less value and is said to be *ex-rights*. Because the market price of the old stock is the chief determining factor in the value of the rights, a slightly different method of calculation is required before the record date than thereafter.

Rights are often traded before they are actually issued. The value of a right on a "when-issued basis" *before* the record date is calculated by dividing the difference between the prevailing market price for the old stock and the subscription price for the new stock by *one more* than the number of old shares required for a subscription to one new share. To illustrate, if new stock is being offered to old stockholders in the ratio of one new share for four old shares at $30 a share, the value of one right, as calculated before the record date with the old stock selling at $40 a share, would be $2 ($40 − $30 = $10 ÷ 5 = $2). The price of the stock would be likely to decline to $38 on an ex-rights basis.

The value of a right as determined *after* the record date, and before it expires, is calculated by dividing the difference between the prevailing market price for the old stock and the subscription price for the new stock by the *exact* number of old shares required for a subscription to one new share. Using the above example, the value of one right, as calculated after the record date with the old stock selling at $38 a share, would be $2 (38 − $30 = $8 ÷ 4 = $2).[6]

If any dividends are payable prior to the expiration date of the rights, one must reduce the market price of the old stock by the amount of the dividend payment before calculating the value of the rights, inasmuch as the new stock will not be entitled to the dividend.

The problem is more complicated when rights to buy new convertible securities are issued to common stockholders. The convertible bonds or preferred have no record of past market price. Until they are issued, they will be traded (if at all) on a when-issued basis. After they are issued, their price will reflect the value, if any, of the conversion privilege. Their price can be quite volatile, as will be the price of any rights still outstanding before their

---

[6]The following formulas may be used for calculating the value of a right, where M = market price, S = subscription price, and R = number of rights required to purchase one new share:

$$\text{Value before ex-rights} = \frac{M - S}{R + 1}$$

$$\text{Value after ex-rights} = \frac{M - S}{R}$$

expiration date. An example of the offering of convertible securities through rights is found on page 189.

Common Stocks as Investments

Although generalizing about the investment qualifications of any group of securities as a class is dangerous because of the wide variation in quality within any one group, certain observations concerning common stocks as investments may be hazarded.

Studies covering long periods before the 1970s showed that, given proper selection and timing, the long-run record of a diversified list of high-grade common stocks had been better than that of bonds from the standpoint of income and capital value.[7] The period selected and the securities making up any such studies have, of course, greatly affected the results obtained. But the overriding advantage of common stocks in general was seen in the actual and potential growth in market value and in dividends, combined in the total rate of return.

Wide differences between individual stocks with respect to quality, income, and price performance exist in any given period, regardless of general economic and market levels and trends.

Advantages to 1973   Let us review the major factors that were responsible for the long postwar rise in the stock averages that reached its peak in January 1973, although interrupted by several periods of weakness:

1. Confidence in the continued expansion of the economy;

2. Rising corporate earnings and dividends;

3. The short-lived nature and mildness of postwar recessions and the increasing potency of government action as a preventive against serious depressions;

4. The steady movement of stocks into institutional hands;

5. The great increase in individual ownership of common stocks (30,000,000 holders in 1970) and so in the demand for this type of investment;

6. The Federal income tax structure that favored investment for capital appreciation by applying lower taxes on long-term capital gains than on current income;

7. The slow increase (and in some very recent years an actual decline) in corporate stocks outstanding as a result of corporate financing policy;

[7]The first of these were Edgar L. Smith, *Common Stocks as Long-Term Investments* (New York: The Macmillan Company, 1926); C. C. Bosland, *The Common Stock Theory of Investment* (New York: The Ronald Press Company, 1937); and D. C. Rose, *Practical Application of Investment Management* (New York: Harper & Row, Publishers, 1934). More modern references include W. J. and D. E. Eiteman, *Common Stock Values and Yields, 1950–1961* (Ann Arbor, Mich.: Bureau of Business Research, Graduate School of Business, University of Michigan, 1962); Lawrence Fisher and J. H. Lorie, "Rates of Return on Investments in Common Stocks," *The Journal of Business*, January 1964, pp. 1–21; and J. H. Lorie and M. T. Hamilton, *The Stock Market: Theories and Evidence.* (Homewood, Ill.: Richard D. Irwin, Inc., 1973.)

8. The improved "quality" of reported earnings as a result of more uniform and revealing accounting methods;

9. The improvement in information and analytical techniques that make for better projections of earnings and more valid valuations;

10. The declining importance of current dividend yields to an increasing number of investors;

11. The continued desire for an inflation hedge.

Not all of these factors continued to be important in the later 1960s and the early 1970s, with the result that common stocks showed a volatile record and failed to reach the previous all-time high. The averages fell dramatically in 1966. Subsequent recovery was halted in the spring of 1969, when a very severe decline rode to 1970. Vascillating rise and fall was characteristic of 1970–1971. The secular expansion of the economy had leveled out. The recession of 1969–1970 did not halt continued inflation. And perhaps most important of all, the rise in bond yields to unprecedented levels in 1970, and the continuation of historically high levels, provided competition for stocks that deprived them of much of their appeal. But in late 1972 and January 1973 (when the Dow Jones Industrial Stock Average reached 1052) the prices of common stocks in general, reflecting the high level of economic activity and the expectation of peace in Viet Nam, reached all-time highs.

Later developments   In January 1973 the sharpest decline in stock prices since 1929 began (see Chart 9-1). By the low point in September 1974 the leading averages and indexes showed these changes (using monthly closing figures):[8]

	Dec. 1972	Sept. 1974	Per Cent Change
Dow Jones 65 stocks	329	189	−43%
Dow Jones 30 Industrials	1020	608	−41%
Standard & Poor's 500	118	64	−46%
New York Stock Exchange index	64	33	−48%
American Stock Exchange index	129	63	−59%
NASDAQ Over-the-counter index	134	55	−59%
Indicator Digest NYSE index	54	22	−60%

Chart 9-1 selects three of these indexes and shows their *relative* changes in value 1969–1977, using prices as of December 31, 1964 as base prices.

There were three main quantitative reasons for the great decline: (1) economic recession evidenced by declining profits, increasing unemployment, and other leading indicators; (2) spectacular increases in interest rates, which forced down price-earnings multiples, especially on "growth stocks," and forced up earnings yields and dividend yields in competition with those on bonds and other fixed-income securities (Table 9-4); and (3)

---

[8]For an explanation of these averages and indexes, see Chapter 13.

THE TEN YEAR "STOCK MARKET" RECORD

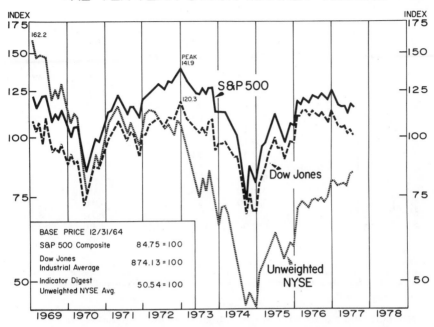

INDEX
175

162.2

150

PEAK
141.9

125

S&P 500

120.3

100

Dow Jones

75

BASE PRICE 12/31/64

S&P 500 Composite	84.75 = 100
Dow Jones Industrial Average	874.13 = 100
Indicator Digest Unweighted NYSE Avg.	50.54 = 100

50

Unweighted
NYSE

INDEX
175

150

125

100

75

50

1969 1970 1971 1972 1973 1974 1975 1976 1977 1978

Source: MacKay-Shields Financial Corporation, New York. Reprinted with permission.

"double-digit" inflation that undermined business costs and outlook, produced spurious inventory profits, and dramatically lowered price-earnings multiples. Other economic, qualitative factors were also involved.

Table 9-4 (using the Dow Jones 30 Industrial Stocks and Standard & Poor's bond index) shows average annual prices, price-earnings multiples and their opposites, the "earnings yields," and dividend and bond yields, 1950–1976, at year-end prices. The relationships among these factors will receive much attention later in this book. But the data reveal that the combination of fluctuating earnings and changing rates of capitalization of earnings produced sharp volatility in prices. The variations would show as even more marked if interim changes were indicated.

Until the 1960s, the advantage of common stocks with respect to dividend yield, as compared with bonds, reflected the premise that the return on equities should exceed that on long-term credit instruments. This advantage declined steadily in the postwar period as common stock prices rose, until in 1959 the "spread" between average high-grade bond and average stock yields became negative. Table 9-4 shows the average annual dividend yields on the Dow Jones industrial average compared with the Standard & Poor's index of high-grade industrial bonds, and the relation of bond and stock yields in the postwar period. The relation between prices, dividends, and earnings remained fairly stable in 1962–1965. Stock prices, on the average, reached their then peak in 1965. After the substantial decline in prices in

TABLE 9-4   Yields on Common Stocks and Bonds (at Year-End)

| | 30 Industrial Stocks | | | | Aaa Industrial | |
	Earnings	P/E Ratio	Price	Earnings Yield	Dividend Yield	Bond Yield	Spread
					(1)	(2)	(2) over (1)
1950	$30.70	7.7	$235.40	13.0	6.85%	2.50%	4.35%
1955	35.78	13.7	488.40	7.3	4.42	3.09	1.33
1960	32.21	18.2	615.89	5.5	3.47	4.22	− .75
1965	53.67	18.1	969.26	5.5	2.95	4.71	−1.76
1966	57.68	13.6	795.69	7.4	4.06	5.22	−1.16
1967	53.87	16.8	905.11	6.0	3.34	6.13	−2.79
1968	57.89	16.3	943.75	6.1	3.32	6.49	−3.17
1969	54.02	14.5	800.36	7.1	4.24	7.62	−3.38
1970	51.02	16.4	838.92	6.1	3.76	7.15	−3.39
1971	55.09	16.2	890.70	6.2	3.44	6.94	−3.50
1972	67.11	15.2	1,020.02	6.8	3.16	7.04	−3.88
1973	86.17	9.9	850.86	10.1	4.15	7.50	−3.35
1974	99.04	6.2	616.24	16.1	6.12	8.41	−2.29
1975	75.66	11.3	852.41	8.8	4.39	8.40	−4.01
1976	95.67	10.5	1004.65	9.5	4.08	7.78	−3.70

Sources: *Dow Jones Investors Handbook;* Standard & Poor's *Trade & Securities Statistics.*

1966, common stock yields and earnings yield improved and price-earnings multiples were reduced, but bond yields also rose, so that the negative spread between bond and stock yields increased. Dividend yields declined with the rise in prices in 1967–1968, and rose somewhat in 1969–1970. But the precedent-setting increase in bond yields in 1966–1970 and the strong stock market in 1972 drove the negative spread between bond and stock yields to record figures in 1970–1972.

The rise in stock yields in 1973–1974, resulting from declining prices, outpaced even the spectacular increase in bond yields and caused the negative spread to decline, only to rise to a new high in 1975 and 1976. (See Chart 9-2.) Through good times and bad, despite renewed interest in dividend-paying equities that reappeared in the middle 1970s, investors (especially institutions) continued to regard price appreciation as the chief appeal and advantage of stocks, granted the wide variety within any general group used for indexes or averages. The concept of "total return," or income plus appreciation, gained increasing acceptance. (See Chapter 23.) And this despite serious limitations and the fact that the long-run return from stocks (footnote 7) has historically been less than the cash yield on bonds in periods of very high interest on bonds such as 1969–1970 and 1973–1976.

Such general movements should not obscure the very important fact that investors have applied, and continue to apply, different values to the earnings and dividends of different stocks. The relation between these factors is discussed in Chapter 25.

Disadvantages of common stocks   The investor cannot overlook the distinct disadvantages involved in commitments in common stocks,

YIELDS ON CORPORATE BONDS & COMMON STOCKS

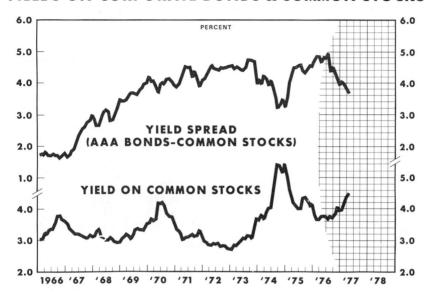

Source: Donaldson, Lufkin & Jenrette Securities Corporation, New York. Reprinted with permission.

although the vast range in quality within the common stocks available for investment makes generalizations somewhat dangerous.

From a *technical* viewpoint, common stocks suffer the double handicap of being junior securities and of having only contingent claims upon earnings. The stockholder faces the probability of a reduction in dividend income and the possibility of a complete loss thereof in periods of economic stress, in contrast to the contractual right of the bondholder to be paid irrespective of prevailing earnings. This is not to say, of course, that *all* common stocks behave worse than *all* bonds in times of adversity.

From an *economic* viewpoint, common stocks suffer the double handicap of being subject, in varying degree, to the vicissitudes of the business cycle and to the adverse influences of industrial trends. In periods of prosperity, when earnings are good, dividends are regular and the price action is favorable; but in periods of recession, when earnings are poor, dividends may be irregular, prices decline, and the situation of the stockholder becomes unenviable. Prices also change because investors change their requirements for price-earnings ratios and dividend yields. All of these factors were in sharp focus in 1969–1970 and 1973–1974. And over longer periods, certain industries grow as others decline, making the selection of an industry as difficult as that of a particular corporation. Alertness and adaptability are essential to protect capital investments under these changing circumstances.

From a *political* viewpoint, common stocks suffer the handicap of public regulation and increased and double taxation (on both the corporate net income and the dividends received by the investor.) Even though the enterprise may not be under the restricting influence of a regulatory commission, as the railroad and utility companies are, the company may face increased costs in the form of heavy taxes and higher wage scales, which cannot all be passed on to buyers of its products and which reduce the amount of income available to the stockholders.

Finally, and most important, the erratic and unpredictable action of the prices and yields of common stocks, that reflect the greater risk of equities both in individual situations and in the market as a whole, makes the problem of valuation of these securities particularly difficult.[9] Too much may be paid for even a good equity, and too little received for it when sold.

In spite of their weaknesses, common stocks do have a place in the portfolios of many investors, *provided*: (1) the risk is lessened by adequate diversification of industries and companies; (2) all but the most skilled investors restrict their purchases to the stocks of large, prominent, and conservatively financed companies with a long record of good earnings and continuous dividends or of price appreciation; (3) the prices paid for the stocks are reasonable in relation to the prospective earnings and dividends of the companies selected; (4) the purchases (and sales when called for) are timed properly or dollar-cost averaging is employed; and (5) most important of all, the investor recognizes and is willing to take the risks that even a well-diversified, well-selected, well-timed portfolio of common stocks inevitably involves. Considerable attention is given to these problems in other sections of this book.

The vast majority of investors should not attempt to "play the market" in short-term trades, and a great many of them would do well to use methods of indirect investment which capitalize to a certain extent on the real advantages of common stocks, and minimize, to some degree at least, their equally real disadvantages. These are discussed elsewhere in this volume. But the decline in the number of shareholders to 25 million (from the peak of 30 million) is some evidence of the disillusionment with the market that has continued through the 1970s.

Marketability A special feature of interest to all investors is the marketability of their holdings; that is, access to ready sale or purchase without loss in value due to an imperfect market. Lightly traded stocks, whether listed or not, suffer from an inflated price when large amounts are ordered, and from artificial deflation when large amounts are offered. And the large institutional investors are handicapped by the market's inability to absorb very large purchases and sales without price reaction.

Convertible Securities

Three types of "sweeteners" are used to increase the appeal of bonds and preferred stock when these lack sound investment quality and/or when the outlook for common stock is promising: (1) the participating feature, now

[9]The problem of valuation of common stocks is discussed in Chapter 25.

rare; (2) the conversion feature; and (3) the stock-purchase warrant. Each of these accompanies the bond or preferred stock with the possibility of gain through rising earnings and dividends on the common stock. But they have different effects on the investor's position. The owner of a participating bond or preferred stock retains his prior status, but may share increased earnings with the common. The owner of a convertible security must give up his senior position if he prefers to own the common. The owner of a warrant must make an additional investment to acquire the common stock, but may choose to retain or sell his original senior securities.

Of the three "sweeteners," only the last two are important today. They add a speculative "equity" quality to the bonds or preferred stock. Their main appeal may lie in this feature. For this reason they are discussed in this chapter along with common stock.

Why corporations issue convertible securities A convertible security is one that may be exchanged, at the owner's option, for common stock at a given price or ratio.

As suggested above, adding the convertible feature to junior bonds or to preferred stock is usually designed to increase the appeal of the issue and thus decrease its interest or dividend cost. Then, when and if the bonds are converted, the debt is retired without a capital outlay. The company has, in effect, sold common stock at a favorable price. In addition, the sale of convertible securities, especially bonds, can tap institutional markets which are not allowed, or may not wish, to buy common stock outright. An ancillary advantage is found in the use of convertible securities in mergers where the selling stockholders will accept them in lieu of common stock. In all cases, convertible bonds have the advantage to the issuer that, until converted, their interest is an expense for income tax purposes.

There is the possibility, of course, that the issue will not be converted. As long as this is the case, the unconverted bonds or preferred stock "over-hang" the market for the common. And actual conversion may dilute the earnings, and possibly the dividends, available to the common stock.

"Convertibles"—a feature of strong stock markets Most convertible securities are issued by financial and industrial companies which can hope for cyclical and longer-term increases in earnings. In rising markets the convertible issues have much of the appeal of common stocks themselves, as demonstrated by the data below. Very few have been issued by railway companies. Some "growth" utilities have found them feasible.

In relation to all corporate bonds issued, convertibles bore the following relationship:[10]

1969	22.0%	1973	2.9%
1970	8.9%	1974	5.3%
1971	12.5%	1975	3.3%
1972	8.6	1976	2.4%

[10]Securities and Exchange Commission, *Statistical Bulletin.*

The dramatic decline in the percentage of convertible bonds to total bonds issued in 1973–1976 indicates their lack of appeal as potential equities in a period of market weakness or uncertainty.

Advantages or disadvantages to the investor   Investors may wish to take an intermediate position, that is, to enjoy the defensive advantage of being a senior security-holder, and at the same time enjoy the possible appreciation of the common stock's price and dividends. And in the meantime, they may obtain a higher yield than is offered by the common stock itself. In return for these advantages, the investor takes a lower yield than a "straight" bond of the same company would provide. This can be expensive if he never chooses to convert. He has paid for a feature that he hasn't used. And if he does eventually convert, he may feel that he should have bought the common stock in the first place. Thus, convertible securities are feasible investments, depending on the needs and risks of the investor, and depending on the timing of purchase, conversion, and possibly resale. They do not necessarily offer the advantage of "eat your cake and have it too." And their market prices can be very volatile.

We should note here that, while conversion is at the option of the bondholder, a corporation may force conversion by exercising the right to call the bonds at a price lower than the market value of the bond or of the stock into which it is convertible.

Provided the investor does not pay too much for the privilege, the convertible feature may have real advantages. The owner of the convertible bond remains a creditor as long as he holds the bond. When it is to his advantage to do so, he may convert into stock with its possibilities for higher earnings and price appreciation. As indicated above, convertible bonds have a special appeal under bull market conditions because of their possibilities for sharing in the upward course of stock prices. The investor should remember that once conversion has taken place, the step cannot be retraced.

Major considerations   The conversion feature gives the investor the option to exchange his bond or preferred stock for common stock at a set price or ratio during a prescribed period. In considering the purchase of a convertible security, these factors should be investigated:

What is the inherent quality of the security? Few "convertibles" are high-grade at the time of issue. They are usually unsecured debentures, often subordinated to other debt. They usually bear ratings of less than "A."

What are the terms of conversion? Conversion may be expressed either as the dollar amount of the face or *par* value of bonds or preferred to be given up for each share of common stock (*the conversion price*), or as the number of shares to be received for each $1,000 bond or each share of preferred stock (*the conversion ratio*). The conversion price of Baxter Laboratories 4s, due 1987, is $17.25; in other words, at a ratio of 57.97 shares per $1,000 bond.

Does the conversion price increase (or the conversion ratio decrease) in stages over the life of the convertible issue? An example of this rather unusual feature is found in the Sinclair Oil Corp. convertible subordinated debenture 4 3/8s, due 1986; the ratio begins at 7.5 shares per $1,000 bond to December 1, 1976, declining to 6.666 shares after December 1981.

When does the conversion option start and when does it end? In most cases the privilege never expires as long as the bond or preferred stock is outstanding; occasionally there is a set date, as in the case of American Airlines debenture 4/4s, due in 1992, which lose their conversion option in 1980.

Is any cash required on conversion? This somewhat unusual feature is found in the U(nited) A(ir) L(ines) Inc. convertible subordinated debenture 4/4s of 1992; the bondholder must turn in $200 cash along with his $1,000 bond in exchange for 16.2 shares of common stock. This conversion option expires in 1981.

What is the call price schedule of the convertible security? The corporation can force conversion by calling in the security at a higher price than the value of the common stock to be received. Where the bond or preferred has a high coupon or dividend rate the investor must be particularly alert in watching for redemption by the issuer.

Is the conversion ratio protected against dilution? It is customary to increase the ratio (decrease the conversion price) in proportion to the increase in outstanding common shares arising from stock splits and stock dividends (the *"anti-dilution" clause*).[11]

What is the "investment value" of the security, that is, its value without the conversion option? This hypothetical value, and its corresponding yield, is calculated by some of the investment services by comparison with other issues of like quality and maturity, but which are not convertible. The market price of the security will not fall below the value of the shares of common stock into which it is convertible (*conversion parity*); this may be at or above the investment value. In June 1976, Sperry Rand 6s of 2000 sold at $122.50 per $100 bond to yield 4 1/2% to maturity, but had an investment value of only $69, so that the *premium over investment value* was over 100%.

How does the current yield of the convertible security compare with the yield on the common stock? The investor seeking a middle position may prefer the convertible security for its yield, and not convert until the dividend rate on the common stock has increased, or until he is forced to convert by reason of the call of the bond or preferred.

What rate does the convertible bond yield to maturity? This is often low. (See the Union Pacific example below.) It can even be a minus quantity where the bond sells high above its investment quality because of the value of the conversion privilege.

What is the amount (or per cent) of the conversion premium (if any) at which the market price of the bond or preferred exceeds the market value of the shares for which it could be exchanged? A premium often occurs when the market value of the common stock is still low; the bond with a low coupon may even sell at a substantial discount. Before they lost their conversion privilege through merger, in June 1976 Susquehanna Corp. 5 1/2s of 1988, priced at 51, had a

---

[11]As shown in Chapters 24 and 26, earnings per share of common stock must be stated in corporate reports on both the regular basis and on a "fully diluted" basis, that is, assuming that all convertibles are exchanged for common.

conversion value of only $8.16 (a premium of 525%.) Occasionally, however, a high premium reflects the high value of a "call" on stock which is expected to perform brilliantly. In June 1977, Union Pacific Corp. 4 3/4s of 1999 sold at 187 per $100 bond, to yield only 2.5% currently and a negative yield to maturity. The conversion value of the common stock per $100 bond was 96.

Classification of convertible securities   With respect to price in relation to conversion value, convertible bonds (and preferreds) may be classified in three groups: (1) Those selling at "investment value" (and above their "conversion value"); the conversion feature (a function of the terms of exchange as well as of the price of the common stock) is deemed to be worthless. (2) Those selling at their conversion value. After a substantial rise in the price of the common stock, and when the bond price has "followed up" the stock's price, the latter will set a possibly high minimum, and the yield on the bond can be low or even a minus quantity. (3) Those selling at a premium above their conversion value. The premium can reflect the fact that the bond, even at a low investment value, is worth substantially more than the common stock that its conversion would acquire; or it may reflect the great promise of the common and represent substantial value in the conversion privilege.

In a weak or falling stock market, especially when interest rates are high, as in 1970–1971 and 1973–1975, the prices of bonds in the second and third groups are particularly vulnerable. For example, DPF (Data Processing Financial) 5 3/4s of 1987 fell from 300 in 1969 to 44 in 1974.

Conditions leading to conversion   Knowledge of the established conversion price or ratio and the prevailing market prices of both the convertible security and the common stock is necessary to determine whether conversion of presently owned convertible securities into common stock would be feasible, how much the common stock would have to rise in order to make conversion feasible if the convertible security were bought at its present price, and the influence of the conversion feature on the price of the convertible security.

If an investor had paid 104 for a bond "convertible at $50 per share" into common stock presently selling at 45, obviously the conversion feature has little or no value to him, and conversion would be unprofitable, regardless of the relative income or yields on the two securities. The value of the bond in terms of common stock is only 90. If he wanted the stock, he would sell his bond and buy the stock. The "conversion parity" would be a value of $52 per share for the stock in this case. Only when the stock rose above $52 in market price would conversion by this investor be likely to take place.

If the investor is interested in a convertible security selling at 96, which is convertible into common at $50 or in the ratio of 20 shares for each $1,000 bond, the common would have to sell at above 48 to make conversion attractive. The investor should calculate the necessary per cent appreciation in the price of the common stock to make conversion attractive. In this case it would be 20% if the price of the common stock is 40.

It is important to remember that the investor should never convert at a loss, that is, take less in market value of common stock than the market value of the security that is turned in. Conversion is likely to take place (1) when the conversion privilege is going to expire, (2) when the conversion price is going to rise, (3) when the convertible security is called at a price that is lower than its conversion value, or (4) because the dividends on the common exceed the income from the bond or preferred stock. But, to repeat, under none of these conditions is a market loss acceptable. Where a loss would be incurred, it would be better to sell the bond or preferred stock and buy the common stock.

Sale of convertible securities through rights   Because convertible securities may eventually be exchanged for common stock, which may result in dilution, they are often offered to present stockholders through subscription rights. (See p. 177.) An example is found in the case of the American Telephone and Telegraph Company. On June 2, 1971, the company offered to shareholders of record as of June 3, 27.5 million shares ($1,375,000,000) of new convertible preferred stock ($1 par), on the basis of 1 new preferred share for each 20 shares of common plus $40 in cash. Each share of the preferred was to be convertible, on or after October 1, 1971, into 1.05 shares of common stock (that is, at a conversion price of $47.50). At that time, the common stock was selling at 45, so that the new preferred stock had no conversion value. After the date of record, and until June 18, the day the rights were issued, the common stock sold ex-rights. Based on the when-issued value of the preferred of $57, the rights sold for 11/32 on June 4. Subsequently, until they expired on July 12, their price ranged from 1/4 to 3/8. The variation reflected the range in price of the preferred of 55 1/8 to 57 3/8.

Investing in "convertibles" through mutual funds   Some investors are attracted to convertible securities as a compromise between ordinary bonds and common stock, but find them difficult to analyze and select. There are a few mutual funds whose portfolios consist of convertible bonds and preferred stock, so that, for a fee, the investor may employ diversification as well as professional management. (See Chapter 11.)

Stock Purchase-option Warrants

General nature   Bonds and preferred stock are sometimes sold with long-term warrants which give the holder the privilege of buying a certain number of common shares per bond or per preferred share, from the company, at a specified *subscription price*. The warrants may or may not be detachable (with or without an independent market), and may be valid for an unlimited or a limited period.

The option-type warrants described here differ in three main respects from those representing rights to buy new common stock under "privileged subscription" described on p. 177:[12] (1) their designated life is long—

---

[12]They also differ from the options (puts and calls) to sell or buy shares of outstanding stock described in Chapter 16.

sometimes perpetual; (2) they are attached to new bonds or preferred shares; (3) the subscription price of the common stock at which they are exercised is higher, rather than lower, than the market price of the common at the time of issue.

The price of stock obtained by exercising the warrant is higher than its market price when the warrants are issued, and so then they have no intrinsic or mathematical value. They become valuable during active stock markets as this "call" on stock takes on value. There is always some chance that the common stock price will rise above the price via the warrant, until the option expires.

Perpetual warrants issued by the Alleghany Corporation in 1952 gave the holder the privilege of buying common stock from the company at the price of $3.75 per share. In September 1973, at a low in the market, these warrants had a market value of $6.00, despite the fact that the market value of the stock was only $8.00 per share. Speculators were willing to buy the warrants on the chance that the future price of the stock would rise above $9.75 ($3.75 + 6.00). In March 1977, when the stock sold at 12 3/4, the warrants sold at 9 1/2, or slightly above their theoretical value of $9.00.

In May 1970, American Telephone and Telegraph Company offered to existing shareholders a package of new debentures plus warrants, through rights. The offering of $1,569,000,000 was the largest single corporate financing then on record. For each 35 shares held, shareholders of record April 10, 1970, received rights to buy, at $100 per unit, $100 in 8 3/4% debentures, plus two warrants to purchase one share of common stock each at $52 a share. The warrants expired on May 15, 1975. At the time of the offering, the common stock was selling at 47, so the warrants had no mathematical value. The price of the common ranged from 40 3/8 to 53 7/8 during the rest of 1972, and so the warrants' market price reflected their possible long-run rather than their immediate term value as options to buy shares. The price of the warrants ranged from 1/8 to 13 in 1970–1975.

Warrant values and premiums When detachable, warrants have their own market. A few are listed on the New York Stock Exchange, many more on the American, and still more are traded over-the-counter. The difference between the market price and the option price of stock is the warrant's theoretical or mathematical value—often zero. Thus, an option to buy a share of stock at $20 has a theoretical value of $5 when the stock has a market price of $25.[13] Should the stock fall to 19, the warrant actually has a negative theoretical value.

When traded, the market price of a warrant is seldom the same as its theoretical value. The latter provides a floor (down to zero). But even when its mathematical value is zero, the warrant may enjoy a substantial demand. Indeed, the market prices of most stock-purchase warrants exceed their theoretical value, in many cases very substantially. In the previous example, even if the theoretical value is zero (when the market price of the stock is 19), the warrant will be quoted. The excess of the market price over the

---

[13]The formula for the theoretical or mathematical value is:

$$V = \text{Market Price} - \text{Exercise Price} \quad (\text{or } V = MP - EP).$$

theoretical value of the warrant is known as its *premium*.[14] In the above case, with the warrant selling at 30 and stock selling at 25, the premium would be $5. Thus, the market price of the warrant will vary with that of the common, but will reflect chiefly its value as a call at a fixed price, that is, the probability that the market price of the stock will exceed its option price and possibly rise very substantially above it. The premium may become very high.

An extreme example of a premium is found in the case of the warrants issued by the Whittaker Corporation at different times, giving the holder of common stock the option to buy new common stock at prices ranging from $7.48 to $50. In March 1977, the market price of the stock was 5 1/2, and that of the warrant was 7/16.

Leverage   One of the chief features of warrants is that they offer a possibly high degree of price "leverage," that is, a warrant may increase (or decrease) in much greater proportion than that of the stock on which it has a call. Suppose a company's stock is quoted at 15, and warrants are outstanding that permit the holder to buy shares at $20. The warrants have no theoretical value. But let us suppose that the outlook for improvement in the company's earnings is such that the warrants enjoy a market value of $5. If the stock subsequently goes to 45—a 200% increase—the warrants will be worth 25—a 400% increase. In 1976, warrants of Walter Kidde, Inc., entitled the holder to buy new class C Convertible Preference stock at 90. During the year, the latter sold as low as 43 and as high as 53. But the warrant's price (even lacking mathematical value) ranged from 3/4 to 4.

Leverage can be expressed mathematically as the ratio of the market price of the common stock to that of the warrant. In the hypothetical case cited above, this is 1.8 (45 ÷ 25). The high premium is accompanied by a low leverage factor. When the warrant price is low in relation to the market price of the common, the premium (if any) is low and the leverage factor high. Such a high leverage factor is theoretically very attractive, because a given amount spent on a warrant will "control" a high amount of stock value. Actually, high leverage is associated with securities whose potential for appreciation is not highly regarded by investors.

The warrants discussed above are those of the "detachable" type and have their own market, usually over-the-counter, but sometimes listed. Where the warrants are "nondetachable" their value is incorporated into that of the securities with which they were offered.

Special Sources of Current Information on Convertible Securities and Warrants

A number of financial services provide current information on convertible securities and stock purchase warrants. Standard & Poor's *Bond Guide, Convertible Bond Reports,* provides two-page reports on individual convertible

---

[14]The formula for the premium is:

   Premium = Warrant Price − Mathematical Value   (or $P = WP − (MP − EP)$).

bonds. Its *Statistical Analysis, Convertible Bonds* (weekly) gives all relevant data on a variety of issues. Other statistical sources are: Kalb, Voorhees & Co., *Convertible Fact Finder* (weekly), *Convertible Preferred Chart Book* (monthly), and *Convertible Bond Chart Book* (monthly); Richard H. Morris Associates, *Warrant & Stock Survey* (weekly); and *Value Line Convertible Survey* (monthly).

REFERENCES

The following sources provide descriptions of the characteristics of stocks, their ownership, and their price action. References on the use of common stocks in investment programming, and methods of their analysis, are cited in the bibliographies of Parts V and VI. The problem of common stock valuation is discussed in Chapter 25.

BOGEN, J. I., ed., *Financial Handbook*, 4th rev. ed., Section 13. New York: The Ronald Press Company, 1968.

CHILDS, J. F., *Encyclopedia of Long-Term Financing and Capital Management*. Englewood Cliffs, N.J.: Prentice-Hall, Inc., 1976.

DEWING, A. S., *Financial Policy of Corporations*, 5th ed., Book I, Chapters 3–6. New York: The Ronald Press Company, 1953.

DOUGALL, H. E., and J. E. GAUMNITZ, *Capital Markets and Institutions*, 3rd ed., Chapter 11. Englewood Cliffs, N.J.: Prentice-Hall, Inc., 1975.

GERSTENBERG, C. W., *Financial Organization and Management*. 4th rev. ed. Chapter 5. Englewood Cliffs, N.J.: Prentice-Hall, Inc., 1959.

GRAHAM, BENJAMIN, D. L. DODD, and SIDNEY COTTLE, *Security Analysis*, 4th ed., Chapters 8, 30, 31. New York: McGraw-Hill, Inc., 1962.

GUTHMANN, H. G., and H. E. DOUGALL, *Corporate Financial Policy*, 4th ed., Chapters 8, 9. Englewood Cliffs, N.J.: Prentice-Hall, Inc., 1962.

HUSBAND, W. H., and J. C. DOCKERAY, *Modern Corporate Finance*, 7th ed., Chapters 4, 5. Homewood, Ill.: Richard D. Irwin, Inc., 1972.

LEFFLER, G. L., and L. C. FARWELL, *The Stock Market*, 3rd ed., Chapter 2. New York: The Ronald Press Company, 1963.

LEVINE, S. N., ed., *Financial Analyst's Handbook*, Vol. I, Chapter 4. Homewood, Ill.: Dow Jones-Irwin, Inc., 1975.

LORIE, J. H., and M. T. HAMILTON, *The Stock Market: Theories and Evidence*. Homewood, Ill.: Richard D. Irwin, Inc., 1973.

MADER, CHRIS, and ROBERT HAGIN. *The Dow Jones-Irwin Guide to Common Stocks*. Homewood, Ill.: Dow Jones-Irwin, 1976.

NEW YORK STOCK EXCHANGE, *Shareownership: 1970*. New York: The Exchange, 1970.

ROSE, D. C., *Practical Applications of Investment Management*. New York: Harper & Row, Publishers, 1933.

SMITH, E. L., *Common Stocks as Long-Term Investments*. New York: The Macmillan Company, 1926.

VAN ARSDELL, P. W., *Corporation Finance*, Chapter 12. New York: The Ronald Press Company, 1968.

VAN HORNE, J. C., *Financial Management and Policy*, 4th ed., Chapter 20. Englewood Cliffs, N.J.: Prentice-Hall, Inc., 1977.

WESTON, J. F., and E. F. BRIGHAM, *Managerial Finance*, 5th ed., Chapters 13, 16. New York: Holt, Rinehart & Winston, 1975.

The following sources have particularly good discussions of "convertibles" and warrants. See also the References at the end of Chapter 8, and the general references on common stocks listed above.

BALDEN, A., *Techniques for Investing in Convertible Bonds*. New York: Solomon Bros. and Hutzler, 1966.

BOLTEN, S. E., *Security Analysis and Portfolio Management*, Chapters 14, 15. New York: Holt, Rinehart & Winston, Inc., 1972.

COHEN, J. B., et al., *Investment Analysis and Portfolio Management*, 3rd. ed., Chapter 11. Homewood, Ill.: Richard D. Irwin, Inc., 1977.

GRAHAM, BENJAMIN, *The Intelligent Investor*, 4th rev. ed., Chapter 16. New York: Harper & Row, Publishers, 1973.

————, D. L. DODD, and SYDNEY COTTLE, *Security Analysis*, 4th ed., Chapters 44, 45, 46. New York: McGraw-Hill, Inc., 1962.

LEVINE, S. N., ed., *Financial Analyst's Handbook*, Vol. I, Chapters 10, 17. Homewood, Ill.: Dow Jones-Irwin, Inc., 1975.

More Profit and Less Risk: Convertible Securities and Warrants. New York: Arnold Bernhard & Co., 1970.

NODDING, T. C., *The Dow Jones-Irwin Guide to Convertible Securities*. Homewood, Ill.: Dow Jones-Irwin, Inc., 1973.

PRENDERGAST, S. L., *Uncommon Profits Through Stock Purchase Warrants*. Homewood, Ill.: Dow Jones-Irwin, Inc., 1975.

STEVENSON, R. A., and E. H. JENNINGS, *Fundamentals of Investment*, Chapters 18, 24. St. Paul: West Publishing Co., 1976.

TENNICAN, M. L., *Convertible Debentures and Related Securities*. Cambridge, Mass.: Harvard University Press, 1975.

VAN HORNE, J. C., *Financial Management and Policy*, 4th ed., Chapter 22. Englewood Cliffs, N.J.: Prentice-Hall, Inc., 1977.

Short-Term Investments

SCOPE: Traditionally, short-term instruments have been given little attention in works on investments, except in sections dealing with commercial bank secondary reserves. But the "money-market" group of investments has now come into its own and deserves special attention from the standpoint of the investor. This chapter, with some slight duplication, builds on the discussion of the money market in Chapters 2 and 3. The order of treatment is : (1) short-term Treasury obligations—Treasury bills, (2) short-term debt of Federal agencies, (3) short-term "tax-exempts," (4) bankers' acceptances, (5) commercial paper, (6) negotiable certificates of deposit, and (6) the course of yields.

Until recent years short-term high-grade (money-market) investment instruments were acquired chiefly by commercial and Federal Reserve banks, and by business corporations seeking a liquid investment for surplus funds. But the rise in short-term yields to record heights in 1969–1970 and 1973–1975, together with the extreme declines in stock prices and the substantial fall in bond prices, gave investment appeal not only to their traditional buyers but to individuals, pension funds, insurance companies and other financial institutions, and to state and local governments. The combination of high quality, limited price risk, high marketability, and high interest rates was irresistible. Individuals and other investors with ample means bought the large denominations that were typical of short-term paper. Individuals of smaller means rushed to purchase shares in the rash of "money-market" funds that were the sensation (and possibly the salvation) of the mutual fund industry in the 1970s (Chapter 11).

The more important types of short-term debt instruments were listed in Chapter 2, with the volume outstanding in selected years indicated in Table 2-2. The discussion in this chapter will omit Federal funds, as not being an "investment" in the traditional sense, and certain other instruments, such as repurchase agreements, brokers' call loans, and Eurodollars, as being too specialized for general investment appeal.

Short-term Treasury Obligations—
Treasury Bills

Although Treasury notes and bonds move into the short-term category as they approach maturity, the chief component of the "money-market" list of investments is the Treasury bill. As of December 31, 1976, bills totalling $164 billion comprised 78% of Treasury debt with less than one year to maturity, and 39% of total marketable debt.[1]

General comparisons Table 10-1 summarizes some of the leading characteristics of the various types of short-term instruments. Short-term Treasury obligations (chiefly Treasury bills) stand highest for quality, followed closely by Federal agency issues. The various issues of Treasury bills differ only in maturity. Short-term Federal agency securities differ in maturity, government guarantee, and tax status. (See Chapter 6.) The highest-grade municipal securities rank closely with those of Federal agencies, but their yields are, of course, considerably lower because of exemption from Federal income tax. Their maturities differ and, even within the same quality group, differences in marketability and therefore in liquidity make for slight differences in yield. Then come bankers' acceptances, and bank negotiable certificates of deposit, where some slight differences in quality (credit) are found. Prime commercial and finance company paper enjoys a high quality rating, but other paper of lesser quality is also available.

The marketability of most of the major types of short-term obligations discussed in this chapter is very good; that of Treasury bills is excellent. In recent years a good secondary market has developed for the negotiable certificates of deposits of major banks, and there is an active acceptance market. Top-grade short-term municipal issues enjoy good marketability, although very large amounts may run into a sticky situation. Lower-rated "tax-exempts" have a lesser degree of liquidity, while commercial paper is not readily marketable.

As for price risk, Treasury bills and Federal agency debt again lead the pack with the lowest vulnerability. Here maturity is the only or major factor. Prices and yields of the other instruments are influenced mainly by differences in both maturity and risk. But the market conditions and rate of absorption introduce some price risk insofar as acceptances, municipal issues, and commercial paper are concerned.

Characteristics The Treasury bill is an unsecured, bearer obligation sold at competitive bidding. It bears no coupon, but is sold at a discount from face value, through the auction technique. Interest is the difference between purchase price and par at maturity or sale. Bills are auctioned weekly (through the Federal Reserve banks) on maturities of three months and six

---

[1] *Federal Reserve Bulletin.*

TABLE 10-1 Money-Market Instruments

	Obligation	Denomination	Maturities	Marketability	Basis
U.S. Treasury bills	U.S. government obligation. U.S. Treasury auctions 3- and 6-month bills weekly 9-month and 1-year bills monthly. Also offers tax anticipation bills through special auctions.	$10,000 to $1 million	Up to 1 year.	Excellent secondary market.	Discounted. Actual days on a 360-day year.
Prime sales finance paper	Promissory notes of finance companies placed directly with the investor.	$1,000 to $5 million ($25,000 minimum order)	Issued to mature on any day from 3 to 270 days.	No secondary market. Under certain conditions companies will buy back paper prior to maturity. Most companies will adjust rate.	Discounted or interest bearing. Actual days on a 360-day year.
Dealer paper 1. Finance	Promissory notes of finance companies sold through commercial paper dealers.	$100,000 to $5 million	Issued to mature on any day from 15 to 270 days.	Limited secondary market. Buy-back arrangement usually can be negotiated through the dealer.	Discounted or interest bearing. Actual days on a 360-day year.
2. Industrial	Promissory notes of leading industrial firms sold through commercial paper dealers.	$500,000 to $5 million	Usually available on certain dates between 30 and 180 days.	Limited secondary market.	Discounted. Actual days on a 360-day year.

TABLE 10-1. (cont'd)

Prime bankers' acceptances	Time drafts drawn on and accepted by a banking institution, which in effect substitutes its credit for that of the importer or holder of merchandise.	$25,000 to $1 million	Up to 6 months.	Good secondary market. Bid usually 1/8 of 1% higher than offered side of market.	Discounted. Actual days on a 360-day year.
Negotiable time certificates of deposit	Certificates of time deposit at a commercial bank.	$500,000 to $1 million	Unlimited.	Good secondary market.	Yield basis. Actual days on a 360-day year. Interest at maturity.
Short-term tax-exempts 1. Project notes of local public housing agencies	Notes of local agencies secured by a contract with federal agencies and by pledge of "full faith and credit" of U.S.	$1,000 to $1 million	Up to 1 year.	Good secondary market.	Yield basis. 30-day month on a 360-day year. Interest at maturity.
2. Tax and bond anticipation notes	Notes of states, municipalities, or political subdivisions.	$1,000 to $1 million	Various, usually 3 months to 1 year from issue.	Good secondary market.	Yield basis. Usually 30 days on a 360-day year. Interest at maturity.

Source: Morgan Guaranty Trust Co., *Money-Market Investments—The Risk and the Return*, New York, 1970. Reproduced by permission.

months, and monthly in nine-month and one-year maturities. Denominations range from $10,000 to $1,000,000. (In March, 1970, offerings of $1,000 and $5,000 denominations were eliminated.) Competitive bids are made by large investors for large amounts. Individuals and others are permitted to purchase up to $200,000 without competitive bids, at the average price of accepted competitive bids. Investors may place orders directly at the Federal Reserve banks or indirectly through brokers and dealers.[2]

Primary market   Institutional investors comprise the original primary market for Treasury bills, with commercial banks, government securities dealers, and U. S. Government trust accounts as principal bidders in the auctions. The Federal Reserve Bank of New York acts on behalf of the Federal Reserve. Banks bid for their own account as well as for their customers. Noncompetitive bids in amounts up to $200,000 are generally concentrated in the three-month (90 days) and six-month (182 days) issues. The high yields in 1969–1970 and 1973–1975 drew thousands of individual investors into the market, and caused the formation of a number of new "money-market" mutual funds.

Secondary market   The highly organized secondary market, consisting of banks and dealers, ensures the ready convertibility into cash that make Treasury bills an ideal investment for the "secondary reserves" of commercial banks. Corporations commit idle or surplus cash to bills after determining their expected cash flows. Maturities are selected that coincide with the corporation's future cash requirements. There is no credit risk and virtually instant liquidity. The Federal Reserve Open Market Committee relies on this secondary market to acquire or sell Treasury securities, including treasury bills, in its efforts to loosen or extend the bank demand deposit component of the U.S. money supply.

Ownership of Treasury bills   The previous discussion explains the pattern of ownership of Treasury bills and other short-term Government debt. The ownership of Treasury bills, at the end of selected years, is shown in Table 10-2.

The big shift during the 1960s was away from commercial bank and corporate ownership towards that of the Federal Reserve banks, which concentrated on short-term Treasury holdings, and new types of investors including financial institutions and individuals. This continued in the early 1970s, reflecting the extremely high yields available in 1973–1975. The decline in yields 1975–1976 saw some return to traditional ownership, but the new market was substantially retained.

Calculation of yield: quotations   Treasury bills do not bear coupons, but are sold on a discount basis. The discount, or difference between the purchase price and maturity (or the resale) value, constitutes the investor's income, and is taxed as such. The rate of return or yield is figured, using a

---

[2]In addition to standard bills, tax anticipation bills are sold to corporations, acceptable in payment of Federal income taxes.

TABLE 10-2 Ownership of Treasury Bills, 1960–1976
(in billions of dollars)

Owner	1960 Amt.	1960 Per Cent	1965 Amt.	1965 Per Cent	1970 Amt.	1970 Per Cent	1976 Amt.	1976 Per Cent
Fed. Res. banks	$3.2	8%	$9.3	15%	$26.0	30%	$41.3	25%
Commercial banks	7.0	18	10.2	17	10.3	12	17.3	11
U.S. Govt. agencies & trust funds	0.6	2	1.0	2	0.7	1	0.4	—
Nonfinancial corporations	5.6	14	4.7	8	1.5	2	9.9	6
State & Local govts. }			4.8	8	3.8	4	5.6	3
Others[a] }	23.0	58	30.2	50	45.6	51	89.5	55
Total	$39.4	100%	$60.2	100%	$87.9	100%	$164.0	100%

[a]Includes other institutional owners and individuals.
Source: Treasury Bulletin.

360-day year, by dividing the discount by par (or sale price) and expressing this percentage as an annual rate.

The formula for the yield (discount rate of return) or for the price is:

$$d = \frac{360}{n}\left(\frac{100 - p}{p}\right) \text{ where}$$

$d =$ the discount rate in percent per annum
$p =$ the price paid for $100 maturity (or sale) value
$n =$ number of days to maturity (or sale).

For example, if a 91-day bill is bought at 98.650 (a discount of 1.350) and held to maturity, the discount *rate of return* would be (on $100 par):

$$\frac{360}{91} \times \frac{100 - 98.650}{100} = 5.341\%$$

or, if the discount rate is known, the price would be:

$$\frac{360}{91}\left(\frac{100 - p}{100}\right) = \frac{5.341}{100} = 98.650$$

Secondary market quotations on Treasury bills are expressed in terms of bid and asked discount rates of returns, not in price. Thus, on Wednesday, July 13, 1977, the following quotations appeared (among others):

U.S. Treas. Bills
Mat.   Bid Ask
Discount
7–26   5.25   4.97
10–27 5.22   5.16

The bill with the longer maturity, three months, bore the higher rate of discount. The corresponding asked prices for the 10-day and 90-day bills would be $98.68 and $98.75, respectively.

The above method of calculating yield differs from that used to figure the yield on a coupon instrument of the same maturity, because the latter (the "bond-equivalent" yield) uses the price rather than par as the divisor, and assumes a 365-day year. In our example, the interest for 91 days is $1.350/98.650 = 1.368\%$. On an annual basis the "bond-equivalent" yield is $1.368 \times (365/91) = 5.487\%$. Since all Treasury bills are sold at a discount, the "bond-equivalent" yield is always higher than the discount yield.

Market yields The difference in the yields on different issues of Treasury bills is almost entirely a function of the difference in maturity, since the quality and marketability are equal. When the general yield curve of Treasury obligations of all maturities slopes upward, the longer the maturity, the higher the yield. The opposite occurs during periods of tight money such as 1969–1970 and 1973–1974; then shorter maturities bore higher yields. Occasionally the special demand for a certain maturity by corporate investors or by the Federal Reserve for credit control purposes will slightly upset the normal spread between yields on different maturities.

The course of yields on Treasury bills will be discussed at the end of this chapter in connection with the general pattern of yields on money-market instruments as a whole. The peculiar conditions since 1965 will be stressed.

Short-term Debt of Federal Agencies

Very close to Treasury bills in quality and marketability are the short-term securities of Federal agencies, including the nonguaranteed debt of the "big five" sponsored credit agencies and the obligations of government-owned agencies such as Government National Mortgage Association (GNMA), Federal Housing Administration (FHA), Export-Import Bank (Eximbank), and Tennessee Valley Authority (TVA). Agencies of both types are described in Chapter 6, with additional comments on those involving mortgage credit in Chapter 12.

Types of securities Unlike Treasury bills, which differ only in maturity, short-term agency securities also differ in characteristics, quality, and tax status. There are two major categories: (1) participation certificates issued against pools of assets (usually loans), originally bearing medium- and long-term maturities, but entering the short-term group as they approach maturity; and (2) conventional notes, debentures, and bonds, of which the first two types are ordinarily issued with maturities of one year or less with interest paid by coupon. Federal National Mortgage Association (FNMA) notes are an exception—they are sold on a discount basis like Treasury bills.

Agency securities also differ in quality in that some (FHA) are directly guaranteed by the U.S. Government; others (CCC, Eximbank, FHA, and GNMA) are indirectly guaranteed, while the others (the sponsored agencies) have no specific Federal support. The status of agency securities with respect to state income tax also varies. (See Chapter 6.) Nevertheless, all agency securities enjoy a very high credit rating.

An interesting feature of most agency securities is that they cannot be called before maturity. This makes those agency securities that bear high coupon rates especially attractive to investors.

Primary and secondary markets   Securities of Federally sponsored agencies are originally issued through separate fiscal agents who assemble selling groups of banks and dealers, and who establish the offering price. Government-owned agencies market their securities in various direct ways and through syndicates.

There is an active secondary over-the-counter market in the sponsored agency issues, and quotations are found in the leading financial papers and special periodicals. Only the securities of the larger government-owned agencies are regularly quoted. Dealers in United States securities are responsible for making the markets. The volume of trading ranks far below that of regular government issues. Smaller agencies have small over-the-counter and dealer activity.

Ownership of agency securities   Agency securities are owned by the same types of investors as Government securities, except that Federal Reserve banks are less important. Large financial institutions acquire the bulk of agency debt, both short- and long-term. Individuals and corporate investors must play a less important role, largely because the typical individual investor is much less familiar with agencies and their financing.

As of December 31, 1976, as shown in Table 10-2, Federal Reserve banks, commercial banks, other financial institutions and municipal governments held about 75% of Treasury bills.[3] These groups held at least 90% of agency issues. Commercial banks were the most important single type of owner. Commercial banks and other financial institutions dealing in large quantities find the yield differentials between direct Government and agency securities attractive. Agency securities are legal investments for all institutions and are legal security against public deposits and trust funds. The interest of individual investors increased somewhat in 1969–1970 and 1973–1974, attracted by the combination of high quality and high yield.

Market yields   Yields in agency securities are only slightly lower than those of direct Treasury issues with comparable maturities. Yields on three-month paper may be 30 to 60 basis points (.30 to .60%) above those on three-month Treasury bills. The differential reflects the difference between actual and moral guarantee, the greater familiarity with Treasury issues, and the latter's better marketability. Yields are, however, lower than on purely private money-market instruments.

Short-term "Tax-Exempts"

Types and characteristics   State and municipal bonds are issued in serial maturities, so that some issues with early maturities are always avail-

---

[3] *Treasury Bulletin.*

able. In addition, there are project notes of local public agencies, and notes of states and municipalities which represent temporary borrowing in anticipation of tax income or of longer-term bond financing.

The appeal of these securities is three-fold: (1) their relatively high quality and liquidity (with some notable exceptions); (2) the exemption of their interest from Federal income taxes and from state income taxes in the state of issue (Chapter 7); and (3) the large array of issues available. The $5,000 denominations of serial bond issues are almost always available; those of project notes and tax anticipation notes range from $1,000 to $1,000,000. The securities are not generally callable.

Range of quality Unlike Treasury bills, short-term "tax-exempts" include a considerable range of quality, which was widened with the troubles of New York City in 1975 and the spreading influence of its difficulties. (See Chapter 7.) Nevertheless, investors seeking high-quality paper can obtain it.

Markets and yields The primary market for new short-term issues is largely confined to commercial banks and nonfinancial corporations seeking liquidity plus income tax exemption. The secondary market for large denominations is moderately active. Some dealers specialize in tax-exempts. The market is a negotiated one, and spreads between bid and asked quotations can be as wide as 250 basis points.

Yields on short-term municipals, adjusted to a taxable rate, tend to vary fairly widely with quality. Rates on those with high quality and good marketability fall above those on Federal issues of the same maturity, and those on prime commercial paper. In contrast to the yield curve for Treasury issues, that for municipal securities is almost always an ascending one, the short maturities bearing the lowest rates. (See Chapter 7.)

Bankers' Acceptances

Definition These are drafts or bills of exchange drawn on businesses or financial institutions which, when "accepted" by the drawee, become two-name paper. The banker's acceptance arises from a transaction in which a bank, having given its customer a letter of credit, accepts a draft drawn on the customer, say, an importer. The draft may then be sold by the drawer in the acceptance market. It enjoys a high credit rating because it is a negotiable obligation of a leading bank whose credit has, in effect, been added to that of its customer. Transactions include U.S. imports and exports and goods shipped or stored in foreign countries. The creation of dollar acceptances is concentrated among the largest and best-known American banks, and foreign banks and their American agencies. Maturities range from 30 to 180 days, with 90 days the most common. Borrowers pay the going rate of discount plus a commission of around 1/2%.

Acceptance markets In addition to a few banks, a small group of dealers in New York City maintain the acceptance market. Most of these are primarily engaged in dealing in Government securities. They earn their profit from the small spread (from 1/8 to 1/4%) between buying (bid) and selling (offered) rates.

Investors in bankers' acceptances include commercial banks, which may use them as collateral when borrowing from the Federal banks or retain the instruments they have accepted in their own portfolios. Other investors include corporations and financial institutions seeking the highest-grade short-term private debt instruments, and the Federal Reserve System (through the Federal Reserve Bank of New York) to expand or shrink bank reserves. Denominations of $25,000 to $1,000,000, as well as a lack of understanding of the market, discourage investment by individuals.

Market yields Because of their high quality and bank guarantee, bankers' acceptances bear lower rates than commercial paper; yields fall slightly above those on Treasury bills for the same maturities. They climbed to record levels in 1968–1969 and 1973–1975. Lending through acceptances reflects the same influences on the supply and demand for bank credit as do the other money-market instruments, plus the added impact of market-export financing. The very substantial rise in acceptances outstanding in 1974 and 1976 reflects the expansion of foreign business and storage of goods in foreign countries.

Commercial Paper

The term "commercial paper" was originally confined to the short-term bearer notes of industrial and commercial firms. It now includes a wider variety of issuers.

Types and characteristics Commercial paper is unsecured, short-term bearer notes issued by well-known business firms, with maturities ranging from a few days to nine months (270 days). The category excludes directly negotiated short-term loans for banks and other lenders.

There are two main types of commercial paper classified by method of sale: (1) directly to investors, or (2) through dealers. (See Table 2-2.) Most of the direct paper is issued by finance companies and bank holding companies. Industrial and commercial companies, utilities, and transportation companies provide the bulk of paper sold through dealers acting as agents for the investors. Directly placed paper saves the borrower the commission charged by dealers and, in addition, being used by the strongest firms, the discount is usually a bit lower than on paper sold through dealers. Most dealer paper is sold outright to the dealer, who assumes the rest of resale. Denominations range from $25,000 to $5,000,000.

Commercial paper notes are sold at a discount like Treasury bills (360-day year). The interest paid is the difference between purchase and sale price. Investors select maturities to match their needs for short-term investments and for liquidity.

Primary and secondary markets   Dealers in paper resold to investors charge a commission of 1/8 to 1/4%, and also receive the interest on the discounted notes for the period held before resale. About a dozen dealers dominate the primary market. There is no secondary market for directly placed sales finance paper. A limited market is made by dealers for finance and industrial paper issued through them.

Commercial banks were the traditional investors in commercial paper, buying notes when funds exceeded the direct demand for loans. In recent years, especially during periods of very high interest rates, other investors have entered the market because of the safety, attractive yields, and liquidity through short maturities. These include individuals, corporations seeking safety and liquidity in the placement of surplus funds, nonbank financial institutions, pension funds, and mutual funds. Commercial paper has also been an important component of the portfolios of the "money-market" funds described in Chapter 11.

Quotations and yields   Like those on Treasury bills, open-market quotations on commercial paper are in terms of discount rate, and are thus slightly lower than on a "bond-equivalent" basis. Rates on "prime" paper, issued by the strongest firms, have traditionally been below the prime bank rate, except in periods of extremely tight money. Paper of less than very high quality, called "desirable" paper, yields about 25 basis points (.25%) less than the prime bank rate (not counting the additional cost of any compensating balance).

Commercial paper has enjoyed an excellent investment record, with few losses until the tragic failure of the Penn Central in 1970. Quality ratings are published by the National Credit Office (a subsidiary of Dun & Bradstreet) by Standard & Poor's in *Commercial Paper Reports*, and by Moody's in *Bond Record*.

Interest rates on prime commercial paper are ordinarily slightly higher than in prime bankers' acceptances of similar maturities, and slightly higher again than those in Treasury bills. Rates rise and fall with those on other short-term instruments in line with money and credit conditions. The tremendous growth of commercial paper in recent years is indicated in Table 2-2, and reflects not only the general increase in short-term debt, but also the increasing dependence on commercial paper in the face of credit restraints, as well as the lower costs of financing by this method, including the avoidance of bank compensating balances.

Negotiable Certificates of Deposit

Large negotiable bank certificates of deposit have been described in Chapter 5, together with the changes in rates in recent years. These instruments, in denominations of $100,000 to $1,000,000 (occasionally higher), range in maturity from one to about 18 months. Four months is the most common term. Interest accrues on a 360-day basis, and interest rates, for the paper of the largest, strongest banks, may run about 1% higher than those on

Treasury bills. Rates are a function of maturities and the issuer's eagerness to attract new deposits.

Owners and markets   Institutional and corporate investors dominate the market for CDs, although individuals' money has been attracted to large portfolios. The latter type of investor has, however, been very much in the market indirectly through his purchase of "money-market" mutual funds. (See Chapter 11.) Although most investors hold their CDs to maturity, a secondary market is found in New York City. Interest rates lie somewhat above those on Treasury bills and slightly below those on bankers' acceptances and commercial paper. Banks' willingness to pay attractive rates, and so attract funds from other money-market paper, has accounted for the great expansion in CD volume in recent years.

The Course of Yields

Table 10-3 reveals the remarkable swings in the volume of money-market investments in recent years. Table 3-6 and Chart 3-1 show the peaks and valleys or shifts in interest rates during the same period, at about the same times. The relationship between the change in volume and the yields is very apparent. In 1969 and into 1970, the credit crunch sent yields on all short-term instruments to their then record highs under pressure for the demand for funds and the restrictions on supply. More "normal" conditions in 1971–1972 soon changed to another crunch in 1973–1974, a period distinguished by very sharp declines in stock prices and a rise in both long-term and short-term interest rates to record new heights. In 1974, the major money-market obligations increased to a record of $64 billion in the face of a Federal tight-money policy.

Table 10-3 reveals the peaks and valleys (at year-end) of the major outstanding short-term investments, 1966–1976. The components change in different proportions. Bank CDs and commercial paper show the greatest volatility, reflecting the greater sensitivity of bank credit to easy or tight credit conditions (*viz.*, 1974 vs. 1976). The big increase in Treasury bills in 1974 and 1975 ($38 billion) reflected the financing of the large Federal deficits in those years and the refunding of debt with short-term issues. In 1976, the increase was more normal at $6.5 billion.

Federal agency debt rose in an effort to loosen the mortgage situation. Bankers' acceptances showed a very sharp rise as a result of the pressure of export-import financing. The expansion of commercial paper and CDs outstanding shows the search for funds by lenders, despite very high interest rates. The whole picture was reversed in 1975–1976 with the beginning of economic recovery and a less restrictive Federal Reserve credit policy.

Yields on short-term instruments revealed in the "short-term credit" group in Tables 3-6 and Charts 3-1 and 10-1 reflect those influences. The downward and upward swings are seen in all of the components. After a momentary rise in the middle months of 1975 and in 1976, short-term rates resumed their downward course. The high bargain yields were a thing of the past.

SHORT-TERM INTEREST RATES

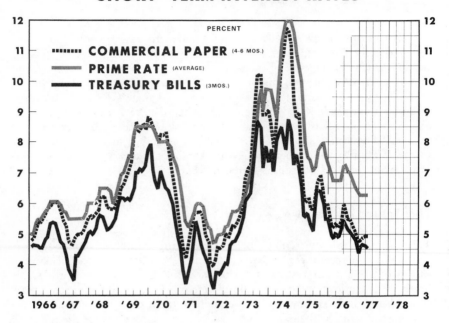

Source: Donaldson, Lufkin & Jenrette Securities Corporation, New York. Reprinted with permission.

TABLE 10-3 Annual Changes in Year-End Volume of Money-Market Instruments Selected Years, 1966–1976 (in billions of dollars)

	1966	1967	1969	1970	1972	1974	1976
Treasury bills	$4.5	$5.2	$5.6	$7.4	$6.4	$11.9	$6.5
Agency paper (short-term)	3.5	-1.7	5.8	-0.5	1.5	5.5	a
Bankers' acceptances	0.2	0.7	1.0	1.6	-0.8	9.6	3.8
Commercial paper	4.3	3.3	11.4	0.5	2.6	8.1	4.3
Negotiable CDs	-0.6	4.7	-12.5	15.2	9.8	28.5	-17.4
Total	$11.9	$12.2	$11.3	$24.2	$19.5	$63.6	$-2.8

aNot available.
Source: Federal Reserve Bulletin (including Flow of Funds).

Portfolio strategy, with respect to the use of short-term money-market investments, is part of investment policy as discussed in Chapters 18 and 19. The aim is to balance risk (price variation) and return (interest plus any price change) so as to fit the needs of the investing individual or institution. At the one extreme, the roll-over of the shortest-term Treasury bills provides the least return and the least risk; at the other, lesser-quality and longer-maturity instruments magnify both risk and return, at the risk of interim price variations.

REFERENCES

DE PRANO, MICHAEL, et al., eds., *Money, Financial Markets, and the Economy*. Belmont, Ca.: Dickenson Publishing Co., Inc., 1970.

Handbook of Securities of the United States Government and Federal Agencies, 27th Edition. New York: First Boston Co., 1976.

HAWK, W. A., *The U.S. Government Securities Market*. Chicago: Harris Trust and Savings Bank, 1973.

HEEBNER, A. G., *Negotiable Certificates of Deposit: the Development of a Money Market Instrument*. New York: Institute of Finance, Graduate School of Business Administration, New York University, 1969.

LEVINE, S. N., ed., *The Financial Analyst's Handbook*, Vol. II, Chapter 15. Homewood, Ill.: Dow Jones-Irwin, Inc., 1975.

Money Market Handbook for the Short Term Investor, 3rd ed. New York: Brown Brothers, Harriman & Co., 1970.

Money Market Instruments, 3rd ed. Cleveland, Ohio: Federal Reserve Bank of Cleveland, 1970.

Money Market Instruments: The Risk and the Return, rev. ed. New York: Morgan Guaranty Trust Co., 1970.

Money Market Investments. New York: Morgan Guaranty Trust Co., 1964.

Money Market Investments and Investment Vocabulary, 4th ed. San Fransisco: Bank of America, 1974.

NICHOLS, D. M., *Trading in Federal Funds*. Washington: Board of Governors of the Federal Reserve System, 1965.

POLAKOFF, M. E., et al., *Financial Institutions and Markets*, Chapter 20. Boston: Houghton Mifflin Co., 1970.

WILLIS, P. B., *The Federal Funds Market: Its Origin and Development*, 3rd ed. Federal Reserve Bank of Boston, 1968.

———, *The Secondary Market for Negotiable Certificates of Deposit*. Washington D.C.: Board of Governors of the Federal Reserve System, 1967.

Investment Company Securities

SCOPE: This chapter describes a very important medium of indirect investment—the investment company—and suggests methods by which its securities may be analyzed. The order of discussion is: (1) general nature and purpose, (2) types of investment companies, (3) scope of the industry, (4) growth of the industry, (5) regulation, (6) unit trusts and other lesser forms, (7) financial statements, (8) capitalization and leverage: closed-end companies, (9) organization and management, (10) distribution and redemption of shares, (11) purchase and sales commissions, (12) investment policy, (13) general factors in selection, (14) specific tests of performance, (15) senior securities, (16) warrants, (17) special uses, (18) tax status, (19) prices, dividends, and yields, (20) recent developments, (21) newer types of funds, (22) criticism of investment performance, and (23) special sources of information.

General Nature and Purposes

The investment company invests the funds of a large number of individual investors in a portfolio of securities so as to obtain advantages that the individual might not enjoy through direct investment in securities of his own choosing. By operating a large collective fund contributed by a number of shareholders and possibly creditors, the investment company can offer each investor a stake in a variety of individual securities at possibly a very low per share outlay.

The investment company issues shares (and in some cases, bonds and preferred stock), the proceeds of which are distributed over a number of securities to obtain a spreading of risk. The aims of these companies differ as to emphasis on income or capital appreciation. They expect to produce results, in one or possibly both of these respects, superior to those the investor could obtain through managing his own funds with his limited capital and lack of expert knowledge.

The purported advantages of the investment company are:

1. Diversification for a small outlay. Through the purchase of one share in an investment company the investor has an interest in a portfolio that may contain a cross section of types of securities, of industries, and of companies.

2. Selection of securities, industries, and companies by experts who have at their disposal research and talent facilities not available to the individual investor. Professional supervision should result in continuous adjustment to changes in market and business conditions.

3. Appropriate timing of purchases and sales within the portfolio, presumably on the basis of seasoned judgment.

4. Installment (periodic) purchase of shares, automatic reinvestment of dividends, periodic withdrawal (liquidation) of shares, and other services, at the investor's option.

5. Convenience through the handling by the investment company of all the details connected with the ownership of corporate securities.

6. Simplicity of estate management and settlement. Equal division of an estate may be made without a possibly disadvantageous conversion to cash.

The first five of these advantages are of special interest to the small investor. The investor of means can obtain them through the employment of investment counsel, and can afford the fees required for such service. (Even so, studies of investment company ownership show an increasing percentage of large accounts.) But the companies differ greatly in some of these respects. Funds vary from widely diversified to highly specialized. The investment record of many leaves much to be desired. The "experts" have by no means always done a good job; some of them have done very poorly. Many funds have not excelled in the appropriate timing of transactions, or in becoming more or less liquid as conditions require. And in addition to the wide differences in performance, companies differ in their objectives (notably in the choice between price appreciation and current income), in customer options and services, and in sales charges. The investor's problem is to select the company or companies with superior records which will achieve for him the investment objectives that he would like to obtain by direct action, but which are difficult or impossible through management of his own funds.

Types of Investment Companies

Investment companies may be classified by a number of criteria:

BY DEGREE OF MANAGERIAL DISCRETION In the *management* investment companies, the management has power to change portfolio securities at its discretion, subject to any specific restrictions contained in their charters or in the law. *Unit* or *fixed* trusts have portfolios in which the power of substitution is either denied or rigidly limited. The fixed trust is an arrangement by which the shareholder purchases shares or units representing a proportional interest in a specific portfolio of securities.

BY ARRANGEMENTS FOR ISSUANCE AND REDEMPTION OF SHARES *Closed-end* companies have a fixed capitalization. The securities they have issued are purchased and sold on the market like those of other companies. They do not make a continuous offering of shares, nor do they agree to redeem their shares on demand. *Open-end* companies (known generally as mutual funds) stand ready to redeem their shares at net asset value, on demand, and make a continuous offering of shares at their net asset value (calculated at least daily) plus (in "load funds") a commission or sales fee.

In late 1966 and early 1967, a new type of closed-end company appeared —the so-called *dual-purpose* funds. While differing in details, these have a common feature: two kinds of shares—participating preferred and common —are issued. The preferred shares, representing one-half of the fund, receive all of the *income* from the total fund, with a minimum annual dividend, and are to be eventually retired. The common shares receive all of the *capital appreciation* from the total fund. Thus, "2-to-1" "leverage" was introduced. Upon completion of the offerings, the shares were listed or traded over-the-counter, and sell at premiums or discounts, depending on their expected performance. (See p. 238.)

Other newcomers to the closed-end group include the "letter stock" fund specializing in a portfolio of restricted (unregistered) securities (p. 000), and fixed-income funds (p. 238).

By Type of Long-Term Capital Structure   *Nonleverage* companies (including all open-end funds with one or two exceptions) have only common stock outstanding, although they may gain some leverage benefit from short-term bank loans.[1] Some *leverage* companies (closed-end) have outstanding senior capital in the form of bonds or bank loans and/or preferred stock. Consequently, any increases and decreases in asset value and in earnings are magnified insofar as their common stock is concerned. The significance of leverage is discussed in more detail later in this chapter.

By Type of Portfolio Securities   The portfolio may consist entirely of common stocks, with various degrees of diversification. (By legal definition a *diversified company* is a management company in which holdings of one company do not exceed 10% of the outstanding voting securities of that company or 5% (at cost) of the investment company's total assets.) Or the portfolio may be *balanced*, that is, may contain bonds and preferred and common stocks of a variety of issuers, with minimum proportions of each type stipulated by the investment company's charter. Some funds contain no restrictions. Other types invest solely in bonds, low-grade or high-grade, in preferred stocks, or in stocks of one industry (*specialized* funds). There are also funds which concentrate on convertible securities, in stocks representing foreign investment, and other special types.

By Degree of Risk, as Measured by Vulnerability to Price Change   Funds range from very conservative to very speculative. On the one extreme are funds invested in high-grade bonds; at the other are those emphasizing low-priced volatile common stocks and special situations. The investor should, of course, determine, from the announced policies of the management and the character of the portfolio, whether the fund is designed for safety or for high but uncertain income or capital appreciation.

[1]Such loans must be covered by at least 300% in asset value.

By Investment Purpose   Closely allied to the foregoing is the classification according to the objectives of the fund. Some are designed for regular or possibly maximum current income, others aim at capital appreciation, while still others hope to produce both reasonable income and growth in market value. Some promise preservation of capital, others do not conceal their intent to take risk. Actual performance, of course, may not fulfill these declared objectives.

By Tax Status   Most investment companies have elected to be classed as *regulated* for tax purposes, in order to obtain the tax concessions provided by the Internal Revenue Act. Classification by tax purpose suggests two groups: (1) companies taxed like other corporations with respect to income derived from interest, dividends, and capital gains; (2) regulated companies choosing to pay out substantially all net income derived from interest and dividends, together with short-term capital gains, and which may or may not retain realized long-term capital gains and pay a tax on the same. The tax status of investment company securities is discussed later in this chapter.

By Type of Purchase Contract   The shares of *unit* or *fixed* trusts, and of management funds, are purchased outright. Another arrangement is now seldom used: the purchase of face-amount installment certificates by which the investor agrees to make regular payments to the company over a period of years, and the company agrees to pay the investor a specific sum of money on a future date. The investor's installments are invested by the company in mortgages and in securities.[2]

By Type of Organization   Unit trusts and some of the earlier management trusts are trusts in fact; however, most investment companies are now organized as corporations. The use of the trust form of organization in the early years led to the expression "investment trust"—a term which has given way to "investment company" or "investment fund" in recent years.

By Method of Sale or Sponsorship (Mutual Funds)   Most mutual funds are distributed through local brokers and dealers, thence to the investor. Some, however, have their own "captive" sales forces, which sell only the particular funds directly to the shareholders. Both of these types charge a sales load or commission. *No-load* funds, for which no dealer or representative system is employed, are offered by investment counselling firms which manage a mutual fund as a secondary activity, or by brokerage firms.

By Actuarial Requirements   As indicated in Chapter 4, variable annuities sold commercially by other than life insurance companies must be registered as investment company securities and their issuers are regulated under the Investment Company Act of 1940. Although legally classified as such, these contracts are not ordinarily included in discussions of investment company instruments.

---

[2]This arrangement should not be confused with the accumulation plans whereby shares in open-end funds are acquired regularly. See the discussion of special uses of investment company shares later in this chapter.

The variety of classifications suggests that the investor has a wide choice on a number of bases. A feasible reclassification by main types would be:

1. Unit investment trusts
2. Management companies
   (a) Open-end or mutual funds, with a range of types of portfolio and purposes[3]
   (b) Closed-end, both leverage and nonleverage, with a similar range
3. Minor types: face-amount installment certificates

The above classifications are not mutually exclusive. On the contrary, certain logical combinations are to be expected. For example, investment purpose, type of portfolio securities, and degree of diversification go hand in hand. The objective of capital appreciation usually involves a portfolio of common stocks, and these have varying degrees of risk in terms of stability of price and dividends. Maximum appreciation as a goal would invariably involve concentration on a specialized portfolio of high-risk equities. Similarly, where current income is the goal, bonds, money-market paper, and preferred stocks, as well as diversified dividend-paying common stocks, are acquired, and much less volatility is tolerated.

Scope of the Industry

Several methods of measuring the scope of the investment company group and its various classifications are available. The largest numbers are indicated by the Securities and Exchange Commission. As of June 30, 1976, 1,286 active companies were registered with the Commission under the Investment Company Act of 1940, with total assets (at market value) of over $80 billion.[4] This represented a growth of over $73 billion since the middle of 1950.

	Number of Active Companies	$ Assets (billions)
Management, open-end	250	$11.3
No load	57	1.3
Variable annuity-separate accounts	479	44.3
Load funds	786	$56.9
Management, closed-end	39	0.3
Small business investment companies	7	0.3
Capital leverage funds	132	8.7
Other	178	$ 9.3
Unit investment trusts	315	13.2
Face-amount certificate companies	7	1.1
Total	1,286	$80.5

[3]See p. 213 for other classifications.
[4]*42nd Annual Report of the S.E.C.* Washington, D. C., 1977.

It should be noted that the above data include small business investment companies and variable annuities. Neither of these types is usually included in discussions of investment companies.

A useful classification breaks down the more important open-end or mutual funds into eight major categories as of the end of 1976.[5]

Type of Fund	Number of Funds	Combined Assets (millions)	As a Percentage of Total Assets
Common stock			
Maximum capital gain	111	$ 5,065	9.4%
Growth	159	15,800	29.2
Growth and income	90	15,576	28.8
Specialized	13	363	0.7
Balanced	22	4,711	8.7
Income	95	7,739	14.3
Bond & preferred stock	8	638	1.2
Money market	42	3,624	6.7
Tax-free municipal bonds	16	559	1.0
Total	556	$54,075	100.0%

Growth of the Industry

The major growth in the industry took place in the open-end or mutual category, where assets increased from $2.5 to $53 billion in the 1950–1968 period, fell off to $48 billion at the end of 1970, and reached an all-time high of $62 billion in 1972. At that time 11 million shareholder accounts were owned by over 8 1/2 million investors. By the end of 1976, the assets of conventional funds had declined to less than $48 billion, reflecting a decline in market value of portfolios in 1973–1974 of more than $12 billion, and the excess of redemptions over sales of new shares in 1972–1976. At the end of 1976 the number of holders of conventional shares had fallen to about 7 1/4 million. The appeal of the new "money-market" funds offset somewhat the decline in the conventional fund segment. But with the reduction in short-term interest rates, these new funds lost much of their appeal, and redemptions about equalled sales in 1976. Shrinkage in both categories continued during 1977. Pertinent data are shown in Table 11-1 where the information on mutual funds is confined to members of the Investment Company Institute, which represent 90% of the industry's combined assets.

The great expansion from 1950 until the early 1970s reflected several factors: the growth of individual savings available for investment, the increased interest in securities investment, the rise in market values of common stocks, and the aggressive promotion of the sale of mutual fund shares as a means of participating in economic growth and (through common stocks) of hedging against inflation.[6] Other factors included the increase in

[5] Wiesenberger Investment Companies Service, *Investment Companies, 1977.* (New York, Wiesenberger Financial Services, 1977), p. 45.

[6] For an analysis of the excess of sales of shares over redemptions, and the asset change attributable to change in market value during 1950–1974, see H. E. Dougall and J. E. Gaumnitz, *Capital Markets and Institutions,* 3rd ed., (Englewood Cliffs, N.J.: Prentice-Hall, Inc., 1975), p. 120.

TABLE 11-1 Investment Companies Assets, Shareholders, and Sales
of New Shares, 1950–1976 (dollar figures in millions)

	Net Assets			Open-End Companies Only			
	Open-End	Closed-End	Total	No. of Shareholder Accts. (thousands)	Gross Sales	Redemptions	Net Sales
1950	$ 2,531	$ 872	$ 3,403	939	$ 519	$ 281	$ 238
1955	7,838	1,199	9,037	2,085	1,207	442	765
1960	17,026	2,084	19,110	4,898	2,097	842	1,255
1965	35,220	3,391	38,611	6,709	4,358	1,962	2,396
1966	34,829	3,163	37,992	7,702	4,672	2,005	2,667
1967	44,701	3,777	48,478	7,904	4,670	2,744	1,926
1968	52,677	5,171	57,848	9,080	6,820	3,839	2,981
1969	48,291	4,744	53,035	10,391	6,718	3,661	3,057
1970	47,618	4,024	51,642	10,690	4,626	2,988	1,638
1971	55,045	5,324	60,369	10,901	5,147	4,750	397
1972	59,831	6,743	66,574	10,635	4,892	6,563	−1,671
1973	46,519	6,623	53,142	10,331	4,359	5,651	−1,292
1974c	34,062	5,294⎤	41,071	9,970	3,091	3,381	− 290
m	1,715	⎦		104	2,229	556	1,673
1975c	42,179	5,861⎤	51,685	9,713	3,302	3,686	− 384
m	3,645	⎦		164	6,749	5,884	865
1976c	47,537	6,639⎤	57,580	8,879	4,226	6,802	−2,576
m	3,404	⎦		176	8,643	8,872	− 229

cConventional funds.
mMoney-market funds.

Sources: Investment Company Institute, *Mutual Fund Fact Book* (New York: The Institute, annually) and *News* (weekly) ; Wiesenberger Services, *Investment Companies.* The data on open-end companies pertain to members of the Investment Company Institute. Data on closed-end companies pertain to larger companies only.

the number and variety of funds to meet different investment objectives, and the availability of a number of convenient features such as accumulation and withdrawal plans and dividend reinvestment arrangements.

The decline in sales of new shares that began in 1962, accompanied by a higher rate of redemption, reflected in part the severe break in stock prices in the first six months of that year. The continued decline in public interest through 1963 reflected the general apathy toward stocks in general and mutual fund shares in particular. In both years mutual companies' sales suffered from the criticism levied on their managements in the original "Wharton Report" (cited in footnote 10), and in the Securities and Exchange Commission's massive study of the securities markets.[7] Net sales recovered in 1964–1965 and reached a new high in 1966.

In 1967 the rate of redemption reflected the economic difficulties of that year and the weakness in the stock market. However, net sales showed

[7] *Report of the Special Study of the Securities Markets of the S.E.C.*, Part 4, Chapter XI, "Open-End Investment Companies," 1964.

increases to record heights in 1969 and 1970 as the equities market flourished into the spring of the latter year. Then followed what was then the sharpest bear market for stocks until May 1970, and disillusioned investors substantially reduced their purchases of mutual fund shares. The increase in redemptions in 1971 reflected renewed dissatisfaction with stocks in general and mutual fund shares in particular.

The industry faced new problems of stagnation and the task of overcoming the disillusionment of investors over fund performance, especially that of the very aggressive funds which had shown the greatest vulnerability to price change. In the latter part of 1971, general stock market strength revived both prices of and interest in mutual funds, but in 1972 sales were again low and redemptions high, resulting in a net loss in sales.

The big drop in mutual fund assets began in 1973 with the extremely sharp decline in security prices accompanied by continued shrinkage through the excess of redemptions over sales of new shares. Market value decline of conventional funds continued in 1974, but was disguised by the sale of shares of the new "money-market" funds. (See p. 240.) Even so, the value of total assets fell to the lowest level since 1966. Market recovery plus a large increase in new money-market fund shares were enjoyed in 1975, but in 1976 redemptions of conventionals again exceeded sales, and money-market funds suffered very large redemptions, reflecting the decline in short-term interest rates. Investors continued to desert the industry and turn to competitive forms of investments, including direct purchases of stocks and bonds, and shares in new types of closed-end investment companies.

The above comments apply mainly to mutual funds. The growth of closed-end funds in the postwar period has been modest as was shown (Table 11-1). The major long-term factor has been the variation in the market value of portfolios rather than the issuance of new securities. A few older companies have done some new financing, and a number of new and specialized forms of closed-end companies such as the leveraged "dual-purpose," "letter stock," and income funds have been promoted in recent years.

Regulation

With a few exceptions, state "blue-sky" laws deal mainly with the distribution of securities rather than with company operation and management. Far more important is the Federal regulation under the Investment Company Act of 1940, which provides for the registration with the Securities and Exchange Commission of every investment company with more than 100 security-holders. Unregistered companies are forbidden to conduct an interstate business and are denied the use of the mails for purchase or sale of securities. The general purposes of the Act are to prevent major abuses and to assure the dissemination of accurate and adequate information. Companies offering shares to the public in interstate commerce or through the mails are also subject to the Securities Act of 1933, and those closed-end companies whose securities are listed must comply with the provisions of the Securities Exchange Act of 1934. Companies must also obtain permission for intrastate sale of shares from the securities departments or commissioners of individual states. Trading in unlisted shares (including all mutual funds) is regulated by the Maloney Act of 1938 which established control of over-the-counter transactions through the National Association of Securities Dealers, Inc.

Major provisions of the 1940 Investment Company Act, together with important rulings of the Commission, are summarized here:

- Registered companies must file with the Commission a registration statement covering their background, mode of operation, management advisory contracts, and intended investment policy. This information must be kept current by periodic revision.

- For management companies, minimum capital is set at $100,000 before stock may be publicly offered; this discourages the formation of small and weak concerns.

- Closed-end companies may issue funded debt or incur a bank loan only if it is covered three times by assets; preferred stock must be covered twice. Only one class of bonds and one class of preferred may be issued, and preferred stock must have voting rights. Open-end companies formed after 1940 may not issue senior securities, and any bank loans must be covered three times by assets. Face-amount certificate companies organized since 1940 must have a minimum capital of $250,000 and may not issue preferred stocks.

- Each management company must clearly declare its basic investment objectives; once stated, these can be changed only with majority stockholder approval.

- Semiannual reports must be issued to stockholders. Some companies now issue reports quarterly. The reports must present balance sheets, income and surplus statements, the composition and value of portfolio items, the aggregate purchases and sales made during the period covered, and the remuneration paid to officers, directors, and advisers. The Commission has the power to require certification of statements by independent public accountants and to promulgate uniform accounting rules.

- Dividends from any source other than undistributed net income must be accompanied by a written statement disclosing the source, so that stockholders may distinguish income and capital gains distributions.

- Sales practices are largely self-regulated through the rules of fair practice of the National Association of Securities Dealers, Inc., an organization subject to the jurisdiction of the Commission. All sales of new securities must be made in compliance with the Securities Act of 1933.

- Sales promotion literature is governed by the Statement of Policy issued in 1950, which deals with methods of stating performance results, claims in regard to management ability, and other items.[8]

[8]Section (h) of the Statement of Policy states that it will be considered materially misleading for open-end company sales literature "to use any comparison of an investment company security with any other security or medium of investment or any security index or average without pointing out: (1) that the particular security or index or average and period were selected; (2) that the results disclosed should be considered in the light of the company's investment policy and objectives, the characteristics and quality of the company's investments, and the period selected; and (3) any factor necessary to make the comparison fair."

Other important provisions of the Statement include: (1) approved method of showing the rate

- Other provisions cover certain standards of conduct and operation, including intercompany investments, self-trading, dealings with sponsors, and custodianship of assets. An important clause is that at least 40% of the directors must be persons who are not officers or employees of the investment company, its investment advisor, or principal underwriter.
- Regulations governing the sales practices, financing, and operations of fixed trusts, installment plans, and face-amount certificate companies are included in the Act. Regulation of management fees and sales commissions, and other rules introduced in 1970, are indicated in the last section of this chapter.
- The Act contains severe penalties for fraud, embezzlement, and willful violation of its provisions.
- Tax exemptions governed by the Act and by the Internal Revenue Code are discussed below.

The Investment Company Institute has had a salutary effect on the attitude of investors toward management companies. This organization has worked closely with the SEC and with state and tax authorities to improve standards and public relations.

Regulation does not assure the investor of success in his use of the investment company, but it does offer him reasonable protection against malpractices, and its disclosure provisions assure him of information on the basis of which he should be able to make his selections with intelligence.

Unit Trusts and Other Lesser Forms

In fixed or unit-type trusts which hold stocks, definitive blocks of certain dividend-paying stocks are purchased and are deposited with a trustee, and against them certificates of ownership are issued in small denominations. Ten shares each of 30 different common stocks of well-known companies might be purchased at a total cost of $12,000 and deposited with a trustee against the issue of 10,000 shares of stock. These shares might be sold at $1.32 each, giving the sponsors a gross profit of $1,200, out of which distribution expenses would be paid. As dividends are received by the trustee, a small fee is retained, and the remainder is distributed proportionately to the shareholders. After the first block of 10,000 shares is sold, the process is repeated indefinitely, the sales price being adjusted each day to prevailing quotations on the deposited securities. Thereafter, the certificateholder can redeem his shares for cash at their net asset value, or accept his proportion of actual portfolio securities.

The provisions of the unit trust usually require that the trustee make a complete distribution of all income received, whether in the form of cash, stock, or rights. Shareholders must distinguish those distributions that are not income, but are return of capital investment.

---

or return that distinguishes investment dividends and capital gains, (2) prohibition of statements concerning future returns, and (3) the prohibition of extravagant statements that concern management ability.

Few unit trusts with common stock portfolios have been formed in recent years. But a number of "tax-free" funds have been formed that own port-folios of municipal securities and sell shares against specific different blocks of such bonds from time to time. (See p. 239.) And beginning in 1971 a number of unit trusts were formed to take advantage of the high yields on corporate bonds. Some of these income funds pay out their earnings monthly.

In the face-amount certificate plan the investor buys a contract that provides for the return by the seller of a lump sum of money at a specific future date. The selling company invests the periodic payments toward this contract in mortgages and securities. The chief disadvantage of this arrange-ment is that if the investor should withdraw during the first few years before the maturity date, the cash surrender value of his contract is less than the accumulated payments that have been made. The Investment Company Act of 1940 requires that companies offering these certificates set up a reserve equal to at least 93% of subscriber payments, and that the cash value of the contract shall never be less than 50% of the reserve.

The remainder of this chapter emphasizes management companies because of the relative unimportance of the lesser forms described above.

Financial Statements

Investment companies are required to issue to stockholders at least semi-annually reports containing detailed financial information. *For closed-end companies*, the statements include: (1) a balance sheet, (2) an income and expense statement, (3) a statement of surplus, and (4) in some cases, a sum-mary of assets and liabilities. *For open-end companies*, the exhibits include: (1) a statement of net assets, (2) an income and expense statement, (3) a state-ment of changes in net assets, and (4) the record of net asset value and distributions per share for at least the three preceding fiscal years.

The balance sheet of the closed-end company usually carries the portfolio at market value (with cost indicated in parentheses). The asset coverage of funded debt, preferred stock per share, and common stock per share, at the date of the statement, is usually shown elsewhere in the report. The statement of net assets of the open-end companies also shows investments at market value, so that, after deduction of liabilities, the net assets applicable to out-standing shares on a per-share basis are revealed.

For both types of companies, the statement of operations must itemize each category of income or expense that represents more than 5% of income or expense. The statement shows dividend and interest income from securi-ties owned, less general expenses, including investment and administrative expenses, and interest on any debt. Federal income taxes may be deducted before the figure for net income, depending on the policy followed with respect to tax status. Gains on securities, realized and unrealized, are excluded from income and are reported in the operations statement.

Statements of the Income Fund of America, an open-end balanced fund, as of December 31, 1976 are shown in Tables 11-2, 11-3, and 11-4.

TABLE 11-2 The Income Fund of America,

Assets and Liabilities, December 31, 1976

Assets:

Investment securities at market (cost: $105,324,128)		$132,382,306
United States Treasury bills		1,486,673
Cash		1,277,815
Receivables for—		
Sales of investments	$ 553,182	
Sales of Fund's shares	460	
Dividends and accrued interest	1,160,199	1,713,841
		136,860,635

Liabilities:

Payables for—		
Purchases of investments	1,942,162	
Repurchases of Fund's shares	70,490	
Management services	56,199	
Accrued expenses	14,693	2,083,544
Net assets at December 31, 1976—Equivalent to $8.37 per share on 16,100,067 shares of $1 par value capital stock outstanding (authorized capital stock— 30,000,000 shares)		$134,777,091

Reproduced by permission of the Capital Research and Management Company

TABLE 11-3 The Income Fund of America

Statement of Operations, Year ended December 31, 1976

Investment Income:

Income:		
Dividends	$ 4,106,582	
Interest	3,950,919	$ 8,057,501
Expenses:		
Management services fee	659,154	
Transfer agent fees	121,033	
Custodian fees	15,162	
Registration statement and prospectus	13,133	
Postage, stationery and supplies	36,859	
Reports to shareholders	12,796	
Auditing and legal fees	25,904	
Directors' fees	21,222	
Taxes other than Federal income tax	31,883	
Other expenses	13,986	951,132
Net investment income		$ 7,106,369

Realized and Unrealized Gain on Investments:

Realized gain on investments:		
Proceeds from sales of investments	$69,720,418	
Less cost of investments sold	68,880,284	
Net realized gain		$ 840,134
Unrealized gain on investments:		
Unrealized appreciation as of December 31, 1975	4,784,283	
Unrealized appreciation as of December 31, 1976	27,058,178	
Net unrealized gain		22,273,895
Net realized and unrealized gain on investments		$ 23,114,029

Reproduced by permission of the Capital Research and Management Company

TABLE 11-4   The Income Fund of America

Changes in Net Assets, Year ended December 31, 1976

From Investment Activities:	
Net investment income	$ 7,106,369
Undistributed investment income included in price of shares sold and repurchased	(138,114)
	6,968,255
Less dividends paid: $0.41 and $0.40 per share, respectively	6 854,067
Remainder	114,188
Net realized gain (loss) on investments	840,134
Net unrealized gain on investments	22,273,895
Increase in net assets from investment activities	23,228,217
From Capital Share Transactions (exclusive of amounts allocated to investment income):	
Proceeds from shares sold: 68,820 and 119,682 shares, respectively	504,557
Proceeds from shares issued in reinvestment of net investment income dividends: 571,259 and 706,135 shares, respectively	4,453,407
	4,957,964
Cost of shares repurchased: 2,263,744 and 1,475,511 shares, respectively	17,506,410
Decrease in net assets from capital share transactions	(12,548,446)
Net increase in net assets	10,679,771
Net Assets:	
Beginning of year	124,097,320
End of year (including undistributed net investment income: $822,803 and $708,615, respectively)	$134,777,091

The statement of changes in net assets found in the mutual fund report itemizes the investment income and dividends paid therefrom, as well as realized capital gains and dividends paid therefrom, and explains the derivation of the total net assets figure exhibited in the statement of net assets. To the net assets at the end of the previous period are added any undistributed realized gains (or loss) on sales of investments (the net income from ordinary operations having all been distributed), the increase or decrease in unrealized appreciation of assets, and the net increase in shares outstanding.

The required reports also include a complete portfolio of securities at market value, usually classified by type and by industry and showing the percentage of each classification to the total.

The surplus statement of the closed-end company shows the derivation of the earned and capital surplus figures on the balance sheet after adding to previous earned surplus the ordinary net income and any profit (or loss) on sale of securities and deducting the dividends paid during the reported period.

In addition to the periodic reports, prospectuses are prepared by the closed-end company when it offers new securities; the open-end company issues a new prospectus regularly because it makes a continuous offering of new shares. The open-end prospectus also contains material concerning the history, functions, investment policies, capitalization, management, provisions for purchase and redemption of shares, price of shares, and dividend record of the company, together with a complete portfolio shown at both cost and market prices.

Capitalization and Leverage: Closed-end Companies

The capitalization of the open-end company (with one or two exceptions) is simple, consisting of one type of stock. Some short-term bank debt may be used. In contrast, some closed-end companies have senior securities outstanding in the form of bonds and/or preferred stock, and may also have incurred bank debt. It is this senior financing that provides leverage. The senior securities have a fixed claim on assets and earnings, so that when these rise, the increases redound to the benefit of the common stock. Likewise, when total asset value and/or income (before interest and preferred dividends) decline, the shrinkage is magnified insofar as the common stock is concerned. Leverage causes the common stock of some closed-end companies to increase or decrease in market value more than the market rises or falls as a whole.[9]

The effect of leverage is accentuated when the portfolio of the company includes common stocks that are themselves junior securities of their issuing companies. Thus, the least total leverage is found in companies with only common stock outstanding and with portfolios that are very conservative, and the highest is found in those which have issued bonds and preferred stock to a high proportion of total capital structure and have a portfolio consisting mainly of junior securities. The closed-end group includes a wide range in this respect.

Organization and Management

Investment companies are ordinarily organized as corporations. All fixed trusts and some management companies use the trust form.[10]

The directors (or trustees), officers, and staff may handle all of the affairs of the company, including general administration, servicing of accounts,

---

[9]A simple illustration will indicate the effects of leverage. Suppose that a fund starts with total assets of $10,000,000 and has a capitalization consisting of $5,000,000 in par value of bonds and preferred outstanding (the preferred having a liquidating preference of par value) and 500,000 shares common stock. The asset value per share of common is $10.00. If the value of the total assets increases 50% to $15,000,000, the equity of the common stock becomes $10,000,000 or $20.00 per share, a 100% increase. If the value of the total assets decreases 50% to $5,000,000, the common stock has no equity at all.

Similar effects would be seen in any increase or shrinkage of total income available for interest and dividends. Variations in the return to the common stock, after fixed interest and preferred dividends, would be determined by (a) variations in the overall earnings and (b) the degree of leverage or ratio of senior capital to total assets.

[10]Of 156 open-end companies that replied to a comprehensive questionnaire for the Wharton study, 117 were corporations and 39 used the trust form of organization. *A Study of Mutual Funds*, prepared for the Securities and Exchange Commission by the Wharton School of Finance and Commerce, 87th Congress, 2nd Session, 1962. (Washington: U.S. Government Printing Office, 1962.)

distribution of shares, and investment management. Ordinarily, however, in the case of mutual funds, the last two functions are performed by the management firm that originally sponsored the fund or group of funds, or by separate subsidiaries of the sponsor, one for underwriting and distribution, the other for investment counsel.[11]

Management companies that underwrite and distribute mutual fund shares may also be classified with respect to method of distribution: (1) those that serve as wholesalers, distributing through local broker-dealers who in turn sell to the public; and (2) those with their own "captive" sales organizations which sell only the shares of the sponsored fund or group of funds. In the latter case, the "complex" or completely integrated corporate organization enjoys the income from both the management fee charged to the fund or funds and the entire sales commission.[12]

The management fee generally runs one-half of 1% of assets (at market value) up to a certain amount, then often graduates to as low as one-quarter of 1% on large assets. In a few cases compensation is a function of investment performance as measured against the market averages.

Most no-load mutual funds are sponsored and managed, for a fee, by investment counsel firms. These do not actively promote sales and charge no initial sales commission. Some charge a small fee for redemption of shares. Other no-load funds are operated by securities brokerage or investment banking firms. In all, about 170 no-load funds are of general public interest.

Closed-end companies are managed by their own officers and staff; they may, however, buy investment management, at a fee, from an affiliated firm or from an independent advisor.

The affiliations and fee arrangements of the investment company with other concerns acting as sponsors, distributors, or investment managers are set forth in the prospectuses of mutual funds and indicated in the annual reports of the closed-end funds.

Distribution and Redemption of Shares

Like those of any corporation, the securities of closed-end companies remain outstanding in the same amount unless the company carries on new financing, retires its senior securities, or purchases common stock for the treasury.

---

[11]Of the 156 companies mentioned in footnote 10, all but 14 were parties to contracts with at least one outside organization that functioned as investment adviser, administrative manager, or both. *Ibid.*, p. 6.

The Wharton Study reports the results of a comprehensive questionnaire filed by 163 advisers of 232 mutual funds with total assets of $15 billion as of 1960. Of these, 73 were "independent" advisers who in some cases also wholesaled the shares, 36 were investment counselors or their subsidiaries, 27 were broker-dealers or their subsidiaries, 5 were subsidiaries of underwriters of shares, and the balance consisted of several minor arrangements. *Ibid.*, p. 27.

[12]In addition to advisory and management fees and distribution income, some management concerns also derive brokerage commissions on the purchase and sale of portfolio securities held by their associated funds. Thus total income is the function of the number of shares sold and value of the portfolio.

The whole matter of sales practices and commissions is very thoroughly explored in *Report of the Special Study of the Securities Markets of the S.E.C.*, *op. cit.*, Chapter XI, Part B, and it also has received special scrutiny by the S.E.C. in its 1966 report.

There is no continuous offering of new shares and no provision for redemption at the option of the investor. In contrast, new shares of open-end companies are, with a few exceptions, continuously offered at their net asset value plus a "loading fee" in the case of "load" funds. The supply of shares is virtually unlimited and the investor can buy any quantity at any time. The shares of the open-end fund may be presented for redemption at any time to the company or its sponsor, at net asset value. (A few "no-load" funds charge a small redemption fee.) The company is obliged to redeem within the period stated in its prospectus, and in no case in more than seven days. In actual practice, most open-end companies repurchase very promptly. However, the investor runs the risk of a loss in net asset value per share if he chooses to redeem during a period of rapidly declining security prices.

The above arrangements give the shares of the open-end company perfect marketability. Those of the closed-end companies that are actively traded on exchanges or over-the-counter have good marketability. The bonds and preferred stock of closed-end funds are usually traded over-the-counter and may or may not have an active market.

Purchase and Sales Commissions

The purchase and sale of securities issued by closed-end companies involve the payment on listed issues of brokerage commissions identical with those charged for trading in any listed securities. For closed-end securities bought in the over-the-counter market, the investor pays the asked price.

In the case of shares of open-end companies, the buyer pays the net asset value per share (calculated daily), plus, in "load" funds, a commission or loading charge in the neighborhood of from 7 1/2 to 8 1/2% of the offering price. On large orders there is usually a graduated scale at lower rates.[13] The bulk of this loading charge is retained by the local dealer as his sales commission or by the fund's allied distributing organization; in the former case, the balance goes to the principal underwriter or distributor. The investment company itself is not expected or allowed to shoulder any selling expenses. Ordinarily no charge is made for redemption.

If the shares are held for a long period, the initial load, amortized over a number of years, becomes a modest percentage of any income or capital appreciation received. But where the investor holds his shares for only a short period, the charge may consume any dividends or increase in capital value that may have been gained.

Investment Policy

As indicated previously, investment companies by no means follow a uniform investment policy. There is a great range in type of portfolio investments held—from the most conservative bond funds to low-priced and specialized

[13]Funds sponsored by investment counselling and brokerage firms apply no sales load, but their shares are usually issued only on application to the company itself or its distributing affiliate.
New legislation pertaining to sales commissions is noted in the concluding section of this chapter.

common stock funds. There is an equally wide range in objectives—from funds seeking regular income to those frankly seeking capital appreciation. Between these two extremes are all sorts of combinations.

The order of thinking on the part of the investor should run as follows: (1) What portion of my funds may appropriately be placed in investment company securities? (2) Which investment company or companies have investment policies, as demonstrated by their announced objectives and their performance, that come closest to meeting my needs?

Registered investment companies must state their broad investment policies in the prospectuses describing their shares. In these statements, and in the actual operations of the company as indicated by their periodic reports, investment policy is revealed by: (1) the general type of portfolio held, (2) the degree of actual diversification, (3) the investment quality of the portfolio, (4) the extent to which the fund remains fully invested, and (5) the relative emphasis on stability of income as against trading profits and/or appreciation.

The general portfolio may consist solely of common stocks, of preferred stocks, or of bonds, or it may be a balanced fund containing all three of these security types. The type of security held and the safety or appreciation prospects of the fund are not necessarily related, for an all-bond fund may be more speculative than an all-common-stock fund, depending on the character of the portfolio. But in general, the funds consisting of senior securities and the balanced funds aim at more stability of income and show less volatility in price action than the all-common funds. There are, however, gradations in all categories.[14]

Policy is also reflected in the actual degree of diversification, measured by the number of companies represented in the portfolio, which may range from 30 to 300, and the percentage distribution of the total dollar value of the fund in different companies and industries. Each fund has its own diversification policy, and this is announced in its prospectus and revealed by its portfolio. If the investment company is registered and publicized as a "diversified" company, it must by law meet the standards of the Investment Company Act. Otherwise, it may concentrate or spread its funds as it wishes, in accordance with announced policy. In general, wide diversification is sought if stability of income is a primary goal. The narrowest diversification is found in those funds that are invested in stocks of one industry or in highly selected "special situations."

Regardless of the type of securities in the fund and the degree of numerical diversification, the choice still has to be made between high-grade securities, speculative securities, or a combination of the two. That is, the fund may or may not be diversified from the standpoint of quality.

Policy must also be made with respect to full employment of funds. Some companies, especially those primarily interested in producing income, remain

---

[14]Keystone Custodian Funds has no balanced fund, but makes available nine classes of designated portfolios: B1, high-grade bonds; B2, good- and medium-grade bonds; B4, high-return discount bonds; K1, medium-grade (income) bonds and preferreds; K2, speculative or "appreciation" common stocks; S1, high-grade common stocks; S2, good-grade "income" common stocks; S3, growth common stocks; S4, low-priced common stocks. Two additional pioneering funds are also available: Apollo and Polaris.

virtually fully invested. Others switch among short-term paper, bonds, and common stocks, depending on the judgment of the management concerning the future course of the financial markets.

The relative importance of income as against appreciation is revealed by the changing character of the assets (shifts between defensive and aggressive positions) and by the source of dividends as revealed in the income and surplus statements. The investor who is investing primarily for regular income should avoid those companies whose distributions depend primarily on realized capital gains.

In the discussion above, no distinction between open-end and closed-end companies was made nor between leverage and nonleverage companies. Although some relation exists between the general type of company, or the way in which it is financed, and its investment policies and objectives (for example, a closed-end fund may seek to magnify speculative gains through high leverage), there are some conservative closed-end companies and some very speculative open-end companies. And a few leverage companies follow a more conservative policy than some companies without senior financing. Possibly because the open-end company is under pressure to sell new shares and must be prepared to repurchase shares on demand, its investment policy is directed toward maximum appeal to the greatest number of investors; hence, investment performance and marketability of holdings are given more emphasis than in the case of the closed-end company.

Most buyers of investment company securities are not willing or able to make a detailed examination of portfolios and portfolio changes. But they should be aware of the general nature of these policies and of their results in terms of actual performance. When an investor buys investment company shares, he is in effect saying, "Here's my money—you put it to work for me." He should know the type of concern to which he is entrusting his funds and whether its objectives and attitude toward risk coincide with his own. And he ought to apply some tests to determine whether, based on its past record, the fund is likely to be good, bad, or mediocre for his specific purposes.

General Factors in Selection

Several important factors (other than investment performance) should be considered in selecting the securities of one or more investment companies.

Objectives and general character of the fund   The first step is to eliminate those companies whose announced purposes do not coincide with the investor's own objectives, and whose general policies and portfolio indicate more (or possibly less) risk than the investor is prepared to take. Investors requiring recovery of principal would avoid all but the most conservative companies. Investors requiring assurance of regular income would select shares in well-managed income, balanced, or tax-free, funds, or senior securities of closed-end companies. Investors seeking capital appreciation would determine what degree of risk (in terms of volatility of price and/or income) they are prepared to take.

Age and size   The size, maturity, and rate of growth of the investment company deserve close scrutiny. The company should be large enough to provide adequate diversification (if this is a consideration) and be able to afford compensation for skilled management without consuming too large a proportion of income for managerial and operating expenses. It should be old enough to be tested under periods of both prosperity and adversity. Any investment company (and most individual investors, for that matter) can show a good performance in a bull market; it is the record during both good and bad times that counts. The rate of growth of the open-end fund is important because it affects the expense ratio. It also indicates the general appeal the fund has had to the investment community.

Very large funds have the advantage of being able to obtain wide diversification in portfolio securities and to devote a large management fee to research and analysis. They are, however, handicapped by the sheer size of individual holdings. To divest a block of stock worth several millions may take weeks to accomplish. And over-diversification leads to mediocre results.

Price volatility   Many investors require high stability of price; they may count on redemption or sale of shares for liquidity. Others are willing to assume price risk for the sake of high income and/or appreciation. The variations in price in periods of unusual general market change—as in the last six months of 1961, before the break, the first six months of 1962, when stock prices fell sharply, and in 1962, 1963–1965, 1966, 1969–1970, and 1973–1975 can be obtained from the Wiesenberger manual and other sources.

Volatility of fund prices during "ups" and "downs" in the stock market is used by some services in comparing funds. This is a way of recognizing that risk as well as performance is a factor to be considered in the choice of funds. In recent years, measures of fund performance have been developed that incorporate risk into the specific tests. In these measures, risk is indicated by the volatility of the total rate of return rather than price alone. (See p. 452.)

Porfolio turnover   This can be defined (as does the SEC) as the value of securities purchased or sold, whichever is less, divided by the average value of assets during the period being measured.[15] For many years a high rate of portfolio turnover activity was considered improper, both as a sign of uncertain and vascillating investment policy, and a cause of higher management costs. It is now recognized that in the search for a higher *total* return, an increase in portfolio turnover may be acceptable to correct past mistakes, to reflect desirable changes in liquidity as market conditions change, and as an indication of frequent reviews and increased intensity of portfolio management. But there appears to be little relation between turnover and investment achievement. The investor would prefer high turnover with superior performance to low turnover and poor performance.[16]

Amount and character of dividends   Because of the tax advantages accruing to investment companies that elect to declare themselves

[15]Short-term paper and U.S. government securities are usually excluded.

[16]For data on common stock activity rates on portfolios of selected institutions, see the New York Exchange *Fact Book* (annual).

"regulated" companies for tax purposes, most investment companies consistently distribute as dividends all net investment income and short-term capital gains, and all or a part of realized long-term capital gains. This may make the total dividend very erratic, since the capital gains portion varies considerably from year to year, depending on the securities market and the rate of turnover of the portfolio. The company is required to state the portion of each dividend derived from each of the two sources. The investor primarily interested in income should select the company chiefly by its ability to earn and distribute regular investment income. He should reinvest rather than spend that portion of the dividend derived from capital gains so as to preserve his capital intact.

Management fee and total expense ratio   The holder of investment company securities pays for the management of his funds. The management fee, together with other expenses involved in operating the company, should bear a fair relationship to income and to the assets managed. For open-end companies, expenses (including management fee) range between 10 and 15% of investment income and between .50 and 2.00% of average net assets. Some new or specialized companies show even higher rates. These ratios should be considered in the light of the size and the objectives of the fund. As a fund grows, its expenses do not rise proportionally. And the objectives of the fund may require unusually high research and management expense, as in those companies that delve heavily into special situations. The investor would prefer a company with a high expense ratio that produces superior results to an economically managed fund that produces only mediocre results.

A high ratio of expense to *income* may result from the fact that the portfolio deliberately includes a number of low or nondividend stocks, acquired for appreciation. In such a case the investor may be more than repaid by a good growth record.

Sales commissions   The investor should not select a fund or funds merely because the original sales commission or "load" is low or even nil. Performance is more important. He should, however, be aware of the initial sales charge and use it as a marginal factor in the selection process, and in calculating return on cost. Short-term trading in shares of "load" funds is expensive, especially when small amounts are involved.

Conveniences and services   The investor should check the availability and terms of special services and arrangements offered by mutual funds.[17] They include

Automatic dividend reinvestment (including income and capital gains distributions) in new shares without a sales commission, that is, at their asset value.

Voluntary accumulation plans, in which the shareholder invests a certain number of dollars at regular intervals, usually along with reinvestment of divi-

[17]Wiesenberger, *Investment Companies*, has a special section where each of these arrangements, along with other information, is indicated for each fund reported in the manual.

dends. The minimum dollar amount of original purchase and of subsequent regular investment in new shares is prescribed. This is an open-account arrangement involving no definite time period or total investment, and the shareholder may withdraw from the plan at any time.

Contractual accumulation plans, whereby the investor agrees to pay a fixed monthly or quarterly payment over a designated period of years. The minimum installment permitted by the Investment Company Act of 1940 is $10 a month. A typical plan involving $3,000 would call for 120 monthly payments of $25 each. In these plans a large portion of the total sales charges is paid in advance as a *front-end load*. Such a load cannot exceed 50% of the first 12 installments. In the previous example, the total sales load at 8% would be $240. Fifty per cent of each of the first 12 payments, or $12.50 per month, totals $150 and comprises 62.5% of the total sales charge. The rest of the total sales load is distributed over the remaining payments at, of course, a much lower per cent of each. In addition, a custodian fee of from 1 to 3% of the total payments is also deducted from the first payments, so that less than one-half the amount of the early payments is "working" for the investor.

The Securities and Exchange Commission has been very critical of contractual front-end-load plans, on the grounds that they do not represent the incentive to savings that is claimed for them, and that many investors do not understand the initial consumption of payments by sales expenses.[18] Legislation governing such plans was passed in 1970. (See p. 218.)

Withdrawal plans. After the investor has made a minimum initial investment in shares (often $5,000 or $10,000), the fund pays a certain amount to him each month. Some of the capital of the account may have to be withdrawn to make up the payments, depending on the earnings on his shares, their increase or decrease in value, and the dollar size of the withdrawals.

Conversion privilege, which enables the shareholder to transfer from one fund to another within a group of funds managed by the same advisor, as his needs change—for example, from a growth to an income fund. A small fee, but no sales commission, may be charged for the transfer.

Specific Tests of Investment Performance

The past performance of investment companies may be measured by applying various specific tests. No one test is applicable to all companies, but should be selected in the light of the objectives of the companies studied. For example, balanced funds could not be expected to record changes in asset values similar to those of common stock funds. Income funds will show different yields and different changes in asset values than growth funds.

Performance should be studied over a period of years. Short periods are not representative of varying business and market conditions. And even average annual performance over a period of years may have been affected by one or two especially good or bad years. The year-by-year and the

[18]*Report of the Special Study of Securities Markets of the S.E.C.*, Chapter 11, Part IV, pp. 115–203.

cumulative performance are most important. And one must recognize that, although the past record is the only significant clue to the future, identical results may not be produced in the future.

The following tests apply to common shares. Senior securities of closed-end companies will be discussed later in this chapter.

Test of total earning power   For both closed-end and mutual funds, the total earning power derived from interest and dividends received on a portfolio is measured by the percentage of such income, after operating expenses, to the average value of the assets held during the year. In the case of closed-end companies, earnings before interest is the numerator. A consistently low rate of return does not necessarily reflect poor management. The fund may consist of high-grade securities that are expected to produce regular rather than large returns. Or the investment policy may be directed more toward capital growth than toward interest and dividend income.

Test of dividend yield   For the holder of mutual fund shares or of common stock in a closed-end company, the important current income test is the annual rate of return produced on the net asset value of his shares from net investment income after all expenses, interest, and taxes, and exclusive of realized capital gains from the sale of portfolio securities. In the case of mutual fund shares, either the beginning or the average net asset value may be used as the base, and the actual investment dividends may be used rather than the net investment income, since virtually all net investment income is distributed. A further refinement would be to employ the offering price (net asset value plus any sales load) as the base.

Income yield based on the average value of the net assets per share has the disadvantage of being affected by change in asset value during the year—higher where asset value has declined, lower where asset value has increased. This complicates the problem of comparing different funds.[19]

The yield on closed-end stocks is calculated like that on any common stocks, namely, by the relationship between market price and dividends.

The actual return and its stability are, of course, affected by the objectives of the fund, the composition of its portfolio, and, in the case of closed-end companies, the degree of leverage and the size of any premium or discount from asset value at which the shares are bought. There is a wide range. The stocks of many diversified mutual common stock growth funds produced (in 1977) less than 2%, some even less than 1%. At the other extreme, yields of 5 to 6% were found in the case of income funds owning common stocks. Until recent years, if shares bought primarily for current income could consistently offer a net investment return of 5% and, in addition, produce modest capital gains, the fund was thought to be doing better than most

[19]Wiesenberger reports the yield from dividend income on the year-end asset value. Using DI for dividend income and NA for asset value, the following model may be useful:

$$\text{Yield on beginning asset value} = \frac{DI}{NA}$$

$$\text{Yield on average asset value} = \frac{DI}{(NA_t + NA_{t+1})/2}$$

investors could do alone. But with the rise of bond yields to record heights in 1969–1971 and 1973–1975, such yields on stocks became competitively unattractive. Managers of common stock income funds were obliged to place more emphasis on appreciation of portfolio value to produce a satisfactory total rate of return. Convertible securities were frequently bought as a compromise. Also, a number of new income funds were formed to take advantage of the high yields, and were restricted to corporate and Federal bonds or to tax-free municipal securities.

Test of growth   Capital appreciation is more important than current income to many investors. This is measured by computing the percentage rate of change in net asset value plus distributed realized capital gains, annually and for various periods. In comparing companies, one must add back *distributed* capital gains to compensate for the fact that the amount of these varies from company to company and from time to time.[20]

Measures of total performance   The total performance of an open-end company for a single year or over a longer period may be measured by combining the change in the net asset value per share and the dividends (from all sources) distributed during the period. If the net asset value per share of an open-end fund or of a nonleverage closed-end fund were $10 at the beginning of the period and it distributed 80 cents in total dividends, and the net asset value were $10.20 at the end of the period, the performance gain was 10% for the period. The performance of an individual company should be compared with that of other companies with similar objectives. The performance of common stock funds may be compared with selected stocks or groups of stocks, and with a stock average or index such as the Dow Jones composite index of 65 stocks or the Standard & Poor's index of 500 stocks as representing the market as a whole.[21]

A more refined measure is used by some services. The percentage change over a period (or alternatively, the growth in value of an initial investment in terms of dollars—say $10,000) is calculated by adding to the change in net asset value of the original shares the cumulative value of shares obtained by reinvesting realized capital gains in additional shares of the fund, plus investment income dividends in cash. Many annual reports of mutual funds display charts showing the results of an assumed investment (including sales

[20]Using NA for net asset value, and DC for distributed capital gains, the model for this test is

$$\frac{NA_{t+1} + DC}{NA_t} - 100\%$$

[21]The index of total performance may be calculated by the investor or found in an advisory service. It cannot be used or furnished by an investment company.

Using NA for net asset value, DI for income dividends, and DC for distributed capital gains, the model for this test is

$$\frac{NA_{t+1} + DI + DC}{NA_t} - 100\%$$

Restrictions in the Securities and Exchange Commission Statement of Policy include: (1) the period covered in any statement of performance must include at least 10 years, (2) the sales charge, or total cost of the investment, must be shown, and (3) dividends from investment income and distribution from security profits may not be combined. However, "capital results" may be shown either by adding back security profit distributions or by assuming that these had been reinvested.

commission) over a given period, calculated in this way. Some also present figures to show the ending value of the original investment, assuming that *all* dividends are reinvested in shares.[22]

More sophisticated measures of mutual fund performance have been developed that may be more widely used in the future, although those just mentioned are likely to dominate the performance data that are available for broad public use. The more refined methods use volatility of rate of return, as the measure of risk of a fund, in relation to the market as a whole.

The concept of risk and its use along with rate of return is discussed at greater length in Chapter 23, where other and more sophisticated measures of performance are described.

The usefulness of any index of performance for comparative purposes is limited by the period chosen for study. Performance in any one year is not very significant; performance over a period of years is affected by the course of the market as a whole. For these reasons, emphasis should be placed on an examination of year-to-year results in the search for consistent superiority, and if a period of some years is used, the performance of the whole period should be viewed in the light of the trend in the market as a whole. A defect of data, charts, and graphs based on a selected period is that an investor cannot determine what his performance experience would have been if other particular stages of the period had been chosen.

Comparison of the performance of an individual company or of a group of companies with a general stock index also has decided limitations. "No one buys the averages." These represent a nonexpense, fully invested, non-managed position in common stocks with no particular policy involved. And in any period of generally rising (or falling) prices, their performance would have an upward (or downward) bias. The performance indexes are useful mainly for purposes of comparison of funds which have substantially the same objectives and types of portfolio. Any other comparisons, or comparisons with the averages, are likely to be misleading.[23]

The basic test   While somewhat intangible, the real test of the appeal of an investment company's shares lies in the answer to the question, "based on its record, is the company likely to do a better job for my purposes than I could do alone with respect to safety, income, appreciation, or other objectives?" A cold-blooded inspection of the records of investment companies reveals that some have fallen far short of the results to be expected of expert management. But there are many whose performance has been very satisfactory indeed, and some whose records have been clearly superior.

Senior Securities

The preceding discussion pertained mainly to the shares of open-end funds and the common stock of closed-end funds. The latter have steadily reduced

[22]For sources that publish performance information, see p. 243.

[23]For the position of the Securities and Exchange Commission in this respect, see footnote 8.

their senior securities in recent years, by mandatory sinking funds or by using the call feature. Most debentures have been retired, but a few preferred stocks are still outstanding.

Five factors should be analyzed in the appraisal of the preferred stocks of closed-end companies:

1. Overall asset coverage, or ratio of assets to the sum of all liabilities plus the preferred stock at liquidating value; this proportion should be at least 400%.

2. Overall income coverage, or ratio of investment income to total interest plus preferred dividends; this proportion should be at least two times.

3. Regularity of dividends derived from investment income as contrasted with realized capital gains.

4. Special features, such as the convertible feature, and the advantages of same.

5. Price history.

An example of a high-grade issue is found in General American Investors Company $4.50 Preferred. The issue is preceded by no senior obligations and is well supported by assets ($13,970 per share at the end of 1975 and by earnings (dividends earned 51 times in 1976). The issue is callable at 105 plus accrued dividends and is nonconvertible. The yield at the early 1977 price of 70 was 6.4%. Dividends have been paid regularly since 1929.

Warrants

At the opposite extreme from the senior securities of closed-end companies are the stock-purchase warrants that have been issued by a few concerns. These warrants carry an option to buy common stock from the company at a stipulated price during a specific period. The value of the warrant is theoretically determined by the excess (if any) of the market price of the common stock over the price at which the warrant may be exercised. (See p. 189.) Actually the warrant may sell at a considerable premium above its theoretical value, and may be in demand even if its theoretical value is zero or negative. This is because any rise or potential rise in the market value of the stock gives value to the option to purchase it at a set price. If the warrant is an option to buy at 10, and the market price of the stock is 10, the warrant has no theoretical value, but may sell for $2 or $3 because, if the stock should rise to 15, the warrant would be worth $5. Variations in the price of the common stock are magnified in the market value of warrants, which tend to have marked price volatility. For example, the warrants of Tri-Continental Corporation, a large closed-end fund, gave (1976) the holder the perpetual option of buying 3.57 shares of common stock at $6.30 per share. The price of the common stock ranged from 18 to 22 during 1976, and the price of the warrants (traded over-the-counter) ranged from 37 to 55.

Special Uses of Investment Company Shares

In recent years much has been made of the advantages of investment company securities to the small investor. Certain other more specialized uses that pertain to investors in general should also be examined.

For dollar-cost averaging   The investor who wishes to avoid making decisions with respect to the swings in the market and who is steadily accumulating funds finds in the shares of investment companies an almost ideal vehicle for the device of dollar-cost averaging that is described in Chapter 19. The problem of selection of the fund or funds for this purpose still remains, but the diversification and management that are obtained are valuable additions to the advantages which the process of dollar averaging may produce. In recognition of this appeal, and in order to acquire a continuous market for new shares, most open-end companies provide "accumulation plans" whereby the investor enters into an agreement to invest a certain number of dollars at regular intervals, and in most cases all dividends and distributions can be automatically reinvested at asset value without a sales load on this portion of the accumulation. The minimum dollar amount of initial purchases and of subsequent regular investment in new shares is prescribed. (See p. 227.)

For provision of a fixed cash income   Most open-end companies offer withdrawal plans whereby the shareholder may obtain a fixed monthly income. Where the dividend income is not large enough to cover the required amount, shares are liquidated for the balance. (See p. 228.) Mutual funds are now permitted to issue literature showing the past results that such arrangements would have produced. Because of the secular rise in common stock prices in the 1960s and early 1970s some funds were able to show that a certain rate of cash income (such as 6%) could have been distributed in the past, from income and liquidation of shares, and the erosion of capital could still have been offset by capital appreciation, leaving the fund larger at the end of a given period of years than at the beginning. Of course, such a performance is not guaranteed. The extremely sharp decline in stock prices in 1973–74 eliminated the appeal of this arrangement for many investors.

For the investment of trust funds   Investment company shares are eligible for trust investment (1) where the trustee is empowered by the trust instrument to purchase investment company shares, (2) in the states where by law or court decision fiduciaries may purchase investment company shares, (3) in the other states that also follow the "prudent man" rule, and (4) where the "legal list" does not include equities, but where general discretionary powers are provided by the instrument. Originally, the main argument against the practice was that the purchase of such shares involved the improper delegation of trust powers to the management of the investment company that selects the portfolio. This is not the case, although the trustee must still apply rules of caution to the selection of the particular securities by investigating the policy, portfolio, and management of each company under consideration.

The development of common trust funds by bank trustees, together with the emphasis on their own investment departments, has retarded the use of investment company shares as trust investments, especially after the relatively poor performance of mutual fund managers in the 1970s.

For the investment of pension and profit-sharing funds. The rapid growth of corporate pension plans in the last 35 years, described in Chapter 4, has opened up another outlet for investment company securities. Where the purchase of equities over a prolonged period is appropriate for such funds, investment company shares provide the opportunity for a small fund (say, under the Keogh and IRA plans) to acquire an interest in a managed and diversified portfolio. Large funds are typically invested and managed as separate accounts.

Tax Status of Investment Companies

If investment companies were taxed as ordinary corporations, triple income taxation would result. The corporation whose securities are held in the portfolio has paid taxes; the investment company would pay a tax on its earnings; and the holder of its shares would pay taxes on dividends received. The Internal Revenue Code recognizes this problem by permitting an investment company to elect to be a "regulated investment company" for tax purposes. To qualify as such, it must: (1) be registered under the Investment Company Act of 1940, (2) derive at least 90% of gross income from dividends, interest, and gains from sale of securities, (3) obtain less than 70% of gross income from sale of securities held for less than three months, (4) have at least 50% of assets in cash, Government securities, and a diversified list of securities, and (5) distribute as taxable dividends not less than 90% of its investment income (interest and dividend income less expenses) and short-term capital gains for any taxable year. It is not obliged to distribute any of its realized long-term security profits. The few "nonregulated" companies pay regular corporate taxes on realized capital gains and the current corporate ordinary and surtax rates on 15% of dividend income and 100% of interest income after deducting expenses and general taxes.

The "regulated" investment company may retain long-term realized capital gains and pay a 25% tax on them, *on behalf of the stockholder.* The stockholder reports this payment on his own income tax return. (If his top tax bracket is less than 50%, in effect he receives a refund.) The shareholder then writes up the cost of his shares by three-quarters of the gain to reflect the fact that a capital gains tax has now been paid on part of the value of his holdings, just as if the net after-tax gain had been distributed and then reinvested. The shareholder, of course, pays taxes on any realized capital gains distributed to him.

When the shareholder of a regulated investment company receives a dividend check, the company indicates that portion derived from net investment income and that portion derived from realized capital gains, so that the investor can report and pay the personal income taxes that apply to him.[24]

Two types of funds have been available to those seeking exemption or postponement of Federal income taxes: (1) funds whose portfolio consists of tax-free state and municipal securities, and (2) tax-free exchange ("swap") funds. "Tax-free" funds have much appeal to investors who can benefit from the exemption from income taxes of municipal securities. (See p. 239 and Chapter 7.) Diversification provides some protection against loss, and attractive rates of return are available. Most such funds are operated as unit trusts. In mid-1976 there appeared the first open-end municipal bond fund. (See p. 239.)

"Swap funds," which first appeared in 1960, were formed to accept the investors' securities in exhange for their shares. No current capital gain was realized by the investor. The tax cost of the fund shares remains the same as that of the investor's original holdings, as does that of the fund itself. Later, if the fund sells portfolio securities, any realized capital gain is taxed on the same basis as that applying to other funds. However, since requests for redemption of fund shares can be honored by delivering portfolio securities instead of cash, the fund can avoid forced realization of capital gains and so these are further postponed as far as the investor is concerned.

Swap funds are closed-end—they do not make a continuous offering of shares; the securities contributed were held in escrow during the organization period, and shares in the fund were exchanged in a single transaction. At the beginning of 1977, 12 such funds were operating. By Federal law, no new registered and incorporated exchange funds could solicit business after April 30, 1967.[25]

Prices, Dividends, and Yields

Open-end shares   As indicated previously, the buying price of a share of an open-end company consists of its net asset value plus, in "load" funds, a selling charge to cover distribution costs. The "bid" price reported in the financial columns is this net asset value. The "asked" price is virtually the net asset value plus the load.[26] The value of the share thus rises and falls with the value of the total portfolio, which is in turn determined by the com-

[24]To avoid impairment of the capital at work, most open-end companies urge their stockholders to take their capital gains distributions in additional shares of stock. The individual shareholder has the same right as any investor to the normal dividend exclusion on *income* dividends received. (See Chapter 17.)

[25]A few unregistered exchange funds have been organized as limited partnerships. Their legal and tax status is in doubt (1977).

[26]Actually, the asked price is found by multiplying the bid price (net asset value) by 100 over 100 minus the load. Thus, if the bid price is 10 and the load is 8%, the asked price is $10(100/92) = 10.87$.

position of the portfolio and conditions in the securities markets. The range of volatility in price action among the whole open-end group is very wide, reflecting the different purposes and objectives of the different funds and the investment policies followed.

Dividends derived from investment earnings on open-end shares likewise differ in amount and in stability, depending on the character of the fund and the policies of the management. Just as with individual securities, the investor has a wide choice among funds emphasizing growth and appreciation, or those aiming at high but variable income, or those directed toward moderate but more stable income. And within any group, there is wide variation in actual performance.

Closed-end shares   The price of shares in closed-end funds is affected by the same factors as the above, plus the influence of a high or a low degree of leverage. But in contrast to mutual fund shares, the difference between asset value and market value per share may be very substantial, just as the market price per share of a business corporation may differ considerably from its book value. Since 1945 the shares of many closed-end companies have sold at considerable discounts from asset value. Wiesenberger reports that at the end of 1976, there was an average discount of 23% on the shares of 10 diversified closed-end companies; the range was from no discount to 32% discount. Including specialized funds and nondiversified companies, 50 sold at discounts and seven at a premium.[27]

A substantial discount does not necessarily represent a bargain. It may indicate large potential tax liabilities on unrealized capital gains. It may reflect lack of confidence in the management, but is more likely to reflect the general condition of the market and the evaluation of earnings and dividends by appropriate capitalization of these factors. Unlike shares of open-end companies, the common stocks of closed-end companies sell for what the market thinks they are worth in terms of future earning power, dividends, and prospects of appreciation.

Because of their more specialized nature, the fact that they can be redeemed only by sale in the open market, and (in some cases) the factor of leverage, the common stocks of closed-end companies in general have more price volatility than those of open-end companies. The greatest volatility is shown by those companies whose portfolios themselves are volatile and which have high leverage in their own capitalization.

The character of the closed-end fund is also reflected in its dividend policy and the yield action of its shares. Here again the investor has a wide choice. Earnings, and hence dividends, are affected by the objectives of the fund, the proficiency of its management, and the relative importance of investment income and capital gains. And the yield on these shares is determined by the factors affecting earnings and dividends, as well as by the market price action.

---

[27]Wiesenberger Investment Services, *Management Results,* Jan. 1977. Prices and premiums or discounts are reported each Monday in *The Wall Street Journal.* See also United Business Service, Inc., *United Mutual Fund Selector* (semi-monthly).

Recent Developments

A number of developments that have taken place in the investment company field in recent years, both in operation and regulation, are summarized as follows.

1970 Amendments to the Investment Company Act   In December 1966 the Securities and Exchange Commission released a comprehensive report on mutual funds, and suggested that a number of important revisions be made in the Investment Company Act of 1940 and in the regulatory power of the Commission under that statute, relative to mutual funds.[28] After long and controversial hearings, in 1970 Congress passed amendments to the Investment Company Act that fell considerably short of meeting the SEC recommendations. The more important of these were

1. "Front-end load" plans were not eliminated, nor was the 50% sales charge in the first year. But the investor can rescind the entire transaction within 45 days, and during the first 18 months the shareholder can get a refund of his payments less 15%.

2. Sales charges were not limited to a specific maximum, but the offering price of mutual fund shares may not include "an excessive sales load." Rules relating to the sales commission are to be formulated by the National Association of Securities Dealers.

3. Management fees are not specified. But fees based on performance are prohibited unless they increase or decrease proportionately with an appropriate index of securities prices used to represent the market as a whole.[29]

4. "Fiduciary duty," that is, the obligation to guard the interests of shareholders with honesty and prudence, is imposed on the officers and directors of investment companies and their advisors. Actions by shareholders to recover damages are enforceable only in a U.S. District Court.

Sale of mutual fund shares by life insurance companies   As indicated in Chapter 4, insurance companies have entered the mutual fund business directly or through affiliates. At the end of 1975, 185 funds organized by insurance companies had assets of $4.3 billion. In addition, insurance companies or their parent companies owned sponsors that managed 80 funds with assets of $5.6 billion, and 56 funds affiliated with insurance companies had assets of $11.9 million.[30] Some of these offer a "funding" arrangement whereby the investor agrees to purchase a certain dollar amount of mutual fund shares and of life insurance, over a period of time, on a regular

[28]*Report of the S.E.C. on the Public Policy Implications of Investment Company Growth,* Report of the Committee on Interstate and Foreign Commerce, 89th Congress, 2d Session, House Report No. 2337 (Washington, D.C.: U.S. Government Printing Office, 1966).

[29]For detailed information and analysis of management fees, see *Institutional Investor Study Report of the Securities and Exchange Commission,* Chapter IV. 92nd Congress, 1st Session, House Document No. 92–64. (Washington: U.S. Government Printing Office, 1971).

[30]Wiesenberger, *Investment Companies* (New York: Wiesenberger Financial Services, Inc., 1977).

basis (monthly or quarterly). The shares are used as collateral for loans to purchase the insurance. The expectation is that the long-term increase in value of the shares will more than pay the interest cost on the loan.

The entrance of insurance companies into the mutual fund area was the result of several factors: (1) the need to meet the competition of equity-type securities that are more attractive than cash reserve life insurance policies in an inflationary setting; (2) as a step in the development of financial conglomerates offering a variety of financial services; (3) as a means of increasing life insurance sales; and (4) to increase agents' income. The sharp market decline in 1973–1974 and the poor performance of many funds have discouraged the growth of such sponsored funds.

Commercial banks and mutual funds   For some time commercial banks have wished to operate their own mutual funds. Their trust departments already manage common trust funds and serve as managers of individual agency accounts and of estates consisting of securities portfolios. In April 1971, in a case involving the First National City Bank of New York, the Supreme Court ruled that, based on the separation of commercial and investment banking required by law, banks may not operate commingled agency accounts.[31] But some bank holding companies have set up new closed-end investment companies as subsidiaries.

Newer Types of Funds

The decline in investment interest in the traditional types of investment companies has been partially offset by the recent appearance or the recent rapid growth of a number of types of funds identified briefly as follows.

Closed-end

"Letter stock" funds appearing in the late 60s and early 70s specialized in acquiring restricted (unregistered) securities and direct private placements. Securities were often bought at substantial discounts from the market prices of requested shares of the same issues. Chief difficulties have been the problem of valuation and of speedy liquidation of portfolio holdings.

Closed-end dual-purpose funds (p. 210) have not lived up to expectations. Their double leverage feature resulted in very substantial declines in the market value of their capital shares in the 1969–1970, the late 1971, and 1973–1975 periods of marked weakness in stock prices. Only a few (1977) are selling at or above net asset values, and in certain cases the latter have been substantially eroded. Income shares were yielding 8 to 10% in early 1977, and their prices had suffered from the decline which corresponded with rising interest rates.

Fixed-income funds. The rise in interest rates and the decline in stock prices encouraged the appearance of a number of funds in the early 1970s, whose objective is regular income. Their portfolios have emphasized corporate bonds, but some have included high-yielding common stocks.

[31]401 U.S. 617 (1971).

Open-end

Hedge funds. At the end of 1968 there were 140 unregistered hedge funds with assets of $1.3 billion. They were typically organized as limited partnerships, and quotations are available on only two or three publicly held funds. Their name derives from the fact that they attempt to hedge the effects of high leverage and margin trading (debt financing) with short selling, arbitrage, and the use of options, in order to take advantage of swings in stock market prices. They ranged in size from $50,000 assets to $118 million. Two features distinguish their common stock portfolios from those of other aggressive funds: emphasis in investment policy on stocks traded on regional exchanges and over-the-counter, and willingness to buy initial stock offerings. The Commission has found their investment performance to be mediocre. The Commission also recommended that they be brought under its regulations.[32]

"Offshore" funds are incorporated in foreign countries and sell shares to foreign nationals. But they were often organized and managed by Americans and invest all or a substantial portion of their portfolios in American equity securities. Because they are not registered under the Investment Company Act and because their shares are not registered under the Securities Act, these cannot be sold in the United States. The reported value of their holdings in American securities, held by American custodians alone, reached $2.35 billion in December 1969, falling to $2.12 billion in February 1970.[33] In its lengthy study of offshore funds the Commission concluded that although they had been a significant vehicle for foreign investment in American equities, their faulty disclosure of operations and investment information, the doubtful quality of their portfolio management, and the substantial losses to investors in some funds all indicated the need for bringing the funds under its regulation. Although the funds themselves would be exempt, regulation could be applied to sales corporations based in the United States that sell shares in offshore funds abroad.[34]

Index funds. Because the average mutual fund, and probably the average pension fund, has failed to do as well as (or less poorly than) the general market averages, in the early 1970s a few funds were launched with the announced aim of providing investment results that correspond to the price and yield performance of the market as a whole, as represented, say, by the Standard & Poor's composite index. The launching of such funds (some using the trust form of organization) reveals an admission on the part of their sponsors that either the market as a whole is efficient or that professional money managers are unable to detect its inefficiencies, that is, to select stocks that will do better than the market.

Municipal bond funds. The usual type of municipal bond fund has been a unit trust type where shares are issued against successive series of fixed portfolios. (See p. 218.) As the underlying bonds are reduced, the series gradually

---

[32]*Institutional Investor Study Report of the S.E.C.*, Supplementary Volume I, Chapter 5. See also *Fortune*, May 1971, pp. 269–270.

[33]*Ibid*, Chapter VII.

[34]For a complete survey of types, structure, management and sponsorship, tax status, and other aspects of offshore funds, including their significance in the balance of payments, see *Institutional Investor Study Report of the S.E.C. op cit.*, Chapter VII.

liquidates. The tax-free income is passed along to the shareholders without a management fee. By mid-1976 such funds had assets of $7 billion. In mid-1976 a new type of municipal bond fund appeared—the first open-end fund. Organized as a limited partnership, it offered the advantages of any managed mutual fund, yet required a lower minimum initial investment than the unit trust type.

Corporate bond funds. In addition to the "money-market" funds described below, a number of income funds restricted to investment in high-grade corporate bonds were organized in 1970–1975 to combine the merits of safety and attractive rates of return.

Government securities funds. The trauma of the 1973–1974 stock market debacle and the attractive yields available on the highest-grade bonds led to the appearance of income funds whose portfolios consisted of medium- and long-term Federal government and agency securities. Soon, however, the new "money-market" funds, invested in short-term instruments, became the more popular new medium.

Money-market funds. High interest rates on high-grade short-term instruments led to the appearance in 1974–1975 of about 50 new "money-market" funds, investing principally in Treasury bills, commercial paper, and negotiable bank certificates of deposit. At the peak in early 1976 their assets totalled almost $4 million. Yields ran as high as 10 to 11% in 1974, but declined to around 5% by early 1977. Their immense appeal stemmed not only from their safety, liquidity, and high yield, but also from the availability of small denominations, in contrast to the large denominations required in direct purchase of money-market paper. (See Chapter 10.) Ease of redemption, monthly payment of interest, lack of a sales load, low required initial investment (as low as $1,000), ease of reinvestment, and even, in some cases, easy transfer by check, were appealing features. Even in the wake of a later decline in short-term interest rates of 40 to 50% from their peak, such funds have retained some of their popularity. (See Table 11-1.) Some funds have used the trust rather than the corporate form of organization.

Money-market/options funds. The appeal of high-grade money-market instruments for safety, plus a burgeoning interest in options, led to the appearance early in 1976 of a new type of open-end fund which invests a limited portion of its assets in a portfolio of call options and the balance in money-market securities. The chief objective is capital appreciation, at limited risk. At this writing (late-1977) the record of this new type had not been revealed.

Criticism of Investment Performance

Unlike pension funds, investment counsels, and bank trustees, the investment record of mutual investment companies is an open book. The asset values of the shares of widely held companies are reported daily, and their dividends are reported regularly. A number of services issue comparative reports on performance. Consequently, mutual funds have been subject to constant scrutiny, with resulting praise and blame. Funds are compared with each other, and with the general market indexes. During strong stock markets, most of them come off well, especially the more aggressive and speculative funds. In periods of weakness, many look bad and criticism mounts.

Two research studies have been especially critical: "The Wharton Study" in 1962,[35] and a Twentieth Century Fund study in 1970.[36] The former concluded that for the period 1953–1958, the average performance by mutual funds was not appreciably better than would have been achieved by a completely unmanaged (general market) portfolio with the same distribution between stocks and other assets. The second study, using the period 1960 through June 1968, compares the rate of return (dividends plus capital gain as a percentage of initial investment) with what could have been achieved by investing equal amounts in a random sample of all stocks listed on the New York Stock Exchange. In this study the factor of risk (volatility of monthly rates of return) was also taken into account and related to performance. The study concluded the following based on elaborate statistical analysis: The funds demonstrated an inability to outperform the stock market; management showed no particular ability to predict market trends; management fees and sales charges were excessive for the results obtained. It is not surprising that a high correlation was found between rate of return and risk.

Such criticisms suggest that it is important to make a careful selection among the many funds that are available, and that the choice of a fund should be made on the basis of long-run results. They also suggest the significance of the period studied and of the choice of the types of companies that are studied for performance. These factors are emphasized by the fact that in two later studies mutual funds were given much better ratings. In a special study for the Securities and Exchange Commission, the National Bureau of Economic Research reported that in the period 1965–1970 the performance of the "growth" funds, measured by traditional methods, was distinctly better than that of the popular stock averages, in spite of the market losses in 1969–1970.[37]

In a thorough study of industry performance, the Commission found that 236 open-end funds with net assets of $30 billion (90% of the industry) were well run in relation to risk. Measuring performance by the difference between the rate of return earned by the funds and that realized by standard portfolios which had shown the same risk (volatility), the group produced a higher return by 0.6% annually in the 10-year period 1960 through 1969.[38]

But it was in the period 1973–1976 that investment companies faced their severest test, and, in the opinion of many, failed. The great collapse in the stock market in 1973–1974 (the sharpest since 1929–1932), accompanied by a severe decline in bond prices, was reflected in investment company performance. The inability of most funds to adjust to radically changing conditions was very apparent. Dozens of comparisons published in special services and in financial journals and the financial press indicated that the industry

[35]See footnote 10 for citation.

[36]Irwin Friend, Marshall Blum, and Jean Crockett, *Mutual Funds and Other Institutional Investors: A New Perspective.* A Twentieth Century Fund Study (New York: McGraw-Hill, Inc., 1970.)

[37]*Institutional Investor Study Report of the S.E.C., op. cit.,* Supplementary Volume I, Chapter 5.

[38]*Institutional Investor Study Report of the S.E.C., op. cit.,* Chapter IV.

had done a below-average job, both in absolute terms and as measured against the market as a whole.

Table 11-5 compares the 1971–1976 annual percentage changes in the leading stock price indexes or averages with the total performance of the Lipper mutual fund and growth fund averages. These latter include reinvested dividends and, therefore, are biased on the positive side as compared to the market series.

TABLE 11-5   Annual Percentage Changes in Market and Mutual
Fund Averages, 1971–1976

Series	1971	1972	1973	1974	1975	1976
Market:						
Standard and Poor's 500	10.8%	14.4%	−17.4%	−29.7%	31.6%	19.1%
Dow Jones 30 industrials	6.1	14.5	−16.6	−27.6	38.3	17.9
NYSE composite	13.9	14.2	−19.6	−30.3	31.9	21.5
Amex composite	13.6	4.5	−22.2	−33.2	38.4	31.6
Mutual funds:						
Industry	18.1	9.3	−22.2	−22.6	29.4	23.6
Growth funds	23.2	14.7	−27.0	−30.0	32.0	16.7

Sources: Market series: Barron's and Federal Reserve Bulletin; fund series: Lipper Analytical Services, Inc., reproduced with permission.

Most funds, especially the growth funds, declined more in 1973 than did the general averages. This reflected the previous emphasis on "performance" stocks in which interest had not been much discouraged by the earlier market decline in 1969. Even income stocks and funds declined, hit by the rise in interest rates. Relative to the market, the industry did somewhat better in 1974, but investors had expected much more. Affected by caution in reentering the market, and by the pressure for liquidity brought by the continual liquidation of shares, the industry failed to enjoy as good a recovery in 1975 as did the market as a whole. The industry data for 1974 and 1975 would have looked different had it not been for the influence of the burgeoning group of "money-market" funds, which provided safety and yield, but not price appreciation.

Conclusions

Investment companies differ widely with respect to basic characteristics, size, rate of growth, investment policies and types of portfolios, income, dividend, and price performance. All of these factors deserve the closest scrutiny. In utilizing this indirect and delegated means of investment, the investor must first be sure of his own objectives. He must then select a fund or group of companies that appear to have the same objectives, keeping in mind that no investment company is "tailor-made" to fit a particular investment situation. He must then examine the statements and performance of these companies and, having selected one or more for a portion of his funds, must make a continued appraisal in order to know whether the company is doing a better job for him, at a cost to him, than he could do alone. He must make intelligent use of performance data. He must not expect spectacular results. On the other hand, he is entitled to full value in services rendered.

Special Sources of Information

The investor has far more information on investment companies than on any other type of institutional investor through which he operates.

Barron's, quarterly section on investment company dividends and prices.

Computer Directions Advisors, Inc., publishes quarterly *Spectrum 1 Investment Stock Holdings Survey* and *Spectrum 2 Investment Company Portfolios*.

Forbes magazine, annual report on comparative performance.

Fund Scope, a monthly magazine devoted to investment company data and performance.

Hirsch Organization, Inc., publishes annually Yale Hirsch's *Mutual Fund Almanac*, defining types and uses of mutual funds and 8-year performance data.

Investment Dealers Digest, annual special section on mutual fund earnings and performance.

Johnson's Investment Company Charts (annual), showing graphically the performance of leading funds.

Lipper Analytical Services, Inc. publishes (weekly and quarterly) performance and ranking of mutual funds classified by size and objectives, and a number of other services. (Available only to professional investment managers.)

Moody's Bank and Finance Manual provides financial statements of mutual funds and (in the blue section) industry data.

Mutual Fund Fact Book, with data on all phases of the industry, published annually by the Investment Company Institute.

Standard & Poor's Industry Surveys, section on investment companies gives data on individual funds and groups.

Trusts and Estates, regular comment on performance of funds.

United Mutual Fund Selector (bi-weekly) provides data on performance results and makes specific recommendations. Published by United Business Service Co.

Vickers Guide to Investment Company Portfolios, published by Vickers Associates.

Wiesenberger Services, Inc. publishes annually the comprehensive *Investment Companies*, providing performance data together with much information on all phases of the industry; also *Charts and Statistics*, annual one-page reports on the leading funds, showing the results of a $10,000 investment over the latest 10-year period; *Current Performance* (monthly), including dividend records; *Management Results* (quarterly) shows performance in various recent periods; *Wiesenberger Report* (quarterly) discusses new developments, sales, and redemptions.

Reports and prospectuses of investment companies, showing portfolios in detail.

Releases and brochures of investment companies and dealers.

Annual reports of the Securities and Exchange Commission, section on regulation of investment companies, with industry data.

REFERENCES

A Study of Mutual Funds, prepared for the Securities and Exchange Commission by the Wharton School of Finance and Commerce, 87th Congress, 2d Session, 1962. Washington, D.C.: U.S. Government Printing Office, 1962.

BULLOCK, HUGH, *The Story of Investment Companies*. New York: Columbia University Press, 1959.

CASEY, W. J., *Mutual Funds Investment Planning*. New York: Institute for Business Planning, Inc., loose-leaf.

DOANE, C. R., and E. J. HILLS, *Investment Trusts and Funds from the Investor's Point of View*. Gt. Barrington, Mass.: American Institute for Economic Research, 1970.

DUKE, E. E., *Selecting Your Mutual Fund*. New York: Exposition Press, 1972.

FERROTTI, A. P., ed., *CFA Seminar on Investment Company Portfolio Management*. Homewood, Ill.: Richard D. Irwin, Inc., 1970.

FRIEND, IRWIN, M. BLUM, and JEAN CROCKETT, *Mutual Funds and Other Institutional Investors*. A Twentieth Century Fund Study. New York: McGraw-Hill, Inc., 1970.

Institutional Investor Study Report of the Securities and Exchange Commission, Chapters IV, VII, and Supplementary Volume No. 1, Chapter 5. 92nd Congress, 1st Session, House Document No. 92–64. Washington, D.C.: U.S. Government Printing Office, 1971.

Investment Company Institute, *Management Investment Companies*, a monograph prepared for the Commission on Money and Credit. Englewood Cliffs, N. J.: Prentice-Hall, Inc., 1962.

———, *The Mutual Fund Shareholder*. New York: The Institute, 1966.

———, *The Money Managers: Professional Investment Through Mutual Funds*. New York: McGraw-Hill, Inc., 1967.

JACOBS, SHELDON, *Put Money in Your Pocket: The Art of Selecting No-load Mutual Funds*. New York: Simon & Schuster, 1974.

JOHNSON, H. A., *Johnson's Investment Company Charts*. Buffalo: Hugh A. Johnson Investment Co., annually.

MEAD, STUART B., *Mutual Funds: A Guide for the Lay Investor*. Morristown, N.J.: D.H. Mark Publications, 1971.

Report of the Securities and Exchange Commission on the Public Policy Implications of Investment Company Growth. Report of the Committee on Interstate and Foreign Commerce, 89th Congress, 2d Session, House Report No. 2337, December 2, 1966. Washington, D.C.: U.S. Government Printing Office, 1966.

Report of the Special Study of the Securities Markets of the Securities and Exchange Commission, Part 4, Chapter XI. Washington, D.C.: U.S. Government Printing Office, 1963.

RUGG, D. D., and N. B. HALE, *The Dow Jones-Irwin Guide to Mutual Funds*. Homewood, Ill.: Dow Jones-Irwin, Inc., 1976.

SPRINGER, J. L., *The Mutual Fund Trap*. Chicago: Henry Regnery Co., 1973.

STRALEY, J. A., *What About Mutual Funds?* 2d rev. ed. New York: Harper & Row, Publishers, 1967.

WATKINS, A. M., *Making Money in Mutual Funds*. New York: Hawthorn Books, Inc., 1973.

Real Estate Securities and Mortgages

SCOPE: This chapter discusses two types of investments related to real estate: *securities* (bonds, shares, and participations in partnerships) and *mortgages*. Home ownership and direct investment in and management of real estate for rental income and capital appreciation are not discussed, save as these relate to securities and mortgages.

The order of discussion is: (1) types of real estate-related investments, (2) characteristics of real estate-related investments, (3) investment in real estate shares and partnerships, (4) real estate investment trusts, (5) real estate mortgages—characteristics and (6) volume. (7) residential mortgages, (8) commercial and industrial mortgages, (9) farm mortgages, (10) the primary mortgage market, (11) the secondary mortgage market, (12) ownership of mortgage debt, (13) recent developments in mortgage financing, (14) mortgage yields, and (15) special sources of current information.

Types of Real Estate-related Investments

To most individual investors the growing equity in a home is the most important single investment. Many have found also that acquisition of real estate for rental income and capital appreciation has much appeal. Nevertheless, direct ownership and management of real estate by individuals is omitted from the discussion in this chapter because such commitments have characteristics that are too special and complex for a book that is devoted primarily to securities investments.

The two major types of real estate-related investments with which we are concerned are real estate securities and real estate mortgages, classified as follows:

    I. Real estate securities
        A. Shares in real estate companies
        B. Participations in syndicates and partnerships
        C. Debentures and shares in real estate investment trusts ("REITs")
            1. Equity trusts
            2. Short-term mortgage trusts
            3. Long-term mortgage trusts

4. "Hybrid" trusts
II. Real estate mortgages, classified
  A. By type of property pledged
    1. Farms
    2. One- to four-family residences
    3. Multifamily dwellings (apartments)
    4. Commercial and industrial property
  B. By level of lien
    1. First mortgages
    2. Junior mortgages (second, third)
  C. By type of lien
    1. Conventional
    2. Government-supported
      (a) FHA-insured
      (b) VA-guaranteed
  D. By use of property
    1. Owner-occupied: residential, commercial
    2. Rental: residential, commercial, industrial
  E. By type of borrower
    1. Consumers
    2. Corporations
    3. Small businesses
    4. Farmers
  F. By purpose
    1. New construction
    2. Acquisition of existing property
    3. General financing
  G. By type of lender
    1. Financial institutions
    2. Governmental agencies
    3. Individuals
III. Securities of Federally sponsored credit agencies
  A. Debentures
  B. Mortgage-backed securities
  C. Participation certificates
  D. Shares

The major investment characteristics of the first two main groups will be discussed. Some attention is given to the Federally sponsored credit agencies, but their security issues are discussed in Chapters 5 and 6.

Characteristics of Real Estate-related Investments

The whole field of real estate and real estate financing is very complex, and generalizations are dangerous. The following brief summary suggests the factors that deserve further investigation.

Advantages   For the investor in securities representing ownership of real estate and in mortgages for which real estate is the collateral, fixed property presents important advantages. Land is scarce and getting scarcer and, therefore, more valuable. Real estate has tangibility and permanence. It offers stability and dependability that is lacking in many other types of investment assets. Real estate credit is usually available, albeit often at high rates. Special income tax advantages are attractive. The after-tax returns from ownership are often higher than those from other equities, and the yields on obligations secured by real estate are often more generous than on most other fixed-income securities. The prospect of substantial increases in value also offers an enticing opportunity to hedge against inflation.

Risks and disadvantages   On the other side of the coin are a number of risks and defects. Real estate values change with regional and neighborhood changes, and with shifts in economic demand. Severe credit shortages and high yields occur, as in 1966, 1969, and 1973–1974. The combined impact of general economic recession and special real estate cycles produces mounting delinquencies and mortgage foreclosures. Soaring land and construction costs, especially in highly inflationary periods such as 1965–1975, affect demand, supply, and profits. Real estate and mortgages suffer from relatively poor liquidity and marketability, in part a result of large denominations and the unique characteristics of individual properties. The markets for real estate and for mortgages are still largely local, although some progress has been made towards a national mortgage market. The whole real estate scene, especially that of housing, sees changes and innovations in architecture and structure, and in the housing shift towards mobile homes, condominiums, and cluster developments that threaten the value and income of more traditional types of improvements. The investor finds it difficult to get wide geographical diversification of risk. And finally, there persists the need of special managerial skill to cope with the wide variety of operating and financial problems unique to real estate.

Delegation of management   In order to capitalize on the advantages and to reduce the risks suggested above, many investors have turned towards some of the types of investments described in this chapter to gain the advantages of professional management and large financial resources. The investors delegate to others the problems of title search and insurance, construction, appraisal, control of rental revenues and leases, control of operating costs, planning of capital expenditures, financing, minimizing income and property taxation, accounting and maximization of cash flow, legal decisions, interpretation of legislation, and dealing with a growing maze of governmental regulations.

The investor should delegate management and control with great care. The safety and the success of the investment can be considerably augmented by the competence and resources of the nominal owner or the responsible debtor. Unfortunately, the risks and losses may also be magnified by inept management and inadequate net worth.

Investment in Real Estate Shares and Partnerships

Three devices for sharing property ownership in small units have been developed: (1) real estate corporations, (2) partnerships or shares in syndicates, and (3) real estate equity trusts. The first are business concerns engaged in either land development or in the leasing or operation of commercial properties, including office buildings, retail buildings, and standardized warehouse and industrial facilities. Their shares, like those of any company, differ in quality and appeal. Investors should understand the specialized nature of the business and the special risks that attend the operation and management of real property. Shares of some of the larger companies are listed on the organized exchanges and enjoy adequate marketability.

Land development companies offer speculative participation in land and in residential communities and recreational projects. Profits depend not only on the cost of the original land and the sales of ultimate parcels, but also on the terms under which land parcels are sold, improvements made, and receivables or contracts collected. Most investors should consider only the largest and most successful concerns, and understand fully whether their returns will be derived from income or from eventual capital gains, that is, from the operation or from the sale of properties. They should have some knowledge of real estate accounting and taxation.

A number of oil, mineral, lumber, paper, railroad, and diversified companies own large acreages which offer possibilities of ultimately sharing in the secular rise in land values. In such cases the investor is not wholly dependent on land development.

In very recent years investors have been offered participation in (limited) real estate partnerships and in syndicates on a unit basis. Formerly these opportunities had been limited to closed groups. In some cases a minimum investment of $5,000 or $10,000 is required. Units are usually offered only to state residents who meet stated net worth requirements. As limited partners, investors can have no voice in management. The investment property may consist of one development, say, a large office or apartment building, or a variety of projects.

As noted previously, the advantages of real estate ownership without management responsibility can be very real. However, as also noted, the wise investor will check the reputation, financial standing, and experience of the general partner(s) with special care. He must also be careful not to be misled by promises of very high projected "rates of return," which may consist of a number of elements, perhaps overlapping, and which are dominated by depreciation payout and eventual capital appreciation. The character and quality of such rates of return are not comparable to the earnings yields on other forms of investments. Even under competent management, shares in land development, leasing, and operating companies tend to have unusual price volatility. The Standard & Poor's real estate stock index (1965 = 10) rose from 9 in 1966 to 52 in 1969, then declined to 6 in 1974, with large interim variations.

Limited partners and syndicates are especially dependent for their success on capital gains with their limited tax burden. Cash flow (especially from depreciation) is relied upon to pay off the debt and increase the equity. The eventual goal is sale of the property in a rising market at a substantial profit and the dissolution of the syndicate.

Real Estate Investment Trusts

An extremely important development in the period from 1960 to the present has been the organization, operation, investment decline, and possible revival of the real estate investment trust—a type of "indirect" investment in properties and mortgages that at its peak in 1974 had combined assets of over $21 billion owned by over 200 organizations.

General nature   Real estate investment trusts are formed under Federal legislation of 1960, and enable the individual investor to obtain an equity in a portfolio of real estate and real estate obligations through purchase of shares of beneficial interest. The problem of large real estate and mortgage denominations is thus avoided. Or the investor may buy debentures supported by the diversified assets.

The trust enjoys the same tax position as the open-end (mutual) fund, that is, if (among other requirements) at least 90% of net income is distributed in dividends, the trust itself avoids income taxation. The trust must have 100 or more shareholders, may not deal (trade) in real estate, and may not be more than 50% owned by five or fewer individuals.

Officers and directors may not engage directly in the management of the assets, which is farmed out to professionals at an annual fee that runs around 1% of assets. Many investment advisors are mortgage banking companies or affiliates of commercial banks and life insurance companies. These institutions have also been the chief promoters and sponsors.

Types of trusts   There are three types of trusts: (1) equity trusts, whose assets consist chiefly of operating property; (2) short-term loan trusts, engaging principally in development and construction loans with maturities ranging from three months to three years; and (3) long-term mortgage trusts. Distinctions among these types have blurred as a large number of "hybrid" trusts have broadened their portfolios away from these original specializations.

Early experience   The big growth of trusts in the late '60s and early '70s was aided by the tremendous demand for mortgage funds, by very aggressive promotion, and by the appeal to small investors of high yields and price appreciation. Through 1968 over 50 REITs were formed, and about $350 million of their securities were marketed. During the 1969–1970 tight money period, when mortgage funds from other institutional sources declined substantially, the trusts continued to grow and reached about $5 billion in assets by the end of 1970. The rapid growth continued through 1974, at the end of which assets reached over $21 billion, in spite of tight money conditions. They made types of loans and investments not sought after by the more traditional lenders and shared in the strong growth in new construction activity. Attractive yields and dramatic price appreciation were generally enjoyed by investors. In 1975 shares of about 50 trusts were listed on the New York Stock Exchange and of about 30 on the American Stock Exchange.

Later experience   In the latter part of 1973 and through 1974–1976, growth, earnings, dividends, and market prices of shares all declined disastrously. The trusts were hard hit by the general economic recession. Most REITs reported large losses. The short-term construction loan trusts were hit the hardest. They were caught between very high short-term interest costs on bank loans and commercial paper and lower rates on loans previously committed to builders. They were also belabored by the combination of overbuilding, inflation, very high interest rates, and overall economic decline that resulted in widespread delinquencies and defaults among real estate builders and developers. Several large trusts sought the protection of the bankruptcy courts. Others, especially those that were affiliates of commercial banks, avoided bankruptcy through assistance from their creditors. By the end of 1974 over 50% of total invested assets before loss reserves were in a nonearning status. Dividends dried up. The whole situation was aggravated by the lack of reserves and retained earnings as a cushion against losses; all trusts had had to distribute at least 90% of net income in dividends, and many had paid out 100%. The market prices of trust shares, which had previously been well above and often several times book value, fell beneath a factor of 1.0. The high leverage that characterized the financing of the trusts contributed to the decline in average net return on assets from 4 or 5% to under 1%. These influences, coupled with a sharp drop in stock prices in general, drove market prices of trust shares to appallingly low levels. (See below.)

Sources and uses of funds   The data for 1968–1976 in Tables 12-1 and 12-2 reveal the growth, decline, and fall of the REITs. The sources of funds show the dependence on short-term credit (especially by bank-sponsored trusts) and the generally high leverage employed. The uses show the allocation of most of the funds to vulnerable assets, including commercial mortgages and real estate. The 1976 figure for increase in real estate reflects foreclosures and repossessions of property.

Table 12-2 shows the distribution of combined REIT assets, in amounts and percentages, at the end of selected years.

The combined figures disguise the specialization in assets by the various types of trusts. But they show the rapid growth of the industry (to over $21 billion of assets in 1974) and the subsequent difficulties as indicated by the decline in home mortgages, the large increase in real estate held (mainly from foreclosure of multifamily and commercial mortgages), and the negative net worth.

Price and yield record   Yields on REIT shares were in the 7 to 8% range in the early 1970s. As the prices of shares fell in 1973, and dividends were continued, yields as high as 15% were available. Then, as earnings and

TABLE 12-1 Annual Sources and Uses of Funds, Real Estate Investment Trusts, 1970–1976 (in billions of dollars)

	1970	1971	1972	1973	1974	1976
Uses						
Home mortgages	$0.4	$0.2	$0.4	$0.7	$-0.2	$-0.3
Multifamily mortgages[a]	0.8	0.9	2.0	2.4	0.2	-1.6
Commercial mortgages[a]	0.7	1.2	1.7	2.5	0.2	-1.5
Real estate	0.3	0.4	1.1	0.7	1.1	1.7
Cash and other assets	0.0	0.2	1.0	0.2	-0.2	0.3
Total	$2.2	$2.9	$6.2	$6.5	$ 1.1	$-1.4
Sources						
Commercial paper	$ —	$0.8	$2.4	$0.7	$-3.3	$-0.2
Bank loans	$0.1	0.6	1.3	4.0	4.4	-1.0
Bonds	0.5	0.4	0.4	0.6	0.2	-0.1
Mortgages on properties owned	0.1	0.1	0.5	0.3	0.2	0.3
Other liabilities	0.1	0.1	0.1	—	—	—
Equity issues	1.5	1.0	1.5	1.0	-0.3	-0.3
Total	$2.2	$2.9	$6.2	$6.5	$ 1.1	$-1.4

[a]Including construction loans.
Some columns do not add to totals due to rounding.
Source: Federal Reserve Bulletin (flow of funds).

TABLE 12-2 Combined Assets of REITs, 1968–1976 (at book value, in billions of dollars)

	1968		1970		1973		1976	
	Amt.	Per Cent	Amt.	Per Cent	Amt.	Per Cent	Amt.	Per Cent
Home mortgages	—	—	$0.7	15%	$ 4.1	20%	$ 1.0	6.0%
Multifamily mortgages[a]	$0.1	14%	1.0	21	3.7	18	3.2	19.3
Commercial mortgages[a]	0.1	14	1.5	32	7.3	36	5.5	33.1
Real estate	0.4	57	0.9	19	3.2	16	8.9	53.6
Other assets	0.1	14	0.6	13	1.9	10	-2.0	-12.0
	$0.7	100%	$4.7	100%	$20.2	100%	$16.6	100 %

[a]Including construction loans.
Some columns do not add to totals due to rounding.
Sources: Federal Reserve Bulletin (flow of funds) ; National Association of Real Estate Investment Trusts, *REIT Fact Book* (annual).

dividends dried up, yields became nil or a very low rate on stock market values, depressed though these were.

REIT shares were among the worst stock performers in 1973–1975. Their price index fell to less than one-sixth of its level at the beginning of 1973. Shares of some trusts rallied in 1976 as their portfolio losses were written off and their earnings increased.

Analysis of trust shares There are still some real estate trusts that deserve attention, although they lack appeal to the conservative investor. Some came through the industry's collapse, scarred but solvent. General economic recovery, improvement in housing starts, the real estate cycle in general, and lower interest rates, gave some trusts new life and hope in 1976. The investor interested in this type of commitment would do well to investigate these factors:

- *Sponsorship and banking connections.* Trusts affiliated with strong bank and insurance companies had set up large reserves for losses. Although these suffered drastic losses, some net worth remained. The same is true of those sponsored by the strongest mortgage banking companies.
- *Per cent of "problem investments" to total.* This ranged from 20 to 40% in 1976. But if weak assets do not increase, some earnings should be available to shareholders.
- *The debt-to-equity ratio.* In the early 1970s, this factor often reached 3 or 4 to 1. As of the time of writing, a ratio of 1 1/2 or 2 to 1 appears reasonable, although the risks of leverage must still be recognized.
- *Equity per share.* Prior to 1973, share prices reached high levels in relation to their book value, reflecting the high multiples that investors applied to earnings. Ratios of 1 1/2 to 2 times book value were common. In the great deflation, prices dropped to a fraction of book value. At the time of writing only when complete reliance can be had in reported asset figures, after loss reserves, would the investor pay book value for REIT shares. The price is, of course, based mainly on prospective earnings and dividends.
- *Earnings (and dividends) per share.* The stronger trusts now produce earnings and dividends, but substantial increases must be expected before this dividend income can be assured.
- *Price-earnings ratios.* Just as the ratios of price to earnings of most common stocks were sharply deflated in the great market decline of 1973–1974, so the shares of REITs felt the general readjustment. Their experience also reflected the peculiar weaknesses of the industry. The investor considering an REIT stock would do well not to pay a higher price in relation to projected earnings than for stocks in general.

Real Estate Mortgages—General Characteristics

Money directly invested in real estate is represented by *deeds*, or instruments that evidence the ownership of real property and by which title is transferred. Money indirectly invested is represented by *mortgages* or other evidences of debt such as real estate bonds. Without going into legal technicalities, a mortgage (or "deed of trust") may be defined as an instrument under which real property is pledged as security for a loan. The owner of the property, the mortgagor, is borrowing money from a lender, the mortgagee, under a contract whereby the property is pledged as security for payment on interest and principal. Title and possession remain with the mortgagor until default occurs, in which event the property is sold through foreclosure proceedings for the satisfaction of the debt.

The mortgage recites the terms of the loan and a description of the property pledged. Covenants are customarily inserted under which the mortgagor promises to pay taxes and assessments and to keep the property fully insured and in good condition. An "acceleration of maturity" clause makes the principal of the loan due immediately in the event of default in payment of interest or any failure with respect to the covenants. Mortgages are customarily recorded in the public records of the community to protect mortgagees against any claims of third parties against the property.

A *first mortgage* has a prior claim upon the pledged property, subject to operating expenses and taxes. First mortgages on properties in the course of construction are also subject to liens for unpaid materials and services. Subsequent mortgages have claims subordinate to the first mortgage claim.

A *second mortgage* is one that has a claim upon the pledged property after that of the first mortgage. As first mortgages are usually placed for the largest amount that conservative investors are willing to lend on the property, the second mortgage (discussed below) is often too hazardous for safe investment.

An *amortized mortgage* is one that is repayable in regular installments for the duration of the loan; monthly payments include principal, interest, and usually taxes and insurance.

A *leasehold mortgage* is secured by a long-term lease of real property and, therefore, is subordinate to the rental contract between the leasor and the owner. Such a mortgage is often placed upon property erected on leased land and, consequently, is in effect a first mortgage on the building and on the lease of the land. Even under this interpretation, the instrument has a junior claim upon the earnings of the property subject to the ground rent.

Most modern mortgages are of the amortized type. Under the amortized loan the borrower agrees to make regular payments on principal as well as interest, and his equity in the property grows steadily as payments are made. The amount of the regular payment depends on the size of the loan, the interest rate, and the term of the loan. To repay $20,000 at 9% in 15 years requires monthly payments of $202.85. A 30-year maturity at the same interest rate requires $160.92. These figures are, of course, exclusive of taxes and insurance. Because of the long-term character of real estate credit, the value of the property pledged is stressed more than the personal credit of the borrower, although this is by no means neglected. The income of the borrower is, however, of paramount importance under the GI bill. The tendency toward high loans in relation to value (as high as 90%) and long maturities (up to 35 or even 40 years) has forced special attention on the property and on accurate appraisal of its value.

Volume of Mortgage Debt

Table 12-3 shows the total mortgage debt outstanding at the end of selected years 1955–1976, classified by major types of borrowers. This period of growth reflects a number of factors: general economic expansion, volume of construction, flow of available funds, rising costs, and propensity to borrow.

At the end of 1976, the volume of outstanding mortgage loans secured by one- to four-family nonfarm homes was $559 billion. The 1945 figure was $19 billion. The enormous rise in this type of debt since the end of World

TABLE 12-3 Mortgage Debt Outstanding at Year-End, 1955–1976 (in billions of dollars)

	1955	1960	1965	1970	1976
Farm	$ 9.1	$ 12.8	$ 21.2	$ 31.2	$ 57.1
Residential					
One- to four-family	88.2	141.3	212.9	280.2	556.4
Multifamily	14.3	20.3	37.2	58.0	104.3
	$102.5	$161.6	$250.1	$338.2	$660.7
Commercial	18.3	32.4	54.5	82.3	171.2
	$129.9	$206.8	$325.8	$451.7	$889.0

Sources: 1955: S. B. Klaman, *The Volume of Mortgage Debt in the Postwar Decade* (New York: National Bureau of Economic Research, Inc., 1958); 1960–1976: *Federal Reserve Bulletin;* Federal Home Loan Bank Board *Journal.*

War II is attributable to the great development of housing that was financed substantially by savings institutions of all kinds on an amortized basis. Consumer incomes, population, prices, and construction costs all rose during the postwar period. Funds flowing into mortgages likewise have risen steadily, save for the years 1956–1957, 1966–1967, 1969–1970, and 1974–1975, periods of "tight money." The result has been a tremendous increase in home mortgage financing. The average annual increase in one- to four-family mortgage debt was $12.5 billion in 1955–1965, and $34 billion in 1965–1976. The figures for multifamily and commercial mortgage debt were $6 billion and $11 billion, respectively, for these two periods. The latter types now constitute about 31% of total mortgages outstanding. Institutional lenders provided the bulk of this financing, and the balance was lent by individuals and others (trust funds, endowments, and mortgage companies); much of this latter volume found its way later into the hands of insurance companies, banks, and savings and loan associations. The importance of institutional lending is indicated in the ownership of mortgage debt in Tables 12-4 and 12-5.

Individuals originate (that is, acquire new mortgages in the "primary market") a substantial proportion of the home mortgage debt. The practice of individual mortgage lending occurs largely in smaller communities, many of which lack immediate institutional facilities. However, a substantial portion of new mortgages acquired by individuals has later found its way into institutional portfolios. And virtually all loans originated by mortgage companies are transferred to institutional lenders. (See Table 12-4).

The three basic types of home (one- to four-family) mortgage loans are: (1) those insured by the Federal Housing Administration, (2) those guaranteed by the Veterans' Administration, and (3) conventional loans.

Residential Mortgages

FHA-insured mortgages FHA loans are insured under the terms of Title II of the National Housing Act of 1934 as amended. Only first mortgage amortized loans on approved properties are insurable. In early 1977 the maximum interest rate on mortgages secured by small family units was 8%, with the mortgagor paying an additional 1/2% to the FHA mutual insurance fund as an insurance premium. On such mortgages, of which there are several classes, the maximum maturities ranged as high as 35 years, with maximum loan-value ratios of 97% of the first $25,000 of value and 95% of total value to a maximum loan of $42,000 on a $44,210 home. Other interest rates, maturities, and loan-value ratios are found in the case of multifamily units. Monthly payments to the lender to cover taxes and insurance charges are added to the regular installments of interest and principal. Equities in the properties, subject to the loans, are transferable.

The original fixed interest rate on FHA loans was 4 1/4%. Successive changes, up and down, have followed variations in general long-term interest rates. FHA's have sold higher (at premiums), but usually lower (at discounts) from face value, and so at lower and usually higher yields than the contractual rate. Changes in the nominal rate (presently made by the Department of Housing and Urban Development) have been made to encourage home financing and to compete with other interest rates. The nominal rate rose to a peak of 9 1/2% in August 1974 near the peak of the "credit crunch," then declined to 8% in 1976 after general interest rates had declined. At that time FHAs sold at substantial discounts so as to yield over 9% (not including the 1/2% insurance charge). The main market is still largely institutional, although individuals have been permitted to buy these loans since 1961. An impetus to indirect ownership by individuals was given by the creation of Government National Mortgage Association mortgage-backed securities in 1970. (See p. 266.)

The influence of FHA insurance in the mortgage field has been reflected in greater standardization of provisions, and has, along with other factors mentioned previously, led to the virtual disappearance of the old straight five-year loan in favor of the long-term amortized type and to loans of high percentages of appraised values. After a notable record for nearly 40 years, the FHA loan has deteriorated substantially in quality and acceptance, in part because of sloppy Federal controls, inadequate appraisals, and the abandonment of strictly economic factors in lending requirements, and in part because of the modification of "social" programs such as insurance of low-income housing and subsidized low-cost housing. The results are seen in the high yields on FHA-insured mortgages. (See Table 12-6.) Under the Housing and Urban Development Act of 1966, the Assistant Secretary of the Federal Department of Housing and Urban Development serves as Federal Housing Commissioner and directs the FHA mortgage insurance programs.

VA-guaranteed loans   The Serviceman's Readjustment Act of 1944, as amended, provides for the guarantee by the Veterans Administration of loans made to qualified veterans by lending institutions for the purposes of home, farm, or business financing. The maximum maturity of these loans is set by the amended law at 30 years for guaranteed home or business real estate loans and 40 years for farm real estate loans. The nominal interest rate was set at 8% (1977).

The law provides a maximum guarantee of $17,500 or 60% of the loan, whichever is less, and lenders may make loans for 100% of the purchase price of the property. Borrowers avoid closing costs in cash since these must be carried by the seller.

The interest rate of 8% represents a substantial increase over the original 4% rate. Like the nominal rate on FHA-insured mortgages, that of VA loans has been adjusted through the years to changes in long-term interest rates so as to make them competitive. It was as high as 9 1/2% in August 1974. VA loans have not been attractive to individual investors, and many institutional investors have preferred the FHA type. The volume of these loans has been in relative decline through the years.

Some of the recommendations of the President's Commission on Financial Structure and Regulation (Hunt Commission), filed in December 1971, bear specifically on the provisions of and market for FHA and VA mortgages, which would make these liens much more attractive to investors. In addition to the broadening of the lending powers of institutions (Chapter 5), the major items are

1. Elimination of ceiling interest rates on Federally sponsored mortgages—a change that has long been recommended by institutions and mortgage bankers.

2. Interest rates on these mortgages to vary with the price level, with limits on the degree of change within stated periods. "Variable mortgages" are now used in interest rates, but present many problems, especially the uncertain position of creditors with respect to income. (See p. 267.)

3. Equalization of income tax provisions for competing financial institutions.

4. Other provisions for strengthening the mortgage credit system include authority of institutions to lend in any part of the country and to make equity investments in real estate developments.

The "Study of Financial Institutions and the Economy" (FINE) was begun in 1973 and has involved extensive hearings on proposed legislation (FIA acts) which have not yet been acted upon by Congress. The study endorsed most of the recommendations of the Hunt Commission and added two highly controversial recommendations with respect to mortgages:

1. Tax all depository institutions uniformly, but provide for a Federal income tax credit for the interest income received from mortgages on housing for low- and moderate-income owners and renters. Authorize direct Federal Home Loan Bank Board loans to any depository institution for use in financing new or existing low- and moderate-income housing at rates to reflect the rates charged by the FHLBB. Permit these rates to be Federally subsidized at below-market costs in times of need. Authorize a new system of low- and moderate-income mortgage reserve credits to offset an equal amount of deposit reserves up to a fixed percentage.

2. Eliminate the supervisory and regulatory responsibilities of the Federal Home Loan Bank Board, three Federal banking agencies, and the National Credit Union Administration. Create a new Federal Depository Institutions Commission to take over these functions. Recharter the Federal Home Loan Bank System to administer the Federal Home Loan Mortgage Corporation and a proposed housing credit incentive program.

Conventional home mortgage loans   The noninsured and nonguaranteed amortized loan has consistently been more important than the two other types of home loans, amounting to 83% of the total in 1976. While generalization is difficult, it is probably correct to say that their maturities have seldom exceeded 25 years, with the most typical term being 15 to 20 years, depending on the property and the borrower's credit standing. Interest rates now (1977) range between 8 3/4 and 9%, depending on the property, the credit of the borrower, the geographical location, and competitive conditions. The loan-market value ratio has run as high as 80% during periods of noninflated real estate prices (95% on privately insured loans), but has tended to be lower—from 60 to 70%—during periods when market values were greatly in excess of appraised values. The various lending institutions have different policies in respect to maturities and loan ratios, and, of course, the terms of a specific loan are determined by the circumstances of the case and the legal restrictions imposed by the laws under which the institution operates. Federally chartered savings and loan associations follow the pattern set by the Federal Home Loan Bank Board, and the lending policies of national commercial banks are governed by the rules of the Comptroller of the Currency.

Until 1972 the conventional loan market was almost entirely local. In that year the Federal National Mortgage Association was authorized to make a secondary market through its new "free market" system. The Federal Home Loan Mortgage Corporation had been doing so since 1970. (See p. 92.)

Since 1966 yields on conventional loans have generally been lower than on Federally supported loans, because of the growing disenchantment of institutional investors for the latter type. (See Table 12-6.) The advent of private insurance of conventional loans in 1970 has also contributed to their investment superiority. Conventional loans of 95% of value are now frequently insured by private carriers.

Multifamily (apartment) loans   Loans secured by multifamily dwellings comprised (1976) about 15% of residential mortgages outstanding, compared with 14% in 1955. The very substantial increase in dollar amount since 1945 reflects the rise in land values, the shift back to apartment living, and relaxed regulations that permit greater institutional investment in this type of loan. Apartment loans are much in demand by savings banks and life insurance companies, and to a lesser extent by savings and loan associations. Their higher yields also give them appeal to many individual investors. In 1976–1977, typical yields ranged from 9 to 9 1/2%, and interest payments were often accompanied by a "sweetener" in the form of a percentage of gross or net income, or an equity interest in the enterprise.

Second mortgages   Second mortgages were a feature of the 1920s and 1930s, but fell into disrepute as a result of the losses that foreclosures brought to their holders in the Great Depression. After World War II the demand for second mortgage money again began to show itself on the real estate scene. Young families and small businessmen lacked the substantial down payments required behind conventional first mortgage loans. As of 1960, $3.8 billion of junior mortgages were outstanding, representing 2.4% of residential debt.[1] This figure was probably in excess of $15 billion in 1977. Owners include mortgage companies, individual investors, sellers of homes, and certain institutions. Banks and savings and loan associations are now permitted to hold them. Net yields of 12 to 14% (resulting from the discounting of the paper) are not uncommon. The modern second mortgage calls for rapid amortization of principal over a short period, often as low as five years. Thus, as the loan is retired (along with reduction of the first mortgage), second mortgages grow in strength in relation to the value of the property. Nevertheless, the owner of a second mortgage, such as a seller who has had to take a junior mortgage in order to make a sale, is always in a vulnerable position. And if he wants cash, he must sell the junior lien at a very substantial discount that may run 8 to 15%. Although rising property values, rapid repayment of junior liens, and higher personal incomes may prevent another major wave of defaults of second mortgages, the investor intrigued by the high yields should understand the nature of the junior lien and all of the factors that can make for its individual strength or weakness.[2]

Commercial and Industrial Mortgages

Loans secured by commercial property such as stores and office buildings represent a highly specialized business involving a knowledge of both real estate and economic factors, and so are made in the main by commercial banks and by life insurance companies and their correspondents. There is no arrangement for government insurance or guarantee.

Commercial mortgages for substantial amounts are almost always amortized and have maturities as long as 30 years. Many of these mortgages belong in the category of "term loans," as indicated in the section on bank investments. (See Chapter 21.) Amortized loans on hotels, apartments, and office buildings have largely replaced the real estate mortgage bond issues so common in the 1920s.

When industrial properties are financed by individual mortgages (as distinguished from corporate mortgage bonds), again the institution, especially the life insurance company, is the chief source of funds. (See Table 12-5.) Such mortgages are too large and the credit problems too specialized for the individual investor. These loans are frequently amortized in as short a period as 10 years, to reflect the special risks attendant to business property. Institutional mortgage lending for industrial purposes is increasingly encroaching on the more traditional method of property financing through corporate bonds.

In recent years, especially during periods of very high interest rates (1968–1976), yields on mortgages secured by income property bumped into state

[1]U.S. Department of Commerce, Bureau of the Census, *Census of Housing* (Washington, D.C.: U.S. Government Printing Office, 1960), Volume V, "Residential Finance," Part 2, page *xxiii.*

[2]A modern version of the second mortgage is found in the so-called "wrap-around" loan under which the buyer of a property on which there is already a modest first mortgage gives the seller a new wrap-around lien for a much larger sum. The seller continues his payments to the holder of the first mortgage.

usury ceilings (often 10%). For this reason, and because they could demand almost any terms during the "credit crunches," life insurance companies have required special "sweeteners" such as equity participation, rent sharing, and other features, in multifamily, industrial, and commercial mortgages.

Farm Mortgages

Farm debt, which totalled $4.8 billion at the end of 1945, rose to $57 billion at the end of 1976. The total includes a wide range of types and maturities.

The ownership of farm mortgage debt is shown in Table 12-5. Life insurance companies have always been important investors, holding 13% of the total at the end of 1976. Commercial banks have always had an important share. The 12 Federal Land Banks, established in 1916 (p. 89), and the Federal Farm Mortgage Corporation, also an important investor, are part of the comprehensive Farm Credit Administration.

The Farmers Home Administration was established in 1946 as an agency of the U.S. Department of Agriculture. It makes operating loans of from one to five years in maturity and farm-ownership loans of as long as 40 years. It insures mortgage loans made by private lenders, and so is in a sense an organization similar to the FHA. It serves as an agency for applicants who are unable to obtain credit from other sources.

Individuals continue to play an important role in farm mortgage lending despite the rapid growth of Federal aid. The inherent qualities of farm mortgages as an investment appeal to many local capitalists and former landowners. Private mortgage companies serve as middlemen between investors and farmers requiring long-term credit.

Such investments are recommended only to investors capable of keeping close watch on farm commodity prices, farm values, and the earning power of individual situations. The replacement of the old five-year loan by the amortized type has introduced many desirable features, but the inherent risks of instability of farm income still persist, along with the disadvantages of poor marketability, inadequate diversification, and others discussed earlier.

The Primary Mortgage Market

Investment in mortgages is accomplished either by (1) original lending by institutions and individuals directly or through intermediaries such as mortgage bankers, or by (2) purchase of outstanding mortgage loans in the secondary market. The former process is dealt with in this section.

Institutional sources of mortgage credit As indicated previously, mortgage loans on residential property are largely institutional, although the holdings of individuals are substantial. Table 12-4 shows the distribution, by type of mortgages, of outstanding mortgage loans on one- to four-family nonfarm homes, as of the end of 1955, 1965, and 1976.

The savings and loan associations hold the largest amount of urban home

TABLE 12-4 Ownership of Nonfarm Home Mortgage Debt—
One- to Four-Family (in billions of dollars)

Held by	1955 Amount	1955 Per Cent	1965 Amount	1965 Per Cent	1976 Amount	1976 Per Cent
S&L Associations	$30.0	34%	$94.2	44%	$260.9	47%
Commercial banks	15.0	17	30.4	14	86.2	16
Mutual savings banks	11.1	12	30.1	14	53.2	10
Life insurance companies	17.7	20	30.0	14	16.1	3
Federal agencies	0.1	—	2.5	1	35.5	6
Mortgage pools & trusts	—	—	0.1	—	42.1	7
Individuals and others	14.3	17	25.6	12	62.4	11
	$88.2	100%	$212.9	100%	$556.4	100%

Some columns do not add to totals because of rounding.

Sources: United States League of Savings Associations, *Savings and Loan Fact Book; Federal Reserve Bulletin* (flow of funds).

mortgages (47% at the end of 1976), and their lead has been steadily increasing. As indicated in Chapter 5, home mortgage financing is still their chief function, although in recent years income property loans have risen to almost 20% of their total mortgage portfolios. (See Table 12-5.) Their investment policies and legal restrictions on lending will be discussed in Chapter 21. We should note here that the bulk of the home mortgages held by these associations are conventional liens. There are several reasons for this: (1) FHA and VA loans, with their ceilings on nominal interest, their many regulations, and their decline in quality (FHAs) have fallen into disfavor; (2) being local institutions in touch with their own borrowers, the associations feel safe in relying on their own portfolio rather than on insurance or a guarantee; (3) they are permitted to lend a higher percentage of value on a conventional loan than other financial institutions are and, hence, they find these relatively more attractive.

Commercial bank investments and the restrictions thereon will be discussed in Chapter 21. Although the volume of home mortgage lending by these institutions is very substantial, banks also make other types of real estate loans, such as those secured by commercial and industrial properties. (See Table 12-5.) However, FHA and VA loans were emphasized; by 1955 such loans comprised 50% of the home mortgage holdings of commercial banks. At that time commercial banks were generally limited by law to a loan ratio of 60 to 66 2/3% and to a maturity of 10 years on conventional home loans; hence, the higher loan ratios and longer maturities of the nonconventional loans had great appeal. The insurance or guarantee features were particularly attractive to a banking institution. However, the relative appeal of nonconventional mortgages has fluctuated with changes in market yields on other investments and with changes in bank regulations. The current yields on Federally underwritten mortgages were still (1977) not competitively attractive. Also, banks may now lend to 80% of appraised value on conventionals, with a limit of maturity to 20 years. Banks are the most important source of interim construction financing.

Life insurance companies have traditionally been large investors in urban mortgages, which bear higher yields than bonds and are appropriate for the investment of insurance reserves. This interest has been encouraged by the "legalizing" of approved real estate mortgages in all states. Mortgages comprise 28% of the assets of the life insurance industry (down from 40% in the early 1960s), amounting to $91.6 billion at the end of 1976—an all-time high. Housing, including single- and multiple-family units, accounts for nearly 33% of all mortgages owned. In the residential field, the life insurance companies have been particularly interested in FHA and VA loans. These permit higher loan ratios than even the conventional 75 to 80% legal limit in some states and are particularly adaptable to the use of the mortgage correspondent system. However, their fixed contractual interest rates are not always attractive compared with high-grade corporate bonds and conventional mortgages. In recent years, however, the trend has been away from house mortgage lending to multifamily and nonresidential loans. (See Chapter 22.) The latter comprised over 53% of mortgages held at the end of 1976.

Although life companies make mortgage loans directly through their branch offices, the bulk are originated and serviced by their mortgage correspondents—local mortgage banking companies which arrange the original transaction and then place the loan with the insurance company, thereafter collecting a service fee as agent of the company.

Sound home mortgages are almost ideal investments for mutual savings banks. At the end of 1976, such liens (including multifamily), totalling $67 billion, comprised about 61% of their combined assets. The great postwar demand for housing credit, the development of Federally underwritten liens, the liberalization of regulations (which permit a loan-value ratio as high as 75 to 80% on conventionals), and the increase in out-of-state lending through mortgage correspondents have all contributed to the banks' emphasis on residential loans. Mutual savings banks are the largest single source of FHA and VA financing. Their mortgage investment policies are discussed in Chapter 21.

The data in Table 12-5 show the relative importance of the various financial institutions as owners of farm, commercial, and industrial mortgages. Most of this volume was acquired in the primary market, although institutions do seek mortgage investments in the open market for outstanding paper (mostly residential) when their own organizations and their mortgage bank correspondents do not fulfill their mortgage investment requirements.

Federally sponsored and other credit agencies in the primary market   Original mortgage loans are made by several Federally sponsored and Federally owned credit agencies, of which four deserve special mention. As we have seen, the Federal Land Banks system raises funds by the sale of debentures and acquires mortgages, through 12 regional Banks, from farmers and ranchers. In 1976, 18.5 billion of such credit was outstanding. The Federal Home Loan Banks provide mortgage credit indirectly by advancing funds to members (mainly savings and loan associations). The Farmers Home Administration makes direct loans to farmers for land and housing. The Government National Mortgage Association among other and more important functions, buys mortgages for which it is committed by the Secretary for Housing and Urban Development. Its main activities, however, are in the secondary market and, more recently, in the guarantee of specific blocks of FHA, VA, and Farmers Home Administration mortgages and their sale through "pass-through" securities. (See p. 266.) It also sells participations in pools of its own mortgage portfolio. At the end of 1976 over $42 billion of mortgages supported such pools and participations, including mainly those offered by GNMA and Farmers Home Administration.

Home mortgages as investments for individuals   A substantial percentage of home mortgages are originated by individuals, who also buy them in the secondary market. But there are several disadvantages of home mortgages as investments for individuals, which may be summarized as:

- *Large denomination.* Individual mortgages represent substantial sums that make diversification impossible except for the institution or the investor of considerable means.

- *Inadequate marketability.* The individual investor has access to the Federal National Mortgage Association only for the resale of FHA-insured or VA-guaranteed mortgages. He is mainly dependent on institutional buyers and local mortgage brokers and mortgage companies. If he wishes to sell a mortgage, he usually does so on a negotiated basis. In recent years "mortgage exchanges" have been established in a few large cities, where mortgages are "traded" at prices reflecting the terms and risk of individual loans. However, the volume of such trading is relatively small, and consists largely of second liens. The secondary market for mortgages is discussed further later in the chapter.

- *Reinvestment.* The amortized mortgage now almost universally used requires much record-keeping and the reinvestment of the small regular payments on principal.

- *Unusual care and management.* Investment in mortgages is a specialized business requiring a knowledge of land values, community and neighborhood changes, and construction standards. Numerous problems, such as checking the title, currency of tax payments, insurance, and proper maintenance and repairs are involved.

- *Foreclosure process.* Although, in case of default, the mortgagor is permitted to buy in the pledged property at the foreclosure sale, the foreclosure process involves considerable time and expense. In addition, many states provide for a period *after* foreclosure, in some cases as long as 18 months, during which the mortgagor may redeem his pledge.

These disadvantages suggest why institutions equipped with staff, technical knowledge, and large funds, have traditionally dominated the mortgage field.[3] However, certain very real advantages may be enjoyed.:

[3]These disadvantages have been substantially reduced to large investors by the availability of mortgage-backed securities issued under the guarantee of the Government National Mortgage Association, a Federal agency described in this chapter and in Chapter 6. But the minimum denomination of $25,000 makes these securities unattractive to the small investor.

• *Yield.* The yield on sound mortgages is at times considerably in excess of that available on high-grade and even good-grade bonds. (See Chapter 8.) And where less-sound and second mortgages are bought at substantial discounts, there is the possibility of substantial appreciation as the debt is reduced or as the value of the security increases.

• *Safety.* Where the margin of safety is adequate, the long-term amortized mortgage offers real safety features to the lender. The growing equity of the homeowner provides a strong incentive against default. And the longer-term and amortized payments prevent the whole debt from falling due at the wrong time for the borrower and during periods of depressed real estate values.

• *Secured Value.* The property securing sound residential mortgages offers the stability, durability, and ready identification that characterize investment in real estate itself.

Other originators of mortgage loans   Among the other primary sources of mortgage money are, to a modest extent, trustees, private pension funds, state and local government retirement funds, and state and local credit agencies. Such owners are steadily increasing the dollar amount of mortgages held, but their relative importance has declined substantially in the last 35 years. Far more important during this period have been the real estate investment trusts, which were described earlier in this chapter. And still more important as originators of mortgages are the mortgage banking firms (mortgage companies) who place their loans on a "take out" basis with institutional buyers, mainly mutual savings banks and life insurance companies. This type of organization is significant enough to deserve separate discussion.

Mortgage companies   Mortgage companies (sometimes called mortgage bankers) play an increasingly important role in the primary market for mortgages. These firms seek out and originate loans, secure interim bank financing, and resell the loans to financial institutions, typically in blocks of $1 million or more. Thereafter they service the loans at a typical fee of $1/2\%$ per year, collecting and remitting the monthly payments of interest plus principal, and seeing that the tax and insurance payments are kept current. Over 750 such companies are in operation, with assets of $500 million. They service approximately $135 billion of mortgages, or 20% of the national total, with emphasis on one- to four-family residential liens, both conventional and underwritten. In 1975, almost one quarter of their servicing volume was for life insurance companies, who used their services for 37% of their mortgages, 13% for mutual savings banks (for 22% of their holdings), 14% for savings and loan associations (for 6% of their mortgages), and 20% for FNMA and GNMA (for 42% of their mortgages).[4]

Mortgage companies make an important contribution to a national mortgage market by originating and servicing loans in capital-starved areas

---

[4]Mortgage Bankers Association of America, *Mortgage Banking*, 1975. Washington D.C.: The Association, Research Committee Trends Reports 18 and 19, 1976.

such as the South and the Middle West, and transferring them to owners in capital-surplus areas such as the East and California.

The scope of activities, the ownership, and the organization of mortgage companies have been changing materially in recent years. Many have been acquired by bank holding companies. Mergers have greatly increased the size and reduced the number of firms operating on a national basis. Ancillary activities, such as the writing of property and title insurance, property management, and real estate sales, and the growing emphasis on special-purpose loans for financing industrial tracts, shopping centers, and other nonresidential properties, have greatly broadened their lending role. The growing practice of insurance companies in originating their own loans through regional offices, the increase in mortgage banking activities by commercial banks, and the gradual reduction of interregional flows of mortgage funds are competitive developments that are leading to fundamental changes in the mortgage banking function.

The Secondary Mortgage Market

In the secondary market, outstanding mortgages are transferred. Individual and institutional investors, mainly Federal agencies, use the secondary market to buy and sell mortgages—chiefly residential—either through their own contacts or through mortgage brokers, which are local concerns acting as middlemen at commissions of $1/4$ to $1/2\%$. Purchases are used to round out mortgage portfolios when new originations are not sufficient.

Commercial banks "warehouse" construction loans for later resale. Savings banks make only minor use of purchased mortgages. Insurance companies prefer to acquire permanent loans from others and seldom resell them. Savings and loan associations originate virtually all of their mortgage holdings. The main contributors to the secondary market have been individuals, Federally sponsored credit agencies, and real estate investment trusts.

Federally sponsored agencies in the secondary market The Federal Home Loan Bank System (described in Chapters 5 and 6) functions through 11 regional banks and is supervised by the Home Loan Bank Board. It provides rediscounting facilities to savings and loan members.

The Federal National Mortgage Association ("Fannie Mae") was established in 1938 to provide a secondary market for institutional holders of FHA-insured and VA-guaranteed mortgages. The chairman of its Board is the Secretary of Housing and Urban Development. "Fannie Mae" obtained the initial funds for mortgage purchases by borrowing from the U.S. Treasury.

As indicated in Chapter 6, the Federal National Mortgage Association is now publicly owned, with its shares traded on the New York Stock Exchange. Its major activity is providing a secondary market for FHA and VA mortgages. It does not originate mortgages, and those it acquires are serviced by the originators—banks, mortgage companies, and other institutions—at an annual servicing fee of $3/8\%$. It acquires its assets by offering forward commitments of announced amounts to purchase eligible mortgages, with the prices (and yields) determined by auction bidding. Net annual purchases have been large in recent years.

Under the Emergency Home Finance Act of 1970, "Fannie Mae" was authorized to serve as a secondary market for conventional residential mortgages, with prices and yields established at periodic auction. The first four-month commitments were made in February 1972.

An additional secondary market for conventional mortgages is provided by the Federal Home Loan Mortgage Corporation ("Freddie Mac"). This agency acquires multifamily as well as one- to four-family loans, and makes commitments for up to two years on the former. A controversial feature was that at the outset, "Freddie Mac" subjected commercial banks to a 1/2% discount below prices paid to savings and loan associations. This was because the latter have invested over $100 million in the new agency. It has not yet (1977) developed a portfolio of any significance.

As noted in Chapter 6, the Government National Mortgage Association ("Ginny Mae") was created in 1968 to take over Fannie Mae's special assistance and management and liquidation functions.[5] Its new activity is to guarantee the timely payment of principal and interest on securities backed by pools of FHA and VA mortgages. The originators of these mortgages—mainly mortgage companies—who issue the securities must meet certain minimum net worth requirements. Three types of securities may be issued against the pooled loans: (1) bond-type securities with fixed interest and maturities, but without interim amortization of principal; (2) "straight pass-through" securities under which GNMA guarantees that the holder will receive timely payment of the amortized principal and of interest *as collected*; and (3) "modified pass-through" securities, under which GNMA guarantees the timely payment of a specific portion of principal installments and a fixed rate of interest, *whether collected or not*. The GNMA guarantee is backed by the full faith and credit of the Federal government.

The chief buyers of mortgage-backed securities have been savings and loan associations, savings banks, pension funds, and insurance companies. It is expected that individual investors of means will become large holders, because of the safety and marketability of the issues. But "small" investors will be discouraged by the minimum denomination of $25,000 (the minimum size of a securities offering is $2 million).

Bond-type and modified pass-through securities have been the chief types of mortgage-backed securities issued thus far. In early 1977 over $35 billion were outstanding. GNMA-guaranteed mortgage-backed securities offer a number of advantages to investors: good yield (8% in early July 1977), highest quality, regular cash flow (in the case of the pass-through variety), and good marketability. They open up possibilities of a large flow of capital into mortgages from institutional and individual investors who were previously unable or unwilling to acquire such instruments directly. For further discussion, see Chapter 6.

---

[5]The Special Assistance Program involves the purchase of or participation in mortgages where established home-financing facilities are inadequate. The management and liquidating function has to do with Federally owned mortgage portfolios. Ginny Mae held over $30 billion of mortgages at the end of 1976.

Ownership of Mortgage Debt: A Summary

At the end of 1976, one- to four-family residential mortgages comprised 62% of mortgage debt outstanding. A breakdown (Table 12-5) of the ownership of *all* mortgage debt outstanding shows the relative importance of other types of liens held by major institutions and individuals, government agencies, and minor institutions, as previously discussed.

TABLE 12-5 Ownership of Mortgage Debt, December 31, 1976 (in billions of dollars)

Type	Savings & Loan Ass'ns	Life Insurance Cos	Commercial Banks	Mutual Savings Banks	Federal[a] Agencies	Individuals and Others	Total
Farm	$ —	$ 7.4	$ 6.7	$ —	$ 22.2	$ 20.8	$ 57.1
Residential							
One- to four-family	260.9	16.1	86.2	53.2	77.7	62.3	556.4
Multifamily	28.4	19.2	8.1	14.2	14.3	20.1	104.3
	$289.3	$35.3	$ 94.3	$ 67.4	$ 92.0	$ 82.4	$660.7
Commercial and other	33.8	48.8	50.2	14.3	2.5	21.6	171.2
	$323.1	$91.5	$151.2	$ 81.7	$116.7	$124.8	$889.0
Per cent of total	36.3%	10.3%	17.0%	9.2%	13.1%	14.1%	100.0%

[a]Includes mortgage pools.
Source: Federal Reserve Bulletin.

The last line of the table shows the proportion of total mortgages held by the various categories of owners at the end of 1976. The very substantial position of Federal agencies in the mortgage market is a development of the past decade.

Recent Developments in Mortgage Financing

In addition to those previously indicated, six important recent developments in the mortgage field should be given brief mention:

• Mobile homes, mobile home parks, and condominiums are now accepted as appropriate security for loans, with necessary safeguards.

• Variable mortgage interest rates, that is, rates on outstanding mortgages that rise and fall with rates on new mortgages, are being used by state-chartered savings and loan associations in a few states, including California. They are already used in Canada and Europe. Their purpose is to mitigate the violent swings in the housing cycle by easing the extremes in yields and encouraging a more even flow of mortgage money. Practical difficulties have retarded the use of variable rates, and special legislation is necessary to expand their use.

• Some mortgage bankers are making available convertible mortgages on income properties under which, at the investor's option, the mortgage debt steadily converts to equity in lieu of cash amortization of the loan. At the end of the term, the investor owns a majority interest in the real estate, and the developer's equity interest has decreased correspondingly. The main purpose is to attract more funds to the building industry by offering the investor a hedge against inflation through the appreciation of his asset.

• In recent years private insurance of conventional loans has been offered by a number of firms. Ordinarily the top 10 to 20% of the loan is covered. The loan originator, such as a bank or mortgage company, obtains the insurance against foreclosure before closing the loan for itself or for a "take-out" client. Applied to loans of a high percentage of value, private insurance has aided in the development of more uniform risk in conventional loans and, therefore, the growth of a national market. The expansion of private mortgage insurance was stimulated by legislation in 1970 which provided that conventional loans bought by FNMA and FHLMC could carry loan-to-value ratios up to 90% if the excess over 75% were guaranteed.

• A new development has been the establishment in some metropolitan centers of local, and in one or two cases national, mortgage exchanges where a market is made in uniform—featured Federally—supported and conventional home mortgages. More recently, a nationwide automatic mortgage market information network (AMMINET) has been established to provide market quotations on packages of mortgage loans. Both of these developments should improve the liquidity and marketability of mortgage investments.

• In October 1975, the Chicago Board of Trade began trading in futures on GNMA certificates, so that a hedge on interest rates is available.[6]

Mortgage Yields

Market yields on FHA and VA mortgages, all of which must meet similar standards, tend to be fairly uniform on a national basis. Those on conventional mortgages, however, reflect variations in risk and geographical influences, so that generalizations on a national basis must be made with caution. Table 12-6 provides information from 1955 through 1976. The crudities of annual averages should be recognized—some variation within the year is, of course, to be expected. For purposes of comparison, the yield on Moody's Aaa corporate bond series is also shown in the table

The table reveals a rough relationship between home mortgage yields and bond yields, as the general supply of and demand for long-term funds rise and fall. Mortgage yields appear in general to be less volatile than bond yields, owing to the lack of a fully national flow of mortgage funds. Yields on Federally underwritten mortgages follow the ceiling rate but reflect the con-

---

[6]Other new developments in the mortgage field include loans with graduated payments, or with partially deferred interest (both designed to accommodate young families), and annuities based on property value.

TABLE 12-6   Mortgage Yields, 1960–1976*

| | FHA Mortgages (sec. 203) | | Conventional Home Mortgages | Aaa Corporate | |
	Ceiling Rate	Market Yield (1)	(National Average) (2)	Bonds (3)	Spread (1) over (3)
1960	5.75%	6.2%	6.2%	4.4%	1.8%
1961	5.75–5.25	5.7	6.0	4.4	1.3
1962	5.25	5.6	5.9	4.3	1.3
1963	5.25	5.5	5.8	4.3	1.2
1964	5.25	5.4	5.8	4.4	1.0
1965	5.25	5.5	5.7	4.5	1.0
1966	5.25–6.00	6.3	6.1	5.1	1.2
1967	6.00	6.5	6.3	5.5	1.0
1968	6.00–6.75	7.2	6.8	6.2	1.0
1969	6.75–8.50	8.3	7.7	7.0	1.3
1970	8.50	9.0	8.3	8.0	1.0
1971	8.50–7.00	7.8	7.6	7.4	0.4
1972	7.00	7.6	7.5	7.2	0.4
1973	7.00–8.50	8.2	7.8	7.4	0.8
1974	8.25–9.50	9.6	8.7	8.6	1.0
1975	9.00–8.50	9.2	8.8	8.8	0.4
1976	8.50–8.00	8.8	8.8	8.4	0.4

*Apply to loans on new single-family dwellings.
Source: Federal Reserve Bulletin.

sistent discounts that have prevailed in recent years. Discounts persisted in 1966–1970, even after successive increases had brought the ceiling FHA rate to 8 1/2% in early 1970. During the following period of credit strain the rate rose to 9 1/2% in 1974—a record high. The increases reflected the effort by the FHA commissioner to make mortgage yields competitive with yields on other fixed-income investments and thus counteract the reluctance of builders and sellers of homes to absorb deeper discounts in order to attract buyers. The rate was lowered by steps to 8% in 1976, when it again became too low to compete with other investments.

Even at the high ceiling rates that prevailed in 1974–1975, discounts prevailed. The chief institutional investors in home mortgages continued to press for the abandonment of fixed nominal ceilings and for completely "free-market" rates that change with changing capital market conditions.

Until early 1976 the FHA and VA ceiling rates on multifamily loans were the same as those on home mortgages. In January 1976 the Commissioner set up a "two-tier" system under which the rate on insured apartment loans remains 1/4% higher.

Since 1966 the yield on conventional home loans has often been somewhat lower than on Federally supported liens, reflecting the preference of institutional investors for the unregulated type. The recent growth of private insurance of conventional loans may aid in preserving the differential.

During the early 1960s the spread between the market yield on FHA-insured home mortgages and high-grade corporate bonds fell somewhat and then leveled off at about 100 "basis points." Tight money conditions prevailed in 1966 and 1969–1970. All interest rates rose, and a spread persisted. The big demand for mortgage money, and the shortage of funds in savings institutions, placed special pressure on commercial banks and Federal credit agency funds and on yields. At the end of 1970 FHAs still yielded 8.8%, and conventional mortgages, with a national average of 8%, produced as much as 9% in the Southwest and the West. Such yields were required when the yield on high-grade bonds reached a record level. In addition, lenders tended to be more selective about types of properties and borrowers, and maturities were shortened.

The short respite from credit strain in 1970–1972 reflected in part the increased flow of funds into savings institutions, and mortgage yields declined relatively more than bond yields. The spread between market yields on FHA mortgages and on high-grade mortgage bonds was reduced to 30 basis points or less, only to rise again as interest rates, driven high by inflation, reached new record levels in 1973. The rise continued in 1974. In December 1974 the market yield on FHA home mortgages reached 9.6%, and conventional loans brought 9.2%. Disintermediation—that is, the outflow of savings funds from thrift institutions—meant that commercial banks and Federal agencies were again relied on to satisfy the pressure. Real estate investment trusts entered a "squeeze" situation between the very high cost of short-term funds and the less mobile rates charged to customers, with disastrous results. (See p. 251.) The flow of mortgage funds improved somewhat in 1975–1976, but mortgage yields remained at a high level. However, the increase in bond yields in 1975 brought the spread to as low as 0.4%, where it remained in 1976.

Yields on conventional mortgages show a wider geographical dispersion than those on the more uniform FHAs. This reflects the differences among states in maximum allowable interest rates, in the mortgage investment powers held by the various lending institutions, on restrictions on out-of-state loans, and in foreclosure procedures and borrowers' rights. And although substantial mortgage funds now flow from areas of surplus to areas of shortage, variations in local supply and demand still contribute to geographical differences in mortgage yields. Although considerable progress has been made, an efficient national mortgage market has not yet been achieved.

Special Sources of Current Information

A large variety of sources of current information is available on construction, housing, and real estate finance. We are concerned here with sources that have to do specifically with the types of investments discussed in this chapter.

SHARES IN REAL ESTATE COMPANIES This is an "industry" for which there are no group data. Individual situations must be studied separately in annual reports and in Moody's and Standard & Poor's corporation services. Standard & Poor's publishes an index of real estate shares in *Standard Trade & Securities Service*. Those of individual companies are covered in the investment manuals and services.

REAL ESTATE INVESTMENT TRUSTS   Sources include:

Audit Investment Research, Inc., *Audit's Realty Trust Review* (New York, biweekly).
National Association of Real Estate Investment Trusts, *REIT Fact Book* (Washington, annual), and *REIT Statistics* (quarterly).

REAL ESTATE MORTGAGES   Information sources also include:

Periodicals: *Federal Reserve Bulletin;* Mortgage Bankers Association of America's *Mortgage Banking* (monthly) and its *Quarterly Economic Report of Trends in the Mortgage Industry.*

Life Insurance Fact Book; Savings and Loan Fact Book.

Federal Home Loan Bank Board, *Journal, Savings and Home Financing Source Book* (annually), *Annual Report,* and *News* (monthly); U.S. Department of Housing and Urban Development, *Statistical Yearbook.*

Mortgage Bankers Association of America, *Mortgage Banking: Trends, Financial Statements, and Operating Ratios* (occasional).

U.S. Bureau of the Census, Census of Housing (1970).

U.S. Bureau of the Census, *Statistical Abstract of the U.S.*

REFERENCES

AMERICAN INSTITUTE OF BANKING, *Home Mortgage Lending.* New York: The Institute, 1963.

BABB, J. B., and B. F. DORDICK, *Real Estate Information Sources.* Detroit: Gale Research Co., 1963.

BEATON, W. R., *Real Estate Finance.* Englewood Cliffs, N.J.: Prentice-Hall, Inc., 1975.

BROWN, R. K., *Essentials of Real Estate.* Englewood Cliffs, N.J.: Prentice-Hall, Inc., 1970.

CANDILLIS, W. O., *Variable Rate Mortgage Plans.* Washington: American Bankers Association, 1971.

COLEAN, MILES T., *The Impact of Government on Real Estate Finance in the United States.* New York: National Bureau of Economic Research, Inc., 1950.

————, *Mortgage Companies: Their Place in the Financial Structure,* a monograph prepared for the Commission on Money and Credit. Englewood Cliffs, N.J.: Prentice-Hall, Inc., 1962.

CONWAY, L. V., *Mortgage Lending,* 2d ed. Chicago: American Savings and Loan Institute Press, 1962.

DOUGALL, H. E., and J. E. GAUMNITZ, *Capital Markets and Institutions,* 3d ed., Chapter 11. Englewood Cliffs, N.J.: Prentice-Hall, Inc., 1975.

FEDERAL NATIONAL MORTGAGE ASSOCIATION, *Background and History of FNMA.* Washington, D.C.: The Association, 1965.

FRESHMAN, S. K., *Principles of Real Estate Syndication,* 2d ed. Los Angeles: Parker & Son, Inc., 1973.

HOAGLAND, H. E., and L. D. STONE, and W. E. BRUEGGEMAN, *Real Estate Finance*, 6th ed. Homewood, Ill.: Richard D. Irwin, Inc., 1977.

JONES, OLIVER, and LEO GREBLER, *The Secondary Mortgage Market*. Los Angeles: University of California Graduate School of Business Administration, 1961.

KLAMAN, S. B., *The Postwar Residential Mortgage Market*. Princeton, N.J.: Princeton University Press, 1961.

————, *The Postwar Rise of Mortgage Companies*, Occasional Paper No. 60. New York: National Bureau of Economic Research, Inc., 1959.

LEVINE, S. N., ed., *The Financial Analyst's Handbook*, Chapters 14, 26. Homewood, Ill.: Dow Jones-Irwin, Inc., 1975.

MADER, CHRIS, *The Dow Jones-Irwin Guide to Real Estate Investing*. Homewood, Ill.: Dow Jones-Irwin, Inc., 1975.

MAIR, GEORGE, and A. R. CERF, *Real Estate Analysis and Taxation*. New York: McGraw-Hill, Inc., 1969.

MAISEL, S. J., and S. E. ROULAC, *Real Estate Investment and Finance*. New York: McGraw-Hill, Inc., 1976.

PEASE, R. H., and L. O. KERWOOD, eds., *Mortgage Banking*, 2d ed. New York: McGraw-Hill, Inc., 1965.

RAPKIN, CHESTER, et al., *The Private Insurance of Home Mortgages*. Philadelphia: University of Pennsylvania, 1967.

Real Estate Investment Trusts: An Industry Profile. Washington: National Association of Real Estate Trusts, 1973.

Real Estate Investment Trusts: A Background Analysis and Recent Industry Developments 1961-1974. Washington, D.C.: Securities and Exchange Commission, February 1975.

RICKS, R. B., *The Role of Federal Mortage Credit Agencies in the Capital Markets*. Washington, D.C.: Federal Home Loan Bank Board, 1970.

RING, A. A. and JEROME DASSO, *Real Estate Principles and Practices*, 8th ed. Englewood Cliffs, N.J.: Prentice-Hall, Inc., 1977.

ROBINSON, R. I., and D. WRIGHTSMAN, *Financial Markets: The Accumulation and Allocation of Wealth*, Chapter 16. New York: McGraw-Hill, Inc., 1974.

ROULAC, S. E., ed., *Real Estate Securities and Syndication*. Chicago: National Association of Real Estate Boards, 1973.

SHENKEL, W. M., *Modern Real Estate Principles*. Dallas, Tex.: Business Publications, Inc., 1977.

TUNITAS, E. J., *Real Estate Investment Trusts*. Boston: Financial Publishing Co., 1972.

UNGER, M. A., *Real Estate Principles and Practices*, 4th ed., Part 4. Cincinnati: South-Western Publishing Co., 1969.

WIEDEMER, J. P., *Real Estate Finance*. Reston, Va.: Reston Publishing Co., Inc., 1974.

Part III

Investment Mechanics

Sources of General Investment Information and Advice

SCOPE: This chapter indicates the major sources of general investment information, starting with the general economic scene and progressing through industries and major categories of securities. The investor is now ready to examine the facts on individual companies. He will then frame his investment policy in the light of general investment and market conditions, and make his specific selections. He must, of course, first understand the way in which securities are priced and quoted, individually and by groups or averages. He may seek personal advice or retain professional management. The topics are: (1) tools of investment, (2) general handbooks of economic information, (3) sources on current economic and business conditions, (4) information on industries—general (5) information on companies and their securities, (6) information on general investment and market conditions, (7) security price indexes and averages, (8) security price quotations, (9) general investment advice, (10) personal investment advice, and (11) professional investment management.

Special sources of information on industries and governments are indicated in the appropriate chapters.

The Tools of Investment

Intelligent investment is to a considerable degree a matter of adequate knowledge. The greater the knowledge the investor has of facts, the more satisfactory his experience should be.

A growing fund of information is available in a wide variety of sources. Some of these deal with the general business situation and outlook; others provide material concerning specific industries, companies, and securities. Some of the information is from primary sources; often it is offered in digested or semidigested form in secondary sources.

All investors use the advice or opinion of others to a certain extent, some merely to confirm or challenge their own ideas. Others depend almost completely on others' advice and counsel. Therefore, sources of information and sources of advice may logically be discussed in the same chapters. Indeed, some sources do two things: Give the investor information, and accompany it with opinion.

General Handbooks of Economic Information

General sourcebooks of economic information are mines of facts covering a very wide range of topics.

Handbook of Basic Economic Statistics, published monthly, quarterly, and annually by the Economic Statistics Bureau, Washington, D.C. Each issue contains more than 1,800 series relative to different aspects of the national economy, collected by government agencies.

Trade and Securities Statistics, published by Standard & Poor's. A wide range of statistics is covered by the "Basic Statistics" section and kept up to date monthly by the publication of "Current Statistics."

Statistical Abstract of the United States, published annually by the U.S. Department of Commerce, Bureau of the Census, includes summary statistics from public and nongovernmental sources on industrial, economic, social, and political subjects. Supplemented by *Historical Statistics of the United States, Colonial Times to 1970.*

Survey of Current Business, published monthly by the Office of Business Economics, U.S. Department of Commerce, includes a wide variety of statistical series that indicate the trend of business; these are combined in a biennial supplement, *Business Statistics.* The July issue of the *Survey* is the *National Income* number summarizing business activity for the preceding year.

Supplement to Economic Indicators: Historical and Descriptive Background, 7th ed., U.S. Congress, Joint Economic Committee, 1967. Historical data and descriptions of the series in *Economic Indicators.*

Economic Report of the President, transmitted to the Congress annually (January), includes a variety of statistical tables on income, employment, and production.

Banking and Monetary Statistics, published by the Board of Governors of the Federal Reserve System in 1943, and supplemented by a series of pamphlets that update the sections of the original volume; for example, *Money Rates and Securities Markets,* Section 12, 1966.

World Almanac, published annually by the Newspaper Enterprise Association, Inc., contains comprehensive information of wide coverage.

Sources on Current Economic and Business Conditions

Of the many papers and periodicals devoted in whole or in part to economic and business conditions, only a relatively small selection can be indicated here. Topical coverage by a much larger number of publications is found in such general indexes (monthly and annual) as *Reader's Guide to Periodical Literature, Public Affairs Information Service, Business Periodicals Index,* and *Applied Science and Technology Index,* available in all good libraries. *Vertical File Index* is an annual and monthly index to selected pamphlet material on a wide variety of subjects. *I.E.P. Index* is a monthly publication listing articles in leading American and foreign business and professional journals. *F&S Index of Corporations and Industries* (weekly, monthly, and annually) indexes articles on companies and industries that have appeared in financial publications and brokerage house reports.

Daily business and financial pages and special papers The investor can follow current developments in the financial section of his daily newspaper. Of these, *The New York Times* has the best coverage. (Another advantage of this source is that it publishes a semimonthly and cumulative index of all important news items.) But the information in most dailies is usually very sketchy. Financial material is better obtained from special daily business and financial papers. *The Journal of Commerce and Commercial* (New York) emphasizes commodities and shipping and commercial news. *The Wall Street Journal* is published in six editions—New York, Washington, Chicago, San Francisco, Dallas, and Asian. In addition to general business news, it emphasizes notes on individual companies and industries and has a fairly complete quotation section. An index of the New York (national) edition is published monthly and annually.

The information contained in the financial sections of the large metropolitan papers and in the special business papers is either statistical or general. The statistical news comprises business and price indexes indicating the state of business, summarized annual and interim reports of corporations, price quotations on commodities and securities, dividend payments, foreign trade and exchange, volume of securities traded, security price averages, and money rates.

The state of business activity throughout the country is measured by a variety of series and index numbers compiled by both public and private agencies. The most widely quoted of these are the monthly figures on Gross National Product, or the value of all goods and services produced in the nation, and the Federal Reserve Board's index of industrial production. Other indexes reveal changes in the cost of living, wholesale and retail prices, employment, and a wide variety of business trends.

In addition to their annual reports of earnings, interim reports on a semiannual or quarterly basis are published by the great majority of important companies. This information, which is summarized in the newspapers, helps investors to act quickly if necessary for the protection of their interests.

Investors should make proper allowance for seasonal influences upon interim reports. Earnings for the first quarter of the year are rarely a dependable guide for the entire year. For example, because of increased volume of crop movements during the harvest months, earnings of certain railroad companies during the second half of the year are generally much better than during the first half.

Price quotations on securities are obtained by the papers, in the case of listed issues, from reporting services using the electronic tapes operated from the securities exchanges. Quotations on unlisted securities are obtained from investment firms which maintain markets in such issues and from the National Association of Securities Dealers. Explanations of price quotations and their sources are given later in this chapter.

The larger newspapers also give daily information concerning the volume of trading on the last day of trading—the volume of stocks in shares and of bonds in dollars—sometimes compared with those for the equivalent day of the previous year.

The day's leaders—the stocks with the most shares traded—are often itemized in a separate table. Also shown are the number of issues traded that day on the particular exchange, the number of advances and declines from the previous day, and the number of new highs and new lows for the year to date. Even on a day of a general rise in shares, some make their new lows for the year. Seldom if ever have all stocks or bonds moved in the same direction on the same day.

A number of indexes and averages have been constructed to represent large groups of securities on the market as a whole. The large metropolitan dailies and the special business newspapers quote one or more of these. Security price averages are discussed later in this chapter.

Of great interest to most investors is the course of interest rates on various categories of loans and investments. Those basic "bellwether" rates frequently indicated in the papers, either in a special section or derived from price quotations, include yields on short-term instruments including Federal funds, Treasury bills, and prime commercial paper, as described in Chapters 6 and 10. The first two are sensitive indicators whose changes may signal changes in other yields and in securities prices. Yields in intermediate- and long-term funds are best represented by those of U.S. Treasury notes and bonds of different maturities, as described in Chapter 6. They provide a continuous standard representing the riskless rental value of intermediate- and long-term capital. The spread between yields on corporate bonds and Treasury bonds of similar maturity represents the current reward for risk. (See Chapter 8.)

A special interest rate of great importance is the Federal Reserve discount rate charged on advances to member banks secured by U.S. Government securities. This is an important tool of credit control, and, along with the rate on Federal funds, indicates the Federal Reserve Board's attitude towards the credit situation and its management of the money supply. Another important interest rate is the "prime rate" charged by the metropolitan banks on unsecured short-term loans to their strongest business customers.

The general news consists of reports on economic, business, and political conditions, with a growing emphasis on government activity and its effect on corporate earnings.

A very wide variety of business and financial news is reported in the daily press. A glance at *The New York Times* or *The Wall Street Journal* reveals information on the outlook for various industries, banking and credit, Treasury and municipal financing, foreign business and economic developments, corporate developments, consumption, trade and transportation developments, new security offerings, shipping news, and notes on business personalities. Opinion and comment often accompany reports on Federal finance, money and credit, prices, production, housing starts, building contracts, carloadings, department store sales, electric power production, employment and payrolls, crop production and prices, business inventories, and business failures.

Regular reading of the financial pages will go far toward explaining the forces that bear upon the investment markets. At the same time, the investor must discriminate between the vital and the unimportant. Sole reliance should not be placed on the rather superficial material that comprises much of the daily financial and business news. Systematic study of the more specialized sources, such as those indicated below, is necessary for sound investment judgment.

Weekly business and financial periodicals   *Barron's* is a very readable source on business trends, industries, companies, and securities. Short analyses of individual situations are emphasized. The central section, "The Market Week," provides a compendium of security prices, earnings, and dividends covering unlisted securities and investment funds as well as stocks listed on the New York, American, regional, and Toronto exchanges.

Business Week covers the changing business scene and has an interesting section devoted to financial developments.

The Commercial and Financial Chronicle is a comprehensive publication containing digests of financial news, articles and editorials on business and finance, and detailed quotations on listed and unlisted corporate bonds and stocks, options, mutual funds, and U.S. Government and agency securities.

The Economist, published in England, gives an excellent survey of British and international economic developments and contains statistics on commodity production and prices.

Financial World is devoted to investment advice and information on a wide variety of securities, companies, and industries; it also publishes *Stock Factographs* annually with data on over 2,000 companies.

Investment Dealers Digest is devoted mainly to reports, lists, and advertisements of new corporate and municipal securities offerings.

The Market Chronicle provides articles and editorials on companies and the securities markets, and a detailed quotation list of over-the-counter stocks.

Media General Financial Weekly, published in Richmond, Va., contains short articles on financial developments, industries, and companies. Its comprehensive statistical section presents weekly price changes, volume of trading, per share earnings, price-earnings ratios, dividends, and other data on listed and unlisted stocks, as well as prices and yields on corporate and government bonds.

The Money Manager provides news, quotations (especially on municipal, corporate, and Federal bonds), and discussion of the money, capital, and foreign financial markets.

United States Investor emphasizes investment news and policy for banks and insurance companies.

U.S. News and World Report covers political and economic developments and trends, and reprints the official texts of important political speeches and government reports.

The Wall Street Transcript reprints the reports of investment firms on companies and industries, and provides the texts of speeches by corporate executives to financial analyst societies.

The Weekly Bond Buyer provides a wide variety of news items related to bonds and interest rates, calendars of offerings, and tables of bond yields.

Two weekly news magazines, *Time* and *Newsweek*, contain good business sections, with emphasis on interesting developments in specific companies. *Kiplinger Washington Letter* is devoted to legislative and official activities related to the economic scene.

Monthly business and financial periodicals   With the exception of the *Magazine of Wall Street*, *Forbes*, and *Investor's Reader*, issued semimonthly, and *Financial Analysts Journal*, issued bimonthly, the following are monthly journals which cover a wide range of interests:

Bulletins of commercial banks, such as the First National City Bank (New York) *Citibank Monthly Economic Letter*, the Cleveland Trust Company *Business Bulletin*, the Morgan Guaranty Trust *Guaranty Survey*, and the Chase Manhattan *Business in Brief*, contain critical and descriptive material on economic and business trends and the capital markets. *Monthly reviews or bulletins* of the several Federal Reserve Banks cover monetary, fiscal, and business conditions.

Conference Board Record surveys the direction of business activity.

Credit and Financial Management is devoted primarily to short-term financing.

Dun's Review, published by Dun & Bradstreet, emphasizes management techniques, trade indexes, and failure data. The Dun & Bradstreet 14 financial ratios are published periodically.

Economic Indicators, published by the Council of Economic Advisors, contains charts and tables on basic economic data. An annual summary is also published.

Federal Reserve Bulletin, published by the Board of Governors of the Federal Reserve System, reviews banking and financial developments and provides a wealth of statistical information, both domestic and foreign, on money, credit, banking, and business. This is a basic source. Also very useful is *Federal Reserve Charts* (monthly and annually) on bank credit, money rates, and business conditions.

Financial World contains articles on companies and securities.

Forbes (biweekly) covers business and financial developments and investments. Its annual survey of American industry rates the management performance of a large number of companies.

Fortune presents in a unique fashion the picture of American business enterprise. Its discussion of domestic and foreign business and economic problems and its articles on industries, businesses, and business executives are colorful and comprehensive.

Harvard Business Review contains scholarly and practical articles on all aspects of business management (bimonthly).

The Institutional Investor discusses the problems and policies of large fund management.

Investor's Reader, distributed biweekly by Merrill Lynch, Pierce, Fenner & Smith, covers investment developments and company reviews.

Magazine of Wall Street (biweekly) discusses industries and companies and makes specific investment recommendations.

Money, published by Time, Inc., contains articles on personal finance, including investments.

Monthly Labor Review, published by the U.S. Department of Labor, Bureau of Labor Statistics, surveys trends in the labor market.

Nation's Business, published by the U.S. Chamber of Commerce, contains articles on general business subjects written from the standpoint of the business executive.

Stock Market Magazine emphasizes reports on growing industries and companies; it also provides current information on mutual funds, mergers, new security issues, and general economic conditions.

Survey of Current Business (see general handbooks above).

Quarterly investment and financial periodicals   *Financial Analysts Journal*, published (bimonthly) by the New York Society of Security Analysts, is devoted to analytical methodology and portfolio management.

The Journal of Finance, five issues a year published by the American Finance Association, contains articles on investment and business finance, money and credit, and international finance, with emphasis on research material.

Pensions and Investments and *Pension World* are devoted to the management and investment problems of private pension funds.

Annual government policy reports   Certain reports indicate the course of Federal public policy on the economic front. These are the *Mid-year Economic Review* and the *Annual Economic Review* of the President's Council of Economic Advisors (the *Annual Review* accompanies the President's Economic Report to the Congress), and the report to Congress of the Joint Committee on the Economic Report.

Information on Industries—General

We cannot indicate here all of the many sources of information concerning industries. The following classifications should, however, prove useful. More specific sources on special classifications of industries and companies are indicated in the appropriate chapters.

Business and financial newspapers and periodicals   (See above.)

Government publications and documents   A mass of information on many industries is available in government releases, especially information of a statistical character and on regulated groups. Special mention should be made of the U.S. Department of Commerce, Bureau of the Census, publications such as *Current Industrial Reports, Business Cycle Developments* (monthly), *Business Conditions Digest* (monthly), *Survey of Current Business, Survey of Manufacturers* (annual), *Monthly Retail Trade Report, Statistical Abstract of the United States, Census of Manufacturers* (latest 1967), *Census of Mineral Industries* (1967), and *Census of Retail Trade* (latest 1972); *Census of Transportation* (1972), and *Census of Governments* (1972). *Minerals Yearbook* is published by the U.S. Department of the Interior, Bureau of Mines. U.S. Business and Defense Services Administration issues (annually) *Industry*

Trend Series, showing recent trends and outlook for over 50 selected industries. *The U.S. Industrial Outlook* is published by The U.S. Bureau of Domestic Commerce (annually). Reports of regulatory commissions having to do with railroads, utilities, and banks will be indicated in the sections, below, which are devoted to these industries. Others include annual reports of the Federal Aviation Agency, Federal Communications Commission, Federal Trade Commission, the Maritime Administration, and the annual and special reports of the Securities and Exchange Commission. Of special interest are the SEC's quarterly reports on *Plant and Equipment Expenditures of United States Business, Net Working Capital of United States Corporations,* and *Quarterly Financial Report: U.S. Manufacturing Corporations.* Special governmental hearings and investigations are useful but irregular in appearance. The reader should consult the monthly and annual catalogs of the U.S. Superintendent of Documents for additional sources.

A valuable source of financial statement data on corporations by groups is *Statistics of Income,* issued annually by the Internal Revenue Service, U.S. Treasury Department.

The *Yearbook of International Trade Statistics* and the *Statistical Yearbook* (annual), published by the United Nations, provide valuable data on foreign business and finance. Other publications concerning foreign economic conditions include the Chase Manhattan Bank *Latin American Business Highlights* (quarterly) and *Europa Year Book* (annually); Citibank (New York) *Foreign Information Service:* and the U.S. Department of Commerce *International Commerce* (weekly).

Trade association publications   Many trade associations publish statistical material that indicates the conditions and trends in various industries. Examples are the annual review or statistical issues of the American Iron and Steel Institute, the Manufacturing Chemists Association, the American Meat Institute, the National Lumber Manufacturers Association, the United States Copper Association, the American Petroleum Institute, and the Rubber Manufacturers Association.[1]

Trade journals   Magazines devoted to special industries are excellent sources of infromation in their respective fields. The following are representative: *American Gas Journal; Automotive Industries; Canner; Chemical Week; Coal Age; Electrical World; Electronics; Food Industries; Iron Age; National Petroleum News; Oil and Gas Journal; Public Utilities Fortnightly; Railway Age; Rayon Organon; Rubber Age; Textile World;* and *Steel.* A number of trade journals publish annual statistical or review bulletins.[2]

Reports of statistical and rating services   The two major statistical and financial services provide considerable information on industries,

---

[1]For lists of trade associations see: *National Trade and Professional Associations of the United States* (Washington, D.C.: Columbia Books, Inc., 1976); *Encyclopedia of Associations: National Organizations of the U.S.,* 10th ed. (Detroit: Gale Research Company, 1976).

[2]See *Statistical and Review Issues of Trade and Business Periodicals* (Boston: Baker Library, Harvard University Graduate School of Business Administration, 1964). See also S. N. Levine, ed., *Financial Analyst's Handbook.* Vol. II, Chapter 34. Homewood, Ill.: Dow Jones-Irwin, Inc., 1975.

along with their other data on companies and securities. (See below.) *Moody's Manual of Investments, Industrials* (annually) contains a central "blue section" that provides ratios and data on industrial groups. Standard & Poor's *Industry Surveys*, divided into basic and current sections, indicates how various industries are performing. The same company's *Outlook for the Security Markets* (weekly) includes short industry reviews, as does its weekly *Highlights*. *Trade and Securities Statistics* provides a wealth of data and index numbers on every phase of business activity and on major industries.

Reports of private agencies   Certain private agencies specialize in statistical information concerning specific industries. Examples are the F.W. Dodge Corporation *Dodge Statistical Research Service, Construction*, the Ward *Automotive Reports and Automotive Yearbook*, and the Alfred M. Best & Co. *Best's Insurance Reports*. Predicasts, Inc., publishes quarterly in *Predicasts* a synthesis of forecasts from over 500 journals, documents, and other sources. Standard & Poor's publishes annually composite corporate per share data, by industries. Commodity Research Bureau, Inc., publishes annually the *Commodity Yearbook*. The Conference Board has issued a series of volumes on various industries, *Statistics of Manufacturing Industries*. Investors Management Sciences, Inc., publishes detailed quarterly and annual computerized data on all major companies in *Financial Dynamics*.

A large number of publications provide operating results and financial data of specific industries. For a complete list, see Robert Morris Associates, *Sources of Composite Financial Data: a Bibliography*, 2d ed. (Philadelphia: Robert Morris Associates, 1971). Additional sources of data on manufacturing, trade, and merchandising industries are cited at the end of Chapter 26.

Reports of investment advisory services   In addition to reports and appraisals of specific companies, industries and their trends are appraised in many specific general investment and business services, such as *United Business Service, Babson's Investment and Barometer Letter, The Value Line Investment Survey, Dow Theory Forecasts*, and others.

Reports and brochures of brokerage and investment banking firms   As part of their service to clients, such firms frequently prepare special industry studies that are available at their offices or by mail.

A special service of great value is provided by the F&S *Index of Corporations and Industries* which lists (weekly and annually) periodical articles and published investment house brochures, classified by industries and companies. An allied publication is the F&S *Index, International* (annually).

Information on Companies and Their Securities

In addition to the general and specialized periodical publications listed in the preceding section, the major sources of information on individual companies include:

Annual and interim reports to stockholders   These vary in detail and value. Some are packed with facts; others meet only minimum standards of accounting and financial information. Interim income statements—quarterly or semiannually—are issued by companies with securities listed on an organized exchange. A few industrial concerns publish monthly earnings; railroads are required to do so. The financial press reproduces the latest figures as they are released.

Prospectuses issued under the Securities Act of 1933   These provide much more detail than annual reports, but appear only when new financing is undertaken. The more comprehensive registration statements required by the same statute are available for examination at the offices of the Securities and Exchange Commission. Prospectuses and registration statements are discussed further in Chapter 14.

Form 10-K   Each company with securities listed on an organized exchange, and unlisted companies which had issued securities under the Securities Act of 1933 in excess of $2 million, must file with the Securities and Exchange Commission on Form 10-K an annual balance sheet and income statement. The data may be more comprehensive than the annual report to stockholders. Form 10-K is available for inspection at the Commission offices and at the securities exchanges where issues are listed. Under a contract with the Securities and Exchange Commission, Leaseco Corporation microfilms Form 10-K and other documents submitted to the Commission. This information is available in good financial libraries.

Statistical services   The two large statistical services—Moody's and Standard & Poor's—are engaged primarily in the publication of statistical data concerning corporations of investment interest. As we shall see below, they also offer opinion and investment advice.

The more important offerings of each of these services, with respect to factual information on companies, are:

MOODY'S

Annual Manuals: *Municipal and Government; Bank and Finance; Industrial; OTC-Industrials* (over-the-counter); *Public Utility; Transportation.* The history, statements, security prices, and dividend records of a very large number of concerns are presented. The central "blue sections" provide valuable data concerning these industrial groups as a whole. The manuals are kept current by weekly or semiweekly supplements.

Bond Survey, information on bond market trends, individual issues, and investment recommendations (weekly).

Bond Record, a guide (monthly) of prices and earnings, including ratings, of some 3,000 bonds.

Dividend Record, issued semiweekly with a yearly base book.

Handbook of Common Stocks, charts and data on over 1000 companies quarterly.

Standard & Poor's

American Stock Exchange Reports, two pages of data on finances, securities, and developments of all Amex listed stocks.

Analysts Handbook, per-share data on 95 industry groups and Standard & Poor's industrials (annually with quarterly supplements).

Bond Guide (monthly), data and ratings on 4,000 corporate and municipal bonds.

Called Bond Record (semiweekly, weekly, and quarterly), current lists of dates and provisions of bond redemptions.

Commercial Paper Reports (intermittently), finances and ratings of companies which have issued commercial paper.

Corporation Records, factual information on 11,800 companies, in loose-leaf form. Latest developments are reported in *Daily News Section*.

Daily Stock Price Records (quarterly), three-month price history of stocks on NYSE and ASE and of daily bid and asked prices of over-the-counter stocks.

Directory of Bond Agents, calls, coupon-paying agents, bonds in default (annually, with five supplements).

Dividend Record (week days and annually), information on dividends and rights issued by nearly 10,000 companies.

Earnings Forecaster (weekly), earnings estimates on over 1,800 companies by leading investment organizations.

Fixed Income Investor (weekly), developments in bond and preferred stock markets; government and corporate issues are rated and recommended.

Industry Surveys (weekly), compilations of group data on leading industry groups and major companies in each industry.

Municipal Bond Selector (monthly) data and ratings on municipal bonds.

New Issues Service (weekly), summaries of prospectuses in advance of offering.

New York Stock Exchange Reports, two-page descriptions and financial data on NYSE listed securities, with recommendations.

The Outlook (weekly), comment on the market, with recommended industries and companies.

Over-the-Counter and Regional Reports, two-page reports on over 1,000 companies traded over-the-counter and on the regional exchanges.

Standard & Poor's Register of Corporations, Directors and Executives (annual with three supplements), lists the officers, directors, and products of over 37,000 companies classified by industry; geographical index.

Standard & Poor's Stock Guide (monthly) shows prices, earnings, dividends and other data, and buy, hold, or switch rankings on nearly 5,000 common and preferred stocks and 400 mutual funds; pocket-size.

Statistical Service (monthly), comprehensive collection of business, industry, stock, and bond statistics in nearly 1,000 different series.

Stock Guide (monthly), a digest on over 1,900 widely traded stocks, showing earnings, dividends, prices, capitalization, etc.

Transportation Securities (weekly), coverage of transportation operations and earnings.

Trendline Daily Basis Stock Charts and *Current Market Perspectives*, chart services.

OTHER SERVICES

Robert D. Fisher, *Fisher Mining Manual.*

Financial Dynamics, 14 volumes; detailed analyses of top companies in over 100 industries; published and kept current by *Investors Management Sciences.*

Financial World, Independent Appraisals of Listed Stocks (monthly) gives summary data and ratings.

Financial World Stock Factographs (annually) provides a summary of basic information on stocks listed on the New York and American exchanges.

Financial Stock Guide Service, *Directory of Obsolete Securities* (Jersey City, N.J., biennially).

Forbes, "Annual Report on American Industry," a feature of the first issue each year.

Fortune 500 and *Second 500*, an annual compilation in *Fortune* showing by size and rank the sales, assets, net worth, return in equity, earnings per share and their growth rate, and total return on investment, of the leading American companies.

United Graphic Guide, 12-year charts published annually by United Business Service Company.

Value Line Investment Survey, one-page summaries for 1,400 stocks of income, earnings and price, projections of earnings and price, and value ratings.

Walker's Manual of Western Corporations (annually), kept current by a *Weekly News Letter* and monthly *Supplements.*

Most of the sources of information on industries listed above refer to manufacturing, merchandising, service, and other "industrial" categories. Sources on transportation, public utilities, financial, and other classifications are found in the appropriate chapters of this book.

Advisory services   United Business Service, The Value Line Investment Survey, Dow Theory Forecasts, Babson's Reports, and many others analyze industries and companies and make recommendations.

Reports and brochures of brokerage firms, security dealers, and investment banks   These reports are issued regularly or intermittently to customers and potential clients. These range from one-page summaries to comprehensive analyses. The information is usually accompanied by investment advice. For an index of such reports, see F&S *Index of Corporations and Industries.*

Lists of information on companies, officers, directors, products, sales, and employees   Dun & Bradstreet's *Million Dollar Directory* (annually with two supplements) and *Standard & Poor's Register of Directors and Executives* (annually with three supplements) list this information.

Information on General Investment and Market Conditions

Many of the sources outlined above provide comment and opinion on the general investment and market outlook. Such opinion ranges from careless to exact, and from condensed to complete. What are the forces at work in the investment market? What is the outlook for the bond and stock markets? Where will the averages go? What is the outlook for general business, and how well are the securities markets reflecting this outlook? The investor can get much free advice on such matters, or he can subscribe to services that purport to give him more expert comment.

The daily financial press (metropolitan dailies and the special business and financial dailies) reports the opinion of newsworthy persons and summarizes the attitude of Wall Street houses.

Certain periodicals such as *Barron's, Commercial and Financial Chronicle, Financial World, Magazine of Wall Street, and Investor's Reader* keep up a running discussion of the outlook on the market.

The statistical or subscription services devote much of certain of their publications to descriptions of the current market situation and prognostications of the near-term and long-term outlook. The following are representative: Moody's *Bond Survey*; Standard & Poor's *Outlook*; and the *United Business Service*.

Special advisory services, as well as investment counsels, keep their clients in tune with the general investment situation.

Brokers, dealers, and the larger bond houses offer a running commentary, oral and written, on the market and its condition. Their brochures and "letters" show interesting but confusing dissimilarities.

Special mention should be made of the many forecasts of market price action, either in general publications or in special letters, advertised in the financial press and sold to clients at a fee. These in the main tend to project the current condition or trend in the market. Some are daring enough to predict change. The usefulness of such advice is limited because different securities have a way of acting differently unless the whole market is in a drastic upward or downward surge. Certain well-known forecasts are based on interpretations of the Dow theory. Such opinions may help the investor avoid the worst mistakes in the timing of purchases and sales. Other methods also exist by which the investor can minimize or even avoid this problem. (See Chapter 19.)

Security Price Indexes and Averages

Stock price averages and indexes A number of price averages and indexes have been constructed to represent large groups of securities or the market as a whole. The most widely published are the Dow Jones averages, the Standard & Poor's indexes, the New York Stock Exchange Index, and Barron's averages. Most good financial pages will show one or more of these. Others are described below.

Dow Jones & Co. publishes four stock price series at the opening and close and at each hour of the New York Stock Exchange day: 30 Industrials,[3] 15 Utilities, 20 Transportation, and the composite of the 65. Such averages enable the reader quickly to observe the trend in prices more reliably than observing the movement of a few leading issues.

The Dow Jones Industrial Average of 30 stocks was originally computed by dividing the unweighted total value of the stocks by 30. Due to stock dividends and split-ups, however, the current (July 1977) divisor has been reduced to 1,504[4]. This explains the high level of the "average" price. Quarterly dividends, earnings, and price-earnings ratios are also calculated for the four averages, again involving the use of the divisor. These are published daily in the *Wall Street Journal* and weekly in *Barron's*.

The Dow Jones averages have often been criticized as not representative of the market as a whole. But they are still widely used and quoted. The Dow Jones Company publishes an annual volume, *Dow Jones Investors' Handbook*, containing historical price, earnings, dividend, and other information on the four stock averages.

Other indexes are said to be more representative of the stock market as a whole. The Standard & Poor's four general indexes were first issued in February 1957: the 500 stock Composite, the 425 Industrials, the 55 Utilities, and the 20 Railroads. The Industrial index was started at 47, which was about the average price of "Big Board" listed stocks at that time. In mid-1976 the composition of the S&P indexes was changed to make them more representative of the modern market: 400 Industrials, 40 Public Utilities, 20 Transportation, and 40 Financial. The new composite 500 and the separate series contain another new feature in that that they include 12 stocks that are traded in the over-the-counter market.

The S & P's are not averages but are weighted indexes; that is, the price of each share is multiplied by the number of shares outstanding. The aggregate value is then expressed as a percentage of the average value in the base period 1941–1943, then divided by 10. Price changes are computed hourly, and daily at the close of the market. Dividends, earnings, dividend yields, and price-earnings ratios for the five series are published in *The Outlook* (weekly). Four supplementary group indexes: Capital Goods, Consumer Goods, High-Grade Common Stocks, and Low-Priced Common Stocks—as well as a large variety of indexes representing the various industries—are also published.

Objections to the misleading high value of the Dow Jones averages, and the need for more representative measures of change in the value of listed stocks, led to the production in 1966, by both the New York and American

---

[3]The companies included in this popular stock average are (1977): Allied Chemical, Aluminum Company of America, American Brands, American Can, American Telephone & Telegraph, Bethlehem Steel, Chrysler, DuPont, Eastman Kodak, Esmark, Exxon, General Electric, General Foods, General Motors, Goodyear, International Harvester, International Nickel, International Paper, Johns-Manville, Minnesota Mining & Manufacturing, Owens-Illinois, Procter and Gamble, Sears Roebuck, Standard Oil of Calif., Texaco, Union Carbide, United Technologies, U.S. Steel, Westinghouse Electric, and Woolworth.

[4]Divisors are also used in calculating the other Dow Jones stock averages.

Exchanges, of daily indexes of all common stocks listed on the respective exchanges. The NYSE Index covers more than 1,330 common issues, and is weighted to reflect the number of outstanding shares of the individual issues. The base index was arbitrarily set at 50 as of December 31, 1965. Hourly changes in the composite are also converted into changes in terms of dollars and cents per share. The Exchange also publishes four separate indexes: Finance, Transportation, Utility, and Industrial.

The original American Stock Exchange index was unweighted. In 1974 it was changed to a weighted basis (by number of shares of each component). It thus became similar to the Standard & Poor's and New York Stock Exchange indexes as a "market value" rather than a "market price" index.

An index based on 35 over-the-counter stocks is prepared by the National Quotation Bureau and is available at dealers' offices and in some financial publications. In addition to this composite, there are five special "NASDAQ" indexes: Transportation, Utilities, Industrials, Insurance, and Banks.

Price averages also indicate the trend of the market by classes of securities. Some newspapers show separate averages for utility, oil, steel, food, motor, and other groups of stocks, and thus enable their readers to compare the prices of any particular group with the general trend of the market. Standard & Poor's *Trade and Securities Statistics* and *Outlook* provide an unusually large number of industrial group price indexes.

There has been much discussion of the "representativeness" of the leading well-known stock averages and indexes. The Standard & Poor's 500 includes about three-quarters of the value of all stocks listed on the New York Stock Exchange, and the Dow Jones about 25%. The weightings used in the Standard & Poor's and the exchange indexes inevitably reflect the great influence of the stocks of the larger corporations. What about stocks as a whole, regardless of size? Two *unweighted* averages are available, and their movements stand in sharp contrast to those of the leading indicators. The *Value Line* (geometric) *Average* of over 1,600 stocks includes representative issues listed on the large and the regional exchanges and traded over-the-counter. The *Indicator Digest Corporate Index* (published twice monthly for private circulation by Indicator Digest, Inc.) also covers the whole range of stocks.

Bond and preferred stock price indexes Although the chief interest in bond movements lies in their changing yields, price action is also important, especially to investors interested in "total return" from price change plus current income, and those with possibly temporary interest in particular issues, especially convertibles, whose current yield is followed quite closely.

Dow Jones produces daily composite price averages of 40 bonds and of its components: industrials, first-grade rails, second-grade rails, and utilities. It also provides an index of prices of railroad income bonds. Standard & Poor's publishes weekly indexes of both corporate bond yields and prices, by rating and for composite, industrials, and utilities groups, as well as weekly price indexes of Federal bonds (long-term, intermediate, and short-term).

A bond index that is increasingly used is prepared by Salomon Brothers, a large New York investment firm. Its high-grade bond index serves as a standard against which to compare stock price movements. Other bond indexes are found in *Barron's* and *The Bond Buyer*. Other indexes of prices of long-term U.S. Government bonds are found in the *Federal Reserve Bulletin* and in the *Treasury Bulletin*. Standard & Poor's computes weekly indexes of preferred stock prices and of yields, found in *The Outlook*, and an index of convertible bonds, published in *The Fixed Income Investor*. Moody's publishes a Utility Preferred Stock Index in the *Bond Survey*.

Security Price Quotations

United States Government obligations United States Treasury bonds are listed on the organized exchanges, but the bulk of the trades is in large amounts and takes place over-the-counter. These bonds are quoted in percentages of par value, with fractions in 1/32 of a point. The unit of trading on the New York Stock Exchange is $1,000 par value, but price quotations are in terms of $100 of principal. For example, the following information on a specified Treasury bond appeared in the financial section of *The New York Times* on March 22, 1977, reporting transactions as of March 21:

			Bid	Asked	Net Change in Bid	Yield
Aug.	'88–'93	7 1/2	99.26	100.26	—	7.42%

These bonds bore a 7 1/2% interest rate and were payable in August 1993 but were redeemable by the Government at any time between August 1988 and 1993. The best bid at the close of trading was 99 26/32 or $99.8125, and the best offer (lowest asked price) was 100 26/32 or $100.8125. The bid was unchanged from the closing bid of the previous day. The yield to maturity (1988) was 7.42%.

Treasury notes, which represent debt of from one to seven years in maturity, are also quoted in thirty-seconds; but Treasury bills, also traded exclusively over-the-counter, are quoted on a percentage-of-yield basis. (See Chapter 10.) For example, on March 30, 1977, the following quotation on Treasury bills appeared:

Date	Bid	Ask	Chg.	Yield
Sept. 1 1977	4.78	4.72	−0.02	4.88

Listed bond price quotations Foreign bonds and domestic corporation bonds that are listed on the New York Stock Exchange and the American Stock Exchange are quoted in percentages of par, in eighths of a point. For example, on the same date as above, the following appeared under the general heading of "New York Stock Exchange Bond Trading":

Corporation Bonds 1977			Sales in				Net
High	Low		$1,000	High	Low	Close	Change
106 1/2	101	Beth Stl. 8 3/8's, 2001	13	102 1/2	102	102	−1

The price of Bethlehem Steel 8 3/8% bonds, due in 2001, ranged from a high of $1,065 ($1,000 principal value) to a low of $1,010 during the period January 3 to March 21, 1977. On March 21, transactions totalled $13,000. The highest price at which a trade took place during the day was at $1,025 per bond, the lowest at $1,020. The closing price of $1,020 represented a decrease of $10 over the closing price on March 18 ($1,010).

Numerous abbreviations are used in bond titles appearing on quotation pages and elsewhere, of which the following are most commonly found:

adj., aj	adjustment
asd., asstd.	assented
clt., col., col. tr.	collateral trust
con., cons.	consolidated
c., cou., coup.	coupon
ct., cv., conv.	convertible
deb.	debenture
div.	divisional
eq., equip.	equipment
ext.	extension
f.	traded flat
g.	gold
gen.	general mortgage
gu., gtd.	guaranteed
imp.	improvement
inc.	income bonds
int. ctfs.	interim certificates
jt.	joint
m., mtg.	mortgage
p.m.	purchase money
perp.	perpetual
pr. ln.	prior lien
re., real est.	real estate
ref., rfg.	refunding
r., reg.	registered
ser.	series
s.f.	sinking fund
st.	stamped
war.	warrants
w.w.	with warrants
x.w.	without warrants
Ist 4's	first mortgage 4% bonds
87	due in 1987
85–77	due in 1985, may be paid 1977 to 1985

Listed stock price quotations   Quotations of listed stocks are fairly well standardized, and until recent years about the same methods were used on all of the exchanges. Two important innovations have appeared in the lists published by *The Wall Street Journal* and some of the larger metropolitan dailies: (1) since October 1972, the price-earnings ratio, calculated daily, and (2) since mid-1976, the "composite" quotations on New York Stock Exchange and American Stock Exchange listed stocks, which combine the volume and price data of all such stocks, wherever traded, including the regional exchanges.

The following information on a leading industrial common stock listed on the New York Stock Exchange is taken from *The New York Times* of March 22, 1977 covering transactions on March 21, 1977.

1977 High	Low	Stocks and Div. (in dollars)	PE	Sales (100's)	High	Low	Last	Net Change
28 7/8	25 1/4	Gillette 1.50	10	237	27	26 3/4	27	+1/8

The price of Gillette common stock from January 3, 1977, to March 21, 1977, ranged from a high of $28 7/8 per share to a low of $25 1/4. The current annual dividend rate was $1.50 per share, based on the last quarterly or semiannual declaration. (Sometimes the dividend is the amount declared or paid thus far in the year and is so indicated by a footnote designation.) The closing price was 10 times the 1976 earnings. The total volume of sales on July 18 was 23,700 shares. The highest price during the day was at $27, the lowest was at $26 3/4, and the last sale before the close of the trading day was at $27. This was $.125 higher than the closing price on the previous trading day.

Unless otherwise designated, the quotation refers to the common stock of the company. Quotations on preferred stocks are indicated by *pf.* Other abbreviations and symbols frequently used in stock quotations and elsewhere are as follows:

A.D.R.	American depository receipts
com.	common
ct., ctfs., vtc.	voting trust certificates
cv.	convertible
ex d., xd.	without dividend
ex r., xr.	ex-rights
gtd.	guaranteed
pf.	preferred
pr. pf.	prior preferred
w.i.	when, as, and if issued
w.w.	with warrants

Quotations on listed stocks (and bonds) not traded on the New York Stock Exchange on a given day are found in a separate section and are in terms of bid and asked prices. The major New York dailies also report closing prices on a selected list of stocks on regional exchanges, as do *Barron's* and *The Commercial and Financial Chronicle.*

Quotations on options On July 12, 1977, the common stock of Ford Motor Company closed at $44 7/8 on the New York Stock Exchange. On the same date certain Ford call options (among others) were quoted on the Chicago Board Options Exchange at these prices (volume traded, in 100s, is also shown):

Option	Price	—Jul—		—Oct—		—Jan—		N.Y.
		Vol.	Last	Vol.	Last	Vol.	Last	Close
Ford	40	141	4 7/8	58	5	43	5 1/2	44 7/8

The buyer of the January option at $550 (100 shares at $5 1/2) would be able to buy 100 shares of Ford at any time until its January expiration for $40 a share.

Over-the-counter quotations A very large number of securities are not listed but are traded over-the-counter. In addition to the Federal obligations previously mentioned, this group includes: bonds of U.S. Government agencies that are fully guaranteed by the Government; bonds of Federally sponsored agencies, such as the Federal Land Banks; state and municipal bonds; railroad guaranteed stocks and equipment obligations; bank, insurance company, and investment company stocks; real estate securities; foreign securities (other than those listed); and a host of industrial, utility, and railroad bonds and stocks.

Quotations of local over-the-counter securities are obtained from dealer-broker houses, and the National Association of Securities Dealers, Inc. makes available daily and supervises the quotations for a large number of securities. The number of quotations varies from a long list in the major dailies and special financial newspapers to a short list in smaller local dailies.

In early 1971, a national automated quotation system (NASDAQ) was inaugurated; desk-top equipment provides instant quotations on several thousand over-the-counter securities to subscribing brokers and dealers.

Over-the-counter quotations are confined to bid and asked prices, and may be accompanied by dividend information (in the case of stocks). The bid price on the previous day is sometimes shown. (The over-the-counter market is discussed in Chapter 15.)

Mutual funds Quotations on selected lists of mutual fund (open-end investment company) shares are found in metropolitan dailies and in such sources as *Barron's*, *Wall Street Journal*, *Bank & Quotation Record*, and the *Commercial and Financial Chronicle*. The *Wall Street Journal* shows the net asset value, the offering price (these two are identical for "no-load" funds), and the change in net asset value from the close of the previous day. *The New York Times* and other dailies cite the "sell" (asset value) "buy" (bid price, or asset value less commission) and (in some cases), change in the buy price. For discussion of prices and quotations of investment company shares, see Chapter 11.

Sources of published price quotations Daily range and close: metropolitan newspapers; *Wall Street Journal.* Standard & Poor's *Daily Standard Price Records* provides three months of daily prices on over 5,600 stock issues.

Weekly range and close: Barron's; *Commercial & Financial Chronicle, Financial Weekly.*

Monthly range: Bank and Quotation Record, published monthly by Dana & Co., New York; Standard & Poor's *Security Owners Stock Guide.*

Annual range: some metropolitan newspapers; *Wall Street Journal;* Barron's (see first issue in January); *Commercial & Financial Chronicle;* Moody's *Manuals* (also "blue sections"), Moody's *Handbook of Common Stocks;* Standard & Poor's *Corporation Reports, Listed Bond Reports;* NYSE *Stock Reports,* and American *Stock Exchange Reports; Over-the-Counter and Regional Stock Reports; Bond Guide.*

Quotations on unlisted securities: available at brokers' offices from National Quotation Bureau, Inc., lists. This firm also publishes *National Monthly Stock Summary* and *National Monthly Bond Summary* (semiannually and monthly), giving quantity of orders and offers, and prices, of unlisted stocks and bonds. Many newspapers and such publications as the *Commercial & Financial Chronicle,* Barron's, and *Market Chronicle* publish quotations as a regular feature.

State and municipal bonds: Blue List of Current Municipal Offerings, Bank and Quotation Record, Moody's Bond Record, The Money Manager.

U.S. Government and Federal agency securities: selected lists in *The Wall Street Journal* and metropolitan dailies, *Commercial & Financial Chronicle, The Money Manager, The Financial Weekly.*

Options: They are now traded on the Chicago Board Options Exchange, the Midwest Exchange, the Philadelphia Exchange, the American Stock Exchange, and the Pacific Coast Exchange. Quotations appear in the *Wall Street Journal,* Barron's, the *Commercial & Financial Chronicle,* and in leading metropolitan dailies. For discussion of options, see Chapter 16.

General Investment Advice

The investor who is unwilling or unable to make his own investment selections has a number of sources of investment advice at his disposal. Some of this advice is aimed at all who read or subscribe; other advice is pointed at particular clients. But even if he relies somewhat on the opinions of others, the intelligent investor should be able to judge the reasonableness of the opinion he seeks.

Periodicals Certain journals are devoted primarily to investment advice. These include *Financial World, The Commercial & Financial Chronicle, Magazine of Wall Street,* and to a limited extent, *Forbes.* Barron's articles suggest the investment position of industries and companies. *Financial Analysts Journal* reports the impressions of professional analysts on industries and companies.

Statistical or subscription services Such services offer advice on industries, companies, and investment policy in their general publications such as Moody's *Bond Survey*, Standard & Poor's *Outlook*, *Bond* and *Stock Reports*, and *Industry Surveys*, and Fitch's (now Standard & Poor's) *Survey of Over-the-Conuter Securities*. Included in the pocket-sized manuals of these services are lists of companies suggested for investment. One weakness of such advice is that securities are often recommended on the basis of their earnings prospects without much regard to their prices.

Security ratings The statistical or subscription services also rate the quality of the more important securities by symbols such as Aaa, Aa, and so forth. Ratings are useful guides in the selection of suitable securities, but investors should find them valuable chiefly in confirming or challenging their own appraisals. Moody's and Standard & Poor's bond ratings are found in Moody's *Manual* and *Bond Survey* and Standard & Poor's *Corporation Descriptions* and *Bond Guide*, respectively. Another organization, Babson's Business Service, rates bonds (and stocks) in its reports to clients.

Standard & Poor's rates stocks in the pocket manuals and in the weekly advisory service. Common stocks bear symbols of A+ to C, preferred stocks AAA to C.

Financial World issues *Independent Appraisals of Listed Stocks* (monthly), in which stocks are rated by symbols. Quality symbols are also used in the *Value Line Investment Survey*.

Investment services The statistical and rating services not only provide advice in their general publications, but also sell investment advisory service to a more restricted group of clients. A large number of other firms are solely in the business of selling investment advice: Babson's, Value Line, United Business Service, and many others. Such services cover general market forecasting, general investment advice, and specific recommendations. The value of such services is difficult to assess. The investor should make a sample test of previous recommendations and discover how well they turned out.

Brokers, dealers, and investment banking houses Investors probably rely more on their security brokers and dealers for advice than on any other source. Some of these maintain research and analytical departments. Many of them publish research bulletins, brochures, and regular "market letters." Some are speculatively minded, and are mainly interested in producing appreciation in their clients' portfolios. And all of them live on commission volume. Nevertheless, the skilled and conscientious broker will strive to serve his customer well.

Personal Investment Advice

One difficulty with the above sources of advice is that their counsel is not often directed towards the special needs and conditions of different investors. This is to be expected, since much advice is free or relatively inexpensive. More personal advice costs money—and it is worth it if gets good results.

Sources of such advice are of four main types: (1) brokers, dealers, and investment houses; (2) banks and trust departments; (3) subscription services; and (4) professional investment counsel.

Brokers, dealers, and investment houses These sources offer personalized portfolio management of large accounts for a separate fee. Many of them are registered investment advisers. (See below.)

Banks and trust departments Many investors rely on their commercial banking connections for investment advice. Such advice is likely to be cautious, in keeping with banking tradition. More specific service, at a fee, is available from the larger banks on discretionary "agency" accounts, ranging from limited to full management. The trust department will also manage securities on a trust basis, individually or pooled in a "common trust fund." (See p. 431.)

The subscription services In addition to their general services, the investment and rating services offer portfolio reviews and management supervision of special accounts. The fee for thorough service for individuals, small banks, pension funds, and other investors may run from 1/4 to 1/2% of the principal, per annum, with a minimum of $500 to $1,000.

Professional Investment Management

Scope of the industry The investment advisory industry has achieved a position of major importance as a result of the growing interest in securities, the development of investment capital in more and more hands, the growth of institutional accumulations of funds and the increasing complexity of the task of investment management. A special impetus to growth has been the great increase in public and private pension funds and the new responsibilities of their managers under the Employee Retirement Income Security Act of 1974.

At the end of 1970, about 3,500 firms were engaged in supplying, at a fee, investment advice to a wide array of corporate, institutional, and individual clients. Assets under advisement totalled $130 billion, divided among 85,000 accounts.[5] (These figures do not include advisers whose sole service consists of the issuance of written reports; bank trust departments and life insurance companies are also excluded from the definition of "investment adviser").

The assets managed by 1,343 firms (constituting the great bulk of the industry's business) were distributed among major clients as shown in Table 13-1.

[5]The factual data in this section are derived from *Institutional Investor Study Report of the Securities and Exchange Commission*, Chapter IV. 92nd Congress, 1st Session, House Document No. 92–64, March 1971. This source provides a wealth of information on investment advisers that was never available before, including size measurements, securities holdings, organization, operations, management fees, expenses, revenues, and other facts. A good deal of the detail is derived from a study of a large sample of firms.

TABLE 13-1 Assets and Accounts of Investment Advisers

Type of Client	Assets ($ bill.) Total	Assets ($ bill.) Common Stock	No. of Accounts
Registered investment companies	$59.1	$48.3	893
Individuals and personal trusts	25.5	20.2	69,623
Employee benefit plans	13.1	8.4	4,337
State and local government pensions	6.5	1.5	191
Corporations	6.5	2.3	2,166
Educational endowments	5.7	3.6	477
Other nonprofit organizations	3.3	2.1	1,614
Insurance companies	4.1	1.3	439
Nonregistered investment companies	2.4	1.7	1,386
Advisers' own portfolios	1.6	1.2	804
Foundations	1.4	1.0	200 (est.)
Other	0.8	0.6	2,841
	$130.0	$92.2	84,971

Source: *Institutional Investor Study Report of the Securities and Exchange Commission,* Chapter IV, p. 150. 92nd Congress, 1st Session, House Document No. 92–64, 1971.

The average size of advisory accounts was highest for investment companies and lowest for individuals. In a sample of 158 advisory firms with 42,118 accounts, 75% of individuals' and personal trust accounts had assets of less than $.5 million.

Investment policy   Of the total assets managed, $92 billion or 71% consisted of common stock. The highest ratio of common was found in nonregistered investment companies (hedge funds, offshore funds) and the lowest in insurance companies. Individuals' and personal trust accounts averaged 79% in common stocks, but within this group there was a wide range of from zero to 100%.

Of the total funds managed, $78 billion or 60% of assets and 61,000 or 66% of accounts were "discretionary," that is, the advisers had full jurisdiction over the portfolios. This arrangement is most pronounced in the case of investment company and individual clients.

Management fees   The average advisory fee ran .46% of assets. Individuals' accounts fees were concentrated between .40 and .60%. Fees based on performance were charged in a number of cases.

Types and affiliations of advisory firms   The term "investment adviser" includes a variety of types of firms. As indicated above, many securities brokers and dealers manage portfolios on a fee basis. The term also includes publishers of advisory services such as bulletins, financial letters, forecasts, industry and company analyses, and investment advice. Our interest here is in a more restricted group, the *investment counsel* firms, whose function is to supply, for a fee, direct investment supervisory services to the type of clients listed in Table 13-1, and particularly those serving individuals.[6] Until recently, counsels have been interested only in fairly large accounts of individuals, but now firms are appearing which accept accounts as small as $5,000–$10,000, with typical fees of 2% with a minimum of $200. The larger firms (about fifty) are members of the Investment Counsel Association of America and operate under strict rules that require the highest level of professional conduct.

Regulation   Investment advisers who use the mails or interstate commerce must register with the Securities and Exchange Commission and are subject to regulation under the Investment Advisers Act of 1940.[7] They must file information with the Commission covering details of organization and operation, affiliations and qualifications of principals, records and contracts, scope of authority over clients' funds, management fees, and other details. Advisory contracts must be in writing. Fraudulent, deceitful, and manipulative conduct is prohibited. There is no requirement to file financial statements or periodic reports of condition with the Commission. The composition of clients' portfolios and the investment performance achieved are not made public. The investor who is considering employing an investment counsel must get any information on its investment competence from the firm or from other clients.

REFERENCES

AD HOC COMMITTEE OF LIBRARIANS, *Sources of Information on Transportation*, published for the Transportation Center at Northwestern University. Evanston, Ill.: Northwestern University Press, 1964.

ANDRIOT, J. L., *Guide to U.S. Government Statistics*, 4th ed. McLean, Va.: Documents Index, 1973.

COMAN, E. T., JR., *Sources of Business Information*, rev. ed. Berkeley, Calif.: University of California Press, 1964.

DANIELS, L. M., *Business Information Sources*. Berkeley, Ca.,: University of California Press, 1976.

D'ARCY, G. M., *Investment Counsel: Profit and Peace of Mind for the Investor*. New York: I. Oblensky, 1964.

FARELL, M. L., ed., *The Dow Jones Averages 1885–1970*. Princeton, N.J.: Dow Jones Books, 1972.

FLUMIANI, C. M., *How to Read the Wall Street Journal for Pleasure and Profit*. Springfield, Mass.: Library of Wall Street, 1967.

FOREST, J. G., *Financial News: How to Read and Interpret It*. New York: The New York Times, 1965.

---

[6]The subscription services qualify as "investment counsels" under the Investment Advisors Act if a "substantial" part of their income is derived from fee accounts.

[7]Investment advisers whose only clients are investment companies have been required to register since December 1971.

HAZARD, J. W., and MILTON CHRISTIE, *The Investment Business*, Chapter 5. New York: Harper & Row, Publishers, 1964.

How to Read and Understand Financial and Business News, 9th rev. ed. New York: Doubleday & Co., Inc., 1963.

Institutional Investor Study Report of the Securities and Exchange Commission, Chapter IV. 92nd Congress, 1st Session, House Document No. 92–64. Washington: U.S. Government Printing Office, 1971.

JOHNSON, H. W., *How to Use a Business Library*, 4th ed. Cincinnati: South-Western Publishing Co., 1974.

LEVINE, S. N., ed., *Financial Analyst's Handbook*, Chapters 32, 33. Homewood, Ill.: Dow Jones-Irwin, Inc., 1975.

McNIERNEY, MARY A., ed., *Directory of Business and Financial Services*, 6th ed. New York: Special Libraries Association, 1963.

SCHMECKEBIER, L. F., and R. B. EASTON, *Government Publications and Their Use*, 2d rev. ed. Washington, D.C.: The Brooking Institution, 1969.

SELECT INFORMATION EXCHANGE, *1970 Guide to Business and Investment Services*. New York: Geo. H. Wein, 1970.

Selected Business Reference Sources. Baker Library, Graduate School of Business Administration, Harvard University, 1971.

STABLER, C. N., *How to Read the Financial News*, 10th ed. New York: Harper & Row, Publishers, 1965.

U. S. DEPT. OF COMMERCE, BUREAU OF THE BUDGET, *Statistical Services of the United States Government*. Washington, D.C.: U.S. Government Printing Office (irregular).

WALTER, H. C., ed., *Investment Information and Advice*, 2d ed. Rochester. N.Y.: Fir Publishing Co., 1964.

WASSERMAN, PAUL, and JOANNE PASKAR, eds., *Statistics Sources*, 4th ed. Detroit: Gale Research Company, 1974.

WOY, J. B., *Investment Information: A Detailed Guide to Selected Sources*. Detroit: Gale Research Company, 1970.

——, *Investment Methods: A Bibliographical Guide*. New York: R. R. Bowker Co., 1973.

New Securities:
Investment Banking

SCOPE: This chapter discusses the origination and distribution of new securities offered to the public. It is chiefly concerned with the work of investment banking firms and with the regulation of their activities in marketing corporate issues. The order of discussion is: (1) economic functions of investment banking, (2) business functions of investment banking, (3) types and organization of investment banking firms, (4) methods of sale of new issues; (5) the buying and underwriting functions, (6) selling the securities, (7) other investment banking services, (8) Federal regulation of new issues, (9) state securities regulation, (10) new developments in investment banking.

Economic Functions of Investment Banking; The Primary Market

In the primary market for securities, new issues are offered to the investing public. The chief institution for this market is the investment banking firm.

The investment banker is a middleman, between the governmental or business issuer of securities and the investing public. Through him, new capital is obtained in large volume. To a large degree he influences the channels into which savings are directed. His responsibilities extend to the issuer for advice, aid in financing, and determination of sound financial practices. To his investor clients he is responsible for thorough investigation of the issuer and its securities, selection of sound issues, formation of investment judgment, and aid in maintaining a market, that is, standing ready to buy the securities he has helped to sell. He thus plays an important role in capital formation, both by making available to business concerns and public bodies the funds required for the operation and growth of the economy and by obtaining these funds from the savings of many millions of investors, directly and through financial institutions. As of 1976 about 3,000 firms regularly or at times acted in some sort of investment banking capacity, of which the core was represented by the 700 members of the Securities Industry Association (formerly the Investment Bankers Association).[1] In the past,

[1]*Directory of the Securities Industry Association,* New York, 1976.

investment bankers have underwritten over 50% of the securities sold in the United States, and aided in the placement of another 20%.[2]

Annual data are available on the gross proceeds of new corporate security issues (over $300,000 in size) offered for cash in the United States. (See Table 14-1.) Most of the issues sold publicly involve some or all of the services of investment bankers; many of those sold *privately*, that is, directly from corporation to institutional investor, are also placed by investment bankers acting as agents.

TABLE 14-1   Public and Private Security Offerings, 1976

Public offerings	
Registered under Securities Act of 1933	$35,908,000,000
Private offerings	16,253,000,000
Total	$52,161,000,000

Source: Securities and Exchange Commission, *Statistical Bulletin.*

Business Functions of Investment Banking

The chief function of the investment banker is the distribution of new issues of securities. He assists the issuer during the entire process of raising its required new capital, from the initial planning of the financing to the final placement of the securities with investors. He performs the same function as the merchant who buys goods on a wholesale basis and sells them at retail. In most transactions he also advises the corporation as to the form and timing of the sale.

In acting as merchants engaged in the distribution of securities, investment bankers differ from commercial bankers, who are primarily the custodians of funds deposited with them. The commercial banks, in loaning these funds, are, in effect, using capital which belongs to other people and which they must be prepared to return at short notice.[3] Investment bankers, who are not allowed to engage in deposit banking, must supply their own funds for purchasing securities, or use short-term bank credit for this purpose. As merchants, they place their capital in inventories for resale.

The investment banker should be distinguished from the *broker*, who is mostly concerned with executing transactions in outstanding securities for the account of others, and from the *dealer*, who buys and sells securities for his own account. Neither of these as such plays any part in the actual origination of new security issues, although they may be involved in the retail distribution of such issues.

Many brokerage houses maintain investment banking departments, and many investment banking firms have brokerage divisions that act as dealers

---

[2]*United States v. Henry S. Morgan, Harold Stanley, et al., Defendants' Preliminary Memorandum*, U.S. District Court for the Southern District of New York (Civil No. 43–757, 1950), pp. 12, 24.

[3]Commercial banks serve as investment bankers in underwriting municipal obligations. They also make industrial "term loans" for maturities as long as 10 years, and thus provide medium- and long-term capital.

in both listed and unlisted securities, and in mutual funds. A number of investment houses act as managers of portfolios for investors, organize and manage investment companies, deal in government securities, and maintain facilities for commodities trading. In recent years several investment banking firms have formed affiliated venture capital partnerships or corporations.

From a functional viewpoint, the work of an investment banking house may be divided into five fields:

The buying function: purchasing, through underwriting or otherwise, new issues of securities to be offered for resale.

The selling function: distributing, either at wholesale through other dealers or at retail to the public, the securities previously purchased.

The advisory function: giving professional advice to issuers and buyers of securities, based on information compiled by the research department.

The protective function: protecting the interests of holders of securities through the provision of secondary markets and aid in the reorganization of companies in trouble.

The service function: performing a number of miscellaneous services for the convenience of the investor.

Types and Organization of Investment Banking Firms

Types   Investment banking firms may be classified as: national or local, depending on their field of activity; partnerships or corporations, depending upon the form of organization; and underwriters or distributors, depending on the relationship with the issuer. Many of the larger investment houses (such as Merrill Lynch and Kidder, Peabody) do a nationwide business with offices in the principal cities; some of the very largest have no out-of-town offices (such as Morgan Stanley and Kuhn, Loeb). Some conduct a purely wholesale business; others are both wholesalers and large retailers. These firms are able to distribute relatively large portions of new issues and usually join in the original underwriting. Others are known as distributors, although the underwriting firms also act as distributors.

Only about 250 firms regularly accept corporate underwriting commitments. Only about 50 firms manage the major issues of securities. Most of these have their headquarters in New York, Chicago, and San Francisco.

Internal organization   The internal organization of an investment banking firm depends chiefly upon its size. The larger houses have three major departments: a buying department, which investigates new clients, originates new issues, and deals with institutional investors in private placements; a syndicate department, which deals primarily with other firms in organizing purchase groups to handle large issues; and a sales department. Large firms also maintain statistical and research organizations. The smaller houses combine many activities into a few operating departments.

Methods of Sale of New Issues

Investment banks participate in the following major types of transactions related to the raising of capital:

1. Private placement of securities with institutions, the investment bank acting as the agent of the issuer.
2. Underwritten negotiated public offerings, where the investment bank obtains the issue, for resale, by direct negotiation with the issuer.
3. Underwritten sealed-bidding public offerings, where the issue is obtained by a successful bid in competition with other bidders.
4. Agency or best-efforts issues, where the firm sells securities to the public as the issuer's agent, without any underwriting risk.
5. Privileged subscription offerings, where the firm guarantees the successful sale by the issuer to its own stockholders.

Direct and private sale of securities   Not all securities are placed in the hands of investors through investment banking houses. Direct selling is employed by the Federal government in the issue of new obligations. Direct selling is also employed by new, weak, and speculative concerns that cannot obtain or cannot afford the services of an investment banker. Sale of securities to employees and executives is also direct, as is the sale of new stock or convertible bonds to present stockholders by privileged subscription. (The offer of stock by rights is described in Chapter 9.) In many cases, however, the issuing corporation may have the successful sale of securities through rights guaranteed or underwritten by investment bankers, under a "stand-by" agreement described later in this chapter. Direct sale of bonds (other than convertible issues) is unusual.

Direct selling also takes the form of *private placements*, whereby a corporation sells securities in large blocks to large investing institutions, chiefly life insurance companies, without utilizing the underwriting services of the middleman. Investment bankers participate in such offerings by acting as the intermediaries for their corporate clients. Their "finding fee" will range from 1/4 to 1 1/2% of the issue. An offering to no more than 25 potential buyers is generally considered a private sale, exempt from registration under the Securities Act of 1933. Most private sales are made to one or a very few buyers. Over 50% of corporate bond offerings, consisting mainly of high-grade industrial securities, are now offered privately. (See Chapter 3.)

The growth of private placement is attributable in part to the requirements of the Securities Act of 1933 with respect to issues publicly offered. It avoids the time, work, expense, and possible liability incurred in registration of new issues and the uncertainty created by the required waiting period that precedes the public offering. Private placement also saves the traditional underwriting commission of the investment bankers. But the chief reason for its growth is the opportunity to tap the great institutional market with "tailor-made" contracts that shape the debt to the needs of both corporation and investor. A technical disadvantage is that such securities are not eligible for resale to the public at a later date until the proper registration procedure is then completed. The major disadvantage, however, is that the investing public is prevented from participating directly in the better new issues which are preempted by relatively few large institutions.

Private negotiation The new securities bought by investment banking houses for resale are obtained either through negotiated sales by the issuer to the bankers, or through competitive bidding. Under the former method, an investment banking house, or more frequently, a group of participating houses, acquires the issue from a corporation in a private deal. The sale may go to a particular banking house because of previous satisfactory services. Or it may result from the search for new issues, or from relations with other bankers. New financing proposals may also reach investment banking houses through the direct application of the corporation seeking funds. Choice of the firm to handle an issue is very important because of the close and confidential relationship that will prevail between the investment banker and his client.

Negotiated underwriting is largely confined to the issues of industrial companies as contrasted with railroad and public utility securities, which are ordinarily acquired by competitive bidding. The lack of uniformity and comparability among industrial companies makes competitive bidding inappropriate for their financing.

Competitive bidding The traditional custom of investment bankers in buying new corporate securities through private negotiation has been considerably undermined by regulation requiring competitive bidding for certain types of securities. Approximately one-half of all corporate bonds, including nearly all railroad and most utility bonds, and virtually all state and municipal bonds, are now sold through this procedure.[4] Few industrial bonds are offered in this manner.

The Interstate Commerce Commission requires this type of bidding for equipment trust issues and other types of railroad debt securities. Certain state utility commissions, such as those of Massachusetts, New Hampshire, Indiana, California, and New York, require competitive bidding for companies under their jurisdiction, as does the Federal Power Commission. The Securities and Exchange Commission requires competitive bidding for security issues of registered holding companies and their gas and electric subsidiaries. Issues of less than $1,000,000 are exempt, as are issues sold pursuant to preemptive rights.

Competitive bidding is necessary and appropriate in the case of municipal bonds. The main reason for its use in the sale of corporate securities has been the desire to eliminate or lessen monopoly in securities underwriting. Advocates of the practice also maintain that securities will be better priced,

---

[4]In 1963, 47.5% of corporate bonds sold to the public for cash were acquired by competitive bidding, of which 44.4% consisted of utility bonds; and 51.9% of the bonds were acquired by negotiation, of which only 8.5% were utility bonds. The remaining bonds were not underwritten. Irwin Friend, *Investment Banking and the New Issues Market.* Cleveland: The World Banking Co., 1967, p. 390. Current data are not available.

commissions more reasonable, distribution wider, and unwise dominance of corporations by their bankers eliminated. The leading arguments against the practice are:

- The investment banker becomes a mere merchant and cannot provide the issuer with advice on the terms of the issue, the timing of the offering, and the appropriate price. However, in some cases the corporation employs an investment banking firm to assist it in designing an issue for public sealed bidding, at a fee for services as a financial expert. Such advisers may not participate as underwriters.
- Issues may become overpriced and consequently run the risk of "stickiness" in anything but a very strong market.
- Small dealers are discouraged from participating through the decline in their portion of the gross commission.
- The investment banker cannot represent the interests of the investor as well as through private negotiations, because of the less complete investigation, lack of advice to the issuer, and possible overpricing of the issue.

Underwriting securities   Large issues involve more risk than a single investment house is willing to assume. Wide and rapid distribution is necessary, and one firm cannot afford to have a large portion of its capital in one issue. While the negotiations are nearing completion, or before a competitive bid is entered, the originating house, acting as group manager, invites a group of investment houses to share in the purchase. The number invited varies with the size and character of the issue and the current condition of the securities market. It may range from as few as two to over 200. The $200,000,000 issue of Communications Satellite Corporation common stock in June 1964 was underwritten by 385 houses. The financial responsibility of the participants, the particular markets in which they specialize, their past records, and their ability to distribute securities are the chief criteria for their selection. The managing or originating house determines the size of the individual participations. Under present practice, the purchase agreement is signed by the originating firm as the representative of all members of the purchase group.

The Securities Act requires a waiting period of 20 days between the filing of the registration statement and the effective date of public offering of the issue. The agreement to purchase is contingent on the registration statement's becoming effective, for without effective registration the purchasers cannot publicly offer the security, if the offering falls under the scope of the Securities Act. This is why the final agreement is not actually signed until just before public offering.

The Buying and Underwriting Functions

The buying department   The buying department of a large investment banking firm is ordinarily organized into two divisions: corporate and municipal. Firms which act as distributors rather than underwriters do not have buying departments; they obtain their wares from underwriting firms through sales agreements.

When a corporate bond issue is sold through competitive bidding, decisions concerning the amount and form of the financing are made by the company's management, which (if required) files a registration statement with the Securities and Exchange Commission and issues an invitation for public bidding after the customary 20-day waiting period. In the case of larger issues, bidding groups are formed to enter joint offers. The bidders make an intensive study of the quality and terms of the issue and of the market for similar securities. A bond or preferred stock issue is awarded to the bid that provides the lowest cost of money; the highest net price per share wins the bid on a common stock issue.

As indicated previously, municipal securities are purchased through competitive bidding. The municipality advertises its issue in a daily newspaper or in *The Daily Bond Buyer*, stating the terms of the issue and calling for sealed bids. Usually the bid showing the lowest net interest cost to the issuer is accepted. When a proposed issue is larger than single firms can handle, bids are placed for a designated part of the issue. The aggregate price obtainable from the best combination of partial bids is frequently less than the price offered by the bidder for an entire issue on an "all-or-none" basis, so buying firms usually offer group bids for an entire issue on joint account.

The work of the buying department in making a bid for a new issue of municipal bonds is chiefly mathematical. After estimating carefully the price which could be received from the sale of the bonds to the public, with due consideration for interest rate and maturity date, a profit differential is subtracted and a bid price is determined. If it is assumed that the bonds could be sold on a 5.70% yield basis, which would indicate a sales price of 103.55($1,035.5 per bond) for 6% bonds with a 20-year maturity, a profit margin of .8 point ($8 per bond) might be subtracted, leaving an indicated bid price of 102.70($1,027 per bond). In a strong municipal bond market, the profit margin might be cut to 1/2 of 1% ($5.00 per bond), indicating a bid price of 102.20($1,022 per bond). As other bidders have probably calculated along the same lines, the actual bids are seldom in simple fractions, but in involved decimals such as 102.175.

As indicated previously, most industrial securities are purchased through private negotiations between the investment house and the corporation. The usual procedure of an investment banking firm may be divided into three major steps. The first is the "office" analysis of the company's finances and management that follows the first discussions. The second is the engineering, legal, and accounting examination. The third is the negotiation conference, at which the final decision is reached.

The purchase agreement between the underwriters (purchase group) and the corporation contains provisions covering: (1) title, amount, and complete description of the provisions of the security; (2) warranties by the issuer, including full compliance with the Securities Act, proper accounting certification, correct financial statements, absence of lawsuits against the issuer, and qualification of the issue under state blue-sky laws; (3) the agreement of the underwriters to purchase and of the issuer to sell the entire issue, usually with several liability on the part of the underwriters, and the amount each underwriter agrees to purchase; (4) the price of the issue, the underwriting discounts or commissions, and the method of payment and delivery; (5) the agreement of the underwriters to make a public offering within a fixed period after the effective date of registration at a stipulated offering price; (6) the agreement of the issuer to pay all expenses in connection with the issuance and delivery of the securities to the purchasers; (7) the agreement of the issuer to deliver copies of the prospectus if required under the Securities Act; (8) the agreement of the issuer and underwriters to indemnify each other against any liabilities under the Securities Act, with certain reservations; (9) any limitation on obligations of the underwriters, such as those arising out of adverse changes in the condition of the issuer or in the market; (10) the furnishing of certified financial statements by the issuer.

The purchase group (also known as the *purchase syndicate* or *underwriting syndicate*) is tied together by an "agreement among underwriters," which is a temporary partnership agreement that sets forth the rights and liabilities of the underwriters among themselves. It authorizes the originating firm to act as agent and manager of the group (for which it is paid a specified sum), stipulates the terms of payment by each underwriter for his share of the issue, and contains provisions for stabilizing the market, disposition of unsold securities, termination of the contract, and the nature of the obligation or liability of the members. The liability of each member is limited to the amount of his participation.

Several days after the public offering the company delivers the securities to the underwriters, or to their representative, and the managing underwriter delivers a check to the company in payment of the agreed price for the entire issue. The firms participating in the purchase group "take down" only that part of their subscription which they plan to sell directly, and leave the remainder for distribution to members of the selling group, from whom they will receive reimbursement through the underwriting managers.

Pricing and the underwriters' spread   An important and delicate task of the investment banker is to set the time and the price at which the issue is to be sold to investors. He is guided by the prices and yields prevailing in the market on comparable issues. Underpricing deprives the issuer of funds that might otherwise have been raised. Overpricing may result in delayed sale and large losses for the underwriters.

The price includes the underwriters' spread or commission.

The factors determining the size of the spread as a percent of issue price are as follows. The factors are not mutually exclusive.

- *Size.* Spreads have an inverse relation to size. (See Table 14-2.)
- *Quality.* This is closely related to size and type of issue.
- *Type of issue.* Lowest spreads are found in bonds, highest for common stocks, with preferred stocks and convertible debentures in between.

• *Principal trading market.* A new unlisted issue costs more to float than a well-known issue listed on the New York Stock Exchange.

• *Method of distribution.* Firm underwriting costs less than "best efforts" or sale through rights.

Keeping in mind that the commission is payment for risk and effort, the lowest spread percent is found in the case of a large, high-grade bond issue with an existing market, firmly underwritten. At the other end of the spectrum comes a small, speculative common stock, without a good existing secondary market, sold on a "best-efforts" basis.

The underwriting spreads, representing commissions and discounts to investment bankers, on various types of securities registered with the Securities and Exchange Commission for public distribution in 1971–1972, are shown in Table 14-2 as a percent of gross proceeds.

TABLE 14-2   Average Underwriting Spreads as a Percentage of Proceeds of Public Sale of Corporate Securities 1971–1972

Size of Issue ($ millions)	"Straight" Bonds	Convertible Bonds	Preferred Stock	Common Stock
Under 0.5	11.51	—	—	13.24
0.5–0.99	5.25	14.56	—	10.48
1.0–1.99	12.98	9.78	8.36	10.60
2.0–4.99	4.02	6.70	—	8.19
5.0–9.99	2.36	3.85	1.88	6.70
10.0–19.99	1.20	2.00	1.37	5.52
20.0–49.99	1.00	1.64	1.37	4.41
50.0–99.99	0.89	1.24	1.35	3.94
100.0–499.99	0.83	1.17	2.25	3.03
Over 500.00	0.88	—	—	—
Average spread[a]	1.14	3.20	1.52	8.41
No. of issues	659	147	150	1599

[a] Average of total issues, not average of classifications shown.

Source: Securities and Exchange Commission, *Cost of Flotation of Registered Issues, 1971–1972.* Washington, D.C.: U.S. Government Printing Office, 1974.

The spread or commission consists of three elements: (1) the management fee of about 20% in negotiated transactions and 5% of the gross spread in most competitive transactions, (2) the compensation for underwriting of about 30% of the gross spread after allowing for the management fee, and (3) the selling commission of about 50%. Thus, in a negotiated deal with 2% overall spread, management might receive 3/8%, 5/8% might be retained by the underwriters, and 1% might be the compensation for selling. (Members of the National Association of Securities Dealers, Inc., are customarily allowed a "trade" concession of 1/8%.) Where an underwriter sells all or part of his participation to his own clients, he receives both the underwriting and selling portions of the spread on all bonds taken up. The amount of the commission or discount to be retained by the underwriters must be fully disclosed in the registration statement and in the final prospectus describing the offering.

In addition to bankers' commissions and discounts, the corporation incurs other expenses of flotation, including preparation of the registration statement and prospectus. For securities registered with the Commission in 1971–1972, these expenses ranged between 3 and 24% of gross proceeds, in inverse relation to size and quality.

In addition to cash compensation, managing underwriters are frequently given warrants on options to purchase common stock at favorable prices. The typical issue bearing such extra compensation is small and lacks quality, and investment bankers must be given a "sweetener" to induce them to take the risk of underwriting, or even to use their "best efforts" to sell the stock, because their reputation is involved.

"Best-efforts" or agency selling   A deviation from outright purchase by underwriters under a firm commitment is an arrangement whereby the investment house takes no risk but merely acts as agent for the company, agreeing to use its best efforts to distribute the securities at the public offering price. Such arrangements are found chiefly in the distribution of stocks, especially smaller unseasoned issues, although very occasionally a high-grade bond or stock issue will be sold under these terms. The typical common stock issue sold by "best efforts" is under $1 million in size with seldom a preexisting market. Best-efforts commissions average about 13% of gross proceeds, compared to 8% on underwritten issues which average $10 million but may run up to $500 million in size.[5]

An example of a large high-grade issue sold by "best efforts" is the offering by American Telephone and Telegraph in June 1976 of 12 million common shares at $54.85 per share, netting $636,300,000 after a commission of $1.85 per share.

"Stand-by" underwriting   In its strict sense, the term *underwriting* refers to an insurance function whereby underwriters agree to take up the unsold portion of an issue that is being offered by the corporation directly to the investor. The definition of an *underwriter* contained in the Securities Act of 1933 includes both this arrangement and outright purchase by investment banks. The term *stand-by* or *pure* underwriting is used to describe the former arrangement.

The most frequent use of the stand-by arrangement is found in the issuance of stock or convertible bonds to present stockholders under privileged subscription.[6] Where the issuer does not wish to incur the risk, an underwriting group is formed to stand by to take any securities not purchased by stockholders. A commission is paid, consisting of a certain rate on the whole issue; an additional commission may be paid on all shares taken up by the banking group. If stockholders subscribe to the whole issue, the underwriters have been paid for their assurance that the funds will be available when

[5]Securities and Exchange Commission, *Cost of Flotation of Registered Issues, 1971–1972.* Washington, D.C.: U.S. Government Printing Office, 1974.
[6]See discussion of convertible securities in Chapter 9.

required, and for advisory services. The additional commission is in the nature of a real purchase-and-resale discount.

Typical minimum commissions for better-grade securities offered through rights will run: (1) convertible debentures of industrial companies, 1.00 to 1.25%; (2) preferred stocks of industrial companies, 1.50 to 3.50%; (3) industrial common stocks, 1.00 to 5.00%; and (4) utility common stocks, .50 to 3.00%. Additional compensation is usually paid on any securities not subscribed and taken up by the underwriters.

Occasionally a corporation will offer securities to present owners, through rights, at a subscription price so far below market price or in such a strong stock market that it dispenses with stand-by underwriting. A spectacular example of this is found in the case of the offering of $713,313,000 convertible 4 1/4% debentures of 1973 by the American Telephone & Telegraph Company in January 1958, at par ($100). Each $100 debenture was to be convertible into a share of common stock by delivery of the debenture and $42 in cash. The market price of the company's common stock at the time was $170 per share. This was the largest single piece of private corporation financing on record until the same company offered the largest bond issue on record in May 1970. The offering of $1,569,000,000 debentures, plus warrants, was made through rights. No underwriters were involved. And in June 1971, the company sold, through rights, $1,375,000,000 of new convertible preferred stock. (See p. 189.) Again, no stand-by underwriting was used.

As illustrated in the above cases, the services of an underwriter are unnecessary where the issuer's stock enjoys broad public ownership, a good and relatively stable secondary market, and when the subscription price is well below market price.

Selling the Securities

Once an issue is underwritten, it must be sold as rapidly and as widely as possible in order to satisfy the issuer and limit the risk of the underwriters. In the case of large issues, the usual device for distributing the issue to the ultimate investor is the *selling group*, which sells that portion of the issue not sold by the underwriters directly to their own clients. The selling group consists of "representative dealers," (sometimes as many as several hundred), who are invited to enter into an agreement entitling them to share in retailing the issue; they are selected on the basis of their ability to obtain permanent placement of the securities. They receive the portion of the gross spread mentioned previously that is allotted to the selling function, on all securities passed along to them. The members of the group are committed financially only for those securities for which they subscribe.

Invitations to participate in a selling group are sent out early, but the actual formation of the group, in the case of securities whose offering is subject to the provisions of the Securities Act of 1933, is delayed until the effective date of the registration statement. In the interim, the dealers are acquainted with the details of the forthcoming issue by means of a preliminary or "red herring" prospectus which differs from the final one in omitting the price at which the issue will be offered to the public and the concession (share of the spread) that will be allowed the members of the selling group.[7]

The arrangements between the purchasing and selling groups are set forth in an agreement in the form of a letter from the manager to the selling group members. It includes, among other matters, the offer of a specific amount of securities to the invited dealer, the public offering price, and the amount of the dealer's concession, together with provisions for terminating the group. The securities cannot be offered to the public below the public offering price during the life of the group, which, under present-day practice, seldom exceeds one month. Some offerings are not quickly absorbed, however, because of market conditions or because they have been overpriced.

Underwriting groups support the market while offering new securities. To avoid the effect of reported transactions at prices lower than that set in the public offering, the underwriting manager places buying orders in the market for purchases at the public offering price. The market price of a new issue is not allowed to fall below the established price during the period of distribution. Such market stabilization has been approved as an essential part of security distribution. However, two rules must be observed: (1) Notice of the intention to support the market must be included in the prospectus, and (2) daily reports of stabilizing operations to facilitate the distribution of a registered security must be made to the Securities and Exchange Commission. After the offering period, unsold securities are sold at their new (lower) value.[8]

New issues of securities are ordinarily sold through direct solicitation by salesmen employed by the investment dealers, who are compensated on a commission basis. Investors should realize that all securities are not of uniform quality and are, therefore, not equally suitable for all buyers. While reputable investment houses naturally avoid poor securities, they do not confine themselves to those of the highest grade. The more conservative houses instruct their salesmen not to offer securities indiscriminately. Investors, in turn, should not assume that all securities offered by a house in which they have confidence are desirable commitments.

Other Investment Banking Services

The advisory function Investment banking firms provide advice to issuers of securities. A corporation that has decided to sell securities will consult with the investment house which usually handles its issues before determining the nature of the offering. The firm is constantly in touch with market conditions and can recommend the type of security that will prove

[7]The term "red herring" is derived from the fact that each page of the prospectus contains a statement, printed in red, that information is subject to correction and that the document is not an offer to sell or a solicitation of an offer to buy the securities described.

[8]Investment bankers are concerned when institutions and hedge funds liquidate large blocks of their own stock against "the syndicate bid," thus disrupting the orderly placement of a new issue. In March 1976, Morgan Stanley Company, acting on behalf of the underwriters, stabilized the one-million-share offering of Union Camp Corporation at $92. Some 160,500 shares were sold against the $92 bid, causing the syndicate to be terminated earlier than planned.

most attractive under existing conditions, the provisions it should include, and the price it should bring. Moreover, it may advise on future needs and market conditions. This advisory function has been explained as follows.

What the issuer is normally interested in, when it selects an investment banker to assist it in raising capital, is getting the required amount of funds at a cost of money that is as low as is consistent with a number of vital considerations: these include the maintenance of a sound capital structure, its credit standing, and its relationships with its securityholders, as well as the imposition of restrictions on its operating flexibility. A form of security which would result in the cheapest cost of money to the issuer at the particular time, for example, may in fact turn out to be far more expensive to the issuer because it is not suited to its overall financial and operating requirements. There is an enormous variety of securities and provisions which can be designed to meet the needs of a particular issuer and the demands of particular markets. In the determination of the proper combination of provisions for the particular security, all the above-mentioned factors must be taken into account.[9]

Another advisory service to issuers is aid in planning mergers. For example, in February 1976, Lehmann Brothers advised Colgate Palmolive on its acquisition of Riviana Foods, and Marcor's merger with Mobil Oil in July 1976.

Many large common stock issues are sold directly to the public without underwriting or even "best-efforts" selling. A group of investment firms is formed to assist the issue in the details of the offering and to solicit subscriptions for a stipulated commission.

Investment houses also advise investors. They are always willing to discuss the suitability of a particular security to the needs of the investor, either in personal consultation or by correspondence. Many houses invite their customers to submit investment lists for periodical examination, on the basis of which recommendations are made for changes they believe will be beneficial. Most houses will cheerfully prepare an analysis of any security in which a customer may be interested, even though the firm may have no interest in the issue.

The protective function Investment houses usually act to protect the interests of customers in securities which later meet default. They form protective committees to represent the securityholders in the reorganization of the company so as to obtain the most equitable treatment.

As an additional method of protecting the interests of their customers, investment houses usually maintain trading departments. The trading department usually "makes a market" in securities previously issued by the house by maintaining bid and asked prices. Orders for the purchase and sale of securities not issued by the house are handled through this department. Requests for price quotations from customers are likewise answered by this division. The work of the trading department is especially valuable in con-

---

[9]*U.S.A. v. Henry S. Morgan, Harold Stanley, et al., Brief on the Service Function of the Investment Banker* (September 28, 1951), p. 52.

nection with unlisted securities, because of the lack of reliable quotations for many issues in this important group. Unlike the trading department of a brokerage house, which is operated for the prime purpose of direct profit, the trading department of an investment house is maintained principally to assist the sales department in the distribution of new issues. As we saw above, during the offering period, the house or selling syndicate operates a trading account through which the price of the securities is stabilized until the entire issue is sold. Such trading is legitimate if it is made known to prospective buyers in the offering prospectus. (See below.)

The service function Investment banking firms perform many minor services of considerable benefit to their customers. They protect securities in their vaults in special safekeeping envelopes. They collect interest and dividend payments when so requested. They notify investors of called bonds and of opportunities to profit from sinking fund offers or conversion options. They keep files of customer security holdings and stand ready to make suggestions for the improvement of portfolios. They maintain analytical departments that produce information available to customers. They advise customers on income and estate tax problems in connection with security holdings. Usually, no special charges are made for these services.

Federal Regulation of New Issues

The Securities Act of 1933 marked the passing of an old order and the beginning of a new epoch in the business of security marketing. As aptly remarked by President Roosevelt in recommending this legislation, the old slogan of "let the buyer beware" has been amended to "let the seller also beware." The obligation of full disclosure in connection with new security offerings has been placed upon the issuing corporation and the distributing investment house.

The Securities Act does not eliminate statutes ("blue-sky" laws) governing intrastate sale of securities, or interfere in the security-approval functions of the Interstate Commerce Commission or the state public utility commissions. The Federal law supplements existing state laws which had not proved sufficiently rigorous in preventing severe losses to the investing public, and which lack uniformity. It applies only to securities offered through the mails or in interstate commerce. In general, the law requires that specific information on new security offerings be filed with the Securities and Exchange Commission prior to sale to the public, and that the issuers be held responsible for the completeness and accuracy of such information.

Exempt securities Certain classes of domestic securities are exempt from the provisions of the Securities Act:

- United States Government obligations and bonds of territories and Federal agencies;
- State and municipal bonds;

- Securities issued by railroads and other common carriers subject to Federal regulation;
  - Receiver's and trustee's certificates, issued with court approval;
  - Issues aggregating less than $500,000 in any one year if regulations of the Commission are complied with;
  - Securities of savings and loan associations and banks;
  - Securities issued in exchange for old securities in a reorganization or recapitalization;
  - Intrastate issues;
  - Securities sold by private placement.

Exempt transactions Certain transactions are exempted from the Securities Act:

1. Transactions in new issues, not through an underwriter and not involving a public offering (that is, sold to 25 or fewer persons),
2. Transactions by persons who are not issuers, underwriters, and dealers,
3. Brokerage transactions, executed upon unsolicited customers' orders, and
4. Offerings limited to the residents of a state by an issuer in that state.

Registration statement Before new securities may be offered to the public, a registration statement, which becomes effective 20 days later— or earlier, as the Commission may determine—must be filed with the Securities and Commerce Commission. Copies must be made available to the public. The Commission may issue a deficiency statement or serve a stop order if the statement is incomplete or inaccurate in any material respect. The registration statement must give specific information on a number of designated points, among which are:

1. General information on the issuer—location, products, and so forth;
2. Purposes of issue;
3. Price at which offered to the public;
4. Price at which offered to any special group;
5. Promoters' fees;
6. Underwriting fees;
7. Net proceeds to the company;
8. Remuneration of any officers receiving over $25,000 annually;
9. Disclosure of any unusual contracts, such as managerial profit-sharing;
10. Detailed capitalization statement;
11. Detailed balance sheet;
12. Detailed earnings statement for three preceding years;
13. Names and addresses of officers, directors, and underwriters;
14. Names and addresses of stockholders owning more than 10% of any class of stock;
15. Pending litigation;
16. Copy of the underwriting agreement;
17. Copy of legal opinions;

18. Copy of articles of incorporation or association;
19. Copies of indentures affecting new issues.

A separate group of requirements is provided in connection with new issues of foreign governments.

The prospectus The prospectus is the document supplied to the investor by which a security is offered for sale. Its information must coincide with that in the registration statement, with the omission of certain technical features, as stated in the law and as determined by the Commission.

Injunctions and criminal proceedings Willful violations of the Act are subject to injunction by the Commission, which may also institute criminal proceedings against the violators in the Federal courts, with possible fines and imprisonment.

Civil liability If the registration statement contains any untrue statement of a material fact or omits any material fact, any purchaser unaware at the time of purchase of such situation may take legal action, within three years, for recovery of loss against the persons mentioned in the statement as officers or directors of the company, as professional advisers, or as underwriters. To escape liability such persons (other than the issuer) must prove that after reasonable investigation they had no reasonable ground for belief that the information was incomplete or inaccurate. Damages may not exceed the price at which the security was offered to the public.

Financial statements In connection with the balance sheets and earnings statements required in the registration statement and prospectus, the Securities and Exchange Commission is empowered to prescribe the forms in which the information is to be submitted, the items to be shown, and the methods to be followed in the preparation of accounts, in the appraisal of assets and liabilities, in the determination of depreciation and depletion, and in the differentiation between charges to capital accounts and to operating expense.

Speculative securities The purpose of the Securities Act is not to prevent the sale of speculative issues, but rather to stop the sale of fraudulent securities and to place before the investor all the facts necessary for intelligent judgment. Investors must rely upon their own or other opinions in arriving at a decision to purchase.[10]

[10]The position of the Commission in this important respect has been officially stated as:

The public should thoroughly understand that the Commission is not authorized to pass in any sense upon the value or soundness of any security. Its sole function is to see that full and accurate information as to the security is made available to purchasers and the public, and that no fraud is practiced in connection with the sale of the security.

Speculative securities may still be offered and the public is as free to buy them as ever.

The Commission's duty is to see that the security is truthfully presented to prospective purchasers. The fact that a description of the security and of the concern issuing the security is filed with the Commission is in no sense and must not be regarded as an endorsement or approval of the security or the concern by the Commission.

Appraisal of the Securities Act   The effectiveness of the disclosure provisions of the Securities Act of 1933 is difficult to evaluate. Many issues of securities never get through the registration procedure, being screened out by the inability or unwillingness of their promoters to disclose the required information. How many other questionable issues are never filed for registration because of inability or unwillingness to disclose the facts will never be known. How much reliance the average investor places on the copious information available in the prospectus cannot be measured. At least it is there for him to use if he wishes to use it and can understand it; but most individual investors do not rely heavily upon it. Large investors and investing institutions, as well as investment managers and counsels, are the chief users of both the prospectus and the registration statement.

The effectiveness of the fraud sections of the Act is also difficult to appraise. An unknown number of persons have been deterred, by fear of possible indictment, from interstate sale of securities or use of the mails. But others have run the risk and paid the penalty. Up to June 30, 1976 the Commission had obtained convictions against 2,846 defendants in the criminal cases developed by it.[11]

Special Federal securities regulation   The issuance of certain securities exempt from the Securities Act, notably that of railroads and other interstate common carriers, is subject to special regulation. The purpose of issue, form of issue, and disposition of funds raised through the sale of securities (with certain exceptions) are subject to the control of the Interstate Commerce Commission. Such regulation, like that of the financing of utilities registered under the Public Utility Holding Company Act of 1935 and those affected by state utility commission control, is largely designed to assure conformity with sound principles of finance. Although railroads are not required to issue prospectuses in the form prescribed by the Securities Act, similar documents are often used to describe railroad issues.

State Securities Regulation

State statutes, popularly known as "blue-sky" laws, exist in all states except Nevada for the purpose of protecting investors from fraudulent security offerings. These laws lay down certain rules for the sale of securities within the state and impose penalties for their violation. About one-half of them require the registration or licensing of distributors; most require that securities be registered. In four states (Delaware, Maryland, New Jersey, and New York) the statutes include antifraud laws that enjoin and prosecute fraud when or after the issue has been sold. State blue-sky laws exempt many types of securities.

Lack of uniformity of state securities laws and the fact that they applied only to issues within the state were among the reasons for the passage of the Federal law in 1933. The Federal law is much stricter generally.

---

[11]*Annual Report of the S.E.C.* (Washington, D.C.: U.S. Government Printing Office, 1977.

New Developments in Investment Banking

Investment banking has expanded markedly from its original function of underwriting and distributing domestic securities. Investment firms have become specialists in arranging private placements. Their advisory services extend to municipal governments as well as to business corporations. They are increasingly involved, from head office and foreign branches, in raising capital abroad. They are entering the fields of lease financing, real estate planning, and venture capital. They face increasing competition from bank holding companies in some of these respects. These developments, in addition to the necessity to cut costs and to protect capital, explain the trend towards reduced numbers and larger size in the investment banking field.

REFERENCES

BLACK, HILLEL, *The Watchdogs of Wall Street*. New York: William Morrow & Company, Inc., 1962.

BOGEN, J. I., ed., *Financial Handbook*, 4th rev. ed., Section 9. New York: The Ronald Press Company, 1968.

CAROSSO, V. P., *Investment Banking in America: A History*. Cambridge, Mass.: Harvard University Press, 1970.

CHILDS, J. F., *Encyclopedia of Long-Term Financing and Capital Management*. Englewood Cliffs, N.J.: Prentice-Hall, Inc., 1976.

CLARK, F. G., and R. S. RIMANOCZY, *Where the Money Comes From*. New York: Van Nostrand Reinhold Company, 1961.

COHAN, A. B., *Cost of Flotation of Long-Term Corporate Debt Since 1935*. Chapel Hill, N.C.: School of Business Administration, University of North Carolina, 1961.

———, *Private Placements and Public Offerings: Market Shares Since 1935*. Chapel Hill, N.C.: School of Business Administration, University of North Carolina, 1961.

COMMERCE CLEARING HOUSE, *Federal Securities Law Reporter*. New York: Commerce Clearing House, Inc., loose-leaf.

DAVEY, P. J., *Investment Banking Arrangements*. New York: The Conference Board, 1976.

DEBEDTS, R. F., *The New Deal's S.E.C: The Formative Years*. New York: Columbia University Press, 1964.

DOUGALL, H. E., and J. E. GAUMNITZ, *Capital Markets and Institutions*, 3d ed., Chapters 9, 10. Englewood Cliffs, N.J.: Prentice-Hall, Inc., 1975.

FRIEND, IRWIN, et al., *Investment Banking and the New Issues Market*. Cleveland: The World Publishing Company, 1967.

GOLDBERG, S. E., *Private Placements and Restricted Securities*. New York: Clark Boardman Co., Ltd., 1971.

INVESTMENT BANKERS ASSOCIATION OF AMERICA, *The Role of the Investment Banker in Arranging Private Financing*. New York: The Association, 1961.

KNAUSS, R. L., *Securities Regulation Sourcebook*. New York: Practicing Law Institute, 1970.

LEFFLER, G. L., and L. C. FARWELL, *The Stock Market*, 3d ed., Chapter 25. New York: The Ronald Press Company, 1963.

LOSS, LOUIS, *Securities Regulation*, 2d ed. Boston: Little Brown & Company, 1961.

————, and E. M. COWETT, *Blue Sky Law*. Boston: Little Brown & Company, 1958.

RAPPAPORT, L. H., *SEC Accounting Practice and Procedure*, 2d ed. New York: The Ronald Press Company, 1966.

ROBBINS, SYDNEY, *The Securities Markets: Operations and Issues*. New York: The Free Press, 1966.

SECURITIES and EXCHANGE COMMISSION, *Cost of Flotation of Registered Issues, 1971–1972*. Washington, D.C.: U.S. Government Printing Office, 1974.

————, *Investigate Before You Invest, A Message for Investors*. Washington, D.C.: The Commission, 1975.

————, *The Work of The Securities and Exchange Commission*. Washington, D.C.: The Commission, 1974.

SHAPIRO, ELI, and C. R. WOLF, *The Role of Private Placements in Corporate Finance*. Boston: Division of Research, Harvard Business School, 1972.

WATERMAN, N. W., *Investment Banking Functions*. Ann Arbor, Mich.: School of Business Administration, Bureau of Business Research, 1958.

WINTER, E. L., *A Complete Guide to Making a Public Stock Offering*, 2d ed. Englewood Cliffs, N.J.: Prentice-Hall, Inc., 1972.

Old Securities:
Exchanges and Markets

SCOPE: This chapter discusses the operations of the "secondary" markets for outstanding securities and how they are regulated for the protection of investors. The order of topics is (1) functions and classes of secondary securities markets, (2) securities exchanges, (3) Federal regulation, (4) special trading arrangements, (5) recent developments in exchange operation, (6) the over-the-counter market, (7) the third market, and (8) the fourth market.

Functions and Classes of Secondary Securities Markets

Securities markets assist buyers and sellers of securities in carrying on transactions in an orderly manner and at fair prices. The marketability that they give to securities, in varying degrees, facilitates the ready conversion of securities into cash at prices that reflect the consensus of investment judgment at any one time. It is important to investors, to industry, and to the public that their markets provide breadth, continuity, and stability to securities transactions.

Several types of secondary securities markets are found in the United States: (1) the organized exchanges—central points where transactions are conducted in listed securities on an auction basis through brokers acting as agents for their customers; (2) the over-the-counter markets for unlisted securities, where prices are determined by negotiations between buyers and sellers of securities on the one hand and dealers on the other, or between dealers themselves; (3) the over-the-counter "third market" for listed securities, and (4) the "fourth market" for transactions between institutions.

The organized exchanges have traditionally been thought to provide numerous advantages and closer prices than the unlisted market, but in recent years the distinction has become less apparent. In the first place, unlisted securities have grown tremendously with respect to both quality and quantity. In the second place, the investment firms provide trading facilities for unlisted issues that are often comparable to the markets for listed issues. In the third place, certain issues of quality cannot, because of either small capitalization or limited distribution, meet the listing requirements of the exchanges. And, lastly, reliable quotations on prices of a large number of unlisted securities are now available without delay.

The preference of investors for listed issues has become somewhat outmoded by these developments. The unlisted market embraces issues of the highest quality, such as Treasury obligations and municipal bonds. Many investors buy common stocks as freely from the unlisted group as from the listed issues. Nevertheless, listing does provide some advantages that are outlined below.

Securities Exchanges

Functions   Securities exchanges are auction markets where brokers for sellers deal directly with brokers for buyers. The broker for the buyer tries to obtain the lowest possible price, while the broker for the seller tries to obtain the highest possible price. Consequently, prices change from sale to sale according to the volume of securities offered and sought.

Members of the securities exchanges generally act as brokers who execute orders for their respective clients. They may, however, act as principals in purchasing and selling for their own account. In this capacity, they are not permitted to take advantage of their position, but must give precedence to orders held for others at the same price. Their principal advantages over nonmembers are the saving of time by their actual presence on the floor of the exchange and the saving in commission charges.

The primary purpose of a securities exchange is to provide a continuous and liquid market for the exchange of outstanding issues.[1] Indirectly, however, the exchanges aid corporations in raising new funds by providing advantages to both the corporation and the investor. To the corporation, the listing of its securities may add marketability, may result in wider distribution of the securities, and may provide publicity that may be of value as long as the corporation is making a good record and the market is stable. And the precise valuation of its securities aids in determining the proper offering price of new issues and in fixing the terms of exchange of securities in a merger.

Listing has some disadvantages to the corporation. Compliance with the registration and reportings requirements for listed securities is time-consuming, expensive, and imposes potential liabilities that are avoided by over-the-counter trading. The dangers of excessive speculative trading are also greater where the securities are readily traded and subject to immediate pressure. And a low valuation known to all may also prove a handicap when the company is planning additional financing or a merger.

Advantage of listing to the investor   Improved marketability is an advantage to the investor as well as to the issuing corporation. A listed secu-

---

[1]Leffler and Farwell suggest three important functions of the exchanges: (a) to create a continuous market, (b) to provide a means for the determination of fair prices, and (c) to aid, indirectly, in financing industry. See G. L. Leffler and L. C. Farwell, *The Stock Market* (New York: The Ronald Press Company, 1963), pp. 71–78.

rity is bought or sold where buyers and sellers meet, where the value of the security is best known, and where the most favorable price is obtainable. Moreover, if the investor is not immediately interested in buying or selling, he can keep in touch with the prices at which the security is being sold. If he is an owner already, a downward trend in price may warn him that an exchange is desirable, and an upward trend may enable him to realize a profit. If he is not now an owner, publication of current prices acts as an invitation to buy, if the price is attractive.

Mere listing on an exchange will not automatically guarantee good marketability in the sense that the volume of trading will be large so that purchases and sales can be made with a minimum of price movement. A number of listed securities are relatively inactive. Other things being equal, however, the continuous market provided by an exchange is an important advantage.

The fact that a security is listed is no assurance that it is has quality. But the investor knows that the listed company (at least at the time of listing) is a substantial going concern with a considerable public following. Some of the guides used by the New York Stock Exchange for an initial listing are national interest in the company and its stock, at least 2,000 owners of 100 or more shares, 1 million common shares in the hands of the public, demonstrated net income before taxes of $2,500,000 at the time of listing, and both tangible assets and common stock outstanding with an aggregate value of at least $16,000,000.

Listing adds to the collateral value of a security. Banks generally prefer as collateral those securities that are readily marketable and which may be readily converted into cash if the loan is not paid. Bankers accept the market quotation as their chief criterion of value.

The regulation of listed issues, the required publicity of the affairs of their issuers and knowledge of price and volume of trading add protection to the holdings in listed securities that may be very valuable to the investor.

Listing has greatest significance in the case of stock. Stocks of leading companies are customarily traded through the exchanges, whereas bonds are usually bought and sold over-the-counter. Although the larger part of the shares of stock traded in New York is handled through the exchanges, less than 10% of bond trading is done through exchange transactions.

Organization of the exchanges A stock exchange provides a securities market open only to members who act chiefly as brokers for the buyers and sellers of the securities traded in that market. The exchange itself does not buy or sell securities nor does it establish their prices. The exchange is an auction market in which the buying and selling of thousands of investors and traders produce a large volume of transactions at the prices established by those transactions. Each sale ends the auction of a certain lot of securities, and a new auction is then started. There are no secret transactions, and complete publicity is given to the bond and stock prices by means of stock and bond ticker tapes.

The New York Stock Exchange, whose origin can be traced back to 1792, is the largest and most important of the exchanges and constitutes a national center for securities trading. It has set the standards by which the other exchanges operate. The second largest exchange, as measured by the number of listings and the volume of trading, is the American Stock Exchange, also in New York. Exchanges exist in other cities to serve mainly as trading places for securities with a more local interest.

Of the 12 exchanges, 11 were (1976) classified as national, being subject to the regulations of the Securities Exchange Act of 1934, while one was exempted. (See Table 15-1.) Exchange activity is indicated by data concerning listings. The figures for the lesser exchanges omit the much larger number of issues admitted to unlisted trading. The importance of unlisted trading shows up in the data on volume of trading.

TABLE 15-1   Data on Exchange Activities (dollars in millions)

	Number of Issues Listed, December 31, 1975		Dollar Volume of Trades during 1975 ($000's)	
	Stocks	Bonds	Stocks[b]	Bonds
New York	2,111	2,632	$133,818,551	$9,079,083
Midwest	35	1	7,604,714	1,443
American	1,197	197	5,678,028	204,193
Pacific	64	21	5,096,042	60,132
Philadelphia	121	3	2,721,893	436
Boston	91	1	1,870,995	—
Detroit	6	—	196,660	—
Cincinnati	9	7	268,393	332
Spokane	27	—	4,457	—
National	—	—	109	—
Intermountain	33	—	552	—
Honolulu[a]	25	3	524	—

[a]Exempted exchange.
[b]Includes rights and warrants.
Source: Securities and Exchange Commission, Annual Report, 1976.

The New York Stock Exchange is a voluntary association of 1,366 individuals who are the exchange *members*. Members comprise three different classes: (1) partners or stockholders in about 490 commission houses devoted to the handling of orders on the exchange, conducting business in about 500 cities across the country; (2) registered traders operating for their own account; (3) capitalists or representatives of estates who maintain membership for the convenience of trading and for the savings on commissions resulting from the ownership of a "seat" or membership. The first group of members represents what are called *member firms* and *member corporations*.[2] The 4,000 other partners or stockholders in these firms are known as *allied members*; they cannot go on the floor of the exchange, they have no voice in its management, and their allied memberships have no monetary value. The value of

---

[2]Corporations were first admitted as member firms in 1953; they must be exclusively in the securities business.

a seat or membership, however, has been as high as $625,000 (1929) and as low as $17,000 (1942). In 1968–1969, a seat sold as high as $515,000, and in 1977 as low as $35,000.

Operations on the New York Stock Exchange   The activities on the floor of the exchange are conducted by its members, classified as follows:

The *commission broker* executes orders for his firm on behalf of its customers, at the agreed commission rates.

The *floor broker* transacts business for other exchange members who have more orders in different stocks than they can handle alone or who wish aid in handling large orders. He shares the commission received by the member firm.

The *registered trader* buys and sells for his own account. He derives his profit (or loss) from trading on relatively small price fluctuations. The *registered trader* succeeds the former "floor trader," and his activities are subject to regulation enacted in 1964 that stemmed from the Special Study of the Securities and Exchange Commission.[3] He must have adequate capital, and most of his trading must be at prices above (for purchases) or below (for sales) the last different price. He must relinquish priority preference and parity to off-floor dealers so that his position on the trading floor will not give him an advantage over the investing public.

The *specialist* acts as both broker and dealer. As a broker, he executes orders in the stocks in which he is registered as a specialist; his work in this capacity is largely confined to limited orders (see Chapter 16). As a dealer, he buys and sells shares in his special stocks for his own account, subject to the rules of the Exchange and of the Securities and Exchange Commission.

Historically, the *odd-lot dealer* bought from and sold to commission firms less-than-100-share lots of stock at prices based on round lots, plus or minus a differential. In May 1976, the odd-lot dealer was eliminated when the New York Stock Exchange acquired the computerized securities processing system of Carlisle DeCoppet and Company, which had been the Exchange's sole franchised dealer in odd-lot orders.

The *bond broker* specializes in trading in bonds on a commission basis, although a few of them operate as dealers for their own account.

Only listed securities can be traded on the floor of the New York Stock Exchange, and, under the Securities Exchange Act of 1934, all of these must be registered with the Securities and Exchange Commission. (On the American and the regional exchanges, trading in unlisted securities provides a substantial volume of business, under conditions explained later in this chapter.) The Department of Stock List restricts the privilege to seasoned issues of established, substantial going concerns in which there is sufficient distribution and trading interest to assure an adequate market. Securities of about 1,576 different companies are on the trading list, including 1,550 common (36 of which are foreign), 608 preferred, and 2,708 bond issues

[3]Report of the Special Study of Securities Markets of the Securities and Exchange Commission, 88th Cong., 1st Sess., House Document 95, (Washington, D.C.: U.S. Government Printing Office, 1965), Part II, Chapter 6. Hereafter called *Special Study*.

(including foreign and government bonds). The market value of all stocks and bonds listed on the Exchange is 1.3 trillion.[4]

American, National, and regional exchanges   The American Stock Exchange (Amex) provides a market for securities of companies not large enough or otherwise not qualified for the "Big Board." Its listing requirements are much less stringent, it encourages the registration of relatively young companies, and its list includes a considerable number of foreign stocks including American depository receipts. A special feature of its organization is the use of associate members who are not entitled to trade on the floor of the exchange but who may transmit orders through regular members at a reduced commission.

The National Stock Exchange, in New York, was opened in 1962. It is still relatively small, with no rigid listing requirements. Unlike the regional exchanges, it does not list stocks that are listed on other exchanges.

The regional exchanges were originally established to provide organized markets for local securities. But with the advent of rapid communications with New York, the growth in size of regional companies, and the expansion of the over-the-counter market, the importance of trading in regional stocks has declined to the point where over 90% of the trading is in stocks either dually listed on the New York Stock Exchange or admitted to unlisted trading privileges (see the discussion below.)

Federal Regulation

Securities Exchange Act   The securities exchanges of the United States were first brought under Federal control under the Securities Exchange Act of 1934. This law created a Federal Securities and Exchange Commission appointed by the President. It provides for the registration with the Commission of any exchange as a National Securities Exchange. It forbids the operation of any unregistered exchange except those which may be exempted by reason of a limited volume of transactions. It places the control of the credit used in the purchasing or carrying of securities with the Board of Governors of the Federal Reserve System. It prohibits the manipulation of security prices and the use of deceptive devices for such purpose. It requires all companies that have securities listed on the registered exchanges, and large companies whose securities are traded over-the-counter, to file comprehensive information of their affairs and to keep the information reasonably current. It imposes severe penalties for violations. In short, it aims to eradicate the more serious abuses in securities trading that characterized the period of the 1920s.

The Securities Exchange Act of 1934 was a logical supplement to the Securities Act of 1933, whose purpose is to provide adequate protection to investors in the purchase of *new* issues. The objective of the Securities Exchange Act is to safeguard investors in transactions involving the purchase

[4]Data as of January 1976. Source: New York Stock Exchange, *1977 Fact Book.*

or sale of *outstanding* securities. Through such legislation, the Federal government has assumed far-reaching regulatory control of the investment markets.

The Securities and Exchange Commission   The Federal Securities and Exchange Commission was created for the purpose of administering the Securities Act of 1933 and the Securities Exchange Act of 1934.[5] This commission, comprised of five members appointed by the President, has wide discretionary powers in the administration of the laws. Registration statements, listing applications, and periodic reports must be prepared according to its requirements. Important exemption powers are granted to the Commission with respect to exchanges, securities, and reports.

Registration and regulation of exchanges   As one of the means toward the securing of fair and orderly markets for securities, the Securities Exchange Act requires that exchanges be registered with the Commission as national exchanges or be exempted from registration. In 1977 there were 11 registered and one exempted exchange.

In the registration statement, the exchange must provide full information concerning its activities, organization, membership, and rules of procedure, and agree to comply with and enforce the provisions of the Act. Registration brings the trading rules of the exchange under the control of the Commission.

Registration of securities   Transactions on the national securities exchanges are restricted to those securities which have been officially registered with the exchange and with the Commission, and which are not exempted under the provisions of the law. The exempted group comprises, in general, Government bonds and shares in mutual investment companies (separately regulated). Companies which wish to list their securities on a national securities exchange must submit detailed information of their affairs at the time of application, and must agree to keep such information reasonably current. This information includes

The organization, financial structure, and nature of the business.

The terms, position, rights, and privileges of the different classes of securities outstanding.

The terms on which securities are to be and, during the preceding three years, have been offered to the public or others.

The directors, officers, and underwriters, and each security-holder of record holding more than 10% of any class of any equity security of the issuer, their remuneration, and their interests in the securities of and their material contracts with the issuer and with any person directly or indirectly controlling or controlled by the issuer.

Remuneration to persons other than directors and officers that exceeds $25,000 a year.

Bonus and profit-sharing arrangements.

Management and service contracts.

Options existing or to be created in respect of their securities.

[5]The jurisdiction of the Commission under other statutes is described in various other sections of this book.

Balance sheets and profit and loss statements for not less than the three preceding fiscal years, certified by independent public accountants.

Trust indentures, underwriting contracts, articles of incorporation, and other documents and agreements as the Commission may require.

Registration requirements also apply to companies engaged in interstate commerce or whose securities are traded over-the-counter by the use of the mails or in interstate commerce. Registration is required of issuers with assets in excess of $1 million for each class of equity security which is held by at least 500 persons. Banks whose deposits are insured by the FDIC are included, but administration of the registration requirement is delegated to the appropriate Federal bank regulatory agency.

The registration statements referred to above should not be confused with those required under the Securities Act of 1933 described in the previous chapter, and which pertain to the offerings of *new* securities.

Regulation of dealers and brokers   Broker-dealers in either listed or unlisted securities must register with the SEC as a condition of dealing across state lines. The Commission prescribes rules with respect to floor trading by exchange members and to prevent excessive trading off the floor by members for their own account that would be detrimental to the maintenance of a fair and orderly market. One of the main problems has been to deal with the situation wherein the same individual acts as an agent for a customer and also trades for his own account as a dealer. Such a conflict of interest may abuse the fiduciary relationship inherent in the brokerage function.

Report requirements   Issuers of securities registered under the Securities Exchange Act must keep the information filed with the Commission "reasonably current" and submit such annual and quarterly reports as may be prescribed. These reports must be prepared in such detail and according to such accounting procedures as are required by the Commission. The Commission prescribes the methods to be followed in the preparation of the reports, in the appraisal or valuation of assets and liabilities, in the determination of depreciation and depletion, in the differentiation of investment and operating income and of recurring and nonrecurring income, and in the matter of separate and consolidated income statements and balance sheets. The rules governing the form and content of the financial statements filed with the Commission under the Securities Exchange Act of 1934 and the Securities Act of 1933 are found in the Commission's Regulation S-X. The registration statements are available for public inspection at the offices of the Commission.

The Securities Act also requires issuers of listed securities and those of larger publicly held unlisted securities to make adequate information available to shareholders in interim and annual reports. The information must be substantially the same as that required in 10-K registration statements.

Trading by "insiders"   Many investors have always been afraid that officers and directors could exercise undue influence over the prices of the securities of their companies and could take advantage of inside information at the expense of the investing public. The Securities Exchange Act provides that each executive officer, each director, and each owner of more than 10% of the equity securities of registered companies must report changes in his holdings monthly. These changes are in turn published by the Commission. To prevent the unfair use of confidential information, such persons must account to the corporation, within six months, for profits realized from any transaction in their company's stock. These profits are recoverable by the company by suit within two years. Short sales by "insiders" are prohibited.

Proxies and their solicitation   To promote more democratic and informed action on the part of company stockholders, the Securities Exchange Act requires that any proxies sent out by registered companies must be accompanied by a proxy statement that discloses fully the matters to be voted upon. Proxies must make provision for voting either yes or no on all matters. Proxies may not be solicited until their material has been submitted to the Commission. Proxy statements are often very revealing. They include, among other matters, the remuneration paid to officers and directors, an annual report for the last fiscal year, and the shareholdings of the management.

Credit control   Under the Securities Exchange Act, two provisions have greatly restricted the use of borrowed funds in the purchasing and carrying of securities: (1) The Board of Governors of the Federal Reserve System now fixes the margin requirements for both banks and brokers. Since January 3, 1974, the minimum margin (or equity) has been 50% on registered common stock and 50% on corporate bonds (margin trading is described in Chapter 16). (2) Exchange members, or brokers and dealers transacting business through them, may obtain brokers' loans only from member banks of the Federal Reserve System or nonmember banks that agree to comply with the restrictions on securities loans.

The precise effect of margins, and of changes in same, is hard to evaluate. Especially in a bull market the volume of trading is curtailed by limitations on margin accounts.

Manipulation of prices   The reported prices of securities must be the result of legitimate and open trading. Whether the price of a security is high or low, fluctuating or stable, it should represent the consensus of buyers' and sellers' valuations without artificial influence. Pool operations and manipulative practices were frequent in the 1920s but, since the passage of the Securities Exchange Act, have largely disappeared from the scene. The Act specifically prohibits five types of manipulation:

Matched orders, or fictitious transactions by two or more persons that create a price without any actual change of ownership.

Wash sales, where one person "paints the tape" by fictitiously buying and selling a stock at the same time, thereby recording a price, but again without any change in ownership.

Pool operations, whose purpose is to raise the price of a security (or depress it by short sales) through the concerted activities of the members of the pool, followed by the unloading of the stock on the public at a price influenced by the manipulation and accompanying information concerning the security.

Dissemination of false information to the effect that the security's price will rise or fall as the result of manipulation.

The spread of false information concerning a security; for example, incorrect information concerning the earnings of a corporation in order to induce its purchase or sale.

Short selling as such is not prohibited, except in the case of officers and directors. However, the price at which a short sale may be executed is regulated. (See Chapter 16.)

Special Trading Arrangements

Buying and selling large orders   Various procedures have been developed, with SEC approval, to facilitate the purchase and sale of blocks of stock within a reasonable time and at a reasonable price. The customer who originates the large block order pays a special commission that may run three or four times the usual auction market rate. The more important of these procedures are

1. *Block transactions.* Transactions involving 10,000 shares or more are executed on the floor of the New York Stock Exchange. The market value of the 1.0 billion shares of such transactions in 1976 was $29.2 billion, or 18% of total reported volume.[6] These figures reflect the participation of institutions and other large investors.

2. *Exchange distribution (or acquisition).* The broker may accumulate orders for sale (or purchase) and then fill the original block order on the floor during regular trading hours, at prices between the current bid and ask quotations.

3. *Secondary distribution.* Under this method, which is used for extremely large sell orders, the member usually acts as a dealer, combining with other members and nonmembers to effect the sale of the large block after trading hours and at a fixed price.[7]

Unlisted trading privileges   The New York Stock Exchange does not admit to trading privileges any securities not formally listed with it. But other exchanges do a very considerable volume of trading in securities that have not been formally listed. On the American Stock Exchange the number of stocks of companies who have never formally applied for listing privileges but which have been of sufficient interest to warrant trading is diminishing. The regional exchanges, however, have relied to a very considerable extent on unlisted trading, especially in stocks not listed locally but already listed on the New York Stock Exchange.

[6]New York Stock Exchange, *1977 Fact Book*, p. 11.

[7]In 1976, on the New York Stock Exchange, only 18.7 million shares were offered through secondary distributions, and only 774,000 shares through exchange distributions. *New York Stock Exchange Fact Book, 1977*, p. 15.

An exchange may be authorized by the SEC to continue unlisted trading in three groups of securities: (1) those that enjoyed such privileges prior to March 1, 1934; (2) those since listed on another exchange and for which there is adequate public distribution and sufficient trading activity in the vicinity of the applicant exchange to justify unlisted trading (this is the dynamic source of new issues for trading on regional exchanges); and (3) a few issues on which there is information substantially similar to that filed for listed companies.[8]

A large portion of the unlisted trading on regional exchanges consists of trading in New York Stock Exchange-listed stocks, especially in odd-lot business. In addition to such trading in stocks listed elsewhere, *multiple listing*, whereby a stock is specifically listed on more than one exchange, has appeared in recent years. However, the practice does not appear to be as significant as that of obtaining unlisted trading privileges on regional exchanges for issues registered on some other exchange.

The American Stock Exchange first permitted trading in stocks listed on the New York Stock Exchange in August 1976. The stock of Varo Incorporated was the first to be dually traded on the two major exchanges.

Trading in options   Four registered exchanges—American, Midwest, Philadelphia, and Pacific—and one special exchange, the Chicago Board of Options Exchange, are currently listing and trading in call options. In June 1977, the Securities and Exchange Commission gave these exchanges permission to begin pilot programs for trading in put options. (See Chapter 16.)

Recent Developments in Exchange Operation

Developments in the 1960s and early 1970s   A number of important developments took place in the 1960s and early 1970s, of which the following are the more important:

The failure and/or merger of over 110 member firms that was caused by the bear market of 1968–1970, lack of capital, "back office" confusion and inefficiency, "fails" (failure of brokers to deliver sold stock or bond certificates to the buyers within the required five days), and very high operating expenses. Most of these problems have been overcome.

Permission of the Board of Governors of the Exchange in 1969 for member firms to "go public," that is, sell shares to the general public. Several leading firms have done so, and their shares have been listed.

Federal chartering of the Securities Protection Corporation in 1970. The members of the Corporation, all of whom are registered broker-dealers and members of national securities exchanges, pay initial assessments of $1/8\%$ of gross receipts (going eventually to 1%). The fund protects each customer-investor against losses of $50,000 (of which no more than $20,000 can be in cash) in the event of the failure of a member firm. The seven-man board of

---

[8]As of June 30, 1976, approximately 2,700 stocks were admitted to unlisted trading on the exchanges (including duplications). *Annual Report* of the Securities and Exchange Commission, 1976.

directors includes representatives of the general public, the securities industry, the U.S. Treasury, and the Federal Reserve Board.

Reconstruction of the Board of Governors of the Exchange in 1972 to include ten "public" directors.

Securities Act amendments of 1975   In June 1975, Congress enacted new legislation governing the operation of stock exchanges. The new laws:

1. Abolished fixed commission rates, at least on large transactions. (See p. 345.)

2. Ordered the SEC to work toward the formation of a national market system. The central market's principal objective would be to provide the most competitive prices via an electronic communications network for all qualified securities, regardless of where the stock is traded. Publication of consolidated quotations is a step in this direction (p. 290.)

3. Directed the SEC to review the Exchange's controversial Rule 394 which requires that member firms must check first on the Exchange's trading floor before taking the orders to the over-the-counter "third" market.

4. Stopped exchanges from reducing the number of seats below the levels prevailing in May 1975.

5. Permitted institutional membership on an exchange. The new test is the 100–0% rule (replacing the old 80–20% rule) which permits institutions such as mutual funds and insurance companies to hold seats on the exchanges provided they do 100% of their business with the public.

Changing role of the New York Stock and other exchanges.   In the last two decades, the ownership and trading pendulum on the NYSE has swung from the individual to the institutional investor. Large insurance companies, pension funds, investment companies, bank-administered trusts, and non-profit institutions held close to one-half the market value of all stocks listed on the NYSE in 1976. Three-fourths of the stock trading volume on many days is traceable to institutions. At the same time, the number of individuals owning shares of publicly held corporations or investment companies fell from 30,800,000 in early 1970 to 25,200,000 in mid-1975. The 18% decline was the first drop in the number of shareowners since the Exchange began compiling figures in 1952.

The individual exodus from stocks is the result of a combination of many factors. The Exchange has cited the following.[9]

1. Disappointing market performance in 1965–1975, accented by two especially steep plunges.

2. Historically high yields on fixed income securities and other alternative investment and trading vehicles.

3. Rampant inflation of 41% over a 5 1/2 year span eroded the discretionary income of every family. Consequently, stocks lost much of their appeal as an inflation hedge.

[9]*Annual Report of the New York Stock Exchange*, 1975, pp. 11, 12.

4. Overall deterioration of public confidence in business, government, and other institutions made people more cautious about the risks associated with stocks.

The totality of these and other factors is that the Exchange finds itself confronted by forces that in large part it cannot control. The Exchange's long-standing ability to furnish a central auction market with market-making handled by specialists is being undermined by forces which require brokers and dealers to compete for business on the basis of price and service rather than location.

The viability of the Exchange is challenged on another front: negotiated commissions. The abolition of fixed commission rates, at least on large orders, on May 1, 1975, means that institutions are now in a position to exact larger discounts from the former posted rates on buy and sell orders. (See p. 345.)

Perhaps more ominous has been the improvement in both communication and computer sophistication which may make a physical exchange "floor" both unnecessary and obsolete. Advances in this technology are found in the hardware of an intricate and elaborate computerized communications network. (See NASDAQ, p. 291.) This permits quotations of any number of market-makers in a single stock to be shown simultaneously, and changed instanteously, on a single screen.

With the likelihood of still more structural changes ahead, it is difficult to define precisely the future role of the New York Stock Exchange. Its traditional role of providing a continuous auction market will be increasingly subject to more competition. Many member firms have begun to diversify their product mix and sources of income away from major dependence on the securities commission business. The shift by many firms towards offering a wide array of services to their customers, including listed options, commodities, bonds, tax shelters, and even insurance, has lessened the importance of an organized exchange to the securities community.

The Over-the-Counter Market

Operation   The majority of security issues are not listed on any of the securities exchanges. Although less important in aggregate value than the listed issues, the unlisted or "off-board" group is much larger, because of the inability or the unwillingness of corporations to gain listing privileges for their securities. In comparison with the approximately 6,670 securities of 1,700 issuers listed on the various national exchanges, there are about 30,000 additional issues in which a market is maintained throughout the country, of which about 11,000 stocks and 2,500 bonds are actively traded. Over-the-counter sales of active stocks (exclusive of mutual fund shares) grew from $4.9 million or 31% of all stock sales in 1949 to $38.9 billion or 37 per cent in 1961.[10] Estimates for 1976 run $80 billion or about 40% of all stock sales.[11]

[10]*Special Study, op. cit.*, Part II, p. 547.
[11]In 1976 the dollar volume of shares traded through NASDAQ/OTC was $24.8 billion. *The NASDAQ/OTC Market Fact Book 1976*, p. 3.

Of the corporate bond business of the country, 80% is carried on over-the-counter. Although many are listed, the over-the-counter market accounts for nearly 100% of the trading in U.S. Government issues. The following types of issues are usually in this classification:

- United States Government and agency issues;
- State and local government bonds;
- Railroad equipment trust certifications and guaranteed stocks;
- Many railroad bonds and stocks;
- Many public utility bonds and stocks;
- Most industrial bonds and stocks;
- Most bank and insurance stocks.

So extensive has the group of unlisted securities become that few intelligent investors now confine their commitments to the listed group. Listing, even on an important exchange, does not assure ready marketability. The activity of many dealers has resulted in the creation of a market in which many unlisted securities have marketability equal to that of the average listed issue.

Firms that provide markets in unlisted securities make no attempt to cover the entire field. One group will specialize in municipals, another in bank and insurance company stocks, and still another in Federal issues. The investor must ascertain the particular firms that "make a market" in issues in which he is interested.

The market in unlisted securities is made by dealers at prices reached through *negotiation*, which means through bargaining bid and offered prices. In most, but not all, transactions, the dealer acts as a principal, not as an agent for his client as the broker does. His compensation is the spread between purchase and resale price. He may have a desired security in his own inventory, or he may acquire it from another dealer. In any event, in transactions with the public his spread may run as high as 5 and 10% and is typically about 3% on common stocks.

The quotation by an unlisted dealer is generally *subject to confirmation* and represents the range in which he is willing to bargain. A quotation of "92–94" means that he is willing to pay at least 92 and does not expect to sell for more than 94. He is usually willing to *close the spread* to secure an order, and in the preceding case might bid 92 1/2 for 100 shares or offer 100 shares at 93 1/2 on a *firm* basis, generally subject to immediate acceptance.

The quotations on unlisted securities which appear in the newspapers are given in the form of bid and asked prices as reported by representative dealers, rather than those of actual transactions. The newspapers publish only a limited number of quotations and usually give preference to local issues. Comprehensive lists of quotations on unlisted securities are available to all investment dealers, however, who can provide an immediate quotation on any important unlisted security from the daily sheets of the National Quotation Bureau, Inc. This organization supplies subscribing houses with daily reports from all over the country of bid and asked prices on the more active securities and the names of dealers who are interested in the securities.

On an average day, as many as 8,000 stocks and 2,000 bonds may be quoted.[12] Since February 1971, the National Association of Securities Dealers, Inc., has operated the NASDAQ automated quotations system which provides instant bid and asked quotations on nearly 2,400 unlisted stocks, supplied by nearly 500 firms making markets in those securities.

Regulation of the over-the-counter market   Regulation of the over-the-counter market is effected through the National Association of Securities Dealers, Inc. (NASD), an organization set up under the Maloney Act in 1938, which constituted an important amendment to the Securities Exchange Act. The association includes about 3,000 dealers and operates under strict rules designed to maintain fair practices among its members. It has the power to expel members guilty of unethical practices. Its rules are filed with the Commission and, in turn, it has adopted the rules of the Commission governing over-the-counter transactions. One of the interesting features of the Association's work has been its sponsorship of a maximum mark-up or spread of 5% of asked over bid prices.

The membership of the Association includes nearly all of the brokers and investment banking houses, and most of the active over-the-counter dealers. One reason for the comprehensive membership is that, under the Maloney Act, registered members of the Association enjoy preferential treatment in a number of respects. For example, price concessions from underwriters or wholesalers to retailers can be given only to Association members.

Under the Securities Exchange Act of 1934, all over-the-counter brokers and dealers other than those whose business is exclusively intrastate, or who confine their activities to tax-exempt securities, must register with the Securities and Exchange Commission. Registration may be suspended or revoked if a broker or dealer or any member of his organization has been convicted of a crime or has been enjoined in connection with a securities transaction, has made a willful misstatement in the registration, or has willfully violated the securities laws and the rules of the Commission. Brokers and dealers are prohibited from engaging in manipulative, fraudulent, or deceptive practices in over-the-counter transactions and from inducing the purchase or sale of any security by willful omission or misstatement of a material fact.

The Third Market

Over-the-counter trading, by nonmembers, in common stocks listed on national exchanges, is known as the *third market*. Although most of the transactions involve large institutional and securities dealers, individuals are increasingly turning to this market also. The chief reason for its use is the possible savings on commissions on large orders. Also, listed securities may be traded off-board without restrictions by broker-dealers who are not members of an exchange. About seventeen firms do the bulk of the business.

---

[12]For sources of quotations on unlisted securities see Chapter 13.

As a result of comprehensive study of the third market by the SEC, in 1965 the Commission proposed rules that would produce more complete information on this market, including an identification of broker-dealers making off-board markets in listed securities, and the filing of data showing the volume of such trading in listed common stocks. Such reporting began in 1965. In 1976, the value of third-market dealings was $22.7 billion, equal to 4.6% of the value of exchange transactions.[13]

The Fourth Market

Large institutions and, occasionally, large individual investors have, for a number of years, directly bought and sold securities, or exchanged securities, with each other. The principal reasons for the "fourth market" are to obtain a better price, to save commissions, and to make portfolio changes without registering with the S.E.C. The volume of such transactions is unknown.

REFERENCES

BACKGROUND AND OPERATIONS OF THE SECURITIES INDUSTRY. *A Program of Self-Instruction.* New York: Association of Stock Exchange Firms and New York Institute of Finance, 1965.

BOGEN, J. I., ed., *Financial Handbook*, 4th rev. ed., Section 10. New York: The Ronald Press Company, 1968.

COOKE, G. W., *The Stock Markets*, rev. ed. Cambridge, Mass.: Schenkman Publishing Company, 1969.

DIRKS, R. C., and LEONARD GROSS, *The Great Wall Street Scandal.* New York: McGraw-Hill, Inc., 1974.

EITEMAN, W. J., C. A. DICE, and D. K. EITEMAN, *The Stock Market*, 4th ed. New York: McGraw-Hill, Inc., 1966.

FRIEND, IRWIN, et al., *The Over-the-Counter Securities Markets.* New York: McGraw-Hill, Inc., 1958.

JENNINGS, R. W. and HAROLD MARSH, eds., *Securities Regulation; Cases and Materials*, 3d ed. Mineola, N.Y.: Foundation Press, 1972.

LEFFLER, G. L., and L. C. FARWELL, *The Stock Market*, 3d ed. New York: The Ronald Press Company, 1963.

LOSS, LOUIS, *Securities Regulation*, 2d ed. Boston: Little, Brown & Company, 1961.

MARTIN, W. McC., *The Securities Markets, a Report with Recommendations.* New York: The New York Stock Exchange, 1971.

MERRILL LYNCH, PIERCE, FENNER and SMITH, INC., *Proposal for a National Market System*, New York: Merrill Lynch, 1975.

————, *How Over-the-Counter Securities are Traded.* New York: Merrill Lynch, 1968.

[13]SEC *Statistical Bulletin.*

NEW YORK STOCK EXCHANGE, *Understanding the New York Stock Exchange*. New York: The Exchange, 1970.

POLAKOFF, M. E., and A. W. SAMETZ, *The Third Market—The Nature of Competition in the Market for Listed Securities Traded Off-Board*. Reprint Series No. 33. New York: New York University Schools of Business, 1966.

PRENTICE-HALL, INC., *Securities Regulations*, 2 vols. (loose leaf). Englewood Cliffs, N.J.: Prentice-Hall, Inc., 1978.

ROBBINS, SYDNEY, *The Securities Markets: Operations and Issues*. New York: The Free Press, 1966.

SHEPARD, LAWRENCE, *The Securities Brokerage Industry: Nonprice Competition and Noncompetitive Pricing*: Lexington, Mass.: Lexington Books, 1975.

SOBEL, ROBERT, *The Big Board: A History of the New York Stock Exchange*. New York: The Free Press, 1965.

WELLES, CHRIS, *The Last Days of the Club*. New York: Dutton Publishing Co. Inc., 1975.

WEST, R. R., and S. M. TINIC, *The Economics of the Stock Market*. New York: Praeger Publishers, Inc., 1971.

WILLETT, E. R., *Fundamentals of Securities Markets*, rev. ed. New York: Appleton-Century-Crofts, Inc., 1971.

ZARB, F. G., and G. T. KERCKES, eds., *The Stock Market Handbook*, Section I. Homewood, IL.: Dow Jones-Irwin, Inc., 1970.

Buying and Selling Securities

SCOPE: This chapter discusses the manner in which orders are placed for the purchase and sale of securities and some of the factors that the investor should keep in mind in connection with the transfer of securities. The order of discussion is : (1) buying and selling orders, (2) buying new securities, (3) buying and selling unlisted securities, (4) types of orders, (5) short selling, (6) options, (7) buying on margin, (8) trading in rights and warrants, (9) buying and selling listed bonds, (10) time of delivery, (11) commission charges, (12) transfer taxes and federal registration fees, and (13) transfer of securities.

Buying and Selling Orders

The method of purchase or sale of a security is determined largely by the type of issue. Orders involving listed issues are normally placed with brokerage firms that are members of the particular exchange involved. Unlisted issues are bought and sold through dealers in such issues. Investors who do not have their own brokers often have their banks place their orders for them.

New issues of securities are ordinarily bought from investment bankers at a fixed price. Subsequent purchase and sales are usually handled by brokerage firms which charge a commission for their service. Investors are occasionally charged commissions for unlisted securities, but ordinarily the dealer's compensation is the spread between bid and asked price.

In addition to the listed and unlisted secondary markets, there is a growing third market (Chapter 15) where listed securities are purchased from the inventories of dealers. Such transactions usually involve substantial blocks of securities.

Buying New Securities

United States Savings bonds, Series E, are purchased at the cost of $75.00 per $100 of maturity value at U.S. post offices, Federal Reserve Banks, savings and loan associations, commercial banks, or directly from the Treasurer of the United States, and are redeemable for cash at fixed redemption values at the same places. Bonds of Series H are purchased at Federal Reserve Banks or from the Treasurer of the United States.[1]

Shares of open-end investment companies are purchased from investment dealers or the company's sales representative at their net asset value at the time of purchase. A loading charge, the bulk of which goes to the dealer or representative as a commission, is added by "load" funds. Shares are redeemable by the company at any time at their net asset value. The quotations of such shares, found in the financial section of the leading papers, are shown as bid and asked prices. The bid price is the asset or redemption value. The asked price is approximately the asset value plus the loading charge of up to 8 3/4%, if required.[2]

Shares in mutual funds offered by investment counsel firms, and other "no-load" funds, are priced at net asset value, without a "load" or commission. This is because little or no sales effort is undertaken by the firm or its distributor.[3]

New offerings of corporation and municipal securities, sold through investment and commercial banks, are purchased at the public offering price which includes the underwriting discount. (The bankers' discount, or spread, as explained in Chapter 14, varies with the size and quality of the new issue.)

Securities purchased directly from the issuing corporation include those of smaller new companies that do not obtain underwriting services, those offered under privileged subscriptions, and those acquired through the exercise of stock-purchase warrants.

Buying and Selling Unlisted Securities

As explained in the previous chapter, the over-the-counter market for unlisted securities is a trading market for thousands of issues of bonds and stocks. Orders for purchase and sale are placed with dealers (including, in the case of U.S. Government securities and municipal obligations, commercial banks), who operate mainly as principals. The customer usually buys directly from the dealer, who fills the order by buying from another over-the-counter house or from his own "shelf" if he is "making a market" or has "a position" in the security. The difference between the price paid by the dealer for the security and the price at which he sells it to the investor is the spread that represents the dealer's compensation. Bid and asked prices on unlisted issues are made available to dealers, for "inside" trading among themselves, on the daily quotation sheets of the National Quotation Bureau, Inc., and by using the electronic desk-top quotation machine. The quotations found on the financial pages are supplied by the National Association of Securities Dealers. Some lists of quotations (often "national" lists) are bids and offers quoted by over-the-counter dealers to each other; they do not include retail mark-up or commission. Other lists (often local) are inter-dealer

[1]See Chapter 5 for further information.
[2]See Chapter 11 for further details.
[3]See Chapter 11.

prices on the bid side, but the asked prices have been adjusted upwards to include approximate markup. Some lists contain both quotation arrangements. Prices at which actual transactions have taken place in the over-the-counter markets are not available.

Types of Orders

Market and limit orders   Orders for the purchase or sale of securities may be placed on a *market* (no price limit) or a *limit* basis. An order "at the market" means an immediate order "at the best price available," but without limitation as to price; on a quotation of 92 bid, 93 asked, an order to buy at the market would be executed at 93, and an order to sell at the market would be executed at 92. On limit orders, the investor places a price limit which the broker may not violate; on a selling order, the broker must not sell for less than the price limit, but may accept more, whereas, on a buying order, the broker must not pay more but may pay less than the price limit. The advantage of the market order is in immediate execution; the chief disadvantage is at times an unsatisfactory price. The advantage of the limit order is the avoidance of an unsatisfactory price; the chief disadvantage is delay in execution and the possibility that the order will never be executed.

Price quotations on securities represent bids and offers for limited quantities. Orders exceeding the established unit of trading (which is usually one $1,000 bond or 100 shares of stock) frequently cannot be filled at the prevailing quotation. An order to buy at the market 1,000 shares of a stock quoted 52 1/2-53 may be filled on a basis of 100 shares at 53 1/8, 100 at 53 1/4, 200 at 53 1/2, and 400 at 53 3/4. An order to sell 1,000 shares under the same conditions might be filled on the basis of 200 at 52 1/2, 100 at 52 1/4, 300 at 52, and 400 at 51 3/4. An order to sell $10,000 of a certain bond issue quoted at 88-90 might be executed on a basis of $2,000 at 88, $2,000 at 87 3/4, $1,000 at 87 1/2, and $5,000 at 87 1/4. So "thin" are the markets on some bonds that an offer of $100,000 may cause the price to drop as much as one to two points.

Day and open orders   Limit orders for the purchase or sale of securities may be placed on an *open* or a *day* basis. The investor may state that the order is to be held until it is executed, which, in the case of price-limit orders, may require several months or longer. Such orders are known as GTC orders, or "good until cancelled." Without specific instructions that the order is to remain open, however, it is understood to be a day order, and is regarded as automatically cancelled if not executed on the day it is placed.

Open orders would seem preferable when the investor is in no hurry to act and is not satisfied with prevailing prices. But this practice will not always work to his advantage. Frequently, open orders to buy at prices below the prevailing market are executed when adverse developments which make the security much less attractive come too quickly to allow the investor to cancel the order. The investor should be in constant touch with his broker if substantial orders are pending.

Stop-loss orders Investors who wish to limit losses sometimes place orders to be executed at prices below the prevailing market. An investor who has bought 100 shares of a certain stock at $50 a share, and who desires to limit his maximum loss to about $5 a share, places an order to sell at "45 stop." This order is not an instruction to sell now at $45, but rather an order to sell at the market "if and when" the price should decline to $45. This type of order is also to protect profits gained from price advances as well as to limit losses on short sales. In the preceding case, the investor holding stock quoted at $60 which cost $50 may place an order to sell at "55 stop," so as to assure a profit of $5 a share. A speculator who has sold "short" 100 shares at $50 per share may place an order to buy at "60 stop" in order to limit his loss to around $10 a share. In a very rapidly declining or rising market, however, such stop prices are by no means guaranteed. A market which has many stop-loss orders just below prevailing prices is technically weak, since a limited volume of selling would bring prices down to the stop limits. The automatic execution of these orders would further depress the price, "setting off" stop orders at lower limits. After the cumulative effect has run its course, the price may rise. Most investors should not place selling orders until they are ready to sell. It is usually safer to place an immediate order to sell at the prevailing price than a deferred order to sell at a lower price.

Function of the specialist Orders which are placed for execution at prices "away" from the prevailing market are customarily turned over by brokers to other members who act as *specialists* in the particular stocks. Every stock on the New York Stock Exchange is assigned to a specialist. These specialists maintain records, known as books, in which these orders are entered in the sequence received.

Table 16-1 shows the specialist's book for orders in a certain stock at prices between 50 and 50 3/4. The highest (best) bid is for 200 shares at

TABLE 16-1   Specialist's Book

Buy		Sell	
50	1 Brown 2 McGill 1 Jones	50	
1/8		1/8	
1/4	2 Ewart	1/4	
3/8		3/8	
1/2		1/2	
5/8		5/8	1 Newton 1 Farmer
3/4		3/4	1 Starr 1 Tomkins
7/8		7/8	

50 1/4, and the lowest (best) offer is for 200 shares at 50 5/8. The quotation would then be 50 1/4–50 5/8. A new order to buy 400 shares *at the market* would be executed: 200 at 50 5/8 and 200 at 50 3/4. An order to sell 600 shares *at the market* would be executed: 400 at 50, and 200 at 50 1/4. However, the specialist, acting as a dealer for his own account, may decide to close the spread between bid and asked by buying at 50 1/2, making the quotation 50 1/2–50 5/8, or by selling at 50 1/2 making the quotation 50–50 1/2. He is more likely, however, to enter his own orders when the spread is much more substantial than in this example, so as to perform his function of maintaining a fair and orderly market.

The specialist provides a convenient concentration point for orders which otherwise could not be expediently handled by the regular brokers. In addition to acting as a brokers' broker, he has the responsibility of maintaining an orderly market in the stocks assigned to him. He does this by buying and selling for his own account when a temporary disparity occurs between supply and demand. In October 1976 competition between two specialists in the same stocks began for the first time since 1967.

Odd-lot orders   An odd-lot is an order of less than 100 shares. For the great majority of stocks on the New York Stock Exchange, the unit of trading is a round lot, or 100 shares. Ten-share markets have been established for a group of stocks in which activity is limited for various reasons, mainly their high prices.

Markets in odd-lots are made by the Exchange specialists or market makers responsible for assigned stocks. The related processing tasks are handled by the Exchange itself. Exchange market-makers levy a 12 1/2 cent-per-share charge on all odd-lot orders executed after the market opening. Two large member firms, Merrill Lynch and Dean Witter, have been making their own markets in odd-lots away from the floor and do not charge any extra fee, other than regular commissions, for such orders.

Odd-lot trading permits the investor of limited means to buy modest numbers of shares in several corporations and thus obtain some diversification. The commission charged on small orders, especially in low-priced stocks, comprises a significant percentage of the purchase and sale price. This disadvantage is maximized if the shares are held for only a short period of time.

Short Selling

A *short sale* is the sale of stock which the seller does not own. Anticipating a decline in the price of the stock, the short seller hopes to make a profit from selling the stock now and buying it back later at a lower price. The broker to whom the order is given arranges to borrow it, either from his own stock or from stock of customers who have allowed their securities to be used for this purpose, or from some other broker who has stock available for lending.

When stock is borrowed by the broker from a customer, the customer continues to receive any dividends paid during the transaction. The customer who lends the stock relies on the broker to return the same number of shares of stock on demand. Where stock is borrowed from another broker, the borrowing broker deposits with the lender of the stock the full market price of the borrowed shares, the money having been obtained by their sale. Thus the lender has the use of cash during the period the stock is lent, and when stocks are freely available for lending, he may pay interest, at the "loaning rate" of, say, 1%. Where not much stock is available for borrowing, it is usually loaned "flat," with no payment for its use. When stock is in much demand for short selling, the lender may even receive a premium for the use of the stock, stated in terms of $1 or a multiple thereof for each day on each 100 shares borrowed. As the price of loaned stock rises and falls, the amount of cash held as security is increased or decreased as either party requests that it be made equal to market price. Any dividends on loaned stock go to the lender.

Loans of stock may be called by either party on three days' notice. The short seller continues his "short position" until he decides to "cover" his short sale by buying an equivalent number of shares and delivering them to the lender in return for the cash.

An order for a short sale must be so designated when placed, and cannot be executed at a price lower than that established in the last preceding regular (as distinguished from short) sale.[4] It can be executed at a higher price, or at the last price, provided this in turn is higher than the next preceding different price. The purpose of these rules is to prevent the use of short sales to depress the market price of the issue.

Some short sales are made "against the box." The short seller owns the security being sold short, but makes delivery by borrowing it, and later covers either by using his own stock or buying in the market. Such operations are usually made for income tax and hedging purposes.

Some believe that short selling should be outlawed as detrimental to investment values. Others claim that it provides a corrective check to abnormally high prices and a protective cushion to declining prices. Short selling is much more prevalent in periods of market weakness or uncertainty than in periods of great strength. Instead of acting as a brake on an advancing market, short selling may actually result in higher prices as short sellers place buying orders to cover their positions when prices advance.

The *short position* in individual listed stocks, that is, the number of shares sold short and not covered as of a particular date, is regularly computed by the New York Stock Exchange and published monthly in the financial sections of the leading newspapers.

Options

Trading in options An *option* is a contract which involves the right to buy or sell securities (usually 100 shares) at specified prices within a stated time. There are various types of such contracts, of which *puts* and *calls* are the

[4]On regional exchanges (outside of New York), the price can be equal to the last sale prevailing on the New York Stock Exchange.

most important. A *put* is a negotiable contract which gives the holder the right to sell a certain number of shares (usually 100) at a designated price within a limited time. An investor holding 100 shares of a certain stock selling at $50 a share who fears that the price may decline substantially because of an impending development, but who otherwise desires to keep his stock, may purchase a put that gives him the right to sell his stock at, say, $45 a share to the seller of the option.

A *call* is a negotiable contract which gives the holder the right to buy a certain number of shares (usually 100) at a designated price within a limited time. An investor considering the purchase of 100 shares of a certain stock selling at $50 who feels that the time is not opportune, but who fears that the price might rise suddenly while he is waiting, may purchase a call giving him the right to buy the stock at, say, $55 a share from the seller of the option.

Historically, put and call contracts have been traded over-the-counter by dealers functioning as market-makers in options. Structural defects of the over-the-counter options market include the relatively higher commission costs (customers have to deal with a put and call dealer in addition to their regular broker), the lack of uniformity in expiration dates, and poor liquidity, as it is very difficult to close out the transaction prior to expiration.

In April 1973, the Chicago Board of Options Exchange opened its doors, and public interest in option trading increased dramatically. By standardizing expiration dates and execution prices, the CBOE allowed call options to be traded as freely as common stocks, with similar liquidity. Call options are now also traded on the American, Midwest, Philadelphia, and Pacific Coast exchanges. Trading in puts began on a pilot basis in June 1977. For an example of option quotations, see Chapter 13.

Factors determining option prices   The level and movement of option prices are the result of the interplay of these forces:

- Supply and demand for the options themselves.
- The relationship between the current market price of the stock and the exercise or (striking) price of the option.
- The relative volatility of the underlying security.
- The amount of time until the option expires.
- The level of interest rates.

Option strategies   While option strategies seemingly are limited only by the imagination of the trader, there are some basic combinations:

BUYING A CALL.   Buyers of calls are seeking option profits from the possible advance in the price of the underlying stock with a relatively small investment compared with buying the stock outright. The most that can be lost is the cost of the option iteslf.

ESTABLISHING A SPREAD.   A spread involves the simultaneous purchase and sale of different options of the same security. A vertical spread is the purchase of two options with the same expiration date but different striking prices. In a horizontal spread, the striking price is the same but the expiration dates differ.

WRITING OPTIONS. A covered option is one written against an owned-stock position. An uncovered or "naked" option is written without owning the underlying security.

Example: Buying a call. Assume that in February, XYZ common is selling at $50 and a July option (entitling the holder to buy 100 shares at $50) is selling at $5.00 per share. Assume further that by April the price of the option has increased to $8 and the underlying stock to $56 a share. Leverage arises from the fact that an outright buyer of the stock has, before commissions and taxes, a paper profit of $600 ($5,600 − $5,000) or a 12% increase, whereas the option purchaser has a paper profit of $300 ($800 − $500) or 60%. The option holder has limited his risk to $500, the price of the option. In contrast, the outright buyer of the stock may lose considerably more.

Example: Establishing a spread. Suppose a speculator believes that XYZ common is likely to increase in value. Instead of buying the stock at its current price of $40 3/8, he buys an October call (giving him the right to purchase 100 shares at $40) for 2 5/8 a share, and simultaneously sells an XYZ October $45 call for $1.00 per share. The maximum loss possible on this transaction is the difference between $262.50 paid for the October 40 call and the $100 received from the October 45 call, or $162.50. Suppose that by October, the XYZ October 40 call had climbed to 9 1/2 (262% increase) and the underlying stock rose to $49 1/4 (22% increase) and the October 45 call increased to $4 (300% increase). In closing out the spread, the speculator sustains a loss of $300 on his written call ($400 − $100) while earning a profit of $687.50 on the purchase call ($950 − $262.50) or an overall net gain of $387.50 (238%).

Example: Writing Options. The covered write is considered to be the most conservative of option strategies. Individuals, and particularly institutions, are now writing options to protect a stock holding considered attractive for long-range retention but vulnerable to near-term price corrections.[5] The income dervied from the sale of a covered option offsets the decline in the value of the underlying security. For example, suppose XYZ Common sells at $50. The investor writes a six-month option receiving a premium of $400. Six months later, XYZ is selling at $45 a share. The 10% drop in the price of XYZ from $50 to $45 causes a $500 loss in the equity portfolio. Since the option produced $400 in income, the net paper loss comes to only $100.

Option risks[6] Various risks are involved in option transactions:

- The purchaser of an option runs the risk of losing his entire investment in a relatively short period of time. If the market price of the underlying

---

[5]A new law permits tax-exempt institutions, such as pension funds and university endowment funds, to write call options on common stocks in their portfolios without risking their tax-exempt status. With these institutions holding common stocks in excess of $120 billion (at the end of 1976) the potential exists for a great surge in option activities by these institutions. (See Chapter 22.)

[6]Prospectus of the Chicago Board of Options Exchange, October 30, 1975, pages 5–7.

security fails to rise above the exercise price, the option will be worthless at its expiration.

• The writer of an option who does not own the underlying security deliverable upon exercise of the option (the "uncovered writer") is subject to risk of loss if the price of the underlying security increases.

• The writer of an option who owns the underlying security deliverable upon exercise of the option ("the covered writer") is subject to the full risk of his position in that security, in exchange for the premium. So long as he remains a writer he has given up an opportunity for gain resulting from an increase in the price of the underlying security above the exercise price.

• Additional risks pertain to the ability of the trading and clearing mechanisms of the secondary market to function effectively. Holders and writers must be able to limit their losses by closing out positions prior to the time when trading in their options ceases.

Options provide challenges as well as potential profits and losses. Since option trading requires sophisticated knowledge of market movements as well as possible adverse tax consequences, prospective option traders should seek professional advice. (The taxation of options is indicated in Chapter 17.)

Buying on Margin

The two main types of accounts with brokers are cash accounts and margin accounts. In a cash account, purchases are made outright for full ownership, and sales are made against immediate delivery of securities. To open a margin account, the buyer deposits with his broker cash or securities equal to a portion of the price of the security (the margin) and his broker advances the balance. To finance this balance, the broker uses his own capital or obtains funds by pledging the securities purchased with a bank as collateral for a loan. If the price of the stock declines, the buyer must keep the margin good by depositing additional cash or securities so that at all times the margin will meet the required minimum percentage of the market price. If the margin falls below this percentage, a margin call is sent to the customer. If the customer fails to provide the additional margin, the broker sells out the account.

The volume and origin of the brokers' loans that arise out of securities transactions are subject to regulations under the Securities Exchange Act of 1934. The *initial* margins which members of security exchanges registered under the Act require from their customers are laid down by the Board of Governors of the Federal Reserve System. A margin of 100% (no loanable value) was in force from January 1946 to February 1947; since that date, the percentage has varied between 50 and 90, and since January 3, 1974, has been 50%.[7] The Securities Exchange Act also provides that members of registered securities exchanges and brokers and dealers who do a security

---

[7]The minimum margin on Federal obligations is 5% of principal, on state and local government bonds, 15% of principal or 25% of market value, whichever is lower, and on registered corporate bonds, 50%.

business through such members may borrow (for securities transactions) only from member banks of the Federal Reserve System and nonmember banks that comply with the regulations pertaining to securities loans.

In addition to the Federal Reserve regulation of *initial* margins, the New York Stock Exchange has certain credit requirements. No person may open a margin account with a member firm without depositing at least $2,000 or its equivalent in securities. Generally speaking, a customer's equity may at no time be less than 25% of the market value of securities carried. Some firms require 40%.

To illustrate the combined effects of the Federal Reserve minimum initial margin requirements and a 25% minimum *maintenance* requirement, suppose a customer of a member firm buys on margin 200 shares of stock at 100. His initial equity or margin is $10,000 and his debt or debit balance is $10,000. The stock could fall to $60 per share before he would be required to deposit additional margin. At $60 the market value of his 200 shares would be $12,000 and his margin one-quarter of that amount or $3,000 ($12,000 – $9,000).

Trading in Rights and Warrants

Rights to subscribe to stock under privileged subscriptions are sometimes very actively traded, and examples of listed rights are usually found in the stock quotations. After the official announcement of their issue, the Committee on Stock List of the New York Stock Exchange announces a date on which the rights may be traded on a "when-issued" basis. Under this arrangement, buyers (and sellers) of rights receive delivery of (or deliver) the rights and make the appropriate settlement after the rights are actually issued. Thereafter, the rights are bought and sold in the regular way until the date of expiration, after which they have no value.

Many companies provide facilities or retain a bank or trust company to assist stockholders in disposing of their rights or in acquiring additional rights so as to round out the number needed to purchase an even number of shares of new stock.

Stock-purchase warrants are attached to bonds or preferred stock at the time of issue or are issued in mergers as payment for services. They entitle the holder to purchase common stock from the issuer at a specified price within a definite period of time or indefinitely. When the warrant is detachable, it may have a separate listing and enjoy an active market. The most actively traded warrants are listed on the American Stock Exchange, but in 1970 the New York Stock Exchange first admitted them to listing.

The methods of determining the value of rights and warrants are explained in Chapter 9.

Buying and Selling Listed Bonds

Although the bulk of bonds are traded over-the-counter, some 2,708 bonds of 1,054 issuers were (1977) listed on the New York Stock Exchange. The other leading exchanges also quote bonds although they have much smaller lists. (See Chapter 15.) The ordinary unit of trading on the exchanges is one $1,000 bond, and quotations are shown as a percentage of face value. Thus, the price of a $1,000 bond quoted at 98 is $980. As explained in Chapter 8, three types of quotations are used: (1) *and interest*, with accrued interest from the last coupon date added to the price; (2) *flat*, with no addition of accrued interest, in the case of bonds whose income is not assured or is in default; and (3) on a *yield basis*, the bid and asked values being expressed in terms of yield rather than price.

Bid and offering prices of bonds are usually in 1/8s, except in U.S. Government securities where the values are expressed in 1/32s. Quotations on the New York Stock Exchange and the American Stock Exchange are sent out over ticker service; the bonds are designated by their coupon rates, and by their maturities if the same company has two or more issues with the same coupon rate. The price of a registered bond, the transfer of which involves time and expense, is usually slightly lower than that of an identical bond in coupon form.

Time of Delivery

Securities bought and sold on the securities exchanges must be delivered within the time specified by the exchange. Under the rules of the New York Stock Exchange, regular delivery is required on the fifth full business day (excluding Saturdays, Sundays, and holidays) following the day of sale.[8] Sales not made in the regular way may be made for *cash*, which means for delivery and payment on the day of sale. Sales may also be made for *delayed delivery*, which gives sellers up to seven days in which to arrange delivery. (Short sellers are not allowed to use the delayed delivery option, which is restricted to actual owners of securities.) Or the seller may have his broker offer the stock *seller's option* and specify the number of days, from five to 60, for delivery. The prices at which stocks are sold on other than *regular-way* delivery are usually slightly lower because these other arrangements operate more to the benefit of the seller than that of the buyer.

In the hectic days of 1967–1969, many brokerage houses suffered from "back-office log jam"; that is, they were unable to manage the massive amounts of securities being bought and sold. "Fails" to deliver reached a peak of over $4 billion in December 1968. Although some share volume was higher in 1970–1976 than in 1968, the volume of "fails" has declined to less than $1 billion, due to improved operations techniques, the larger size of transactions on the Exchange, and the installation of the Central Certificate Service. This service centralizes and applies modern clearing-house methods to interhouse transfers of stock certificates. Since 1970 much

---

[8]An exception is found in the case of Government bonds, for which regular delivery is the next day.

thought and research has been devoted to the possibilities of doing away with stock certificates altogether, substituting electronic bookkeeping and transfer of ownership units.

When unlisted issues are bought or sold through dealers, the time of delivery is set more by informal agreement than by formal rules. In general, however, the practice closely conforms to that of the listed group.

Commission Charges

Recent developments When listed securities are purchased or sold directly from or to investment dealers, no commission charge is ordinarily made, since both parties usually act as principals in the transaction. When securities are bought or sold through brokerage houses, a commission charge is paid by both the buyer and the seller.

During its entire life until 1971, the New York Stock Exchange fixed the commissions charged on stock transactions; that is, commissions were established at posted (and graduated) rates, which were revised from time to time. Under institutional pressure the Securities and Exchange Commission ruled in 1971 that orders of $500,000 or more were to be negotiated. The figure was subsequently lowered to $300,000 or more. On May 1, 1975 ("May Day"), costs of all transactions were, at least nominally, placed on a negotiated basis. In fact, only large transactions (over $100,000) are (1977) ordinarily negotiated however. Others are charged posted rates which in some cases are higher than before "May Day."[9] The small investor has not received the benefit of negotiation.

Standard commissions on purchases and sales of listed bonds in relatively small amounts remained the same. The reader should realize, however, that the bulk of bond sales are large over-the-counter transactions at a net price filled from dealers' inventories, rather than on an agency (commission) basis.

Another development since May 1, 1975 has been the appearance of the "discount broker" who charges substantially lower commissions on securities transactions (as low as 50 to 55% of the nondiscount rate), where only the trading service is rendered.[10] No investment advice, custodial service, or sales service is rendered. Some commercial banks will also process customers' transactions (through brokerage firms) at less than the typical posted broker's rates.

Commissions before "May Day" Commission rates for bonds and stocks traded on the New York Stock Exchange before May 1, 1975, were:

---

[9]Some brokerage houses give a 10 to 15% discount on commissions on orders of a certain size and with certain conditions of timing and delivery. See p. 246.

[10]A rate of $4 per $1,000, with a minimum of, say, $74, is charged on bonds, in contrast to the $5 per thousand on trades of listed bonds.

Bonds

Price per $1,000 of Principal	Commission per $1,000 Bond
Less than $10	$ .75
$10 but under $100	1.25
$100 and over	2.50

Stocks

Single Round Lot Orders		Multiple Round Lot Orders	
Money Involved in the Order	Minimum Commission	Money Involved in the Order	Minimum Commission
$ 100–$ 799	2.0% + $ 6.40	$ 100–$ 2,499	1.3% + $ 12.00
800– 2,499	1.3 + 12.00	2,500– 19,999	0.9 + 22.00
2,500 and Above	0.9 + 22.00	20,000– 29,999	0.6 + 82.00
		30,000– 500,000	0.4 + 142.00

Subject to the provision that the minimum commission on single round lot orders is not to exceed $65.00.		Plus	
		First to tenth round lot	$6.00 per round lot
		Eleventh round lot and over	$4.00 per round lot

Plus on any order involving an amount not in excess of $5,000, the commission computed in accordance with the foregoing provisions is increased by 10%, and on any order involving an amount in excess of $5,000, the commission computed in accordance with such provisions is increased by 15% and then 8%.

The minimum commission on a 100-share order or an odd-lot order need not be more than $71.50/80.73 (based on amount of money involved) The minimum commission per round lot within a multiple round lot order is not to exceed the single round lot commission computed in accordance with the rate for 100 share orders.

Examples of pre-"May Day" and current commissions
The total purchase price (exclusive of taxes, fees, insurance, and postage) for buying on March 15, $10,000 in face value of a 7% bond with interest payable April 1 and October 1, at 105 is computed as follows:

	At Pre-May 1975 Bond Rate	At Current Bond Rate	At Current Discount Rate
Principal: $10,000 at 105%	$10,500.00	$10,500.00	$10,500.00
Interest: $10,000 at 7% for 5 months and 19 days	328.60	328.60	328.60
Commission: 10 bonds at $5.00	50.00	50.00	
Commission: 10 bonds at discount			40.00
Total cost	$10,878.60	$10,878.60	$10,868.60

The accrued interest is computed up to, but not including, the day of delivery, which would be March 20. The entire payment of $328.60 for accrued interest would be recovered on April 1, when interest amounting to $350.00 would be collected for the six months thus ending. The net cost to the buyer would, therefore, be $10,550.00.

348

The total purchase price (exclusive of taxes, fees, insurance, and postage) for buying 100 shares of a common stock at $45 is computed as follows:

	Pre-May 1975 Stock Rate	Post-May 1975 Typical Rate	Discount Example
Principal: 100 shares at $45	$4,500.00	$4,500.00	$4,500.00
Commission +$22.00	68.75	77.00	34.38
Total cost	$4,568.75	$4,577.00	$4,534.38

Commissions on options These range typically from $25.00 for one call at $1 per option to $213.62 for 10 calls at $10 per option. Discount brokers charge about 50% of these rates.

Transfer Taxes and Federal Registration Fees

The purchase or sale of securities involves the payment of a broker's commission by both buyer and seller. In addition, the *seller* has deducted from the proceeds of the sale: (1) the Securities and Exchange Commission's registration fee, (2) a state transfer tax levied in some states (including New York) on stock transactions made within the state, and (3) insurance and postage. The SEC registration fee is imposed on the exchange and is collected from its members, who in turn charge the seller of the security, at the rate of 1 cent for each $500 or fraction thereof. New York State imposes an excise tax on transfer of stocks *within the state* on a graduated scale ranging from 1.56 cents a share on stocks selling under $5 a share to 6.25 cents on stocks selling above $20.[11] There is no New York tax on bond transfers. Insurance and postage runs about 40 cents per $1,000 of value.

Transfer of Securities

Bonds are negotiable instruments, and stocks are in effect negotiable under modern stock transfer laws. Title may be transferred by simple delivery, in the case of coupon bonds which are payable to bearer, or by endorsement or assignment and delivery, in the case of registered bonds and all classes of corporate stock. Endorsement in blank converts an instrument payable to a specified party into an instrument payable to the holder. The law generally upholds the title of an innocent purchaser to a negotiable instrument, so that buyers and sellers of securities should be most careful in arranging transfers. Because dividend payments are made only to stockholders of record, new owners arrange for transfer to ensure the receipt of future payments. In the event of loss through delay, such owners may recover only from the former owners.

[11]Nonresident rates range from .79 ¢ to 3.13 ¢.

Each seller of a negotiable instrument gives three implied promises in the transfer to a buyer: (1) that the instrument is genuine, (2) that the seller is not aware of any defect in its validity, and (3) that the seller is the legal owner with full power to sell.

Stock certificates are registered in the names of the owners or their brokers ("street names"). Sometimes, owners prefer to have their stocks registered in the names of nominees, who have the right of transfer. Certificates can be transferred by endorsement or by attached written assignment.

Each certificate is numbered, states the total number of authorized shares and the number of shares represented by the certificate, and bears the name of the registered owner, the signature of two properly designated officers of the company, and the respective authentications of the registrar and transfer agent. On the reverse side of each certificate appears a transfer order which represents a combination of a bill of sale and a power of attorney with authority to transfer.

The signature on the assignment must correspond with the name written on the face of the certificate. The endorsement must be guaranteed by a responsible financial institution. The actual transfer on the books of the company is usually arranged by the new owner or his broker, but the seller sometimes makes the transfer to be assured that his name no longer appears as a stockholder.

The transfer of stock held by a corporation, or in the name of a decedent or an estate, or in the name of a trustee or guardian, or by an alien or nonresident requires additional documents of a nature too technical for discussion in this volume.

REFERENCES

ANSBACHER, M. G., *The New Options Market*. New York: Walker and Co., 1975.

BOGEN, J. I., ed. *Financial Handbook*, rev. ed. New York: The Ronald Press Company, 1968.

CLASING, HENRY K., JR., *The Dow Jones-Irwin Guide to Put and Call Options*. Homewood, Ill.: Dow Jones-Irwin, Inc., 1975.

COOKE, G. W., *The Stock Markets*, rev. ed. Cambridge, Mass.: Schenkman Publishing Company, 1969.

EITEMAN, W. J., C. A. DICE, and D. K. EITEMAN, *The Stock Market*, 4th ed. New York: McGraw-Hill, Inc., 1966.

Encyclopedia of Stock Market Techniques, rev. 2d ed. Larchmont, N.Y.: Investors Intelligence, Inc., 1965.

ENGEL, LOUIS, *How to Buy Stocks*, 5th rev. ed. Boston: Little, Brown & Company, 1971.

FINLEY, H. M., *Everybody's Guide to the Stock Market*, rev. ed. Chicago: Henry Regnery Co., 1968.

GROSS, LEROY, *The Stockbroker's Guide to Put and Call Option Strategies*. New York: New York Institute of Finance, 1974.

LEFFLER, G. L., and L. C. FARWELL, *The Stock Market*, 3d ed. New York: The Ronald Press Company, 1963.

MATTLIN, E. B., *Understanding and Using the Language of Wall Street*. New York: Dreyfus Publications, Inc., 1973.

MILLER, J. T., *Options Trading*. Chicago: Henry Regnery Co., 1975.

MITTRA, SID., *Inside Wall Street*. Homewood, Ill.: Dow Jones-Irwin Co., 1971.

NEW YORK STOCK EXCHANGE, *Understanding the New York Stock Exchange*. New York: The Exchange, 1970.

———, *Crisis in the Securities Industry: A Chronology, 1967–1970*. New York: The Exchange, 1971.

SARNOFF, PAUL, *The Wall Street Thesaurus*. New York: I. Obolinsky, 1963.

SECURITIES AND EXCHANGE COMMISSION, *The Future of the Securities Market*. Washington, D.C., February 2, 1972.

———, *White Paper on the Structure of a Central Market System*. Washington, D.C., March 30, 1973.

STONE, J. M., *One Way for Wall Street: A View of the Future of the Securities Industry*. Boston: Little, Brown and Co., 1975.

Understanding Options. Chicago Board Options Exchange, 1974.

WEAVER, MARK, *The Technique of Short Selling*. Palisades Park, N.J.: Investors' Library, 1963.

WILLETT, E. R., *Fundamentals of Securities Markets*, rev. ed. New York: Appleton-Century-Crofts, 1971.

WYCKOFF, PETER, *The Language of Wall Street*. New York: Hopkinson and Blake, 1973.

———, *Wall Street and The Stock Markets*. Philadephia: Chilton Book Co., 1972.

Taxation of Securities Investments

17

SCOPE: This chapter discusses the degree to which securities investments and investment income are taxed and the influence of taxation on investment policy. The order of discussion is: (1) taxation and investment policy, (2) Federal personal income taxes, (3) yields on tax-free bonds, (4) capital gains and losses, (5) Federal personal income taxes on dividends, rights, and options, (6) corporate income taxes, (7) state and municipal income taxes, (8) Federal estate and gift taxes, (9) state estate and inheritance taxes, (10) estate planning, (11) personal property taxes, (12) transfer taxes on securities, and (13) taxation of insurance proceeds, annuities, and pensions.

The discussion gives effect to the changes made by the Tax Reform Act of 1976 and the Tax Reduction and Simplification Act of 1977.

Taxation and Investment Policy

Protection against taxation, especially that imposed on income, is becoming a major requirement in the investment programs of individuals and taxed institutions. Indeed, for many investors, it is the dominating influence.

A wide variety of tax levies must be given careful consideration. The Federal government imposes income, gift, and estate taxes; state governments impose income, estate or inheritance, and (in a few cases) property taxes; local county and municipal bodies impose property taxes.[1] The incidence of these taxes does not apply uniformly to all investment media, nor to all investors, individual or corporate, nor in all localities. The importance of taxation to the individual investor varies with his income, the size of his estate, the place of his residence, the number of his dependents, the location of his commitments, and any special tax advantages or disadvantages that apply to him. The small investor has little or no interest in tax factors; the large, wealthy investor has a major interest. To a large middle group they supplement other more important factors. To corporations and institutions the significance of taxes varies from none at all to being a matter of major investment importance.

---

[1] In addition, a few states levy gift taxes, and a few municipalities (for example, Philadelphia) levy income taxes. But these are of minor significance.

The term *tax-exempt*, frequently used in connection with securities, usually refers only to income taxes and generally to Federal income taxes. The bonds of states and municipalities are known as tax-exempt or "tax-free" issues. Thus, if bonds of Boston are owned by an investor in Albany, N.Y., no Federal tax is imposed upon the interest, but the New York State income tax applies, as well as the Federal and New York State estate taxes in the event of the death of the holder. Tax-exemption, therefore, applies primarily to income taxes and not to estate, gift, and property taxes.

The tax position of the investor is complicated by overlapping taxes. The income available for dividend payments by a corporation is substantially reduced by corporate income taxes, which in 1977 were imposed at rates as high as 48%. The dividend income of the stockholder is further reduced by personal income taxes, which were imposed at rates as high as 70%.[2] The estates of investors are subject to both Federal and state death taxes.

Federal Personal Income Taxes

Federal income taxes comprise the heaviest tax burden for most investors. In 1977, the Revenue Code required that single taxpapers with taxable income of $20,000 or less and married taxpayers with a taxable income of $40,000 or less use special tax tables showing actual taxes on a large number of amounts. On taxable income in excess of $20,000 (after deductions and personal exemptions), a single taxpayer uses a rate schedule with taxes beginning at 38% on the first $2,000 and rising by graduated brackets to 70% on taxed net income in excess of $100,000. The maximum *total* rate on taxable "earned income" is 50%.[3] Married persons filing separate returns, heads of households, and married persons filing joint returns are subject to different rates than the above. Using the rates applicable to earned income for the calendar year 1977, an investor with a gross income of $50,000, with a wife and two children, would calculate his tax as follows (assuming a joint return):

Gross income	$50,000
Exemptions ($750 × 4)	3,000
Taxable income after exemptions	47,000
Tax thereon	13,964
Less special credits	180
	$13,784

The Federal income tax of $13,784 is about 29% of the taxable income. The tax rate on the highest income bracket in this case is 48%, which is the lowest effective rate on any new investment income of the taxpaying couple.

[2]Less the $100 dividend exclusion described later in this chapter.

[3]"Earned income" (now called "personal service income") includes wages, salaries, professional fees, and other recognized income for personal services rendered, as well as pensions and annuities. Income not classified as "earned" is taxed at a maximum *total* rate of 60%.

The Federal income tax levy increases rapidly with the size of the annual income. To investors in the higher tax brackets, securities that are exempt from ordinary Federal income taxes naturally make a strong appeal. These now (1977) include bonds of Puerto Rico; bonds of states and political subdivisions (municipalities); revenue bonds issued by authorities that operate public facilities under the egis of a municipality or state; and other non-guaranteed municipal bonds, such as those issued to finance municipal utility operations.[4]

The income from all obligations of the United States and its instrumentalities, issued after March 31, 1941, is fully taxable by the Federal government, but not by state or local governments.

Some securities bear "tax-free" covenants under which the issuing corporation pays part of the state or Federal income tax imposed on the holder. As the amount paid is usually "up to 2%," the advantage to the holder is almost insignificant. Federal laws do not recognize such covenants for obligations issued since 1934.

Yields on "Tax-free" Bonds

An investor subject to a tax rate of 30% on new income pays a $24 tax on the $80 received annually from an 8% taxable bond; this payment reduces his income to $56. The purchase of a tax-exempt 5.6% bond at par produces the same net return to that individual. The purchase of a tax-exempt 5% municipal bond at par affords the same return as a taxable 10% corporate bond bought at par to an investor subject to a tax rate of 50% on the income from the additional investment.[5]

Investment policy with respect to Federal income taxes depends on the size of the annual personal net income. The total tax rate of investors of limited means is small, and they should buy taxable securities and pay the tax. Investors with very substantial incomes find the purchase of tax-exempt securities more advantageous. As shown in Table 17-1, a married investor with a taxable income of $45,600 (separate return) would have to receive a yield of 11.9% on a taxable bond to equal a yield of 5% on a tax-free bond.

The effective tax rate to an investor is the one that applies to his highest income bracket, inasmuch as income from investments is reported in addition to income from other sources. The highest bracket of an investor with a

---

[4]See Chapter 7. The Federal government imposes a minimum tax that is designed to make certain that affluent taxpayers do not avoid taxation altogether. A special 15% tax (after exemption of the greater of $10,000 or 1/2 the regular tax) is levied on "preference items," including the untaxed half of capital gains, excess depreciation on real estate, excessive deductions for intangible drilling costs in oil and gas shelters, and exceptionally high contributions and interest. (See tax services for the complete list of these preference items.)

[5]The illustrations on this and the previous pages deal with relief from Federal income taxes. Any state income taxes paid on the interest on municipal bonds are deductible from taxable income for Federal tax purposes.

Given the Federal tax bracket applying to income *adjusted for state incomes taxes*, the equivalent pre-tax yield of a 5% municipal bond yield for an investor in the 50% bracket is

$$\frac{0.05}{1 - 0.50} = 10\%$$

TABLE 17-1 Equivalent Yields on Tax-Free and Taxable Securities (rates applying in 1977)

Individuals & Married
(*Filing Separate Returns*)

Selected Taxable Income Brackets	Highest Bracket Rate	Tax-Free Yields					
		4.0%	4.50%	5.00%	5.50%	6.00%	6.50%
$21,000– 23,600	48%	7.69	8.65	9.62	10.58	11.54	12.50
23,600– 27,600	50	8.00	9.00	10.00	11.00	12.00	13.00
39,600– 45,600	58	9.52	10.71	11.90	13.10	14.29	15.48
61,600– 71,600	64	11.11	12.50	13.89	15.28	16.67	18.06
91,600–101,600	69	12.90	14.52	16.13	17.74	19.35	20.97
Over 101,600	70	13.33	15.00	16.67	18.33	20.00	21.67
Corporations (on income over $25,000)	48	7.69	8.65	9.62	10.58	11.54	12.50

taxable income of $101,600 (married and filing a separate return) is 69%. Hence, he must receive 16.13% from a taxable bond in order to have 5.00% remaining after the tax.

The appeal of tax-exempt bonds to investors in the higher tax brackets is reflected in their yields in relation to those on taxable bonds. The yields in the various Moody's bond groups, in October 1977, are shown in Table 17-2.

TABLE 17-2 Yields by Bond Group

	October 1977
Corporate bonds (composite)	
Aaa	8.00
Aa	8.20
A	8.45
Baa	8.85
Long-term municipals	
Aaa	5.30
Aa	5.45
A	5.65
Baa	5.85
U.S. Treasury. long-term	6.65

Source: Moody's *Bond Survey.*

To obtain an after-tax yield on corporate bonds equal to the tax-free yield on municipals, the investor in the upper brackets would have to take considerable risk. In October 1977 he could get a return of 5.30% on the best municipals, and 5.85 on good-grade municipals. If he were to purchase a corporate bond, and its interest fell into the 50% bracket, such a bond could have only very poor quality.

The advantage to be gained from the purchase of tax-exempt bonds varies from time to time with the changing spreads between yields on different securities. (Comparative yields are discussed further in Chapters 7 and 8.)

The investor should also consider the alternative yields on common stocks. In the postwar period until 1959, the yield on representative stock averages consistently exceeded that on high-grade municipal bonds. Whether the after-tax yield was relatively attractive depended on the effective tax rate that applied to particular investors. In 1950, when the dividend yield on the Dow Jones 30 industrial stocks averaged 7.5%, the average yield on Moody's Aaa municipals was 1.56%. Only investors in the very highest brackets would have preferred the latter for income. However, as stock yields declined in subsequent years, accompanied by a rise in state and local government bond yields, the advantage of stocks, with respect to current income, first disappeared and then became negative. In 1964 the yield on Moody's Aaa municipal bond series averaged 3.09%, while that of the industrial stocks was 3%. In January 1970, at the then peak of interest rates, the municipals series yielded 6.4%, while the industrial stock average yielded 3.60%. In September 1974, when interest rates peaked again, the rates were 6.49% and 5.45%, respectively. Even after the subsequent decline in municipal bond yields, only part of the gap had been closed. In October 1977, the rates were 5.3% and 4.75%.

Such figures suggest that stocks have been preferable, over the long run, to tax-free bonds for price appreciation rather than for income. Certainly the investor of means who held good stocks through the whole of great postwar bull market that reached its peaks in 1966, 1973, and 1976 would have been much further ahead from the combination of income plus appreciation on stocks than by holding municipal bonds, especially when the lower income tax rates on capital gains are considered. However, in the latter half of the 1960s, in 1970–1971, and in 1976 stocks failed to exceed the high level set in 1966, and the shorter-run risks of holding equities became very evident in the falling markets of 1966, 1970, and 1973–1974. The high yields on municipal bonds that characterized the more recent period mean that such investments would have outperformed common stocks in total rate of return, especially on an after-tax basis.

Generalizations concerning the appeal of stocks versus tax-exempt bonds must be tempered with the reminder that different investors bear different tax rates, and that yields change through time. Under rates applying to 1977 income, the first $30,000 of taxable income (unmarried individuals) was taxed at as high as 45%. To equal a tax-free yield of 5%, the investor whose income hit the 45% bracket would have to receive 9% current income from stocks. To do this with equivalent safety is impossible. A good case can be made for stocks as a component of many portfolios along with municipal bonds. But the investor must realize that his return from many stocks must come mainly from appreciation rather than from dividends and that substantial risks must be assumed. He must also recognize that the differential between gross yields on tax-free bonds and on stocks will continue to change.

The investor seeking the tax advantage of municipal bonds, but also seeking professional management, may buy shares in unit trusts or mutual funds whose portfolios consist of a diversified list of state, local, and revenue bonds. The income exceeds that on the highest-grade tax-free bonds, is free from Federal income taxes, but may not be exempt from state income taxes, depending on the geographical composition of the list. (See Chapter 11.)

Other methods of reducing income taxes Other methods of reducing Federal income taxes on family income from investments, in addition to the purchase of tax-free bonds (or of shares in funds whose portfolios consist of tax-free bonds), are:

- The use of the joint return (mentioned above) whereby a married couple can split combined income and thus move each half of the income into a lower tax bracket.
- Irrevocable gifts of securities to members of the family (but subject to gift taxes) and to trusts with a minimum duration of 10 years.
- The use of family partnerships and corporations (under certain conditions).
- Postponement of some income until retirement through participation in pension plans whose income is accumulated taxfree; rates applying after retirement will presumably be lower.
- Purchase of bonds at a discount. (See below.)
- The acquisition of securities whose income is taxed as capital gains or is a return of capital and so not taxed. (See below.)
- Investment for appreciation so as to enjoy a possibly reduced rate on capital gains (discussed below); this includes appreciation in bonds bought at substantial discounts.
- Use of the income-averaging option to reduce the impact of unusually large income or capital gains in any one year.
- Use of the so-called tax shelters. (See below.)
- Special services on taxes and estate planning indicate additional tax-reducing measures.

"Tax shelters" There are a number of "tax shelters," mainly the use of the limited partnership in such investments as: oil and gas drilling and exploration; real estate (to take advantage of the depreciation allowance); farming, including cattle-feeding; and equipment leasing. The limited partner's loss is limited to his investment, but gains are not taxed by the partnership but flow through to the partners. Risks can be very substantial. The choice of the shelter, and of its management (general partners) can be complicated. The Tax Reform Act of 1976 introduced very substantial changes in tax-shelter possibilities.[6] The investor is advised to seek the most competent and unbiased advice on all the facets of the available opportunities such as special risks, possible tax savings, and real returns.

---

[6]The chief change was the elimination of the "nonrecourse note," a device that had permitted limited partners to get first-year deductions in excess of their cash investment.

Capital Gains and Losses

The fact that capital gains receive special treatment is of considerable interest to many investors in the upper brackets. Profits and losses on the sale or exchange of capital assets held for more than nine months (one year in 1978 and after) are long-term capital gains and losses, those on the sale or exchange of capital assets held for not more than nine months (one year in 1978 and later) are short-term capital gains and losses. In calculating taxes, capital gains and losses are offset against each other. First, short-term gains are applied against short-term losses, and long-term gains against long-term losses. Then the results are combined. If a net short-term gain remains after deducting a net long-term loss, it is added to ordinary income and taxed at regular rates. If a net long-term gain remains after deducting long-term losses and any net short-term loss, it is taxable at a maximum rate of 25% on the first $50,000 of such gains ($25,000 in the case of a married individual filing a separate return) and 35% on any gains in excess of such an amount. The taxpayer then calculates the tax by adding to ordinary taxable income one-half of the net long-term gain and applying the appropriate rate.[7]

A net short-term capital loss (with no long-term loss) is applied against any net long-term gain, and the balance may be used as a deduction of up to $2,000 ($3,000 beginning in 1978) from the year's ordinary income. Any loss still remaining can be carried forward. A net short-term loss in excess of any long-term capital gain, or a net long-term loss, may be applied, up to $1,000 in a joint return, against the year's ordinary income, but taken into account at only 50%. That is, it takes $2,000 of net long-term loss to obtain a $1,000 deduction. Any remaining net short-term or net long-term losses that are carried forward to a future year retain their original character.

The 25% to 35% limitation on the tax on net long-term capital gains provides a special impetus to investors in the higher tax brackets to seek appreciation rather than regular income, and may thus greatly influence the composition of the portfolio. The purchase of low-yield growth stocks that offer promising appreciation, emphasis on oil, mining, natural gas, and other natural resource investments, and the purchase of real estate for appreciation, are all encouraged by the capital gains provisions.

Investors should be acquainted with some of the special measures by which the capital gains tax can be used to advantage (apart from the timing factors discussed below). The more important of these are:

- Purchase (in the market) of corporate and Federal bonds at a discount. Upon later resale or call, any appreciation is taxed as a capital gain. The greatest advantage is derived from bonds where most of the yield is represented by a deep discount rather than by the income on low-coupon bonds. (An

---

[7]Or he may use an alternative method by calculating the tax without including the long-term gain, and adding 25% of the amount (up to $50,000) by which net long-term gains exceed net short-term losses, and 35% of the amount in excess of $50,000. However, unless the unmarried or head-of-household taxpayer's income is over $40,200 (or $27,600 if married and filing a separate return, or $55,200 in the case of a joint return) the alternative computation is not feasible.

exception is found in the case of U.S. Savings bonds, Series E, whose entire yield is represented by the discount and is taxed as ordinary income when the bond is redeemed. (See Chapter 6.)

• The purchase of state and local government bonds at a discount. Any realized appreciation is taxed at the capital gains rate, but because their coupon income is tax-free, the preferable municipal bond is the one whose yield, or most of it, is represented by coupon income.[8]

• Depending on the investor's tax bracket and the sums involved, selling one security at a capital loss may be preferable to disposing of another at a gain, since the tax saving from the loss, plus the net proceeds of the sale, may exceed the after-tax proceeds from the profitable security. This is especially true if excess net capital losses are used to offset ordinary income.

• Investment in certain categories of stocks where dividends consist in whole or in part of distributed capital gains or of a return of capital rather than ordinary investment income. (See below.)

The timing of purchases and sales of securities is also affected by this special influence. Without discussing the subject in detail, the following practices should be considered, especially by those benefiting by the 25% to 35% top tax rate on net long-term gains:

1. Hold appreciating capital assets over nine months (one year beginning in 1978) so as to gain the reduction applying to long-term gains.

2. Use capital losses to offset short-term gains or ordinary income, rather than long-term gains. Short-term loss can be used 100% as an offset to ordinary income, but long-term loss only 50%. The unused portion of loss can be carried over and applied against ordinary income until exhausted.

3. Take long-term gains before unused loss carryovers expire.

4. Take losses and profits in different years so as to obtain the best results from matching gains and losses attributable to different years.

5. Realize on reinvested earnings by sale before large dividend payments are made; the latter enter the stream of ordinary income that may be taxed at a higher rate.

6. Use short sales to postpone realized gains, by selling short those stocks showing long-term paper gains and closing out such sales by delivering the holdings in the following year.

7. Record capital gains that can be offset by capital losses, by buying back the same or a similar security at once (at the cost of the brokerage commission). Also, record capital losses now and repurchase 31 days or more later, or buy a similar security now. (Or double up on the original shares so as to have the same securities after the sale.)

---

[8]When municipal bonds are bought at a premium, the premium must be amortized against the coupon income and deducted from the cost basis in computing any subsequent capital gain or loss. It may be to the advantage of the investor to handle corporate bonds in the same way; his taxable income is reduced, but although the cost basis is likewise reduced, any later realized gain will be taxed at the capital gains rate.

Additional suggestions on the timing of purchase and sales, offsetting gains and losses, and using the carryover provisions to take full advantage of the special treatment of capital gains and losses are available from security dealers and brokers and from tax services and tax consultants.

The reader is reminded that realized capital gains on all types of securities —corporate, municipal, and Federal—are subject to the Federal tax on capital gains.

Federal Personal Income Taxes on Dividends, Rights, and Options

Cash and property dividends are fully taxed (with certain exceptions noted below) as income. The corporation also pays a tax on the net income from which the dividends are derived, and the result is, of course, double taxation on the original corporate profits.

There is, however, partial relief from the double taxation of corporate profits. The first $100 of "qualified" dividend income received during the year ($200 in a joint return where husband and wife each received $100 dividend income) is excluded.

Some "dividends" are, in whole or in part, a return of capital, representing liquidation rather than earnings. One example is found in the case of "wasting assets" companies whose distributions exceed earnings after depletion. In the calculation of any later realized capital gain or loss, the cost basis of the stock is reduced accordingly. Another type is found in certain electric and gas utilities whose dividends are wholly or partially a return of capital because, for tax purposes, their income has been reduced by deferred depreciation.

All or part of some dividends represent capital gains distributions rather than ordinary income. The chief examples of this type are the realized capital gains distributions of regulated investment companies. (See Chapter 11.)

Dividends in the form of stock have special treatment. Where the stockholder has periodic choice between cash or stock dividends, he pays a tax on receipt of either type. He also pays a tax on stock dividends that discharge dividend arrearages of the current or preceding year. But if the dividend is an ordinary common stock dividend paid on common stock, it is not taxed on receipt. Upon subsequent sale, only the gain is taxed, and at the capital gains rate that applies to the taxpayer. In calculating the amount of gain (or loss) on sale of the shares, the cost basis of the original shares is adjusted to reflect the increased number of shares. Thus, if the investor had bought 100 shares of common stock for $1,000, and subsequently received 25 additional common shares as a stock dividend, the cost basis of the 125 shares would become $8 per share. Subsequent purchases, sales, stock dividends, and stock splits present problems of identification. A careful record of the specific blocks of shares bought and sold, and of shares to which the dividends have applied, is necessary to calculate the cost basis of each share sold in order to determine any capital gain or loss. Invoices of all purchases and sales should be retained, otherwise the "first-in, first-out" rule may be applied, to the possible detriment of the investor.

Stock rights also receive special Federal income tax treatment. They are not taxable on receipt. Unless the market value of the rights is more than 15% of the value of the outstanding stock at the time of distribution (an unlikely event), the cost basis of stock acquired through rights is the subscription price, and that of the original stock remains unchanged. If the rights are subsequently sold, the cost basis is zero and the entire net proceeds are considered capital gains, either short- or long-term. The holding period of the new stock begins on the date the rights are exercised; that of the rights begins at the time the underlying stock was acquired.

The tax aspects of gains from put and call options are complicated. In general, the income is not recognized until the option is either utilized or expires. The reader should consult up-to-date tax manuals for details. Treatment of corporate stock-purchase options was drastically revised by the Tax Reform Act of 1976.[9]

Corporate Income Taxes

The investor is, of course, considerably affected by the corporate income taxes that reduce his earnings and dividends, and by the influence of taxation on the prices and yields of corporate securities. Under rates applying to 1977 income the ordinary corporation is subject to the following rates:

On taxable income under $25,000	20%
On taxable income $25,000–$50,000	22%
On taxable income over $50,000	48%

This means that for larger companies, the effective rate is virtually 48%.[10]

High corporate tax rates, followed by even higher rates on dividends as personal income, provide a strong motive for retention rather than distribution of profits by many corporations. To prevent undue retention, a tax on the improper accumulation of surplus of from 27.5% to 38.5% is imposed on that portion of the earnings (over $100,000) retained but not necessary for the reasonably anticipated needs of the business. Use of earnings for expansion, or to provide for reasonable contingencies or to retire prior obligations, is not penalized. This section of the Internal Revenue Code applies mainly to closely held corporations.

Corporations are subject to taxation of capital gains. For virtually all corporations the effective rate is 30% on net long-term gains. Ordinary corporations pay a tax on dividends received on common and preferred stock

[9]The Act virtually eliminates the former qualified stock-purchase option as a type of executive compensation. Profit on sale of shares acquired through options and granted under a company plan adopted before May 21, 1976, is still taxed as a capital gain rather than as ordinary income. But those granted after that date lose the qualified status, and ordinary income tax is paid on any realized gain.

[10]To prevent splitting businesses into two or more companies to reduce the individual corporation's net income below $25,000, there are special regulations governing multiple-corporate operations.

investments, but after an 85% deduction. This gives stocks a special appeal to business corporations holding stocks as general investments and to certain taxed institutional investors for which stocks are eligible assets. The special tax advantage of investment in high-grade preferred stocks to business firms, insurance companies, and other taxed institutions accounts in part for the fact that the yields have been as low as and, in some cases, lower than those on high-grade bonds.[11] Institutional investors such as approved pension funds and college endowments, whose income is tax-exempt, find no advantage in purchasing preferred stocks (unless convertible) rather than bonds, and, of course, such funds avoid investment in state and local government bonds whose yields are unattractive.

Taxed corporations, such as banks and insurance companies, find a major advantage in investing in tax-free state and local government bonds, whose yields greatly exceed the yields on Federal and on high-grade corporate bonds after the application of a high tax rate. (See Table 17-1.)

Certain types of corporations are subject to special income tax rates or provisions. Life insurance companies are taxed under a special formula that reduces the effective tax rate on investment income to between 20 and 25%.[12] Other insurance companies are taxed at the regular corporate rate, less allowed reserves against losses, as are savings banks, savings and loan associations, and commercial banks. Public utility companies are allowed a special deduction from taxable income for dividends paid on nonparticipating cumulative preferred stock issued before October 1942. Investment companies may obtain tax-exemption by complying with the provisions of the Investment Companies Act of 1940 and the Internal Revenue Code that qualify them as "regulated investment companies," including the important requirement that they distribute in dividends at least 90% of each year's net investment income and short-term capital gains.[13]

Ordinary corporations find many ways to reduce the impact of income taxation. Among these are the use of carrybacks and carryforwards, the application of special depletion rates for tax purposes by "wasting asset" companies, the use of accelerated depreciation and amortization which reduces and postpones (possibly indefinitely) part of the tax bill because of increased depreciation expense, the use of the investment credit for equipment purchased, and the use of debt financing to take advantage of the deductibility of interest as an expense for income tax purposes. These devices are described in works dealing with business finance and accounting.

State and Municipal Income Taxes

Some 45 states now levy personal income taxes. The exemption limits are generally higher than those permitted by the Federal returns, and the rates, while graduated, run much lower. Thus, in California (1977 returns) the

[11]See Chapter 9, Table 9-2.
[12]See Chapter 30.
[13]See Chapter 11.

rates on taxable net income after exemptions and deductions, single person, graduate from 1% on the first $2,000 to 11% on taxable income over $15,500. The state income tax is a deduction from income in computing the Federal income tax.

State and higher Federal rates in the upper brackets combine to impose a very substantial levy on investment income. Some relief is found in those states that permit the splitting of income (and exemptions) to bring the respective portions of a joint state return into the lower brackets. In 14 states the Federal income tax is a partly or wholly deductible expense.

State tax regulations differ considerably in the treatment of such items as capital gains, dividend and tax deductions, medical expenses, and many other items. The trend, however, is towards more similarity with the Federal rules in respect to such details.

Where taxable income is derived in more than one state, duplicate taxation is avoided in those states which have entered into reciprocal agreements. For example, California has (1977) such agreements with 28 other states.

About 46 states now impose income taxes on corporations, with the rates typically 5% to 6%. In addition, some municipalities, mainly in Pennsylvania and Ohio, impose income taxes on wages, salaries, and business profits; investment income is ordinarily exempted, however.

Interest on Federal obligations is exempt from state income taxes in all states. The interest on state and local government bonds of the state of issue is exempt "at home." Further discussion of this subject is found in Chapters 6 and 7.

Interest on the obligations of certain Federal agencies is exempt from state income taxes; that of others is taxed (Chapter 6). Interest on international organization bonds is taxable at both state and Federal levels.

As in the case of Federal taxation, state capital gains taxes apply to realized capital gains on all types of securities, including stocks and Federal, state, and corporate bonds.

Federal Estate and Gift Taxes

Before 1977, separate Federal rate schedules applied to estates and gifts. Graduated estate taxes were levied on sums in excess of certain exemptions, a marital deduction, and a specific exemption. Rates ran from 3% on the first $5,000 of the net estate to 77% on the net estate over $10,000,000, less a credit for state inheritance taxes paid. A graduated gift tax was placed on all gifts after a cumulative lifetime exemption of $30,000 plus $3,000 to any person in any one year, at rates uniformly three-fourths of the corresponding estate tax rates (2 1/4% to 57 3/4%).

The Tax Reform Act of 1976 changed these provisions drastically. A uniform rate schedule applies to both estates and gifts made after 1976. The donor's lifetime gifts are added to his estate. A "unified credit" of $30,000 (increasing to $47,000 in 1981) replaces the previous exemptions. The marital deduction for property left to a spouse is $250,000, or 50% of the adjusted gross estate, whichever is greater. Starting in 1981, estates up to $425,000 can be passed to heirs free of any estate and gift taxes. Under the old law, gift tax rates were 75% of estate tax rates. The new law created a single 18% to 70% schedule, effective 1977, to apply to both estates and gifts.

The first $100,000 of lifetime gifts to a spouse (above the $3,000 annual exclusion) is now tax-free. The unified rate is applied to gifts to the spouse of between $100,000 and $200,000 and is 50% of such gifts over $200,000.

The 1976 legislation requires that the fair market value as of December 31, 1976, or the decedent's original cost, whichever is greater, becomes the tax basis of "carry-over" inherited property. The basis for other property and for losses remains the decedent's basis at death.

Federal tax regulations governing estate and gift taxes include many other provisions. They are very complex and should be interpreted by investors or their advisors with extreme care, using accurate information.[14]

State Estate and Inheritance Taxes

With the exception of Nevada, all states in the United States now impose some form of death tax. The *estate tax* is levied directly against the net estate as an entirety, generally on a graduated scale. Such a tax is used alone by a dozen states, including New York. The *inheritance tax* is levied on the individual shares of the beneficiaries after the net estate has been divided. Most states levy this type of tax. In all states except Nevada, an additional estate tax is levied to take advantage of the credit for state death taxes that is allowed against the Federal estate tax.

To avoid tax duplication, the Federal law allows a credit for state death taxes based on a special table. No credit is allowed on the first $40,000 of the taxable estate. The *maximum* credit graduates from 0.8% on $40,000 to $90,000 to 16% on any excess over $10,040,000. For example, on a $240,000 adjusted taxable estate (taxable estate reduced by $60,000), the maximum credit is $3,600. If the state tax were $1,500, the credit would be $1,500, and the states have increased their taxes to at least equal the Federal credit. Most states also set smaller deductions and exemptions from the gross estate and so tax many estates which are not subject to the Federal tax.

Some 15 states levy gift taxes patterned after the former Federal legislation.

Estate Planning

Estate planning involves the planning of liquid assets, investments, life, health, and property insurance, and the terms of wills so as best to serve the needs of the investor and his family and to minimize current and future taxes. It involves the judicious use of insurance arrangements, *inter vivos*

---

[14]The face value of certain issues of Treasury bonds called "flower bonds" is acceptable in payment of Federal estate and gift taxes. These bear low coupon rates and sell at substantial discounts. Their appeal for estate tax purposes causes them to sell at lower yields than those on other Treasury bonds with the same maturities. About 13 issues were (1977) outstanding.

gifts, life estates, short-term and testamentary trusts, the marital deduction, and charitable beneficiaries. A major goal in many cases is to prevent death taxes from depleting capital in each generation to which the estate may pass.

Heavy Federal and state taxes of the estate or inheritance type prove a special problem for investors of large means who have been able, in spite of high income taxes, to accumulate a substantial estate. A very substantial portion of the estate must be held in cash or highly marketable securities lest the sudden need for cash for the payment of levies coincide with a period of depressed security prices. Or, where the estate consists of assets that are not readily marketable, special insurance is often taken to provide tax funds and preserve the estate for the heirs.

The whole subject of estate planning is complex, and generalizations are dangerous. Each situation requires its own solution. It is best to consult special works on the subject, such as those listed in the references to this chapter, and to make no important moves without competent legal advice.

Personal Property Taxes

Taxes on real and personal, tangible and intangible properties are imposed by some 15 states and by virtually all municipal governments. Investors are especially interested in those taxes that apply against securities which are regarded as personal intangible property. Some states impose taxes specifically against security holdings. For example, the Pennsylvania tax is 0.4% annually (the 4-mill tax) on the value of securities (other than stocks of corporations domiciled in the state) held by residents of that state. The more general practice is to impose on securities the same tax rate as that levied on tangible real property such as land and buildings.

The significance of such taxes to the investor depends upon the seriousness with which they are regarded in the community in which he is a resident. The location of the issuer of the securities and the domicile of the security instruments are also factors to be considered in the assessment of these taxes.

Although some states impose personal property (as well as income and estate) taxes on securities held within those states for the account of non-residents, the general practice is to the contrary. The constitution of New York State guarantees that the state will not impose any property, income, or estate tax on any securities held within the state for nonresidents of the state, in safe-deposit boxes or in safe-keeping, custodian, or trust accounts.

Transfer Taxes on Securities[15]

The New York State transfer tax applies only on sales of stock. In 1977 it was 6.25 cents per share on stock selling at or over $20, 4.69 cents per share on stock selling between $10 and $20, 3.13 cents on stock selling between $5 and $10, and 1 5/6 cents on stock selling at less than $5. The tax can be

---

[15]See also Chapter 16.

avoided by trading at brokerage offices outside of the state. The tax is reduced by 50% for nonresidents.

Taxation of Insurance Proceeds, Annuities, and Pensions

The proceeds from life insurance policies received by a beneficiary or by the insured when "cashed" are subject to special Federal income tax treatment. The proceeds of a lump-sum payment of the full face value of a policy are generally free from income tax. Installment payments spread over the expected life of the beneficiary or over a fixed number of years are taxed only if they exceed the installment period's portion of the principal plus a spouse's exclusion of $1,000. In the case of installment payments when there is no lump-sum option, the discounted value of the policy at the date of the insured's death is used as the principal amount. However, when proceeds of policies are left on deposit, the interest on the proceeds is fully taxed, as is the interest on retained "dividends" from participating policies during the life of the insured.

The income tax status of annuities is quite complex. The taxability of the proceeds depends on the life expectancy of the beneficiary or beneficiaries, whether there are any refund features in the policy, and the period over which benefits are to be received. The Internal Revenue Service provides life expectancy tables that apply to refund annuities and joint life and survivor annuities, for calculating the share of each year's payments that is a return of the original investment. The tax regulations or Master Tax Guides provide the details of the procedure.

The 1976 tax law gave executives and others who take their pension benefits in a lump sum a new option. The law permits a taxpayer to treat the entire lump sum as ordinary income, with 10-year forward income averaging.

A particularly drastic feature of the 1976 Act stipulates that appreciation in value after December 31, 1976 of non-carryover property left by death will generally be subject to income tax when sold by the decedent's estate or beneficiaries.

The growing importance of pension and retirement plans, including deferred profit-sharing plans, was indicated in Chapter 4. Company contributions while the investor's account is being accumulated are tax-free provided the plan meets the requirements of the Internal Revenue Code. The tax on the retirement income depends on how the benefits are distributed, the proportion of the investor's own previous contributions, and other factors. The tax status of pensions is complex and difficult to summarize.

Special "tax-free" retirement plans for self-employed persons and individuals are described in Chapter 4. The Tax Reform Act of 1976 substantially increased the allowable contributions under the "Keogh" and "IRA" plans. Deferred salary and profit-sharing plans have the general advantage of reducing income until after retirement when the investor's total income is presumably lower and taxed at lower rates. Social Security retirement income is tax-free.

REFERENCES

BOWE, W. J., *Estate Planning and Taxation*, 3d CLU ed. Homewood, Ill.: Richard D. Irwin, Inc., 1972.

BROSTERMAN, ROBERT, *The Complete Estate Planning Guide*, rev. ed. New York: New American Library, 1970.

CASEY, W. J., *Estate Planning*. Larchmont, N.Y.: Institute for Business Planning, Inc., loose-leaf.

————, *Tax Planning*. Larchmont, N.Y.: Institute for Business Planning, Inc., loose-leaf.

CLAY, W. C., JR., *The Dow Jones-Irwin Guide to Estate Planning*. Homewood, Ill.: Dow Jones-Irwin, Inc., 1975.

COMMERCE CLEARING HOUSE, INC., *Federal Tax Course*. New York: Commerce Clearing House, Inc., annual.

DROLLINGER, W. C., *Tax Shelters and Tax Free Income for Everyone*. Ann Arbor, Michigan: Epic Publications, 1972.

ENBERG, H. W., ed., *Tax Sheltered Investments*. New York: Practicing Law Institute, 1973.

FARR, J. F., *An Estate Planner's Handbook*, 3d ed. Boston: Little, Brown and Co., 1966.

GORDON, G. B., *You, Your Heirs, and Your Estate*. Rockville Center, N.Y.: Farnsworth Publishing Co., 1973.

HAFT, R. J., *Tax Sheltered Investments*. New York: C. Boardman Co., 1973.

KAPLAN, PHILIP, *Tax Savings to Increase Your Income the Year Round*. Larchmont, N.Y.: American Research Council, 1962.

LASSER, J. K., *Lasser's Your Income Tax*. New York: Simon & Schuster, Inc., annual.

LASSER TAX INSTITUTE, *How to Save Estate and Gift Taxes*. New York: Simon & Schuster, 1974.

LOWNDES, C. L., et al., *Federal Estate and Gift Taxes*, 3d ed. St. Paul, Minn.: West Publishing Co., 1974.

MERRILL LYNCH, PIERCE, FENNER AND SMITH, *Investing for Tax-Free Income*. New York: occasional.

PRENTICE-HALL EDITORIAL STAFF, *Federal Tax Course*. Englewood Cliffs, N.J.: Prentice-Hall, Inc., annual.

SUMMERFELD, R. M., *The Dow Jones-Irwin Guide to Tax Planning*. Homewood, Ill.: Dow Jones-Irwin, Inc., 1974.

U. S. TREASURY DEPARTMENT, INTERNAL REVENUE SERVICE, *A Guide to Federal Estate and Gift Taxation*. Washington, D.C.: U.S. Government Printing Office, 1971.

————, *Your Federal Income Tax*. Washington, D.C.: U.S. Government Printing Office, annual.

Part

The Investment
Program

Investment Objectives: Quality Risk and Its Control

SCOPE: Up to this point the material in this book has provided the background and information needed by the investor to design an intelligent investment program. Following a discussion of the general economic setting of the subject (Part I), the major general types of investment media were described (Part II). Then came a series of chapters (Part III) dealing with the mechanics of investment: the financial language, the sources of investment information and advice, the origin of new securities, the market for outstanding securities, the techniques of purchase and sale, and the tax treatment of various types of investments. We are now ready in Part IV to consider the development of the investment program. Chapters 18 and 19 outline the general principles that govern investment policy. The application of the principles to individual investment programs is found in Chapter 20 and to institutions in Chapters 21 and 22.

The order of discussion in Chapter 18 is: (1) steps in investment planning, (2) budgeting for investment, (3) determination of investment objectives, (4) financial requirements, (5) allied questions, (6) types of investment risk, and (7) loss of (safety) quality.

Steps in Investment Planning

Investing is a serious business. It should be based on a well-considered plan that takes into account the needs of the investor and the degree of risk he is willing to assume. The development of a plan involves six steps: (1) budgeting and allocation of funds for investment; (2) determination of the investment goals in the order of their priority; (3) determination of the types and level of risks to be assumed; (4) choice of the general types of investment media to meet the objectives and control the risks; (5) selection of specific investments; (6) measurement of investment performance and revision of the program. This approach appears complicated, but it is better to err on the side of careful planning than to hazard the hard-earned savings of a family or the funds entrusted to institutions.

This chapter and Chapter 19 deal with the first three of these steps, Chapters 20 to 22 with the fourth, and Parts II and V contain descriptions and methods of analysis of the different types of investment media. The sixth step is discussed in Chapter 23.

Budgeting for Investment

We saw in Chapters 1 and 2 that the financial savings of individuals are represented by a variety of investment media. The origin of these savings is disposable income after consumption expenditures and repayment of debt.

The individual family budget usually includes certain involuntary investments such as the regular payment of mortgage principal, the "savings" element in life insurance premiums, and payroll deductions for Social Security. Less obligation is involved in regular contributions to pension plans, payroll deductions for Savings Bonds, and stock purchase plans.

Many families have little or no additional savings available for investment after the above disbursements have been made, at least for some time. Others can invest in a variety of media on a purely voluntary basis. A regular plan that shows the allocation income to each investment goal, in order of priority, should be drawn up as part of the general family budget. As indicated in Chapter 20, the circumstances of each individual or family differ widely, so that no set plan will be widely appropriate. But budgeting for investment to take care of important objectives is as important as budgeting the unit's consumption expenditures.

Institutions have no choice but to provide for their obligations to savers and other holders of contracts. Their financial plans and budgets are mainly devoted to this end.

Determination of Investment Objectives

A "good" investment is one that is appropriate; that is, one that fulfills the objectives of the investor or investing institution and involves as much or as little risk as can appropriately be assumed. A "safe" investment may or may not be appropriate from either standpoint; the same is true of a "risky" one. For example, a very wealthy individual whose whole estate consists of Treasury bonds would be making a "safe" investment if he purchased additional Treasury bonds with new funds. But such a policy might not be "good," because this investor can take advantage of the tax-exempt features of municipal bonds, take the risks involved in owning equities, and direct at least a portion of his funds towards the riskier goals of capital appreciation and preservation of purchasing power. The purchase of additional Treasury bonds would be intelligent only if he needed high liquidity and was satisfied with a relatively low rate of return. At the opposite extreme, an investor of limited means with dependents to provide for, and whose funds are already wholly invested in common stocks, might make a relatively safe investment (as stocks go) if he purchased additional shares of strong, prosperous industrial corporations enjoying regular earnings and paying regular dividends; but such a policy might hazard his need for recovery of principal and for highly dependable income, and he would be incurring risks that he is in no position to take. Using an institutional example, the purchase of short-term money market instruments by a pension fund might be safe and desirable as a temporary lodgement for cash, and, in some periods, as a source of income. But continuous allocation of a large portion of a fund to this medium would not protect participants against inflation.

Whether a certain investment is "good" depends, then, on the circumstances of the investor, on the goals toward which savings or institutional funds should be applied, and on the amount and kind of risk that can be assumed.

Types of investment objectives Investment objectives may be expressed in two ways: first, in terms of the general purposes to be fulfilled; second, in terms of the financial requirements to be achieved so as to implement these purposes. For example, an individual may have provision for the education of his children as one of the purposes of saving and investment. If the need is some years away, he may decide that growth of capital is required. Education is the general purpose, growth of capital is a requirement. If another of this individual's objectives is to provide for sudden emergencies, liquidity or immediate recovery of principal is a requirement.

Similarly, the purposes or functions of institutions involve certain financial requirements. For example, the major function of a life insurance company is to provide for the beneficiaries of its policy-holders. To fulfill this objective requires little immediate recovery of principal. More important requirements are longer-term capital preservation and income sufficient to cover the rate at which contractual reserves have to be accumulated.

The various goals of individual investors and their accompanying financial requirements are discussed in Chapter 20, those of institutions in Chapters 21 and 22.

Financial Objectives or Requirements

The following discussion deals with the major financial objectives or requirements: (1) immediate recovery of principal, (2) eventual recovery of principal (capital preservation), (3) growth of capital, and (4) assurance of income. Their order of priority will vary from individual to individual and from institution to institution.

Immediate- or short-term recovery of principal For the majority of individual investors and for many institutions the protection of dollar value is of prime importance. Savings accounts involve no risk of immediate loss provided the savings institution remains solvent and financially liquid. The principal of securities may be recovered through resale only if the instrument is readily marketable and enjoys price stability; those with a fixed maturity provide eventual recovery of principal at maturity, except in case of default. But recovery in the short term is assured only through the purchase of very short maturities.

Emergency funds require complete liquidity at no loss, and this is usually achieved only at some sacrifice of income. The same is true of the investments of institutions, such as banks, that must meet payments on demand or on very short notice. Immediate recovery of funds held as protection against the death of the income-producer is likely to be necessary for only part of the estate. Funds accumulated for an equity in a home in the near future must also be protected against shrinkage.

Investments made for purposes such as education of dependents may require complete availability, depending on when the funds are needed. Funds earmarked to produce supplemental income for the individual investor before retirement can be invested by some families so as to risk change in market value, provided the income produced is satisfactory. The same is true of investing for retirement.

The creation of an eventual estate (other than through insurance) is impelled by a wide variety of reasons. The estate may have to provide for dependents, or it may be planned as a gift to endowed or charitable institutions, or for many other purposes. In many cases, however, immediate recovery of principal is not required, save for the payment of estate taxes, other expenses, and debts of the deceased.

Immediate recovery of principal (liquidity at no loss) is extremely important to some investors, as in the case of a commercial bank for its secondary reserves, but much less so for others, such as a life insurance company for its long-term insurance contracts.

Eventual recovery of principal   Although funds may not be immediately required, safety of principal, or more accurately, ultimate recovery of principal, may be an important requirement. Funds held for emergencies must be available, without shrinkage, 5 or 10 years from the present. Funds provided against the death of the income-producer are assured mainly through life insurance. The importance of avoiding loss of principal varies greatly from case to case. Purchase of a home on a long-term amortized mortgage plan avoids the problem of investment in instruments with fluctuating values, as payments on principal are made from current income.

Generalizing about provision for urgent family needs, such as education, is difficult. In many cases, the family can assume considerable risk if it has confidence in the eventual payout of its portfolio. The steadily rising costs of education suggest that well-selected common stocks or mutual fund shares are appropriate in many plans to offset inflation and participate in a growing economy. Whether the family will wish to accept the inevitable fluctuations in the value of stocks is an important decision. Funds accumulated to produce supplemental income before retirement can be invested at some risk unless other sources of income are inadequate.

The degree of risk to capital is again a matter of individual choice. The creation of a substantial estate imposes the least pressure on eventual recovery of principal. However, after the very sharp decline in both bond and stock prices in 1973–1974, new emphasis on "capital preservation" was given in the investment management of many large funds.

Growth of capital   All investors would like to see their capital grow. The conservative method of growth is through the compounding of income from savings types of investments. Growth by price appreciation involves risk. The acceptable level of risk of loss of capital is, in turn, a function of willingness or temperament and adequacy of resources. Unwillingness or inability to assume the risk associated with growth requires a sacrifice of return and loss of purchasing power.

The types and measurement of risk are discussed later in this chapter, and the extent to which risk of loss of principal and income by individuals is involved in accomplishing objectives is discussed in Chapter 20, and for institutions, in Chapters 21–22. The concept of risk-reward relationships runs through the discussion in many sections of this book.

Assurance of current income   For many investors this requirement has even greater importance than recovery of principal. Except in the cases where total income is already very large in relation to need, or where income from sources other than investments is very substantial, or where capital appreciation is important, current income is likely to take a senior place in the priority of investment considerations.

Whether the dollars of income will be assured depends on the solvency and earning power of the user of the funds, and, in the case of corporate stocks, on the dividend policy of the corporate management. Methods of determining these factors comprise much of the material in Part V of this book. But the need of assured income is determined prior to the selection of the investments. Emergency funds that must be available on short notice have historically produced a relatively low rate of income, as in the case of savings deposits or Savings Bonds cashed well before maturity. In recent years, however, savings deposits have yielded substantial rates. If policy loans are made on the cash-surrender value of insurance, the income is likely to be negative because the rate charged will exceed the return produced on the insurance company's reserves. Many investors need income at a minimum of risk immediately and continuously; in other cases, such as for retirement purposes, it may not be needed until the remote future. Generally speaking, the smaller the fund and the greater the importance of each dollar of income, the less the risk that can be assumed and the lower the rate of income that can be obtained with required safety. If assurance of income is paramount, income must be sacrificed. The same is true for many institutional investors. In other situations, however, regularity and certainty of income may be much less important than capital preservation or appreciation, or protection against inflation.

In the preceding discussion, *current income* means regularly received income in the form of interest or dividends. The concept of income can also include capital gain or loss derived from the change in market value of the portfolio. (See Chapter 23.) In comparing the returns on bonds and common stocks, it is necessary to include both current income and change in price, because only a portion of profits is declared in dividends, and yields on stocks are typically lower than those on bonds. (See p. 182.) This concept of "total return" is perfectly legitimate provided the source of appreciation is growth in real value. Much impetus to the choice of capital gains as against income in the traditional sense has also been given by the special tax treatment of such gains.

Such a transfer of emphasis from present income to future income and, hence, to future total returns is appropriate only for investors who do not need assured current income and who can afford the risks' of price change. The important thing is that the risks be recognized and that the selection and timing of the purchases and sales be made intelligently and at prices that do not overvalue present assets and income and future prospects.

The use of the "total return" concept by institutional investors will be discussed in Chapters 21–23. The very sharp decline in stock prices in 1973–1974 and the delay in reaching the previous peak suggest the danger of the concept when commitments are made on the basis of unrealized gains.

Allied Questions

Associated with the task of determining investment objectives and financial requirements are other very important decisions which may color the whole program: What legal restraints influence the choice of investments that are selected to fulfill investment objectives? Should the investor manage his own affairs or delegate management to others? How important are tax considerations in determining investment policy? How important is the need of protection against inflation?

Legality   Institutional investors, especially those in a fiduciary position, must arrange their programs and make their selections within the framework of Federal and state restrictions. These restrictions change through the years. They apply with special strictness in some situations, for example, in the investment of savings bank funds, and allow considerable latitude in others, as in the case of fire insurance companies and investment companies. But in all cases, what the institution would *prefer* to do is heavily influenced by what is *permitted* by law.

Legality is important to individuals as well as to institutions. In the first place, indirect investment through the medium of a savings or investment institution is *ipso facto* affected by the legal requirements bearing on that institution. Thus, the participant in a pension plan which does not permit the company to purchase common stocks might find the rate at which his reserve is accumulated lower but less volatile than it might be if such investments were made. In the second place, the investor in certain securities, notably those issued by states and municipalities, must be satisfied that the security conforms to the legal restrictions on the borrowing government.

Freedom from management   Many investors must be as carefree as possible, either in the sense that safety of principal and stable income are important or in the sense that they wish to assume little or no responsibility for investment decisions. Others are willing to undertake the tasks of selection, timing, and supervision of the portfolio.

Freedom from care through safety can be obtained by making investments that are subject to little or no shrinkage in dollar value and income, but such freedom is obtained only at the sacrifice of income. The holder of an insured passbook deposit in a strong bank or savings and loan association has freedom from care—and (at the time of writing) 5% to 5 1/2% interest and up to 7 1/2% to 7 3/4% on time deposits. The holder of a Series E Savings Bond has freedom from care—and 6% return if the bond is held to maturity. Release from responsibilities of investment management requires the transfer of such responsibilities to others—either investing institutions which operate a portfolio of investments, or investment advisors.

The importance of freedom from care depends on the size of the fund, the need of assurance of income and recovery of principal, and the amount of attention and skill that the investor is able to devote to his investment affairs.

Investments in savings institutions, including deposits, life insurance, and annuities, involve delegation of authority. Investments in very high-grade securities involve a minimum of effort and supervision. Investments of all other types require delegation of responsibility unless the investor himself is willing to select, appraise, time, and supervise the funds. In many cases the investment of funds by individuals for emergencies, home ownership, or essential goals such as education and retirement, should be as carefree as possible, in both the senses in which we use the term. Investing institutions are usually large enough to employ financial managers, using either in-house or outside professional counsel.

Tax considerations   The higher the investor's income, the more will matters of taxes determine the character of his portfolio. Indeed, for individual investors of means and for some institutions, it may be the dominating influence. The subject of taxation of investments is treated in Chapter 17 and in various other chapters where pertinent. We need only suggest here that the prospects for continued high personal and corporate taxes and for substantial estate and inheritance taxes will continue to have a major influence on many portfolios. Two devices for minimizing income taxes—the purchase of tax-exempt state and municipal bonds, or "tax-free" funds, and the use of the special capital gains provision—are especially significant.

Protection against inflation   Inflation has followed all of the wars in which the United States has been involved and is a dominating and disconcerting feature of our economy. Experience with inflation to date, and the prospects for its continuation, mean that it will persist as an important influence on investment policy. The means by which attempts to offset inflation may or may not be feasible and successful are given full treatment at various points in this volume. At this point it is necessary to suggest four problems in connection with the matter of hedging against inflation, each of which will be further developed elsewhere:

· Cash and savings deposits provide no hedge at all.

· Fixed-income obligations have rarely provided protection save in periods such as 1975–1977 when the rate of interest on some investments exceeded the rate of price inflation.

- In making his choice between the safety of *dollars* of principal and income and the preservation of the *purchasing power* of those dollars, the small investor must select the first alternative. He cannot afford the risk that equities (with the possible exception of home and business properties) inevitably involve. One of the discouraging facts of economic life is that the investor who most needs protection against rising prices can least afford it.

- Common stocks and real estate offer an inflation hedge only in varying degrees, depending on the timing of purchase and sale, and the selection of the particular securities or property.

The need for and ability to hedge varies among different types of investors. As has been indicated, the investment plans of some investors, especially institutions with fixed-dollar obligations, can ignore inflation; some investors are affected by inflation but can do little or nothing about it; some investors and institutions make the problem of offsetting the decline in the value of the dollar a dominating influence in their investment planning. This last point of view is based on the assumption of continued inflation.

The traditional discussions of inflation in works on investments have dealt chiefly with choices of media that will offset its erosion of purchasing power. Our discussion in Chapter 19 will involve the influence of inflation on the media themselves, with new emphasis on bond yields and prices. The "double digit" inflation of the 1973–1975 period brought home the fact that the outlook for yields in all long-term securities markets is, in part, a function of the outlook for inflation and estimates of its rate of increase or decline.

Types of Investment Risk

The preceding discussion suggests that there is a wide variety of investment objectives, expressed in either explicit or in general terms, and that these will differ in relative importance from case to case. Furthermore, in seeking to meet these objectives, a number of types of risks must be confronted. Before a definite program can be constructed, the nature of these risks, and the methods of minimizing or avoiding them, should be well understood. Some investors can incur considerable risks of various kinds, others cannot. The important thing is to relate the objectives and the risk-taking in a rational way.

Whatever the investor does, some kind of risk will be present. The central problem of investment is to work out a program that will meet the objectives without incurring more risk than can be afforded, and that will produce a return that will compensate for this risk. Too often investors ask themselves, "What return would I like?" Then they frame their investment program accordingly. The more sensible approach would be, "What are my objectives, what financial requirements must be considered in order to acheive these goals, what risks will be encountered, and how much risk should I take?"

The two major types of investment risk are possible loss of dollars of income or principal of the fund, and possible loss of its purchasing power.[1] These can be further classified as follows:

1. Loss of dollars of income and/or principal value owing to:
   (a) Lack of quality of the enterprise ("internal risk")
      (1) Loss of interest and dividend income and of maturing principal.
      (2) Resulting loss of market value of securities.
   (b) Changes in interest rates ("money-market risk")
      (1) Bonds
      (2) Preferred stock
      (3) Common stock
   (c) Volatile and/or secular stock prices in securities markets as a whole ("market price risk")
2. Loss of purchasing power of income and/or principal ("purchasing power risk")

Changes in quality (ability to pay interest, principal, and dividends) are reflected in changing market prices of individual securities. Indeed, before actual default on interest or principal takes place, the real loss is recorded in price. Possible or actual declines in dividends have the same effect.

The second and third types of risk of loss of dollars (1(b) and 1(c)) are not associated with the quality of the individual security, but with market forces —changing interest rates and changing levels of stock prices in the market as a whole.

The risks that threaten the dollar value of the principal or income may be encountered separately or in combination: The worst losses are suffered when several risks have their effect simultaneously. Thus, an inherently weak stock, in a cyclical industry, in a period of recession in security prices, will suffer the worst price decline. On the other hand, a high-grade high-profit concern, with earnings and dividends strong even in a recession period, may have a price decline in a real bear market, but will recover fast and pay dividends in the meantime.

The loss of purchasing power due to rising consumer and business prices (inflation) also affects securities prices, especially those of bonds.

Loss of Quality ("Safety")

Quality may change because of problems besetting the whole economy as they affect a particular industry, or because of factors associated with individual governmental units or companies. The risk of loss of dollars of income or principal is, of course, reflected in the market price.[2]

---

[1]In discussions which use variations in price as the surrogate for the risks as classified, category 1(a) is known as "unsystematic" risk, that is, associated with a particular stock; and categories 1(b) and 1(c) as "systematic" risk, or variations stemming from changes in market prices in general. See Chapter 23.

[2]Other factors than quality affect the prices and yields of securities. For a list of these, see Chapter 8.

There are three major and allied methods of reducing the quality risk at the level of the investor's risk aversion and in relation to his objectives: analysis, valuation, and diversification.

Analysis Careful analysis of the economy, of industries, and of individual issues, both corporate and other, is designed to reduce the uncertainty of future investment returns and, therefore, of market price. If high-risk investments are not appropriate to the investor's portfolio, analysis eliminates them. It helps in the selection of investments that fit the investor's risk level. It helps to reveal the deterioration of investments that have lost ground in respect to quality. It aids in the selection of investments that are appropriate for the investor's needs and objectives, whatever these may be. As indicated in Chapter 24, the depth and scope of analysis varies from superficial to exhaustive, depending on a variety of factors. The whole of Part V is given over to analysis of corporate securities. Tests of other media are explained in Chapters 4–11.

The importance of analysis varies with different types of investments. In general, the savings types discussed in Chapters 4 and 5 require little work on the part of the investor, save for an understanding of their characteristics. Mortgages are highly specialized and should be avoided by individual investors who lack training and experience in this field; institutional investors are better equipped to deal with this category. Very high-grade bonds, including government issues, pose few difficulties if they are held to maturity, save for an understanding of their characteristics and the influence of money rates on their prices and yields. But even high-grade corporate and municipal bonds may not remain high grade, so that continual inspection of quality is necessary. It is in the selection of lesser-grade bonds, preferred stocks, and common stocks, that very careful analysis becomes vital. And the investor must decide whether to undertake this task himself or rely on the judgment of others.

Intelligent valuation When securities are to form a part of the investment program, *the price at which a security is to be bought (or sold) is as important a decision as the selection of the security itself.* One of the disadvantages of concentrating purchases of stocks in the "growth" group is that these stocks often sell at a premium resulting from their popularity; furthermore, the unwary investor may fail to recognize that they have lost their quality of growth until after that condition has become evident. Possibly the most difficult task in the field of investments is that of determining what a security, especially a common stock, is really worth. Chapter 25 is devoted to this problem, and aids to this task are suggested in Part V. In passing, we should note, however, that valuation of securities, especially of equities, can be made only within a considerable range. Since such securities are ordinarily purchased and sold on the basis of going-concern value, no one can tell precisely what they are worth. The common stock of the General Electric Company may be undervalued at 60 and overvalued at 70. To decide that it is worth precisely 65, and not 64 or 66, however, leaves no room for all of the uncertainties of the present and the future which confront any stock.

Intelligent valuation of investments will aid in minimizing the several types of price risk. All of these risks are magnified if the investment is over-priced when purchased or underpriced when sold.

Diversification   The investor cannot control the course of the general market, that is, the "systematic" risk of loss associated with price changes in classes of securities in general. But, by diversification, he can reduce the "unsystematic" quality of economic risk associated with particular industries, governments, and securities. In this sense of the term, diversification can mean spreading the investment fund over a sufficient number of selected components (say, corporate stocks) so as to reduce substantially the uncertainty of future returns, or spreading the fund to produce returns similar to the general market index. In this discussion we shall use the former concept.

Diversification can be used at any level of risk. The higher the general quality, the smaller the need for diversification, but the lower the rate of return. An investor can dispense with diversification altogether if all components of his portfolio are riskless (with respect to quality), as where the fund consists of Federal government bonds. But the lower the quality, the greater the need for diversification, although this will reduce the returns below their possible maximum level.

The principle of diversification can also be applied to interest payment dates and maturity dates, to timing of purchases, to general types of media used, and to marketability.[3] We are concerned here with the applications from the standpoint of quality risk, involving chiefly limitations of the amounts or percentages to be invested in one type of security, or in any one company or industry.

Portfolios can consist of a wide spectrum with respect to grade (from blue-chips to new speculative issues) or purpose (from secure income to aggressive growth), but most funds are specialized in some respect, within which diversification to reduce quality risk is still useful.

The investor should not go so far in diversifying by industries and companies as to obtain mediocre results. Studies have shown that the funds that have produced the best performances are not those that have spread their funds over hundreds of separate issues. Moreover, as more and more individual companies diversify their own activities, a smaller number of securities provides a greater amount of economic diversification. The investor in Goodyear is investing in tires, tubes, individual rubber products, chemicals, and plastics. The owner of Philips Petroleum stock has a stake in oil, natural gas, petrochemicals, and nuclear energy.

In recent years a new approach to industrial portfolio diversification has been widely adopted, namely, to classify companies and "industries" by their major markets rather than by specific products. For example, the portfolio might include groups of "housing" stocks, "consumer service" stocks, "finance" stocks, "international" stocks, "natural resource" stocks, "energy" stocks, and so on. Different industries are found within each of these securities groups. The housing group could include cement companies, appliances,

---

[3]Diversification as a means of spreading the risks associated with changes in interest rates, pricing, and timing is discussed in Chapter 19.

and mobile home manufacturers. The finance group could include banks, savings and loan holding companies, and commercial credit companies. "Leisure time" and "antipollution" stocks are examples of very modern groups within which a diverse selection of traditional industries may be included but which enjoy a common economic demand.

The diversification of an investment fund according to geographical boundaries affords more theoretical than actual advantages. The investor who practices national distribution finds the task complicated because of limited opportunities in certain sections and because of the nationwide activities of the more important companies. Only in the cases of investors with extremely large funds, such as life insurance companies, is geographical diversification of practical value. Securities of the American Telephone & Telegraph Company represent national diversification in themselves, just as securities of the General Electric Company represent international diversification.

"Efficient" portfolios   In recent years much attention has been given to portfolio diversification on a quantitative basis. That is to say, how can the portfolio mix be so selected as to produce the most "efficient" portfolio? The efficient portfolio either (1) maximizes the expected return at a given (and acceptable) level of expected risk, or (2) minimizes the expected risk at any acceptable rate of expected return. The concept involves *expected* return and risk because the portfolio manager makes his decisions on the basis of estimates of the future.

The rate of total return is measured by change in value, plus any distributions in a particular period, and risk is measured by the volatility of rate of return. The degree of risk is the extent to which the actual (weighted average) rate of return is likely to differ from its expected level; the variance is measured by the standard deviation of expected variations around the expected return. (See Chapter 23.) The higher the standard deviation, the greater are the probabilities that the rate of return will in fact not be achieved. The risk on a Treasury bill is very low. That of a speculative stock can be very high. The efficient portfolio combines selected assets so as to produce the desired combination of risk and return.

In the case of stocks, variations in the rate of return are, under present conditions, chiefly the result of changes in market value. As we have seen, there are two types of change: (1) "systematic" variations in general market prices; (2) "unsystematic" or independent changes associated with the portfolio itself. (See Chapter 23.) If a portfolio were to consist of all stocks in the market, the second type of risk would be zero. A very widely diversified portfolio would have almost the same result. If a portfolio consisted of a few stocks, the independent risk could be very high, but the rate of return could likewise be high.

Wide diversification reduces the "unsystematic" risk. But diversification can be overdone, even when low risk is desired. A relatively small list can involve relatively low risk and produce an acceptable rate of return if the components are carefully selected. The problem here is to avoid "correlated" securities—those that can be expected to act alike, such as those in the same industry, or those which have the same characteristics, such as the same cyclical pattern. Under a cautious policy, risk could be reduced below the systematic level, but the manager would wish not to reduce the return in the same proportion. Under an aggressive policy, the manager would be willing to assume possibly high risk, but would wish to be compensated with a return that is even higher in proportion.

All this means that each portfolio manager has a very wide array of possible portfolios from which he is to select the one expected to bear an acceptable rate of return, but which has the least risk exposure at that rate. Consider the following attainable portfolios:

Portfolio	Expected Rate of Return Percentage	Expected Risk (Standard Deviation)
A	12	5
B	16	14
C	6	3
D	9	4
E	5	4
F	6	10
G	12	14
H	12	10
I	16	15
J	9	7

A, B, C, and D are the efficient portfolios because they offer the highest expected returns at particular levels of risk. No one would consider E. A is better than H and G. B is better than I. C is better than F. D is better than J. The choice among A, B, C, and D would depend on a number of factors in the particular fund situation.

Markowitz pioneered in developing the "efficient portfolio" concept.[4] Others have refined the technique. A number of decisions are necessary, not the least of which is the choice of the period during which past risk and return are deemed to be portents of the future. Few individual investors have access to the mass of statistics relating to hundreds of securities, the computer equipment, or the skill in programming that are necessary to produce the most efficient funds. Institutional investors have these resources and may adopt the approach if they approve its basic assumptions.

The achievement of satisfactory diversification by direct investment of a relatively small fund is practically impossible. Fortunately, several media exist for indirect investment of small funds, such as the investment company and the common trust fund, that enable the investor of limited means to obtain diversification that he could not obtain alone.

REFERENCES

See end of Chapter 19.

[4]H. M. Markowitz, *Portfolio Selection: Efficient Diversification of Investments.* New York: John Wiley & Sons, Inc., 1959.

Other Types of Investment Risk and Their Control 19

SCOPE: This chapter continues the discussion of investment principles begun in Chapter 18. The order of discussion is: (1) risk of changing interest rates ("money-rate risk"); (2) market-price risk, common stocks; (3) risk of changes in purchasing power; (4) modern approaches to risk measurement, and (5) management of investments by others.

Risk of Changing Interest Rates

The prices of all fixed-income securities rise or fall, reflecting the decline and rise in interest rates. This is the most important influence on the price of "riskless" Treasury obligations.[1] Long-term Treasurys have sold as high as 102.5 and as low as 57.4 (annual average) in the last 35 years as shown in Table 6-6. However, because coupon rates affect price but are only one influence on yield, the yield more accurately portrays the interest or "money rate" risk.

Bonds As bond interest rates rise and fall, their prices fall and rise, to reflect the shifting forces of supply and demand for funds. The influences of supply-demand forces is most evident in the general level of yields, as shown in Table 3-6 at peak and low points in the capital and money markets. Table 6-7 shows the fluctuations in yields on Treasury obligations, and Table 8-5 shows those on corporate bonds. The "money-rate risk" shows up clearly in the variations in prices of long-term issues. To use a corporate illustration, a $1,000 7% bond due in 30 years is worth par in a 7% market; whereas in a 9% market, the price of a $1,000 bond of the same maturity is only $793.60.

The "interest-rate risk" is a function not only of changes in the general level of interest rates, but also of the shifting spreads between yields on lower- and higher-maturity obligations. Table 6-5 shows yields on Treasury securities with different maturities, at interest rate peaks and lows. Ordi-

---

[1]Some Treasury bonds have special features or sell at such discounts as to be influenced by their income tax advantages. See Chapter 6.

narily the larger the maturity, the higher the yield, quality being equal. This reflects investors' time preference. But in times of "tight money" (1966, 1969–1970, 1973–1974) short- and intermediate-term rates push up to and even exceed long-term rates. Short-term interest rates are much more volatile than long-term, but their changes have a much smaller effect on price. An increase of 2% per annum in the rate on a one-year obligation selling at par would lower the price (for the same maturity) only from 100 to 98.

Interest rates (hence, bond prices) have traditionally had a cyclical pattern related to variations in business and credit expansion. Typically, high rates (and low bond prices) have appeared in tight money situations during business expansion, followed by a sharp decline in rates (and a rise in price) during periods of recession or stagnation when demand for borrowed money subsides. The period 1973–1975 saw a reversal of this situation however. Interest rates rose and bond prices fell along with those of stocks. The chief explanation was the influence of historically high prices ("double-digit" inflation). Investors demanded that compensation for loss in purchasing power be added to the price of money. Yields on bonds and "earnings yields" (reciprocals of P/E ratio) on stocks had moved together.

The yield of a bond is comprised of two main elements: the long-term riskless (as to quality) rate of interest, and (except for Treasury bonds) a premium for quality risk.[2] Recently the riskless rate has had to include a varying but substantial factor to compensate for inflation. If the long-term riskless rate were 3%, and 5% is added for inflation protection, an A-rated utility bond would have to yield 9 to 10% to include the risk factor. See Chart 19-1.

Traditionally, an investor could attempt to forecast cyclical swings in interest rates and prices mainly by forecasting the ups and downs in general business activity. Until recent years, stock prices and changes in bond yields and prices coincided fairly closely with the business cycle. Bond yields rose to reach their peak towards the peak of economic activity, then declined (as prices rose) during recession, reaching their lows (and price highs) just before new economic advances began. Since 1965 this pattern has not prevailed because of the influence of actual and expected inflation on the required rate of return. Bond yields spiralled upward in 1967 and again in 1969–1970 despite declining industrial production. Another sharp rise occurred in early 1971 as fears of renewed inflation persisted. Still another very sharp rise in yields (and decline in prices) occurred in 1973–1975 in spite of recession conditions in 1974–1975. With recovery in 1976–1977, bond yields then declined (and prices rose) as inflation subsided. This combination of industrial, monetary, and inflationary factors produced a situation that has made the forecasting of interest rates and bond prices extremely difficult.

If changing interest rates could be forecast accurately, investors would buy or sell bonds confidently, that is, go from a 100% invested position to a lesser position, or the reverse. Large funds can afford bond managers; but even these cannot skillfully time either purchase or sale. They can and do

---

[2] An additional premium for lack of good marketability is added in many cases. See p. 156.

"play the yield curve" (Chapter 8) by estimating the changing spreads between long- and short-term rates, then shifting maturity percentages in their bond portfolio accordingly. Individual investors can also reduce risk and actually take advantage of fluctuating bond prices by dollar-cost averaging in good bonds or shares in bond funds over a period of years.

Diversification of a bond fund by maturity dates can be used to minimize the interest-rate risk, even without playing the yield curve. Long maturities are uneconomical in years of low interest rates, since the new securities bought with the proceeds of maturing obligations produce a lower rate of return. Large investors distribute maturity dates in order to avoid concentration in any particular years and generally refer to their *maturity calendars* before buying new issues. The average investor will usually find it more convenient to distribute his holdings of bonds into the three chronological groups of short-term (up to five years), medium-term (five to 10 years), and long-term (over 10 years). He can limit his commitment in any group to, say, 40% of his bond fund, or better still, he can buy long-term bonds when yields are high; and when interest rates are low, he can put any new money into short-term maturities. As interest rates decline, the prices of long maturities increase, and the risk of price loss in the event of an increase in rates is minimized with the purchase of short maturities.

The desire of investors to obtain a favorable rate of return frequently results in the assumption of risk beyond a reasonable limit. The highest-grade issues afford the lowest yields because they are exceptionally well secured and have the greatest price stability. The lower-grade issues afford higher yields because they are less secure and are more subject to fluctuations in market value. In September 1974, at the peak of interest rates, medium-grade bonds provided only a modest additional yield over high-grade obligations—Moody's Aaa bond series yielding 9.3% and Baa bonds yielding 10.4%. Such a small differential is attractive only to large institutional investors to whom every "basis point" (.10% yield) is important.

Second-grade bonds should be bought only by persons who can afford to assume the commensurate high degree of risk. An axiom of the investment business holds that the higher grade the securities, the smaller will be the potential market depreciation, so that while high-grade bonds sometimes prove to be weak investments, low-grade bonds seldom prove to be safe.[3]

Preferred stocks   Changes in money rates also affect the prices of preferred stocks. Those of the very highest-grade preferreds, with their fixed dividend income virtually assured, rise and fall like bonds. The yields on lesser-grade preferred stocks reflect not only changes in money rates, but changing prospects of earnings and, thus, of dividend payment. Low-grade preferreds act more like common stocks with respect to price. Theoretically, the highest-grade preferreds, whose dividends are earned many times over, should provide a higher yield than high-grade, long-term bonds because they represent ownership, not debt. Their income is a distribution of profit, not

[3]One or two investment companies hold portfolios of "junk" bonds bought at large discounts. Diversification, selection, and clever timing may lower risk and still produce a relatively high return.

interest. However, in October 1977, the yield on Moody's Aaa industrial corporate bond series was 7.80%, whereas the yield on the same service's high-grade industrial preferred series was about the same —7.90%. This anomaly is explained by the fact that taxed corporate investors find preferred stocks advantageous (85% of the dividend being tax-exempt) and so drive down their market yields. (See Chapter 9.)

Common stocks   Prices of common stocks are also affected by changing interest rates, although their effect is usually overshadowed by the even more important influence of earnings and dividend prospects. The rate at which the market capitalizes the earnings on a common stock (the "earnings yield") includes the basic interest rate plus an additional increment that reflects the risk in the situation. Stated in an oversimplified fashion, the value of a share of common stock reflects principally the expected future earnings capitalized at a rate that is commensurate with the risk involved, adjusted for the actual dividend prospects. (See Chapter 25.) The value, therefore, changes when either or both of the two components (earnings and capitalization rate) change, and the most drastic change in value, of course, occurs when the two components change in opposite directions—that is, when expected earnings decline (or increase) and the rate of capitalization increases (or declines). A simple hypothetical example will serve to illustrate this point. If the antici- pated earnings on a share of common stock are $5 and the rate of capitaliza- tion demanded by the market is 10%, the value of the stock is $50. If the earnings remain the same, but the rate is reduced to 5%, the value is $100. The value of a share of stock may thus change through the influence of the

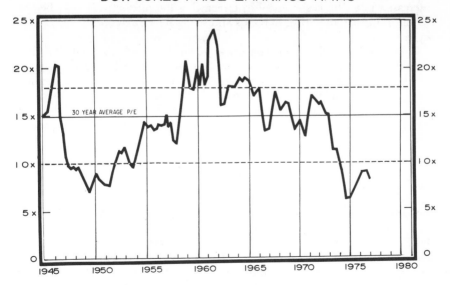

DOW JONES PRICE-EARNINGS RATIO

Source: MacKay-Shields Financial Corporation, New York. Reprinted with permission.

going rate for the risk in the particular situation even though the outlook for earnings remains the same. Moreover, if the earnings are increased to $10 and the rate reduced to 5%, the value is $200.

The custom in financial circles is to express the relationship between earnings and price in terms of a price-earnings ratio or multiple of earnings, that is, the reciprocal of the rate of capitalization. Thus, where the market capitalizes $5 of earnings at 10% to produce a value of $50, the stock sells at 10 times earnings; capitalization of $5 of earnings at 20% means that the stock sells at five times earnings. The actual record of the 30 stocks making up the Dow Jones Industrial Average shows how market price may be influenced principally by the rate of capitalization or its reciprocal, the multiple of earnings. In December 1961, the average stood at 739, which was 23 times estimated earnings for 1961. In September 1963, the average stood at 740, an almost identical figure, but this was only 18 times expected 1963 earnings. Between the two dates, the ratio, or multiple, that satisfied traders in these common stocks as a group had changed so materially that even the very substantially higher earnings on the group of stocks produced only the same average value. In February 1966, the average was 996, a figure that capitalized expected 1966 earnings at almost 17 times. The high price level reflected a combination of higher dollar earnings, and a lower multiple, than had prevailed five years earlier. In January 1973, at the peak of the market, the Dow industrials sold at 1050 or 15 times 1972 earnings. In October 1974, the decline in the earnings multiple to 6, coupled with a small decline in earnings themselves, sent the price to 570. See Chart 19-1 and Table 25-10.

Thus, an investor in common stocks must be prepared to suffer from declining market values even though earnings remain stable or actually increase, unless he is successful in forecasting the interest rate risk. Because of this influence, the prices of bonds and stocks have risen and fallen together in recent years.

The preceding discussion concerns the stock market as a whole. Price-earnings ratios of individual stocks change with those in the market as a whole (the "systematic risk"), but are also influenced by investors' estimate of quality. Within the general market, individual stocks go their separate ways. In the stronger "bull" and "bear" markets, the majority of stocks do move in the same direction but in different degrees. Some stocks ignore the general trend altogether.

Market Price Risk—Common Stocks

Types of price movements　　There are four types of movements in the prices of common stocks: (1) long-term or secular; (2) cyclical (bull and bear markets); (3) intermediate, or within the cycle; and (4) short-term. Any chart of stock prices for a number of years—say, 15 to 50—will reveal the secular trend. The explanation of this trend can be oversimplified by saying that it reflects the secular growth in national product and income and of corporate profits, together with the influence of inflation in the economy and a steady rise in the demand for common stocks in the face of a somewhat limited supply. But it is small satisfaction to most investors to understand the secular trend when cyclical variations in price are so violent. An investor is more interested in these "bull" and "bear" markets and the risks and opportunities they offer.

The buy-low- sell-high approach to cyclical swings is difficult, because stock prices reflect basic business and monetary conditions and trends which are hard to forecast beyond a few months.[4] Historically, peaks and troughs in stocks prices have led peaks and lows in business activity by 5 to 9 months (depending on the indexes chosen), so that analysis of economic fundamentals should permit decisions based on cyclical turning points in the market. But the relationship between the economy and stock prices is crude at best. There are sharp *intermediate* movements within the market cycles. In the main, these reflect changing attitudes towards the future course of the cycle and the timing of change from the current phase. Such contrary movements were evident in 1957–1958, 1962, 1966–1967, 1970, 1969–1970, 1975, and 1977. (See Table 19-2.)

A second difficulty is that most investors would like to do much better than "the market," which requires unusual skill in selecting and timing the purchase of industries that have their own cycle. And even among these, individual companies will fare differently. (See Chapter 26.) Thus, in 1976, the profits of 1890 manufacturing corporations rose 29% compared with 1975.[5] Noting a few examples, profits of auto and trucks rose 230%, textiles 146%, and glass products 86%. But profits of sugar declined 63% and those of iron and steel declined 10%. In the financial field, earnings of property-casualty insurance companies rose 255% while those of bank holding companies rose only 8%.

"Growth" industries offer a special appeal over the long run. But even these have to be selected carefully, and much patience may be required over a considerable period. Companies with aggressive management, that follow a program of research to develop new products and markets and enjoy steady increases in sales, strong finances, and a continued high or increasing return on invested capital, fit best into the growth pattern. One difficulty with "growth stocks" is that the investor may have to pay too high a price for the growth factor. As shown in Chart 19-2, changes in the price-earnings ratios of the "growth" stocks so popular in the 1960s and early 1970s have been much more pronounced than those of the Dow Jones industrial average. Their valuation is discussed in Chapter 25.

The prospects for an individual company, like those for an industry, can best be determined by analytical methods. The investor can take advantage of the cyclical swings in the general market by purchasing securities, notably equities, when they appear undervalued, except when the whole general market is in an extreme range and even the most promising situations are vulnerable to a general collapse in market price. And he can use the market

[4]Stock prices are themselves one of 12 leading indicators of cyclical changes used by the National Bureau of Economic Research to identify the current phase of a business cycle.

[5]*Citibank Monthly Economic Letter*, April 1977, pp. 8, 9.

PRICE/EARNINGS RATIOS*

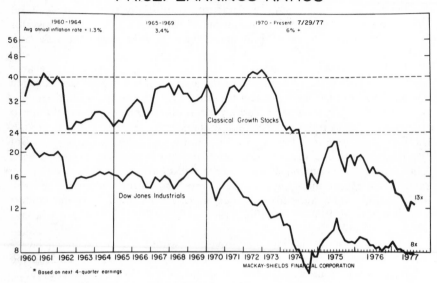

Source: MacKay-Shields Financial Corporation, New York. Reprinted with permission.

level for determining the points at which to sell securities when they are overvalued marketwise.

Within any stock average, individual industries and stocks go their own way. In March 1974, two-thirds into the great bear market period that began in January 1973, the 30 Dow Jones Industrials stock average had declined 47%. Twenty-one stocks had declined (Chrysler the most—54%), but three remained unchanged, and six had actually increased (Allied Chemical as much as 55%). In 1976, Standard & Poor's 400 industrials rose from 101 to 119, or 18%, but air conditioning stocks rose 79% while brewery stocks fell 13%. Restaurant chain stocks as a group fell 7 1/2%, yet within this group the range was from an increase of 76% (Church's Fried Chicken) to a decrease of 17% (Marriott).

The problems of timing of purchase and sale of individual securities have led to the appearance of "index" funds whose portfolios are so diversified as to move in price like the general stock indexes. (See Chapter 11.) These appeal to investors who are content with the longer-run rise in stock prices and are willing to tolerate cyclical variations of the market as a whole. Indeed, many institutional investors failed to achieve even this record in 1973–1976.

But many investors prefer to use technical devices that may aid them in calling the turns by study of the market itself rather than the study of underlying causes of price change; or to take advantage of price changes by one or more fairly automatic procedures such as dollar-cost averaging and the use of formula plans.

Dow theory   The many technical devices that look at the action of the market itself as the indicator of its direction and of the direction of business can first be illustrated by one device that has had considerable use, the Dow theory.

Stated in its simplest form, the Dow theory is a mechanism designed to indicate the major bull or bear trend of the market without forecasting the extent of the movement in time or degree. It is based on the premise that stock price averages, reflecting the activities of thousands of investors, discount all important economic and financial factors that could affect the supply and demand for stocks.

According to the theory, stock prices have three basic movements: (1) the major or primary trends lasting for a year or more in which a general change of more than 20% occurs, (2) secondary trends (within the primary) which may last from three weeks to three months and which may retrace as much as one-third to two-thirds of the preceding primary movement, and (3) daily fluctuations.[6] A comparison of the successive high and low points reached in secondary fluctuations of the stock market enables an observer who notices that the successive high and low points are advancing to determine the primary trend of the market. If the price average should rise from a low point of 920 to a high point of 960, then fall to 940 and advance to 965, an upward primary trend was indicated when the decline stopped at 940, and was confirmed when the new advance went above 960. If the upward trend continues until the price average reaches 975, a subsequent change in the direction of the market trend would not be indicated until a decline from that level was followed by a recovery to *less* than 975 and a subsequent decline to a lower point than on the preceding decline. In an advancing market, a change in the direction of the trend is indicated when an advance fails to carry higher than the preceding advance and when a decline goes lower than the preceding decline. In a declining market, a change in the direction of the trend is indicated when an advance goes higher than the preceding advance and when a decline does not go as low as the preceding decline.

The Dow theory is based on the use of both the Dow Jones industrial and transportation averages and is valid only when the movements of both averages are confirmatory. When all fundamental forces in the market are bullish, both averages will advance, and new high points will be made by both averages, each confirming the other. If either average consistently refuses to confirm the other, a major movement is probably near its end.

The Dow theory does not pretend to forecast the duration and degree of price movements; often it does not indicate a change in the direction of the primary trend until some time after a change has taken place. Thus, on December 11, 1972, the transportation average reached its peak of 240, as did the industrial average on January 11, 1973, with its peak of 1052. On April 24, 1973, the transportation and industrial averages both penetrated their intermediate low point of 189 and 922 respectively, nearly four months

[6]The Dow theory is not concerned with secular trend.

after the bear market began. After the low in the market (industrials at 577) in early December 1974, stocks rose. But it was not until January 27, 1975, that both averages surpassed their previous intermediate peaks (with industrials at 692) to signal a bull market. These illustrations indicate the chief flaw in the technique. While waiting for the industrial and transportation averages to confirm the trend, much of the major up or down markets may have already passed.

The Dow theory is also faulty because it places too much faith in the particular stock averages used. Common stock prices in general do not discount all economic factors; the Dow Jones averages are not truly representative of the market; and, finally, no one "buys the averages." All common stocks do not rise and fall together. The typical investor is far more interested in his own portfolio rather than in the securities that comprise particular market averages or indexes.

Such "mechanical" devices as the Dow theory may serve the investor by offering warnings that may prevent disaster.[7] To the extent that the opinion of general market movements induces the investor to review the composition and values of his own portfolio, such approaches as the Dow theory have some merit.

Technical devices: charting The Dow theory is used to identify trends *after* they have begun. Other technical approaches attempt to *predict* changes in trends of price averages or of individual stocks. Charting involves (1) bar-charting the daily (or other interval) price as a vertical line showing the range from high to low, with the closing price indicated as a crossline on the bar, or (2) point-and-figure charting of price change, using "x's" for price increases and "o's" for declines, on paper that is marked off into square blocks. In each type the left-hand or vertical scale indicates price. In the bar-chart the horizontal scale indicates time, and below the bar-chart is a separate scale showing volume of trading. Prediction for both types involves the recognition of formations that are similar to previous patterns and that, therefore, signal price change.

Charting can be highly technical, and the interested reader is advised to consult special works on the subject such as those listed in the references for this chapter. A major criticism of the validity of charting is found in the "random walk" theory, which holds that stock markets are efficient so that prices respond to all new information at any point in time. Analysis of past price action data is invalid. In other words, stock prices have no memory, and the actual prices are good estimates of value. Successive price changes are statistically independent.

[7]For a study of the indicated results from the Dow theory applied to the Dow Jones Industrial Average, 1897–1963, see Benjamin Graham, *The Intelligent Investor*, 3d rev. ed. (New York: Harper & Row, Publishers, 1965), pp. 32–34. Other studies are as follows: for 1897–1967, with a chart of all signals 1917–1967, William Gordon, *The Stock Market Indicators*, Chapter 2 (Palisades Park, N.J.: Investors Press, Inc., 1968); for 1896–1938 and 1938–1967, P. H. Greiner and H. C. Whitcomb, *The Dow Theory and the Seventy-Year Forecast Record* (Larchmont, N.Y.: Investors Intelligence, Inc., 1969); for 1923–1964, H. M. Finley, *Everybody's Guide to the Stock Market*, rev. ed., Chapter 8 (Chicago: Henry Regnery Company, 1968).

It is possible that, when accompanied by the study of other information such as trading volume, charting can aid in the detection of short-run price movements. But indicators of longer-run movements must still depend on "fundamental" analysis of earnings, dividends, interest rates, economic and political conditions, and the other factors examined in the analytical section of this book.

Other "technical" approaches Of the other technical approaches to the problem of market timing, only a few will be indicated here.

Odd-lot trading On the assumption that the "little fellow" is usually wrong, the ratio of odd-lot sales to purchases is said to signal general market change. For example, a ratio of over 100% is thought to forecast a rise in the market as a whole.

Breadth of market The daily difference between the number of advancing and declining issues is cumulated over a period of time to detect the direction of the market. The index is used in connection with one of the market averages such as the Dow Jones Industrials.

Volume of trading Inspection of data on the number of shares sold is expected to reveal the impending end of a bull market, as volume increases to the saturation point.

Short position The number of shares sold short, or the dollar amount of short sales, is studied in relation to total market volume. Short selling is "bearish" in that it anticipates declining market prices. However, short sales must eventually be covered, and some believe that a rise in prices will trigger large buying.

Confidence index This is based on the ratio of high-grade to low-grade bond yields. As confidence in the economy improves, the spread in yield is reduced. *Barrons* publishes this index in its "Market Laboratory" section.

Each of these techniques has been the subject of much study, and the findings are by no means conclusive. The reader is advised to consult special books and articles for technical details and the reasons for differing conclusions. Regardless of their imperfection, such techniques may be useful in signalling the market's reactions to developments that have not yet been exposed by fundamental analysis.[8]

Dollar-cost averaging Another method of dealing with the timing problem—in fact, of avoiding it—is known as *dollar-cost averaging*. This is useful to investors who are accumulating capital and who wish to avoid always buying common stocks when they are too high and to benefit from the expected variations in market price. Stated in its simplest terms, this involves regular purchase of securities in equal dollar amounts, regardless of their unit price. As the price of the security or securities bought declines and rises, a greater or smaller number of shares can be bought with the same amount of money. Over a long period of time, as long as the market price

---

[8]Other "market barometers" are: the "speculative index," (ratio of the American to the New York Stock Exchange volume of trading); mutual fund sales and redemptions; and stock versus bond yields.

rises and falls, the average *cost* of shares purchased will be lower than the average *price* at which the shares are bought. These elements may be illustrated by a simple example (Table 19-1). Suppose that $1,000 is invested in the shares of a company at regular intervals, beginning at $50 per share, with a subsequent decline to $20 and recovery to $50.

TABLE 19-1   Dollar-Cost Averaging

Purchase	Price	Shares Purchased Each Interval	Total Shares Purchased	Total Amount Invested	Value of Total Investment
1	$50	20	20	$1 000	$ 1,000
2	40	25	45	2,000	1,800
3	30	33.3	78.3	3,000	2,350
4	20	50	128.3	4,000	2,567
5	30	33.3	161.6	5,000	4,850
6	40	25	186.6	6,000	7,467
7	50	20	206.6	7,000	10,334

At the end of the period, the average cost of all shares purchased is $33.88, whereas the average price is $37.14. The reason is, of course, that more shares have been bought at the lower prices. While the example is extreme in that it is based on a very sharp decline and recovery in a short period, three points are worth noting: (1) While the loss at the low point is 36%, the stock had to advance to only a little over 30 to recover the entire loss, and from then on profits mounted rapidly; (2) as long as prices eventually recover from their lows, a wide fluctuation in price is advantageous; (3) the ending rather than the starting prices are important. Even better results would be obtained if there had been a secular rise in the stock.

If followed regularly and courageously, dollar averaging is likely to produce far better results than attempts to "buy low and sell high." The investor must, of course, be prepared to commit funds regularly over a considerable period of time, say, 10 or more years, so as to include several market cycles. He must have the nerve (and the capital) to keep buying as the market declines, and at relatively short intervals, at least several times a year. He must choose his stocks with great care, preferably those with volatile price action but long-term growth. And he must be prepared to change his portfolio—the favorite stocks of today may be poor choices 10 years from now. The program of many investors should consist of the regular purchase of shares of well-managed investment companies. Some of these offer plans whereby dividends are automatically reinvested in new shares.[9] The compounding of dividends, coupled with the regular investment of new principal, produces a very substantial accumulation over a period of years, provided the period is long enough and provided the investor has the fortitude, funds,

[9]See Chapter 11.

and emotional poise to continue buying through all phases of the price cycle.[10]

Formula plans Another method of attacking the timing problem is by the use of a formula plan by investors who have already accumulated a substantial fund and who wish to preserve and increase their capital over the years, and at the same time avoid the use of judgment concerning the course of the market. The formula plan substitutes an automatic device for emotional and erroneous decisions concerning the best buying and selling points. It offers a compromise by which the investor can take some advantage of the swings in the market. Formula plans differ considerably, but they all have in common the use of two funds—the *aggressive fund*, consisting of common stocks, and the *defensive fund*, consisting of high-grade bonds and/or cash. Under the constant-ratio type of plan, the investor determines in advance the proportions of aggressive and defensive securities that he wishes to maintain. When the market moves up and down sufficiently to alter this ratio by a predetermined amount, he switches funds from one to the other of the type of securities to restore the original ratio. Thus, a plan could start with a "normal" ratio of 50% in common stocks and 50% in bonds. In a rising market for common stocks, the common stock portion is permitted to rise until it reaches 60% of the value of the fund; it is then cut back to 50%. In a falling market, after the common stock portion reaches 40%, stocks are bought to raise this portion to 50%.

Under the variable-ratio type of plan, the proportion of stocks is reduced in a rising market and increased in a declining market, the decisions being based on predetermined levels in a selected market index. When the market reaches a predetermined point on the up-side, stocks are gradually sold and all or part of the proceeds are placed in cash or bonds. When the stock market reaches a certain point on the downward cycle, bonds are sold or cash is used to purchase stocks on a gradual basis. Such a procedure is a compromise application of the "buy-low, sell-high" principle. To produce satisfactory results, the following conditions must be met: (1) A satisfactory formula must be devised. (2) Stock prices must have moved up and down sufficiently to bring the plan into action. (3) The common stocks must be carefully selected (shares in well-managed investment trusts are recommended). (4) The price action of the particular securities selected must not deviate substantially from that of the market as a whole. (5) The market for stocks must not remain on a permanently high or low level. (6) When either bonds or stocks are sold, the other type of security must be expected to remain level or to rise. (The plan will not work if, as in 1973–1974, prices of both bonds and stocks decline at the same time, and subsequently rise together. Under these conditions cash rather than bonds is the best medium

[10]Using the Standard & Poor's Index of 500 Stocks, an annual investment of $2,000 a year started on January 1, 1962, including all dividends and after brokerage fees and taxes, would have produced a market value of $27,930 in January 1971 from an investment of $20,000, despite the fact (or owing to the fact) that several reactions were experienced in the market, including the very severe last six months of the 1968–70 bear market. Individual stocks would, of course, have shown widely different results.

for the defensive fund.) (7) The investor must exercise patience and fortitude by selling when stocks are rising, buying when they are falling, *waiting out* the greater peaks and valleys that may appear after his action has been taken. The average individual is not likely to possess sufficient skill to observe all of these conditions. And it is also necessary for him to forecast the longer-term trend of stock prices.

Risk of Changes in Purchasing Power

Even though the dollars of principal and income may remain the same, their value in terms of purchasing power rises and falls with changes in the price level. This fact is becoming increasingly important as prospects for rising prices are confirmed. The dollar has lost over 70% of its purchasing power in the period of inflation since World War II. Protection against the purchasing-power risk, or inflation hedging, thus becomes an increasingly important consideration for investors who can assume the risks that such protection inevitably involves. It is the basis for much of the current discussion concerning the position of an investment fund that should be placed in "aggressive" securities or other investments of the equity type.

The loss of value of both principal and income that results from rising prices and a rising cost of living is easily illustrated by referring to the changes that took place in the period 1945–1976. As Table 19-2 shows, the Bureau of Labor Statistics Consumer Price Index stood at 53.9 for the year 1945 (1967 = 100). In December 1976, the index was 174.3. Thus, the buying power of $1.00 cash or principal in securities was reduced to 30 cents in the 31-year period. An investor who had bought a $100 Series E Savings Bond for $75 in mid-1945 and retained it for 30 1/2 years could redeem it for $245.44 in December 1976, but he was repaid only $73.60 in 1945 purchasing power, including 31 years' accrued interest. Similarly, any fixed income has been reduced 70% in effective value over this period.

Investments in real estate and common stocks offer the best possibilities of an inflation hedge. The former represents a highly specialized type of commitment and one that requires considerable management, knowledge of land values, and knowledge of community development. It also has the disadvantage of inadequate diversification. Common stocks, on the other hand, are easily bought and sold, and in large or small amounts. Much has been written and said about the practicability of common stocks as protection against rising prices. And this protection is, in fact, afforded over long periods of time, but subject to decided limitations. The 31-year period 1945–1976 again provides an illustration of the fact that over a considerable period commodity prices and the cost of living, on the one hand, and common stock prices, on the other, do move in the same general direction. Table 19-2 shows (1) the Consumer Price Index (1967 = 100), (2) the Index of Wholesale Prices (1967 = 100), and (3) the price, earnings, and dividends of Standard & Poor's Index of 400 Industrial Stocks. In each case, the average for the year is shown.

TABLE 19-2   Price Indexes and Common Stocks

	BLS Consumer Price Index	BLS Wholesale Commodity Price Index	Standard & Poor's Industrials		
			Price	Earnings	Dividends
1945	53.9	57.9	$14.70	$ .82	$ .61
1950	72.1	81.8	18.30	1.93	1.53
1951	77.8	81.9	22.70	2.55	1.45
1952	79.5	88.6	24.80	2.46	1.44
1953	80.1	87.4	24.80	2.59	1.47
1954	80.5	87.6	30.30	2.89	1.57
1955	80.2	87.8	42.40	3.78	1.65
1956	81.4	90.7	49.40	3.53	1.78
1957	84.3	91.3	47.60	3.50	1.84
1958	86.6	94.6	49.40	2.95	1.79
1959	87.3	94.3	61.50	3.53	1.90
1960	88.7	94.9	59.00	3.39	2.00
1961	89.6	94.5	70.00	3.37	2.08
1962	90.6	94.8	65.50	3.87	2.70
1963	91.7	94.6	73.40	4.24	2.78
1964	92.9	94.7	86.20	4.83	2.60
1965	94.5	96.6	93.50	5.50	2.85
1966	97.2	99.8	91.10	5.89	2.98
1967	100.0	100.0	99.20	5.66	3.01
1968	104.2	102.5	107.50	6.15	3.18
1969	109.8	106.5	107.10	6.17	3.27
1970	116.3	110.4	91.30	5.43	3.24
1971	121.3	113.9	108.40	6.82	3.18
1972	125.3	119.1	131.80	6.83	3.22
1973	133.1	134.7	120.50	8.86	3.48
1974	147.7	160.1	92.90	9.69	3.72
1975	161.2	174.9	96.50	8.34	3.78
1976	174.3	187.1	117.68	9.91	4.25

Sources: Federal Reserve Bulletin; Standard & Poor's *Trade and Securities Statistics.*

Over the whole period the increase in stock prices and dividends far outran the increase in the cost of living. Stocks rose 700%, dividends 600%, and consumer prices 223%. But within this period, marked discrepancies appeared. In six periods—1956–1957, 1959–1960, 1961–1962, 1965–1966, 1969–1970, and 1973–1974—while the cost of living continued to rise, stocks declined. From the middle of 1963 to October 1974, while consumer prices rose 44%, industrial common stocks in general, as measured by Standard & Poor's Industrial Average, began and ended at the same level. To be an effective hedge against inflation, dividends on stocks should increase faster than the price level. This has not happened in the 1970s. Chart 19-3 again shows clearly the *long-run* relationship between stock prices and the cost of living. But in recent years investors have become disillusioned about the efficacy of stocks in general as a counter-influence to inflation.

INFLATION AND STOCK PRICES

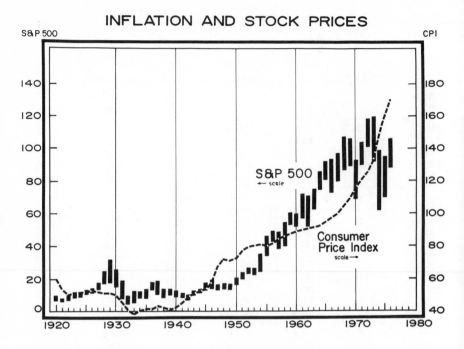

Source: MacKay-Shields Financial Corporation, New York. Reprinted with permission.

Limitations of common stocks as an inflation hedge are summarized:

• A hedge works only over a considerable period of time; and this period has had to be lengthened greatly because of the market situation in the 1970s.

• To enjoy the greatest advantage, stocks must be purchased at depressed levels within this period.

• All stocks are not equally good for inflation protection. Various industries, and hence their common stocks, act differently with respect to earnings. Subgroups of stocks go in different directions even during a period of general rise. So the problem of *selection* still persists.

Modern Approaches to Risk Measurement

The various types of risks discussed in this and previous chapters are reflected in price changes or, perhaps better, in variations of the total rate of return (income plus price change). In modern portfolio management, the risk of an individual security or of a portfolio is measured (1) in absolute terms by the variability of price (or of total return), and (2) in relative terms by variability in relation to that of the market as a whole. As we have seen, "systematic" or "undiversifiable" risk is that portion of a stock's (or a portfolio's) movement that can be attributed to the movement of the market

398

as a whole; the "unsystematic" or "diversifiable" risk is that portion of the movement that is attributable to a specific security or portfolio.

These measures of risk are used both in the selection of securities and portfolio construction, and in later evaluation of portfolio performance. For this reason the explanation of modern risk measurements is found in Chapter 23, together with a discussion of their merits and limitations.

Management of Investments by Others

The responsibility for selection, diversification, and timing of investments so as to meet objectives and fulfill their allied requirements can be undertaken by the investor or passed along to others.

Insofar as investment in securities is concerned, the common trust fund (Chapter 22), the investment company (Chapter 11), and the insurance company (Chapter 30) relieve the investor of management, except that in the case of the last two, decisions concerning the selection of the fund and the timing of the purchase or sale of its shares must still be made. The natural inclination of most trustees to operate a common trust fund conservatively gives the beneficiary lower income and less appreciation than he might possibly obtain alone. But diversification, superior stability, and some protection against inflation, together with freedom from care, give the common trust fund a strong appeal to many investors seeking these requirements. The portfolios of these funds are seldom published and the results of their management can be obtained only by direct inquiry. On the other hand, the portfolio and record of insurance companies and investment companies are always available. As indicated in Chapter 11, investment companies differ widely with respect to investment goals and policy. Some seek reasonable income and considerable stability. Others are operated for capital appreciation. The goals of the investor, the investment requirements that should be fulfilled, and the risks that can be undertaken are factors that must be considered, together with the record of its management, in the choice of any fund. The great growth of investment funds until very recently attests to the desire of many investors to transfer their investment problems to others.

The investment counsel also stands ready to take the responsibility for investment management, but at fees which are likely to make his services prohibitive for the small investor. For those who can afford their advice, the investment advisers are prepared to tailor the investment programs of their clients to their individual needs, balancing the several factors of income, recovery of principal, appreciation, tax protection, diversification, and inflation hedging (and the possibility of subsequent deflation) in one coordinated pattern. For the most part, the well-established counsel firms are careful not to promise too much and lean toward long-run results rather than toward spectacular performance. (See Chapter 13.)

Other methods of transferring managerial responsibility on a fee basis include the agency accounts and advisory services of large banks (Chapter 21) and the supervisory services of some of the larger stock exchange firms.

In any case, an investor should know his own needs and level of risks so that he can understand and approve the decisions of the experts to whom he transfers the main responsibility for investment management.

REFERENCES

BABSON, R. W., *Business Barometers for Profit, Security, Income*, 10th ed. New York: Harper & Row, Publishers, 1961.

BARNES, R. M., *The Dow Theory Can Make You Rich*. New Rochelle, NY.: Arlington House, 1973.

BISHOP, G. W., JR., *Charles H. Dow and the Dow Theory*. New York: Appleton-Century-Crofts, 1960.

BREALEY, R. A., *An Introduction to Risk and Return from Common Stocks*. Cambridge, Mass.: The M.I.T. Press, 1969.

CHISHOLM, R. K., and G. R. WHITAKER, JR., *Forecasting Methods*. Homewood, Ill.: Richard D. Irwin, Inc., 1971.

COHEN, A. W., *Technical Indicator Analysis by Point and Figure Technique*. Larchmont, N.Y.: Chartcraft, Inc., 1970.

COOTNER, P. H., ed., *The Random Character of Stock Market Prices*. Cambridge, Mass.: MIT Press, 1964.

COTTLE, C. S., and W. T. WHITMAN, *Investment Timing: The Formula Plan Approach*. New York: McGraw-Hill, Inc., 1953.

———, SIDNEY, and W. T. WHITMAN, *Corporate Earning Power and Market Valuation*. Durham, N.C.: Duke University Press, 1959.

DAUTEN, C. A., and WILLIAM VALENTINE, *Business Cycles and Foreacasting*, 4th ed. Cincinnati: South-Western Publishing Co., 1974.

EDWARDS, R. D., and JOHN MAGEE, *Technical Analysis of Stock Trends*, 5th ed. Springfield, Mass.: John Magee, Inc., 1966.

EITEMAN, W. J., and D. S. EITEMAN, *Common Stock Values and Yields, 1950–61*. Ann Arbor, Mich.: Graduate School of Business Administration, 1962.

Encyclopedia of Stock Market Techniques. Larchmont, N.Y.: Investors Intelligence, Inc., 1970.

FOSTER, E. M., *Common Stock Investment*. Lexington, Mass.: Lexington Books, 1974.

GORDON, WILLIAM, *The Stock Market Indicators*. Palisades Park, N.J.: Investors Press, 1968.

GRANVILLE, J. E., *Granville's New Key to Stock Market Profits*. Englewood Cliffs, N.J.: Prentice-Hall, Inc., 1963.

GREINER, P. H., and H. C. WHITCOMB, *The Dow Theory and the Seventy-year Forecast Record*. Larchmont, N.Y.: Investors Intelligence, Inc., 1969.

HICKMAN, WALTER B., *Corporate Bond Quality and Investor Experience*. Princeton, N.J.: Princeton University Press, 1958.

HOMER, SIDNEY, *A History of Interest Rates*. New Brunswick, N.J.: Rutgers University Press, 1963.

JILER, WILLIAM, *How Charts Can Help You in the Stock Market*. New York: Commodity Research Publications Corp., 1962.

LEVINE, S. N., ed., *Financial Analyst's Handbook*, Vol. I, Chapter 44, Homewood, Ill.: Dow Jones-Irwin, Inc., 1975.

MARKOWITZ, H. M., *Portfolio Selection: Efficient Diversification of Investments*. New York: John Wiley & Sons, Inc., 1959.

MOORE, G. H., ed., *Business Cycle Indicators*. Princeton, N.J.: Princeton University Press, 1961.

RUSSELL, RICHARD, *The Dow Theory Today*. New York: Russell Associates, 1961.

SMITH, E. L., *Common Stocks and Business Cycles*. New York: William-Frederick Press, 1959.

TURNER, J. P., and R. C. TURNER, *Business Conditions Analysis*, 2d ed. New York: McGraw-Hill, Inc., 1967.

WESSMAN, LUCILE, *Practical Formulas for Successful Investing*. New York: Willard Funk, 1955.

WIESENBERGER INVESTMENT SERVICE, *Investment Companies*, 1977 ed., Part II. New York: Wiesenberger Services, Inc., 1977.

WILLIAMSON, J. P., *Investments: New Analytic Techniques*, Chapter 7. New York: Praeger Publishers, Inc., 1971.

———, *Performance Measurement and Investment Objectives*. New York: The Common Fund, 1972.

Individual Investors

SCOPE: This chapter applies the material in earlier chapters concerning investment media and principles to the problems of investment by individuals. The order of discussion is: (1) review of investment media, (2) individual differences, (3) application of investment principles, (4) illustrative situations, and (5) a word of explanation.

Review of Investment Media

The media of investment were classified in Chapter 1 and described in Chapters 4–11. Bank stocks and shares in insurance and other financial companies were omitted from that discussion. The description of these types is combined with the techniques of analysis applied to them in Chapters 29 and 30, which are directed particularly to these groups.

Investment media include a surprising variety of types. No one type is likely to suit the needs and purposes of one investor, though various combinations may satisfy his requirements. With a few exceptions, such as insured deposit accounts and Federal obligations, it is not possible to generalize about the merits of any class of investment media because of the range of quality within each class. An investor must be able to choose discriminately *within* the group or groups that are most feasible for his particular program.

Individual Differences

Individuals and their needs are affected by such a wide variety of factors that one cannot generalize concerning their investment objectives or the means by which these may be accomplished. No fixed policies or rules apply to all. Factors, in different combinations, that determine one's investment objectives and programs include:

> Total wealth or resources
> Present funds available for investment
> Current and expected income

Income tax status
Age
Health
Dependents and their ages

Temperament
Willingness to assume risk (degree of "risk aversion")
Social and personal ambitions

Education
Time available for investment management
Knowledge of investment fundamentals and techniques

Such individual and family differences suggest that each investor's program will differ in some degree from that of others. But certain general principles can serve as guides. Some objectives are common to a large proportion of situations. As indicated in Chapter 19, these personal goals involve the fulfillment of certain financial requirements.

Application of Investment Principles

The following discussion is centered on certain widely held investment objectives and the application to these aims of the general principles of investment management discussed in previous chapters. The order of priority and the portion of the savings to be devoted to each objective will vary from case to case. Obviously, the amount of funds available for investment restricts or widens the objectives that can reasonably be attained. In budgets allowing for very modest savings, the only objectives that can be obtained are those at the top of the suggested list. As annual savings increase or are accumulated, the objectives can be widened and more risk can be taken. And the objectives themselves will change through the years with the changing circumstances of the investing individual or family.

Using the approach suggested in Chapter 19, the investment requirements (recovery of principal, assurance of income, etc.) associated with each major objective will be indicated, followed by suggestions as to appropriate types of investment media (with their attendant risks) that should be included in the portfolio. The appropriateness of these types varies with changing conditions in the securities markets as well as with shifts in the various attributes and circumstances of the investing unit.

Reserve funds   A reserve of from three to six months' take-home income to take care of sudden hazards or drains that confront many investors is high on the priority list. Together with life insurance, it enjoys first place in most programs. The possibility of sudden stoppage of income (other than through the death of the income-producer), sudden expenditures not covered by casualty and property insurance, unexpected personal expenses, and many other items suggest that some savings be maintained in highly liquid form. The inherent conservativeness of the investor will also affect his feeling concerning the need for resources that are available on very short notice.

This portion of the portfolio is held in the form of bank savings deposits, accounts in savings and loan associations, and Savings Bonds. The cash-surrender value of life insurance policies should never be relied on as a regular segment of an emergency fund; it may have to be withdrawn or borrowed in case of dire need, but this threatens the continuation of protection.

Certain reservations concerning these investments are indicated. When very high rates are available in money market instruments, as in 1974–1975, either these high-grade and safe media, or mutual funds holding short-term instruments, are appropriate for an investor who is able to acquire large denominations.

The investment requirements to be fulfilled by the cash reserve are: (1) recovery of principal on short notice, (2) such income as the safe investments will provide, (3) in most cases, freedom from management care, and (4) satisfactory denomination. Tax status is unimportant, or at best a secondary consideration. Nor should an emergency fund be expected to provide any hedge against inflation.

Protection against death of the income-producer   For the majority of investors, the death of the income-producer constitutes a threat that can be met only by adequate life insurance. Insurance provides an estate that would be difficult for most investors to provide through any other means.

The investment attributes of life insurance and the main types of policies were discussed in Chapter 4. The amount of needed protection depends on circumstances that vary from case to case: the number and age of dependents, the funds available for premiums at the age of the insured, the living standards desired for dependents, and the size of the estate exclusive of insurance. An insurance plan providing for maximum protection when most needed and retirement income when the need of death benefits has been reduced, can be worked out for each individual family.

The investment requirements fulfilled by insurance are: recovery of principal (in the event of death); income for the beneficiaries through any one of several methods of distributing the face of the policy, and possible retirement income for the assured; complete freedom from care and management; satisfactory denomination and diversification; and favorable income tax status (with respect to proceeds). No protection is provided against rising prices, because the obligation of the insurance company is to pay a contractual dollar sum. Because insurance promises to pay in terms of dollars rather than in purchasing power, the insured must increase his insurance protection against the prospect of cheapened dollars at the time of death or retirement. Some argue that if the life insurance company were permitted to invest heavily in common stocks, the higher return obtained would permit lower premiums (more insurance) and more generous "dividends" or rebates that would help to offset rising prices.[1] To obtain such results at the expense of

[1]See Chapter 22 for discussion of investment policies of life insurance companies.

safety would threaten the basic purpose of insurance. It would be sounder for most investors to supplement an insurance estate by purchase of equities if the risks of such commitments can be assumed.

Factors such as the degree of management required, tax status, and inflation hedging will bulk large or small, depending on an individual's circumstances. For a wealthy investor, estate and inheritance tax considerations are a major consideration.

Over and above the minimum protection provided by life insurance, pensions, and Social Security, funds accumulated for the support of dependents in the event of death of the insured can be invested in a variety of media, depending on the risks that can be assumed. A wide range, from income-producing high-grade bonds to common stocks, can be utilized.

Since protection of dependents is high on the list of priorities, most investors should begin to build this portion of the fund through the use of insurance, even in the face of continued decline in the purchasing power of the fund. Regardless of how astute an investor may be, to rely on market appreciation of securities to provide the *minimum* essentials for dependents is to flirt with disaster.

Home ownership The purchase of a home is the largest single investment made by the majority of families. Funds accumulated for eventual home ownership should be relatively risk-free. The investment requirements to fulfill this objective are recovery of principal, possibly modest income until the home is acquired, considerable if not total freedom from care, and risk-avoidance by diversification until the home is acquired. If the purchase is considerably in the future, and if the family can afford the risk of equities, the growth of a fund invested in high-grade stocks or mutual funds, using dollar-cost averaging, may offset the rising costs of real estate. An important risk is that at the time of purchase, stock prices may be depressed.

The modern method of amortizing the purchase of a home through a long-term mortgage solves many of the problems in investing for this purpose and relieves the home buyer of the responsibilities of management of the funds in the meantime. The required payments of interest plus principal are a budget item that ranks in importance only second to food and clothing. The hazard of loss of savings held by the investor against eventual purchase of property is eliminated, at least as long as he is able to meet the terms of the loan.

Once a substantial equity has been acquired, the investor has a considerable sum tied up in fixed property. This portion of his savings is subject to the risks of changing land values, obsolescence, neighborhood decline, and the swings in the real estate market. The denomination is large and diversification is sacrificed. To offset these perils, the owner of well-selected, well-maintained property may derive a considerable imputed income from this part of his funds, may achieve an income tax expense in the property taxes and interest paid, and may enjoy a valuable hedge against inflation. Ownership of such property provides the most important way of hedging that many investors enjoy.

Education and other family needs A variety of special objectives
are found in every family's investment plan. Among these, the education of
children plays a prominent part. Funds saved for this purpose should be
invested so as to accumulate a certain definite sum when needed. For such
a purpose, regular investment in Savings Bonds can play a leading part.
These can be bought in large or small denominations to mature during the
period when the funds are needed, and, if the plan is begun early enough,
the compounding of the 6% yield to maturity will add considerably to the
size of the fund. When interest rates are high, income from high-grade bonds
will produce even better results, although some price risk is involved here.[2]
A certain portion of life insurance should also be earmarked for education
and similar vital purposes so that these goals may be fulfilled whether the
head of the family survives or not.

The previous paragraph suggests that little or no risk should be assumed
in the investment of funds for education. Conservative investors would agree.
However, the constantly rising costs of education pose a serious problem.
When the fund is begun many years before need, the purchase of sound
common stocks may, over the years, provide a hedge against rising costs.
Decisions with respect to timing and selection may be avoided by dollar-
averaging in the shares of well-managed mutual funds.

Housing and education are only two of a number of basic family needs to
be financed by savings. Accumulation of funds to buy into a business is
important in some cases. The degree of liquidity and safety required, self-
management versus delegation of investment responsibility, and the need
for tax avoidance, will vary from case to case. Compounding of secure
income provides peace of mind. But investors willing to put up with fluctuating prices will find that well-selected growth stocks acquired at sensible
multiples of earnings may produce even more gains, in the long run.

Retirement income In many cases the next investment objective is
the provision of retirement income. Young families will give this little attention during the early years when other needs are more pressing. But with the
passage of the years, the need for taking care of retirement begins to loom
large. Most investors will rely substantially on Federal Social Security benefits and on public or private pension plans. Many can supplement these
plans with accumulations under their own control.

For investors to whom a minimum of risk and complete freedom of management are important, the fixed-dollar annuity should be considered,
especially by the elderly. But modern annuity contracts are written at very
modest "guaranteed" rates of accumulation—some as low as 2 1/2% to 3%.
In the face of a secular rise in the cost of living, a much larger outlay for
annuity protection is required to produce the same real income at retirement.

Variable annuities (described in Chapter 4) are available commercially
in some states. The proceeds of these contracts reflect changes in common

[2]At 6% compound interest, money doubles in 12 years; at 8%, in 9 years.

stock values and, if well managed, may, in the long run, provide a hedge against the rising cost of living.

Social Security benefits are adjusted periodically for the cost of living, but require an increasing levy on both employees and employers. Special arrangements that provide tax-deferment by self-employed investors ("Keogh" plans) and for those not covered by a corporate plan (IRAs), as described in Chapter 4, can involve the accumulation of stocks or mutual fund shares.

A growing number of investors seek additional provision for retirement through a long-range program of direct security purchases, using a balanced fund of bonds and stocks or the regular purchase (possibly dollar-averaging) of carefully selected investment company shares. The value of such a fund will rise and fall with the course of the security markets, but over the long run the result should be an accumulation considerably in excess of the value of a fixed-dollar annuity. This is especially the case if current income is reinvested and compounded over a considerable period of time, at the generous yields available in 1977–1978. Investors with sufficient time and skill to manage their own funds may emphasize the direct purchase of sound growth stocks; others would be well advised to rely on good-grade corporate bonds and Savings bonds and the shares of investment companies which have produced a better-than-average record. The proportions of the retirement fund to be devoted to bonds and to equities depend on the size of the fund and the skill and knowledge of the investor. In the past few years, disillusionment with the performance of growth stocks for capital gain, together with generous rates of interest on bonds, have led to increased emphasis on income securities and the very satisfactory results that can be obtained from compounding their returns through the years. The character of this type of fund will be influenced by the relative importance of suitable denomination, tax status, and the need for offsetting the declining value of the dollar.

"Income securities" are not the only avenue to increasing returns, however. Many solid growth stocks, properly bought, become income stocks over time. Their rising dividends can produce a very attractive return on their original cost.

To an increasing extent, corporate and public pension funds, with their growing emphasis on equity investments, are relied upon for retirement income and hedging against inflation. Such funds provide freedom from care and management, tax relief, and the benefits of compounding of interest and of economic growth. Their investment aspects are discussed in Chapter 4, and their own investment policies in Chapter 22.

Supplementary income before retirement When the primary objectives outlined above have been fulfilled or portfolios are being regularly built up for their eventual fulfillment, the remainder of the investment program can involve more risk-taking. Recovery of principal can be given less importance, and current income can be stressed. Investors who have achieved their early and important goals may consider a balanced fund of bonds and stocks (or other equities) to supplement their regular income.

The need for a "second income" derived from investments grows as the price level rises. Such an income can be obtained in a haphazard fashion by the occasional purchase, at opportune times, of income-producing securities. Here the investor faces the problems of selection, valuation, and timing that require considerable skill and experience. He must decide either to direct his own investment buying and selling, with the aid of services and other sources of advice and information, or to turn his affairs over to others. Even if the latter course is taken, an investor should be well acquainted with investment principles so that he can understand and review the decisions made on his behalf.

The types of investments for supplementary income will vary with the individual case. Where modest but secure income is the goal, bonds at their present generous yields, and stocks with unusual dividend records, are indicated. Complete freedom from management can be obtained through the establishment of a living trust or the purchase of an immediate annuity. The business or professional man may take advantage of the higher average yields on diversified liberal-dividend common stocks and fairly good bonds or purchase shares of investment companies that invest primarily for income. The investor of means may take advantage of the tax-exemption feature of state and municipal bonds for a substantial section of his fund. Such an investor is, of course, likely to place more importance on preservation of capital and on estate planning than on current income.

A major problem in the 1970s is to obtain a respectable income from common stocks. Dividend yields on many high-quality stocks are low in relation to the rates on alternative investments. The investor in quality equities must sacrifice current returns for potentially higher future returns by selecting good stocks with increasing dividend payouts.

Creation of an estate   The final goal of some investors is the creation of an estate for dependents (over and above minimum insurance and Social Security), charities, and other beneficiaries. Estate planning is a complex problem involving income and estate tax considerations, drafting of an adequate will, selection of executors and trustees, gift planning, insurance, and general investment policy. The investor who has provided for the more important needs can retain the services of firms making a specialty of estate planning. These firms employ or retain attorneys, tax experts, insurance advisers, and investment counsel. The investor should, however, be well acquainted himself with everything that is done for him.

The investment requirements in planning for a substantial eventual estate are: (1) tax relief on current income; (2) a substantial degree of liquidity for estate and inheritance tax purposes, through either insurance or a liquid segment of the portfolio; (3) minimizing the estate and inheritance tax burden; (4) growth of the fund over the years by compounding the returns derived from the portfolio; and (5) provision against dissipation of the fund by loss of dollars and of purchasing power. Practically all of the media of investment described previously might be involved in such a program, the amounts and proportions of each being determined by the individual circumstances.

Illustrative Situations

Investments of the young family   The young family consisting, say, of husband, wife, and two small children, with an annual income of $20,000 before taxes, is likely to be able to make only a start on the more fundamental investment objectives outlined previously. Under present-day conditions, provision for an emergency fund, a modest amount of low-cost insurance (say, three times annual income), and payments on a home are likely to absorb most available savings. Funds for education and other family needs may be accumulated through the purchase of Savings bonds, or high-grade corporate bonds as income increases, and a start toward retirement income is made through Social Security and company or public pension plans. For some years deposit-type investments, U.S. Savings bonds, and other safe and liquid sources with modest income will probably dominate the program.

Since a young family's need of funds for education and similar requirements will not be felt for several years, its initial investment program should include a segment, possibly small, of sound growth stocks, and their continued purchase over the years on a dollar-averaging basis, thus taking advantage of the secular increase in common stock values and enjoying compounding of those values through reinvestment of dividends. However, the rewards of successful investment in common stocks are available—or should be—only to those able to assume their risks and possibly their management. Unless the young family is temperamentally and economically equipped to try its hand at risk-taking, it had better follow a conservative policy. But if it is, and when extra savings are available, regular purchase of high-grade stocks on an averaging basis can produce good results over the long run. The goal should be "a total return" (annual income plus appreciation) of at least 10%. Less than this does not reward adequately for the risks of price fluctuation; good-grade corporate bonds with much lower price risk could be had (late 1977) to yield 8 1/2% to 8 3/4%.

Dollar-cost averaging is recommended because of the difficulty of detecting the low and high levels in the market. Theoretically, a young family should accelerate its purchase program in low periods, such as the fall and winter of 1974. But from a psychological point of view, this is too much to expect. Investment services can provide lists of basic portfolio stocks that are particularly suitable for averaging. High quality plus growing earnings and dividends are a must.

The New York Stock Exchange's Monthly Investment Plan, providing for the purchase through Exchange members of any "Big Board" stock or stocks (by payment of from $40 quarterly to $999 monthly) is a convenient device for dollar-cost-averaging by the small investor.[3]

Many young businessmen participate in stock-purchase and stock-option plans that may prove very valuable over the years. Eventual retirement

---

[3]Local "investment clubs," in which individuals pool and manage small monthly purchases of common stocks, provide experience in investing as well as possible diversification. See Arelo Sederberg. *The Stock Market Investment Club Handbook*. Los Angeles: Sherbourne Press, Inc., 1971.

income of substantial proportions can be obtained through participation in company profit-sharing plans.

The established professional man The professional man well launched on a prosperous career is likely to have provided for the prime essentials at the top of the list of investment priorities and may assume considerable risk. Such an investor would put major emphasis on: (1) additional current income, (2) provision for eventual retirement, and (3) the creation of a substantial estate over and above that provided by insurance. Investing for capital appreciation is involved in the last two of these goals. The investment program should include a fund of seasoned bonds to provide a backlog of less volatile securities, and a steady accumulation of common stocks over the years, which will produce a substantial "total return." Proportions will vary with the times. If his fund is very substantial, he can afford to employ an investment counsel; otherwise, he should consider buying shares of investment companies with clearly superior records. (See Chapter 11.) His absorption in professional activities is likely to leave little time and provide little opportunity for training in security analysis and the management of his own funds. He may be a shrewd direct investor, but he is ordinarily out of touch with business and financial affairs and may be tempted to make sudden and possibly ill-advised investment decisions.

Depending on the size of the accumulated fund and the annual savings available for investment, the age and health of the investor, the number of dependents, and numerous other considerations, the degree of risk that can be undertaken will vary greatly. In many cases the professional man had better lean to the conservative side, lest his time and attention be diverted from his main line of activities.

Unless averaging is used, the problem of timing is confronted. The less willing or able an investor is to deal with this problem, the more the emphasis on stocks of basic, large, strong concerns. The 1973–1975 period reveals the sad fate of many high-multiple "aggressive" or "capital gains" stocks, especially those of new and untried ventures.

Under conditions prevailing in the latter 1970s, good-grade corporate bonds should not be ignored. For many years these securities had little or no appeal for the individual investor. But the attractive yields available in 1975–1978 have caused many persons to turn to bonds. Compounding the interest in 8% bonds can double the principal of a fund in nine years, with modest price risk. A compromise position could be taken with the purchase of convertible bonds at prices at or not much above their conversion values. In many cases these produce higher current income than the common stocks of the same companies, and yet have the "downside" protection of bonds. (See Chapter 9.)

Depending on the tax bracket in which any new income would fall, this investor may be interested in tax-exempt municipal bonds for that portion of his retirement fund devoted to high-grade securities. Other tax-saving devices are suggested in Chapter 18.

Retirement arrangements under the "Keogh" and "IRA" plans are available and offer very substantial advantages to professional investors. Fixed trust and/or mutual "tax-free" funds offer tax benefits.

The established businessman The frequently used expression "businessman's risk" or "businessman's investment" implies two things: (1) that this type of person can assume considerable risk, and (2) that his business training and experience equip him to keep a close eye on economic and financial conditions and to exercise unusual acumen in the selection and management of securities. These qualities may or may not exist. Furthermore, preoccupation with his own affairs may not leave enough time for adequate investment management. On the other hand, he may be in close contact with and be able to interpret and use sources of investment information that will produce better-than-average results.

Many businessmen have fulfilled the important initial objectives, and their investment policy can be directed to supplementary income before retirement, building a retirement fund, and estate creation. Supplementary income before retirement can be obtained in part from short-term trading in securities, although here again timing is as important as selection, and expert advice (often hard to find) is recommended. If liquidity is important for special purposes, "money-market" mutual funds are available, or the affluent investor may purchase money-market instruments directly. Provision for retirement will begin with Social Security, but will depend more on a lucrative company pension plan, supplemented by portfolio. Businessmen with relatively modest means can take advantage of a "Keogh" plan arrangement. In any case, more "aggressive" securities, both for higher income and for appreciation, are appropriate. Investment counsel can be obtained. (The fee is an expense for tax purposes.)

If our successful businessman has no need of large current income from his portfolio, and if he is in the upper tax brackets, he should pay particular attention to the production of long-term capital gains. He is also likely to be interested in short-run or speculative activity and in investment "bargains," including undervalued stocks and special situations.

This type of investor can devote some portion of his stock fund to new and promising ventures; the balance of his equities should consist of stocks or convertible securities selected for their long-run merits. An honest appraisal of past experience will suggest his real ability to make sound decisions concerning the selection and timing of purchases and sales, and determine whether at least a portion of his aggressive portfolio should be placed in the hands of others with more experience and more facilities for appraisal of the market and of individual securities.

The "businessman type" includes such a variety of investment situations that generalizations concerning ability to assume risk, to gauge market trends, or to select and manage a securities portfolio, are dangerous. Tax considerations will vary in importance with each case. The need for liquidity will also vary, depending especially on the type of business in which he is engaged and whether his own business is stable or uncertain. If a substantial portion of his savings is tied up in his own enterprise at considerable risk, his investment portfolio should lean toward the conservative. The established businessman, if he is a corporate officer, can likely participate in a company stock-option plan and in a program of deferred compensation based on company contributions. Such programs provide tax relief and may result in a very substantial accumulation of equities.

The widow or retired couple   A growing number of persons, both in absolute terms and as a percentage of the population, depend on a fixed-dollar income after the working years have passed. The extension of Social Security and pension benefits to an enlarged list of the elderly, plus the increase in their dollar amount, has made a substantial provision for retirement. But the *maximum* Social Security retirement income (mid-1977) is $474 a month for an individual and $830 a month for a widow with two children.[4] To supplement these benefits, and to be independent of relatives and charity, retired persons need supplemental income from private pensions and investments.

For purposes of this discussion, we assume that the retired investors we have in mind no longer need to provide for dependents and that other objectives, such as home ownership, have been reached. The main problem is the maintenance of an income for their own needs. Once the sum of $100,000, or even $50,000, invested in high-grade securities could provide for reasonable living standards. Just prior to World War I, for example, an investment of $100,000 in high-grade bonds provided $5,000 tax-free income. After World War II, allowing for the decline in interest rates (to 2 3/4%), for income taxes, and for the lowered buying power of the dollar (45% of 1913), it took $500,000 to provide the same real income.[5] In 1977, much higher interest rates were available, but the dollar had less than 22% of its 1913 buying power. Using the postwar period, the buying power of the dollar declined 70% from 1945 to 1977. Thus, a real dilemma is posed for the *rentier* class—whether to live on modest income, or to take greater risk and try to magnify income through investment in equities, or to consume principal.

Table 20-1 shows the pretax dollar return from a $100,000 fund invested in various media, under conditions prevailing in September 1977. At that time interest rates were still high, and a fund of $100,000 invested then would produce $8,750 annually from good-grade corporate bonds and $8,000 from very high-grade bonds. Preferred stock yields also outranked deposit-type yields by an ample margin. The latter brought a lower return than on long-term Treasury bonds but involved no price risk. Savings bonds were relatively more attractive than they had been for some time. Common stock yields in general stood at the bottom of the yield scale. But within the common stock group, the actual range was from zero to perhaps 10%. The general stock averages are heavily influenced by stocks that are more attractive for growth than for current income.

---

[4]These benefits will not be payable for several years. To receive these benefits, the average salary of the worker, excluding the lowest five years, would have to be $16,500.

[5]Benjamin Graham, *The Intelligent Investor*, 3d ed. (New York: Harper & Row, Publishers, 1965), p. 6.

TABLE 20-1   Yields from Selected Investment Media
September 1977

Medium of Investment	Representative Yield—Per Cent	Dollar Income
"Blue-chip" industrial common stocks	5.00%	$5,000
Commercial bank passbook account	5.00	5,000
Mutual savings bank passbook account	5.25	5,250
Savings and loan association passbook account	5.25	5,250
"Income" mutual funds	6.00	6,000
U.S. Savings bonds, Series H	6.00	6,000
Certificates of deposit (6 months)	6.50	6,500
Long-term U.S. Treasury bonds	7.50	7,500
High-grade corporate bonds	8.00	8,000
Public utility common stocks	8.00	8,000
High-grade utility preferred stocks	8.25	8,250
Medium-grade corporate bonds	8.75	8,750

To the majority of retired investors, the avoidance of loss must be the major consideration. The dilemma involved in this choice between good income with low risk and possibly high income with high risk can best be solved by utilizing *both* income and principal to maximize annual cash returns (1) through annuities established as such or based on the proceeds of life insurance policies, (2) through gradual liquidation of high-grade securities not subject to material market fluctuation, (3) through the establishment of a living trust providing for regular payments of interest and principal, and (4) through using the withdrawal privilege offered by mutual funds.

As indicated previously, a growing number of retired investors participate in private or public pension plans. These differ widely in terms and benefits. A very substantial (but declining) percentage of pension benefits is derived from investment in equities and offers some protection against inflation. (See Chapter 22.) Other investors will receive the proceeds of "Keogh" and "IRA" plans. A number of investment services periodically publish "retirement portfolios," which in 1977–1978 contained a high percentage of corporate bonds or mutual income funds.

Continuing inflation works a hardship on retired persons whose incomes do not increase with the cost of living. Social Security benefits are now adjusted to the cost of living, but this provides only modest relief. To achieve safety, with steady and adequate income, and inflation protection, continues to be an insoluble dilemma. Imperfect though they may be in market return, sound common stocks with known dividend prospects and good chances for appreciation offer some hope for investors who are willing and able to assume the risks of equity ownership.

The wealthy investor   The wealthy investor enjoys several distinct advantages with respect to investment policy: He can afford the risks that equities inevitably involve. He can obtain ample diversification in his own portfolio. He can take advantage of the tax-exemption feature of state and municipal bonds and should substitute these for other high-grade corporate and Federal obligations in the bond section of his portfolio. He has a variety of other tax-reducing options at his disposal. He can make full use of capital gains provisions of the Federal income tax law. He can afford the services of competent investment counsel to "tailor" a program that will combine his needs for income, capital appreciation, and estate tax protection. He can use some of his principal if he wishes to do so.

For such investors, matters of income and estate tax planning bulk even larger than purely investment considerations. Apart from a substantial fund in high-grade short-term securities held for the purpose of meeting estate and inheritance taxes, together with any specific investments that represent business commitments, the wealthy investor's portfolio will consist substantially of tax-exempts, a varying defensive balance in money market securities or high-grade bonds, and aggressive common stocks. Whether he manages such a portfolio himself, utilizes an investment company, or employs professional management, will depend on his investment competence and confidence and on the complexities of the particular situation.

The wealthy investor can achieve a considerable degree of freedom from care through the medium of a living trust, through holding investment company shares, or through the use of counsel. However, he should always review and check the decisions of others.

A Word of Explanation

In the preceding suggestions for different types of investors, recommendations of specific lists of securities have been avoided. This is because investment portfolios have a way of becoming inappropriate or even obsolete. The circumstances of the investor, the appeal of industries and companies, and rates and prices in the investment market all change through time. Investment is a dynamic art and no program can remain static. Nor can any itemized array of securities or plan involving certain proportions of different types of investments be applicable to any large number of situations even within a general type. Constant vigilance and willingness to change are required of the investor or of those to whom he entrusts his investment problems.

Sources of current information which aid in the process of changing and revising both policy and portfolio are indicated in Chapter 13 and in the chapters on the major types of securities.

REFERENCES

BABSON, T. E., and D. L. BABSON, *Investing for a Successful Future.* New York: The Macmillan Co., 1961.

BELLEMORE, D. H., *The Strategic Investor: Individual Portfolio Management.* New York: Simmons-Boardman Publishing Co., 1963.

COBLEIGH, I. U., *All About Stocks.* New York: Weybright and Talley, 1970.

COHEN, J. B., and A. W. HANSON, *Personal Finance: Principles and Case Problems,* 4th ed. Homewood, Ill.: Richard D. Irwin, Inc., 1972.

CRANE, BURTON, *The Sophisticated Investor: A Guide to Stock Market Profits*, rev. ed. New York: Simon and Schuster, Inc., 1964.

EDITORS OF FORTUNE, *Fortune's Guide to Personal Investing*. New York: McGraw-Hill, Inc., 1969.

ENGEL, LOUIS, *How to Buy Stocks: A Guide to Making More Money in the Market*, 5th rev. ed. Boston: Little, Brown & Company, 1971.

FINLEY, H. M., *Everybody's Guide to the Stock Market*, rev. ed. Chicago: Henry Regnery Company, 1968.

FISHER, P. A., *Common Stocks and Uncommon Profits*, rev. ed. New York: Harper & Row, Publishers, 1960.

————, *Paths to Wealth Through Common Stocks*. Englewood Cliffs, N.J.: Prentice-Hall, Inc. 1960.

GRAHAM, BENJAMIN, *The Intelligent Investor*, 4th rev. ed. New York: Harper & Row, Publishers, 1973.

HARDY, C. B., ed., *Dun & Bradstreet's Guide to "Your Investments,"* 19th ed. New York: Thomas Y. Crowell Co., 1973.

LASSER, J. K., and SYLVIA PORTER, *Managing Your Money*, new rev. ed. New York: Doubleday & Co., 1963.

LOEB, G. M., *The Battle for Stock Market Profits*. New York: Simon and Schuster, Inc. 1971.

LYONS, J. T., ed., *Personal Financial Planning for Executives*. New York: American Management Association, 1970.

MARION, L. F., *Understanding Investment: A Primer for Wives, Widows and Other Capitalists*. Seattle, Wash: University of Washington Press, 1964.

PREGER, PAUL, JR., and D. A. LOCHWING, *The Professional Man's Money: A Guide to Investment Profits*. Englewood Cliffs, N.J.: Prentice-Hall, Inc., 1973.

ROSENBERG, CLAUDE JR., *Stock Market Primer*. Cleveland: The World Publishing Company, 1970.

SCHEINMAN, W. X., *Why Most Investors are Mostly Wrong Most of the Time*. New York: Weybright and Talley, 1970.

"SMITH, ADAM," *Supermoney*. New York: Random House, Inc., 1972.

STILLMAN, R. J., *Guide to Personal Finance*, 2d ed. Englewood Cliffs, N.J.: Prentice-Hall, Inc., 1975.

WEST, D. A., *The Investor in a Changing Economy*. Englewood Cliffs, N.J.: Prentice-Hall, Inc., 1968.

WIDICUS, W. W., JR., and T. E. STITZEL, *Personal Investing*. Homewood, IL.: Richard D. Irwin, Inc., 1971.

Institutional Investors: Banking Types

SCOPE: This and the following chapter discuss the investment policies of the more important financial institutions through which the savings of individuals are put to work. The order of discussion in Chapter 21 is: (1) magnitude of institutional investment, (2) restrictions on institutional investment, (3) commercial banks, (4) mutual savings banks, and (5) savings and loan associations. In Chapter 22 the order is: (5) bank trusts, (6) endowments and foundations, (7) life insurance companies, (8) uninsured private pension funds, (9) state and local government retirement funds, and (10) Federal retirement funds. Discussion of the investment policies of two other types of financial institutions—investment companies and fire insurance companies—is found in Chapters 11 and 30. They lack the trust characteristics of the other institutions, they have much more leeway in the selection of their investments, and their own investment policies determine to a large extent the appeal of the securities they themselves have issued. Thus, the management of the funds of these institutions is more appropriately discussed in connection with the analysis of their shares.

Commercial banks, savings banks, and savings and loan associations as locations for savings have already been discussed in Chapter 5. The material in the present chapter is, therefore, confined to the management of their investment portfolios.

Magnitude of Institutional Investment

Savings flow into the capital and money markets through a variety of institutions that play a constantly increasing role as owners of investment instruments. Individuals are, therefore, concerned with institutional investment policy for two main reasons: (1) Institutional supply and demand is a major influence on the market prices and yields of investments. (2) Individuals depend on the portfolio managers of the savings institutions to protect and increase the value and income of their savings. The importance of the institutions we have discussed or will discuss is indicated in Table 21-1. Bank trustees are included in the table, although they do not own the securities they manage, nor do they issue securities obligations against such assets. But they have a large influence though their control of tremendous portfolios.

The policies that determine the distribution of the investment assets of the

416

TABLE 21-1   Institutional Ownership of Securities and Mortgages, December 31, 1976 (in billions of dollars)

	U.S. Govt. and Agency Securities	Domestic State and Municipal Bonds	Domestic Corporate Bonds	Corporate Stocks	Mortgages
Commercial banks*a*	$138.3	$104.7	$ 7.2	$ 1.6	$151.2
Mutual savings banks	9.1	2.4	26.4	4.4	81.7
Savings and loan associations	*d*	*e*	—	—	323.1
Life insurance companies	7.7	5.4	113.5	34.3	91.5
Noninsured private pension funds	14.9	—	37.9	108.5	2.2
Bank administered trusts*b*	14.1	16.5	17.8	94.3	2.8
State and local govt. retirement funds*c*	8.6	4.4	67.6	26.1	8.5
Federal trust funds	124.0	—	—	—	—
Investment companies (mutual)*f*	2.1	*e*	7.2	43.0	*e*
Non-life insurance companies	8.6	38.9	13.5	15.0	0.3

*a*Includes trading-account securities.
*b*Data for 1975, exclusive of pension trusts and agency accounts.
*c*Book value.
*d*Not available.
*e*Less than $100 million.
*f*Includes money market funds.
Sources: See citations in Chapters 4, 5, 10, 22, 29, 30; *Federal Reserve Flow of Funds.*

above institutions are discussed in this and the following chapter and in Chapters 4, 5, 10, 29, and 30.

Restrictions on Institutional Investment

The common characteristic of the institutions discussed in this and the following chapter is that they act in a position of trust, investing the funds of others entrusted to their care. Such a position requires a greater degree of prudence and caution than the depositors might employ in the selection of their own commitments.

The latitude within which such institutions may exercise investment discretion depends on the nature of the contract or trust, the powers granted by the contract or by the maker of a trust, and the Federal and state laws governing the investment policy of fiduciary institutions. Commercial banks, savings banks, savings and loan associations, trustees, and life insurance companies are obliged to observe strict regulations concerning their investments, although in the case of trustees, the individual trust arrangements may provide considerable latitude. Pension fund managers have wide latitude, depending on the fund objectives, but the Pension Reform Act of 1974 imposes new responsibilities on the companies and fund managers as fiduciaries. On the other hand, educational and other endowments are governed mainly by their own investment policies or self-imposed conditions.

Commercial Bank Investments

Commercial banks as investors Commercial banks form a very important segment of the investment market. As of December 31, 1976, commercial banks in the United States owned $102.5 billion of direct and guaranteed Federal debt, or 15% of the total then outstanding, $35.8 billion or 42% of Federal agency debt outstanding, and $105 billion of state and municipal obligations or about 46% of the total outstanding. They held $151.2 billion, or 17% of total mortgage debt outstanding.[1] Bank management bears a particularly grave responsibility in investing depositors' funds so as to provide safety and adequate liquidity as well as earnings and at the same time protect the solvency and flexibility of the bank credit system.

Types of bank assets The assets of commercial banks consist of three major types: primary reserves of cash and balances with other banks, including legal reserves; earning assets, consisting of loans and investments; and fixed assets. The earning assets can be divided into four other categories: (1) secondary reserves, consisting of highly liquid money market investments, such as bankers' acceptances, prime commercial paper, and short-term Treasury obligations; (2) the bond investment account; (3) securities held for trading; (4) other earning assets, consisting of commercial, industrial, consumer, and real estate loans. The secondary reserve should be of such high quality and liquidity that it can be converted into cash at any time without material loss.

In determining the relative proportion of assets in each group, the bank faces the problem of maintaining adequate liquidity and at the same time deriving a reasonable income. The primary reserves are completely liquid but produce no income. The secondary reserves are extremely liquid and ordinarily yield a relatively low rate of return. But in times of credit stress, their rates of interest have exceeded those of long-term securities. The investment account consists mainly of Federal, Federal agency, and high-grade municipal and corporate obligations. The municipals yield the highest after-tax return, but lack the liquidity and marketability of the Federal obligations. Corporate bonds are relatively unattractive for after-tax income. Commercial loans produce higher yields, but are not dependable sources of funds on short notice. Real estate and consumer loans provide favorable yields, but are the least liquid of the entire portfolio.

Investment restrictions The investment policies of the commercial banks that are members of the Federal Reserve System are governed by Federal statute and the rulings of the Comptroller of the Currency. Non-member state banks are governed by the banking laws of the state where they are located. The member banks comprise 39% of all commercial banks in the country, but hold 74% of the total commercial bank deposits; the following discussion emphasizes their policies.

---

[1]*Federal Reserve Bulletin*; Federal Deposit Insurance Corporation, annual reports.

Commercial banks are not permitted to participate as principals in the underwriting of corporate securities, but may do so with respect to Federal and general obligation municipal bonds. They are not permitted to purchase stocks, with the exception of certain specific types.[2] They may not buy convertible bonds at a price above their value without the conversion feature.[3] They may buy no securities which are in default. They are prohibited from purchasing securities in which the investment characteristics are predominantly speculative.

All securities held by a bank which are not specifically exempted from regulation (such as Federal, Federal agency, state, and local bonds—except revenue bonds) or which are not prohibited must qualify as *investment* securities and must be readily marketable, that is, have such a market as to render sales at fair values readily available. Evidence of marketability must be either public distribution of the particular issue, or public distribution of other issues of the obligor. If there has been no public offering, eligible bonds are limited to 10-year (or shorter) obligations of established enterprises, having sound values, with an acceptable sinking fund. Where the above tests are met, not more than 10% of the unimpaired capital and surplus of the bank may be invested in the securities of any one obligor. If the purchase price is above par, the premium must be regularly amortized. Profits from the sale of securities must not be considered as earnings until adequate reserves for actual or estimated losses have been provided.

Bank examiners classify securities in four groups according to quality. All eligible securities are placed in Group I and are valued on the basis of cost, less amortization of any premium. Securities of investment quality include general market obligations rated in the first four groups by the recognized investment services: Aaa, Aa, A, and Baa or A1 + , A1, A, and B1 +. (While such ratings are valuable, they should not be a complete substitute for a bank's own judgment concerning quality.) Securities in Group II are predominantly speculative in character and are valued at the average market price for the 18 months preceding the examination. At least 50% of the net depreciation, if any, must be deducted from the capital of the bank in determining its solvency. Group III consists of securities in default; these must be immediately written down to market value. Group IV consists of stocks and similar holdings. All market depreciation on them is considered a loss and must be written off against capital immediately. (A bank may have acquired stock through foreclosure of a collateral loan.)

Significance of investments   The role of bank investments has changed greatly in the past two decades, as indicated by the figures in

[2] Up to 15% of capital and surplus may be invested in the stock of a company engaged in the safe-deposit business. Stock of a company holding property necessary for banking purposes or providing accounting services may be acquired, as well as stock in small business investment companies. Under certain circumstances, up to 10% of capital and surplus may be invested in the shares of corporations engaged in foreign banking. In addition, all member banks must subscribe to Federal Reserve Bank stock. (Bank holding companies are exempt from these rules.)

[3] As explained in Chapter 9, the holder of a convertible bond may exchange it for common stock at a ratio fixed in advance. When the common stock rises sharply in value, the bond will also rise, often above its investment value as a bond alone.

Table 21-2. In examining the figures, one should note the changes in absolute amounts, as well as the relative importance of the various categories. The classification of earning assets referred to above is not used in the official reports.

TABLE 21-2   Earning Assets of Commercial Banks as of
             December 31 (in billions of dollars)

	1955	1965		1970	1976	
	Amt.	Amt.	Per Cent	Amt.	Amt.	Per Cent
Loans						
Commercial and industrial[a]	$ 33.2	$ 71.9	23.4%	$113.4	$182.9	22.1%
Agricultural	4.5	8.2	2.7	11.2	23.3	2.8
For purchasing and carrying securities	5.0	8.6	2.8	9.9	15.5	1.9
Real estate	20.8	49.7	16.2	73.3	149.5	181
Individuals	17.2	45.7	14.9	66.3	118.4	14.3
Other	3.1	22.8	7.4	42.6	105.4[b]	12.7
Total loans[c]	$ 82.6	$202.8	65.9%	$310.6	$576.2	69.6%
Investments[d]						
U.S. Govt. obligations	$ 61.6	$ 59.7	19.4	$ 62.0	$102.5	12.4
Bonds of Federal agencies	1.9	4.6	1.5	13.5	35.8	4.3
Municipal obligations	12.7	38.7	12.6	69.8	104.7	12.6
Corporate bonds	1.6	0.9	0.3	2.6⎱	8.5	1.0
Other	.5	0.8	0.3	0.5⎰		
Total investments	$ 78.3	$104.7	34.1%	$148.4	$251.5	30.4%
Total loans and investments	$160.9	$307.5	100 %	$459.0	$827 7	100 %

[a]Includes open-market paper purchased.
[b]Includes Federal funds sold ($48.3) and loans to financial institutions ($42.4).
[c]Totals show net of reserves.
[d]Includes trading-account securities.
Sources: Federal Reserve Bulletin; Federal Deposit Insurance Corporation, Annual Reports.

During the 1930s the dearth of commercial loans and the banks' desire for liquidity following the banking crisis led to a market shift from loans to investments, especially U.S. Government obligations. During World War II, despite an increase in business loans, the trend toward Government securities was accentuated by the role of the banks in financing the war effort. By the end of 1945, total investments were 79%, and Federal obligations 73%, of commercial banks' earning assets. Since World War II, bank lending to finance business, real estate, and consumers has grown at the expense of investments; at the end of 1976, Federal bonds had fallen to 12.4% of total loans and investments. Federal and agency obligations were 4.2%.

Factors determining investment policy   The investment policy of a commercial bank is governed by regulation and by considerations of income and risk. In the purchase of securities other than U.S. Government obligations, the main objective is to obtain a higher after-tax return than that available in the comparable maturities in the Government market. But such a return carries increased risk of unwise selection and subsequent market declines. The factors that help to shape investment policy may be outlined as follows.

REGULATION   The types and quality of investments are heavily influenced by regulation. In addition to the factors noted previously, liquidity position is regulated directly or indirectly by the Federal Reserve. This results in shifts in the proportions of short-, medium-, and long-term securities held.

SIZE   Large banks can afford expert investment management, and can maintain a flexible portfolio policy. Small banks rely on advice for investment services and tend to stress high quality, such as Federal and agency securities and Aaa or Aa municipal and corporate bonds.

TAXATION   Commercial bank profits are fully subject to corporate income taxes. Tax-free bonds are especially attractive investments.

THE NATURE OF DEPOSIT LIABILITIES   Banks which normally carry large demand deposits, especially those which act as depositories for other banks, must maintain a higher degree of liquidity than those whose time deposits predominate or whose demand deposits are unusually stable. Liquidity is reflected in cash position and in the proportion of short-term Government securities and other high-grade "secondary reserve" items among the earning assets.

THE RELATIONSHIP BETWEEN DEPOSITS AND CAPITAL FUNDS   Banks normally have a very small net worth in relation to assets, as compared with business firms. The capital (stock), surplus, undivided profits, and contingency reserves that comprise the net worth represent the protection afforded by the owners to the depositors. The lower the ratio of net worth to deposits, the greater the risk and, hence, the greater the need for liquidity and safety through high quality and short maturity. The appropriate capital funds-to-deposits ratio was formerly considered to be in the neighborhood of 10%. At the end of 1976, the ratio stood at 9.3% for all commercial banks in the United States. National banks showed a ratio of 8.7%. Because of their importance as correspondent banks, member banks in New York City showed a ratio of 9.5%.[4] Such ratios are justifiable only as long as commercial banks remain very liquid.

THE PATTERN OF ASSETS   Closely allied to the previous factor is the amount and character of the bank's assets other than its highly liquid investments. If assets *at risk*—that is, loans and discounts exclusive of open-market paper, and longer-term investments—bulk large among the earning assets, the risk element in the investment program must be kept at a minimum through emphasis on higher quality and shorter maturities in the bond account. Assets, deposits, and net worth are related by the supervisory authorities

[4]Compiled from group data in *Federal Reserve Bulletin*.

and by bank management. The less liquid the assets, the greater proportion net worth must bear to deposits. The bank with a maximum of loans and a minimum of liquid investments must have a higher cushion of owners' equity.

As noted in Chapter 29, in the mid-1970s a number of banks, including some large metropolitan institutions, suffered from the severe decline in value of New York City bonds and from large losses on loans to real estate investment trusts which they had sponsored. Some without adequate net worth were classified by the Federal Reserve examiners as "problem banks."

The character of bank loans is also important. A high proportion of term loans in the loan portfolio requires more liquidity in investments.

THE BANKS' EARNINGS REQUIREMENTS   This factor is placed last because a bank's investment policy must always be based more on considerations of safety than of income. A bank has the objective of earning an attractive rate on the investment of its stockholders, but its first responsibility is to its depositors. High risk and high earnings go hand in hand (at least until disaster strikes); low risk-taking produces low returns. To strike the proper medium between these extremes is the central investment problem of banking. The relation of capital funds to deposits, the character of the deposits, and the types of services rendered by the bank all affect the degree of risk it assumes; the same factors also determine its earning power. When, in order to produce satisfactory earnings, the cash position of a bank is reduced, or loans and investments of longer maturity or of lower quality are acquired, or deposits are greatly increased, the interests of the stockholders and those of the depositors must be balanced with unusual ingenuity.

The market value of the bonds—even those of "money bonds" of the highest quality—in a bank's investment account may decline, either through a decline in their investment standing or through a rise in prevailing money rates that is reflected in declining prices.[5] Banks can guard against the first of these risks by purchasing and holding bonds of the highest credit standing, but they have no control over the second influence. Ideally, banks should hold short-term securities when interest rates are likely to rise and move to longer maturities when lower rates are expected. But such shifts depend on successful forecasting of the business cycle, and are easier said than done. Banks can deal with the problem by a system of staggered maturities, that is, the proper distribution of their holdings in short-, medium-, and long-term obligations. As time passes, securities move steadily into the short-term category. However, in recent years banks have made a practice of concentrating on relatively short maturities (up to 10 years) so as to be able to shift funds into their growing loan portfolios without material market loss. The shape of the yield curve, with attractive yields on short- and medium-term issues, especially in 1969, 1971, and 1973–1975, has also encouraged such concentration. (See p. 156.)

Investment earnings vary in importance from bank to bank. In 1976, interest on investments was 18% of gross revenues of all insured banks. Large banks tend to manage investment portfolios so as to maximize earnings.

---

[5]See Chapters 3, 6, 7, 8, and 19 for discussions of changing bond yields.

Smaller banks are, or should be, more conservative. All banks, however, dislike losses on portfolios and tend to resist policies that will substantially reduce investment income, such as selling bonds during periods of high interest rates.

Types of securities investments The bank's investment portfolio includes securities not classed as secondary reserves, and consists of obligations with medium and long maturities. Investments provide a residual account that varies with the demand for the higher-yielding loans.

U.S. GOVERNMENT OBLIGATIONS   Commercial banks are the largest institutional owners of Federal debt. At the end of 1976, their holdings of $102.5 billion comprised 15.6% of direct Treasury debt. Their holdings of $78.3 billion of marketable Government debt comprised 19% of the amount outstanding.

Federal obligations bulk large in bank portfolios because they possess several attractive features: (1) They involve the least credit risk; (2) they involve the least risk of substantial market price fluctuation; (3) with the exception of certain types, they have perfect marketability; (4) they may be used for bank borrowing at the Federal Reserve banks without payment of penalty rates; (5) they are preferred over other investments by bank examiners and other supervisory authorities. Within its Government bond portfolio, of course, a bank has the problem of distributing maturities. Its policy in this respect will affect its liquidity and its income. In recent years the great bulk of Government holdings has been in maturities of five years or less, as shown in the following schedule for December 31, 1976:

	Amount ($ billions)	Per Cent
within a year	$31.2	39.8%
1–5 years	40.0	51.1
5–10	6.3	8.0
over 10 years	0.8	1.1
	$78.3	100 %

STATE AND LOCAL GOVERNMENT BONDS   Commercial banks are also the largest institutional owners of municipal securities. At the end of 1976, their holdings of $105 billion comprised about 41% of total state and local debt. (See Chapter 7.) Investment in such securities has increased so substantially that at the end of 1976, they represented 42% of total bank investments. Banks are permitted to underwrite municipal securities (other than revenue bands), whose tax-exempt yield is very attractive in relation to the yield on corporate bonds. Holdings of municipals are adjusted with changing demand for loans, the banks' reserve position, and yields on alternative investments.

CORPORATE BONDS   Banks' interest in corporate bonds has declined steadily in recent years. The after-tax yields of the bonds of required quality are not attractive compared to those on high-grade tax-exempt municipals, and they lack the price stability and liquidity of Federal obligations. Direct term loans to corporations, with their higher yields, are the modern substitute. Convertible bonds are not attractive; banks are not allowed to pay more than the investment or "straight" value for such securities.

Profits and losses on securities   Bonds should be bought by banks for income, not for capital gain. This does not mean that banks hold all bonds to maturity. Constant reappraisal of bond holdings and the need to diversify maturities, as well as the liquidation of bonds to feed the secondary and primary reserves when necessary, create a certain turnover in the bond account. Banks thus incur profits and losses in securities even though short-term trading is ordinarily avoided.

The regulations of the Comptroller of the Currency require banks to use any profits realized in the sale of securities to offset actual losses before such profits may be included as income.[6]

Other bank earning assets   Discussion of the loaning activities of commercial banks would involve a digression into commercial bank management too extensive for our purposes. However, because of their longer maturity, two types of loans properly belong in a discussion of bank investments, namely, term loans and real estate mortgages.

Term loans are business loans running from one to 10 years in maturity and amortized by regular installments. The typical term loan is expected to be repaid out of future cash flow. It contains written covenants on the part of the borrower to conduct his financial affairs in a manner agreed upon by the borrower and the lender, such as restrictions on other debt and on dividend distributions. It is usually secured, although the larger term loan is less likely to be secured than is the small one.

Studies of term loans reveal that these credits, which first appeared in the latter 1930s, have become a very important factor in the credit supply. At the beginning of 1977 they totalled $45 billion, or nearly 48% of the aggregate industrial and commercial loans of the large banks that hold 65% of all bank business loans.[7] This means that for the banking system, the total was between $65 and $75 billion—equal to about 30% of total securities investments and many times the holdings of corporate bonds. The larger loans are used most frequently by businesses such as metals and metal products, petroleum, coal, chemicals, rubber, transportation, and communication, which have a heavy fixed investment with a relatively long service life. The smaller loans, for working capital purposes, are used mostly by retail trade and service concerns.

Term loans are a substitute for two other types of bank earning assets that have declined in importance (for banks) in recent years. One is the short-term loan that was almost automatically renewed if the borrower's credit standing remained satisfactory. The other, as indicated previously, is the corporate bond. While loans with maturity of from one to 10 years violate

[6]See Chapter 29 for a discussion of bank earnings derived from investments.
[7]*Federal Reserve Bulletin,* monthly tables.

the traditional theory of bank liquidity, experience has shown their usefulness provided they are made wisely, they are followed and collected carefully, and the bank is otherwise liquid.

Real estate loans, along with term loans, are appropriate investments for saving deposits which have much less volatility than those in the demand category. They have played an increasingly important role in commercial bank portfolios. At the end of 1976, commercial banks held a total (before reserves) of $151 billion in mortgages, or 17% of mortgage debt outstanding, consisting of $6.7 billion in farm mortgages, $86.2 billion in one- to four-family residential, and $58.3 billion in multifamily, commercial, and industrial mortgages.

The experience of banks with real estate mortgage loans in the 1930s was not a happy one, especially for smaller banks. Since that time, practices have been greatly improved by experience and by regulation. National banks may buy any FHA-insured or VA-guaranteed mortgage. In addition, they may acquire conventional first mortgages on improved real estate not exceeding 66 2/3% of appraised value, in the case of 10- to 20-year amortized loans, and 90% for a term of 30 years if the entire principal will be amortized within that period. Single-maturity loans are limited to 50% of appraised value and a maturity of five years. A national bank may make aggregate mortgage loans up to either the amount of its unimpaired capital and surplus or 70% of its time and savings deposits, whichever is the greater.

The amortization feature of modern real estate loans, together with the insurance or guarantee by Federal agencies of loans qualified for such insurance, have done much to put mortgages back into the class of respectable bank assets. Their lack of liquidity is mitigated by the fact that banks can obtain special four-month advances against mortgages from the Federal Reserve Banks, and by the fact that FHA-insured mortgages may be sold to the Federal National Mortgage Association. In case of default, insured mortgages are exchanged for Government-guaranteed debentures of the Federal Housing Administration.[8]

Banks again had problems with real estate loans in 1973–1976. In this case, investment in loans to real estate trusts was the culprit. Very heavy losses were incurred. (See p. 251.)

Consumer loans have increased greatly in recent years. This category includes personal loans and loans made for financing automobiles and other durable consumer goods. For the most part this type of loan is repayable in installments and so offers little liquidity, but if made soundly and with adequate diversification it is an appropriate investment of savings deposits.

Summary of investment requirements Recovery of principal through safety and marketability of investments are the foremost considerations in bank investment policy. Second in importance is assurance of income; the high-grade and relatively short-term bank investments produce a modest but certain yield. Other important requirements are legality (the banks' investments must conform to legal and regulatory requirements), diversifica-

---

[8]A more complete discussion of mortgage loans is found in Chapter 12.

tion (especially for smaller banks), freedom from management in the case of banks without specialized investment managers, and tax status (the bank is taxed at corporate tax rates and finds municipal bonds attractive). Although the bank's expenses rise in periods of rising wages and prices, its obligations are dollar obligations, and it is, therefore, not concerned about protecting its depositors against inflation.

Savings Bank Investments

General factors determining investments The general characteristics of savings banks described in Chapter 5 help to explain why these institutions need less liquidity than commercial banks, and therefore, why their cash and reserve requirements are lower and why their investments include a greater proportion of longer-maturity instruments. The savings bank can invest savings funds in securities of limited marketability and in home mortgages that are adequately safe and ordinarily pay a higher rate of income than do the more marketable and short-term securities.

But safety in the investment of savings bank funds must not be compromised. The purposes for which these banks were established have led to restrictions on their investment powers. They may hold high-grade investments only, including real estate mortgages, government bonds, and prime corporate issues. Such a selection may provide safety but lack flexibility.

Legal investments in New York State No two states have identical laws regarding the eligibility of securities for savings banks. Because the New York law is representative of fairly conservative legislation and has served as a model for a number of other states, the present *legal list* in New York is set forth below. The solvency record of New York savings banks is testimony to the efficiency of the law. No savings bank has failed in New York in over 70 years, and no depositor in a New York State savings bank has lost money by reason of the failure of the bank during the present century.

An official list of the specific eligible securities is issued by the State Banking Department at the beginning of July in each year.[9] The following is a summary of major types, without spelling out the specific requirements to be met in the case of corporate and municipal bonds:

1. Direct and guaranteed obligations of the United States;
2. Bonds of New York and other states based on full faith and credit;
3. Direct obligations of New York State municipalities;
4. Obligations of municipalities in other states meeting certain population and debt-to-property standards;
5. Obligations of the Dominion of Canada and Canadian provincial and municipal bonds meeting specified tests of debt-to-property value;
6. World Bank bonds;

[9]A convenient reference on New York and other states is provided in *Encyclopedia of Banking Laws.* Boston: The Banking Law Journal, 1964, with Supplements.

7. Mortgages on improved real property in New York State up to 75% of the appraised value of residential and business property, up to $25,000 or 90% of the appraised value of one- or two-family owner-occupied residences, to a maturity of 30 years on an amortized basis;

8. Mortgages on unimproved real property in New York State to 50% of appraised value, with certain limitations;

9. Conventional mortgages meeting New York State requirements secured by property outside the state, to 20% of the bank's assets;

10. Insured FHA and VA-guaranteed mortgages, if $20,000 is guaranteed.

11. Bonds of railroad, electric, gas, and telephone companies that meet specified tests of interest coverage and of debt in relation to net worth;

12. Consolidated debenture bonds of the Federal Land Banks, Federal Home Loan Banks, and Federal Intermediate Credit Banks, and bonds of the Federal National Mortgage Association;

13. Stock in a Federal Reserve Bank and a Federal Home Loan Bank in the amount required for membership;

14. Stock of New York State housing corporations under certain conditions;

15. Obligations of various New York State revenue authorities;

16. Preferred stocks showing specified coverage of fixed charges plus preferred dividends;

17. Common stocks listed on registered exchanges that have 10-year dividend records.

The maximum proportion of total assets that may be invested in certain of the preceding groups is as follows: real estate mortgages, 75% (exclusive of FHA-insured and VA-guaranteed mortgages); railroad obligations, 25%; electric and gas bonds, 25%; telephone bonds, 25%; real estate (for transaction of business), 25% of surplus; housing projects, 15% (or 50% of surplus). The limitations on investment in stocks are indicated below.

In two states (Maryland and Delaware), the "prudent man" investment rule applies. Theoretically, this permits broad discretion away from a legal list. In fact, however, even in these states strict policies still apply.

Actual investment policy   During World War II, Federal obligations became the banks' most important investment; at the end of 1945, these comprised 63% of total assets. With the expansion of residential building in the 1950s, 1960s, and early 1970s, a great move out of Government securities and into the higher-yielding mortgages took place, so that at the end of 1976 the banks held only $5.8 billion of Treasury obligations, or less than 5% of their combined assets. The emphasis has been on short- and medium-term maturities to provide the liquidity needed to offset the growing emphasis on mortgages.

Although mutual savings banks pay the same Federal income tax rate as other corporations (on income after approved reserves for losses), tax-free state and local government bonds have played a minor role as investments. At the end of 1976, their total was only $2.4 million or 2% of combined total assets. Holdings of corporate bonds have increased moderately in the postwar period, comprising $26.4 billion or about 20% of total assets at the end of

1976. The banks vary their investment in these securities with the demand for mortgage loans. (See Chapter 5.)

At the end of 1976 savings banks held $82 billion of mortgages (net after reserves), comprising 61% of their total assets. This reflects the great demand for housing credit, relatively attractive yields on mortgages, the liberalization of rules governing mortgage investments such as increases in loan-to-value ratios, the growth of out-of-state lending, and the appeal of FHA-insured and VA-guaranteed liens, of which banks are the largest owners.

A startling change in the principles of savings bank investment policy took place in 1952 when banks domiciled in New York were permitted to purchase common stocks. The holdings of stocks must be kept to a very modest level (one-third of surplus and undivided profits or 3% of assets, whichever is less), and must meet high qualifications of marketability and earnings.[10] The purpose of this change was to increase the earnings of the banks at a time when interest rates were low and dividend yields were high, a situation that no longer prevails. The purchase of common stock by mutual savings banks was also given impetus in 1951 by the imposition of income taxation. Dividends (with their 85% exemption) took on special appeal. Despite this advantage and the liberalization of state laws, at the end of 1976 corporate stocks totalled only $4.4 billion or 3% of total assets.

The limited liquidity required of savings banks is obtained through modest cash balances and holdings of high-grade marketable bonds. (See Chapter 5.) Safety is also fostered by deposit insurance. As of June 30, 1976, 331 or 70% of the 473 savings banks were members of the Federal Deposit Insurance Corporation; all of the others participated in special state deposit insurance systems.

Summary of investment requirements   The savings bank's liabilities are longer-term and less volatile than those of the commercial bank; hence, less emphasis is placed on liquidity and more on income. Their portfolio emphasizes longer-term bond issues, along with amortized real estate loans. Like commercial banks, they are taxed at corporate rates. Nevertheless, municipal bonds have played an unimportant role in their investment policy.

The larger banks are able to manage their own investment affairs. Smaller organizations obtain freedom from care by more emphasis on Government bonds and by using investment services. Like commercial banks, protection of depositors against inflation is unnecessary, so that substantial investment in equities is not necessary or permitted.

Investments of Savings and Loan Associations

General investment characteristics   The general nature of savings and loan associations was indicated in Chapter 5. We saw that their major functions are to act as a location for savings, and to lend on home mortgages.

---

[10]Including preferred stocks, the restrictions become one-half of surplus and undivided profits or 5% of assets, whichever is lower. Investments in the stock of one corporation are limited to 2% of the outstanding shares of the company and to 1% of the assets of the bank.

At the end of 1976, funds aggregating $336 billion were "deposited" in the savings and loan associations throughout the United States. Their assets must be sound. However, because the association does not accept demand deposits, the need for liquidity is not so urgent as in the case of commercial banks. Loans from regional Federal Home Loan Banks are available to take up variations in cash flow.

Actual investment policy   The combined statement of all associations, showing the breakdown of assets by major classes of investments at the end of 1976, is given in Chapter 5. Mortgages comprised 82% of total assets. The bulk of these were amortized conventional loans on one- to four-family housing units, resulting from the associations emphasis or local lending at high loan-to-value ratios. The associations' share of the national total of home loans reached 47% at the end of 1976.

Principal and interest on conventional loans to finance new single-family properties are paid in monthly installments, with maturities ranging from 15 to 30 years, at interest rates (1977) averaging about 9%. The loan-to-value ratio now runs as high as 95%—substantially higher than is allowed on most conventional loans by banks and life insurance companies. Although the maturities of individual home mortgages are long, the turnover of the mortgage portfolio is about 15 1/2% a year, arising from the steady amortization of loans. Loans to finance existing homes, and to provide interim construction financing, usually bear a lower loan-to-value ratio (up to 80%) with maturities of 15 to 20 years.

In recent years the mortgage lending powers of savings and loan associations have been expanded to include loans on multifamily and commercial properties and mobile homes, loans for home repair and modernization, and loans for acquisition and development of residential land. As of the end of 1976, $62.2 billion or 19% of mortgages held were for multifamily and commercial purposes. The lending powers of associations have also been extended beyond their immediate areas through use of correspondents and through participations in first mortgage loans held by other institutions. Of the $90 billion of mortgage loans made in 1976, $12.7 billion or 14% were for one- to four-family home construction, $44.7 billion or 50% for home purchases, and $32.4 billion or 36% for all other purposes.[11]

In addition to qualified mortgages, associations can invest in Government obligations and those of certain Federal agencies, and (since 1964) Federally chartered firms may acquire the four top grades of state and municipal bonds. Treasury bonds are held for liquidity; their proportion of total assets has run around 5 to 6% in recent years, with emphasis on short and intermediate maturities to offset the long maturities of the mortgage portfolio. At the end of 1976, cash and U.S. Government bonds totalled $35.7 billion or 9% of total assets.

Secondary markets   The concentration of investments in mortgages might appear to be dangerous to the solvency of savings and loan associa-

---

[11]United States League of Savings Associations, *Fact Book,* 1977.

tions. But the type of loans made, the amortization feature, and the availability of a secondary market all contribute to soundness. This secondary market exists in insurance companies and in the Federal agencies which stand ready, as in the case of the Federal Home Loan Banks, to lend on mortgages or, as in the case of the Federal National Mortgage Association, to buy them. The latter organization, privately owned, was formed for the purpose of establishing and maintaining a market for mortgages on homes, including large-size housing projects, insured by the Federal Housing Administration and the Veterans' Administration. "Fannie Mae" is also empowered to provide a secondary market for conventional mortgages, as is the Federal Home Loan Morgtage Corporation. The Government National Mortgage Association ("Ginnie Mae") is an instrumentality of the U.S. Government operating within the U.S. Department of Housing and Urban Development. It buys mortgages and also provides an indirect secondary market by guaranteeing securities backed by FHA and VA mortgage loans.[12]

Summary of investment requirements Savings and loan associations need less liquidity than savings banks. The legal and economic character of their "deposit" accounts permits a very heavy concentration in mortgages. Normal cash requirements are light, and need for adequate and stable income predominates. Loans from the Federal Home Loan Banks help to fill the seasonal and cyclical cash requirements. Security investments are almost exclusively Federal obligations, which are generally short- and medium-term maturities to support the small cash balance. Legal regulations are liberal, and income taxation presents no problem because, after "dividends," earnings go largely into authorized reserves and make taxes nominal. No inflation hedge is required for the protection of creditors.

The chief problem of the associations in recent times has been to attract deposits in competition with other types of depositaries. Rates on passbook savings as high as 5 1/2% were being offered in 1977; rates as high as 7 3/4% were paid on term deposits. To pay such rates, high yields on mortgage investments are necessary. Under such conditions, maintenance of quality in the mortgage portfolio places severe demands on management.

REFERENCES

AMERICAN BANKERS ASSOCIATION, *The Commercial Banking Industry*, a monograph prepared for the Commission on Money and Credit. Englewood Cliffs, N.J.: Prentice-Hall, Inc., 1962.

———, *The Role of Investments in Bank Asset Management*. New York: The Association, 1965.

AMERICAN SAVINGS AND LOAN INSTITUTE, *Lending Principles and Practices*. Chicago: American Savings and Loan Institute Press, 1971.

BRADLEY, S. P., and D. B. CRANE, *Management of Bank Portfolios*. New York: John Wiley and Sons, 1975.

[12]See Chapters 6 and 12 for further discussion of FNMA, GNMA, and FHLMC.

CROSSE, H. D., and G. H. HEMPEL, *Management Policies for Commercial Banks*, 2d ed. Englewood Cliffs, N.J.: Prentice-Hall, Inc. 1973.

DOUGALL, H. E., and J. E. GAUMNITZ, *Capital Markets and Institutions*, 3d ed., Chapters 2, 3. Englewood Cliffs, N.J.: Prentice-Hall, Inc., 1975.

HAYES, D. A., *Bank Lending Policies*. Ann Arbor, Mich.: Graduate School of Business Administration, University of Michigan, 1971.

HEMPEL, G. H., and J. B. YAWITZ, *Financial Management of Financial Institutions*. Englewood Cliffs, N.J.: Prentice-Hall, Inc., 1976.

HENNING, C. N., W. PIGOTT, and R. H. SCOTT, *Financial Markets and the Economy*. Englewood Cliffs, N.J.: Prentice-Hall, Inc., 1975.

HESTER, D. D., and J. L. PIERCE, *Bank Management and Portfolio Behavior*. New Haven, Conn.: Yale University Press, 1975.

HODGMAN, D. R., *Commercial Bank Loan and Investment Policy*. Champaign, Ill.: University of Illinois Bureau of Business Research, 1963.

Institutional Investor Study Report of the Securities and Exchange Commission, Supplementary Volume I, Chapter 5. 92d Congress, 1st Session, House Document No. 92–64. Washington: U.S. Govt. Printing Office, 1971.

KENDALL, L. T., *The Savings and Loan Business: Its Purpose, Functions, and Economic Justification*, a monograph prepared for the Commission on Money and Credit. Englewood Cliffs, N.J.: Prentice-Hall, Inc., 1962.

KLAMAN, S. B., *The Postwar Residential Mortgage Market*. Princeton, N.J.: Princeton University Press, 1961.

NATIONAL ASSOCIATION OF MUTUAL SAVINGS BANKS, *Mutual Savings Banking: Basic Characteristics and Role in the National Economy*, a monograph prepared for the Commission on Money and Credit. Englewood Cliffs, N.J.: Prentice-Hall, Inc., 1962.

NICOLS, ALFRED, *Management and Control in the Mutual Savings and Loan Association*. Lexington, Mass.: D.C. Heath & Co., 1972.

PROCHNOW, H. V., and R. A. FOULKE, *Practical Bank Credit*, 2d rev. ed. New York: Harper & Row, Publishers, 1963.

REED, E. W., *Commercial Bank Management*. New York: Harper & Row, Publishers, 1963.

ROBINSON, R. I., *The Management of Bank Funds*, 2d ed. New York: McGraw-Hill, Inc., 1962.

——, and D. WRIGHTSMAN, *Financial Markets: the Accumulation of Wealth*. New York: McGraw-Hill, Inc., 1974.

WELFING, WELDON, *Bank Investments*. New York: American Bankers Association, American Institute of Banking, 1963.

Institutional Investors: Trustees, Endowments, Life Insurance Companies, Pension Plans

Trustee Investments

Nature of a trust A *trust* involves the passing of title to property by deed or will (the estate) from an owner (the settlor—or testator, in the case of a trust created by will) who creates the trust, to a trustee who is to hold the property for the benefit of another, the beneficiary. The trust principle has many applications. We are concerned here with trusts designed to produce income for the beneficiary, who may be the trustor or another person or persons. The relationship between the trustee and the beneficiaries is strictly fiduciary, and involves the highest degree of good faith and fidelity on the part of the trustee and of confidence on the part of the creator and the beneficiary.

Trusts are created for a wide variety of purposes—to support dependents, to educate children, to support educational or charitable organizations, to manage pension and profit-sharing plans, to relieve the creator of the burden of management of funds, and many others. Any legally competent person may set up a trust by an agreement setting forth the identity of the trustee or trustees, the manner in which the funds shall be invested, the distribution of the income from the estate, and the disposition of any principal to the remainderman when the trust terminates.

Types of personal trust A trust created by will and which becomes effective upon the death of the testator is a *testamentary* trust. *A living* or *inter vivos* trust is created by deed or declaration and becomes effective during the life of the maker who may even designate himself as the beneficiary. The trust may be revocable or irrevocable. In a *life insurance trust*, the body of the trust consists of life insurance policies on the life of the creator, the proceeds of which are payable to a trustee when due. The purpose is to relieve the dependents of the responsibility of investing and possibly mismanaging substantial sums of money. As an alternative, the funds may be left with the insurance company and distributed under various settlement options, or the proceeds may be made payable to the estate of the insured and pass into a testamentary trust created under his will.

Corporate trustees   Although individuals may be named as trustees, the responsibilities of the trust function and the growing complexity of security and property management have influenced a trend toward the appointment of banks or trust companies as trustees. State banks have long been permitted under special state laws to act as trustees and to engage in other fiduciary activities. National banks received this right in 1918, but not until they were given perpetual existence in 1972 was it practical for them to engage in trust activities. Most large state and national commercial banks have trust departments that perform a wide variety of functions for individuals and corporations. Trust companies as such were originally formed to act as incorporated trustees, but in most states they are now permitted by law to perform all the functions of a bank. Today, few trust companies are without banking powers.

The corporate trustee offers a number of advantages over the individual trustee:

Perpetual existence   Continuous administration of a trust is important because the trust may extend over a long period of years, and because the interruption of the performance of trust duties, say, by the death of an individual trustee, involves legal and accounting complications, as well as possible changes in investment policy.

Financial responsibility   The corporate trustee, with its substantial resources, strict regulation, and segregation of trust assets, provides financial assurance that most individual trustees cannot offer.

Business responsibility   A trust institution prospers only if it provides satisfactory service, and so it has a compelling incentive to efficiency and aggressiveness in caring for the trust that an individual trustee may not have.

Specialization   The bank or trust company is experienced in the handling of trust business. It also offers the services of specialists in a large department as well as the ancillary facilities of the banking department.

For some years the Comptroller of the Currency has revealed the size and composition of the assets for which the trust departments of national banks have investment responsibility, both as trustees and agents. Since 1968 the Comptroller has joined in measuring the trust department assets of all commercial banks. As of the end of 1975, these totalled $397 billion, of which $305 billion were in trust. The composition of the aggregate figures in shown in Table 22-1.

Legal restrictions on trust investments   The investment policy of the trustee is governed by the instructions, if any, in the trust instrument. If investment powers are not specified, the trustee is restricted to investments permitted by the laws of the state of domicile. The instrument itself may designate the types of securities to be purchased or may impose restrictions. Or it may provide for discretionary powers authorizing the trustee to buy any securities he wishes, subject only to the exercise of prudent judgment. A fourth alternative is the restriction to specific securities turned over at the inception of the trust or to be purchased by the trustee. Testamentary trusts must provide the greatest flexibility in investment policy so that the trustee may fit the trust to the needs of the beneficiaries and under changing conditions obtain reasonable income commensurate with safety. A trust must also provide the trustee with adequate power of sale and purchase.

State laws governing trust investment are far from uniform. In some the legal list is strictly defined by a state board or commission. In others only the general qualifications of "legals" are set forth. In most states, however, the laws have been liberalized or court decisions have been rendered to permit the trustee to buy any securities, subject only to the prudent man rule first set forth in Massachusetts over a century ago:

"All that can be required of a trustee to invest is that he shall conduct himself faithfully and exercise a sound discretion. He is to observe how men of prudence, discretion, and intelligence manage their own affairs, not in regard to speculation, but in regard to the permanent disposition of their funds, considering the probable income, as well as the probable safety of the capital to be invested."[1]

A modern statement of the prudent man rule is: "To make such investments and only such investments as a prudent man would make of his own property having primarily in view the preservation of the estate and the amount and regularity of the income to be derived.[2]

Prior to 1950, New York State represented an example of the "legal list" type of statute. Trust investment was limited, with certain minor exceptions, to the same kinds of securities and mortgages in which savings banks of New York State were authorized to invest, unless other forms of investments were specifically sanctioned by the trustor. In 1950, New York followed the lead of 24 other states, including Illinois, California, and Massachusetts, in adopting, in part at least, the "prudent man" rule. This gave a considerable impetus to the use of common stocks for trust investment. As of 1976, the rule had been adopted in some 45 states. Today, large banks are rarely restricted by "legal lists."[3]

Distribution of trust investments With the exception of Massachusetts and a few other states where equities have been looked upon with favor for many years, the traditional attitude of trustees toward common stocks was that they lacked the stability of income and market value required in a trust fund. The trend toward the prudent man rule and greater holdings of stocks is explained by three factors: (1) the low yields traditionally derived from high-grade bonds and other legals, (2) the rise in the cost of living and the need for protecting the principal and income of the fund from the effects of inflation, and (3) the assumption that in the long run a well-selected list of common stocks will provide greater income than high-grade bonds, where both cash income from dividends and change in market value are included in the concept of "total return." None of these influences has had much validity since 1965. Bond yields have been much higher—at times phenomenally higher—while yields on stocks in general have remained low. A sub-

---

[1]*Harvard College v. Amory*, 9 Pickering 446 (1830).

[2]A. W. Scott, et al., *Restatement of Law of Trusts*, Section 227.

[3]For detailed information on the size, growth, operations, legal environment, and compensation of bank trustees see *Institutional Investors Study Report of the Securities and Exchange Commission*, Chapter V. 92d Congress, 1st Session, House Document No. 92–64, March 1971.

stantial improvement in stock prices will be necessary to restore faith in the "total return" concept.

The New York State law permits fiduciaries to invest up to 35% of restricted trust funds in "such securities as would be acquired by prudent men of discretion and intelligence in such matters who are seeking a reasonable income and the preservation of their capital." Subject to the interpretation of prudence, funds may be placed in bonds not on the legal list, as well as in preferred and common stocks of domestic corporations. Except for bank and insurance company stocks, only those common stocks fully listed on a national securities exchange may be considered.

The distribution of the market value of assets of trust departments of insured commercial banks over which investment responsibility is exercised is shown in Table 22-1. Employee benefit funds, being free from income taxes, include no state and local government bonds, so that they account for the bulk of the corporate bonds held. The large proportion of trust assets represented by common stocks reflects (1) a changing attitude toward the appropriateness of such assets by trustees and by their clients, and (2) the rise in the market values of stocks until recent years.

TABLE 22-1 Distribution of Assets of Insured Commercial
            Bank Trust Departments, December 31, 1975
            (in billions of dollars)

	Amount	Per Cent
Cash assets	$ 16.6	4.2%
U.S. Govt. and agency securities	36.1	9.1
Municipal securities	23.9	6.0
Other bonds	71.4	18.0
Common stocks	214.4	54.0
Preferred stock	5.4	1.4
Mortgages	7.1	1.8
Other assets	22.3	5.5
	$397.2	100.0%

Source: Board of Governors of the Federal Reserve System, Federal Deposit Insurance Corporation, and Office of the Comptroller of the Currency, *Trust Assets of Insured Commercial Banks—1975* (Washington, D.C.: U.S. Government Printing Office, 1977). Agency and advisory accounts ($92 billion) are included.

At the end of 1972, total holdings of bank trustees stood at $404 billion, with common stocks of $277 billion. The decline in 1974 to $325 and $168 billion, respectively, reflects the extreme break in stock prices in 1973–1974, which even the professional managers of trust portfolios were unable to anticipate. The year 1975 showed substantial increases in most assets, especially common stocks.

At the end of 1975, $239 billion, or 60% of total bank trust assets, were held in five states, $123 billion in New York alone. The investment policies and portfolios of the New York trustees are followed with international interest.

Such aggregate figures are, however, quite misleading. There is a wide diversity of trust investment policy, ranging from the very conservative to the aggressive. Some trust accounts are wholly invested in common stocks. The new concept of "prudence" is not so much risk avoidance as the construction of an investment account that will meet the necessary objectives, assume as much risk as is appropriate, and achieve a risk-reward relationship that is suitable for the particular situation, with much attention to protection of purchasing power.

Fiduciaries are still limited by a long line of court decisions, precedents, and experience that cause them to select mainly seasoned high-grade stocks with long dividend records and above-average market stability. Trustees are still obliged to exercise "prudent" care; but their ability to keep their funds productive has been enhanced by the expansion of the legal list and by increased powers of discretion. Some banks have allocated specific proportions of certain trust funds to "glamorous" common stocks that are speculative in the traditional sense. Such securities are, however, usually found in pension trusts rather than in individuals' accounts. Another recent development is the investment in shares of small business investment companies so as to allocate trust funds for "venture capital" purposes.

Common trusts   The handling of small trusts on a profitable basis while obtaining safety and diversification has long been a problem for trustees. Safety and liquidity may be obtained by restricting such funds to high-grade bonds, with emphasis on U.S. Government obligations. But such a policy sacrifices income and protection against inflation. Another alternative that is growing in favor is the use of the *common trust*, in which a number of trust funds are combined for purposes of economy, diversification, and efficiency of administration. Such consolidated funds are permitted by legislation or court decision in all 50 states. State banking institutions must operate common trusts in accordance with the laws of the state in which the bank is located; national banks must follow a uniform plan as laid down by the Board of Governors of the Federal Reserve System. The trust may not invest more than 10% of its assets in any single enterprise other than U.S. Government securities. Cash and readily marketable securities, defined as subject to frequent dealings in ready markets, should comprise about 40% of the trust. Participations and withdrawals are permitted only on quarterly valuation dates. Funds may not participate in a common trust if any assets in the trust are illegal for the fund to hold or if the trust agreement does not expressly sanction the arrangement.[4]

The common trust fund provides diversification and flexibility not otherwise obtainable in small trusts, as well as the possibility of a larger income. A survey of 481 funds, holding $9 billion in assets as of 1976, showed that $3.5 billion or 39% was invested in common stocks and convertible securi-

---

[4]For regulatory history, legal background, and management practices of common trust funds see *Institutional Investor Study Report of the S.E.C., op. cit.*, Chapter V, pp. 444–450. This source also reveals the investment performance of a large sample of pooled employee benefit trusts and common trust funds in the period 1960–1969. In the aggregate, the trusts showed a lower rate of return than the rate that would have been obtained by a hypothetical unmanaged portfolio having the same volatility. But many of them individually showed lower volatility.

ties, $2.4 billion or 26% in straight corporate bonds, $1.9 billion or 21% in municipal securities, $0.5 billion or 6% in U.S. Government and agency securities, and $0.8 billion or 8% in cash assets, mortgages, and other assets. But the proportions varied among the four main types of funds: (1) 175 common stock funds with $2.5 billion in assets, almost all common stocks and convertibles; (2) 88 diversified (balanced) funds with $1.4 billion in assets, of which 70% was common stock and convertibles and 22% straight corporate bonds; (3) 160 income funds with $3.1 billion in assets of which only 8% was in "equity securities"; and (4) 58 tax-exempt funds whose assets of $1.9 billion were almost all municipal bonds.[5] Total assets of all common trusts ran about $21 billion in 1976, including about $7 billion in common stocks[6].

Investment procedure The investment policy of a trustee is complicated by the fact that the wishes of two and often three parties must be respected—the trustor, the present beneficiaries (*life tenants*) entitled to the income, and the ultimate beneficiaries (*remaindermen*) who will receive the principal at the expiration of the trust. The present beneficiaries desire as high a rate of income as might reasonably be expected, and their best interests may not be served if the trustees buy only the very safest securities, with a relatively low rate of return. On the other hand, the trustee must be mindful of the ultimate beneficiaries who are entitled to the principal of the fund as nearly intact as conservative stewardship can preserve it, plus protection against inflation. Between the opposing viewpoints, the trustee must steer a middle course. Because ultimate safety of principal is paramount, however, he must go below medium-grade issues only rarely and should prefer the higher-grade issues. In a market where the yield on the best grade long-term corporate bonds is about 8%, an average current rate of return of over 9% would be an unreasonable expectation from a conscientious trustee. But appreciation of principal could still be enjoyed.

Trustors often make restrictions that hamper the trustee. In some cases, he is required to hold certain securities which might better be sold. In other cases, he is not given the power to purchase securities which in his judgment would be appropriate.

Traditionally, the trustee was regarded as a conserver of capital, with little or no obligation to increase the value of a fund. The argument in favor of common stocks for trust accounts, at least until recent years, was twofold: (1) the eventual higher income that stocks often (but not always) produce in comparison with bonds, and (2) their inflation hedge possibilities. Under conditions that prevailed in the latter 1960s and the 1970s, these arguments lost much of their validity. Where the risk-taking permits, the duty of the trustee is to preserve purchasing power as well as dollars, but this responsibility must always be secondary to that of maintenance of dollar safety.

The high interest rates on bonds in the 1970s enabled trustees to enjoy good income and still preserve principal. Coupled with the discouraging

[5] *Trusts and Estates*, May 1977, pp. 314–323.
[6] *SEC Bulletin*, April 1977.

record of common stocks, this situation led to a very substantial switch out of equities. The trend would have been greater had it not been for trustees' reluctance to report realized capital losses.

Summary of investment requirements   Generalizations concerning the investment policy of trustees are difficult because of differences in trust size and requirements. Many variations in investment policy must be expected. Trust officers, by the very nature of their fiduciary position, must always lean to the conservative side.

The importance of diversification depends on the size of the fund and the requirements of the case. As we have seen, the common trust fund has been developed to provide diversity for smaller estates. Tax status is very important for larger funds. And especially in large discretionary accounts, protection against inflation is sought through investment in equities including common stocks, convertible securities, and real estate. Legality must always be strictly observed, but the spread of the prudent man doctrine has released trustees from strict adherence to the specific legal lists.

Bank agency accounts   Although banks are not permitted to operate mutual funds as such, they have become increasingly active in the management of agency and advisory accounts. In the case of agency accounts, the trust department holds the clients' securities and has an agreed amount of responsibility for investment decisions. In the case of advisory accounts, the bank has the status of an investment counsel. Both types of accounts can be terminated by the investor.

In neither of these accounts does the bank serve as trustee. Title to the assets remains with the investor. And the bank is not restricted by regulations governing trust investments. Because individual portfolios vary widely, depending on the investors' preferences, there are highly aggressive common stock portfolios, balanced portfolios, and accounts invested in high-grade bonds, so that generalizations on investment policy are not possible. Performance results are similarly varied.

Investments of Endowments and Foundations

The endowed funds of charitable, religious, and educational institutions are administered by trustees who are limited by their fiduciary responsibility and by the provisions of specific grants. But "fiduciary responsibility" is an elastic concept. The trustees generally enjoy considerable flexibility in managing the portfolio, and their policies range from strict preservation of principal with a safe return to maximization of income.

The typical endowment fund needs little liquidity, or marketability, save where a portion of principal is to be currently used. The traditional investment policy of most college and university endowment trustees or managers emphasized bonds, preferred stocks, and mortgages, to achieve safety of income and principal. And income included only current cash interest, dividends, and rents. But in recent years, there has been a decided shift toward common stocks, so that these now comprise as much as 80% of some portfolios; other portfolio managers still adhere to the more historically orthodox investment ratios.

The rising costs of college operation, the decline in the ratio of endowment income to total income, and the threat of continued inflation have led the trustees of a number of institutions to a more aggressive investment policy.

The emphasis on preservation of dollars of capital and current income gave way to the goal of maximized earnings as measured by total return (income plus or minus changes in market value, realized or unrealized).

This trend was stimulated by a very critical report from the Ford Foundation in 1969.[7] The report concluded, in general, that: (1) The investment record of endowment management had been poor. (2) The time-honored distinction between income and capital appreciation should be abandoned, and trustees should seek, within clearly defined risk limits, to maximize *total* return. (3) Total return should be figured as mutual funds measure their total performance, namely, by calculating the percentage of income plus appreciation to beginning market value. (4) The portfolios should be put on a unit basis, that is, the total should be divided into a number of units and the value of each unit calculated at regular intervals, and as new funds are received. This would enable a comparison with other endowments and with the performance of mutual funds. (5) Trustees should set the general investment policy, including a desired rate of total return and the risk to be assumed, but employ professional investment management to operate the fund (a practice already followed by some institutions). (6) Moneys that may have to be used within, say, five years should be invested in short-term obligations. (7) The bulk of the list should consist of growth stocks, save for some bonds held as a reserve against periods of distress. (8) A certain percentage of market value should be moved over to income each year.

The high yields on bonds, especially in 1969–1971 and 1973–1975, and the generally flat *secular* price record of common stocks in 1966–1976 cast considerable doubt on the feasibility of the growth stock and total return approach, except over the very long run. The 1960s and 1970s did not produce the 8 or 9% overall return from stock that had been achieved in previous long periods. By early 1977, with Aa corporate bonds yielding 8 1/4% and income stocks from 6 to 9%, aggressive portfolio management that emphasized growth stocks lost much of its appeal.

The advice to move a certain percentage of market value over to income in each year was based on the firm assumption that a substantial secular rise in stock values was assured. The colleges which adopted this policy beginning in the latter 1960s had not anticipated the depreciation in the daily market averages of the 40 to 50% in 1973–1974. The concept of using total return to determine spendable income received a rude blow.

Exact figures on the amount and composition of college and university

---

[7] *The Ford Foundation Advisory Committee on Endowment Management, Managing Educational Endowments* (New York: The Foundation, 1969). A second edition appeared in 1972.

endowments are not available. An estimate for 1976 was $16.1 billion, of which common stock comprised $10.4 billion or 64%.[8] As of March 1977, 454 institutions, each with portfolios worth more than $3 million, had assets totalling $15.2 billion.[9]

In recent years a number of smaller endowments have been pooled under professional management. The New York-based Common Fund organization offers three separate funds—equity, bond, and short-term. About 30 institutions were participating in 1977.

In addition to college endowments, many thousands of nonprofit foundations are established for a variety of social, educational, and charitable activities. The Patman Committee Study of the 1968 annual reports of 20,616 private foundations showed market value of assets at $29 billion. The Securities and Exchange Commission found that at the end of 1976 foundations had assets of $38.6 billion, of which 26.6 billion or 69% was in common stocks.[10]

Investment requirements of foundations differ widely. In some cases, only the income is spent, and as this (including capital appreciation) varies through time, so does the payout in support of beneficiaries. In other cases, steady income is essential to meet commitments. In some instances, liquidity is important; in others, immediate recovery of principal is not required. The degree of risk assumed depends on purpose and management philosophy. Taxes are not a problem.

Life Insurance Company Investments

Scope of the industry   The life insurance company is the most important single type of savings institution. At the end of 1976, the domestic legal-reserve life companies had combined assets of $322 billion. The growth of the life insurance company group is indicated in Table 22-2. The "life insurance industry" is no longer an accurate designation in view of the growth of health insurance and corporate pensions in the activities of the "life" companies. The following discussion will, however, stress the life insurance aspects of the industry.

At the end of 1976, life insurance companies owned less than 1% of the Federal debt, 5% of domestic state and municipal bonds, 34% of domestic corporate bonds outstanding, and 10% of all mortgages outstanding. Their assets are currently growing at the rate of over $30 billion per year.

At the beginning of 1977, 51% of life insurance in force was accounted for by mutual companies, owned by the policyholders and managed by directors elected by them. The balance was outstanding from stock companies operated for their owners like other corporations. Most of the insurance sold by mutuals

---

[8]*S.E.C. Statistical Bulletin.*
[9]*Barron's,* April 18, 1977.
[10]*S.E.C. Statistical Bulletin.*

TABLE 22-2 Selected Data on Life Insurance Companies
(in millions of dollars)

Year Ending	Total Assets	Policy Reserves	Total Income	Life Insurance in Force in U.S.
1950	$ 64,020	$ 54,946	$11,337	$ 234,168
1955	90,432	75,359	16,544	372,332
1960	119,576	98,473	23,007	586,448
1965	158,884	127,620	33,167	900,554
1970	207,254	167,556	49,054	1,079,821
1976	321,552	259,166	83,558	2,530,767

Source: American Council of Life Insurance, *Life Insurance Fact Book* (annual).

and much of the stock company business is the participating type in which the policyholders share in the net earnings of the company through rebates or "dividends."

Sources of funds for investment   The funds available for investment by life insurance companies are derived from three principal sources: (1) premium income over and above that portion allocated to cover expenses and current payments on policies, (2) net income from the existing investment portfolio, and (3) maturing principal of mortgages, term loans, and bonds. Total cash flow for investment purposes runs over $25 billion annually from the net inflows from insurance after payment of benefits, and from net investment income.

As indicated in Chapter 4, most life insurance policies require an annual premium that is more than sufficient in the earlier years to meet death losses. The excess is represented by a policy reserve to cover claims in later years when the annual premium is insufficient. This reserve is accumulated at a rate of interest specified in the insurance contract. The investment requirement is to earn this rate, maintain sufficient liquidity to meet death claims and withdrawal or borrowing of the reserve, and produce a surplus. Under conditions in the 1970s, in the industry as a whole, companies were earning substantially more than this rate.

If the premium payments plus the income on investments exceed death claims and expenses and the necessary additions to reserves, a surplus arises which may be distributed to the holders of participating policies or, in the case of stock companies, to the stockholders.

Factors determining investment policy   The nature of the life insurance business requires a conservative yet somewhat flexible investment policy determined by the following factors: (1) The liabilities are essentially long-term, thus permitting investment in longer-term, less marketable issues with attractive rates of return. (2) The steady cash flow from premium payments based on actuarial calculations, investment income, and redemption of securities and mortgages provides liquidity adequate for death claims and for emergency needs arising from a sudden demand for policy loans. (3)

Because the timing and amount of life insurance benefits can be predicted with considerable accuracy, the need of liquidity is further reduced. (4) The "guaranteed" rates of earnings which help to determine life insurance policy costs are modest, and higher earnings from less-than-Aaa investments can be passed along to holders of participating policies in "dividends," and to the shareholders of stock companies. (5) The ultimate safety required for the protection of policyholders requires investments that meet high standards; diversification is also a means of protecting against losses of principal. (6) Actuarial commitments require the companies to remain fully invested save for working cash balances. (7) Since contracts are in terms of dollars, inflation hedging through investments is unnecessary, save to offset higher operating costs. (8) Strict rules of valuation of assets and regulation of permitted assets must be observed.

Regulation of investments   The public interest with which life insurance companies are vested, arising from their commitments to millions of policyholders and their role as savings institutions, requires strict regulation of operations in general and of investment policies in particular. The companies operate under 50 state charters and are regulated by the insurance commissioners of the various states in which they do business. Companies that operate on a national scale must comply, to some extent, with the investment laws of all states in which they operate. Thus, the requirements of the most stringent of these states determines the level of investment quality for the particular company. State regulation varies considerably, but in general runs as follows: (1) Federal and state government obligations are approved without limit; (2) bonds of municipalities in the state of domicile, and bonds of subdivisions in other states, must meet certain qualifications; (3) corporate bonds and direct business loans are restricted to the higher-grade issues—limitations are imposed with respect to the percentage of total assets so invested, as well as requirements for adequate earnings in relation to fixed charges; (4) first mortgages are generally approved, subject to certain limitations on the amount lent in relation to the value of the real estate mortgaged (from 60% to 90%); (5) common and preferred stocks are prohibited in a few states, and where permitted, are restricted to a small percentage of total assets, and strict asset and earnings standards are required; (6) investment in real estate, other than company-used property, is generally restricted, although most states now permit investment in rental housing, redevelopment projects, and certain types of commercial and industrial property, up to a modest percentage of total assets; (7) loans to policyholders equal to the reserve value of their respective policies are authorized in every jurisdiction.

Return on investments   Such provisions would appear to give life insurance companies sufficient flexibility and scope in their investment policy without any need to depart from the traditional forms of securities and other investment media. Although in recent years the earnings rate produced on investments has tended to increase, following closely the interest rates on U.S. Government securities and high-grade corporate bonds, it is still modest.

The net after-tax rate of return earned by U.S. life insurance investments on their aggregate mean ledger assets is shown in Table 22-3. The relatively high rates in the middle 1970s reflect the higher yields enjoyed on bonds, and the increasing investment in apartment and commercial mortgages. Although the "guaranteed" rate on life insurance policies has remained low, a much higher return is necessary to offset the greater risks involved in health insurance underwriting. In recent years the assumed interest rates in new policies have increased modestly. But they are still considerably below the average rate of return actually earned on operating assets, with resulting benefit to policyholders receiving "dividends" and to stockholders in stock companies, and as an offset to higher operating costs.

**TABLE 22-3 Net Rate of Return on Invested Assets
of Life Insurance Companies**

1950	3.13%	1972	5.56%
1955	3.51	1973	5.88
1960	4.11	1974	6.25
1965	4.61	1975	6.36
1970	5.30	1976	6.68

Source: American Council of Life Insurance, *Life Insurance Fact Book.*

Investment policy An examination of the assets of domestic life insurance companies indicates some significant changes in investment policy. Table 22-4 shows the breakdown of the assets of legal-reserve companies at the end of 1955, 1965, 1970, and 1976.

At the end of 1945, the investment in Federal securities totalled over $20 billion or nearly 46% of total assets. Life insurance companies subsequently reduced their holdings very substantially in order to provide more funds for business capital and mortgage financing and to improve their rate of earnings. At the end of 1976, the holdings of direct and agencies securities totalling $7.7 billion represented only 2.4% of life insurance company assets. The emphasis was on intermediate- and long-term maturities.

Holdings of domestic state and local government bonds actually declined after 1960, and at the end of 1976 comprised only 1.7% of total assets. With the increase in yields on taxable bonds, tax-free municipals have become less attractive to the insurance companies, which pay income taxes at only a 20% to 25% rate. Nearly three-fourths of the domestic municipals held by life insurance companies were revenue bonds; these offered very attractive yields and generally long maturities. Canadian local and provincial bonds became very attractive in the mid-1970s, owing to their high yields.

Corporate bonds remained a very important element in the total portfolio —over $120 billion in 1976. Life insurance companies are the largest institutional holders; they owned (1976) 34% of all domestic corporate bonds outstanding. Although no industry data on their bonds' quality are published,[11] the average is likely to be A or slightly lower. Ability to diversify

[11]The recent *Life Insurance Fact Books* do not show the major categories of corporate bonds.

TABLE 22-4 Assets of Legal-Reserve Life Insurance Companies (in billions of dollars)

Assets	1955 Amt.	1965 Amt.	1965 Per Cent	1970 Amt.	1976 Amt.	1976 Per Cent
Bonds						
U.S. Govt. and agency	$ 8.6	$ 5.3	3.3%	$ 4.5	$ 7.7	2.4%
Domestic municipal	2.0	3.5	2.2	3.3	5.4	1.7
Foreign government	1.2	2.8	1.8	3.2	7.0	2.2
Corporate[a]						
Railroad	3.9	3.3	2.1⎫			
Utility	14.0	17.0	10.7⎬	73.1⎫	120.9	37.5
Industrial and misc.	18.2	38.3	24.1⎭	⎬		
Total bonds	$47.9	$ 70.2	44.2%	$84.1	$141.0	43.8%
Mortgages						
Farm	2.3	4.8	3.0	5.6	7.4	2.3
Residential	18.0	31.2	19.7	26.7	35.3	11.0
Commercial and other	9.1	24.0	15.1	42.1	48.8	15.2
Total mortgages	$29.4	60.0	37.8%	74.4	$ 91.5	28.4%
Preferred stocks	1.7	2.9	1.8	3.5	8.6	2.7
Common stocks	1.9	6.2	3.9	11.9	25.7	8.0
Real estate	2.6	4.7	3.0	6.3	10.5	3.3
Policy loans	3.3	7.7	4.8	16.1	25.8	8.0
Cash and misc.	3.7	7.2	4.5	10.9	18.5	5.7
Total assets	$90.4	$158.9	100.0%	$207.2	$321.6	100.0%

[a] Includes foreign bonds.
Source: American Council of Life Insurance. *Life Insurance Fact Book.*

and the pressure for competitive returns act against the necessity of a very high-grade bond portfolio. A large investment in utility bonds reflects the postwar expansion of the utilities industries, and the high investment status of utility bonds. This group has declined in relative importance, however, owing to even greater emphasis on industrial securities. Furthermore, most high-grade utility bonds are sold through competitive bidding in which insurance companies seldom participate.

The industrial bond group has shown a great absolute and relative increase. This reflects the substantial upgrading of investment quality enjoyed by manufacturing and commercial companies, and expansion of legal lists to include debts of industrial concerns that meet rather stringent earnings requirements. Life insurance companies acquire the bulk of such securities by direct placement. (See Chapter 3.)

The industrial bond category includes instruments that are not bonds in the technical sense. These are long-term notes representing direct lending, similar to, but with longer maturities than, bank term loans. Such financing permits the "tailoring" of loan arrangements to suit each particular situation and provides a vehicle for financing smaller concerns which do not have access to the bond market.

Real estate mortgages have always formed a significant segment of life insurance company investments, but their relative importance has changed greatly over the years. The low point was reached in 1946, when they accounted for less than 15% of total assets. Since that year, the great expansion in housing, a growing emphasis on multifamily, commercial, and industrial loans, and the more attractive yields on mortgages brought these investments to a record high in 1976. At the end of that year, life insurance companies were second only to commercial banks in their holdings of commercial and industrial mortgages ($49 billion or 29% of the national total), and they held $7.4 billion or 13% of total farm mortgages. The $91.5 billion total of all mortgages represented 28% of their total assets. High-grade mortgages are attractive to insurance companies because of their relatively attractive yields, their general ultimate safety, their long maturities, the constant turnover of principal through regular amortization, the variety of types available, and the use of mortgage company correspondents to gain geographical diversification.[12] The lack of high marketability is no problem. The specialized nature of mortgages is no obstacle to the company well equipped with trained staff, and a large part of the portfolio is acquired from mortgage banking companies that have done the preliminary screening.

A special influence that led to increases in commercial and industrial mortages was the high level of yields reached in the 1970s. To earn, say, 10%, special "kickers" such as a share in the profits, warrants, and other features have been attached to such liens.

Real estate investments include property used in operations, and, with rather strict legal limits, property held for income. Of particular interest is the ownership of commercial and industrial properties leased back to their users. The net return on such investments may run as high as 12%. Life insurance companies have also pioneered in construction and operation of large-scale housing projects.

Policy loans reach their highest levels during depressions, when they serve a useful purpose in helping to tide policyholders over periods of stress. That they do not vanish entirely in good times is indicated by the $25.8 billion outstanding at the end of 1976, reflecting the need for funds by policyholders in periods of high interest rates. Rates charged ran 6 to 8%.

Preferred stocks, which totaled $8.6 billion or 2.7% of total assets at the end of 1976, are attractive for their low-tax yields.

A notable development in recent years has been the increase in life company holdings of common stocks, which totalled $25.7 billion or 8% of industry assets at the end of 1976. Most states now permit the purchase of common stock by life insurance companies. New York-domiciled companies are allowed common stock investments up to 10% of admitted assets, or 100% of surplus, whichever is the smaller.[13] Since surplus is usually less than 10% of assets, the legal limit is provided by the surplus for most companies. Holdings of the common stock of any one corporation are limited to 1% of the life insurance company's assets and 5% of the issuing corporation's outstanding stock. To be eligible for insurance company investment, the stock must meet the following requirements: (1) The stock—except bank

[12]See Chapter 12 for additional discussion of mortgage loans by life insurance companies.

[13]Limitations on common stock holdings do not apply to segregated pension fund accounts.

and insurance company shares—must be listed on an exchange registered with the Securities and Exchange Commission; (2) dividends must have been paid for seven years prior to acquisition, and the company must have earned during such period an average annual rate of at least 4% of par or of the issue price; (3) all of the bonds and preferred stock, if any, of the issuer must be eligible for insurance company investment.

Much of the original appeal of common stocks grew from the need for a higher rate of return than bonds could earn, rather than for an inflation hedge. Modern stock yields are, however, much lower than those on bonds. (See Chapter 9.) An even greater problem is the need for adequate outlets for the vast sums being accumulated by the insurance companies. In each year, between $25 and $30 billion of new money needs to be invested, together with $100 to $110 billion of funds from maturing assets.[14] What shall be done with this money? High-grade corporate bonds are appropriate in character, and yield substantially more than Federal obligations. Housing financing has fallen off. (See Chapter 12.) Loans to business and investment in housing projects and commercial income-producing real estate offer high yields, but the managerial costs are high. Common stocks appear to offer intriguing possibilities for insurance investment, although since 1972 their volatility has made them suspect. The sharp decline in common stock assets from 1970 to 1976 is explained mainly by the write-down of holdings to market value.

A special reason for including common stocks in the investment portfolio is the growth of variable-annuity contracts which permit departure from a set actuarial return on the total contract and assume the risks of common stock investment in order to gain a higher total return. (See Chapter 4.) Net acquisitions of common stocks for all purposes were (1977) running about $2 billion per year.

As indicated in Chapter 30, the capital, surplus, and contingency reserves of life insurance companies are a small (as low as 9) per cent of total assets. This explains in part why long-run protection of principal is a major investment requirement.

Summary of investment requirements   Eventual recovery of principal, adequate yield, and only moderate liquidity are the keynotes of life insurance investment policy. Skilled management can be employed, and wide diversification enjoyed. Tax savings are important, but less so than for fully taxed institutions. Legality is of prime importance, and since the insurance obligations of the life insurance company are in terms of a definite number of dollars, a hedge against inflation is not necessary, save to offset higher operating costs. Inflation protection is, however, vital in the case of variable annuity and pension contracts.

---

[14]Common stocks are valued for reporting purposes at market price as of December 31. Government securities, as well as corporate bonds (if they are not in default), are carried on an amortized basis (adjusted each year so as to produce face value at maturity). For a detailed study of investment organization and portfolio management practices of life insurance companies with emphasis on their holdings of common stock, see *Institutional Investor Study Report of the S.E.C., op. cit.*, Chapter VI.

Uninsured Private Pension Funds

Investment policy   The great growth of corporate pension funds, now at a rate of $25 to $35 billion a year, was discussed in Chapter 4. At the end of 1976, $250 billion in market value of assets or reserves had been accumulated by these funds.

The investments of insured funds are commingled with those of company resources in general. The assets of uninsured private funds (including profit-sharing plans) are shown in Table 22-5. The figures are for all private pension funds, including the multiemployer plans and those of nonprofit organizations.

TABLE 22-5   Assets of Uninsured Private Pension Funds[a]
(in billions of dollars, at market value)

	1955	1965		1970	1976	
	Amt.	Amt.	Per Cent	Amt.	Amt.	Per Cent
Cash	$ 0.4	$ 0.9	1.2%	$ 1.8	$ 2.2	1.3%
U.S. Govt. and agency securities	2.9	3.6	4.9	3.9	14.9	8.5
Corporate bonds	⎱ 7.9	21.2	29.1	24.0	37.9	21.8
Preferred stocks	⎰ 6.1	0.8	1.1	1.6	1.2	0.7
Common stocks		40.0	54.8	65.5	108.5	62.4
(Own company)		(4.4)	(6.0)	(5.9)	[b]	[b]
(Other companies)		(35.6)	(48.8)	(59.6)	[b]	[b]
Mortgages	0.3	3.4	4.7	3.6	2.2	1.3
Other assets	0.7	3.0	4.1	4.3	7.0	4.0
Total	$18.3	$72.9	100.0%	$104.7	$173.9	100.0%

[a]Data may not add due to rounding.
[b]Not available.
Sources: Federal Reserve Bulletin (flow of funds) ; S.E.C. Statistical Bulletin.

The group figures hide differences in investment policy among individual funds. But taking the group as a whole, the shift into common stocks has been marked. At the end of 1976, these comprised 62%, at market value, of total assets. Liquidity, as represented by cash and Government securities, has declined in relative importance, as have corporate bonds, although the latter remain important. Mortgages are becoming attractive for their higher yields.

The return earned on the assets of a pension fund is very important. The generally upward trend of interest rates on corporate bonds, Government securities, and short-term investments (1973–1975), and the big decline in stock prices in 1973–1974, encouraged a switch to fixed-income securities and guaranteed-interest contracts with insurance companies.

This conservative policy was also greatly influenced by the Employment Retirement Income Security Act of 1974 (ERISA, see Chapter 4) which placed companies and fund managers or advisors in the status of "named fiduciaries." Each fiduciary must exercise his duties "with the care, skill, prudence, and diligence under the circumstances then prevailing that a prudent man acting in a like capacity and familiar with such matters would use in the conduct of an enterprise of a like character and with like aims."

The lack of clear-cut regulations under the Act, and its joint administration by the Labor and Treasury Departments, also produce uncertainities that have encouraged more conservative investments.

Other requirements of ERISA that contribute to a more cautious investment policy include:

- Fiduciaries must monitor investment performance regularly.
- Assets must be so diversified as to minimize large losses.
- Holdings of the employer's securities or real estate are generally limited to 10% of assets (with certain exceptions).
- In addition to the requirement of prudence, fiduciaries incur civil liability for engaging in specifically prohibited transactions.
- Reporting requirements may eventually require complete disclosure of portfolio assets.
- Funding of pension (not profit-sharing) obligations is required. Liquid funds must be available to pay benefits when required.

Investment principles Uninsured (trusteed) corporate and other private pension funds differ in size, type of management, whether they produce a fixed actuarial benefit, the proportions of company and employee contributions, vesting provisions, whether they include profit-sharing benefits, and in many other respects. Thus, it is difficult to generalize concerning appropriate investment policies, but the following discussion will apply to a majority of cases. The funds are usually in the hands of bank trustees as custodians and are invested within the framework of trust investment regulation; however, since the trust agreements usually provide for discretion, a wide latitude in policy is permitted. Many pension portfolios are managed by investment counsel firms, which sometimes share the fund and compete for the best performance. Others are internally self-managed.[15]

This partly explains much of the aggressiveness of financial management reaching for high returns in the late 1960s and early 1970s. This attitude extended to profit-sharing trusts as well as to funded pension funds. With high bond yields available in the latter 1970s, and in the light of the extreme suffering from the stock market decline of 1973–1974, many funds turned to high-grade bonds. A number of them added or substituted income-guaranteed contracts with insurance companies. Many nonactuarial plans have recently given participants the option to have their account balances invested in fixed-income or in equity portfolios. The investment requirements of uninsured plans follow.

Assurance of income has paramount importance. The reserves accumulated over the years are expected to grow through the compounding of income as well

[15]At the end of 1975 the investment management of the $146 billion of assets of private noninsured pension funds was distributed as follows: self-managed, 15%; banks and trust companies, 64%; broker-dealers, 2%; other investment advisers, 19%. *S.E.C. Statistical Bulletin*, November 1976, p. 553.

as through increased contributions. Where the benefits are computed actuarially as definite liabilities, certainty of income is especially vital. At the same time, yield should be maximized within the boundaries of sensible investments. A difference of one percentage point in average yield (say, an increase from 7 to 8%) can mean a difference of 25% in the size of the eventual accumulation or a reduction in corporate contributions.

Preservation of principal, or the avoidance of dollar loss, is important in the long run. Theoretically, temporary variations in the market value of the portfolio are not. And even these can be minimized through regular dollar-cost-averaging with the new receipts into the fund. But the necessity to report fund assets to beneficiaries at market value, and the increasing tendency to compare investment performance with that of mutual funds and other pension funds, has made investment managers much more sensitive to changes in securities prices. This attitude is due in large part to the great decline in both stock and bond prices in 1973–1974 and to the generally impressive investment record of funds in the 1970s.

Immediate recovery of principal is unimportant for most funds. In most cases, payments into the fund, together with earnings and proceeds of maturing bond issues, will exceed withdrawals for many years to come. Both retirement benefits and payments are subject to fairly predictable forecast. There is little compulsion to liquidate sound securities in unfavorable markets. Nevertheless, estimates of retirements are required to determine those periods when some liquidation of pension fund assets may be required, and investment policy adjusted accordingly, especially during periods of low market prices of securities.

Skilled management can be hired if it is not available at the company or through the trustee, in the person of investment counsel. For smaller funds, investment in mutual investment company shares can provide management for the major portion of the fund.

Diversification is available in all but the smallest funds, and these can obtain it individually through investment company shares or even in common trust funds. A good general principle is to stay out of the stock of the company itself. The employee has enough at stake in his job in the company without tying his retirement income to the fortunes of the same firm.

Tax considerations are unimportant. A properly drawn pension trust, in which the employer's contributions are irrevocably beyond company ownership and are to be distributed in a nondiscriminatory manner, qualifies as a tax-exempt organization. Hence tax-exempt municipal bonds have no appeal as pension fund investments. And except during periods of unusually high dividend rates, preferred stocks also lack appeal. Their chief market is the taxed corporate and institutional investor.

Protection against inflation is very important. This is a recognized goal of many funds, and explains much of the emphasis on common stocks as investments in the 1960s and 1970s. A substantial rate of return, compounded through the years, is a better way of offsetting the rising cost of living than a haphazard investment in equities.

Much disillusionment with common stocks was caused by the drastic decline in market prices in 1973–1974. Managers put new funds into high-yielding, high-grade, short-term investments. Even with the recovery in stock prices in 1975–1976, caution still prevailed, especially since attractive yields on bonds were still available, and guaranteed returns of 8% to 9% were offered by insurance companies.

Legality is most important from the standpoint of conformance with state trust law, with the Internal Revenue Code, and with ERISA.

Insured pension funds   As indicated in Chapter 4, there has been a substantial increase in pension funds placed with insurance companies. This has been the result of several factors, notably the use of "deposit administration" group contracts, including those represented by separate accounts. Investment of the latter is not restricted by the rules applying to life insurance company "general accounts," and so these reserves can be, and often are, invested 100% in equities. The same is true of accounts representing "Keogh plan" and other "tax-sheltered" arrangements for individuals and small groups. (See Chapter 4.)

State and Local Government Retirement Plans

The emphasis that has been placed, in investment circles, on corporate and other private pension plans should not obscure the importance of those operated for the employees of state and local governments. At the end of 1975, about 2,500 such plans were in effect, covering some 10.8 million persons.[16] The recent annual rate of growth of assets is $12 to $20 billion, so that total assets at the end of 1976 were about $117 billion (at book value).[17] Table 22-6 shows the composition of the assets of state and local funds for selected recent years, at book value.

The relative investment in Federal government securities has steadily

TABLE 22-6   Assets of State and Local Government Retirement Plans (in billions of dollars)

	1955	1965		1970	1976	
	Amt.	Amt.	Per Cent	Amt.	Amt.	Per Cent
Cash	$ 0.2	$ 0.3	0.9%	$ 0.6	$ 2.0	1.7%
U.S. Govt. and agency securities	4.7	7.6	22.9	6.7	8.6	7.3
State and local government bonds	2.7	2.6	7.8	2.0	4.4	3.8
Corporate bonds	2.5	16.6	50.0	33.1	67.6	57.7
Corporate stocks	0.1	1.6	4.8	8.0	26.1	22.3
Mortgages	0.3	3.7	11.1	6.9	8.5	7.2
Other assets	0.2	0.8	2.4	2.4	—	—
Total	$10.7	$33.2	100.0%	$59.7	$117.2	100.0%

Sources: U.S. Department of Commerce, Bureau of the Census, *Finances of Employee-Retirement Systems of State and Local Governments* (annual) ; *Federal Reserve Bulletin; S.E.C. Statistical Bulletin.*

[16]See Chapter 4.
[17]*S.E.C. Statistical Bulletin.*

declined, as has that in state and local government bonds. The latter are inappropriate in funds whose income is free from both Federal and state income taxes; they are owned presumably to meet archaic statutory requirements. Corporate bonds have become the biggest single assets, accounting for 58% at the end of 1976. In an increasing number of states, common stocks are now eligible, in recognition of the need for an increasing number of inflation hedging and long-term growth. Mortgage investments are growing rapidly with the search for higher yields and the increase in available funds.

The investment requirements of such funds are similar to those of corporate pension funds, except that statutory restrictions curtail somewhat the latitude in types of investments and the purchase of equities, and encourage Federal Government and corporate bond holdings. But there are signs that equities will continue to play an increasingly important role as state laws become revised and liberalized. The share of annual cash flows devoted to stocks has been rising steadily as equities are made legal in an increasing number of states and as previous limits on common stock investment, now usually 30% of portfolio when permitted at all, are raised. Some states are now allowing outside professional managers to handle a portion of the equity funds.

Federal Retirement Funds

The Federal government collects receipts and disburses payments from a variety of trust funds which support Federal pension plans. The most important of these are the Railroad Retirement Fund (administered by the Treasury), Federal Employees' Retirement Fund (Civil Service), and Disability Insurance Trust Fund. The income of the funds is derived from taxes (including individual and employer contributions), premiums, and investment income. Net receipts after payments are entirely invested in Federal securities, with emphasis on special nonmarketable issues. At the end of 1976, the funds held $52.3 billion of Government and agency bonds, or about 8% of total Government debt then outstanding. (See also Chapter 4.) In addition, the Federal Old Age and Survivors Insurance Fund (Social Security) had reserves totalling $35.4 billion, also invested in Federal securities.

Other Federal trust funds that are invested in (special) Federal government and agency securities include Hospital Insurance, Unemployment, Highway, and National Service Life Insurance.

Combined investments of all Federal trust funds as of December 1976 totalled $130 billion of special Federal and agency securities.

REFERENCES

AMERICAN BANKERS ASSOCIATION, *Proceedings, Seminar on Fiduciary Responsibility.* Washington, D.C.: The Association, 1970.

BANKERS TRUST COMPANY, *Study of Industrial Retirement Plans.* New York: Bankers Trust Company, 1976.

BLEAKNEY, T. P., *Retirement Systems for Public Employees*. Pension Research Foundation, Wharton School of the University of Pennsylvania. Homewood, Ill.: Richard D. Irwin, Inc., 1972.

BRIMMER, A. F., *Life Insurance Companies in the Capital Market*. East Lansing, Mich.: Bureau of Business and Economic Research, Graduate School of Business Administration, Michigan State University, 1962.

CARY, W. L., and C. B. BRIGHT, *The Law and Lore of Endowment Funds*. New York: The Ford Foundation, 1969.

DOUGALL, H. E., and J. E. GAUMNITZ, *Capital Markets and Institutions*, 3d ed. Englewood Cliffs, N.J.: Prentice-Hall, Inc., 1975.

ELLIS, C. D., *Institutional Investing*. Homewood, Ill.: Dow Jones-Irwin, 1971.

THE FORD FOUNDATION ADVISORY COMMITTEE ON ENDOWMENT MANAGEMENT, *Managing Educational Endowments*. New York: The Foundation, 1969.

FRIEND, IRWIN, et al., *Private Capital Markets*, research studies prepared for the Commission on Money and Credit. Englewood Cliffs, N.J.: Prentice-Hall, Inc., 1964.

GARDNER, E. B., ed., *Pension Fund Investment Management*. Proceedings, CFA Research Seminar, 1968. CFA Monograph Series, No. 3. Homewood, Ill.: Richard D. Irwin, Inc., 1969.

GOLDSMITH, R. W., *Financial Institutions*. New York: Random House, Inc., 1968.

HEMPEL, G. H., and J. B. YAWITZ, *Financial Management of Financial Institutions*. Englewood Cliffs, N.J.: Prentice-Hall, Inc., 1976.

HORVITZ, P. M., et al., *Private Financial Institutions*, research studies prepared for the Commission on Money and Credit. Englewood Cliffs, N.J.: Prentice-Hall, Inc., 1963.

Institutional Investor Study Report of the Securities and Exchange Commission, Chapters V, VI, VIII, and Supplementary Volume No. 1, Chapters 2, 5. 92d Congress, 1st Session, House Document No. 92–64. Washington, D.C.: U.S. Government Printing Office, 1971.

JONES, L. D., *Investment Policies of Life Insurance Companies*. Boston: Division of Research, Graduate School of Business, Harvard University, 1968.

LEO, MARIO, et al., *Financial Aspects of Private Pension Plans*. New York: Financial Executives Research Foundation, 1975.

LIFE INSURANCE ASSOCIATION OF AMERICA, *Life Insurance Companies as Financial Institutions*, a monograph prepared for the Commission on Money and Credit. Englewood Cliffs, N.J.: Prentice-Hall, Inc., 1962.

LORING, A. P., *A Trustee's Handbook*, J. F. Farr, rev. 6th ed., Chapter 8. Boston: Little, Brown & Company, 1962.

MACKLIN, JOHN P., *Protecting Purchasing Power in Retirement: A Study of Public Employment Retirement Systems*. New York: Fleet Academic Editions, Inc., 1971.

METZGER, B. L., *Investment Practices, Performance and Management of Profit Sharing Trust Funds*. Evanston, Ill.: Profit Sharing Research Foundation, 1969.

NELSON, R. L., *The Investment Policies of Foundations*. New York: Russell Sage Foundation, 1967.

NIELSEN, W. A., *The Big Foundations—A Twentieth Century Study*. New York: Columbia University Press, 1972.

Non-Profit Institutions—Their Role as Institutional Investors. New York: New York Stock Exchange, 1968.

Personal Trust Investment Management. Proceedings, CFA Research Seminar, 1967. CFA Monograph Series No. 2. Homewood, Ill.: Richard D. Irwin, Inc., 1968.

Proceedings, The Endowment Conference, sponsored by Donaldson, Lufkin & Jenrette, Inc. New York, 1969, 1970, 1971.

Property and Liability Insurance Investment Management. C.F.A. Monograph Series, No. 5. Homewood, Ill.: Richard D. Irwin, Inc., 1971.

SILBER, W. L., *Portfolio Behavior of Financial Institutions*. New York: Holt, Rinehart and Winston, 1969.

"SMITH, ADAM," *The Money Game*. New York: Random House, Inc., 1967.

SOLDOFSKY, R. M., *Institutional Holdings of Common Stock 1900–2000*. Ann Arbor, Mich.: Bureau of Business Research, Graduate School of Business, University of Michigan, 1971.

STEPHENSON, G. T., and N. A. WIGGINS, *Estates and Trusts*, 5th ed. New York: Appleton-Century-Crofts, Inc., 1973.

Tax-Exempt Foundations and Charitable Trusts: Their Impact on the Economy. Prepared for the Subcommittee on Domestic Finance of the Committee on Banking and Currency, House of Representatives, 92d Congress, 2d Session, August, 1972.

TUCKER, J. R., *State and Local Pension Funds*. Washington, D.C.: Securities Industry Association, 1972.

WILLIAMSON, J. P., *Performance Measurement and Investment Objectives for Educational Endowment Funds*. New York: The Common Fund, 1972.

ZURCHER, A. J., *The Management of American Foundations*. New York: New York University Press, 1972.

Reviewing Investment Results 23

SCOPE: The last (but continuing) step in the investment program is a review of investment results. Have the returns been adequate? Has too much or too little risk been taken? Have the objectives been accomplished? What new conditions related to both the investor and the investment markets require changes in goals and in portfolio strategy?

The order of discussion in Chapter 23 is: (1) measuring financial results, (2) measuring risk performance, (3) review of general objectives. Although the discussion pertains mainly to institutional investors, the concepts can be used by individuals with substantial portfolios.

Measuring Financial Results

Investment objectives may have been stated in nonfinancial terms to provide for a specific need, but those are often translated into quantitative goals. For example, an investor may seek "supplementary income before retirement," then express the desired income in specific dollars or in investment yield per annum. A pension fund with the objective "to provide retirement income over and above the rate of inflation" may choose a desired rate of return that will satisfy this goal. So periodic appraisal of actual financial results is necessary to determine whether the program has been successful. The first step is to measure the actual results. The second is to determine if the performance has been satisfactory. Three important appraisals are involved: (1) investment income, (2) growth of capital value, (3) total return.

Investment income Actual income results, in terms of portfolio dividend or income yield (on market price), are not difficult to determine. Some investors require a certain level of current income, or at least seek to maximize it at a given level of risk. They will ask: "Is the income or yield as good as projected?" and "Could I have done better (at the same or lower risk) with a different portfolio, a different type of media, or an income mutual fund?" Plenty of comparisons with similar institutions are available to the managers of pension funds and other aggregates of capital.

Growth of income is often more important than current results. Three situations will illustrate. An investor may seek protection against inflation through rising dividend income rather than capital appreciation. Stocks that offer steady increases in income over the years (based on past performances) may be preferable to those with high current yields but with no prospects for dividend increases. Or investors may compare current and prospective yields on stocks and bonds (as in the middle 1970s) and determine that the latter have a competitive advantage at less risk. Or a fund that has promised a payment on an actuarial basis (insurance company or pension fund) must make sure that the required return is produced with some to spare.

Capital growth When this is the financial objective, actual results (from cost) are measured and compared with those on alternative investments. The performance is judged adequate or not, depending on the stated objectives—inflation protection, creation of an estate, ultimate bequests of capital, and others. Individuals may have difficulty making comparisons with the results obtained by others, and indeed, so different are needs, objectives, and risks that such comparisons might have little meaning. Institutions' performances are subject to continuous scrutiny and, where like is compared with like, relative performance is a valid technique of analysis. The temptation is strong to ask: "Have I done as well or better than the market as a whole?" The validity of this question depends on the length of the period studied, the risk level of the investor, and the basic objective in mind.

A simple model of capital growth measurement by investment companies is given in Chapter 11, and can be used by individuals as well.

Total return Total performance of an investment fund involves income, any capital gains distributions, and unrealized capital gains or losses. The concept is referred to in a number of sections of this book. Where goals are stated in terms of total return, the projected or desired income plus the desired or expected change in market value are combined in a rate that will fulfill the basic objectives of the investor.

Calculation of total rate of return can be simple or sophisticated. On a one-period basis, the "single-internal" rate of return on a single security or on a portfolio can be illustrated by a case in which a stock with an initial value of 50, with a market value of 55 at the end of a period, and having paid $5 in dividends, would show a total return of 10% for the period. This could be annualized if necessary. The following model is similar to that suggested for measuring the performance of mutual funds in Chapter 11. Where the fund is static, a crude "internal" rate of return can be measured by the difference between ending asset value plus interest and dividends received, and beginning value, taken as a percentage of beginning value:

$$\mathrm{R} = \frac{(V_{t+1} + I_t) - V_t}{V_t}$$

The previous calculation assumes that all (net) income is received at the end of a period or spread over the period, and that no new capital is received during the period. The receipt of new capital can be recognized by calculating the unweighted average of returns at different intervals, say, four quarters a year, from different starting and ending values; thus, the magnitude of varying contributions to a fund or withdrawals from a fund can be taken into account.

These previous methods ignore the time value of money as applied to varying flows within a period. However most funds do not remain static. They increase in value by receipt of income and by market appreciation, and decrease in value by payments or withdrawals and by decline in market value. The "internal" or *dollar-weighted* rate of total return is a weighted average of the return on different sums invested at different times, and held for different lengths of time, during the period being measured.

This approach to total return is also called the "discounted cash flow method" because it involves the principle of present value. The return is calculated by finding at what rate the discounted present value of the fund's assets at the end of a given period is equal to the value at the beginning of the period plus the values of each intervening cash inflow (or payment) during the period. The model that denotes the "internal" or "*dollar-weighted*" *rate of return*, and incorporates money flows and the amount of assets at work during each period, is:

$$V_e = V_b(1 + r) + C(1 + r)^j$$

That is, the value of the fund at the end of the measuring period (V_e) equals the value at the beginning of the measuring period (V_b) plus the value of net contributions (C) during the period, compounded at the rate of return. The symbol j is that fraction of the measuring period during which each portion of the net contributions is available to the fund. This measurement of rate of return can be applied to individual periods (normally quarters, half-years, and years) and to cumulative results over several years. A feasible arrangement is to assume that contributions are received quarterly.

The "internal" or "dollar-weighted" rate of return shows the average or overall growth of a fund due to investment returns, given the fund's peculiar cash flow. Since this cash flow is beyond the control of the actual manager of the fund, unless he is permitted to invest or to withhold cash, another measure of performance—that of the manager—must be used.

To derive this rate of return, the fund is valued whenever new money is received by the manager, and the return in each period that begins with the new valuation is calculated. The amount of new money and the length of the periods may be large or small. The rate of return for a given arbitrary period, say, for the fund's fiscal year or for calendar years, is then calculated by taking the geometric mean of the intermediate-period rates of return. The result is called the "time-weighted" rate of return. Only when the cash flows tend to be small in relation to the value of the fund, or where they are uniform in size and periodicity, are the "dollar-weighted" and the "time-weighted" rates of return the same. Use of the "time-weighted" rate is, of course, necessary where different funds are being compared.[1]

Useful as the concept has come to be, "total return" has an inherent weakness that should cause investors and portfolio managers to use it with caution. Total return is a combination of actual (or expected) cash income and actual (or expected) change in market value. Thus, it includes an element of *unrealized* profit or loss that in many cases makes up the bulk of the total rate. Yet many managers compare bond yield and total return as if they were the same, and many have used total return as the only measure of performance. For example, a decision to switch from bonds to equities because the bond yield is only 8% while stocks *may* produce a total return of 10% or more, overlooks the fact that the gain portion of the total return may never be realized, except perhaps over a long period of time. The drastic decline in common stock market values in 1973–1974 should have taught a vivid lesson to this effect, especially to the managers of endowment and pension funds who relied on "total return" to fulfill commitments. The conservative position that profit is not profit until it is realized deserves careful attention.

Measuring Risk Performance

Risk is a factor not only in determining investment policy, but also in measuring investment results. Investors and professional investment managers have always been concerned with the several kinds of risks that affect values and income, and which must be appraised and dealt with in investment policy. Methods of minimizing these risks, or of obtaining satisfactory rewards for the risks that are deemed appropriate for a given program, play an important role in investment policy and management. (See Chapters 18 and 19.)

The various types of investment risk—business and financial "internal" risk, money rate risk, and purchasing power risk—are reflected in the amount and stability of corporate earnings, which in turn are capitalized in the market place. Changes in market value, plus income, are combined in the total rate of return. Variation in the rate of return, then, becomes the specific definition of risk. This concept has been especially used in pension fund management after the refined measurements of rate of return, discussed previously, were developed. Pension fund committees and fund managers turn to the variation in the time-weighted rate of return to measure risk and to appraise and compare investment results.

Measuring variability The degree of variability in the rate of return may be measured in different ways. One of these is to calculate the average deviation of quarterly time-weighted rates of return from the mean, or, in other words, the absolute value of the deviations from the average return, whether these be positive or negative. The following example is illustrative:

[1]The pioneer work that emphasized these refined rates of return was done by the Bank Administration Institute. See References, end of this chapter.

| | 1977 Quarterly Rates of Return | | Deviation of Quarterly Rates |
	Actual	Annualized	from Mean
1st quarter	+6.5%	+26%	26 − 4 = 22
2nd quarter	−5.0	−20	20 − 4 = 16
3rd quarter	0	0	0 − 4 = 4
4th quarter	+2.5	+10	10 − 4 = 6
Sum		+16%	48
Mean		+ 4%	12

In the above illustration the fund had an average quarterly return of 4% in 1977 and an average variation of 12% about that average. Another fund with a 4% rate of return, but with a mean absolute deviation of 24%, would be considered as having shown twice the risk. The goal of fund management is to maximize the return from a portfolio that is permitted a certain level of risk, or, conversely, to minimize the risk that is permitted a portfolio designed to produce a certain rate of return. It is widely accepted that, over the long run, risk and return are positively correlated.

The beta concept   Committees in charge of fund management like to make regular comparisons of the performance of their fund(s) with that of other funds, taking into account the general differences in the funds and the degree of risk assumed. There are services that provide such information. But the question almost always arises (rightly or wrongly): "How have we done in comparison with the market as a whole?" Fund managers are often expected to outperform the market regardless of the objectives of the fund, and regardless of the fact that they all cannot do so.

The "beta" concept (shown below) is used to determine the action of a particular fund (and of individual securities). "Beta" is the average rate of change in rate of return relative to that of the general market. This "systematic risk" is obtained by plotting the rates of return in a series of periods for a fund (or for individual securities) on the vertical axis Y, in relation to the rates of return for stocks representing the market (ordinarily the Standard & Poor's 500) for the same periods, on the horizontal axis X. Then a line of best fit is drawn to indicate the relationship of the two variables. The slope of this line is the "beta volatility coefficient." The line can be drawn by sight but for greater precision a regression line is used, based on the equation $Y = \alpha + \beta X$. Y is the dependent variable.

Beta quantifies the change in a fund's rate of return that was experienced in the past, and can be expected in the future, from a series of general market changes. A beta of 1.00 is assigned to general market movements. The closer the individual stock or fund moves in relation to the market, the closer its "beta" is to 1.00. The further away, the greater the degree of variation of its rate of return from that of the general market. For example, a beta of 1.50 would mean a (past) movement one and a half times as great, on average, as that of the general market. Translated into expectations for the future, a portfolio with a beta of 1.50 will be expected to increase or decrease

7 1/2%, on average, with a 5% change in the general market. A beta of
0.50 should show a variation of only one-half (and therefore, risk of only
one-half) that of the general market. If beta is 1.0, market and fund return
are expected to be equally volatile.

This approach enables an investor or a pension committee to decide first
in quantiative terms what risk it is willing to take, then to select investments
accordingly, to measure the actual results, and to make comparisons with
other funds where the data are available. Certain investment services provide
"betas" for a wide list of stocks.[2]

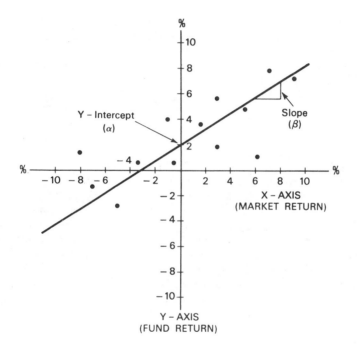

"Beta" does not represent *total* risk, but only the market-related portion.
If beta is 1.0, market return and fund return are equally volatile, and any
difference in the return is attributable to the fund's own characteristics, that
is, to the fund management. The difference between a fund's return (Y)
and the risk-adjusted market return (β times X) is alpha ($\alpha = Y - \beta X$).
On the preceding diagram, alpha is the point at which the sloped line inter-
cepts the Y axis. Alpha represents the extra influence exerted by the fund
management over and above mere co-movement with the market (the
"unsystematic" risk).

[2]A refinement of the beta technique is to calculate how much variation from its average change
during a period a stock (or a portfolio) may have, using the standard deviation as the measure.
Two securities or two portfolios may, for example, both have a beta of 2.0 and an average change in
value of, say, plus 10% during a series of periods. But if one stock has a 5% standard deviation and
the other an 8%, the former is less likely to vary from its average performance.

Another method of comparing fund management with the market uses "excess return" as a measure of performance. It is computed by mixing appropriate portions of "risk-free" assets (such as Treasury bills) and assets presumed to be invested in the general market (say, as measured by the Standard & Poor's 500 stock index). The proportions are selected so as to produce the same beta coefficient as historically shown by the actual portfolio being measured. For each subsequent time period, comparison of the real and the imaginary ("standard") portfolios shows whether actual management performance, after adjustment for volatility, was better or worse, on average, than that of the unmanaged portfolios. For example, if the average period change for the real portfolio were 0.10% and the imaginary portfolio with equivalent volatility (beta) had an average of 0.42%, the "alpha," as calculated in the manner described, would be minus 0.32%.[3]

The use of the alpha-beta approach forces portfolio managers having discretion to adopt a specific standard of risk and return, and to run the fund accordingly. It can be a useful tool in after-the-fact analysis and in policymaking. But the approach has its limitations. It is based on past performance, and future performance is not likely to be the same.[4] Many funds would be advised to aim for something short of the maximum return so as to avoid vulnerability to larger variations in the future value of the fund than have occurred in selected periods in the past. A more basic criticism is that the approach overemphasizes the importance of market value change. In a growing pension fund considerable variation in market values can be absorbed. Possibly more important than temporary changes in value are the risks of changes in the basic quality and in the marketability of the securities that comprise the portfolio. In any event, the investor or manager must have a clear concept of the purpose of the fund; the need for safety of principal; the importance of current income; the projected growth of the fund; the timing and size of contributions and withdrawals; the degree of liquidity required; the level of risk that should be assumed; the need to meet actuarial requirements; and other features that are peculiar to a particular fund.

Many pension fund committees employ securities houses to provide information on the comparative performance of funds classified by size and portfolio mix. Some of these services use simple, others use sophisticated measurements. The houses are compensated with brokerage business. A criticism of the use of such services is that they emphasize short-run results. This in turn leads to the temptation to invest in high-flying investments. The managers of most funds should, theoretically at least, take a long-run point of view. The real basic test of portfolio management is whether the

---

[3]The Securities and Exchange Commission recommends the use of such a measure of performance, and suggests that the results of institutional managers be disclosed. The Commission actually applied it to mutual investment companies, to separate pension accounts of life insurance companies, and to bank commingled trust funds. *Institutional Investor Study Report of the S.E.C.*, *op. cit.*, Chapters IV, V, and VI.

[4]A technical criticism of "beta" is that it can be calculated differently by using different long-term time periods and different intervals within those periods (longer-term vs shorter-term swings). A beta coefficient calculated to two or three decimal places borders on the ridiculous.

management meets its *own* investment objectives within the degree of risk deemed appropriate to the situation.

Summary The investor should review the actual performance of his portfolio, determine the reasons why his requirements and expectations may or may not have been fulfilled, and hopefully make the changes that will produce more satisfactory results. In so doing he may be measuring the effects of his own decisions; in the modern world he is likely to be measuring the effects of decisions of others to whom he has delegated the task of managing his money.

A number of statistical measures of actual performance are available. These range from the simple to the highly sophisticated:[5]

- Comparison of the actual price action, income, and total return with the estimates or expectation he or his advisor had in mind at the beginning of and throughout the period under consideration.

- Comparison of the actual risk incurred with the risk he has initially agreed to assume, as measured by inspection of basic information or by sophisticated indicators such as those defined in the preceding section.

- Comparison of the price and return performance of his fund or portfolio with that of the market as a whole. Did he do better or worse than the market? Did his decisions with respect to selection, diversification and timing produce the hoped-for results? Such comparisons require the comparison of like with like: bond portfolios with bond indexes, stocks with stock indexes, etc., and over a sufficient period of time to be meaningful. The various market averages and indexes and their different trends and movements are discussed in Chapter 13.

- Comparison of his own portfolio's performance with that of funds—such as mutual investment funds—that he might have selected in lieu of running his own affairs, or, in the case of institutional portfolios, comparison with other funds of the same type—viz., one mutual fund versus others, one pension fund versus others.

Review of General Objectives

Few investment programs remain static. All of the conditions suggested in Chapters 18 and 19 that determine objectives and policy are likely to change through time. And, even if the investor's resources and needs do not change, market conditions do. Thus, taking a regular inventory of objectives, of investment policy and strategy, and of results is indicated. Investment management is a continuous process.

[5]Among the more sophisticated methods of measurement of portfolio performance are those suggested by Sharpe, Traynor, and Jenson. Although they are concerned with mutual funds, the techniques could be used in the management of any large fund. W. F. Sharpe, "Mutual Fund Performance," *Journal of Business*, Supplement on Security Prices, January 1966, pp. 119–38; J. L. Traynor, "How to Rate the Management of Investment Funds," *Harvard Business Review*, January-February 1965, pp. 63–75; M. C. Jenson, "The Performance of Mutual Funds in the Period 1945–1964," *Journal of Finance*, May 1968, pp. 389–416.

REFERENCES

BREALEY, R. A., *An Introduction to Risk and Return for Common Stocks*. Cambridge, Mass.: M.I.T. Press, 1969.

COHEN, K. J., et al., *Measuring the Performance of Pension Funds for the Purpose of Inter-Fund Comparison*. Park Ridge, Ill.: Bank Administration Institute, 1968.

DIETZ, P. O., *Pension Funds: Measuring Investment Performance*. New York: The Free Press, 1966.

FAMA, E. F., *Risk and the Evaluation of Pension Fund Portfolio Performance*. Park Ridge, Ill.: Bank Administration Institute, 1969.

THE FORD FOUNDATION ADVISORY COMMITTEE ON ENDOWMENT MANAGEMENT, *Managing Educational Endowments*. New York: The Foundation, 1969.

FOSTER, E. M., *Common Stock Investment*. Lexington, Mass.: Lexington Books, 1974.

FRANCIS, J. C., *Investments: Analysis and Management*. New York: McGraw-Hill, Inc., 1972.

———, and S. H. ARCHER, *Portfolio Analysis*. Englewood Cliffs, N.J.: Prentice-Hall, Inc., 1971.

FRIEND, IRWIN, MARSHALL BLUME, and JEAN CROCKETT, *Mutual Funds and Other Institutional Investors*. New York: McGraw-Hill, Inc., 1970.

Institutional Investor Study Report of the Securities and Exchange Commission, Chapters V, VI, VIII, and Supplementary Volume No. 1, Chapters 2, 5. 92d Congress, 1st Session, House Document No. 92–64. Washington, D.C.: U.S. Government Printing Office 1971.

LEVINE, S. N., ed., *Financial Analyst's Handbook*. Volume I, Chapter 44. Homewood, Ill.: Dow Jones-Irwin, Inc., 1975.

Measuring and Reporting Investment Performance of Pension Funds. National Foundation of Health, Welfare, and Pension Plans, Inc., Milwaukee, Wisc.: 1966 and 1967.

METZGER, B. L., *Investment Practices, Performance and Management of Profit Sharing Trust Funds*. Evanston, Ill.: Profit Sharing Research Foundation, 1969.

SHARPE, W. F., *Portfolio Theory and Capital Markets*. New York: McGraw-Hill, Inc. 1970.

WILLIAMSON, J. P., *Investments: New Analytic Techniques*. New York: Praeger Publishers, Inc., 1970.

———, *Performance Measurement and Investment Objectives for Educational Endowment Funds*. New York: The Common Fund, 1972.

WOOD, N. R., *Measuring the Investment Yield of Pension Funds*. New York: Alexander and Alexander, Inc., 1964.

Part V

Analysis
of Corporate Securities

General Tests of Quality: Corporate Securities

SCOPE: This chapter provides an introduction to the problems of analysis of corporate securities. The specific applications are reserved for subsequent chapters. The order of discussion is: (1) general purposes of analysis, (2) quality of investments, (3) tests of internal risk or quality (4) qualitative factors, (5) characteristics of the particular security (6) other influences on price and yield, and (7) sources of analytical information.

General Purposes of Analysis

The basic purpose of securities analysis is to make good investment decisions in the selection and valuation of portfolio assets. The scope and depth of analysis will depend on a number of factors: (1) the investment objectives —tests of recovery of principal will emphasize different factors than tests of assurance of income, purchasing power protection, etc; (2) the quality of the security as observed by preliminary inspection—a Aaa bond requires much less scrutiny than a dubious common stock; (3) the degree of risk the investor is willing to assume—for example, at one extreme complete freedom from risk of default would limit the investor to Federal obligations and savings types; (4) the procedures taken to avoid risk, such as wide diversification and dollar-cost averaging lessen the responsibility to make an exhaustive investigation; (5) the amount and types of information available; and (6) the investors' willingness and/or ability to do the analytical work.

The "Quality" of Investments

The meaning of "investment quality" The first of the types of investment risks discussed in Chapters 18 and 19 is the internal risk of the enterprise, that is, the ability of the issuer to pay principal and interest on bonds when due, to pay dividends on preferred stock, and to produce growing and stable earnings (and dividends) on common stock. The other types of risks are external to the company, that is, are factors other than its own strength.

The term "quality" has traditionally been used to indicate the degree of internal risk. Quality is rated by investment services by using such symbols as Aaa, Aa, etc. Or securities are said to have "high quality," or "average quality," etc. Or some securities are labelled "investment grade," others "speculative."

All of these designations suggest the relative "safety" of the issue. In the traditional sense, investment "quality" has been synonymous with investment "safety." A "good investment" has been said to offer safety of principal and safety of income, or the assurance of a reasonable return. And because a "good investment" is usually thought to involve little risk of principal or income, it would, therefore, produce a relatively low rate of return while a poor investment would involve high risk and require the possibility of a high return or capital appreciation to compensate for lack of safety.

Limitations of the traditional concept of quality   This chapter is concerned with the general measurement of internal risk or quality. But the concept has important limitations.

The first limitation is that the degree of safety can be measured only approximately. Accurate analysis of all of the forces—economic, political, and managerial—that affect asset values and earnings is impossible. Especially difficult is the task of predicting future events. And even the known facts can be variously interpreted. To a considerable extent, investment analysis remains an art, involving qualitative factors, rather than a science. The task of the analyst is to apply such tests as indicate relatively rather than absolutely the degree of internal risk involved in any corporate security.

A second difficulty of the concept is that the longer the maturity of the investment, the more difficult it is to estimate how assured are the principal and the income. The future always holds a number of uncertainties. Examination of the past record and prevailing condition of the issuer is helpful; knowledge of prevailing business and economic conditions and estimates of the future are essential. But these can never be infallible guides to the future. Who can say how "safe" is the principal of a bond due in 50 years? How "safe" are the dividends of a corporation 10 years from now? How can the "safety" of preferred or common stocks, which are redeemable only in the market or in liquidation, be measured?

Finally, the return of principal and the amount and rate of income are affected by factors other than those associated with the issuer and with the inherent quality of the instrument. Even if one were satisfied that the issuer of a bond would not fail to pay full principal and interest when due, the market value of the bond will be influenced by factors, such as the trend of interest rates (and others listed in Chapters 8 and 9), that may profoundly affect the recoverable value before maturity. Except in cases of extreme strength or weakness, it is difficult to segregate the factor of internal "safety" from the other influences and types of risk that affect market price and yield.

Although payment of income and recovery of principal would appear to require separate analysis, the two are inextricably woven. Where income is assured, the recovery of principal is assured, save for intermediate market fluctuations owing to changing maturity, interest rates, and other influences.

Inability to produce income seriously impairs the value of the principal. The two factors must be measured together.

The degree of quality or amount of internal company risk in any investment security is indicated—sometimes exactly, sometimes only approximately—by the examination of certain important factors. This does not constitute the whole of investment analysis; it pertains solely to the quality of the issue being examined. Of equal importance are an understanding of the investor's objectives, the proper timing of purchase and sale, and the important matter of valuation. A particular security may demonstrate quality, but for some reason it may not be appropriate in a particular portfolio. Or the purchase of this security may not be feasible at a particular time. Or the investor might like everything about a security but its price. And quality is only one of several influences on price.

Tests of Internal Risk or Quality

In examining an investment security for those internal risk elements that in the main determine its strength and the adequacy of the income that should compensate for that risk, a logical approach is to proceed from the general—the industry of which the company is a part—to the specific—the particular security that is being examined. The order will run (1) the nature of the enterprise—its basic characteristics, long-term trends and cyclical patterns, (2) tests of the issuer's financial strength as revealed by examination of its financial statements, (3) tests of operations and earning power, (4) qualitative factors, and (5) features of the particular issue. The discussion in this chapter is confined to basic tests that apply to most corporate issuers. More specific tests and those that pertain to different industrial groups are explored in the chapters that follow.

Secular and cyclical character of the industry An investor should attempt to define the stage in the "life cycle" in which the industry belongs—pioneering, expansion, maturity, stagnation. This is done by an examination of production, sales, and earnings, preferably in comparison with the course of the economy as a whole. The "business" risk associated with a particular company is in part determined by its ability to keep its share in an expanding or maturing industry, or to show superior strength in a declining industry. "Growth industries" are those whose earnings have increased in the past, and are expected to increase in the future at an above-average rate. (A few examples are electronics, computers, technical services, health and medicine, drugs, chemicals, oil exploration, and processed foods.) But a particular company can belong in a growth industry and not share in that growth. (See Chapter 26.) Similarly, some companies in maturing industries exhibit great strength, while others are mediocre. Although there are few strong companies in a stagnating industry (such as railroads), the issues of some do have "quality."

Industries also differ widely with respect to cyclical variations in earnings. Table 24-1 shows the years of highs and lows for major groups. Some

TABLE 24-1 Corporate Profits after Income Taxes
(in millions of dollars)

Group	1950	1952	1955	1958	1959	1961	1966	1970	1974	1975
Mining (including oil)	$ 1,115	$ 846	$ 1,046	$ 778	$ 607	$ 842	$ 822	$ 633	$ 2,551	$ 2,857
Contract construction	325	305	266	395	343	292	1,096	1,105	1,279	1,226
Manufacturing	13,290	9,566	14,453	10,299	13,986	12,046	24,670	15,069	33,447	28,806
Transportation	1,107	846	704	316	452	314	1,393	-615	1,206	-22
Communication	406	465	810	1,073	1,308	1,496	2,539	2,262	2,319	2,145
Electric, gas, and sanitary services	884	999	1,280	1,336	1,583	1,864	2,826	2,175	1,519	2,141
Wholesale and retail trade	3,743	2,267	2,802	2,414	3,160	2,882	5,571	6,718	16,212	17,166
Finance, insurance, and real estate	2,597	2,854	3,711	3,653	4,791	4,851	6,302	6,709	3,684	2,907
Services	326	297	336	318	433	322	1,154	847	1,693	1,741

Source: U.S. Department of Commerce, Survey of Business, July issues.

industries, such as gold, tobacco, packaged foods, and electric utilities, are defensive in that their revenues and earnings suffer little decline during economic recessions. Others, such as durables manufacturing, some transportation, and some financial concerns like banks, are vulnerable in a period such as the early 1970s. But this is not to say that the securities of companies with cyclical characteristics cannot offer quality. The senior securities of many are well secured. The common stocks of even the strongest exhibit instability in earnings and dividends, however. But diversification and dollar-cost averaging through the years can produce good results in so-called growth-cyclical stocks.

The secular and cyclical characteristics of different types of enterprises will be examined in greater depth in Chapters 26–30, where other industry features will also be noted.

Issuer's financial strength   The analysis of the financial strength of the issuer is explained in considerable detail in subsequent chapters, with emphasis on the features that are pertinent to the respective fields. At this point, the more important general tests are discussed.

The tests of capital structure or leverage show the amounts and relative importance of the various sources of long-term funds. Capital structure (sometimes called invested capital or long-term investment) includes the *capitalization* (or securities outstanding) plus the surplus accounts.[1] The most conservative capital structure includes only common stock and surplus; no "senior capital" has been issued. Where substantial amounts of bonds, preferred stock, or both are included, the company has committed itself to fixed or contingent charges through the issuance of senior securities. Such a practice may or may not be dangerous, depending on the assets and earnings support to such securities. The nature of the enterprise is a governing factor in this regard; companies with relatively stable earnings may safely issue a larger proportion of bonds. (Standards of capital structure will be suggested in succeeding chapters.) Conservative investors seeking high quality in securities should favor those companies with the smaller percentages in bonds and preferred stock. But others may prefer companies with high leverage, which will result in earnings being magnified in good times; by the same token, such investors must accept the fact that; in periods of low earnings; leverage may severely reduce the earnings on common stock.

Some suggest that the degree of leverage used in long-term financing reveals the "solvency" of a firm, in contrast to its liquidity or cash and working capital position. The two can be combined by relating *total* debt to assets and earnings.

The *tests of working capital position* indicate the short-term liquidity of the business. The importance of liquidity depends on the nature of the business, the rate at which assets are converted into cash through operations, and the need of the company for working funds. The (net) *working capital* is the difference between current assets and current liabilities. The relationship of current assets to current liabilities, and the turnover and valuation

---

[1]The term "capitalization" is often used to denote total securities plus surplus.

of individual current asset items, should be examined carefully. The use of these tests is discussed in more detail in Chapters 26–28.

In addition to these general tests, the relation of working capital to long-term debt and to capital stock indicates the liquid protection behind each layer of securities.

The *tests of total asset value* show the protection that is provided the various issues of outstanding securities. Bonds and preferred stock should be supported by ample tangible assets. The value of common stock, which represents the residual equity in the business, often reflects superior or inferior earning power, and hence its *tangible book value* (total tangible assets less all liabilities and preferred stock) seldom coincides with its market value. This phenomenon is also in part attributable to the arbitrary fashion in which assets are carried on the balance sheet.[2]

Assets are carried at book values, ordinarily at cost (less accumulated depreciation and other valuation reserves) for fixed assets, and at cost or market value for current assets. Except for financial companies, book value seldom indicates liquidating value and, with respect to fixed assets, is often arbitrary.

The *test of fixed assets* measures the relationship between the value of the fixed assets (less any reserves) and the face value of the securities outstanding. Even assuming that the properties have been properly maintained and adequately depreciated, the value of the fixed assets should substantially exceed the long-term debt. The relationship between fixed assets and net worth should also be noted, to determine whether the owner's investment is represented by illiquid assets. The conservative analyst usually ignores the intangible assets in such tests, as these are likely to shrink in value with any decline in earning power, and their balance sheet value is usually arbitrary.

As indicated in succeeding chapters, the importance of fixed assets and their valuation varies among different industries. Currently there is much pressure in accounting and financial circles to reveal their "replacement value" so as to indicate the effects of inflation.

Operating competence and earning power The income (profit and loss) statement shows the earnings of the company for the period indicated—annual or interim—as disclosed in the revenue and expense figures. Each major item of revenue and expense, and the relationships between them, and between investment and earnings, must be given very close scrutiny. The final figure of net income, that is, the earnings produced for the owners of the business, is the addition to the net worth (before any cash dividends) produced during the period.

The income statement is more "reliable" than the balance sheet in that most of the items are statements of fact. Nevertheless, the reported earnings figures are subject to considerable control, that is, are affected by accounting decisions. The expenses of depreciation and depletion may not reflect the actual rate of decline in the physical value of fixed assets, especially when

[2]Some suggest the following ratios as prior indicators of possible corporate bankruptcy: working capital/total assets; retained earnings/total assets; earnings before income taxes/total assets; market value of equity/total debt.

tax considerations dominate the calculations. Inventories can be valued in different ways. Nonrecurring items of both income and expense, the treatment of charges representing a variety of special reserves, policy with respect to charging deferred income taxes, and a number of other factors make the earnings figures reported for a particular period somewhat arbitrary. For these reasons long-term rather than short-run information should be emphasized.

Reported earnings, of course, reflect trends and relationships of revenues and expenses, whose analysis is discussed in later chapters. Such analysis uncovers the *reasons* for the size and rate of change of the earnings figures.

Analysis of operating competence includes the study of asset utilization, as revealed by turnover calculations (sales divided by assets being studied). As we shall see, turnover of plant is especially important in the heavy manufacturing, transportation and communications, and electric and gas utilities. Operating competence is also indicated by the trend and stability of sales and by profit margins (gross operating profit, net operating profit, and net income, as percent of sales). These and other tests are discussed in detail in Chapters 26–28.

The *tests of earning power* are possibly the most important financial tests used in investment analysis. These include the trend, volatility, and size of the return on capital investment, the coverage of interest on bonds and other long-term debt, the coverage of preferred stock dividends, and the company's capacity to pay current and future dividends on the common stock. These are basic criteria of investment quality.

The rate earned on the *total* long-term investment or capital structure is computed by dividing income before any bond interest, but after income taxes (or net income with interest added back) by the average total capital structure. This shows the productivity of the business without regard to the methods of long-term financing that have been employed, save for the influence of interest on the income tax bill. A similar test of the earning power of operating assets is found in the ratio of operating income to net plant plus net working capital.

The rate of return on total net worth or owners' investment (return on "equity capital") is calculated by dividing the average net worth (at book value) into net income after taxes. The figure is, of course, influenced by any leverage resulting from the use of debt.[3]

The earnings protection to bondholders is revealed by the comparison of the annual interest charges (and other fixed charges such as fixed rent) to the total income available for their payment. The computation of this "times earned" figure can use either earnings before fixed charges, or before fixed charges and after income taxes. Both calculations are valid—the first because interest and rent are expenses in determining taxable income, and the second because, once the tax bill is computed, it has a prior claim over payments to creditors and lessors. The coverage of fixed charges can also be calculated on a "cash flow" basis by using, as the numerator, earnings before deprecia-

---

[3]The expression "rate of return" includes a variety of types. A special use of return on investment is found in the "fair return" on the "fair value" or rate base used in utility regulation. Other "rates of return" are associated with market value of securities such as bond yield, dividend yield, and "total return," or income plus price change as a percent of investment. (See Chapters 8, 9, and 23.)

tion and interest. Coverage of "total debt service" involves the "cash flow" coverage of interest plus sinking fund payments; this can be used as a test of total bond safety. Refinements of these tests and their application in various industries are discussed in Chapters 26–30.

The protection given to the preferred stock dividends is revealed by comparing the total income and the preferred dividend requirements (plus bond interest, if any). The *coverage* may also be calculated by dividing income (before interest) by interest plus two times the preferred dividend. The reasoning is that, assuming a 50% rate of income taxes, the company will have to earn the interest plus twice its preferred dividends to cover the latter once.[4] The appropriate margin of safety required to assure the payment of bond interest and preferred dividends will, of course, differ with the nature of the enterprise, the character of its assets, and the stability of its earnings.

The coverage of preferred stock dividends is sometimes indicated by dividing the net income by the number of shares outstanding. If a company reports net income of $12 per preferred share, and if the dividend is $4, preferred dividends are said to have been earned three times in the given period. A similar result is obtained by dividing net income by the annual preferred dividends. These methods are misleading for companies with both bonds and preferred stock outstanding because they conceal the existence of prior deductions in the form of fixed charges that do not vary with changes in total income. As indicated above, the better method of indicating preferred dividend coverage is to calculate the number of times that total fixed charges *plus* dividends have been earned in the period. Otherwise, the preferred stock might, under certain conditions, show higher coverage than bonds senior to it! Table 24-2 shows the chief methods of calculating the coverage of charges indicated above.

The past earnings and the estimated future earnings on the common stock

TABLE 24-2 Coverage of Charges

	Year A	Year B
Available for fixed charges	$200	$60
Fixed charges (interest and fixed rent)	40	40
Income before income taxes	$160	$20
Income taxes (at 50%)	80	10
Net income	$ 80	$10
Preferred dividends	10	10
Times fixed charges earned (before taxes)	5	1.5
Times fixed charges earned (after taxes)	3	1.25
Times interest plus preferred dividends earned	2.4	1
Times interest plus twice preferred dividends earned	3.3	1
Times preferred dividends earned	8	1

[4]"Overall" coverage of preferred dividends where the applicable rate of income tax is known is determined by

$$\text{EBIT} \div \text{Interest} + \frac{PD}{1 - \text{tax rate}}$$

where EBIT = earnings before income taxes
PD = preferred dividend

are the most important factors of concern to its owners or potential owners and are the most important determinants of its value. The expected earnings should be commensurate with the risks of the enterprise. Their amount and stability determine the dividends to be received as well as the growth from retained earnings that will enhance the investment quality of the stock through the years. The productivity of the common stockholder's stake in the business, in terms of the size and trend of the rate earned on the common equity (net income after preferred dividends divided by average common stock plus surplus), is a basic factor in choosing among alternative equity investments, and is the chief influence on the value placed by the market on each dollar of profits (the price-earnings ratio or multiplier).

The *dividend payment test* involves an examination of the common stock dividend record of the company over a period of years: the amount of earnings available for dividends, and the proportion of earnings ("payout ratio") that has been and may in the future be distributed in dividends. Such dividends are contingent not only on earnings but on the management's policy as to the portion of those earnings that is to be distributed. In many growth situations, retained earnings are more valuable to the stockholder than are dividends, because they add to investment that earns a higher rate than the investor could earn, after income taxes, on alternative commitments. Indeed, in a market such as in the 1960s–1970s, investors have been willing to pay more, in the case of growing companies, per dollar of earnings that are retained than are paid out.

Traditionally, earnings on common stock have been reported as so much per outstanding share, based on the average number of shares for the period, or on the shares at the end of the period. In recent years, however, the accounting profession has recognized that where a company has issued convertible securities and/or warrants, the number of shares will be increased when and if the options are exercised. So the "fully diluted" earnings are computed by adding to the present shares the number that may be issued for conversion or for sale through warrants and dividing this number into the adjusted earnings. (See Chapter 9.)

In recent years investors have paid increasing attention to *cash* earnings per share. This is derived by using earnings before depreciation and other noncash expenses, and after income taxes. "Cash flow per share" would be a better term, because the exempted expenses are indeed real. The cash flow figure reveals the total internally generated funds that are available for expansion if needed; in burgeoning situations such funds, invested at a high rate, can compound to the advantage of the stockholders. The investor is cautioned, however, not to substitute cash earnings for real earnings in appraising the value of a stock. Such a practice has too often been used to rationalize a very high market price.

Qualitative Factors

The tests just described are statistical in nature, using company reports and other data. But there are a number of "qualitative" factors which, while not subject to precise measurement, are very important. Some of these are: (1) special influences that affect the growth and stability of earnings, such as development of new products, change in market share, control of raw materials, vulnerability to price competition, patent control, technological progress, labor relations, and influence of public policy and regulation; (2) the general character and competency of management, its other corporate connections, and the outlook for adequate management succession; (3) perhaps most important of all, the long-term outlook or trend in the future, which must be based in part on doubt or trust and can be estimated only in very uncertain quantitative terms. Other "qualitative" factors that are difficult to measure will be indicated in subsequent chapters.

Characteristics of the Particular Security

The type of security and its peculiar terms and characteristics obviously have an important bearing on its quality. We saw in the earlier chapters describing the various classes of corporate securities that these range from prior-lien bonds with very wide safety margins of both assets and earnings to common stocks representing a very thin equity in the corporate property and income. One cannot generalize about whole groups of securities; many exceptions make it impossible to say that all senior mortgage bonds are safer than junior mortgages, all secured bonds are safer than debentures, all debentures are safer than preferred stocks, or all preferred stocks safer than common stocks. The quality of an issue depends not only on its relative rank but on the resources and earnings of the issuer.

The preferred stock of one company may exhibit more real strength than the first mortgage bonds of another company. The strength of the issuer, the support given its various security issues, and the particular provisions of those issues must be closely inspected. Only within the financial structure of an *individual* company can one safely expect the type and ranking of an issue to determine its relative quality.

Notwithstanding the above comments, the inherent differences between debt and equity, between senior and junior debt, and between preferred and common stocks require that the junior issues present a wider margin of protection if they are to be considered as having real investment quality.

The chief features that affect *relative* position and, thus, relative safety *within* the company's capitalization are: (1) Rank: in the case of bonds, priority of any lien on assets and the value of the pledged assets; in the case of debentures, whether or not these are subordinated to other unsecured debt; in the case of preferred stock, whether the issue is equal to or has precedence over other preferred issues. (2) Sinking fund or purchase provisions and the rate of required retirement of bonds and preferred stock. (3) Restrictions on additional or equal debt. (4) Provisions designed to protect the total debt and working capital position, as well as limitations on common stock dividends. (See Chapters 8 and 9.)

Other Influences on Price and Yield

A number of other characteristics or features pertaining to specific security issues influence their prices and yields, but these are not associated with quality in the sense we have been using this term. They include the call provision, any convertible or warrant features, special tax status, the marketability and seasoning of the issue, and its appeal to special groups, especially to institutional investors. These are discussed in Chapters 8 and 9 and elsewhere where pertinent.

Other factors affecting price and yield reflect the types of risks other than the business or internal risk. These include the risk of price variations in the securities markets as a whole, the "interest rate" risk, and the risk of loss of purchasing power (see Chapter 19).

Sources of Analytical Information

The most useful general sources for the analysis of quality of investment securities are indicated in Chapter 13. In other chapters special sources pertaining to specific media and industries are separately listed.

REFERENCES

BADGER, R. E., *The Complete Guide to Investment Analysis*. New York: McGraw-Hill, Inc., 1967.

BERNSTEIN, L. A., *Financial Statement Analysis*. Homewood, Ill.: Richard D. Irwin, Inc., 1974.

BOGEN, J. I., ed., *Financial Handbook*, 4th rev. ed., Sec. 8. New York: The Ronald Press Company, 1968.

FOULKE, R. A., *Practical Financial Statement Analysis*, 6th ed., Part I. New York: McGraw-Hill, Inc., 1968.

GRAHAM, BENJAMIN, D. L. DODD, and SIDNEY COTTLE, *Security Analysis*, 4th ed., Chapters 2, 7. New York: McGraw-Hill, Inc., 1962.

————, and CHARLES McGOLRICK, *The Interpretation of Financial Statements*, 3d rev. ed. New York: Harper & Row, Publishers, 1975.

HELFERT, E. A., *Techniques of Financial Analysis*, 3d ed. Homewood, Ill.: Dow Jones-Irwin, Inc., 1972.

Institute of Chartered Financial Analysts, *C.F.A. Readings in Financial Analysis*, 3d ed., Part I. Homewood, Ill.: Richard D. Irwin, Inc., 1970.

JAEDICKE, R. K., and R. T. SPROUSE, *Accounting Flows: Income, Funds and Cash*. Englewood Cliffs, N.J.: Prentice-Hall, Inc., 1965.

KENNEDY, R. D., and S. Y. MCMULLEN, *Financial Statements*, 6th ed., Part I. Homewood, Ill.: Richard D. Irwin, Inc., 1973.

LEV, BARUCH, *Financial Statement Analysis: A New Approach*. Englewood Cliffs, N.J.: Prentice-Hall, Inc., 1974.

LEVINE, S. N., ed., *Financial Analyst's Handbook*, Vol. I, Chapters 21–23, 25. Homewood, Ill.: Dow Jones-Irwin, Inc., 1975.

MARIELLO, J. A., *Accounting for the Financial Analyst*. Homewood, Ill.: Richard D. Irwin, Inc., 1967.

MILLER, D. E., *The Meaningful Interpretation of Financial Statements*, rev. ed. New York: American Management Association, 1972.

MYER, J. N., *Financial Statement Analysis*, 4th ed. Englewood Cliffs, N.J.: Prentice-Hall, Inc., 1969.

WIXON, RUFUS, ed., *Accountants Handbook*, 5th ed., Sec. 3. New York: The Ronald Press Company, 1970.

Valuation of Corporate Securities

SCOPE: In this chapter we are concerned with the important problem of valuation of securities. The subjects discussed are: (1) significance of valuation, (2) general problems of valuation (3) valuation of corporate bonds, (4) valuation of convertible securities, (5) valuation of preferred stocks, and (6) common stock valuation.

The discussion emphasizes the corporate securities group of investments. Regarding other investments, marketable Federal government obligations bear no risk of default of interest or principal. Their value depends on the interest rate applying to a particular maturity at a particular time. Price rises and falls conversely with this rate, but always equals investment value. Decisions with respect to the purchase and sale of Federal obligations, therefore, are made on considerations other than value. Obligations of state and local governments are valued on the basis of risk, adjusted for the influence of exemption from income taxation. (See Chapter 7.) Because the importance of tax- exemption varies among different investors, these securities are worth different amounts to different investors. Yet there is only one market price for a particular issue. The valuation of investment company shares was discussed in Chapter 11. Real estate securities present peculiar problems, as indicated in Chapter 12.

Significance of Valuation

In contrast to that of a trader, whose chief interest lies in short-term price changes, the portfolio of an investor in corporate securities for income or for long-term price appreciation should consist of the best values chosen from the large number of available bonds and stocks. Why pay too much? Why hold a security if others offer more value for the money? The answers to these questions present difficult problems, especially in the case of common stocks. An investor may avoid these problems by seeking out securities that may perform the best in the *market*, regardless of value. But here he is relegating the choice of his investment portfolio to the market, that is, to the decisions of others.

An investor may believe in valuation, but avoid making valuation decisions himself. He may buy investment company shares, place funds in a common trust fund, or use other means of indirect investment. Or he may simply rely on the advice of others in the direct purchase or sale of securities.

But even if he elects to emphasize value in his own operations, he can ease his task in two ways: (1) by dollar-cost-averaging, counting on the swings in the market above or below value to produce good long-run results; (2) by diversification, so that, within a total list, too much paid for one security may be offset by underpayment for another. Many funds, individual and institutional, combine these approaches.

The following discussion is based on the assumption that value is important and that the investor will use swings in market prices to his advantage. Sharp changes in market price may bring a security into or out of its value range. The task of the investor or his adviser is to recognize when price and value coincide or differ.

General Problems of Valuation

One may like everything about a security but its price. Indeed, to buy (or sell) a security at too high (or too low) a price is almost as bad as to buy (or sell) the wrong security. While this may be an exaggeration, it suggests that within the host of alternatives the investor may always find some securities that are suitably priced. Or if the ones in which he is interested are overpriced, later market corrections may bring some or all of them into a proper buying range.

All securities have one thing in common: they are worth the present value of their expected future income or, in the case of bonds, the present value of future interest plus the present value of the principal at or before maturity. (See Chapter 8.) Except in sale or liquidation, corporate assets in general are worth what their future earnings are worth. Very liquid assets are, of course, a special factor because they may be used to fill the gap between temporarily low earnings and interest or dividends.

The basic problem of valuation is to estimate future cash income and to pay a price for it that properly reflects the degree of uncertainty of that income. Even a careful analysis cannot predict the future with accuracy; but it can diminish uncertainty and prevent some purchases at grossly excessive prices, and some sales at the very worst time.

The discussion in the previous and following chapter reveals that all security analysis is pointed either directly or indirectly at future income. The financial strength (current and long-term) of a company, its asset values, its management, and the other elements involved in security investigation, relate to the size and regularity of earnings and of income.

Certain problems arise from this approach. The income of ordinary bonds and preferred stocks consists of interest or dividends, and these can be discounted to present value at a rate that reflects the risk of default. In the case of common stocks, however, the estimated dividends may range from none at all (at least in the short run) to 100% of earnings. And where a certain holding period is assumed, value at some "terminal" date must be estimated, theoretically based on present value at that time. Thus, a controversy develops as to whether dividends or earnings determine the value of a common stock. The case for dividends is strong. Retained earnings can be realized only in eventual dividends or in price appreciation, which is itself, theoretically, a function of dividends from the time of sale.

However, the complexities of dividend estimation, and the uncertainties of long-period forecasting make a strong case for using three-to five-year future earnings as the basis of valuation. And special situations such as valuation for merger, or large liquidating dividends, or possible payments of deferred interest or dividends, may affect market value or require special valuation approaches in particular cases.

Many securities do not lend themselves to valuation because future earnings and dividends cannot be estimated. These include securities of small, new companies, those with unusually large earnings fluctuations, those affected by special factors such as a drastic change in management, product lines, or public policy, and those whose prospects depend mainly on foreign operations. Such *qualitative* factors may so outweigh the measurable factors as to make any attempt at valuation a mere guessing game.

A second problem is to determine the reliability of *past* earnings (and of interest or dividend payments) and past price history as the basis for estimates of the future. The past record is the only *known* clue to the future. It reveals past earnings, asset values, and the quality and intentions of management, as well as relationships between earnings and price. To this record must be added an appraisal of any changes that can be anticipated. At best, a study of the past record can aid in diminishing the uncertainty of future prospects.

A third problem is to weigh those forces affecting value that are external to the particular company or security, such as changes in interest rates in the capital market, features of the tax structure, institutional demand, and market efficiency. Changes in security values reflect not only changes in the estimated risk associated with a particular company, but sometimes more importantly, factors that affect all securities or specific types of securities.

A final general problem of valuation is to account for those characteristics that are not associated with inherent risk or quality, including such special features of bonds and preferred stocks (call prices and convertible clauses), marketability, and tax status, as discussed in previous chapters. The valuation should be made first on the basis of quality; then, the incidence of the other factors is taken into account.

Valuation of Corporate Bonds

The *price* of a (straight) bond is the present value of future coupons plus the present value of principal at maturity, discounted at the yield rate. "The price goes where the yield sends it." The methods of price calculation, given the yield requirement, are presented in Chapter 8.

The *value* of high-grade and good-grade corporate bonds is determined by the yield rate that properly reflects the difference between certainty of income and the risk involved. The analyst seeks to answer this question: "Is the yield sufficiently above the riskless rate (for an equivalent maturity) to reward the buyer properly for the risk of nonpayment of interest (and principal)?" If a 20-year Treasury bond yields 7%, does a corporate bond yield of 8, or 8 1/2, or 9% provide a sufficient spread (1, 1 1/2, or 2%) to compensate for the risk? The decision is made after the analysis of the industry, company, and security, along the lines outlined in Chapter 24 and succeeding chapters, has been completed. If the bond is rated, the powerful influence of this factor, representing professional opinion of quality, must also be recognized.

An investor should also compare the yield on a corporate bond with those on high-grade bonds *of the same maturity*, in the same industrial category. Yields on various high-grade bond series are published regularly by Moody's and Standard & Poor's. Suppose, for example, that the average yield on long-term high-grade industrial bonds is 8 1/2%. Such bonds have been appraised twice—by the rating agency and by the market. But the careful investor should satisfy himself that the yield properly reflects the risk. Is the bond high-grade?

In the 1970s the factor of inflation became a very important consideration. Payment of interest and principal in purchasing power became almost as important an issue as payment in dollars. When the long-term riskless return on money, an additional reward for financial risk, and a premium for inflation (purchasing power risk) were combined, it was no surprise to find corporate bonds of poor quality yielding over 10%. (See Chapter 19.) And care must be taken to compare similar maturities and to recognize the special factors, apart from quality, that influence yield. (See Chapters 8 and 19.)

The valuation of high-grade bonds presents few difficulties. The chief problem is to detect later deterioration in quality, and this requires watching. Medium-grade bonds take more care, because the spread between the riskless rate and their yields is wider and more variable, and they may move both up and down in quality.

A low-grade bond, where payment of interest and/or principal is in doubt, should be analyzed like a common stock. Where only a very rough estimate of future earnings can be made, future interest payments are a matter of conjecture, and these should be considered in the category of dividends (unless liquidation, sale, or reorganization is in prospect). Yield *to maturity* is almost meaningless, and current yield must be used and possibly compared with the dividend yields on common stocks. Where no current income is available, the bond sells flat. (See Chapter 8.)

Valuation of Convertible Securities

The value of convertible securities (described in Chapter 9) is based on two elements: (1) the "investment" value of their future interest coupons or dividends, and principal (bonds) at maturity, at an appropriate yield rate determined by analysis, plus (2) the value (if any) of the conversion feature. The latter may send the price of a convertible security above, and the yield below, that which it should bear as a "straight" security. After conversion point is reached, the price will continue to rise (and the yield at market price to fall) with the rise in the value of the shares into which each bond or preferred share is convertible. After this point, their analysis involves that of the stock itself.

As indicated in Chapter 8, current yield receives special attention in the analysis of convertible bonds, because the bond is not expected to remain unconverted.

Valuation of Preferred Stocks

The valuation of sound preferred stocks is similar to that of bonds, but without the influence of maturity. The price should produce a yield that is sufficiently above either the riskless rate, or the rate on the very highest-grade preferreds of the same industry, to compensate for the risks as analyzed. Two factors that differentiate preferred stocks from most bonds should be reemphasized: (1) Their income is not a fixed charge; it is *dividend* income— dependent on earnings and dividend policy; (2) they have no maturity (save for possible call or redemption by the issuer). Because preferred stocks are *equity* securities in the legal sense, the yields of even the strongest ones should exceed those of high-grade bonds. However, as we have seen, the income tax appeal of preferred stocks to taxed corporate investors has a special influence on their prices and yields.

Where the investor assumes that he may not hold his preferred stock indefinitely, either because it may be called by the issuer or because he expects to sell it, his evaluation should include its terminal value as well as its dividends. In the strict mathematical sense, the valuation is the present value of a stream of dividends plus that of the redemption or sale price, using the appropriate yield rate as the discount rate.

The value of the very strongest preferred stocks is influenced by some of the same "nonrisk" factors that affect the yield on bonds—the probabilities of change in interest rates, and the required reward for loss of purchasing power due to inflation. The influence of any conversion feature, marketability, seasoning, and taxes must also be taken into account.

The valuation of good-grade preferred stocks involves determining the higher rate at which future dividends are capitalized. Again, the increment over and above the bond rate reflects the strength of the issue, primarily as determined by the assets that support each share and the estimated coverage of the dividend by earnings.

Very weak preferred stocks are valued like common stocks, plus the possible additional value of any accumulated preferred dividends. With respect to the latter, the investor must estimate the chances of (1) full cash payment, sooner or later; (2) part cash payment; (3) payment in securities rather than cash, by a "recapitalization"; and (4) complete default.

Common Stock Valuation

Principles The basic criteria of common stock values are the amount, reliability, and stability of future earnings and, therefore, dividends. Tests of financial condition, operating efficiency, asset values, and management, as suggested in the previous chapter and in succeeding chapters, all bear on these fundamental factors. The main problem of common stock valuation is twofold: (1) to estimate future earnings (and dividends), and (2) to apply a rate of capitalization (or its counterpart, a price-earnings or price-dividends ratio) that will compensate for the risks as analyzed. With the necessity of combining the variables the resulting valuation can be approximate at best and is subject to regular reassessment and possible correction.

A holder of common stock may obtain the earnings of his company in only two ways (other than through liquidation): (1) by receipt of cash dividends, and (2) by *realized* appreciation in market value that reflects the retention of earnings. Where the bulk of earnings is distributed in dividends, and where such dividends have been and are expected to be regular, the chief basis of valuation is the estimated stream of future cash dividends. The investor demands a dividend yield sufficiently above the bond rate to reflect the uncertainty in the amount and stability of the future dividend stream. Under normal conditions for the average stock, an appropriate yield on current market price should be about 50% above the riskless bond rate. Thus, if the rate on long-term Treasury bonds is 7%, the stock should yield over 10%. But inspection shows that only the weakest issues afford such a rate, even in periods of very high bond yields such as 1973–1975. (See Chapter 9.) The explanation is two-fold: (1) The company is expected to retain a substantial portion of its earnings and gain the advantages of earnings plough-back; (2) both earnings and dividends are expected to increase. The basic criterion of value is *future* returns.

If earnings are not distributed but are retained in the company, they may do little more than temporarily strengthen a weak situation. On the other hand, they may compound at such a good rate (as in the case of attractive "growth" stocks) as to increase the net worth rapidly. Under these conditions the anomaly appears: the lower the cash dividends, the higher the value. This is the case where the company can earn a much more attractive rate than the investor can find in a sound income-producing investment, net after taxes. The tax treatment of capital gains adds additional worth to retained earnings under these circumstances, so that the valuation of current earnings is high (the price-earnings ratio is high) and any modest cash dividends produce a very low yield on market price.

These concepts explain the high price-earnings multiples of the late 1960s and early 1970s that were applied to "glamour" growth stocks. The great decline of stock prices in 1973–1974 saw the collapse of the "two-tier" market in which the multiples of current earnings of many growth stocks, ranging from 30 to 50 times earnings or even higher, were much higher than those of slow-growth or primarily income stocks. (See Chart 19-2.) Nevertheless, after the big break, although stock yields in general rose considerably, they still remained substantially below bond yields. (See Chapter 9.) With the yield on high-grade corporate bonds well over 9%, even "income stocks" produced only 6 to 8%, and many "growth" stocks sold at 15 to 30 times earnings. *Future* earnings and dividends still determined value.

In the long run, then, the high appraisal of "growth" stocks stems from the possibility of *ultimately* high dividend distributions. In the shorter run, undistributed earnings may be worth much more than earnings paid out.

What about asset values? The book or "net asset" value of common stock has usually been given only modest consideration in the valuation of stocks other than those of utilities (where, through regulation, earnings stem from investment), financial companies (where book values represent realizable liquid values), and real estate companies or trusts with realizable properties. In other cases a share of stock is worth what it can earn, not what was spent for the assets it represents. (See Tables 9-1 and 25-1.) However, two uses

TABLE 25-1   Data on Dow Jones 30 Industrial Stocks 1950–1976

Year	Earnings	Price Range	Average[a]	Price-Earnings Ratio[b]		Dividends Amt.	%
1950	$30.70	197–235	219	1.6	7.1	$16.13	7.4%
1955	35.78	388–488	454		12.7	21.58	4.8
1960	32.21	566–685	612		19.0	21.36	3.5
1961	31.91	610–735	698		21.9	22.71	3.3
1962	36.43	536–726	625		17.2	23.30	3.9
1963	41.21	647–767	721		17.5	23.41	3.2
1964	46.43	766–892	849		18.3	31.24	3.8
1965	53.67	841–969	836		15.6	28.61	3.4
1966	57.68	744–995	914		15.8	31.89	3.9
1967	53.87	786–943	890		16.5	30.19	3.4
1968	57.89	825–985	905		15.6	31.34	3 5
1969	57.02	770–969	856		15.0	33.90	4.0
1970	51.02	631–842	767		15.0	31.53	4.1
1971	55.09	798–951	893		16.2	30.86	3.5
1972	67.11	889–1036	961		14.3	32.27	3.3
1973	86.17	788–1052	910		10.6	35.33	3.9
1974	99.04	568–897	718		7.2	37.72	5.3
1975	75.66	632–882	823		10.9	37.46	4.5
1976	96.72	859–1015	999		10.3	41.40	4.1

[a]Average of quarterly closing prices.
[b]Using annual earnings and average price.
Source: *Dow Jones Investor's Handbook.* Homewood, Ill.: Dow Jones-Irwin, Inc., annual.

may be made of the book value figure. First, where it is much lower than appraised value based on earnings, the investor must be confident that the current high rate of earnings on book investment will continue. Second, where it is much higher than appraised value, a bargain is suggested, provided: (1) analysis reveals that earnings—and dividends—may be expected to increase in a "turnaround," or (2) complete or partial liquidation is a possibility. Stocks that sell at or near the net *current* asset value per share (which means that the buyer is paying little or nothing for plant and equipment) offer a low base price that should be considerably enhanced by even a modest increase in earnings. Otherwise the company is "worth more dead than alive," and ripe for a "take-over."

With the above general concepts in mind, more specific approaches to common stock valuation can now be outlined. We should recognize, however, that only a *range* of value, not a precise figure, can be developed. A stock with such regularity of earnings and dividends as to resemble a bond can be valued fairly precisely. A stock presenting great uncertainties can be valued, if at all, only very crudely.

Valuation of near-term earnings   Either   because   the   investor cannot or does not wish to project earnings and/or dividends he often values his stock or decides to purchase, hold, or sell it on the basis of its price in relating to this year's or next year's earnings per share. Whether the price-earnings multiples are too high, too low, or just right depends on comparisions with other stocks or with the market as a whole. This practice is fostered by the publicity given to price-earnings ratios that are now published daily, along with prices, in the leading newspapers.

Use of relative values   Individual common stocks are often considered under- or overvalued in relation to the market as a whole, or to other securities of the same industry. Thus, if the Dow Jones 30 industrial stocks were selling at 11 times current earnings, and at a 4.00% yield from current dividends, a particular industrial stock selling at 8 times earnings and producing a 6% yield might at first sight be deemed undervalued. But if a comparison is to have any merit, the sophisticated investor should compare the projected rate of growth of earnings and/or dividends of "the Dow" with that of the individual stock.

Another use of the relative approach is to compare the price-earnings ratio and the dividend yield of a particular stock with those of other firms in the same industry or with the industry average. This may reveal differences that deserve an explanation and may suggest interesting investment possibilities.

Although such approaches are not real valuation, a comparison within the general market may provide a clue to an over- or undervalued situation which can be confirmed by the investor's valuation after he has completed his analysis. The same is true of comparisons within an industry. The relationships in the market as a whole, that is, how investment-grade common stocks in general and in specific groups are valued by the consensus of investment opinion, provide benchmarks that have considerable usefulness when followed by real investigation of the particular situation.

Use of price-earnings multiples   One often hears such statements as: "The Dow Jones industrials are selling at only x times earnings, compared to ratios of up to 25 that they have enjoyed in the past." Or, "The present multiplier of x for the S & P 500 is the lowest since 19—." Or, "This stock has historically sold at x times earnings; now the multiple is only y." Or, "The stock seems overvalued; its multiple is too high in relation to its past average."

Table 25-1 shows the historical relationship between earnings and price for the Dow Jones 30 Industrial stocks, 1950–1976. Over the period, the annual earnings ranged from $31 to $99, the price from 199 to 1052. High prices usually resulted from the combination of high earnings and a high price-earnings ratio as in 1964–1966. Low prices combined these two factors at low levels, as in 1974–1975.

Comparison with the past may indicate *possible* over- or undervaluation, and thus lead to more searching evaluation. But for common stocks as a whole, for those of an industry, or for an individual stock, past conditions may not repeat, and new factors and relationships may emerge. In 1973–1975, for example, short- and long-term interest rates were very high, the economy was in a recession, and inflation ranged from 6 to 12%. The low price-earnings multipliers reflected this unprecedented combination for which the past was an unreliable guide.

The previous approaches are crude methods of valuation based on current or short-term earnings. They may be the only available procedures, however, especially when future earnings and dividends are highly uncertain or where pertinent information is lacking. And the "bloodless verdict of the market-place," past and present, should not be ignored, especially for trading purposes. But where possible, "intrinsic" valuation using future earnings and/or dividends is the wiser course.

Basic factors in determining "intrinsic value"   Ideally, a real valuation involves the determination of "intrinsic" value or real worth, which can then be compared to market price in making decisions to buy, sell, or hold. Such a valuation is justified on the grounds that stocks are often over- or undervalued in the market, and that valuation not based on market opinion, past or present, will help to identify the correct course of action.

"Intrinsic" valuation recognizes that *future* earnings and/or dividends are the main determinants of real value. This in turn involves two basic problems: (1) estimates of a number of variables, including trends in earnings, dividend payout ratios, stability of earnings and dividends, asset values, the influence of leverage, and corporate liquidity; and (2) evaluation of qualitative" factors such as "management," industry trends, and the "powerful influence of the level of interest rates. All of these affect the estimates of earnings and dividends and the choice of the multiple to be applied.

Valuation using the time value of money   If the value of common stock depends on the course of future earnings and/or dividends, it follows that such returns should be discounted to their present value at an appropriate rate, just as in the case of bonds. The more sophisticated approaches to common stock valuation involve application of the concept of the time value of money.[1]

Exclusive of highly complicated methods, there are four chief valuation approaches that involve the determination of present value:

1. Discounting perpetual dividends in a no-growth situation.
2. Discounting changing rates of dividends.

---

[1]The pioneering work in this field is J. B. Williams, *The Theory of Investment Value* (Cambridge, Mass.: Harvard University Press, 1938).

3. Discounting changing dividends plus terminal value.
4. Discounting future earnings.

VALUATION OF PERPETUAL LEVEL DIVIDENDS   If it is assumed that a common stock may distribute about the same dividend in perpetuity, as in the case of a perpetual noncallable bond or a preferred stock, its present value is the dividend divided by a rate of capitalization that combines the riskless bond rate plus a premium for risk. The model is:[2]

$$V = \frac{D_0}{K}$$

where K is the capitalization rate. This will vary through time as interest rates and risk change just as bond yields and values change. This type of situation is unrealistic insofar as the vast majority of common stocks are concerned, but it forms the basis for the appraisal of more likely conditions.

VALUATION OF DISCOUNTED CHANGING FUTURE DIVIDENDS   In theory, the intrinsic value of a share of stock is the present value of *all* future dividend payments. Future price appreciation will represent the value of future dividends from any point in time. Such an approach applies to stocks the same valuation concept as would be applied to a bond. The formula is:

$$V_0 = D_0 + \frac{D_1}{(1 + K)^1} + \frac{D_2}{(1 + K)^2} + \frac{D_3}{(1 + K^3)} \cdots$$

$$= \sum_{t=1}^{\infty} \frac{D_t}{(1 + K)^t}$$

Where dividends are expected to increase in the future at a constant rate, and are considered perpetual, a simple formula for approximating their present value is:

$$V_0 = \frac{\text{Current dividend rate}}{(1 + \text{discount rate}) \div (1 + \text{growth rate}) - 1}$$

This model is derived from the following equation, where g represents the expected (constant) rate of growth of dividends:

$$V_0 = \sum_{t=1}^{\infty} \frac{D_0(1 + g)^t}{(1 + K)^t} = \frac{D_0}{K - g}$$

Again, K is the rate of capitalization based on risk and other factors, that is, the investor's desired rate of return. This can be derived either by adding a premium to the bond rate or (less acceptably) by using a "normal" rate reflecting the company's growth and stability in relation to that of the economy. The premium added to the bond rate would reflect primarily the expected stability of earnings and dividends. This in turn requires a careful analysis of all pertinent factors that affect earnings, dividend policy, financing, and balance-sheet strength.

---

[2]In more detail:

$$\sum_{t=1}^{\infty} \frac{D_t}{(1 + K)^t} = \frac{D_0}{K}$$

Another approach to deriving the appropriate rate at which dividends are discounted is to start with the "historical" long-term rate of dividend return on stocks and add a premium for expected growth in dividends that exceeds the normal rate, or deduct a penalty for lesser expected performance. The difficulty with this approach is that the historical rate is a function of the period selected. Some use a 20-, 30-, or even 50-year rate. In a world of change, what rate is "normal"?

More complicated applications of this approach assume that there will be various rates of growth through different future periods, such as a transitional period, a period of stability, and then possibly a period of decline. And to reflect the increased risk of the future, the discount rate applied to future dividends is increased at either a fixed or variable rate.[3] Growth-rate tables are used to locate the factors in the individual case.

Such complexity is unrealistic in a changing economic world. It is impossible to make a reliable projection of dividends over a long period of years based on the projected rates, levels, and duration of earnings growth. In addition, the choice of the multiplier at which projected dividends are capitalized is very much a matter of opinion. Writers using this approach who suggest multipliers based on historical average dividend yields for high-grade stocks adjusted for risk, are in part turning to the past market to determine intrinsic value. This value should be free of market influence and be based on future returns.

VALUATION OF DIVIDENDS PLUS TERMINAL VALUE A strict application of valuation based on cash flow must include the present value of any future sales price. A stock is worth what the owner will get from all sources. Hence, the value of a stock is the discounted present value of future dividends plus the discounted present value of estimated sales proceeds at a given future time. Accordingly, to the previous formula one would add $P_t(1 + K)^t$, where P is the terminal value.

This approach involves not only estimating future earnings and then payout, but also the multiplier that the market will apply to those earnings at the time of sale. The uncertainty is compounded, especially if one is making projections over a number of years.

VALUATION OF DISCOUNTED (LONG-TERM) PROJECTED EARNINGS A more refined application of the dividend-valuation approach pays specific attention to retained earnings and their effect on dividends. Corporate earnings can be either distributed or reinvested, and the payout is a function of earnings growth. The valuation process then becomes one of capitalizing projected *earnings* per share as they are affected by the retention of profits. Historically, the combination of dividends and price appreciation reflecting earnings growth was 8 to 9% for common stocks in general, (as of studies in the 1960s). Tables have been constructed to show the multipliers to be applied to "normal" earnings. The multipliers are a function of (1) the estimated trend of earnings growth for a constant growth period followed, say,

---

[3]See citations to Clendenin, Bauman, and Soldofsky in the References at the end of this chapter.

by a diminishing growth period, and (2) of the investor's desired rate of return. The latter will have been chosen by considering alternative investments or by using the historical average return, which is a perilous guide, as we have seen. As an example, suppose the "normal earnings" of a company, derived from past and current earnings, are $6.00 a share, that its projected rate of earnings growth is 6% (for a constant growth period of seven years, followed by a diminishing growth period of 10 years), and that the investor's desired rate of return is 8%. One set of tables shows that the appropriate multiplier is 14.5. Applying this multiplier to $6.00 produces a value of $87.

This approach would have to be amended for changing estimates of the total return on common stocks, for the stability of the company's earnings, and for changing rates of growth, and so would require a different multiplier than the tables assume.

Valuation by simpler methods   The difficulties in estimating all of the variables that are involved on longer-range projections suggest that, in many situations, more elementary approaches to valuation are more feasible:

1. Valuation of short-run dividends of income stocks.
2. Valuation of projected earnings without discounting.
3. Valuation based on the bond rate.

These involve projections of three to seven years—certainly long enough in a world and an economy of rapid change. They also avoid the illusion that very precise figures have some magic validity.

SLOW GROWTH INCOME STOCKS   Common stocks that offer the prospect of only very modest growth of earnings, and which are expected to distribute all or most of their earnings in dividends, are attractive for income rather than for price appreciation. Their value is determined by capitalizing their expected short-run (three- to five-year) dividends at a rate that compensates for risk. This rate is constructed by adding to the *bond rate*, that is, the rate on "riskless" money as represented by the return on long-term Treasury bonds, a premium reflecting the assurance of payment, as determined by analysis. As an illustration, consider a sound company whose dividends grew from $1.20 to $1.60 per share in the past 10 years, and for which a reasonable expectation of average dividends for the next five years is $1.75, reflecting modest growth of earnings and a high payout ratio. Using a bond rate of 7%, plus 1 1/2% for risk, a capitalization rate of 8 1/2% is derived which, applied to $1.75, produces a value range of 19 to 22. Such a valuation, involving a low premium over the bond rate, reflects an appraisal that the stock has high general quality and that dividends will likely continue to grow at the same modest rate *after* the five-year period. Otherwise, a high-grade bond yielding 8 1/2% would be preferable.

Instead of using the "riskless" rate as a base, some recommend the yield on high-grade corporate bonds or the dividend yield on sound income producing public utility stocks. The flaw here is that other people's opinions of value must be accepted. In addition, in the case of the utility stocks, market prices are involved, so that the investor is using the market to determine intrinsic value. Neither of these defects is involved when the Treasury bond rate is used.[4]

In many cases a dividend cannot be projected beyond one year, and even the income for the current year may be questionable. In such cases the current dividend should be capitalized at a high rate to reflect the uncertainty. Under these conditions however, it would be better not to attempt a valuation at all.

Where substantial increases in dividends can be expected in the future, and if, based on past and current policy, the company can be expected to pay out most of its earnings, the valuation of income stocks becomes similar to that of other stocks as discussed above.

VALUATION OF PROJECTED EARNINGS WITHOUT DISCOUNTING Some valuation approaches assume that making long-range earnings and/or dividend projections is feasible. But in a world of change, projecting earnings for even a few years in the future becomes difficult if not impossible. This situation can be met by basing the valuation on a projection of *average* future earnings for a *limited* number of years. The price-earnings multiplier, or the rate of capitalization, is adjusted for the likelihood of continued earnings growth beyond that period.

One commonly used application of this simpler approach involves estimating average future earnings for, say, five to seven years, and applying to such earnings the multipliers that have been typical of the stock in the past. The past relation between price and earnings reflects the judgment of many buyers and sellers. If a stock has always sold at a high multiple, this is because a high opinion of the company has been registered in actual transactions. Where this opinion has not always been borne out by the actual record, the price will have been readjusted to the facts of the case. Granted that the market-earnings relationship may have often been in error, and that the *future* of the company may not resemble the past, such past opinion should not be overlooked. The average multiple based on several years of record can thus be applied to estimated earnings to produce a current valuation. However, as indicated previously, in using this approach the investor must realize that past price-earnings relationships in the market as a whole may not recur for some months or even years. Similarly, substantial changes in interest rates may affect the rates at which stock earnings are capitalized and hence produce new price-earnings multiples for *all* grades of stocks as illustrated by the decline in the prices of most stocks in 1966, 1969–1970, and 1973–1974, when interest rates on fixed-income obligations rose to record heights.

Applying *past* price-earnings multipliers to *future* earnings also has a technical defect. The past multipliers were based on the then *current* earnings, but reflected future earnings growth. To apply these to *future* increased earnings in order to derive a current valuation involves a double counting

---

[4]In any use of the yield on Treasury bonds, the investor must be careful to employ an average yield on long-term issues that are not affected by "deep-discount" prices. Both Moody's and Standard & Poor's publish acceptable representative yield figures, as does the *Federal Reserve Bulletin*.

of growth. Such earnings should be discounted to the present if this approach is used. Or this method should be used to estimate *future* rather than current value.[5]

Another approach is to estimate the rate of growth of future earnings per share, and to apply to the average of, say, seven years' future earnings a multiplier that is itself a *function of the rate of growth of earnings*. The multiplier is based on a modification of the historical norm for the market as a whole, adjusted for the individual situation. To cite an example, if the average rate of growth of earnings over the next seven years (fourth-year earnings) is estimated at 3.5% (the very long-run rate of the Dow Jones 30 industrial stocks), a multiplier of 13.5 is applied, reflecting conditions in 1960-62. If the annual rate of growth is estimated at 5% or 7.2%, the multiplier becomes 14 times and 15 times, respectively, and so forth, to a top limit of 20 where earnings will grow 20% annually.[6]

In such an approach, because *both* the projected earnings per share and the multiplier are a function of growth of earnings, the problem of double counting again occurs. This is dealt with by the assumption that the growth will continue *after* the seventh year, and that this multiplier incorporates this factor. We should also note that this system assumes that the stocks being valued are all of investment grade. Lower multipliers would have to be applied to stocks falling below this standard, and revisions would be made to reflect newer estimates of growth.

VALUATION BASED ON THE BOND RATE   Some of the valuation methods previously described rely, at least in part, on the record in the market itself to help establish the value of a share of stock. What is needed is an approach that is *independent* of the stock market. The *bond-rate method* is suggested as a means to this end.

The investor always has the alternative of buying riskless bonds and enjoying the "pure" rate of interest available at the time of purchase. Equities present more risk than Treasury bonds. Thus, in the long run the *earnings yield* on common stocks should be substantially higher than the bond rate. How much higher? This depends on the risks in the situation.

With a long-term riskless rate of, say, 7%, the average stock should sell at an earnings yield of 10 to 11%, that is, at about 9 1/2 times average *future* earnings. Assuming an 8% rate of growth of earnings (or 7% compounded), about equal to the long-term growth of the Gross National Product, this would mean a price of about 11 1/2 times *current* earnings. If 60% of the earnings were distributed in dividends, this price would produce an average five-year dividend yield of 6 1/4% on the original price. A lower dividend payout would be compensated by a higher rate of growth. As an example, suppose an average-grade stock were currently earning $6 per share, and

---

[5]A sophisticated method of determining future value based on projected three- to five-year earnings (and dividends) by applying past "normal price/cash-earnings relationships and past "normal" dividend yields is found in the Value Line investment service. The method is explained in Arnold Bernhard, *Investing in Common Stocks with the Aid of the Value Line Rankings and Other Criteria of Stock Value* (New York: Bernhard & Co., 1975).

[6]See Benjamin Graham, D. L. Dodd, and Sidney Cottle, *Security Analysis: Principles and Techniques*, 4th ed., Chapter 29 (New York: McGraw-Hill, Inc., 1962).

that the price were $70, or 11 1/2 times current earnings. This is equivalent to about 9 1/2 times the average five-year *future* earnings of $7.35 (assuming a 7% compounded rate of growth). A 60% payout would produce a $3.60 dividend in the first year and $5.00 in the fifth year.

The investor would be willing to pay more than 11 1/2 times current earnings only if future earnings were expected to rise at an above-average rate. He would be willing to pay 20 times current earnings, or even more, if future earnings growth were expected to be exceptionally high.

A given stock should be classified for quality as belonging to one of five categories, based on analysis of earnings growth and stability, short- and long-term financial strength, dividend record and prospects, asset values, and management. (See Table 25-2.) An earnings yield based on expected average five-year *future* earnings, ranging from 1 to 2 times the bond rate, is appropriate for a given category. The average stock belongs in category 3.

TABLE 25-2   Valuation Based on Bond Rate

		Using Five-Year Average Future Earnings		
Quality Category	Bond Rate	Earnings Yield X Bond Rate	Earnings Yield	Price-Earnings Multiple
1	7%	1	7.0 %	14
2	7	1 1/4	8.75	11
3	7	1 1/2	10.50	9–10
4	7	1 3/4	12.25	8
5	7	2	14.0	7

By using average projected five-year earnings as the basis of valuation, a growth stock of great strength could be worth 30 times current earnings, but only if it will *double* its *average* annual earnings in the next five years. A stock of lesser quality is worth 20 times present earnings only if its *average* earnings are expected to increase 50% over the next five years, and so forth.

Let us take three or four hypothetical examples. Suppose a company is presently earning $4.00 per share. The company "has everything." An extraordinarily high rate of growth is expected that will send the annual earnings to $12.00 a share five years hence, for an average of $8.00. It has great financial strength and superlative management. It is placed in category 1. (See Table 25-2.) With the bond rate of 7%, this stock would be worth $8 × 14 = $112, or 28 times present earnings. Very few companies belong in such a category. Or take a company with high but less stable earnings growth prospects, good financial strength, steadily increasing dividends, and good management. Earnings per share *may* grow from $2.00 to $4.00 in five years (average $3.00), but some uncertainty exists. It is placed in category 2. A rough valuation becomes $33 a share. This is over 16 times *current* earnings. Or take a public utility company that has prospects for only modest growth. The current earnings are $4.00 per share and may grow to $5.00 in five years. Dividends are currently $3.00. The stock is valued largely on an income basis and is placed between categories 3 and 4.

A rough valuation is 35, or about 9 times *current* earnings, to yield 8.6% from the current dividend. Or take a growing but highly cyclical industrial company whose current earnings are $5 per share. Depending on economic conditions, the company will earn between $3 and $8 per share during the next five years. The stock is placed in category 4 and valued at 35. A nongrowth utility company would also belong in this category. Or lastly, take a mediocre situation. The current earnings per share are $2.00. But these are not expected to increase. Indeed, they may well decrease. Financial strength is only fair. Management is only so-so. It is placed below category 5. A rough valuation is 12 or less.

In recognition of the inability to read the future with accuracy, we might better cite *ranges* of value for the above situations such as 100 to 120, 30 to 35, 32 to 39, 33 to 40, and 10 to 14. This would allow for the fact that both variables—earnings and multiplier—are subject to error.

Note that in the rough method of valuation used above, earnings five years from now are not being bought at face value. In effect, they are roughly discounted. Yet credit *is* given for any expected growth. Likewise, if a company's earnings are on the decline, such decline would produce a still lower valuation.

The method just described might appear deceptively simple. Actually, the category in which a company is placed—that is, the quality rating that determines the appropriate multiplier of future earnings—is chosen only after thorough analysis. The estimate of future earnings is also based on the analysis and projection of all of the factors that will affect earnings. Very accurate results are not to be expected. For these reasons the number of quality categories is limited to five. Where one or both of these analyses cannot be made with reasonable assurance, a valuation should not be attempted.

The above valuations are based on an assumed riskless bond rate of 7%. As interest rates fall or rise, this rate will change, producing different value results. The relationship between interest rates and stock prices was dramatically illustrated in 1966 when much of the decline in stock prices could be attributed to rising interest rates, and later in 1967 when stock prices rose as interest rates declined. In 1969–1971 the general stock averages fell nearly 35% as bond yields rose to then unprecedented heights, and in 1973–1974 fell 40 to 50% as yields rose even higher. Much of the subsequent recovery can be attributed to declining bond yields. Events of recent years have shown conclusively that stock prices and bond yields are competitive, and therefore interrelated. This is why analysts of general stock price movements pay so much attention to the money supply, the flow of institutional savings, and other factors affecting interest rates.

It is suggested that the investor use several of the various methods of valuation, including both simple and more sophisticated methods, as cross-checks on each other.

Methods of Projecting Earnings   Most of the methods of valuation involve a projection of per-share earnings. One approach is to project the earnings-per-share figure itself, using past trends and future growth expectations. However, the net income figure is the result of all previous items on the income statement, and a projection of net income may overlook very important changes in items that have a powerful influence on the final earnings-per-share figure. A sounder approach is to project the sales, and apply to this basic figure the gross and net profit margins, estimated nonoperating income, fixed charges, and income taxes, that analysis suggests will apply in the future. Care should be taken to eliminate nonrecurring items and such invalid items as inventory profits due to inflation that may have disguised the real past earnings and so interfere with a valid projection of future results.

The following chapters indicate the analytical approaches that will aid the investor to size up the rate, stability, and prospects of earnings, the long- and short-term financial strength, the value of the assets, and the quality of management, in various types of industries. Such approaches provide the basis for intelligent investment decisions.

REFERENCES

AMLING, FREDERICK, *Investments*, 4th ed, Chapter 7. Englewood Cliffs, N.J.: Prentice-Hall, Inc., 1978.

BAUMAN, W. S., *Estimating the Present Value of Common Stocks by the Variable Rate Method*. Ann Arbor, Mich.: Bureau of Business Research, University of Michigan, 1963.

BERNHARD, ARNOLD, *Investing in Common Stocks*. New York: Bernhard & Co., 1975.

BREALEY, R. A., and C. PYLE, *A Bibliography of Finance and Investments*, Part 7, "The Valuating of Equities." Cambridge, Mass.: MIT Press, 1973.

CLENDENIN, J. C., *Theory and Techniques of Growth Stock Valuation*. Los Angeles: Bureau of Business and Economic Research, University of California, 1957.

COHEN, J. B., E. D. ZINBARG, and ARTHUR ZEIKEL, *Investment Analysis and Portfolio Management*, 3d ed., Part II. Homewood, Ill.: Richard D. Irwin, Inc., 1977.

COTTLE, SIDNEY, and TATE WHITMAN, *Corporate Earning Power and Market Valuation, 1935-1955*. Durham, N.C.: Duke University Press, 1959.

ELTON, E. J., and M. J. GRULIER, eds., *Security Evaluation and Portfolio Analysis*. Englewood Cliffs, N.J.: Prentice-Hall, Inc., 1972.

FOSTER, E. M., *Common Stock Investment*. Lexington, Mass.: Lexington Books, 1974.

FRANCIS, J. C., *Investments: Analysis and Management*, Chapter 8. New York: McGraw-Hill, Inc., 1972.

GORDON, M. J., *The Investment, Financing and Valuation of the Corporation*. Homewood, Ill.: Richard D. Irwin, Inc., 1962.

GRAHAM, BENJAMIN, *The Intelligent Investor*, 4th rev. ed., Chapter 11. New York: Harper & Row, Publishers, 1973.

———, D. L. DODD, and SIDNEY COTTLE, *Security Analysis*, 4th ed., Part IV. New York: McGraw-Hill, Inc., 1962.

LEVY, HAIM, and M. SARNAT, *Investment and Portfolio Analysis*, Chapters 4, 5. New York: John Wiley and Sons, Inc., 1972.

LORIE, JAMES, and R. BRADLEY, eds., *Modern Developments in Investment Management.* New York: Praeger Publishers, 1972.

McCARTHY, C. D., and R. E. HEALY, *Valuing a Company: Practices and Procedures.* New York: The Ronald Press Company, 1971.

SOLDOFSKY, R. M., and J. T. MURPHY, *Growth Yields on Common Stocks; Theory and Tables,* rev. ed. Iowa City: Bureau of Business and Economic Research, State University of Iowa, 1963.

WILLIAMS, J. B., *The Theory of Investment Value.* Cambridge, Mass.: Harvard University Press, 1938.

WILLIAMSON, J. P., *Investments: New Analytic Techniques,* Chapter 6. New York: Praeger Publishers, Inc., 1971.

A number of articles on common stock valuation have appeared in *The Financial Analysts Journal* over the years. Convenient selections of the more useful of these articles from this and other publications are found in the following collections of readings:

BALL, R. E., ed., *Readings in Investments,* Part II. Boston: Allyn & Bacon, Inc., 1965.

FREDERICKSON, E. B., ed., *Frontiers of Investment Analysis,* rev. ed., Part IV. Scranton, Pa.: International Textbook Company, 1971.

LERNER, E. M., ed., *Readings in Financial Analysis and Investment Management,* Publication of the Institute of Chartered Financial Analysts, Inc., Sections V, VI. Homewood, Ill.: Richard D. Irwin, Inc., 1963.

LORIE, J. T., and R. A. BREALEY, eds., *Modern Developments in Investment Management: A Book of Readings.* New York: Praeger Publishers, Inc., 1972.

THE INSTITUTE OF CHARTERED FINANCIAL ANALYSTS, *C.F.A. Readings in Financial Analysis,* 3d ed., Part V. Homewood, Ill.: Richard D. Irwin, Inc., 1976.

WEST, D. A., *Readings in Investment Analysis,* Part IV. Scranton, Pa.: International Textbook Company, 1969.

WU, H. K., and A. J. ZAKON, eds., *Elements of Investments: Selected Readings,* rev. ed., Part III. New York: Holt, Rinehart and Winston, Inc. 1972.

Securities of Industrial Companies

SCOPE: This chapter discusses the investment position of securities issued by industrial enterprises. The order of discussion is: (1) field of industry, (2) accounting problems, (3) industrial characteristics, (4) economic characteristics, (5) economic analysis of the industry and company, (6) analysis of income, (7) analysis of assets and financing, (8) working capital changes and flow of funds (9) ratio analysis of industrial statements, (10) use of consolidated statements, (11) special problems of conglomerates, (12) multinational companies, (13) industrial securities: bonds, preferred stock, common stock, and (14) special sources of composite industry data.

The Field of Industry

Industrial companies are engaged in the production and sale of commodities and services under competitive conditions. They comprise the great extractive, manufacturing, and distributive agencies of the nation. The extractive industries include mines, oil, timber, and fisheries.[1] The manufacturing industries cover all phases of manufacture, from automobiles and airplanes to textiles and typewriters. The distributive industries include merchandising operations of all kinds, wholesale, retail, and direct selling by mail. The term *industrials* also includes construction and service concerns. The industrials group includes all forms of private industry not formally classified as transportation, public utilities, financial, or real estate companies.

As a group, the industrials provide in large measure the economic life of the country. Important as the railroad, utility, and financial enterprises are, they serve subordinately as facilitating agencies for the industrial companies.

Accounting Problems

In contrast with the comparability of financial statements of railroad and public utility companies, analysis of industrial companies is complicated by a lack of uniform accounting procedures. Within the boundaries of accept-

---

[1]Natural gas companies, which also belong in the extractive group but which are regulated public utilities, are discussed in Chapter 27.

able accounting practice room still exists for variations with respect to: (1) Annual depreciation and depletion allowances, especially the differences between calculations for book and for tax purposes. (Such variations affect both the reported net income and the balance sheet valuation of assets.) (2) Valuation of investments in securities held as assets. (3) Inventory valuation, as reflected in the balance sheet and in the calculation of cost of sales on the income statement. (4) Balance sheet valuation and income statement amortization of intangible assets. (5) Capitalization, or setting up as an asset to be amortized over the years, versus charging to annual expense, such items as organization and financing costs, promotion and research expenditures, and intangible items such as drilling costs in the oil industry. (6) Location and classification of reserves as current liabilities, long-term liabilities, or net worth, and the charging of expenses (that are credited to reserves) to net income or to retained earnings. (7) Accounting for deferred income taxes ("flow-through" versus "normalizing") that affects the reported net income and the handling of deferred tax credits as liabilities or as net worth. (8) Treatment of nonrecurring gains or losses either as influences on reported earnings or on the surplus account. (9) Revision of earnings per share to account for possible dilution resulting from the conversion of bonds and preferred stock. (10) Consolidation of assets and earnings of subsidiaries and affiliates.

Lack of uniformity is also found in annual financial reports to stockholders. Some companies present detailed and fully explained balance sheet and income statements; they also provide useful comparative annual figures for a number of years. Others are miserly with facts. They present only the minimum information required by their auditors. Fortunately, the trend is toward more complete and uniform information as a result of corporate policies to "open up" their affairs to stockholders, investment analysts, and the public. Regulation such as that imposed by the Securities Act of 1933 and the Securities Exchange Act of 1934 is also responsible for improvement of reports, as are progress in accounting and auditing standards through the activities of the Financial Accounting Standards Board and the influence of professional security analysts.

Industrial Characteristics

An important factor in the industrial field is the growing tendency on the part of companies to diversify their activities. This is apparent in various forms, such as: (1) the manufacture of a more diversified list of products, (2) integration of operations from extraction of raw materials to sale to consumers, and (3) the purchase of control of other companies in a variety of fields. Agricultural implements no longer comprise the major part of the sales of International Harvester; this company has become one of the largest makers of motor trucks. Carborundum Company derives only 40% of its sales from abrasives and related machinery systems. Textron Corporation has five major groups of subsidiaries: aerospace, consumer, industrial, metals, and financial; each group includes a number of companies producing a large variety of goods and services. International Telephone & Telegraph derives only about 30% of its revenues from communications. It is "into" industrial, food, automobile, consumer products, hotels, business services, natural resources, defense, and space. Kodak has engaged in textile manufacturing. General Electric has built up an enormous appliance business in addition to its manufacture of industrial apparatus. Thus, conglomerate companies with diversified activities are difficult to compare. (See. p. 516.)

Economic Characteristics

Industrial enterprise has certain characteristics whose analysis is important to interested investors. *Economic* features include: greater cyclical variation in prices, sales, and profit; competition for the business available; lack of special regulation; a greater variety of lines produced or sold; greater emphasis on new product development and research; greater dependence on foreign markets; and greater dependence on management. *Financial* characteristics (in addition to instability of earnings) include: greater investment in current assets and working capital; faster turnover of operating assets; higher operating ratios and lower profit margins; higher average rates of return on investment; greater importance of intangible assets; special hazards of inventory and credit losses; and more conservative methods of financing. These characteristics vary greatly from company to company. Yet the group has sufficient homogeneity to warrant some generalizations.

Industrial operations are notoriously unstable, being affected not only by changing conditions in each industry but also by swings in the general business cycle. A variation of from 10 to 20% in annual revenues is unusual in utility operations; in contrast, annual sales of industrial companies may move in a much wider range. Such variation has a magnified effect upon earnings through both operating and financial leverage. An impressive margin of safety during prosperous times may dwindle or even disappear during times of recession.

The yearly variation in industrial earnings is indicated by the data in Table 26-1 showing the results of operations of leading manufacturing corporations on the stockholders' book investment (net worth) and net income after taxes. While the dollar figures are not strictly comparable because of the annual variation in the number of companies, the annual financial results indicate the general pattern and trends. However, in such aggregate data the extremes—high or low—experienced by the best and poorest companies and industries in the group are not revealed, but the figures do show some important relationships. In general, falling sales were accompanied by declining net income margins and declining return on owners' investment (1949, 1958). The leverage of rising sales accompanied by a rising margin produced a sharp rise in rate of return (1959, 1963–1966, 1968, 1973). But a rise in sales accompanied by a level margin increased the return on owners' equity only modestly (1962), and in 1969–1971 the lower margin produced a lower rate of return despite increased sales. The cyclical decline in earnings is very evident in 1975. Any general statement concerning the variations in sales

TABLE 26-1 Net Earnings of Leading Manufacturing Companies
(dollars in millions)

	No. of Cos.	Net Income	Net Worth Jan. 1	Return on Net Worth	Sales	Net Income as a Percentage of Sales
1946	1,511	$ 4,091	$ 33,674	12.1%	$ 68,180	6.0%
1947	1,571	6,317	37,062	17.0	88,970	6.9
1948	1,680	8,063	43,607	18.9	107,510	7.5
1949	1,710	6,998	50,656	13.8	103,220	6.8
1950	1,693	9,288	54,403	17.1	120,620	7.7
1951	1,763	8,711	60,617	14.4	140,500	6.2
1952	1,788	8,093	65,990	12.3	149,870	5.4
1953	1,781	8,781	70,218	12.5	165,680	5.3
1954	1,778	9,280	74,825	12.4	157,290	5.9
1955	1,765	12,373	82,599	15.0	184,670	6.7
1956	1,843	12,724	91,659	13.9	212,070	6.0
1957	1,835	12,903	100,545	12.8	218,690	5.9
1958	1,852	10,643	108,140	9.9	204,670	5.2
1959	1,944	13,327	114,446	11.6	229,770	5.8
1960	2,034	12,810	121,720	10.5	237,220	5.4
1961	2,138	12,891	128,002	10.1	238,720	5.4
1962	2,316	14,681	134,145	10.9	267,000	5.5
1963	2,280	16,261	141,922	11.5	285,280	5.7
1964	2,328	18,774	148,385	12.7	307,770	6.1
1965	2,298	22,001	158,061	13.9	343,760	6.4
1966	2,279	24,074	170,405	13.0	381,120	6.3
1967	2,292	23,307	186,380	12.5	408,900	5.6
1968	2,250	26,066	198,730	13.1	457,300	5.7
1969	2,068	26,650	212,793	12.5	493,520	5.4
1970	2,128	23,413	232,025	10.1	508,980	4.5
1971	2,319	26,971	248,584	10.8	573,850	4.7
1972	2,414	31,518	264,417	12.1	618,000	5.1
1973	2,136	41,247	279,200	14.8	736,550	5.7
1974	1,866	45,669	296,786	15.4	878,250	5.2
1975	1,757	39,611	320,602	12.3	900,250	4.4
1976	1,890	53,816	358,153	15.0	1,055,220	5.1

Source: First National City Bank of New York, Monthly Economic Letter, April issues. Since March 1976, Citibank, Monthly Economic Letter.

and profits must be qualified by recognition that some groups—notably those supplying low-priced consumer necessities—have fared much better than the average in periods of recession, while others—notably the capital goods industries—have fared much worse.

The industrial field is characterized by a high degree of competition in a wide number of forms influencing product prices, volume of business, and operating costs. Competition within industries is often limited by integration, control of raw materials, patents, trademarks, brand names, tariffs, and other advantages such as product monopoly through research and development.

Yet actual or potential competition always stands as a threat to the sales and *earnings* of industrial enterprises.

Industrials in general are not subject nearly to the same degree of special regulation that is imposed on public service companies with respect to prices, wages, service, financing, and other activities, except when the national policy dictates, such as during the price-and-wage "freeze" of 1971–1972. However, different types are, of course, subject to various laws that restrict their activities and impose requirements (viz., drugs and automobiles). The relative absence of regulation in normal times permits a high rate of earnings under conditions of brisk business. But industrials lack the protection that regulation affords railroads and utilities. This is one of the many factors that contribute to the general instability of industrial sales and rates of profit.

In the industrials group, the production of a very wide variety of goods and services, combined with sales at changing prices, makes for a lack of uniformity in methods of operation and accounting. It thus becomes extremely difficult to make comparisons of operating performance. Even the statements of two steel corporations may reflect the difference in output between heavy and light or specialty steels. This problem is further aggravated when the same corporation or a parent and its subsidiaries are engaged in a number of different lines of business. Application of the basic tests of financial condition and earning power is about the only practical approach to the analysis of such "conglomerates." (See p. 516.)

The changing economic and technical scene in which business operates requires a constant program of research and new product development. The heavy expenses of such effort are capital expenditures and are mandatory for progress in a competitive age. Farsighted firms are also developing foreign markets, either through foreign subsidiaries or affiliates or by direct sales effort from home. But foreign operations do present a number of special problems. (See p. 517.)

All of the above characteristics combine to give "qualitative" factors of *management* unusual importance in industrial analysis. Unlike the public utility companies, where the range of decision-making is limited by regulation, management policies have wide scope in the industrial field. Efficiency of management is shown in a variety of ways, such as quality of the product, improvements in production and marketing methods, rate of growth, development of new products, and strong finances. But the outstanding test is the rate and growth of earning power.

In addition to their economic characteristics, industrials display certain common financial traits as a group, although without any marked degree of uniformity. (See Table 26-2.) In general, current assets and short-term sources of funds, as represented by current liabilities, play a much more important role in the industrial than in the public service balance sheet. Merchandising concerns may show as high as 60 to 70% of assets in current form; heavy goods manufacturers and mining companies may show a predominance of fixed assets, but not to the same extent as the typical utility or railroad. This condition reflects the large investment in inventories and receivables of the industrial corporation and its greater need of a substantial cash balance. This emphasis on current assets explains in part why many industrial companies rely heavily on bank loans, trade credit, and other current sources of funds.

Another financial feature of industrials is their generally more rapid turnover of investment, as indicated by the relation of sales to operating assets. A public utility may have from $3 to $5 invested for every dollar of sales; a manufacturing company, however, may turn its investment once or twice a year, and a merchant as many as seven or eight times a year, taking all operating assets into account. Accompanying the faster turnover of investment is a higher operating ratio and lower margin of operating earnings and net income (earnings in relation to sales). But even a low ratio of profit to sales may produce a high rate of return on investment. (See below.) Such a return is necessary in order to attract capital in the face of the greater variation in earnings.

A special feature of the competitive industrials is the frequent importance of patents, brand names, goodwill, and other intangible assets, including expenditures on research, trade position, and the like. In fact, the common stocks of many industrials are supported primarily by such intangible values. The practice of carrying valuable intangible assets on the balance sheet at a conservative figure—often as low as $1—produces a low book value for the common stock, but recognizes the fleeting value of this type of property, which depends, in the last analysis, on the *earning power* of the enterprise.

With its large investment in inventories and receivables, the industrial company is subject to the risk of loss in the value of these assets as a result of declining prices and depressed business conditions. And during periods of inflation a substantial portion of reported profits reflects rise in inventory value not attributable to normal operations. The "quality" of earnings is diminished. These risks may be diminished by conservative methods of valuation, adequate reserves, and use of "last-in-first-out" costing of inventory. (See p. 500.)

All of the special hazards to which industrial companies are exposed require a conservative capital structure in which senior securities play a much less important role than in the utilities. Although few prominent companies now avoid long-term debt financing altogether, in most cases the burden of interest is modest. While such a policy overlooks the possible advantages of greater leverage, it produces much greater stability in the net income and in the dividend payments.

The preceding description of financial features is illustrated in Table 26-2 by reference to 1976 figures of selected groups of industrial corporations. The wide variation in ratios is very apparent. Note that these are aggregate figures, and that individual companies may differ considerably within their respective groups. Group data, however, provide a point of reference.

Economic Analysis of the Industry and Company

Economic characteristics   The first step in the study of a company is to describe the industry to which it belongs: that is, its market structure or major divisions and products, its size in terms of sales and possibly number of

TABLE 26-2 Financial Characteristics, Selected Industry Groups, September 30, 1976

	Gross Plant Turnover	Per Cent of Assets		Current Ratio	Inventory Turnover	Long-term Debt Per Cent Cap. Str.	Per Cent of Sales	
		Current Assets	Inven-tories				Cost of Sales	Net Income before Inc. Taxes
Automobile manufacturing	2.4	53.5%	27.9%	1.6	5.3	14.6%	89.9%	3.5%
Chemicals—major	1.1	42.4	17.4	2.1	4.4	28.6	69.3	11.3
Coal—bituminous	1.4	32.4	8.8	1.7	10.2	26.7	69.7	22.0
Containers—paper	1.4	37.2	17.5	2.2	5.5	26.0	76.8	9.1
Copper	0.8	23.0	13.5	2.2	3.0	26.8	86.7	1.1
Drugs—proprietary	2.8	60.7	23.7	2.6	2.3	17.3	41.5	12.8
Electrical equipment	3.0	68.3	32.7	2.2	2.6	15.9	68.7	10.4
Food—canned	2.7	61.1	36.5	2.5	2.9	20.6	71.3	7.6
Food—meat packers	5.2	44.0	20.5	1.9	15.2	34.0	91.0	2.8
Forest products	1.1	27.9	14.6	2.1	4.7	37.2	76.0	7.6
Machinery—industrial	3.0	72.6	41.3	2.6	2.0	21.8	68.1	11.9
Office and business equipment	1.2	52.8	14.6	2.9	2.3	16.6	36.3	17.3
Oil—crude producers	0.8	28.1	6.5	1.7	10.2	36.1	69.7	6.8
Publishing—books	2.2	70.4	24.4	2.9	1.8	34.4	41.8	7.4
Steel—major	0.8	33.3	16.1	2.0	6.2	25.8	85.3	6.7
Tire and rubber goods	1.5	52.6	26.9	2.1	4.5	33.5	75.7	4.8
Tobacco and cigarette manufacturing	2.4	56.8	44.0	2.2	1.4	28.6	60.2	16.7
Eating places	1.9	23.8	5.5	1.5	20.4	40.9	77.5	8.0
Retail department stores	3.8	60.0	21.6	1.7	4.8	23.4	67.4	6.2
Retail food chains—national	8.7	58.0	42.9	1.6	10.6	20.9	81.1	1.5
Wholesalers	7.5	62.0	32.6	1.8	90.9	22.7	86.3	3.1
Standard & Poor's 400 Industrials	1.6	43.3	18.6	1.8	4.7	26.6	72.2	10.1

Source: *Financial Dynamics Industry Composites*, by permission of Investors Management Sciences, Inc.

employees, the location of its operations, and the degree of concentration or number of major companies involved. This information provides the setting for identifying a company within its group and noting its relative importance.

The next step is to examine the economic characteristics of the industry and compare the company with the group to which it belongs. Among the more important economic factors to be considered are: (1) the rate of growth or stage in the life cycle, (2) the stability or cyclical performance of sales and earnings, and (3) the special factors that characterize the industry.

Industries pass through life-cycle stages from infancy to senility, although wars have a way of giving some of the older groups (such as steam railroads and coal) a new lease on life. (See Chapter 28.) The investor should be satisfied that the long-term trend of the industry, as measured by production and sales, at least keeps pace with the rate of growth of the economy as measured by GNP, disposable consumer income, and other indicators. But he should note that rapid growth alone does not necessarily produce immediate high earnings, and that a long period of maturity, after the stage of early growth, may bring its reward in terms of stability, as in the case of the tobacco companies. Examples of growth industries are found in the chemicals, electronics, office machines, ethical drugs, and container industries, to name only a few. An exact definition of a "growth industry" or a "growth company" is difficult. Growth in the investment sense is not mere growth in size (assets, sales, employees), but rather growth in the rate of earnings on invested capital that is in turn reflected in growth in market value of shares. The leading characteristics of a *growth stock* are: (1) continuing increase in sales that produces a continuing increase in earnings and a high rate of return on invested capital, (2) reinvestment and compounding of the bulk of profits, and (3) high earnings attributable chiefly to research, product development, and forward-looking management. These characteristics cause the prices of growth company shares to rise much faster than the average, and to sell at higher-than-average multiples of earnings. We should also note that some growth industries are highly vulnerable to the business cycle (paper, for example). Their secular or long-run expansion makes them interesting for investment, but not necessarily stable. They could be called "cyclical growth" situations.

Some of the basic indicators of growth, and the stage in the life cycle of an industry and of the companies within it, that explain the increase of earnings are growth of markets in terms of geography and products; increased labor productivity as measured by labor costs in relation to product prices; development of patents, processes, and products or services that preserve the competitive position; gains in efficiency as represented by per-unit production and sales costs; preservation and expansion of raw material resources; continuous expansion of capital expenditures without a sacrifice of earnings; and attraction of farsighted and aggressive management personnel. Sales, production (in units of product), and earnings of the industry and of individual companies can be related to the basic indicators of the progress of the economy as a whole.

The stability of an industry and of its constituent companies is vital to investors. The more important indicators of stability are: degree of cyclical variation in sales and earnings, rate of growth or stage in the life cycle, degree of competition within the industry and between the industry and its rivals, labor relations and wage policy, prices and inventory value, tariff and other political influences, and availability of managerial skills. Cyclical variations in sales, production, and earnings are studied in relation to the general economy. Among the chief causes of such fluctuations are dependence on sales to the capital goods market, vulnerability of prices in relation to operating costs, and dependence on other cyclical industries.

Special factors   Among the many special factors affecting industry (and company) results and prospects are the following: degree of inter- and intra-industry competition, labor relations and wage policy, special inventory risks, dependence on tariffs, "political" risks, reliance on foreign markets, dependence on new products, and dependence on defense contracts.

As was mentioned previously, industrial companies are characterized by a high degree of *competition*. The extent to which different types are subject to competition from within or without, and whether the competition is cut-throat or healthy, varies widely. Competition is, of course, important in respect to its effect on the rate and stability of earning power. Healthy competition, as seen in the automobile industry, may actually tend to stabilize earning power. Extreme competition, as in the meat-packing group, may so reduce the margin of profit as to prevent any member from producing a satisfactory return, or may eliminate earnings entirely for some firms. Efforts to limit or minimize competition, and so produce an advantage at least within the group, are found in the use of valuable patents and processes, brand names, favorable channels of distribution, progressive research, successful advertising, control or ownership of raw material sources, tariff protection, and control of unusual managerial and technical talent. However, the more successful a particular company or group of companies becomes in dominating the field by any of these methods, the more exposed it becomes to government antitrust action, as is illustrated by developments in motion pictures (divorce of production and distribution through exclusive dealer contracts), aluminum (compulsory separation of stock ownership interests in the major American and Canadian companies), and automobiles (divestment of General Motors stock by Du Pont).

Labor relations and wage policy have become increasingly important in recent years because of the growing ability of organized labor to introduce pressure on costs and profits, especially in such industries as steel and automobiles, where wages constitute a large proportion of the cost of the product. The investor should be satisfied that labor relations are amicable and that the industry has a good strike record.

As was noted earlier, as a class, industrial concerns are characterized by a relatively large investment in *inventories*. The data previously presented indicate that, as a percentage of total assets and of current assets, inventories vary in importance from one industrial subgroup to another. The greater the investment in inventory, the greater is the special risk from sudden declines in price, and the greater the "artificial" profit achieved as a result of price increases. Efforts to eliminate inventory risks are illustrated by the hedging operations of milling companies, which carry inventory for which there is a constant market at published prices. Other concerns minimize the effects of fluctuations in the value of both raw materials and finished goods by using the "last-in, first-out" (LIFO) method of inventory accounting in calculating cost of goods sold.[2] Others set up special reserves against inventory fluctuations. A rapid turnover is, of course, the best protection of all.

Some industries derive special protection from *foreign competition* by tariffs, as in the case of nonferrous metals and wool. Such protection is not a dependable assurance of profits in a world that may become increasingly free-trade minded. The automobile industry provides an example of a stronger situation, namely, such a level of large-scale production as to compete successfully with low-cost foreign producers. The same ability to achieve the economies of mass production permits this industry to compete abroad with producers having low wage scales. (The increase in the sale of foreign cars in the United States has made this illustration less valid than formerly.)

A host of special political factors are faced during periods of national emergency, such as excess profits taxes, price controls, materials allocation, and the like. Such factors affect the short-run outlook for an industry but (one hopes) do not disturb its long-run earning power.

Many industries and companies are expanding their *foreign markets*, which offer great potential, but are fraught with unusual political, economic, and exchange market risks. (See p. 517.)

The astounding march of *technical progress* in the postwar period is reflected in the great emphasis on research and new product development on the part of industrial firms. To keep up in the competitive race, such expenditures must not only be ample, but ultimately productive. The mere allocation of large sums to research and development is not enough. New product sales and earnings must be forthcoming.

The *defense activities* of the Federal government constitute the biggest economic activity in this nation, with an annual budget of over $100 billions. Whole industries depend on their share of this total, and the fate of thousands of companies hangs on their participation as successful contractors.

All these risks and changing conditions in industry place a premium on *management*. While good management is important to the success of every business, the greater the special hazards to which it is subjected, the greater the emphasis that should be placed on analysis of management in the investment appraisal.

One method of testing management competency is to compare the relative status of the company in its field—whether it is improving its trade position or share of the available market and of the total industry earnings over a period of years. More specific tests are indicated in the discussion that follows.

After examining the economic factors, attention is given to tests of financial strength and earnings as revealed by analysis of company statements.

---

[2]Under the LIFO method, cost of goods sold is charged with the cost of the latest additions to inventory, so that in a period of rising prices, gross profits from operations are reduced over those that would have been reported under FIFO (first-in, first-out).

Analysis of Income

Income statements The income statement (Table 26-3) shows the earnings of a hypothetical manufacturing company for a given period. Revenues and expenses for the period are matched to reveal the net profit from operations. Interest, income taxes, and any special losses in asset values attributable to the period are then deducted to determine the net income transferred to retained earnings (earned surplus). The illustrative statement is designed to show the most useful and representative presentations of items, and suggest the form in which the actual statements of an industrial company may be rearranged for analytical purposes.

TABLE 26-3 Industrial Company Income Statement

		Percentage of Sales
Statement of Profit and Loss		
Net sales (gross sales less returns, discounts, and allowances)	$150,000,000	100.0%
Cost of goods sold	$120,500,000	80.3
Depreciation, depletion, and amortization	2,500,000	1.7
Selling, general, and administrative expenses	14,500,000	9.7
Net operating profit	$ 12,500,000	8.3
Other income	1,500,000	1.0
Gross income	$ 14,000,000	9.3
Deductions from income		
Interest on funded debt	1,800,000	1.2
Other deductions	200,000	.1
Net income before income taxes	$ 12,000,000	8.0
Provision for income taxes	6,000.000	4.0
Net income before special items	$ 6,000,000	4.0
Special items (adjusted for related income taxes)	$ 150.000	.1
Net income	$ 5,850,000	3.9%
Statement of Retained Earnings		
Balance, end of previous year	$ 25,000,000	
Net income for year	5,850,000	
	$ 30,850,000	
Cash dividends paid		
Preferred stock, $3.25 per share	800,000	
Common stock, $4.00 per share	2,000,000	
Balance, end of year	$ 28,050,000	

Special factors affecting reported net income All figures in the income statement combine to determine the "bottom-line" figure of net income. This figure is a function of operations, tax influences, nonoperating and extraordinary income and expense, and accounting decisions. The more important of these that pertain to industrial companies are:

VALUATION OF INVENTORIES The method of inventory valuation affects the cost of sales and therefore affects the reported net income as well as the balance sheet asset figure. The use of the LIFO method helps to minimize the effect of price changes on profits. (See footnote 3.)

DEPRECIATION, DEPLETION, AND AMORTIZATION   Depreciation expense, representing the estimated wear and tear on the physical property during the period, is one over which management has considerable discretion. Its over- or understatement can substantially affect the end-profit results. The adequacy of depreciation is measured by comparing the depreciation expense as a percentage of gross plant with similar figures for other companies and for the industry. Accelerated depreciation has tended to increase the current rates of most companies. The growing practice is either to segregate depreciation and show operating profit before and after this item, or to indicate by a footnote the amount charged to cost of sales. In either case, comparisons of operating results with the industry and with other companies is facilitated.

Depletion, or the allowance for actual loss of assets, as in mining and oil companies, is a major item on many statements. For *book* (annual report) purposes, it is usually calculated at the investment cost of the units sold. Higher depletion for income tax purposes may (temporarily, at least) reduce the current income tax, helping to make this figure appear small in relation to earnings before taxes.

Amortization of intangible assets whose value is used up in production, such as the write-off of intangible drilling costs by oil companies, is affected by policy with respect to the expensing of such costs. Some companies capitalize the outlays and amortize them over a period of years; others charge them as incurred. Comparisons of this item must be made with care.

SPECIAL INFLUENCES OF INFLATION   The almost continuous inflation of recent years has made comparisons of economic performance over time very deceptive. From one point of view, reported corporate earnings that are based on historical cost are overstated if depreciation allowances are insufficient to replace assets at higher prices. The 1976 profits of all nonfinancial corporations were reported at $127 billion. When adjusted for the higher costs of replacing inventory and other productive assets, "real" profits shrank to $99 billion.

The Financial Accounting Standards Board (FASB) and the Securities and Exchange Commission (SEC) have advanced proposals to show the inflationary impact on financial statements.[3]

The FASB approach would restate historical dollars in terms of the general purchasing power of current period dollars. One way of expressing the dollar's loss is the use of index numbers such as the GNP Deflator index. The base year is 1972, or 100.00 for this index. In 1977 the index was 140.5. If a machine had been purchased in 1972 for $10,000, its 1977 cost would be restated as $14,050.

$$\$10,000 \times \frac{140.5(1977)}{100.0(1972)} = \$14,050$$

---

[3]Financial Accounting Standards Board, *Exposure Draft, Financial Reporting in Units of General Purchasing Power.* Stamford, Conn., 1974; Securities and Exchange Commission, *Accounting Series Release No. 190,* 1976.

If the machine had been purchased in 1965 (index 74.3), the restatement calculation in 1977 would be:

$$\$10,000 \times \frac{140.5(1977)}{74.3(1965)} = \$18.909$$

The FASB proposal is still under review, and its implementation has been delayed (1977).

The SEC proposal became effective on December 25, 1976. It requires firms with inventory, gross property, plant and equipment exceeding $100 million and comprising more than 10% of total assets to provide *replacement cost data*. Four items are affected: (1) current replacement cost of inventories; (2) the effect on cost of sales if goods and services had been calculated at current replacement cost; (3) the replacement cost of depreciable, depletable, and amortizable assets which represent the firm's productive capacity; and (4) the effect on depreciation charges if depreciation had been calculated on replacement rather than historical cost.

The following hypothetical example shows how replacement cost adjustments would affect a firm's financial statements.

Income Statement		Historical Cost Basis		Replacement Cost Basis
Revenues		$600,000		$600,000
Cost of sales	$500,000		$530,000	
Depreciation	28,000		34,000	
Other expenses	20,000		20,000	
Total expense		548,000		584,000
Pretax income		$ 52,000		$ 16,000
Income taxes (50% of historical pretax income)		26.000		8,000
Income		$ 26,000		$ 8,000
Balance Sheet				
Inventory		$120,000		$160,000
Plant assets at cost	$ 60,000		$ 80,000	
Less accumulated depreciation	20,000		30 000	
Book value of plant assets		40,000		50,000
Other assets		120,000		120,000
Total assets		$280,000		$330,000
Total liabilities		80,000		80,000
Shareholders' equity		$200,000		$250,000
Return on equity		13.0%		3.2%

The SEC requirement is not without its hazards. The reliance on subjectivity, the absence of a common methodology, and lack of precision in estimating replacement cost requires a high degree of professional competence. The SEC warns investors and others not to reach fallacious judgments by a routine conversion of affected data. Hopefully, the requirement is the beginning of an evolutionary approach that will be refined over time.

OTHER INCOME AND EXPENSE   Many companies derive substantial earnings from activities outside their regular operations, and from rentals, royalties, and interest and dividends on investments. On a consolidated statement, the holding company's share in the earnings of nonconsolidated affiliates is separately reported. Special attention should be given to nonrecurring items, such as loss or gain on the sale of capital assets, legal judgments, write-downs of land or other assets below book value, tax assessments attributable to prior years, and adjustments for depreciation and for uncollectable accounts set up in prior years. Where such items affect the net income, the *clean surplus* theory is being followed, that is, all gains and losses are reflected in profits (net of taxes involved). Otherwise, all or part of them may be charged to the retained earnings (earned surplus) account.

INCOME TAXES   Income taxes are the estimated levy to be paid on profits. In case of a net operating loss, the tax refundable through carryback to a prior year, or the carryforward against profits in a future year, reduces the tax expense for the period.

The tax expense shown on the income statement is associated with the financial income reported on that statement, but is derived from the income on the company's tax return. The two income figures may be very different. For example, suppose a company computes depreciation for income tax purposes on an accelerated basis (the fixed-percentage-of-declining-balance method or the sum-of-the-digits method) but, in its reports to stockholders, charges ordinary straight-line depreciation. It now has two choices. On the assumption that depreciation will decline in later years and taxable income will rise, it may "normalize" its current reported net income by charging deferred tax expense and crediting (on the balance sheet) a deferred liability for taxes payable in the future. Or it may allow the temporarily higher pre-tax net income to "flow through" to final net income. The former system has been widely accepted.[4]

A special influence on net income is the *investment tax credit*. For industrial companies, a full credit of 10% applies to purchases of business equipment placed in service in a given year and serviceable for 10 years. Equipment with useful lives of between three and seven years qualifies for a reduced credit.

Net income per share   This is the amount earned for the stockholders of the corporation and is the final measure of success or failure. Unfortunately, the "net" figure is never accurate, because the actual gain or loss of a business over a period can be determined precisely only when the business is liquidated. As we have seen, the reported net income for a going concern is the result not only of the actual receipts and payments but of a variety of estimates.

---

[4]For special application to utility companies, see Chapter 27.

Earnings per share are found by dividing net income after income taxes by the average number of shares outstanding during the period. Where convertible securities or warrants are outstanding, per share earnings are also reported on a "fully diluted" basis. (See p. 187.)

It is important to determine the influence of different factors on per share earnings, including change in sales, changes in and policy with respect to cost of sales (including inventory valuation and depreciation), selling, general and administrative expense, changes in tax rates or in accounting for taxes, extraordinary income or expense, and changes in the number of shares outstanding of course.[5]

Growth in earnings per share is a function of increasing returns on not only the initial net worth but on the retained earnings reinvested at a good rate of return. "Growth" companies with a small dividend pay-out offer the advantage of compounding the owners' share when a high rate of return on reinvestment is maintained. The investor realizes this return when he sells his shares, with the advantage that any gain representing ploughed-back earnings is taxed at capital gains rates.

Analysis of Assets and Financing

The balance sheet   The balance sheet (Table 26-4) shows the total assets or resources of the company, carried at values that reflect the methods of accounting used. The total *book value* of the assets will not coincide with their liquidating value, cost of reproduction, or sales value as a going concern. Offsetting the assets are the sources from which the resources have been derived, in two main categories—liabilities or debts, and the net worth section showing the owners' investment.

Certain aspects of the industrial balance sheet deserve special attention.

MARKETABLE SECURITIES   These are temporary investments, chiefly U.S. Government securities, that are held pending the need of more cash for operations. The preferred method of valuation is at cost, unless market value is substantially lower. Where large sums are being held for specific purchases or investments at a later date (after one year), such amounts are not ordinarily classified as current assets.

Sometimes U.S. Government securities held for meeting income tax liability are offset against the liability. The net working capital remains the same, but the current ratio is increased (if above one to start with).

INVENTORIES   Inventories represent the value of merchandise on hand. In manufacturing companies, the item is divided into finished goods, work in process, and raw materials. Supplies are sometimes included. In merchandising concerns, the inventories consist of goods for resale.

---

[5]It is difficult for most investors to isolate all of these influences. Some services do it for them: for example, *Financial Dynamics*, published by Investment Management Services, Inc., a subsidiary of Standard & Poor's Corporation.

TABLE 26-4 Industrial Company Balance Sheet

Assets		Liabilities and Stockholders' Equity		
Current assets		Current liabilities		
Cash	$15,000,000	Accounts and notes payable, trade		$ 9,500,000
Marketable securities	1,000,000	Notes payable, bank		700,000
Receivables (net)	28,000,000	Accrued salaries and wages		1,200,000
Inventories	27,000,000	Accrued interest		250,000
Prepaid expenses	500,000	Provision for income taxes		5,000,000
		Accrued other taxes		1,250,000
		Cash dividends payable		2,000,000
		Long-term debt due within one year		100 000
Total current assets	$71,500,000	Total current liabilities		$20,000,000
Long-term investments and receivables	5,500,000	Deferred credits to income		200,000
Property, plant, and equipment	29,000,000	Long-term liabilities		
Less depreciation	7,000,000	Mortgage bonds		20,000,000
	$22,000,000	Term loan		900,000
Deferred charges	700,000	Special reserves		1,500,000
Intangible assets	100,000	Deferred Federal income taxes		500,000
Other assets	200,000	Stockholders' equity		
		Preferred stock	$15,000,000	
		Common stock	4,000,000	
		Capital surplus	3,000,000	
		Earnings reinvested	34,900,000	
				$ 56,900,000
Total	$100,000,000	Total		$100,000,000

The basis of valuation of inventories is very important. The most widely used method is *cost or market, whichever is lower.* The basis of cost is usually indicated—last-in first-out, average cost, or some other method. Since inventories bulk very large on industrial statements, their balance sheet valuation should meet reasonable standards, as revealed by tests that will be explained later in this chapter.

PERMANENT INVESTMENTS   These include holdings of securities that are not readily marketable, and investments in subsidiaries and affiliates. The item may bulk very large if the company is a parent or has substantial control of other corporations. The basis of valuation (ordinarily cost) should be clearly indicated. A clue to the real value of investments is found in the amount reported as "other income" on the income statement. If other income is, say, 25% of the book value of investments, undervaluation is suspected.

THE PROPERTY ACCOUNT   *Fixed assets* include land, buildings, and equipment, and occasionally improvements to leased property. The customary method of valuation is cost less the accumulated allowance for depreciation (and sometimes depletion) (except in the case of land). The book value of such assets may be far removed from their real value to the business. Reserves may be inadequate or overstated, and periodic appraisals may distort the comparability of successive balance sheet figures.

Depreciation is calculated by various methods, of which the most important are:

Straight-line   Cost, less estimated salvage value, is divided by the estimated years of life, producing (for each type of fixed asset) a uniform depreciation expense each year—for example, 10% each year for 10 years—as long as the asset remains unretired.

Declining-balance   The cost value is reduced by a constant rate to produce a successively lower depreciation expense each year. For tax purposes, this rate may be as high as twice the straight-line rate. At a rate of 20%, assets with a cost of 100 would be valued at 80, 64, 51.2, and so on.

Sum-of-the-digits   Asset cost is multiplied by reducing fractions whose denominator is the sum of the digits of the years and whose numerator is the digit for each year of life in reverse order. Thus, for an asset having a five-year life, the denominator is 15 ($1 + 2 + 3 + 4 + 5$), and the numerators are 5, 4, 3, 2, and 1 for each year, in that order. The result is a progressively lower depreciation expense (5/15, 4/15, 3/15, 2/15, and 1/15 of cost).

Unit-of-production or service   The asset cost is divided by a rate per unit of output or service (tons, miles, flying hours) multiplied by the units for a particular year. This produces a varying annual depreciation expense.

Accumulated depletion represents the amount of original cost of "wasting" assets that have been sold off through inventory. Successive book values are divided by successive estimates of remaining units of oil, minerals, or timber to arrive at the remaining capacity.

The *accumulated depreciation* shows the total amount by which the original cost of the fixed assets has been reduced by annual charges to depreciation expense. The amount may be quite different from the actual sum that would be necessary to replace the assets.

INTANGIBLE ASSETS These include such items as patents, trademarks, copyrights, franchises, and goodwill. These are often carried at purely arbitrary values, not infrequently at some nominal sum such as $1, even though they may be very valuable. With the exception of goodwill, they may properly be amortized against income over their legal lives. Conservatism is to be desired in valuing such items, as they would depreciate greatly in case of liquidation resulting from failure, and would be worth very little in the case of prolonged deficits.

RESERVES Reserves represent either provisions for specific claims or losses, or appropriations of retained earnings. The former ordinarily appear just above the net worth section, and include such items as provision for foreign investment and exchange losses, pending lawsuits, self-insurance, employee benefits, and workmen's compensation. *Reserves for contingencies* that relate to nebulous or undetermined hazards should be found in the net worth section as "earmarked" earned surplus.

DEFERRED FEDERAL INCOME TAXES As explained previously, when a company charges accelerated depreciation for tax purposes, but uses straight-line depreciation in its report, it may charge tax expense on the income statement and credit deferred income taxes on the balance sheet, in the amount of current tax saving. The accumulated deferred income tax item on the balance sheet represents a type of reserve to be used in later years when depreciation charges for tax purposes may be lower than the straight-line charges made on the books. Considerable argument occurs on whether this item is a true liability or is part of the net worth. The conservative position favors the former treatment, although in a company that is expanding and continues to add to its fixed assets the item is likely to become permanent.

Working Capital Changes and Flow of Funds

Neither the balance sheet nor the income statement directly reveals the factors causing change in particular categories of assets. Two special statements are often employed in industrial annual reports to explain changes in liquidity: the statement of changes in financial position, and the cash flow statement. The latter is actually an extension or refinement of the former.

The "working capital" statement in Table 26-5 shows that during the fiscal period the firm distributed more dividends than it earned (presumably using retained earnings), that it acquired new plant in excess of depreciation charges, and that it raised funds by new long-term securities financing in excess of the debt and stock retired. But it does not show the changes in the individual *components* of working capital. This can be done by comparing

TABLE 26-5 Statement of Changes in Financial Position

Period _____

Increases		Decreases	
Net income	$ 840,000	Purchase of fixed assets	$ 480,000
Depreciation	320,000	Retirement of term loan	80,000
Sale of fixed assets	80,000	Purchase of treasury stock	40,000
Sale of bonds	1,000,000	Cash dividends	1,440,000
Sale of common stock	1,000,000		
Total	$3,240,000	Total	$2,040,000
Net increase in working capital:	$1,200,000		

the balance sheets at the beginning and the end of the given period. Or, as is often the case, a report may do the work, as in Table 26-6.

As Table 26-6 shows, the company increased its working capital, but at the expense of cash position and investment in inventories. The growth of plant and of receivables was the culprit. A check on the collection period (or turnover of receivables) and of the turnover of plant would be in order. The notes payable have also increased, suggesting a "freezing" of the open accounts owed to suppliers, even though the firm may have reported a

TABLE 26-6 Changes in Components of Working Capital

	Increase (Decrease)
Changes in current assets	
Cash	$ (250,000)
Marketable securities	(180,000)
Receivables	2,260,000
Inventories	(460,000)
Prepaid expenses	30,000
Total	$1,400,000
Changes in current liabilities	
Notes payable	$ 200,000
Accounts payable	(240,000)
Federal income taxes payable	240,000
	$ 200,000
Change in working capital	$1,200,000

profit and paid substantial income taxes. Long-term debt (bonds) has increased, but the stockholders have also made a substantial new investment in common stock. The decrease in cash of $250,000 is the result of all the other items noted above. (See Table 26-7.)

The *net internal cash flow* from operations is the sum of net income and depreciation, or $1,160,000. This could be used to calculate the cash flow per share. However, we note that such funds were more than offset by drains on cash. Cash flow should never be used as a substitute for earnings.

TABLE 26-7 Cash Flow Statement

Increases in Cash		Decreases in Cash	
Item	Amount	Item	Amount
Net income	$ 840,000	Purchase of fixed assets	$ 480,000
Depreciation	320,000	Retirement of term loan	80,000
Sale of fixed assets	80,000	Retirement of treasury stock	40,000
Sale of bonds	1,000,000	Cash dividends paid	1,440,000
Sale of common stock	1,000,000	Increase in receivables	2,260,000
Decrease in marketable		Increase in prepaid expenses	30,000
securities	180,000	Decrease in accounts payable	240,000
Decrease in inventories	460,000		
Increase in notes payable	200,000		
Increase in income			
taxes payable	240 000		
	$4,320,000		$4,570,000
		Decrease in cash—	$250,000

Ratio Analysis of Industrial Statements

Short-term creditors, such as banks and trade suppliers, long-term investors in bonds and stocks, and corporate management are all interested in the financial health and earnings of the company, but each group emphasizes different aspects of analysis. Current creditors are primarily concerned with liquidity or the ability of the firm to meet its current obligations promptly. Long-term investors do not neglect working capital position, but emphasize ultimate solvency and earning power. Management is interested in all aspects of the company's performance.

Statement analysis is not solely a matter of calculating and comparing ratios, although these are useful tools provided their limitations are kept in mind. A ratio may have considerable value in its own right, but it is most revealing (1) where it is compared with similar ratios of other companies in the same industry or with industry composites, and (2) where it is computed for a period of years to reveal the trend.[6] Furthermore, a ratio is the relationship between two variables, and it disguises the actual dollar amounts involved. Thus, two companies may show the same current ratio (see below), say, 2:1 or 200%, but one may have 10 times as much working capital.

Ratios of working capital position and liquidity The time-honored test of current position is the *current* or *working capital ratio* of current assets to current liabilities. A relationship of 2 : 1 is often offered as a standard, but no ideal ratio is applicable to all industries. A 2 : 1 ratio simply indicates that the current assets could shrink 50% in value before the current creditors would be in jeopardy.[7] Some industries require a much higher degree of

---

[6]Sources of composite industry data are given at the end of this chapter.

[7]The *acid test* ratio, computed by dividing current assets less inventories by current liabilities, shows the ability of the company to meet current debts without relying on the least liquid of the current assets. A ratio of 1:1 is often considered a minimum standard.

protection. (See Table 26-2.) Furthermore, the adequacy of this ratio depends on the types of the current assets, the liquidity of those other than cash, and seasonal requirements.

A company may show a favorable current ratio but be in a weak position because assets other than cash either form a large portion of current assets or are not liquid. One must therefore examine the quality of these other current assets. The *collection ratio* is a crude test of the quality of the receivables. It is found by dividing annual credit sales (when such information is available) by 360 to obtain credit sales per day; this figure is divided into the receivables on the books (less reserve for bad debts) to give the collection period or number of day's sales uncollected. If terms of 30 days are allowed customers, the ratio should be not much more than 30.[8]

The liquidity of the remaining important current assets is roughly measured by calculating the *inventory turnover*: cost of goods sold divided by average inventory at cost. This figure varies greatly among different industries. Its trend is perhaps more important than its amount. Another test of inventory is its relationship to net working capital. The higher this ratio, the greater the dependence on inventory for solvency and the greater the risk from a sudden decline in its value.

Tests of fixed assets The investor in securities is specially interested in the long-term financial health of the business as represented by the support offered by fixed assets and the character of the capital structure. (See Chapter 24.) The ratio of *total liabilities to tangible net worth* reveals the burden of debt, both fixed and current, in relation to the owners' equity—exclusive of intangible assets, which are subject to uncertain valuation and rapid shrinkage. Rarely, if ever, should the ratio exceed 100%, to avoid excessive maturities and interest charges. A similar test is the ratio of *net worth to total assets*.

The relationship of *net fixed assets to (tangible) net worth* measures the degree to which the owners' investment is "tied up" in a permanent form. Fixed assets require large maintenance and depreciation allowances and possibly large interest charges on borrowed money; in addition, funds are not available in liquid form to take advantage of cash discounts and other current needs. A maximum of 75% is suggested for most manufacturing companies; the ratio would be considerably less for merchandising concerns.

Capital structure proportions Ratios of bonds and other long-term debt, preferred stock, and common stock plus retained earnings, to total capital structure (sometimes called "capitalization" or "invested capital") vary greatly in the industrial field. Some companies have no senior securities outstanding and rely solely on common stock and reinvested earnings as long-term sources of funds. Others use substantial leverage and incur heavy interest charges and large preferred dividend requirements. Generally speaking, the investor will favor those industrial concerns with a modest

---

[8]A similar ratio is the *turnover of receivables*, found by dividing net credit sales by average receivables. A turnover of 12 would be expected if terms of 30 days are allowed.

amount of bonds and preferred stock outstanding in relation to tangible net worth. In few cases would the 40 to 50% debt ratios of utilities be acceptable in the industrial field.[9] Where funded debt and preferred stock each exceeds one-third of capital structure, unusual stability of earnings and of asset values would be required for these securities to enjoy a respectable status.

A supplementary test of the quality of industrial bonds and preferred stocks is to use the *market* value of the common stock instead of stated common stock and surplus on the balance sheet. This test indicates the market's valuation of the common equity as a cushion for senior capital and is often a more realistic basis of comparison in the case of companies whose earnings bear only small relation to balance sheet figures of fixed or current assets. Examples can be found in chemicals, drugs, electronics, and other growth industries where the book value of the common stock is typically low compared to average market price.

More specific asset tests of the burden of funded debt are found in the ratio of such debt to net (depreciated) fixed assets and to net working capital. The long-term debt should be adequately supported by plant and equipment; a maximum ratio of debt to net plant of 50% is suggested for manufacturing concerns; merchandising companies with smaller fixed assets may show a higher proportion, but the debt must be supported by a greater amount of working capital. The long-term debt should also be supported by liquid assets to ensure continuation of interest payments; long-term debt in excess of (net) working capital is not recommended for industrial concerns.

The asset support behind the preferred stock is measured by the ratio of preferred stock to tangible net worth, which should not exceed 50%. A similar approach is to compute the book value of the preferred on a per share basis. If this is $400, each share of preferred is protected by net tangible assets (after all liabilities) considerably in excess of its preference in liquidation over the common stock.[10]

The *book value* of a common stock is found by subtracting from total assets (or, preferably, from total tangible assets) all liabilities and the liquidating preferences of the preferred stock, including any accumulated preferred dividends. The net tangible assets applicable to the common stock, divided by the number of shares of common stock outstanding, gives the tangible book value per share. While not nearly so important as earnings per share, the figure indicates the investment in tangible properties that may, under proper conditions, produce a reasonable return on the common stock. Common stock may sell at several times book value, either because the assets are carried at very conservative figures or because of unusual earnings; they may sell at a fraction of book value where the opposite conditions prevail. (See Table 9-1.) Indeed, some common stocks even sell at a price below the per-share equivalent of *current* assets less all liabilities and preferred stock. Here, the investor is paying nothing for the fixed assets, but these have little investment value as long as the company is not expected to produce satisfactory earnings, or is not going to liquidate.

---

[9]See Table 26-2.

[10]The "book value" of preferred stock indicates the assets that support each share, not, as in the case of common stock, what each share would receive on liquidation of assets at their book value.

Chart 26-1 shows that industrial common stocks fell 50% in relation to book value in 1973–1974.

S & P 400 INDUSTRIALS - PRICE VS. BOOK VALUE

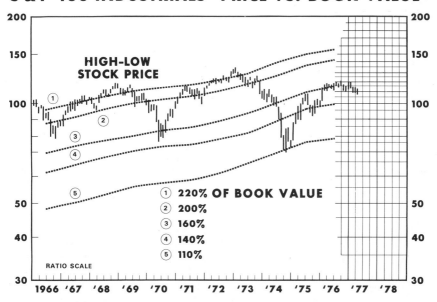

Source: Donaldson, Lufkin & Jenrette Securities Corporation, New York. Reprinted with permission.

Tests of operations or performance As we saw in Chapter 24, the effectiveness of management is revealed by ratios of various income and expense items to net sales, taking the latter figure as 100%. The use of such "common-size" statements enables the comparison of annual figures that differ in dollar amounts, and of the statements of different companies within the same industrial group. Among the more important relationships are the *gross profit margin* (gross profit from operations as a per cent of sales), the *net profit margin* (net profit from operations as a per cent of sales), the *operating ratio* (cost of sales plus expenses as a per cent of sales), and the *net income ratio* (net income either before or after taxes, as a per cent of sales), together with the ratios of important single expense items, such as depreciation, to sales.[11] Illustrative figures of the last two of these main relationships for different indentures are found in Table 26-2.

The net income ratio is especially significant in comparative analysis. It reveals the proportion of sales brought down to net income to provide the return on the owners' investment. But a high net income ratio is not the final measure of profitability. It is the rate earned on the investment that is important. A low net income ratio may provide a high return if net worth is small.

[11]In Table 26-3, the gross profit margin is 100%—80.3%, or 9.7%. The net profit margin is 8.3%, and the operating ratio is 100.0—8.3%, or 91.7%. The net income ratio is 3.9%.

Or, by operating at a low net income ratio a concern that turns its investment many times during the year may produce the same per cent return on that investment as another firm that requires a high investment and operates at a high ratio. The following hypothetical figures illustrate this situation:

	Company X	Company Y
Sales	$100	$100
Net worth	$ 50	$ 10
Net income ratio	5%	1%
Return on net worth	10%	10%

Ratios of operating profits and of net income to sales should be accompanied by others that reveal whether the assets, and the investment of various classes of creditors and of the owners, have been effectively used. The *turnover of operating assets* is calculated by dividing net sales by assets exclusive of long-term investments and intangibles. This reveals the comparative efficiency of the resources devoted to producing sales. The *turnover of working capital* (sales to net working capital) suggests the productivity of the funds supplied by short-term creditors. A fast turnover contributes to both liquidity and earning power and may logically offset an otherwise weak current position. The utilization of plant investment is shown by *plant turnover*, or gross plant divided into net sales. The effectiveness of the total long-term investment in producing revenues is measured by the *turnover of capital structure*, and that of the owners by the *turnover of net worth* (net sales to average stockholders' equity).

Tests of earning power   The profitability of the *total* long-term funds is measured by the rate of return on invested capital, that is, the ratio of income before interest (and after income taxes) to the total capital structure. The trend of this "overall" rate of return through a period of years and comparisons among different companies are very revealing. A chronically low ratio indicates overinvestment, poor competitive position, or generally poor management. A high return is to be desired, of course, but stability is of equal importance.

The overall rate of return is affected by the degree of leverage in the capital structure, because interest is a cost in determining taxable net income. To compare companies *without considering the effect of their financial policy*, the rate of return should be calculated on a pretax basis.

Tests of earnings in relation to the senior elements in the capital structure are: (1) For bonds it is *times interest charges earned*. To achieve a high-grade status, industrial bonds should show a regular coverage of between five and six times, and the figure should not drop below three times in the poorest year (after taxes). An accompanying test is the *factor of safety*, or percentage of sales earned after bond interest and before taxes. This shows how much sales could decline and still leave interest charges covered once. (2) For preferred stock, it is *times interest charges plus preferred dividends earned*. High-grade industrial preferred dividends should show a regular coverage of at least four times.[12]

For common stock, net income is shown as so much per share. *Cash earnings per share* is increasingly used to reveal the internal funds generated for expansion and general corporate use. *Sales per share* relates the output of the business to a possibly changing number of shares outstanding. In the analysis of oil companies, barrels of reserves per share is a useful comparative figure. But the fundamental figure that reveals how effectively the business is being run for its owners is the rate of *return on common equity*, found by dividing the average common stock plus surplus by net income after preferred dividends. A company can show increasing earnings per share, but a declining rate of return if earnings are not growing at the same rate as shares are increased.

The investor in common stock is interested in three other relationships involving earnings: (1) the *price-earnings ratio*, or ratio of net income per share to market price; (2) the *payout ratio*, or ratio of dividends to net income; and (3) the *dividend yield*. The last is, of course, the result not only of price and earnings but also of dividend policy. In October 1977, the companies comprising Standard & Poor's industrial stock index produced a dividend yield of 4.67% from expected dividends of $4.94 or 50% of $9.90 earnings. These stocks, as a composite average, were selling at 10.7 times earnings (or at an earnings yield of 9.3%). The price-earnings ratio of individual stocks varies widely, being influenced by many factors, including (1) the trend and stability of earnings, (2) dividend record and prospects, (3) the market's appraisal of the management and future prospects of the company, (4) financial strength, (5) the level of interest rates, and (6) the general psychology of investors and speculators at any given time.[13]

Use of Consolidated Statements

A growing number of companies are becoming holding or parent companies through the control of voting stock of other corporations. This is a favorite method of external expansion, as a substitute for extension of operating divisions. Where more than 50% of the voting stock is held, the annual report usually includes consolidated statements of the group treated as one company, with intercompany items eliminated. Such statements should nearly always be used by the investor rather than those of the parent company alone. Certain unique features and ratios should be noted:

- On the balance sheet, the assets of fully consolidated subsidiaries are commingled with those of the parent. The cost of shares of affiliates or of nonconsolidated subsidiaries is shown as a long-term investment.

- Where the parent owns less than 100% of the controlling stock of subsidiaries, the minority interest, consisting of the book value (stock plus its share of surplus) of the subsidiary's stock held by outsiders, is shown separately.

---

[12]See Chapter 24 discussion of methods of calculating interest and preferred dividend coverage.

[13]Further discussion of the price-earnings ratio is found in Chapters 19 and 25.

• The consolidated capital structure of a parent and subsidiaries consists of (a) bonds of the subsidiaries, (b) bonds of the parent, (c) preferred stock of subsidiaries, (d) preferred stock of parent, (e) minority interest in subsidiaries, (f) common stock of parent, and (g) consolidated surplus. The last five items comprise the consolidated net worth.

• On the consolidated income statement, sales, expenses and net income of parent and consolidated subsidiaries are combined. The equity or share in the earnings of nonconsolidated subsidiaries and affiliates appears as a separate income item.

• In calculating earnings per share, the figure derived from the consolidated statements should be increased by the parent's share of undistributed subsidiary profits.

Special Problems of "Conglomerates"

The bringing together under one corporate banner of nonrelated firms engaged in disparate activities is one way to describe a conglomerate. City Investing Company, a large conglomerate, is engaged in insurance, savings and loan, oil and gas exploration, home building, mobile homes, motels, water heaters, and publishing.

In the ebullient markets of the 1960s, conglomerate stocks were often the object of frenzied speculation. Prices reached lofty heights, often selling at multiples of 40 to 70 times earnings. The belief was widespread that the profits of two or more firms in joint ventures would always be greater than the total results obtained by these firms working independently. Accordingly, a fast-paced acquisition policy was required to keep the momentum going. For example, Gulf and Western, another conglomerate, acquired 49 companies in one year alone. Unconventional accounting practices (now banned), and a promotional posture that often bordered on the fictional, encouraged the notion that conglomerate growth was unstoppable. When the realization dawned that some of these acquisitions were both unprofitable and unmanageable, the inevitable market correction followed. LTV (formerly Ling-Temco-Vought) reached 169 1/2 in 1967. By 1971, the shares were down to 7 5/8. Litton Industries reached 120 3/8 in 1967 only to plummet to 8 1/2 in 1973. Both have since enjoyed some recovery.

Conglomerate issues, virtually shunned in the 1968–1975 period, have slowly but selectively come back to favor. The Standard & Poor's Stock Price Index of 10 conglomerates rose 56% in 1976 versus a 16% gain for the total industrials group.

In evaluating conglomerate stocks, investors should pay particular attention to the quality of management. Because of the difficulty of analyzing each controlled subsidiary or group, the investor asks "what earnings and growth have the management produced with the resources at its command?" Tests should include actual and relative growth of sales, earnings per share, return on total invested capital, and return on the common stock equity. The debt-to-equity ratio is particularly important as a measure of solvency.

Multinational Companies

Investors in multinational firms are confronted with an array of very special risks. The growing sense of nationalism in both developed and underdeveloped countries makes the threat of a foreign take-over of American ventures more ominous. The Canadian province of Saskatchewan, for example, has nationalized the potash industry, affecting some American firms. Relations between the host country and the American firm can be strained by overt actions such as bribes and illegal political activities.

The profitability of foreign investments can be threatened by limits placed on capital transfers, profit repatriation conditions, and tax offset regulations, as well as by political instability. American unions, concerned about possible loss of jobs, have called for import curbs on textiles, shoes, and other products as a means of restricting overseas manufacturing by multinational firms. Profits have been adversely affected in some foreign countries by the slower rate of economic growth. Floating foreign exchange rates present another uncertainty. Fluctuations between the dollar and other currencies have been frequent and large enough to cause concern. Foreign exchange instability is compounded by a new accounting rule that alters the practice of setting up reserves to smooth out the volatility in foreign earnings. Adverse changes in rates of exchange now flow directly to the "bottom line."

A recital of these special hazards might suggest that multinational firms should be avoided by investors. But all multinational firms are not the same. The successful ones are managed by experienced executives. Rather than avoid all multinational firms, a prudent alternative would be to seek out those with special characteristics. Multinationals operating in countries with prospects of above-average development may offer investment opportunities. Firms which export goods from the United States, rather than make them abroad, may be insulated against currency fluctuations. Some advisors suggest the virtue of multinationals which are diversified, both geographically and by products, and which are thus in a position to avoid the vulnerability created by operations in one or two countries. Some products may always be wanted even in countries with lower economic growth, such as pharmaceuticals, technology-oriented products such as computers, medical instruments, and relatively low-cost, discretionary products such as cigarettes.

Industrial Securities

Bonds Industrial companies are subject to a variety of risks suggested earlier in this chapter, and thus, as a class, would not be expected to rely on bonds as a means of financing to the same extent as would public service companies. However, few large corporations are now without funded debt of some sort, and many have large lease obligations which are in effect equivalent to funded debt. Their (discounted) present value is noted in footnotes in the corporate reports. Some analysts suggest that this be added to bonds in calculating the leverage in the capital structure.

The reasons for avoidance of publicly offered bond issues by concerns that could meet all tests adequately are: (1) a conservative attitude toward long-term debt financing; (2) the adequacy of internal funds, that is, retained earnings and depreciation, to finance expansion; (3) the growing use of intermediate-term loans from banks and insurance companies; and (4) the increasing practice of privately placing high-grade bonds with insurance companies and other institutional investors. Those industrial concerns that have issued bonds, in spite of the risk of debt, have seized the opportunity to finance at low cost and gain a tax advantage, or have been reluctant to rely on the sale of stock issues at relatively low multiples of earnings. Or sometimes when a concern needs money badly, it may have to offer its premier security.

The most common type of industrial bond is the unsecured debenture. Sinking funds or other repayment provisions have become almost universal in the modern longer-term industrial issues, and, because of the possibilities of high returns in common stock, the convertible feature (and subordination) is found much more frequently than in the case of utilities and rails.

Bonds of industrial companies include a wide range of quality. At one extreme, issues of very strong companies supported by very large asset values and demonstrated earning power under a variety of business conditions command great investment respect; when the highest standards are met, such bonds sell at yields as low as those on high-grade utility issues. In October, 1977, the yield on Moody's high-grade industrial bond series was 7.89%, as compared with 8.19% for public utilities. The very top-grade industrial bonds are the prime corporate obligations in the market. Where the highest standards can be met, industrial bonds are eligible for investment by trustees and other fiduciaries in a large number of states.

But the number of very high-grade industrial issues is relatively small, and from this peak the group extends over a wide number of issues that lack, in general, the safety of operating utility bonds. While generalizations are dangerous, we may probably say that, as a *class*, industrial bonds below the very high-grade do not enjoy the investment standing of the utility group as a whole.

A good industrial bond should meet the following tests:

• The industry should exhibit characteristics of stability and growth and freedom from unusual cyclical and other risks. Where such a condition is not found, the debt should be modest.

• The company should be a demonstrated leader in its field, with superior management and prospects as revealed by careful analysis.

• The working capital position should be very strong to permit interest payments during possible periods of low earnings and to allow management flexibility in uncertain times.

• The total long-term debt should not ordinarily exceed one-third of the capital structure. This limit may be exceeded only when interest and lease coverage is more than ample.

• The total bonds should not exceed 50% of depreciated fixed assets or, where the latter are small, should more than meet the working capital test next indicated.

• In any case, total bonds should not exceed net working capital.

• Where not secured by a lien on valuable assets, the issue should contain the protective provisions outlined in Chapter 8.

• The average total income for the five preceding years and for the previous year (after taxes) available for the payment of interest charges should be at least four to five times the fixed charges.

• The maturity of the issue should not exceed 30 years, and a sinking fund or repurchase provision should be provided that is adequate to retire a substantial portion of the bonds before maturity.

• The issue should be at least $10,000,000, well seasoned (see Chapter 8), and should be listed or traded actively to assure reasonable marketability.

Preferred Stocks   Preferred stocks of industrial companies are entitled to investment recognition only on the basis of demonstrated earning power of the issuing company. As with industrial bonds, the group includes a wide range, from high-grade to those little better than weak common stocks. In June 1977, when high-grade industrial bonds were yielding 7.77%, high-grade industrial preferreds were yielding 7.00% and medium-grade issues 7.70%. These yields were lower than those of high-grade rail and utility preferred issues; but again we should note that the number of very strong industrial preferred stocks is limited, and that the standards for a high-grade rating are higher than for rail and utility preferreds.

The low yield on high-grade industrial preferreds is, however, chiefly explained by their appeal to taxed corporate investors such as insurance companies, because 85% of dividend income is tax-free to corporations. This demand, together with a shrinking supply, has sometimes forced the yield on strong preferred issues below that of high-grade bonds. Under these conditions, the best preferred stocks have traditionally had little appeal to individual investors.

At the opposite extreme are stocks that are preferred in name, but are in reality supported by little or no common stock equity, and so are in fact similar to common stocks in quality, but (unless convertible) without the potential of common stocks with respect to income and price appreciation.

Where relative stability of price and assurance of income are required, an industrial preferred stock should meet these tests:

1. See first test for industrial bonds.
2. See second test for industrial bonds.
3. See third test for industrial bonds.
4. The preferred stock should not exceed one-third of the total capital structure.
5. The preferred stock should not exceed 50% of the tangible net worth.
6. The issue should contain the protective provisions described in Chapter 9 designed to prevent the deterioration of its position from the issuance of prior

securities and debt or from the excessive payment of dividends on common stock.

7. The average income before interest (and after taxes) for the five preceding years and for the previous year should be at least four times the preferred dividend requirement, plus bond interest if any bonds are outstanding, and four times the preferred dividend requirement if no bonds are outstanding.

8. Where the issue is convertible into common stock, it should either be strong in its own right without such a feature, or an excessive premium for this feature should be avoided.

9. The issue should be large, well seasoned, and listed on an organized exchange if ready marketability is important.

The investor should never lose sight of the fact that a preferred stock represents ownership in the corporation, that dividend payments are optional (even if cumulative), and that neither a larger corporate surplus nor a long dividend record assures the continuation of dividends in years of poor earnings.

Common Stocks It is extremely difficult to generalize about the investment position of industrial common stocks. The group includes the widest range of issues—from those that have a long and honorable earnings and dividend record and relatively good price stability, to the wildest speculations. Few if any carry absolute assurance of income, but a well-diversified list of industrials is likely to produce a modest return even in times of adversity. No industrial common stocks offer price stability, and their price action is likely to be much less stable than that of operating utility issues. Yet through adequate diversification and wise selection and timing, the worst effects of the stock price cycles may be avoided. (See Chapters 18 and 19.) The most that the investor can hope to obtain is reasonable stability, unless he is prepared to risk the chance of no income at all and wide variation in price for the possibility of unusual capital gain. If income is the primary goal, the investor may achieve it through a list of sound dividend-payers, but he cannot avoid considerable variation in market value.

A special caution concerning "growth stocks" should be repeated here. In the 1960s and early 1970s these sold at very high multiples of earnings in the top layer of what was called the "two-tier" market. In the great collapse of stock prices 1973–1974, the premier growth stocks were especially vulnerable to the decline to acceptable price-earnings ratio. (See Chapter 19.)

No summary list of specific tests of an industrial common stock is included in this final discussion. The investor must be satisfied that the price, return, and appreciation prospects from a given stock or group of stocks adequately compensate for the risks of the issues as measured by careful analysis. He must also be satisfied that such risks are appropriate in his own investment policy and program. As indicated previously in this volume, many methods exist by which, through careful selection, diversification, and timing, or through the use of indirect means of investment, the common stock investor can reduce the risks involved and gain the real advantages that sound common stocks may offer in a balanced program.

Special Sources of Industry Composite Data

Chapter 13 provides a large number of sources of information on industries and industrial companies. The following special sources offer *composite data*—financial statements and/or key ratios—for a large number of industries. A number of other sources, each for a different industry or line, are cited in Robert Morris Associates, *Sources of Composite Financial Data: A Bibliography*, 4th ed. Philadelphia: RMA, 1976.

ACA (Accounting Corporation of America), *Barometer of Small Business*. San Diego, Calif. 1975.

Dun & Bradstreet, Inc., *Cost of Doing Business Ratios, Corporations*, and *Cost of Doing Business Ratios, Partnerships*, New York, annual.

———, *Key Business Ratios*, annual. (Same ratios as described in R. A. Foulke, *Practical Financial Statement Analysis*.

Financial Dynamics, *Industry Composite Supplement*. New York: Investment Management Services, Inc. (a subsidiary of Standard & Poor's Corp.), annual.

Robert Morris Associates, *Annual Statement Studies*. Philadelphia, PA, annual.

TROY, LEO, *Almanac of Business and Industrial Ratios*. Englewood Cliffs, N.J.: Prentice-Hall, Inc., annual.

Standard & Poor's *Analysts Handbook: Composite Corporate Per Share Data by Industries* (annual).

REFERENCES

ADAMS, WALTER, ed., *The Structure of American Industry*, 4th ed. New York: The Macmillan Company, 1971.

ANALYST'S HANDBOOK (A Guide to Industry Publications for Security Analysts). New York Society of Security Analysts, Inc., 1972.

BELLEMORE, D. H., *The Strategic Investor*, Part V. New York: Simmons-Boardman Publishing Corp., 1963.

BOWYER, J. W., JR., *Investment Analysis and Management*, 4th ed., Chapters 9–11. Homewood, Ill.: Richard D. Irwin, Inc., 1972.

COHEN, J. B., E. D. ZINBARG, and ARTHUR ZEIKEL, *Investment Analysis and Portfolio Management*, 3d ed., Part II. Homewood, Ill.: Richard D. Irwin, Inc., 1977.

FOULKE, R. A., *Practical Financial Statement Analysis*, 6th ed. New York: McGraw-Hill, Inc., 1968.

FREDRICKSON, E. B., ed., *Frontiers of Investment Analysis*, rev. ed., Part III. Scranton, Pa.: International Textbook Company, 1971.

GOODMAN, S. E., ed., *Financial Market Place*. New York: R. R. Bowker Co., 1972.

GRAHAM, BENJAMIN, D. L. DODD, and SIDNEY COTTLE, *Security Analysis*, 4th ed., Chapters 9–18. New York: McGraw-Hill, Inc., 1962.

————, and CHARLES McGOLRICK, *The Interpretation of Financial Statements*, 3rd ed. New York: Harper & Row, Publishers, 1975.

HAWKINS, D. E., *Financial Reporting Practices of Corporations*. Homewood, Ill.: Dow Jones-Irwin, Inc., 1972.

LEVINE, S. N., ed., *Financial Analyst's Handbook*, Volume II. Homewood, IL.: Dow Jones-Irwin, Inc., 1975.

PLUM, L. V., ed., *Investing in American Industries*. New York: Harper & Row, Publishers, 1960.

ROBERT MORRIS ASSOCIATES, *Source of Composite Financial Data—A Bibliography*, 4th ed.

WEISS, L. W., *Case Studies in American Industry*, 2nd ed. New York: John Wiley and Sons, Inc. 1971.

WESTWICK, C. P., *How to Use Management Ratios*. New York: John Wiley and Sons, 1973.

See also references, Chapter 24.

SPECIAL REFERENCES ON CONGLOMERATES AND MULTINATIONALS

BAGLEY, EDWARD R., *Beyond the Conglomerates*. New York: American Management Association, 1975.

BERNSTEIN, L. A., *Financial Statement Analysis*. Homewood, Ill.: Richard D. Irwin, Inc., 1974.

EELS, RICHARD, *Global Corporations*. New York: The Free Press, 1976.

FATEMI, N. S., and C. W. WILLIAMS, *Multinational Corporations*. Cranbury, N.J.: A.S. Barnes & Co., 1975.

GILPIN, ROBERT, *U. S. Power and the Multinational Corporations*. New York: Basic Book Publishers, Inc., 1975.

LYNCH, HARRY H., *Financial Performance of Conglomerates*. Boston, Mass.: Division of Research, Graduate School of Business Administration, Harvard University, 1971.

MANTZ, R. K., *Financial Reporting by Diversified Companies*. New York: Executives Research Foundation, 1967.

PHATEK, A. V., *Managing Multinational Corporations*. New York: Praeger Publishers, 1974.

STEPHENSON, HUGH, *The Coming Clash*. New York: Saturday Review Press, 1972.

STONE, DAVID, *An Economic Approach to Planning the Conglomerate of the 70's*. Princeton, N.J.: Auerbach Publishers, 1970.

TUGENDHAT, CHRISTOPHER, *The Multinationals*. New York: Random House, 1972.

VANCE, STANLEY C., *Managers in the Conglomerate Era*. New York: Wiley-Interscience, a division of John Wiley and Sons, Inc., 1971.

ZENOFF, DAVID B., *International Business Management*. New York: The Macmillan Company, 1971.

Public Utility Securities

SCOPE: This chapter discusses the investment position of the securities issued by privately owned public utility companies. The order of discussion is: (1) the utility industries (2) the franchise, (3) regulation, (4) the territorial analysis (5) the management factor, (6) public ownership, (7) balance sheet analysis, (8) types of securities, (9) income statement analysis, (10) electric light and power, (11) the gas industry, (12) the telephone industry, (13) the domestic telegraph industry, (14) the water industry, (15) the holding company and its regulation, (16) investment outlook, and (17) special sources of information on the public utilities industries.

The Utility Industries

Public utility companies are engaged in a business (1) with a public interest, that is, supplying services regarded as indispensable to the consuming public; (2) requiring a large capital investment so that duplication of competing facilities is not feasible; (3) operating under a franchise from a political authority that provides exclusive right to perform the service in the territory served; and (4) as a result of these characteristics, subject to regulation of rates, service, and other functions.

Financial characteristics of utilities include (with some exceptions) a preponderance of investment in fixed assets, large investment in plant in relation to revenues, relatively stable earnings, heavy use of bonds and preferred stocks as sources of funds, and rapid growth.

The utilities group includes electric light and power, gas distribution and transmission, telephone, telegraph, and water. *Operating* utilities provide the actual service; holding companies control groups of operating companies serving several territories.

The importance of public utility companies in the investment field is clearly indicated by Table 27-1. The progress of the utilities stands in sharp contrast to the more static condition of the railroads. Whereas the development of the railroads has been chiefly in betterment of existing facilities, the growth of the utilities continues in extensive expansion into new fields of

527

TABLE 27-1 Assets and Revenues of Privately Owned Public Utilities, 1976 (in millions of dollars)

Group	Assets	Revenues
Electric light and power	$173,000 (est.)	$49,300
Gas		
Distributing	8,840	7,380
Transmission	26,440	15,400
Integrated	11,700	7,800
Telephone	95,000	35,640
Telegraph (domestic)	1,350	530
Water (private)	1,100 (est.)	240 (est.)

Sources: American Gas Association; Federal Power Commission; Federal Communications Commission; *Moody's Public Utility Manual.*

operation. But utility progress has not been uniform. As will be shown later, signs of retrogression have appeared in some divisions of the group.

The Franchise

A franchise is a contract between the company and the area served.[1] From the standpoint of the investor, the more important agreements relate to type of service rendered, competition, territory, duration, and rates. Franchises may be *nonexclusive* or *exclusive*. The former type of award that allowed private competition has been largely replaced by the more satisfactory noncompetitive form. The chief threat of competition is from municipal operation. The territorial limits in the franchise may prevent an operating company from extending its service to rapidly growing contiguous territory.[2]

Franchises may be *perpetual, limited, or indeterminate*. Public sentiment has favored the limited duration basis (10 to 50 years); more recently the indeterminate, or indefinite, type, under which the franchise remains in effect as long as service is satisfactory, has come into favor. In the event the municipality purchases the property, the company is compensated by a valuation set by an independent board of appraisal. It is important that any bonds of the company mature before the franchise expires.

Rate restriction clauses, under which a maximum charge per unit of service is stated, appear in many older franchises. Unfortunate experience with such clauses has led, in newer franchises, to the substituting of flexible rates based on cost of service; in most cases, however, rates are authorized by a state utility commission rather than by the franchise.

The franchise position is important. Vague statements to the effect that "the franchise situation is satisfactory" should not satisfy the investor. The

[1]In many large cities, the utility companies operate under a group of franchises granted at various times to separate companies which are eventually merged into a single group. Where a utility serves a number of communities, it will operate under a number of separate franchises.

[2]Originally, the franchise of Commonwealth Edison Company confined it to the corporate limits of Chicago. In 1953, by a merger with a subsidiary, Public Service Company of Northern Illinois, the company acquired franchises in a number of communities to the north and west of Chicago.

most favorable type of franchise is exclusive and indeterminate with a flexible rate provision; the least satisfactory is the short-term, limited type with a maximum rate restriction.

Regulation

Utilities are regulated by Federal, municipal, and state authorities. Federal regulation is based on the interstate commerce section of the U.S. Constitution and the right to control the use of navigable waters. Its scope with respect to regular operations may be summarized as:[3]

The *Federal Power Commission* licenses power projects in navigable waters and regulates utility companies that transmit electric power and gas across state lines. Its jurisdiction extends to wholesale power and gas rates, cost of natural gas, accounting systems, and financial transactions. It prescribes a uniform system of accounts for all companies engaged in interstate power and gas operations.

The *Securities and Exchange Commission* has jurisdiction under the Public Utility Holding Company Act of 1935 over electric and gas holding companies that control subsidiaries in more than one state. (See the discussion at the end of this chapter.) Regulation covers the security offerings, capital structures, accounts, control, recapitalization, and reorganization of registered holding companies and their subsidiaries. Competitive bidding for their bonds is required.

The *Interstate Commerce Commission* has broad powers over the rates, service, financing, and accounts of electric railway, trucking, and bus companies that operate in interstate commerce.

The *Federal Communications Commission* prescribes the rates and practices of telephone and telegraph companies that are engaged in interstate and foreign communications. It has developed a uniform system of accounts for telephone companies.

Local regulation is generally restricted to powers delegated by the states. Such powers may be limited or very far reaching, extending to "home rule" over certain utility activities, as in Minnesota, Nebraska, South Dakota, and Texas with respect to electric light and power. The franchise is the vehicle for such regulation.

State regulation of companies that conduct intrastate business is the most comprehensive. All of the states except those just mentioned have a public service commission with broad and varying powers. While these powers are by no means uniform, certain leading principles and practices apply in the majority of cases.

Rate regulation The traditional theory of rate regulation has been to approve rate schedules that provide a "fair return" on the rate base, or "fair

---

[3]Other Federal bodies with jurisdiction are: the Nuclear Regulatory Commission, which is responsible for licensing and regulation of the nuclear industry; the Environmental Protection Agency, which controls environmental statement requirements; the Energy and Development Administration, which directs the major Federal activities relating to energy research and development.

value" of property used in the public service (value of the plant plus an allowance for working capital). Regulation is designed, on the one hand, to protect consumers from exploitation and, on the other, to permit a return to the company that will support the investment and attract necessary new capital. Historically, original cost (less depreciation) constituted the rate base or "fair value," although cost of reproduction (less depreciation) has been argued by utility companies during periods of increasing costs of construction. But no consistent and universal agreement existed on what "fair value" meant. More recently, the *prudent investment theory*, which uses original cost plus cost of permanent improvements as the base (after depreciation, and plus working capital) has been adopted in a number of states. Finally, in the *Hope Natural Gas case*,[4] the "fair value" principle was virtually abandoned in favor of a widening of the discretion of the commission so as to permit earnings sufficient to attract capital: that is, cover the cost of capital adequately. A number of states still use original cost as the base; some have adopted prudent investment; still others consider all elements or follow the principal of "fair value" without defining it specifically, but take replacement cost into consideration.

In any case, the state commissions have in mind the earnings (after operating expenses and taxes, but before interest and dividends) that will support the investment and attract capital in the light of prevailing conditions in the capital market. Recently the prevailing range has been 6 to 9% for electric and 8 to 9% for natural gas companies.[5]

The investor in utility securities is deeply concerned with the attitude of the commissions concerning such matters as valuation and fair return. Except in four or five very liberal states, a utility that consistently earns in excess of 8% on valuation is not likely to have its rates increased. One that earns less than 6% has reason to expect a favorable response to a request for a rate increase. However, even if a company earns only a modest rate on its total investment, by using senior securities (leverage), it can produce a respectable return and adequate dividends for the common stock. In some jurisdictions the per cent earned on equity capital is given separate emphasis in rate-making. The average is about 12.5%, with 14% and above considered excellent. The earnings on the common stock of a well-managed utility under fair regulation can be very substantial, but the theoretically

---

[4]*Federal Power Commission v. Hope Natural Gas Co.*, 370 U.S. 591 (1944).

[5]A close approximation of the rate of earnings as calculated for rate-making purposes may be had by dividing net operating income by depreciated property plus about 3% for working capital. A more detailed procedure is described in Federal Power Commission, *Statistics of Privately Owned Electric Utilities in the United States*, 1974 (Washington, D.C.: U.S. Government Printing Office, 1976, p. 731). This source shows the following range of rates of return for 197 companies in 1970:

Less than 5%	9.1% of companies
5 to 5.99%	6.1% of companies
6 to 6.99%	14.7% of companies
7 to 7.99%	35.5% of companies
8 to 8.99%	16.3% of companies
9 to 9.99%	12.2% of companies
10% and above	6.1% of companies

Flow-through accounting was used for liberalized depreciation.

unlimited opportunity that exists for industrial company earnings is not to be expected. Stability and the steady growth of earnings may, however, compensate for such a limitation.

The regulatory setting is vitally important to the investor. A number of investment services rate the various electric utility companies in a scale of 1 to 5 with respect to the attitude of the governing commission towards keeping rates in line with costs. A rating of 3 or above suggests that the stock is continuing to suffer from "regulatory lag."

The reported earnings of the company and the allowed rate of return on total investment and/or equity capital are also affected by the commission's attitude towards two special factors discussed below: (1) flow-through versus normalization of accelerated depreciation, and (2) allowance for funds used during construction.

Competition The commissions protect the interests of investors in utility securities by refusing *certificates of convenience* (which must be obtained by any new companies entering the field) to undeserving applicants. On the other hand, they may require forfeiture of franchise grants for nonuse. Certificates are issued only when the operations of the new company will not infringe upon the vested rights of any company already in the area, when the new company has capital adequate to carry out its plans, and when the organizers of the new company evidence their prior successful experience as utility operators.

Securities In most states new securities can be issued only with the approval of the commission. A limited number of purposes are acceptable: (1) to construct new property, (2) to buy existing property, (3) to better existing property, or (4) to refund existing debt. The amount issued must be reasonable for the purpose. The form of issue, whether bonds or stock, must be in harmony with a balanced capitalization. The terms of the underwriting (the cost of distribution) must not be excessive. While such control does not assure complete investment protection, it undoubtedly does reduce the risk of loss. Some states, such as Massachusetts and California, require competitive bidding for new utility bond issues.

Accounts and reports In most states, the commissions require a uniform procedure. Standard classifications for the more important branches of the industry have been adopted by large groups of states.[6] This results in a more accurate portrayal of financial condition and also facilitates the comparison of companies. The commissions also require detailed reports, which are submitted annually and are open to public inspection. The information forms the basis for the summary sent to the securityholders in the form of the annual report.

---

[6]Through adoption of the classifications developed by the Federal Power Commission or the National Association of Railroad and Utilities Commissioners.

Territorial Analysis

One of the most important factors in the selection of public utility securities is the nature of the territory served. Unlike the railroads, which cover wide areas, and industrial enterprises, which may seek markets anywhere, a public utility company may operate only in a prescribed territory. The opportunity to prosper is definitely limited to a restricted area. Careful attention should, therefore, be given to features such as geographical location, population, and resources.

Geographical location has economic as well as physical influence. The harbors of New York, Boston, Los Angeles, and San Francisco, among others, give those cities a natural advantage. With excellent water and rail facilities, Chicago, Cleveland, and Detroit are splendidly located. Proximity to established channels of trade is an economic advantage from a market viewpoint, just as nearness to waterfalls is helpful from a production standpoint. Marked seasonal variations in climate produce instability of sales. Companies located in certain sections of the country encounter public sentiment unfriendly to private utility operation.

The population of the territory that is served greatly affects the size and the importance of the company. Investors should prefer the securities of companies located in large areas that show a favorable rate of growth.

The economics of the territory should also be carefully considered. Some areas are primarily industrial; others are commercial, agricultural, or residential. The great advantage of the large community lies in the diversity of resources, which makes for stability of demand for utility service. Industrial and commercial territories offer better markets than do agricultural and residential districts, but industrial and commercial demand is subject to greater instability than is residential demand.

In very recent years two special geographical factors have come to the fore: (1) The type of fuel—coal versus natural gas used in steam-generated production of electric power, and the cost and availability of natural gas by gas distribution companies. The "energy crisis" has given a superior status to coal-using plants and those near adequate supplies of gas. (2) The economic and political strength of the territory. Utilities serving large metropolitan areas that have declined in strength—for example, New York and Boston—have lost top ranking. Growing areas and diversified territory are regarded as more favorable.

The decision of Consolidated Edison of New York in April 1974 to pass up its dividend (since resumed) was a severe shock to the status of utility securities and indicates that mere size is not a certain criterion of quality.

The Management Factor

The regulation of such important matters as rates, service, accounts, and financing has restricted the scope within which the management of the utility company exercises decision-making powers, and operating techniques have become fairly standardized within various branches of the utility group. Although a utility company is not faced with all of the problems that face competitive industrial business, sound management is still important. Such matters as operating economies, new fuel sources, engineering of new plants, forecasting of demand, provision of adequate plant and equipment at the proper time, and sound financing require a considerable amount of managerial skill.

Public relations are also important. Investors prefer the securities of those companies whose rate schedules are liberal and whose public relations are favorable. To adopt a maxim, utility companies must live with their customers. Companies with high rate schedules and indifferent public policies do not make good neighbors. The securities of such companies are especially vulnerable in periods of economic recession or political change, as revealed by the New York City situation.

Public Ownership

Gas and telephone properties are seldom publicly operated, but most waterworks are owned and operated by municipalities rather than by private companies. The relatively large amount of capital required, the routine nature of the operations, and the ability of the municipality to borrow at low rates are the chief factors explaining this situation. In the local transit field, inadequate returns or failure of private companies have forced municipal operation in many communities.[7] In the electric field, municipal ownership has been adopted by choice in some communities, such as Palo Alto and Seattle; in others, municipal plants have been constructed to provide service where profitable operation by private capital was questionable. There are more than 2,000 local public electric companies, and nearly 1,000 rural electric corporations. But these enjoy a small share of the business as measured by generating capacity, of which the approximately 500 "investor-owned" companies control about 80%.

The investor should examine the political climate and the attitude toward public ownership in the territory served, and insist on clauses that would provide adequate compensation in the event of recapture. Good public relations between the utility and the community are the best protection against the threat of municipal purchase.

Another major development has been the rise of Federal power projects of which there are now five: Tennessee Valley Authority (the largest power system in America), Bonneville Power Administration, Boulder Canyon Project, Southwestern Power Administration, and Southeastern Power Administration. Such projects have resulted in the purchase by the authority of many private companies in the neighboring territory, the sale of public power to existing companies instead of the expansion of their generating

[7]For many years the street railway services in Cleveland, Detroit, and Seattle have been publicly owned. In 1940, New York City "recaptured" rapid transit facilities formerly leased to the Interborough and Brooklyn-Manhattan companies. In 1947, Chicago set up a Transit Authority to operate a coordinated system of elevated, street car, and bus lines.

facilities, and pressure for lower rates by applying the "yardstick" of public power costs.

Balance Sheet Analysis

The condensed corporate balance sheet of all privately owned electric companies (Table 27-2) illustrates the characteristics of the utility balance sheet. The bulk of the assets is in the form of fixed plant. Current assets play a relatively minor role in the absence of a large cash balance and of inventories. Similarly, the sources of funds are long term, as represented by stocks, bonds, and surplus; current liabilities have relatively minor importance.

TABLE 27-2 Condensed Balance Sheet of Privately Owned
Electric Companies, December 31, 1975
(in millions of dollars)

Assets		
Electric utility plant	$160,782	
Other utility plant	13,096	$173,878
Less provision for dep'n and amort.		$ 35,585
Net plant		$138,293
Other property and investment		2,133
Current assets		13,080
Deferred debits		2,180
Total assets		$155,614
Liabilities		
Common stock		$ 19,520
Preferred stock		16,852
Other paid in capital		10,358
Retained earnings		16,238
Long-term debt		69,927
Current liabilities		15,256
Deferred federal income taxes		4,727
Reserves (operating) and deferred credits		2,692
Contributions in aid of construction		44
Total liabilities		$155,614

Source: Edison Electric Institute, *Statistical Yearbook of the Electric Utility Industry*, 1975. (New York: The Institute, 1976).

Gross electric plant per dollar of revenue is about $4.00, indicating an annual gross plant turnover of about 25%. Gross plant rather than net plant after depreciation is used in this efficiency test because the volume of service rendered is related to the plant in use rather than to its valuation. From a financial standpoint, the productivity of the investment may be measured by using the net plant figure to produce a turnover of about 30%. The investment in gross assets per dollar of revenues is higher, possibly $5 in the case of an all-hydroelectric company, and lower, around $1.50 for natural gas distributing companies. The relationship between plant and revenues provides a rough check on the validity of the important figure of investment in plant and the adequacy of the depreciation reserve.[8]

The ratio of long-term debt to net property is very important. It shows the assets support to the utility's bonds, and is related to earnings support also. If the utility earns a reasonable return on its property as valued for rate-making purposes, this return will provide adequate support to funded debt of, say, 50% of net plant. A return of 8% on total investment would provide interest coverage of 2.5 times on bonds equal to 50% of property, at an average interest cost of 7%. For the combined electric utilities whose statement is Table 27-2, the ratio of long-term debt to net plant was 50% as of 1975. In its regulation of holding companies and their subsidiaries, the Securities and Exchange Commission has established 50% of net plant as a debt standard. Certainly, 60% should be considered a maximum for electric companies.

The pattern of long-term financing is revealed by the capital structure proportions. For the electric industry, long-term debt comprises 52.6%, preferred stock 12.7%, and common stock plus surplus 34.7% of total capitalization (bonds, stock, and surplus). Utilities of all types rely heavily on senior securities for two reasons: (1) the relative stability of earnings makes feasible the use of such sources without undue risk; (2) by using bonds and preferred stock, whose interest and dividend rates are substantially less than the overall rate earned on total investment, the return on the common stock can be magnified sufficiently to attract junior equity capital. This is important, since unlike a competitive industrial company, the public utility cannot rely on reinvested earnings as a major source of funds. In 1975 the net operating income of the electric utilities referred to in Table 27-2 produced a return of 7.2% on average capital structure. After interest and preferred dividends, earnings available to common stock were 13.7% on the average book value of the common stock.

Book value, and its relation to market value, has special significance in the analysis of public utility common stocks. Earnings are directly related to investment. Where stock sells above book value, new financing with stock will increase earnings per share. Sold at book value, there is no effect. Sold below book value, earnings per share are diluted. Under those latter conditions, senior financing with bonds or preferred stock is indicated, even at high dividend or interest rates.

A final balance sheet test is found in the relation of current assets to current liabilities. This familiar ratio is much less important for the public utility company than for the industrial concern because its current items are relatively unimportant and because maturing current liabilities can be met with the steady cash income or funded into long-term obligations. For a strong and growing company, a ratio of less than one is not alarming; where earnings are weak, the ratio should be one or higher to permit the continued payment of bond interest.

---

[8]Plant includes construction in progress, but this is allowed in the rate base in only a few states. Similarly, permitted depreciation allowances are niggardly in some jurisdictions.

Types of Securities

The capitalization of most utilities is relatively simple, consisting of a single large, open-end mortgage bond issue with perhaps several series outstanding, preferred stock, and common stock. Variations from this pattern are frequently observed, however. Some have never issued preferred stock; others, especially in the telephone and natural gas groups, have relied on debenture bond financing because of the lack of mortgageable assets. The open-end mortgage bonds contain the protective provisions described in Chapter 8 that are designed to prevent dilution of assets and earnings from excessive new series.

Provision for rapid retirement of bonds through generous sinking fund or serial redemption requirements is still somewhat unusual, although modest sinking funds of 1 to 2% are found in modern bond issues.[9] The typical utility company assumes that it will always be in debt. The conversion feature often used in industrial financing is not used frequently, though the practice is growing; the call or redemption feature is, customarily included in bonds and preferred stock, however. During periods of high interest rates, investors demand protection against early redemption.

Income Statement Analysis

The main items found on the utility statement are illustrated by the combined income statement in Table 27-3. The operating revenues are the product of the number of units sold (kilowatt-hours, cubic feet of gas, and so forth) and the rates charged. The customers are classified, in the case of private electric companies, into the categories shown in Table 27-4.

The regulatory authorities establish the general level of the utility's net operating revenues; the company determines the rate or rates charged different classes of customers that will produce the permitted income.

The investor should compare the level of a company's rates with national, state, or local average figures. In 1976 the average residential electric bill in the United States was $288, at an average rate of 3.11 cents (3.73 for residential) per kilowatt-hour. Comparatively high rates are profitable, but may render a company vulnerable to rate reductions or to slower rate increases. Comparatively low rates suggest a miserly attitude on the part of the commission, but may also reflect types of fuel used and operating conditions.

Stability and growth of revenues are extremely important. Stability stems from the degree of diversification of the sources of revenue. In 1976, for the electric power industry as a whole, residential consumers accounted for 38% of revenues, but their consumption of kilowatt-hours was only 32%. Conversely, sale of kilowatt-hours to commercial and industrial customers was 65%, but accounted for only 58% of revenues because of the lower average rates per kilowatt-hour. Utility companies relying primarily on

---

[9]An exception is found in the large sinking funds of natural gas companies made necessary by the wasting character of their assets.

TABLE 27-3 Combined Income Statement of Privately Owned Electric Companies—December 31, 1975 (in millions of dollars)

Operating revenues	$48,236
Operating expenses:	
Operations	25,502
Maintenance	2,757
Depreciation and depletion	4,129
Income taxes (including deferred)	3,568
Other taxes	4,188
	$39,144
Operating income	9,092
Other (non-operating) income (net)	416
Allowance for funds during construction	1,694
Total income before interest changes	$11 202
Interest charges	5,200
Net income	$ 6,002
Dividends declared	
Preferred stock	$ 1,143
Common stock	$ 3,272

Source: See Table 27-2.

TABLE 27-4 Sources of Revenues of Privately Owned Electric Power Companies (based on 1976 data)

	Sales		Revenues	
Class of Service	Kilowatt-hours (millions)	Per Cent	Amount (millions)	Per Cent
Residential	453,774	31.7%	$16,920	38.0%
Commercial	355,555	24.8	13,137	29.5
Industrial	569,134	39.8	12,689	28.5
Others	52,327	3.7	1,173	4.0
Total	1,430,790	100 0%	$44,480	100.0%

Source: See Table 27-2.

industrial customers are vulnerable to changes in both volume of sales and of revenues. Growth stems from increased population and industrial activity, but may be unbalanced because of overdependence on one industry or a few major industrial consumers.

The residential load is ordinarily more stable than that of the commercial and industrial users, whose demands tend to vary more with business conditions. Futhermore, while industrial and commercial loads may be very large, their average rates are considerably lower. But such demand can contribute to a higher *load factor* (average consumption to peak consumption) by building up demand in off-peak hours or seasons, and thus produce lower unit costs and higher profits. The higher the load, the less the idle plant capacity. The load factor can be determined for any period—a day, a month, or a year. Consider an electric light and power company with a peak load of 100,000 kilowatts. If its annual output is 525,600,000 kilowatt-hours or 60,000 kilowatts per hour, its annual load factor is 60% or about average for the industry.

In examining the operating revenues of a company, one should note the extent to which they are derived from the main activity of the company, such as electric light and power, and the extent from collateral services such as gas. Good results from one type of activity may be offset by the greater risks of another. However, a mixture of revenues distorts the comparability of the ratios with those of other companies.

A basic test of operating efficiency is the familiar operating ratio: that is, the ratio of all operating deductions, including taxes, to operating revenues. Even more useful as a clue to management's control of everyday operations is the ratio of direct operating expenses (all expenses less depreciation and all taxes) to operating revenues. Typical ratios for various categories of utilities, on both bases, are shown in Table 27-5.

TABLE 27-5   Utility Operating Ratios, 1976

	All Expenses and Taxes	Direct Operating Expenses
Hydroelectric	73%	42%
Steam electric	83	46
Natural gas distribution	92	71
Gas transmission	90	73
Telephone	84	53
Domestic Telegraph	87	67
Water	70	50

In addition to being affected by the type of industry, type of consumer, load factor, cost of fuel, and other factors, the operating ratio is greatly influenced by the depreciation and maintenance expense, over which management has some control from year to year. A low operating ratio may be the result of undermaintenance. Maintenance and depreciation *combined* should not be less than 17% of gross revenues for steam electric companies and 13% for hydroelectric. Annual depreciation expense as a percentage of gross plant (exclusive of land) should run about 2 3/4% for gas distribution, 4 1/4% for gas pipeline companies, 2 1/4 to 2 1/2% for electric companies, and 4 1/2% for telephone companies.

The net operating revenues plus the income from investments and other sources comprise the total income available for interest; this is used to compute the coverage of fixed charges and of fixed charges plus preferred dividends. In 1975, for all private electric companies combined, interest was earned 2.1 times after taxes[10] and 2.6 times before income taxes. This is in contrast to an after-tax ratio of 3.8 times in 1965, and reflects the sub-

---

[10]In these calculations, interest on short-term as well as long-term debt is included. "Allowance for funds during construction" is added back to net operating revenue in calculating the amount of total income available for interest coverage.

stantial rise in interest rates and outstanding debt since that year. Within the whole group, wide variations appear; nevertheless, the relative stability of utility earnings (save electric railway and telegraph companies) and their general ability to earn their fixed charges adequately have put their bonds in a relatively preferred investment position. The investor is satisfied with a lower record of interest coverage for a sound utility than for a railroad or an industrial company.

Another method of testing the ability of the company to earn its fixed charges is to compute these as a percentage of operating revenues. For an efficient and conservatively financed steam electric company, the ratio should not exceed 10%. Thus, if a company had net plant of $75,000,000, operating revenues of $27,000,000, and outstanding bonds of $37,000,000 with an average interest rate of 7%, its interest charges would be about $2,600,000 or about 10% of revenues. And if operating expenses, taxes, and depreciation consumed 80% of revenues, interest would be covered 2.1 times after taxes.

In the 1970s the rise in interest rates sent the cost of new long-term borrowing to over 9% for some companies, and raised the average cost on all outstanding debt substantially. As older debt bearing lower coupons has been retired or refinanced, coverage of total interest has declined.

The relatively stable earnings of utilities enable them to declare most of their net income in dividends. The typical payout is about 70%. "Growth" utilities distribute a lower percentage, and their retained earnings, reinvested at good rates, contribute to gains in earnings per common share and to increases in the dividend rate. Slower-growing companies rely on a higher payout to give their common stock market appeal.

Special problems in income analysis   When examining and interpreting the income statements of utility companies and calculating important ratios, certain special influences on reported earnings should be noted. These are especially important, although not confined to electric power companies.

1. The influence of accelerated depreciation. For income tax purposes, utilities compute depreciation on an accelerated basis. For their own reports they may chose either to let the resulting tax savings "flow through" to earnings, or to "normalize" by charging deferred tax expense and crediting a "deferred income tax" liability account. The latter practice produces lower reported earnings. About half of the state commissions permit "flow through" for rate-making purposes. The conservative analyst prefers the earnings figures under normalization and favors companies in states where the commissions accept normalized earnings and adjusts rates with this in mind.

2. Similarly, the 10 to 11 1/2% (1976) investment tax credit for capital expenditures may be reported either on a flow-through or a normalized basis.

3. Utility companies "capitalize," or include in cost of plant, the actual and/or imputed cost of funds tied up during construction. Because they are capitalized, these financial costs, called "allowance for funds used during construction" are added to operating income before fixed charges. They

increase therefore both the coverage of interest charges and the reported earnings per share. These allowances (1976) ran about 4% of revenues and some 30% of reported earnings svailable to common stock. The analyst prefers companies with a lower percentage of "AFDC" to earnings. A high level of construction in progress with resulting high AFDC has not yet added to real cash earnings.

Electric Light and Power

The electric light and power companies comprise the largest as well as the most popular utility group from the investment viewpoint. In the 90 years of its history, the electrical industry has grown from the small local station to the modern power plant serving thousands of customers over a wide area through an elaborate transmission and distribution system. So successful have the companies been in building up a daytime load that the hours of darkness now represent the *valley* rather than the *peak* of demand. The growth of the industry has been the result of more extensive, as well as intensive, use of electrical energy.

Electricity now occupies a monopoly in the field of illumination, and new uses of power, including appliances and air conditioning, are improving the load factor. The growth of space heating, especially through the use of the heat pump, offers prospects of more vigorous competition with coal, oil, and gas. The relative growth of the industry is indicated by the data in Table 27-6. In recent years this growth has slowed from its former rate of 10% to 6 to 7% per year, reflecting cyclical conditions, customers' resistance to higher rates, and efforts to conserve energy.

The stability of earnings of the electric utilities has enabled most com-

**TABLE 27-6 Growth of the Private Electric Light
and Power Industry, 1950–1976**

	Installed Capacity (millions of kilowatts)	Production (billions of kilowatt-hours)	No. of Customers (millions)	Revenues (billions)[a]	Net Income (millions)
1950	$ 55.2	266.9	$35.1	[b]	$ 831
1955	86.9	420.9	41.5	$ 6.9	1,257
1960	128.5	578.6	46.5	9.7	1,747
1965	177.7	809.5	51.5	12.9	2,556
1970	262.7	1,183.2	56.9	18.8	3,333
1976[c]	415.8	1,582.0	65.0	47.1	6,990

[a]Electric departments only
[b]Not available
[c]Preliminary

Source: Edison Electric Institute, *Statistical Year Book of the Electric Utility Industry* (New York: The Institute, annual).

panies to show adequate coverage of interest charges, although the combination of high operating and capital costs reduced this factor from about 3.5 times in 1960–1965 to less than 2.5 in 1975. Substantial differences among companies reflect a growing diversity of quality.

Although the past rate of growth of over 10% annually is not being maintained, the burgeoning power needs of the country, stemming from population growth, industrial expansion, and increased per capita residential use, will sustain the industry's earning power, although at a lower level.

Six major problems facing the industry are: (1) The lag between rising costs of operation and of capital, and rate revisions reflecting inflation, capital market conditions, and changes in rate of return and valuation standards by the courts. (2) Public concern over the development of nuclear power. In 1976, 65 nuclear projects were in operation or construction, but much uncertainty prevailed with respect to the future growth of this source of energy because of public concern. (3) The threat of even higher cost of oil and gas fuels. (4) Increasing costs of pollution control. (5) Increasing costs of new capacity. (6) Continuing high cost of capital, and the dilution effect of sales of common stock below book value. All these combined to keep the rate earned on net property unsatisfactory for many companies and to discourage new financing with common stock. Securities of electric companies will, as always, continue to include some of mediocre quality. But, on the whole, the quality status of electric bonds and stocks should be maintained, although substantial variation in the market prices of common stocks will continue as price-earnings ratios and yields move up and down in reflection of changing interest rates. (The data on p. 552 show how these have changed in the period 1965–1976.)

The range in quality of utility bonds has widened as a result of the industry's problems in recent years, so that the investor must examine the trends in revenues, operating and financial costs, and return on capital of individual companies with unusual care. Bonds of some companies that formerly enjoyed premier status no longer enjoy that rank. The decline in pre-tax interest coverage in recent years (from over 5 times in 1965 to an average of less than 3 in 1976–1977) has resulted in the lowering of the ratings of a number of electric utility bonds.

Summary of power company tests The balance sheets and income statements of an electric power company should be analyzed carefully. The better-managed companies report financial operations within recognized ranges, as indicated in the following comments. All of the following suggested tests will not be met at the same time. Each is a suggested maximum or minimum and should be considered separately.

With respect to the balance sheet:

1. The value of the fixed assets (land, buildings, and equipment before depreciation) should not exceed 4 times the operating revenue in the case of a steam plant and 5 times in the case of a hydroelectric plant. (Using net plant, the suggested relationships are 3 times and 4 times, respectively.)

2. The amount of bonds outstanding should not exceed 50 to 55% of the net value of the fixed assets or 50 to 55% of total capital structure.[11]

3. The depreciation reserve should be at least 25% of the value of the gross fixed assets for steam electric, 15% for hydroelectric.

4. The preferred stock outstanding should not exceed 10 to 15% of capital structure.

5. The common stock and surplus should represent at least 35% of capital structure.

6. Unless the company is growing rapidly, the working capital ratio should be at least 100%.

With respect to the income statement:

• The ratio of total expenses, including provisions for maintenance, depreciation, and taxes, to operating revenues should not exceed 83% for a steam plant and 73% for a hydroelectric plant.

• The ratio of depreciation plus maintenance to operating revenues should not be less than 17% for steam, 13% for hydro.

• The ratio of operating income, before the payment of interest charges, and after income taxes, to the net investment in plant and equipment should be between 7 and 9% to show a fair return earned on the rate base.

• The ratio of interest charges to the operating revenues should not exceed 7 1/2%. The total income (after all taxes) available for the payment of these charges should average at least 2.0 times the requirement over a representative period of years (2.5 times before taxes).

• The sum of the interest charges and the preferred dividend to operating revenues should not exceed 11%.[12] The total income available for the payment of these charges should be at least 1 3/4 times the "overall" requirement over a representative period of years.[13]

• The balance available for dividends on the common stock should be at least 10% of the operating revenues.

• The rate earned on average common stock equity should be at least 10%.

• For a nongrowth utility, the common stock dividend should be at least 70% of available earnings.

The Gas Industry

The production and distribution of gas on a commercial scale has been a major public utility enterprise in the United States for considerably more than a full century. The industry has shown continued but erratic progress

---

[11]Depending on preferred stock proportion. Debt of 50% and preferred stock of 15% of capital structure total 65%. If a company has no preferred stock outstanding, a higher debt ratio is appropriate, say to a maximum of 60%.

[12]If the preferred stock is to be considered high grade, the coverage of bond interest plus preferred dividends should be as high as the required coverage of bond interest. This means that for a given company, if the preferred is high grade, the bonds more than meet the standard.

[13]The allowance for funds used during construction should not exceed 30% of earnings available to the common stock.

despite almost constant competition of alternative services. As electricity gradually gained supremacy in the lighting field, the gas companies turned to the heating field, with most successful results. The physical characteristics of gas make it an ideal fuel for heating purposes. As a result, the output of the industry has continued to grow faster than the general economy.

The great bulk of the gas sold by the American companies was once produced by the destructive distillation of coal. Although natural gas was used extensively in certain districts, for the main part it was available only to customers located near the producing wells. Extensive petroleum prospecting brought in many rich natural gas wells, especially in the Southwest. To find a market for this gas, companies built pipelines, extending hundreds of miles, bringing natural gas to metropolitan areas including Chicago, Cleveland, Detroit, St. Louis, Washington, Atlanta, New Orleans, Los Angeles, San Francisco, and New England industrial centers.

Investors are interested in three types of gas companies: natural gas distributing companies, natural gas pipeline or transmission companies, and integrated companies performing both functions. The growth of the industry is shown in Table 27-7.

TABLE 27-7 Growth of Gas Industry, 1950–1976

	Proven Reserves (billions cu. ft.)	Production (billions cu. ft.)	Number of Customers (millions)	Sales (trillions of Btu's)	Revenues[a] (millions)
1950	184,585	8,480	24.0	4,209	$ 1,948
1955	222,483	11,720	28.5	6,659	3,450
1960	262,326	15,088	33.1	9,288	5,617
1965	286,469	17,963	37.3	11,980	7,406
1970	290,746	23,863	41.5	16,044	10,282
1976	216,026	20,944	44.9	14,814	23,701

[a]Sales to ultimate customers.

Source: American Gas Association, Inc., *Gas Facts* (New York: The Association, annual).

Only about 34% of the consumption (but about 44% of the revenues) of gas distributing companies is residential (cooking and heating). The commercial and industrial demand introduces an element of instability which to a large extent was, until very recent years, offset by continued growth. (See Table 27-8).

Special problems of the industry   The investor should be aware of the special problems of the gas industry and how they apply to individual companies. These include:

1. *Inadequate supply.* The supply of gas has lagged discovery and consumption. The ruling of the Federal Power Commission in July 1976 increasing the ceiling price of gas in the interstate market will help relieve the supply problem of the interstate pipeline companies, but the (unlikely) decontrol of the wellhead price of gas is also necessary to bring new discovery ahead of consumption.

TABLE 27-8 Gas Utility Revenues (based on 1976 data)

Class of Service	Sales		Revenues	
	Btu's (trillions)	Per Cent	Amount (millions)	Per Cent
Residential	5,014	33.8%	$ 9,941	41.9%
Commercial	2,423	16.4	4,075	17.2
Industrial	7,107	48.0	9,374	39.6
Other	270	1.8	311	1.3
Total	14,814	100.0%	$23,701	100.0%

Source: American Gas Association, Inc., *Gas Facts* (New York: The Association, annual).

2. Instability of sales caused by cyclical and seasonal (weather) influences are a problem for those companies that are heavily dependent on commercial and industrial revenues.

3. Increasing competition from electric heating and appliances exists in the residential and commercial areas.

4. A shift to other energy and power by commercial and industrial users continues.

5. The sluggish growth of housing in recent years has affected the residential demand for gas.

6. Market prices of many companies' common stocks are below book values, thus discouraging equity financing of expansion.

Positive aspects of the industry   There are, however, certain encouraging elements:

• The Federal Trade Commission is inclined to allow higher returns to offset the increased cost of capital of interstate companies.

• The Commission permits the use of normalization of accounting for accelerated depreciation and also accepts higher depreciation rates. Both of these have resulted in increased cash flow.

• Local (state) utility commissions have produced prompter action on rate requests. Most distributors are able to pass on to consumers the higher cost of gas quickly, through automatic or adjusted clauses in their rate schedules. Purchased gas constitutes 70 to 75% of distributors' total expense.

• In spite of lower earnings, the ratio of debt to total capital structure has remained moderate. Preferred stock financing has been successfully substituted for some debt and common stock financing, and convertible preferred issues have a special appeal.

Gas company analysis: distribution companies   Analysis of the financial condition of a gas distributing company involves the application of recognized standards of acceptability to the figures shown in the published financial statements.

With respect to the balance sheet:

- The value of the fixed assets (before depreciation) should not exceed 1 1/2 times the operating revenue (1 1/4 times after depreciation).
- The depreciation reserve should be at least 24% of gross plant.
- The amount of bonds outstanding should not exceed 50% of the capital structure or 45% of the net plant.
- The preferred stock, common stock, and retained earnings should represent at least 50% of the capital structure.
- The ratio of current assets to current liabilities should be at least 100%.

With respect to the income statement:

- Total operating revenue deductions, including depreciation and taxes, should not exceed 90% of operating revenues.
- Operating revenue deductions, exclusive of depreciation and taxes, should not exceed 75% of operating revenues.
- The ratio of depreciation plus maintenance to operating revenues should not be less than 7%.
- Gross income before interest charges should be 9% of the net fixed assets or capital structure.
- The ratio of interest charges and other deductions from gross income to operating revenues should not exceed 4%. The interest charges should be earned 2 1/2 times (after taxes) over a representative period of years.
- The ratio of the sum of fixed charges and preferred dividends to operating revenues should not exceed 5%. Fixed charges plus preferred dividends combined should be earned 2.4 times over a representative period of years.
- The balance available for common stock should be at least 5% of operating revenues.
- The return on common stock equity should be at least 12%.

Gas pipeline company analysis   Rapid though its growth has been, the gas transmission industry presents special elements of risk due to: (1) the uncertain regulatory status of the industry, and (2) the unusually large use of debt as a source of funds. The latter risk would be negligible if the former were removed, because the producing and transmission companies (who produce or buy gas in the field and sell it to retail distributing companies) enjoy resale contracts with large retailing utilities that justify a heavier debt financing than would be appropriate for a local company.

Regulation of natural gas in interstate commerce was given to the Federal Power Commission by the Natural Gas Act of 1938. The Commission's policy was to allow the average field price to be the guide in setting the value of a pipeline's own production. This encouraged the exploration and production of owned reserves. In 1954 the Supreme Court ruled that the Commission had jurisdiction over all sales of natural gas for resale in interstate commerce.[14] The control of the Commission over the cost of gas in the

---

[14]*Phillips Petroleum Co. v. Wisconsin*, 374 U.S. 672.

field is accomplished through area pricing procedures, under which ceilings on prices at which new gas can be sold are established in twenty-two separate areas. The Commission increased the well-head price in 1976.

The Commission has established standard accounting procedures for interstate companies. Of special interest is the rule that accelerated depreciation be utilized and that the resulting tax deferrals be passed through to the consumer in the form of lower rates.

With respect to the balance sheet:

1. The value of the gross fixed assets should not exceed 2 times the operating revenue (1 1/4 times after depreciation).

2. The depreciation reserve should be at least 40% of the gross plant.

3. The amount of bonds and other long-term debt outstanding should not exceed 65% of the net plant, or 55% of the capital structure.

4. The preferred stock, common stock, and surplus should represent at least 45% of the capital structure.

With respect to the income statement:

1. The ratio of total operating deductions, including depreciation and taxes, should not exceed 88% of operating revenues.

2. The ratio of operating expenses, exclusive of depreciation and taxes, should not exceed 70% of operating revenues.

3. The ratio of depreciation plus maintenance to operating revenues should be not less than 8%.

4. Gross income before interest charges should be at least 9% of the capital structure or 10% of the net plant.

5. The ratio of interest charges and other income deductions to operating revenues should not exceed 5 1/2%. Fixed charges should be covered by gross income at least 2.5 times over a representative period of years, after taxes.

6. The ratio of the sum of fixed charges and preferred dividends to operating revenues should not exceed 6%. Interest plus preferred dividends should be earned at least 2 times over a representative period of years.[15]

7. The balance available for common stock should be at least 9% of operating revenues.

8. The return on common stock equity should be at least 15%.

Standards for integrated companies should fall between those given above, depending on the proportion of revenues and assets devoted to each function. Since these are not readily available, the most conservative of the ratio limits stated above may be used as guides.

Still different are the "combination" utilities that provide more than one service, for example, electric and gas. The investor can determine approximate standards by noting the proportion of revenue that is derived from each service.

[15]These figures assume that the company has some "other income" in addition to net operating income.

Market action of gas securities   The price action of gas company securities has been quite volatile, reflecting the market as a whole and the outlook for the industry. From a high of 129 in January 1973, the Standard & Poor's price index of gas pipeline stocks declined 46% to 70 in 1974, and rose to 140 in early 1977. The gas distributors index fell 42%, from 72 to 42, but climbed to above 80 in early 1977. But even the latter prices were depressed on a price-earnings and yield basis. In early 1977, pipeline ratios ranged from 5 to 8. Yields ranged from 3 to 9.7%, with an average of 6.4%. Multiples for distributing companies ranged from 6.6 to 11, with an average of 7.4, and yields ranged from 2 to 10%, with an average of 7%. With a few exceptions, gas stocks sold below book value, thus impeding new equity financing. The uncertainties in the industry continued to depress their investment appeal.

The Telephone Industry

The telephone industry has become an integral factor in the everyday life of the nation. In any age which puts a premium upon speed, instantaneous communication has inestimable value. Progressive policies on the part of operating management in the form of quicker service (automatic dials), promotional rates (at off-peak hours), universal connections (long-distance lines), and teletype service have caused an extraordinary growth in this field.

Although there are 1,600 telephone companies in the United States, the Bell System, consisting of the parent American Telephone & Telegraph Company and its subsidiaries and affiliates, operates 80% of the nation's telephones, services 75% of the calls, and controls over 80% of the industry's assets. General Telephone & Electronics Corporation is the leading domestic independent, operating 33% of the telephone. International Telephone & Telegraph Corporation is important abroad.

American Telephone & Telegraph Company owns and operates the connecting long-distance lines. It controls, through stock ownership, 21 regional operating "Bell" companies and has a minority interest in two others; it also owns Western Electric Company, manufacturer of telephone equipment for the system, and Bell Telephone Laboratories, Inc., a research subsidiary. Its income is derived from toll-service revenues, license-contract revenues received for services furnished to the companies of the system, and dividends and interest on securities of subsidiaries. The growth of the Bell System during the past 21 years is indicated in Table 27-9.

Investment interest in Bell System securities is centered in the bonds and preferred stocks of the regional Bell companies, and the bonds, preferred stock, and common stock of the parent company. In general, the associated companies provide examples of able business management. The senior securities of the regional companies command high investment respect. The volume of debentures of the parent company has increased greatly in recent years. In 1970, $1,569,000,000 of debentures (with warrants) were sold. This was the largest single piece of corporate financing on record. Although

TABLE 27-9 Growth of Bell Telephone System 1955–1976

Items	1955	1960	1965	1970	1976
Telephones (1,000)	46,218	60,735	75,866	96,561	123,100
Average daily conversations (1,000)	168,936	219,093	279,686	368,000	500,000 (est.)
Plant, before depreciation (millions)	$15,340	$24,072	$35,334	54,813	94,167
Operating revenues (millions)	$5,297	$7,920	$11,062	$16,955	32,816
Employees (1,000)	745	736	795	1,005	927
Stockholders, parent (1,000)	1,409	1,911	2,841	3,053	2,900
Net income, parent (millions)	$664	$1,213	$1,796	$2,189	$3,829
Earnings per share, parent	$2.18	$2.77	$3.41	$3.99	$ 6.05

Source: American Telephone & Telegraph Company, annual reports.

the debt ratio has become less conservative, the company's debentures (including the convertibles) command the highest investment rating.

For the first time in its history, in 1971 the parent company sold preferred stock, issuing 27,500,000 convertible shares with par value of $1,375,000,000. Additional preferred stock was sold in 1973. In 1975 the company sold 12 million shares of common stock at 54 7/8 ($658,500,000). The ratio of "senior capital"—bonds and preferred stock—to the consolidated capital structure stood at 51% at the end of 1976. (See Table 27-10.)

TABLE 27-10 Consolidated Capital Structure, Bell System (in millions of dollars)

Items	1955 Amt.	1955 Per Cent	1965 Amt.	1965 Per Cent	1976 Amt.	1976 Per Cent
Funded debt						
Subsidiaries	$ 2,340	18%	$ 5,592	19% ⎫	$32,525	47%
AT&T	2,036	16	3,490	12 ⎭		
AT&T Preferred stock[a]	—	—	—	—	2,862	4
Minority interest in subsidiaries	248	2	647	2	899	1
AT&T capital stock[a]	7,118	56	13,927	47	17,332	25
Retained earnings	1,081	8	5,811	20	16,126	23
Total	$12,823	100%	$29,467	100%	$69,744	100%

[a]Includes premium on shares.

Sources: American Telephone & Telegraph Company, annual reports and *Statistical Report*.

For many years, the common stock of American Telephone & Telegraph was regarded as a premier equity. Its unbroken dividend record partially explains why it was held by over 3 million investors as of 1977. Its appeal (and its market price) was increased considerably by a 3-for-1 split in 1959 and a 2-for-1 split in 1964. Earnings per share rose to $6.05 a share in

1976, and dividends rose from $2.00 in 1965 to $3.40 a share. The lag of rates behind costs and the pending rate investigation (see below), together with the great increase in senior financing, have given the stock a more uncertain outlook and a volatile price record in recent years. In 1965 the stock sold as high as 70, and in 1970 as low as 41, but rose to 65 in early 1977. The company's rate of return has remained below 7.5% and has lagged behind the earning power of "growth" companies in the electric power industry and of some of the independent telephone companies.

AT&T stock continues to enjoy a firm place in the income category. Its convertible preferred stock offers a combination of secure income and possible appreciation. But adequate and timely rate relief will be necessary to overcome inflationary operating and capital costs.

Recent developments The American Telephone and Telegraph Company serves the entire industry in appeals for rate increases. It also leads in innovations in service, including more efficient equipment, data communication, and electronic switching. In October 1965, the Federal Communications Commission ordered a general investigation of interstate rates that will take years to complete. In November 1974, the Justice Department filed an antitrust suit charging AT&T with monopolizing the market for telecommunication services and equipment, and seeking divestiture of Western Electric and the splitting off of AT&T's long lines department. Many years are likely to elapse before these issues are settled.

Communications Satellite Corporation (Comsat) was established in 1963 to provide global transmission service. Comsat is owned in part by a variety of communications and equipment concerns, and its shares are traded on the New York Stock Exchange.

The half-dozen important independent telephone companies serve roughly one-half of the geographic area of the United States and have enjoyed somewhat greater growth than the Bell System because they serve expanding rural and suburban areas. In 1976 their rates of return generally exceeded that of the Bell System, their shares typically sold at somewhat higher price-earnings ratios, and their dividends yields were lower, reflecting a smaller payout of earnings on common stock.

Investors in the telephone industry thus have three choices with respect to both bonds and stocks: The parent AT&T; the Bell subsidiaries, which have bonds and some publicly held common stock; and the independents.

Telephone company analysis Analysis of the financial condition of a telephone company requires the application of standards of acceptability differing somewhat from those used for electric power and gas companies. With respect to the balance sheet:

1. The value of the fixed assets before depreciation should not exceed 3 times the operating revenue (2 1/2 times after depreciation).

2. The retirement (depreciation) reserve should be not less than 24% of the gross fixed assets.

3. The amount of bonds outstanding should not exceed 48% of the capital structure.

4. The comments with respect to preferred stock, common stock, capital structure, and surplus previously made in connection with power company balance sheets are applicable to telephone company statements, except that smaller proportions of debt and of preferred stock are appropriate, in order to recognize the greater volatility of telephone company earnings.

5. Current assets should at least equal current liabilities.

With respect to the income statement

1. The ratio of operating expense (including income taxes) to operating revenues should not exceed 83% (70% exclusive of income taxes).

2. The ratio of depreciation plus maintenance to gross revenues should be at least 30%.

3. The ratio of income available for fixed charges (after income taxes) to capital structure should be at least 8%.

4. The ratio of interest charges to operating revenues should be not more than 7%, and total income should be at least 2 1/2 times the interest charges for a representative period of years.

5. The comments with respect to preferred dividends and balance of earnings remaining for the common stock previously made in connection with power company income reports are equally applicable to telephone company statements, except that interest plus preferred dividends should be earned more generously in the latter group.

Market position   Telephone bonds and preferred stocks enjoy premier status in their respective markets. The yield on AT&T common stock is somewhat lower than the average yield for electric utilities stock; that of the independents is comparable to the electrics. Telephone earnings available to common stock have not been plagued by as much cost inflation, and their growth has not slowed down. The "regulatory lag" is not as extreme. But they are still subject to cyclical variation and to competition from other means of communication. Telephone stocks still lack the prospects of the "growth" electric power companies.

The Domestic Telegraph Industry

Western Union Corporation   The domestic telegraph industry of the United States is controlled by a single company, Western Union. Profits reached a then all-time high in 1959. Net income declined in 1960–1962, but by 1965 was again setting new levels. Fortunately a substantial rise was enjoyed in the 1970s. But the future of the company, and of its securities, is still open to conjecture. The radio, the teletypewriter, the long-distance telephone, and airmail have diverted a substantial part of the business which formerly went by telegraph and cable. Revenues from telegram messages continue to decline, and although those from lesser systems, teleprinter, and exchange services have contributed to a substantial increase in total revenues, a high operating cost ratio keeps the return on total capital and on equity distressingly low. (See Table 27-11.) Net income is unstable, but the dividend yield is not unattractive. The future of the company lies in continuous research and in innovations in communications such as its launching of the first domestic satellite (Westar I) in 1974.[16]

TABLE 27-11   Western Union Financial Analysis

	1965	1976
(Gross) plant turnover	44%	33%
Capital structure proportions		
Long-term debt	32%	48%
Preferred stock	7%	11%
Common stock and surplus	61%	41%
Reserve for depreciation as a percentage		
of gross plant	35%	40%
Current ratio	1.5	1.3
Operating raio (including taxes)	88%	87%
Depreciation and maintenance as a percentage		
of revenues	27%	28%
Return on average capital structure	5%	6%
Times overall charges earned (after taxes)	3.5	1.75
Percentage earned on common equity	3%	6%
Earnings per common share	$2.30	$2.10
Dividends per common share	$1.40	$1.40

Source: Western Union Corporation, annual reports.

Table 27-11 shows pertinent financial data for Western Union in 1965 and 1976. The high operating ratio, the vulnerability to economic recession, and the relatively low return on total investment suggest the necessity of caution with respect to long-term debt, the maintenance of adequate working capital, and a conservative dividend policy.

The Water Industry

Investment interest in the securities of water companies is quite limited, owing to the prevalence of municipal ownership in this field. The supply of private water company securities is limited. Others are available in the municipal "revenue bond" category.

Relatively few large communities, notably Indianapolis, Birmingham, and San Jose, are served by private companies. A number of smaller cities, such as New Haven, and New Rochelle, N.Y., have private service. Certain companies serve rather wide groups of communities. One—American Water Works—is the parent of 45 companies operating in 20 states. The industry

[16]COMSAT's *Comstar* is leased to AT&T.

is the oldest of the utilities and for centuries has retained its essential simplicity of a "pump and a pipe." However, to reach adequate sources, the "pipe" has had to be lengthened in many cases.

Historically, water has almost always been obtainable in unlimited quantity at little or no cost, and its use has quite invariably been proportionate to population. Population growth in the United States is a little over 1% yearly, and so the growth of water companies is equally slow. If, however, the water companies are handicapped by slow growth, they enjoy a compensating advantage in stability of revenue. The use of water, at least for domestic purposes, is seldom contingent upon cost; consequently, the output of water companies is remarkably steady. Stability of earnings is the outstanding advantage of water securities as investments and justifies a relatively high proportion of bonds in the capital structure.

Certain operating characteristics of water companies are worth noting. The investment in fixed assets is large in relation to revenues; in other words, the plant turnover is slow. However, this disadvantage is offset by a correspondingly low operating ratio.

Water company analysis   With respect to the balance sheet:

1. The value of the fixed assets (before depreciation) should not exceed 5 times the operating revenues.

2. The retirement (depreciation) reserve should be at least 15% of the value of the fixed assets.

3. The amount of bonds outstanding should not exceed 60% of the depreciated value of the fixed assets, or 65% of the capital structure.

4. The preferred stock outstanding, together with the bonds outstanding, should not exceed 75% of the capital structure.

5. The common stock and retained earnings should be at least 25% of the capital structure.

With respect to the income statement:

1. The ratio of operating expenses, including all taxes, to operating revenues should not exceed 70%. Direct expenses should not consume more than 50% of revenues.

2. The ratio of depreciation plus maintenance to operating revenues should be at least 15%.

3. Operating income after taxes should be at least 8% of the capital structure.

4. The ratio of interest charges to operating revenues should not exceed 15%. The total income after taxes should be at least 1 3/4 times the interest charges.

5. The preferred dividend requirement, plus the interest charges, should be earned at least 1 1/2 times on an overall basis.

6. The balance available for the common stock should be at least 8% of the operating revenues.

The Holding Company
and Its Regulation

Reference has been made previously to the importance of the holding company in the public utility field, especially in the electric, gas, telephone, and water services. The "pure" holding company's chief asset is the common stock of subsidiary operating companies. The "holding-operating" company owns and operates property in its own right and also controls subsidiaries through stock ownership.

The holding company was used widely in the utility field in order to give to the subsidiaries the advantages of combined management of operations, construction, public relations, and financing which they might not enjoy as separate local concerns. The use of the device also made possible the control of very large properties with small investment, and also made possible (under favorable conditions) a large return to the owners of the holding company common stock. The operating companies typically issued substantial nonvoting senior securities bearing fixed rates of interest and preferred dividends. Thus, they could be controlled by the purpose of common stock only. This application of the "trading on equity" or leverage principle magnified the earnings on the subsidiaries' common stock and, thus, the earnings of the parent.

The benefits of this system to the holding company's owners could be increased by carrying the leverage through an additional step, namely, the use of senior securities by the parent itself. A hypothetical example may serve to illustrate these ideas. Suppose two operating utilities are each financed with 7% funded debt equal to 50% of assets, and 6 1/2% nonvoting preferred stock equal to 25% of assets. The ownership of all or of a substantial portion of the common stock of each operating company gives the holding company control with a minor investment. If each operating company earns 8% on total investment, after payment of bond interest and preferred dividends, 11 1/2% is earned on the common stock equity. Now, if the holding company has obtained its own funds partly through the issuance of its own bonds and preferred stock, the return on its common stock, which represents a still smaller fraction of the assets of the group, is further magnified. But, in times of depression, of course, if the subsidiaries' earnings shrink even modestly, the return on the common stock is reduced in even greater proportion, if not eliminated. In the worst overpyramided situations, holding companies found themselves without revenues in the early 1930s and many failed as a result.

The senior securities of the holding company are actually junior securities within the consolidated group, and the common stock has a very thin equity in the earning power of the operating subsidiaries. This condition is even more attenuated when several intermediate holding companies intervene, each of which issues bonds and preferred stocks.

All holding company securities are not weak. Some companies are conservatively capitalized. Some control very valuable subsidiaries. Some enjoy advantages from control of contiguous properties. By and large, however, investors should realize that, as a class, holding company securities are fundamentally weaker than operating company obligations.

Analysis   Holding companies issue two different types of financial statements. The *corporate* statements refer to the holding company only. *Consolidated* statements include the combined finances of parent company and subsidiaries, eliminating intercompany transactions. For anayltical purposes, the consolidated statements are used because they provide a comprehensive picture of the performance of the entire group.

The tests outlined previously should be applied to the consolidated statements of the group. However, two important refinements are necessary in recognition of the junior position of the (pure) holding company's securities:

1. The components of the *consolidated* capital structure of the holding company and subsidiaries should be arrayed in order of priority, and the percentage of each item to total should then be calculated. The order is:

> Subsidiaries' funded debt
> Subsidiaries' preferred stock
> Minority interest in subsidiaries' common stock and surplus
> Holding company funded debt
> Holding company preferred stock
> Holding company stock
> Consolidated surplus

2. Interest coverage is calculated by dividing the consolidated gross, or total income before interest and after taxes, by the interest on subsidiary debt plus dividends on subsidiary preferred plus interest on holding company bonds. Preferred dividend coverage is calculated by adding to the above the holding company's preferred dividend requirements.

Where the corporate group includes companies providing more than one utility service, say, both gas and electricity, the analysis of the consolidated statements must adjust for the varying tests indicated previously. This is also the case where a single "combination" company is engaged in more than one type of business.

Public Utility Holding Company Act of 1935   The abuses that appeared in the management and financing of operating and holding companies led to the passage of an important Federal statute in 1935. Its major provisions may be summarized as:

1. Holding companies (and their subsidiaries) controlling gas and electric companies in more than one state are subject to the jurisdiction of the Securities and Exchange Commission.

2. The Commission must approve all security issues of the registrants, including new financing, refinancing, reorganizations, readjustments, and mergers; holding companies were to be confined to secured bonds and common stock. In passing on new financing, the Commission considers the appro-

priateness of the security to the earnings, asset values, and capital structure to the issuer; a general limit of bonds to 50% and preferred stock to between 20 and 25% of net plant is imposed. This requires a review of the values paid for assets and the adequacy of depreciation reserves.

3. All intercompany transactions must have Commission approval, including dividends, accounting, intercompany loans (with "upstream" loans prohibited), service charges (which must be at cost), and purchase and sale contracts. Registered companies may not acquire any securities or utility assets or any other interest in a business unless the transaction would work towards a more integrated utility system.

4. Proposals to alter the preferences or voting rights of securityholders are subject to Commission review; unfair or inequitable distribution of voting is prohibited.

5. Competitive bidding is required for the purchase of obligations of companies subject to SEC jurisdiction.

Investment Outlook

The relative stability of earnings produced by public utility companies, their growth tendencies (telegraph excepted), and their established place in the American economy have created a firm position for utility securities in the investment field. The sounder utility bonds find a ready market in the portfolios of institutions. Utility preferred stocks are in demand on the part of investors (especially taxed institutions) seeking relative safety and generous yield. Utility common stocks, while lacking the possibilities of spectacular earnings and market appreciation of some industrial equities, provide a respectable income that is relatively stable through the vicissitudes of the business cycle. The fast-growing companies located in states such as Florida and Texas, where a high rate of return is permitted, have taken on the characteristics of "growth" companies, that is, higher price-earnings multiples and lower dividend yields. Some utility common stocks have a special tax appeal in that all or part of their dividends are exempt from income taxes as a result of higher depreciation charges for tax than for report purposes.

Notwithstanding these general comments, it is important that the investor recognize the changing investment position of utility common stocks in recent years. This is indicated by the record of their prices, price-earnings ratios, and dividend yields. The following data are Standard & Poor's *year-end* averages for utility companies. These stocks shared the general stock market decline in 1973–1974. Because their main appeal has been for income, they were also hard hit by the rise in interest rates. The price-earnings ratio fell to less than one-half of that of 1970. Dividends declined only slightly, but dividend yield almost doubled, and reached 10% in 1974. The year 1976 showed some improvement in earnings, but prices did not recover like those of industrial concerns, and yields remained relatively high. Telephone stocks showed less decline in 1973–1974 and more recovery in 1975–1976. The main appeal continues to be for income, and most utility stocks will continue to rise and fall with interest rates.

The record of individual companies may differ widely from that of the industry average, depending largely on whether the stock is characterized by growth or by stability of income and dividends. And the data do not reveal higher or lower figures within the annual periods.

	1965	1970	1971	1972	1974	1975	1976
Earnings per share ($)	3.89	4.67	4.92	5.24	5.38	5.70	6.32
Market price per share	76	62	60	61	34	44	54
Price-earnings ratio	19.5	13.2	12.2	11.6	6.2	7.8	8.5
Dividend per share ($)	2.49	3.17	3.25	3.31	3.46	3.59	3.76
Dividend yield (%)	3.3	5.1	5.4	5.4	10.3	8.1	7.0

Factors in stock selection   The following important factors should govern the selection of utility stocks. Others have been previously suggested.

• Growth in earnings and dividends sufficient to compete with other equities. In addition to increases resulting from increased production and rates, earnings per share also grow from the plough-back of earnings. The rate base is increased, and as a fair return is produced on the expanded investment, and if the number of shares outstanding remains constant, earnings per share rise. This explains why the stocks of "growth utilities" with lower dividend payout sell at higher multiples of earnings and lower dividend yields than do the "income" stocks. Stock sale above book value also improves earnings per share as the rate base increases and earnings rise more than the number of shares.

• A strong cash flow. This factor has become increasingly important as utilities face the financing of huge capital requirements.

• A constructive regulatory environment. Rate increases should reflect rising costs. Regulatory commissions should also recognize earnings figured in depreciation accounting using "normalized" deferred depreciation and deferred investment credit, as well as allowance for funds during construction.

• In the case of electric power companies, a shift from increasingly expensive oil and gas to coal and nuclear fuel.

• Strong finances, both short- and long-term.

Special Sources of Information on the Public Utilities Industries

GOVERNMENT SOURCES

Securities and Exchange Commission, annual and special reports; Federal Communications Commission, annual reports, *Statistics of Communications Common Carriers* (annually), *Statistics of Telephone Carriers* (annually), *Operating Data from Monthly Reports of Telephone Carriers* (monthly), *Statistics of Communications Common Carriers* (annually); *Statistics of Domestic and Overseas Telegraph Carriers* (annually). Federal Power Commission, annual reports, *Statistics of Electirc Utilities in the United States, Class A and B* (annual volumes on private and publicly owned systems), *Statistics of Natural Gas Companies* (annually), and *Electric Power Statistics* (monthly and annually); U.S. Department of Interior, Bureau of Mines, *Minerals Yearbook* (section on natural gas); annual reports of the respective state public service commissions.

PRIVATE SOURCES

Periodicals, including *American Gas Association Monthly; Electrical World; Gas Age; Oil and Gas Journal; Public Utilities* (fortnightly).

Annual report on the output and capacities of the principal electric power companies, compiled by *Electrical World*.

Weekly and monthly reports on the outputs of the larger electric power systems compiled by the Edison Electric Institute. See also the Institute's annual *Statistical Yearbook of the Electrical Utility Industry, Advance Release*, and *Historical Statistics* (data 1920–1960).

American Gas Association, *Gas Facts* (annually) and *Gas Data Book* (a summary of *Gas Facts*).

Bell Telephone Securities, an annual publication of the American Telephone and Telegraph Company covering all securities issued by the Bell System.

Annual *Proceedings* of the National Association of Railroad and Utilities Commissioners.

Moody's Public Utility Manual (blue section) devoted to output and services, earnings and expenses, financing and regulation.

Standard & Poor's *Industry Surveys* (electric utilities).

REFERENCES

An Evaluation of Electric Utility Bonds. Chicago: Halsey, Stuart & Co., 1975.

BARY, C. W., *Operational Economics of Electric Utilities.* New York: Columbia University Press, 1963.

BERLIN, EDWARD, et al., *Perspective on Power: A Study of the Regulation and Pricing of Electric Power.* Cambridge, Mass.: Ballinger Publishing Co., 1974.

BONBRIGHT, J. C., *Principles of Public Utility Rates.* New York: Columbia University Press, 1961.

Electric Power and the Environment, a Report Sponsored by the Energy Policy Staff, Office of Science and Technology. Washington, D.C., 1970.

FARRIS, M. T., and R. J. SAMPSON, *Public Utilities.* Boston: Houghton Mifflin Co., 1972.

FOSTER, J. R., and B. A. RODEY, *Public Utility Accounting.* Englewood Cliffs, N.J.: Prentice-Hall, Inc., 1951.

GARFIELD, P. J., and W. F. LOVEJOY, *Public Utility Economics.* Englewood Cliffs, N.J.: Prentice-Hall, Inc., 1964.

GRAHAM, BENJAMIN, D. L. DODD, and SIDNEY COTTLE, *Security Analysis*, 4th ed., Chapters 20, 21. New York: McGraw-Hill, Inc., 1962.

GUTHMANN, H. G., *Analysis of Financial Statements*, 4th ed., Chapter 14. Englewood Cliffs, N.J.: Prentice-Hall, Inc., 1953.

————, and H. E. DOUGALL, *Corporate Financial Policy*, 4th ed., Chapter 16. Englewood Cliffs, N.J.: Prentice-Hall, Inc., 1962.

HAWKINS, C. A., *The Field Price Regulation of National Gas*. Tallahassee, Fla.: Florida State University Press, 1969.

HOOLEY, R. W., *Financing the Natural Gas Industry*. New York: Columbia University Press, 1961.

HUNT, F. E., *Public Utilities: Information Sources*. Detroit: Gale Research Co., 1965.

KENNEDY, R. D., and S. Y. McMULLEN, *Financial Statements*, 5th ed., Chapters 28, 29. Homewood, Ill.: Richard D. Irwin Inc., 1968.

LEVINE, S. H., ed., *Financial Analyst's Handbook*, Vol. 2, Ch. 30. Homewood, Ill.: Dow Jones-Irwin, Inc., 1975.

PHILLIPS, C. F., *The Economics of Regulation*, rev. ed. Homewood, Ill.: Richard D. Irwin, Inc., 1969.

Statistical Materials on the Electric Utility Industry. Prepared for the use of the Subcommittee on Energy and Power and the Committee on Interstate and Foreign Commerce, U.S. House of Representatives. Washington, D.C.: U.S. Government Printing Office, 1976.

U.S. CONGRESS, JOINT ECONOMIC COMMITTEE, *Public Utility Industry*. Hearings, 93rd Cong., 2nd Sess., pursuant to Senate Congressional Resolution 93. Washington, D.C.: U.S. Government Printing Office, 1974.

VENNARD, EDWIN, *The Electric Power Business*, 2nd ed. New York: McGraw-Hill, Inc., 1970.

YOUNG, H. H., *Forty Years of Public Utility Finance*. Charlottesville, Va.: The University Press of Virginia, 1965.

Transportation Securities

SCOPE: This chapter discusses the investment position of the securities of transportation companies. The order of discussion is: *Railroads*—(1) development, (2) regulation, (3) size and location, (4) operations and performance, (5) income statement analysis, (6) balance sheet analysis, (7) railroad stock prices and yields, (8) railroad consolidations, (9) recent legislation, (10) review of railroad problems, and (11) outlook. *Domestic Air Transportation*—(1) scope and development, (2) operations, (3) financial characteristics, (4) regulation, (5) future outlook, (6) airline securities. *Motor Carriers*—(1) industry characteristics, (2) development, (3) regulation, (4) financial characteristics, (5) motor industry stocks. Special sources of information, transport industries.

Because a much larger total of their securities are outstanding, railroads are stressed in this chapter. Enough attention is paid to airlines and motor carriers to suggest their special features.

RAILROADS

Development of the Industry

By the end of the 1920s, after 90 years of proud history, the railroad industry had apparently reached maturity, perhaps even the beginning of economic senility. Passenger revenues in 1929 were lower by one-third than in 1920, reflecting competition from the private automobile. Highways, intercoastal and inland waterways, and pipeline carriers were becoming more prominent as competitors for freight traffic, and their competition was fostered by continued railway rate increases. Railway gross revenues fluctuated wildly from their peak of over $6 billion in the late 1920s to half of that figure in the early 1930s. The loss of its monopoly position and its growing susceptibility to economic fluctuations, together with reliance on funded debt as a source of funds, brought the industry to a state of financial collapse and a wave of failures in the depression of the early 1930s. And although a modest recovery was made in postdepression years, permanent damage had been done to the investment position of the industry's securities.

World War II brought enormous demands for transportation. Restrictions on the use of the private automobile returned passenger traffic to the rails.

Heavy demands for freight shipping brought the industry's per cent of total tonnage to approximately 85% during the war production boom, compared with 70% in the mid 1930s.This increased traffic, coupled with higher rates, brought railroad gross revenues to their then all-time peak in 1943–1944. Revenues declined modestly in 1945. The rate of return on investment, which reached an all-time peak of 6.36% in 1942, declined to 3.70% in 1945 as a result of relatively high operating expenses.

Postwar years have not treated the industry very kindly. Railroads now carry only 37% of the nation's intercity freight tonnage, and their share of intercity passenger traffic is now only 6%. From 1945 to the present, the rate of return on net property investment never reached 4.5%, fell below 2% in 1961 and 1970, to 1.2% in the 1975 recession, and rose to 1.5% in 1976. The industry is still sharply affected by the business cycle and by increasing competition from other types of carriers. The late 1960s and early 1970s have seen a new wave of company failures, and attempts at rescue by the formation of the Federally managed systems, Amtrak (passenger) and Conrail (freight). The years 1976 and 1977 show prospects of some improvement.

Some of the shifts that have taken place in the industry in the past 35 years are indicated in Table 28-1. Railway mileage has been gradually shrinking. The industry has succeeded in keeping its long-term debt fairly stable, in spite of increases in equipment obligations. Equipment has decreased numerically, but product per unit has increased with more efficient assets, fuel, and operations. Freight traffic has been maintained, and at progressively higher rates, but the loss of passenger traffic has not been offset by higher rates. The rate of earnings on total investment is extremely low.

Railways are no longer major employers of labor. Their annual capital expenditures, together with the huge volume of securities outstanding, suggest their continuing economic and financial importance.

Regulation

Most important railroads carry both interstate and intrastate traffic and are subject to the regulations of the Interstate Commerce Commission and the public service commissions of the various states. The powers of the Commission have been gradually increased, until they now comprise a wide scope of regulatory authority over all railroad operations. Many of these powers directly affect the investment position of railroad securities.

The outstanding power of the Interstate Commerce Commission is that of rate regulation. The Commission is no longer required to give the companies a fair return upon a fair value, but approves rates sufficient to provide adequate and efficient service at the lowest reasonable cost.

The Commission has broad regulatory powers with respect to new financing. New securities may be issued only with the approval of the Commission after investigation of the purpose of the issue, the amount required, the

TABLE 28-1   Development of Class I Railways, 1940–1976[a]

Items	1940	1950	1960	1970	1976
Miles of first main track	232,524	226,101	217,552	206,265	195,000
Property investment, after depreciation[b]	$23,168	$24,952	$27,474	$27,425	$26,500[e]
Capitalization (net):					
Capital stock[b]	$ 7,020	$ 6,980	$ 5,761	$ 5,280	$ 4,896[e]
Long-term debt[b]	$10,609	$ 8,638	$ 8,389	10,848	$11,834[e]
Total[b]	$17,629	$15,618	$14,150	$16,128	$16,730
Freight cars in service[c]	1,654	1,721	1,658	1,424	1,332
Locomotives in service	41,721	40,036	28,278	27,086	27,573
Revenue ton-miles[b]	373,253	588,578	572,309	764,809	791,413
Av. revenue per ton-mile	.965¢	1.329¢	1.403¢	1.428¢	2.194¢
Revenue passenger miles	23,762	31,760	21,258	10,740	6,009
Av. revenue per pass.-mile	1.75¢	2.56¢	3.01¢	3.91¢	5.86¢
Operating revenues[b]	$ 4,296	$ 9,473	$ 9,514	$11,992	$18,560[d]
Operating ratio	71.90%	74.52%	79.52%	80.56%	80.00%
Rate of return earned	2.94%	4.23%	2.13%	1.73%	1.49%
Net income, ordinary[b]	$ 189	$ 784	$ 445	$ 227	$ 230
Average employees[c]	1,027	1,221	780	566	483
Payroll[b]	$ 1,964	$ 4,594	$ 4,894	$ 5,711	$ 8,278
Capital expenditures[b]	$ 429	$ 1,066	$ 919	$ 1,351	$ 1,744

[a]Class I companies are those whose operating revenues exceed $10,000,000 annually ($50,000,000 beginning January 1, 1978.) They operate 96% of total railroad mileage (1976).
[b]Millions
[c]Thousands
[d]Excludes Amtrak
[e]1975 data

Sources: Association of American Railroads, Economics and Finance Department; I.C.C., *Transport Statistics in the United States, Part I, Statistics of Railways in the United Sales.*

nature of the security, and the cost of distribution. The effect of changing economic conditions on the market values of railway securities over a period of time is another matter.

The authority of the Commission with respect to accounting procedure and periodical earnings statements is also helpful to the investor. All railroad companies must keep accounts under a standard uniform system that assures reliable statements and permits ready comparison. All carriers must submit monthly statements of earnings, which are published in the newspapers and keep investors in close touch with operations of the companies.

New railroad mileage may be constructed and existing mileage abandoned only with permission of the Commission. Holders of securities in unprofitable lines are not protected against continued losses incurred in the operation of such properties, save for subsidization of passenger traffic.

Competing railroad companies are allowed to consolidate only with the approval of the Commission. This veto power has become a potent factor in recent years, although numerous important consolidations have been approved in the 1950s, 1960s, and early 1970s.

The authority of the Commission has been somewhat curtailed by 1976 legislation. (See below.)

Size and Location

Railroad systems and diversification Railway mileage has become increasingly concentrated in fewer major systems. And the original strictly railroad activities have been expanded by the formation of a number of holding company-subsidiary groups of which the railroad is only one, although ordinarily the chief, member.[1] Nonrailroad activities include manufacturing, oil production, land development, and truck and bus transportation. As a result, the consolidated financial statements of such groups have become increasingly unlike railroad statements and are difficult to analyze by traditional tests of operations and earnings. Fortunately, the parent companies must still report separately on railroad operations.

Geographical influences Geography plays an important part in railroad prosperity. The size of the territory served, its growth, physical features, density of population, natural resources, manufacturing plants, and commercial activities directly affect earning power.

The size of the territory limits the distance over which traffic may be carried. Because freight traffic contributes the bulk of railroad earnings, because freight rates vary with the distance carried, and because the transportation cost varies more with terminal expense than with distance, long-haul traffic is relatively more profitable than short-haul shipments. Companies serving extended areas, such as the Union Pacific and the Atchison, have an operating advantage over those serving smaller districts.

The topography of the territory has a distinct influence on operating conditions. Companies that serve relatively level areas, such as the Mississippi Valley region, operate more economically than those serving the mountainous districts.

The density of the population also has a bearing on earnings. In a thickly populated region, passenger traffic is large—a negative factor in most instances, since passenger traffic is relatively unprofitable, requiring expensive terminals and careful train operation.[2] Concentration of population, however, usually means a higher-than-average rate of commercial and industrial activity, both of which bring lucrative freight traffic.

In many districts the prosperity of the entire region, including that of the carriers, depends heavily on a few commodities. Shipments of these commodities are usually carried profitably in bulk over long distances. Economic distress in any commodity, however, seriously harms the earning power of the railroad companies dependent on it. The railroads have, of course, shared in the tendency of industries to diversify their locations. The industrialization of the South and West has made the companies

---

[1]Burlington Northern, Illinois Central Industries, Kansas City Southern Industries, Rio Grande Industries, Santa Fe Industries, Seaboard Coast Line Industries, Union Pacific Corporation, and Western Pacific Industries are leading examples.

[2]According to the Interstate Commerce Commission computations, the passenger-operating expense ratio for Class I railroads in 1970 was 142%. This is the main explanation for the creation of "Amtrak" in 1970. (See p. 568.) Without Amtrak, the ratio was 97% in 1976.

serving these regions less dependent on a few important commodities. A high degree of activity and a broad diversification of enterprise make a satisfactory background for railroad traffic.

Operations and Performance

The average investor should concentrate attention on a relatively small group of items among the operating data. These include:

Miles of line operated. Longer-haul roads are regarded as better. Important exceptions are found in the case of roads in Pocahontas (eastern coal) territory.

Traffic density. This major indicator of volume of traffic is very important in measuring earning power. It is measured most simply by the revenue ton-miles and revenue passenger-miles carried per mile of line. In normal times, a freight density of between 3 and 4 million ton-miles per annum would be average. A road with relatively light freight traffic density derived from high-rate traffic may be as productive as one with heavier density consisting of low-grade traffic.

Commodity tonnage. These figures show the nature of the traffic handled and are usually shown on a percentage basis. Each company reports commodity statistics in major groups, as well as in separate detail. As freight rates are based upon the general principle of charging *what the traffic will bear*—that is, proportionate to the value of the shipment—valuable commodities produce higher gross revenues, and the companies favored by shipments of higher value have an advantageous position. Profits are not directly proportionate to revenues, however, as the low-grade commodities can be moved more economically. That road is in the more favorable position which shows a fair percentage of the high-grade commodities (to gain a better average revenue per ton) and reasonable diversification (to derive stability of earnings).

Average length of haul. Although lower rates per mile are received, long hauls are made at a relatively lower cost, since terminal costs can be spread out over a longer distance. Furthermore, long-haul traffic is less vulnerable to truck competition. For the year 1975 the average haul of revenue freight was 515 miles for all roads as a system.

Performance ratios. Various performance ratios are available for the railroad systems and (in the investment services) for individual carriers. Only a few will be mentioned here. *Net ton-miles per freight train-hour* is the best single measure of freight transportation efficiency since it combines the speed factor with the weight of the load (total and freight) behind the locomotive and tender and reflects the average performance for each hour of transporation. The figure was 39,100 ton-miles for all Class I railways in 1975. *Car-miles per car-day* measures the extent to which cars are kept moving and so contributing to revenue. The figure for freight cars in 1975 was 57 miles, an increase from 52 in 1965. *Average speed of freight trains* increased to over 20 miles per hour in 1976. Other measures of efficiency are described in more detailed discussions of railway analysis.

Income Statement Analysis

The profit and loss report of a railroad company differs materially from that of an industrial company in the way in which revenue and expense items are presented. The combined income statement for all Class I railways in 1940–1976 (Table 28-2), is used as a reference.

TABLE 28-2 Condensed Income Accounts—Class I Railways[a]
for Selected Years (in millions of dollars)

	1940	1950	1960	1965	1970	1976
Total operating revenues	$4,296	$9,473	$9,514	$10,208	$11,992	$18,560
Freight	3,537	7,817	8,025	8,836	10,922	17,422
Passenger	417	813	640	553	420	330[a]
Mail, express, and other	342	843	849	819	650	807[a]
Total operating expenses	$3,089	$7,059	$7,565	$ 7,850	$ 9,660	$14,948
Maintenance of way and str.	497	1,287	1,192	1,236	1,613	3,069
Maintenance of equipment	819	1,708	1,760	1,775	2,165	3,215
Traffic	108	192	258	262	285	337
Transportation	1,501	3,491	3,833	4,020	4,873	7,345
General and miscellaneous	164	381	522	557	724	982
Net operating revenue	$1,207	$2,414	$1,949	$ 2,358	$ 2,332	$ 3,612
Railway tax accruals	396	1,195	999	916	1,068	1,935
Railway operating income	$ 811	$1,219	$ 950	$ 1,442	$ 1,264	$ 1,677
Hire of equipment (Debit) ⎫		140	321	443 ⎫	778	1,247
Joint facility rents (Debit) ⎭	129	39	45	37 ⎭		
Net railway operating income	$ 682	$1,040	$ 584	$ 962	$ 486	$ 430
Other income	169	265	346	365	482	667
Total income	851	$1,305	$ 930	$ 1,327	$ 968	$ 1,097
Miscellaneous deductions	$ 28	$ 48	$ 63	$ 71	122	92
Income available for fixed charges	823	1,257	867	1,256	846	$ 1,005
Fixed charges ⎫		$ 427	$ 373	$ 401	$ 589	$ 656
Contingent charges and ⎬	634					
other deductions ⎭		46	50	41	33	33
Net income (ordinary)[b]	189	$ 784	$ 445	814	226	$ 316
Cash dividends	$ 159	$ 312	$ 385	$ 471	$ 421	$ 430

[a]Excludes Amtrak.
[b]Excludes extraordinary and prior period items.
Sources: Interstate Commerce Commission; Association of American Railroads.

Operating revenues These include all receipts from railroad operations as such. For all railroads, freight traffic contributes about 94% of the total; passenger traffic, about 2% (excluding Amtrak operations); and miscellaneous services, such as mail and express, about 4%. The percentages for many individual roads differ considerably from the group aggregates.

Study of railway data shows the relation of freight revenues to general business conditions. Volume of freight traffic, or, more specifically, traffic density, is heavily influenced by the volume of production of heavy industry. During World War II both freight and passenger revenues soared to record heights; the immediate postwar years saw substantial declines, especially in passenger revenues. Save for declines in the recession years of 1954 and 1958, freight revenues levelled off at $9 billion in the middle 1950s, declining to $7.7 billion in 1961, and breaking through $10 billion in 1969. In the period 1970–1974 the level reached $15.8 billion. The year 1975 saw a decline which, coupled with a higher operating ratio, and higher fixed charges, drove ordinary net income to the lowest level since 1940—$111 million compared with $730 millions in 1974, in spite of substantially higher rates. Freight revenues and net income rose modestly in 1976. Passenger revenues have continued to decline. In 1976 they were $330 million or less than 2% of total operating revenues,[3] and are now substantially exceeded by mail, express, and miscellaneous revenue.

Volume of traffic is one determinant of revenues; the other is the rate level. The price of railway service is best measured by *average revenue per ton-mile* and *per passenger-mile*. For Class I railways as a whole, the former figure was 2.2 cents and the latter 5.9 cents in 1976, as compared with 1.3 cents and 3.2 cents, respectively, in 1965. Such figures, especially for freight traffic, vary considerably among districts and companies, depending on the type of commodities hauled. Carriers handicapped by a low average revenue on a ton-mile basis (caused largely by low-grade shipments) face a formidable obstacle unless they enjoy unusually high traffic density or unusually long hauls.

In using such indicators of operations and earnings, care must be taken to compare companies in the same geographical area and operating under substantially the same conditions, including vulnerability to competition from other carriers.

Operating and financial expenses   Table 28-2 shows the great importance of maintenance and transportation expense. The former is subject to some control, the latter is dominated by wages and fuel costs.[4] The ratio of maintenance expense to revenues (now about 32%) is a criterion of maintenance policy.

Transportation expense is the largest item of operating expenses, comprising chiefly the wages of stationmen and trainmen and the cost of fuel. For the average railroad, this item runs about $36,000 per year per mile of line operated and represents about 40% of operating revenues. Management has little control over this item, as wages are fixed largely by Federal authority, and fuel prices depend on economic conditions and the type used. A low transportation expense ratio is an excellent commendation.

The relation of total operating expense to operating revenues is the *operating ratio*, now (1976) 80%. This is a time-honored measurement of operating efficiency. Table 28-1 shows its modest rise through the years. In judging the operating ratio of an individual carrier, the maintenance

---

[3]Excluding Amtrak and Auto-train, whose passenger revenues were $262 million in 1976, or 80% of those of Class I railways. Total national revenue of $592 million compares with $420 million in 1970, reflecting something of a return to the use of the passenger train.

[4]Wages are included in all of the major categories of expense rather than shown as a single expense. In 1976, salaries, wages, and health and welfare benefits of all Class I railroads consumed 52% of operating revenues. Average number of employees has declined steadily and was only 483,000 in 1976. But payroll cost has grown steadily with the substantial increases in wage rates.

and transportation expense must be considered. A low ratio may be the result of skimping on maintenance. High maintenance ratios accompanied by a low transportation ratio that combine to produce a low operating ratio in comparison with carriers operating under similar conditions indicate superior performance. All lines, especially the weak ones, suffered from inflationary increases in costs in the 1970s.

Taxes   Taxes of all kinds are grouped together on the income statement, and represent over 10% of revenues. Technically, income taxes should be shown as deductions from net income. However, to the railroad they represent expenses that should be covered by revenues so as to leave a fair return, and so are placed in the operating section of the statement. The analyst should keep in mind that in calculating coverage of fixed charges, he is using after-tax income.

Net railway operating income is the balance produced for the security holders after operating expenses, taxes, and facility and equipment rents. Stated as a percentage of net property investment (after depreciation, plus cash, materials, and supplies) is the "rate of return" referred to by the railroads as indicating their overall earning power, and its unsatisfactory level in most years is the chief argument against "unfair" regulatory conditions and subsidization of competing forms of transport. A review of the rate earned by the industry clearly reveals its inadequate earning power and explains its decline in investment status. In only one year from 1921 to 1971 inclusive (1942) did the rate exceed 6%. In only six of these years was it 5% or above. In 21 of the years the rate was less than 3%. A return of 5% on investment is adequate to cover all fixed charges and leave a reasonable balance for dividends, but a return under 3% provides inadequate coverage of fixed charges. Since 1960 the return has averaged about 2.35% and was only 1.73% in 1974 and 1.49% in 1976. The failure of the industry to show a good rate of return does not mean, however, that individual companies have not done so. As in other respects, a wide range exists within the whole group. But few show a respectable record.

Other income, also called *nonoperating income*, includes all revenues from sources other than direct operations, chiefly income from securities of other railroad companies and from nontransportation operations. It means a great deal, for example, to Union Pacific, which usually derives over 40% of its total income before fixed charges from this source. (See below.) It is important also to the lines that are large holders of securities, although it is not always a reliable source of revenue when derived from dividends on stocks of other companies.

Interestingly enough, "other income" was $237 million more than net operating income in 1976, reflecting the erosion of railroad earning power and the growing importance of nonrail sources as means of meeting fixed charges and paying dividends.

Fixed charges include: (1) rent for leased road, usually in the form of guaranteed interest or dividends; (2) interest on funded (long-term) debt; (3) interest on unfunded (short-term) debt; and (4) amortization of discount on funded debt. Where fixed charges exceed 4% of operating revenues and are not earned (that is, covered by total income) at least twice over a representative period of years, investment weakness is indicated, even for the senior securities of a company.

The industry's fixed charges rose very substantially in the 1970s, reflecting high interest rates in general and the decline in railroad credit that was reflected in yields in bonds and equipment trust certificates. (See below.) In 1976 railways as a group earned their total fixed charges 1.5 times after income taxes.[5] But within the industry performance varies widely. Less than a dozen roads show coverage of over 3 times before taxes.

Net income and dividends   Net income is reported as "ordinary" and "extraordinary" (nonrecurring). The chronic instability and inadequacy of railway net income has been very much in evidence in the 1970s. A relatively good year was 1974, with "ordinary net income" exceeding $750 million, which produced a return of 4.8% on average stockholders' equity. But 1975 was a recession disaster.

Some improvement was enjoyed in 1976. Such instability is the result of two main influences: (1) the fluctuations in net railway operating income, aggravated by (2) the presence of large fixed charges. Net results for individual carriers may differ greatly from those of the industry as a whole. In a number of years, nonrecurring items distort the final outcome. Including these, 1976 produced $273 million net, in contrast to 1971's deficit of $436 million after extraordinary items of $680 million.

Dividends distributed in recent years have been relatively stable, considering the fluctuations and low level of earnings. With the exception of 1974, the industry as a whole distributed substantially more than it earned. This is because deficits of some roads reduce the industry's combined profits.

The steady retirement of preferred stock has been partly responsible for maintenance of dividends on the common stock in years of low profits. Aggregate figures are, however, somewhat deceiving. Policy with respect to dividends varies widely among individual companies. Some have ploughed back most of their earnings or have reduced funded debt and fixed charges. Others have distributed virtually all of their profits. In 1970–1976 the low-earning carriers greatly outnumbered those that earned and paid dividends.

Balance Sheet Analysis

Railroad balance sheets differ from those of other corporations in the terms used, the order of the items, and the relative importance of various items. Table 28-3 is a summarized statement for all Class I line-haul steam railways for 1975.

[5]Another method of showing the earnings protection of bondholders is the *factor of safety*: that is, the percentage of operating revenues earned after fixed charges but before income taxes. This is the "cushion" of earnings underlying the fixed charges—the proportion by which the revenues could decline without reducing the interest coverage to less than one. A factor of 6 or 7 is desirable, but this has been accomplished by only a few roads.

The factor of safety may also be computed by using the percentage earned after fixed charges and twice preferred dividends, and before income taxes, to show the margin of safety for preferred dividends. Doubling the preferred dividend recognizes a 50% corporate rate.

TABLE 28-3   Combined Balance Sheet, Class I Railways
December 31, 1975 (in millions of dollars)

Assets		
Road and equipment property		$36,322.2
Improvements on leased property		591.7
		$36,913.9
Less depreciation and amortization		10,053.7
		$26,860.2
Miscellaneous physical property, net		457.0
Investments—affiliated companies and other, net		4,533.2
Current assets		4,706.4
Special funds		514.0
Deferred charges		458.1
Other assets		247.3
Total assets		$37,776.2
Liabilities and Stockholders' Equity		
Capital stock		
Preferred	$ 582.7	
Common	4,313.5	$ 4,896.2
Long-term debt after one year		
Funded debt[a]	7,165.1	
Equipment obligations	4,669.1	11,834.2
Current liabilities[b]		4,631.8
Reserves		687.0
Deferred credits (including deferred taxes)		5,682.6
Surplus		
Capital	$4,144.2	
Retained income	5,900.2	10,044.4
Total liabilities and stockholders' equity		$37.776.2

[a]Includes amounts payable to affiliated companies and long-term debt in default ($2,831.9 million).
[b]Includes long-term debt due within one year, $738.7 million.
Source: Interstate Commerce Commission, *Transport Statistics in the United States, Part I, Railroad Companies.*

Fixed assets   Fixed assets, including investments in affiliated companies, dominate the balance sheet, comprising nearly 85% of total assets. Using the gross figures of total physical property in relation to operating revenue, the gross plant turnover is 50%. In other words, for the industry as a whole, an investment of $2 in gross plant is needed to produce $1 of revenue. From an investor's viewpoint, however, the condition of a property is more important than its book value. Since personal examination is usually impossible, one must rely on careful analysis of maintenance figures.

Depreciation is accrued by all companies on road and equipment. The annual expense charge is included in the maintenance account. The need to provide for ultimate retirement of equipment is greater than in the case of road.

Investments in affiliated companies   These consist of holdings of stocks, bonds, and notes of associated companies. Although the investment is represented by securities, one may assume that the amount represents investment almost as fixed and permanent as road and equipment. The amount involved in some cases is of major importance. The Southern Pacific reported $137 million in such securities in 1976.

In addition to securities investments in other companies, there is often a substantial direct investment in nonoperating properties, such as hotels, oil lands, and mining properties, that produce important income. Such income appears as *nonoperating* or *other income* on the income statement unless it is consolidated.

Current assets   These comprise principally cash, temporary investments, accounts receivable, and materials and supplies on hand. These items have much less significance in the railroad field than in the industrial field. The regularity with which cash revenues are received assures a steady inflow of funds for current bills.

A current ratio of less than 2:1 is not alarming. A higher ratio and a generally healthy working capital position is needed, however, by companies operating at a deficit or facing substantial bond maturities. The maintenance of stable dividends also requires that working capital be built up in times of good earnings. A disturbing sign of the declining liquidity of the industry as a whole has been the steady elimination of net working capital (after debt due in less than a year).

Funded debt   Including equipment obligations, the long-term debt comprises about 44% of the capital structure. This ratio has not varied much through the years, although the bond portion has steadily declined with the decline in railroad credit. (The relative strength of the equipment issues was explained in Chapter 8.) Actually the real debt is much larger when capitalized rentals are taken into account.

Within the total industry funded debt of $11.8 billion, bond quality ranges from fairly high grade to those in default. Some A-rated bonds are available, chiefly the first mortgage bonds of the strong lines, and a number of equipment issues, but even the latter have fallen in investment status. In October 1977 "A" bonds yielded 7.90%, and equipment certificates 8.00%. Second-grade bonds include the junior issues of prosperous companies and some senior issues of weaker companies. There are too many third-grade and unrated issues, but a review of recent earnings history provides the explanation. Yields as high as 9.00% are available, but the narrow margin of interest coverage suggests their unusual risk and reveals the reason for the wave of bankruptcies in recent years, one result of which was the formation of Conrail. (See below.)

Application of the analytical methods suggested in Chapter 24, plus the use of efficiency and other tests suggested in this chapter, should permit an investor to discern the real quality of individual railway bond issues.

Net worth   At the end of 1975, capital stock comprised 18.3% of the industry's capital structure. Of this only 2.2% was preferred. No new common stock has been offered to the public for over 45 years, and only one of convertible securities—by Burlington Northern in 1972. Retained earnings and other surplus comprise 37.5% of capital structure. The former is twice the capital stock account, but this gives no assurance of dividends unless cash position and current earnings are adequate.

Railroad Stock Prices and Yields

Railroad stock prices have shown marked volatility, reflecting the general stock market cycle and the industry's own problems. Standard & Poor's index of railroad stocks (1941–1943 = 10) reached its modern peak of 52 at the beginning of 1969, and fell to 26 during 1970 when generally low price-earnings ratios prevailed. The next peak of 50 was reached in 1973 and, interestingly enough, again in 1974, contrary to the industrial indexes. But by late 1974 the general market weakness drove the rail figure down to 30. The price-earnings ratio, which had been as high as 15.8 in 1972, dropped to a low of 5.2 in 1974, reflecting both the generally high interest rates and the low esteem of the railroad industry. Fears with respect to both the general and the railroad cycle were confirmed in 1975 when earnings per share dropped to $4.80, in contrast to 1974's $5.63. Earnings per share rose to an (estimated) $5.80 in 1976. The price-earnings ratio increased to 7.7 and the index to over 50 late in that year. The multiplier was still substantially lower than that of industrials. (See Table 9-4.)

Part of the improvement in earnings in 1976 reflected the fact that passenger traffic had, to a large degree, become the problem of "Amtrak" (p. 568) which lost over $350 million in 1975.

Dividend yields on railroad stocks remain relatively low, considering their risk, averaging about 5% in 1976 as compared with 6 to 9% for utilities, but exceeding the rates on most industrials. But the group figure is deceiving. It reflects the fact that many lines pay no dividends at all and includes the low yields of some companies, such as Southern Railway and Union Pacific, whose appeal is for growth rather than for income.

Such data do not reveal the varying experience of individual stocks. Chessie System and Norfolk & Western enjoy a healthy rating among the investment services; but their appeal is largely for income. The stocks of very large companies, such as Chicago & North Western and Milwaukee, are more attractive for speculation than for investment. Those of certain companies, such as Seaboard Coast Line, Rock Island, and Milwaukee, emerged from reorganization in the 1930s and have gained investment recognition, but have been characterized by wide price and earnings fluctuations. Several "good-grade" companies, such as Santa Fe Industries, Kansas City Southern Industries, and Southern Pacific, are appropriate in portfolios seeking above-average current cash dividends. A few companies, such as Union Pacific Corporation and Southern Railway, qualify as growth situations, in the former case because of its nonrail potential.

"Investment-quality" preferred stocks are available in the railroad field, but again only in a limited number of instances. And investors demand a higher yield on these than on utility and industrial issues. In October 1977, such stocks yielded from 7.00 to 9.00%; the lower yields were found on convertible preferred stock of some of the holding companies. Investors able to undertake the risk find attractive opportunities in the preferred stocks of the very strong carriers.

Railroad Consolidations

Joint control of competing lines is now permitted under the Transportation Act of 1920 as amended in 1940. Consolidations, whether by lease, stock purchase, or otherwise, must provide for the preservation of competition and the maintenance of existing routes and channels of trade and of commerce. The arrangement must be in the public interest, and the terms must be approved by the Interstate Commerce Commission. The merger process is long and complex.

A wave of railroad mergers began in the early 1950s. Carriers sought the economies of large-scale operation and the reduction of duplicating facilities. Each of the consolidations finally approved by the Commission have been the result of long negotiations between the companies and protracted hearings before the ICC.

Combinations hold possibilities of substantial economies, but they have not all succeeded, as witness the dramatic bankruptcy of Penn Central in 1970. Investors must examine with great care any estimates or claims of economies of scale and improved earnings made by companies that are proposing to merge.

Recent Legislation

The Railroad Revitalization and Regulatory Reform Act was passed in February 1976. Described as the most comprehensive piece of rail legislation of this century, the new bill was designed not only to rehabilitate and modernize physical properties but also to improve the industry's financial stability. Congressional intent was to strengthen the industry's viability by seeking a private sector solution to its many problems.

The Act contained these provisions:

1. Railroads were given rate-making flexibility by allowing them to raise or lower charges up to 7% for two years without regulatory interference.

2. Subsidies were provided for states and local governments that insist on retaining local lines that the railroads would like to abandon.

3. Federal funds, through loans and loan-guarantees, were made available to upgrade facilities.

4. The Secretary of Transportation was required to complete, within one year, a study of the impact on railroads of government subsidies to all modes of transportation.

5. The new law changed ICC procedures affecting mergers. Union Pacific's application for merger with the Chicago, Rock Island & Pacific consumed 12 years of study and hearings. While the proceedings dragged on, the Rock

Island entered bankruptcy. The new bill provided the Transportation Secretary with broader powers in recommending mergers, intervening in such proceedings, and mandating a strict timetable for merger decisions.

6. The bill also provided substantial funding ($2.1 billion) for the newly organized and now operating Consolidated Rail Corporation (ConRail). This government-backed corporation was created under the 1973 Regional Rail Reorganization Act to take over the properties and personnel of six bankrupt Eastern carriers.[6] Conrail's responsibilities embrace 17,000 miles of track serving 100 million people from Boston to St. Louis and containing 55% of the nation's manufacturing plants.

Review of Railroad Problems

The industry is capital intensive to a very high degree. A considerable amount of specialized, costly, and long-life equipment is required. Table 28-1 shows that over $26 billion is invested in net fixed assets. As a result of this concentration, railroads must pay attention to fixed costs, break-even sales volume, and the adequacy of internally generated cash flows. Recently, capital spending exceeded internal cash generation, leaving a net deficit in working capital. The industry's dependence on fixed assets requires heavy reliance on debt and lease arrangements. Borrowing or leasing results in turn in high financial and operating leverage. In a period of increased asset utilization, volume and income will tend to rise faster proportionately than fixed expenses, thus increasing earnings per share. But diminished railroad volume creates the opposite effect.

Although the industry uses less labor today than formerly, wages consume over half of the revenue dollar. (See p. 561.) Some progress has been made in moderating make-work rules, but flexibility in achieving the potential of new technology is hampered by time-encrusted work rules.

The deplorable situation of unprofitable and unattractive passenger service has been substantially relieved by the operation of the National Railroad Passenger Service Corporation, created in October 1970. This quasi-public company, "Amtrak," has taken over the management of most of the intercity passenger service and has developed a network of routes that should speed up passenger service and eliminate unnecessary runs. Participating railroads buy common stock in the corporation. They turn over to it their intercity operations and are reimbursed for providing rights of way and for operating costs. Amtrak is financed by Federal grants, and Federal loans are available to the companies that operate the trains under contract with the managing organization. Better service should result, and much of the passenger deficit will be transferred to the government. In 1976, Class I railroads without

[6]Penn Central, Erie Lackawanna, Reading, Central of New Jersey, Boston and Maine, and Lehigh Valley. The terms of transfer were laid in the Final System Plan developed by the U.S. Railway Association (a government agency) pursuant to the Regional Rail Reorganization Act of 1973.

Conrail's initial financing was in the form of government purchase of $230 million of debentures and preferred stock on which no interest or dividends will be paid until cash flow is adequate. In October 1976, another $350 million was authorized. Net income (before interest) is expected to exceed $200 million in 1980.

Amtrak received $330 million in passenger revenues from 6.0 billion passenger-miles. Amtrak's record was $297 millions and 4.1 billion, respectively.

With Amtrack assuming responsibility of passenger trains, the industry is principally engaged in moving freight. Some lines are still required to maintain short-haul commuter service however.

While overall industry profitability in recent years has been dismal, some roads are capable of making profits, reflecting optimal freight conditions, better regional prospects, longer hauls, or more aggressive management. The trend toward diversification into nonrailroad activities, such as real estate development and oil and mineral activities, continues.

The industry has long chafed under what are described as discriminatory policies by governments with respect to rights-of-way. Railroads must maintain and pay taxes on their rights-of-way while competing carriers use facilities provided by public funds. Approximately 15% of their rail revenue is spent for maintenance of railroad ways. Comparable costs paid by regulated motor carriers take less than 5% of revenue. Airline passengers pay 8%, and airline shippers 5% into the Airport and Airway Trust Fund. Waterway users pay nothing.

Although most observers believe that railroads are in the mature stage, there have been significant innovations in recent years. Among these are trains that by-pass yards, trains that carry a single commodity, piggyback, containerization, and the use of sophisticated computer procedures in classifying freight movements.

Because of their disappointing profits, railroads may find it difficult to attract new capital. Capital estimated at $2 to $3 billion is required annually to buy new equipment, to replace or renovate wornout ties, rails, bridges, tunnels, and signal systems. The industry will almost certainly experience a cash shortfall, possibly as much as $5 billion, during the next 10 years.

The industry presently suffers from duplication of service in parts of the United States. For example, five rail lines operate between Chicago and Omaha, and nine between St. Louis and Kansas City. This situation might be redressed by increased merger activity.

Railroads also suffer from inter-industry competition. Trucks, airlines, and busses compete vigorously for the light and high unit value package business and for making short hauls. Extremely heavy and bulky materials, especially the products of mines and the materials used in durable-goods industries, still travel by rail. These shipments can be cyclical, however. Although the volume of intercity freight is growing, railroads are receiving a declining percentage of it.

Outlook

Historically, the industry's profitability depends on the general level of business activity. Future profit prospects of individual common carriers will continue to reflect route structures, competition with private and contract carriers, financial strength, and overall managerial efficiency in implementing productivity gains to offset increasing costs. In the years ahead, motor carriers are expected to continue to compete actively for their share of the transportation dollar and to make continued inroads into the railroads' share of intercity freight traffic, which is now limited almost exclusively to the movement of trailers and containers (piggyback).

For many years to come, the railroads will provide the main medium of freight transportation. Self-interest alone will compel public policy eventually to give the carriers fair consideration. The future of the industry will depend upon the ability of management to improve service, to adjust to changing conditions, and to persuade Congress and government regulatory bodies (Federal and state) to adopt a policy toward the railroads that will enable them to earn an adequate return on the value of their net investment in properties. For the near term it appears that only a few major companies will achieve this objective. But this does not mean that attractive opportunities for investment are lacking. The stronger railroad holding companies, with their diversified operations, deserve attention. The ICC is conducting a special study of their role in the industry.

DOMESTIC AIR TRANSPORTATION

The airline industry consists of various sectors: international, domestic, regional, air taxi firms, all-cargo carriers, and supplemental or nonscheduled airlines. Each sector reflects its own degree of entry conditions, profitability, traffic mix, competition, seasonality, and levels of service. Our concern is directed towards the domestic (trunk) public carriers.

The characteristics of capital intensity, high utilization of debt with resulting financial and operating leverage, cyclical profit performance, and strict regulation apply to airlines as well as to railroads. To this list could be added the fact that airlines, unlike railroads, receive the bulk of their revenues from passengers, with freight a growing but still minor revenue contributor. Both industries deal with space—a product that cannot be stored. If not sold, its earnings are lost forever.

Scope and Development

In 1976 domestic public air carriers flew more than 130 billion passenger-miles, or nearly 70% of total intercity passenger traffic, compared to 9 billion, or less than 2%, in 1950. Plant investment grew from $500 million to more than $9 billion. As shown in Table 28-4, the earning power of the industry from the mid-50s to the mid-70s did not accompany its physical growth to a system spanning more than 300,000 route-miles.

The data in Table 28-4 tell this story of growth without large earnings. A key figure is the load factor (per cent of revenue passenger-miles to available seat-miles) which was 64% in 1950 and 55% in 1975. After an operating deficit in 1975, the year 1976 produced some profits and a modest return on common stock equity.

**TABLE 28-4 Development of the Domestic (Trunk)
Air Transportation Industry, 1955–1976**

	1955	1965	1976
Revenue—miles flown (millions)	565	940	1.750 (est.)
Revenue—passenger miles (millions)	19.206	48.987	131.400
Available seat-miles (millions)	29,979	88,731	235,500
Operating revenues ($ millions)	$1,132	$3.264	$11,875
Operating expenses ($ millions)	$1,008	$2,847	$11,403
Operating ratio	89.1%	87.2%	96.0%
Net income ($ millions)	$ 63	$ 222	$ 276
Net plant investment ($ millions)	$ 508	$2,648	$ 9,000 (est.)
Return on total investment	a	11.9%	7.5%
Return on common equity	a	21.6%	8.6%
Average revenue per passenger-mile	5.4¢	6.1¢	7.8¢

aNot available

Sources: Civil Aeronautics Board, *Air Carrier Traffic Statistics, Air Carrier Financial Statistics;
Moody's Manual, Transportation.*

Operations

Special operating characteristics   Overall airline profitability is
affected by revenues generated and expenses incurred. The anatomy of this
relationship can be understood by the following:[7]

traffic × yield = revenues

capacity × unit cost = operating expenses

Traffic is measured in revenue passenger-miles (RPM), which is defined as
one revenue passenger transported one mile. Some analysts also use revenue
ton-miles (RTM) which covers the total weight carried, including cargo.
Yield (in this special sense) is computed by multiplying the revenue aircraft
miles by the number of revenue passengers carried on that flight. Capacity
refers to available seat-miles (ASM) or the miles flown in each interairport
flight multiplied by the number of seats available on that flight for revenue
passenger use. One of the most frequently cited airline statistics is the load
factor defined above. An important corollary statistic is the breakeven load
factor (53.7% in 1976) which refers to the number of seats or tons which must
be sold to cover expenses. The determination of unit costs results from breaking down total costs by major category or functions.

Regardless of the number of passengers boarded on a particular flight,
the bulk of operating costs is relatively fixed. Costs such as crew wages,
fuel, direct and indirect maintenance, insurance, landing fees, and depreciation, comprising about 80% of total costs, must be paid whether the depart-
ing plane is full or half empty. Once the breakeven load factor is exceeded,
the contribution to profits from the incremental business will rise dramatically. If not exceeded, losses are incurred.

[7]S. N. Levine, ed., *Financial Analyst's Handbook*, Vol. 2. Homewood, Ill.: Dow Jones-Irwin, Inc, p. 233.

The income statements   Table 28-5 shows the combined (condensed) income statements of domestic trunk air carriers (their domestic operations only) in two recent years, 1974 and 1976—which offer considerable contrast with respect to profitability.

TABLE 28-5   Condensed Income Accounts, Domestic Operations of Trunk Air Carriers, 1974, 1976 (in millions of dollars)

	1974		1976	
	Amount	*Per Cent*	*Amount*	*Per Cent*
Operating revenues	$8,510.2	85.6%	$10,241.8	86.2%
Passenger				
Freight	575.3	5.8	721.1	6.1
Mail	158.3	1.6	182.3	1.5
Charter	133.4	1.3	214.8	1.8
Other	171.5	1.7	100.6	0.9
Non-transport	394.1	4.0	414.2	3.5
Total	$9,942.8	100.0	$11,874.8	100.0
Operating expenses				
Flight operations	$2,875.0	28.9	3,803.0	32.0
Maintenance	1,275.1	12.8	1,535.4	12.9
Passenger Service	937.6	9.4	1,146.0	9.7
Aircraft traffic servicing	1,675.7	16.8	2,006.8	16.9
Promotion & Sales	1,031.9	10.4	1,309.8	11.0
General & Administrative				
expense	395.8	4.0	475.8	4.0
Depreciation, etc.	794.3	8.0	834.8	7.0
Other expenses	277.4	2.9	291.5	2.5
Total	$9,262.8	93.2	$11,403.1	96.0%
Operating profit	680.0	6.8	471.7	4.0
Non-operating income	146.2	1.5	152.5	1.3
Interest	264.2	2.7	232.1	2.0
Net before income taxes	$ 562.0	5.6	$ 391.6	3.3%
Income taxes	238.4	2.4	(123.8)	(1.0)
Special items	—	—	8.3	—
Net income	$ 323.6	3.2%	$ 276.1	2.3%
Dividends	$ 123.1		$ 75.5	

Source: Civil Aeronautics Board, *Air Carrier Financial Statistics.*

Cyclical characteristics   Business travelers account for about two-thirds of U.S. domestic air travel. As a result, traffic and profit patterns are extremely elastic and are quite affected by changes in business conditions. This cyclical sensitivity has created a good deal of instability in the industry. In an effort to get a larger share of the increasing market in good times, airlines increase schedules. In an expanding, optimistic environment more equipment is required; orders for new planes are placed. Because of the long production cycle of new equipment its delivery often coincides with a recession-induced drop in traffic demand. So capacity expands faster than traffic buildup, and load factors and profit margins begin to decline.

In a recession, as in 1975, air traffic tends to fall off; earnings and share prices plummet. The environment of excess capacity and subnormal earnings is marked by employee layoffs, stringent cost-reduction, and deferred equipment purchases. The holding pattern continues until the rate of traffic and profit revives. Forces are then set in motion which in time cause the cycle to be repeated. This cyclical instability is often exacerbated by the tendency of the Civil Aeronautics Board to slice up existing routes by certifying new carriers. In the late 1960s for example, five new carriers were added to the Mainland-Hawaii run, making a total of eight carriers vying for the traveler's dollar. As a result, some carriers serving this route are experiencing lowered load factors and reduced profits.

Industry sensitivity to economic setbacks, as well as resiliency in bouncing back from adversity, is illustrated by 1975 results. In that recession year, the domestic trunk group lost $67 million. Aided by improving business conditions, fare hikes, and some respite from higher fuel increases, in 1976 the 11 major trunk lines earned $472 million before interest and taxes, a return on total investment of about 6.7%. But to attain the CAB-allowed rate of return of 12%, industry profits would have to climb very substantially.

Financial Characteristics

The balance sheet of a typical domestic air carrier shows the following major items in per cent of total assets:

Assets	
Current assets	19.5%
Investments and special funds	9.4
Operating property and equipment (net)	68.4
Other assets	2.7
	100.0%
Liabilities	
Current liabilities	18.2%
Long-term debt	41.2
Deferred taxes etc.	9.6
Preferred stock	.2
Common stock equity	30.8
	100.0%

The large fixed assets present a constant risk of declining property values. The capital structure proportion of long-term debt considerably exceeds the equity of stockholders, and, as in the case of railway companies, works a hardship through high leverage in poor years, but greatly magnifies the profits on common stock in occasional good years such as 1974. The rate of return earned on common equity by 11 domestic carriers in 1976 ranged between deficits for one firm (Pan Am) to as high as 34% for Western.

Regulation

Airlines are subject to the regulations of the Federal Aviation Administration (FAA) and the Civil Aeronautics Board (CAB). In addition, U.S. airlines that operate international flights are subject to regulations of the State Department, their foreign counterparts, and the rate-making powers of the International Air Transport Association (IATA).

FAA regulations are concerned primarily with operational matters—safety regulations, traffic control and navigation and the construction, maintenance, and operation of airports, and airways.

The focus of CAB regulation is economic, prescribing conditions of entry and exit, what routes may be flown, the rates charged, accounting and reporting procedures, and in general defining the minimum level of service that must be maintained. Although the various carriers are certified by the CAB, their route certifications are not exclusive. Unlike electric light and power companies, the airlines do not operate under monopoly conditions.

A contemporary political issue about which there is considerable debate is the extent to which domestic airlines should be regulated. CAB policies have come increasingly under attack. An argument presented by free-market advocates and consumer interest groups suggests that the present regulatory climate is economically inefficient. These critics allege that the absence of price competition has resulted in unnecessarily higher fares for the traveling public.

Congress is studying proposals that would revamp CAB's regulatory powers and increase industry competition.

Future Outlook

Airline stocks are not for every investor. The industry's cyclical characteristics and erratic profit performance make their shares unattractive for those seeking capital preservation and stability of income. The outlook for sustained profitability is clouded by a number of uncertainties. Fuel and wage costs are matters of continuing concern. The domestic carriers paid $1.87 billion for fuel in 1975, up 29% from 1974, although consumption increased only 2.4%. Fuel costs in 1976 ran about 15% over those of 1975, with the expectation that they would be higher in 1977. Existing labor contracts call for wage increases of about 10% annually.

There has been an enormous increase in the cost of equipment. In the late sixties, a B-747 cost about $25 million. Today, it runs closer to $35 million. Many airlines would like to replace their 707s and DC-8s because of noise and fuel efficiency problems. Their replacement will cost about $10 million each.

The most critical financial problem is the necessity to lessen the industry's top-heavy debt load. Pan Am, for example, with a stockholders' equity of $352 million, had (1976) a long-term debt of $780 million. TWA's long-term debt was $907 million with an equity of $377 million. Many carriers have financed with convertible issues. Although the prices of these securities are currently below their conversion points, the possibility exists of a massive equity dilution at some future time. With an estimated $60 billion needed for replacement and growth in the 1980s, the industry must strengthen its finances and improve profitability if it is to attract strong investment interest.

Airline Securities

The market price action of airline stocks has reflected the factors outlined above, together with the general market situation. Prices of airline stocks reached their peak in 1966. In 1973 they were 30% lower, then fell 72% from that level. However, in 1976 they doubled their 1974 value. The high volatility of airline stocks make them more attractive as trading vehicles than as components of most investment portfolios. But, as is the case with all industry groups, some companies present stronger finances and earnings trends than do others. Selection and timing remain the watchwords. The highly specialized character of the airline industry suggests that most individual investors would do well either to ignore it or seek advisers who are specially qualified to deal with a combination of economic and political uncertainties.

MOTOR CARRIER INDUSTRY

This industry has four divisions: local cartage, intercity common carriers, intercity contract carriers, and private carriers. Local cartage is a "for hire" carrier providing pickup and delivery service within a given area. Intercity truck lines offer their services to all shippers, operate over prescribed routes and under posted tariffs. Intercity contract carriers limit their activities to selected shippers. Private carriers are owned and operated by firms and others for their own needs. The data and discussion in this chapter refer to intercity common carriers.

Industry Characteristics

Growth and cyclicality By 1975 common carrier trucks handled over 21% of the ton-miles of intercity freight traffic. But their higher per-ton-mile rates resulted in their share of regulated carrier freight revenues reaching over 50%. Over the years, by stressing speed and service, the trucking industry has captured a growing proportion of general merchandise and manufactured freight.

Industry growth has paralleled the population shift to the suburbs, the decentralization of industry, the almost completed Interstate Highway System (about 90% of the planned 42,500 miles of routes are now open to traffic), and the virtual discontinuance of less-than-carload service by the railroads. Growth has also been aided by the carriers' aggressiveness in providing service to shippers. They are especially flexible in accepting shipments at a later hour than railroads, while still striving for earlier morning deliveries. For those shippers with requirements of pickups and deliveries of one or more times a day, trucks offer a special advantage.

Development of the Industry

Table 28-6 shows the salient features of the industry's growth, both physical and financial, since 1955.

TABLE 28-6 Development of the Motor Carrier Industry, 1955–1975 (Class I Intercity Carriers[a])

	1955	1960	1965	1970	1975
Ton-miles intercity freight (millions)	[b]	[b]	359,000	412,000	441,000
Average revenue per ton-mile (cents)	5.8	6.3	6.5	7.5	9.5 (est.)
Operating revenues	$4,030	$4,763	$7,112	11,137	$16,266[d]
Operating expenses	$3,870	$4,645	$6,736	$10,762	$15,539[d]
Operating ratio[c]	96%	97%	95%	97%	96%
Net operating revenue[c]	$ 160	$ 119	$376	$375	$627[d]
Net income	$ 82	$ 37	$209	$140	$308[d]

[a]As of 1973, carriers with 3-year average revenues of $3 millions or more.
[b]Not available.
[c]8 millions.
[d]All Class I Carriers.

Source: ICC, *Transport Statistics in the U.S.,* Part 7 (annual).

A growing volume of traffic at increased rates is necessary to produce adequate profits from the low net income margin that reflects ever-increasing costs. Earnings results vary considerably within the industry. In good years, such as 1972 and 1974, the group earned over 18% on total equity. Earnings fell off substantially in 1975, to recover sharply in 1976 when about 20% was earned in net worth. The industry's market share of intercity freight traffic continues to make inroads into that of the railroads.

Financial Characteristics

As of 1975, the industry's balance sheet showed this structure:

Assets	
Current assets	33.5%
Operating property less depreciation	48.7
Other assets	17.8
	100.0%
Liabilities	
Current liabilities	29.9%
Funded debt	17.9
Reserves	6.8
Net worth	45.4
	100.0%

The industry runs at a low current ratio, but depreciation and retained profits provide a large cash flow for debt reduction and expansion. Funded debt is modest, consisting mainly of notes secured by equipment. Such conservative financing is required to protect against the cyclical variations in revenue and earnings.

Regulation

The Interstate Commerce Commission has jurisdiction over Class I, II, and III interstate carriers. Entry is controlled, and certificates of convenience and necessity are required over specified routes. Rates and service are regulated. Interstate carriers are also subject to taxation, licensing, safety, and weight regulations of the various states.

Over the years, by stressing speed and service, the trucking industry has captured a substantial portion of general merchandise and manufactured freight relative to other modes of service. The motor carriers' steady revenue growth has been greater than that of any other ICC-regulated carrier.

Motor Carrier Stocks

Stocks of intercity common carrier firms have suffered from market price volatility, reflecting the cyclical character of earnings and the general market situation. From a low in 1973, Standard & Poor's index of trucking stocks more than quadrupled by 1974, fell almost 50% in 1974–1975, then rebounded to an all-time high in 1976 with the recovery of earnings and general market strength. Earnings per share for the group rose substantially in 1975–1976. The price-earnings multiple remains modestly lower than that of the industrial indexes, averaging 8.4 times earnings in 1976. Typically, less than one quarter of earnings are distributed in dividends, and dividend yields average about 3%, with a range from zero to 6%.

Special Sources of Information, Transport Industries

GENERAL:

Transport Association of America, *Transportation Facts and Trends*, annual, with quarterly supplements.

U.S. Department of Transportation, *Summary of National Transportation Statistics*, annual.

Moody's Transportation Manual (blue section), annual with weekly supplement.

Standard & Poor's *Transportation Service, Weekly Transportation Outlook*.

Transport Economics, published bimonthly by the ICC.

Bureau of Census, *Census of Transportation*, 1972.

RAILWAYS:

ICC: *Transport Statistics in the U.S.* Part I, *Railroads* (annual); *Financial and Operating Statistics of Class I Railroads*, semi-annual.

Association of American Railroads: *Statistics of Railroads of Class I*, annual; *Yearbook of Railroad Facts* (annual); *Year-end Review and Outlook* (annual); *Information Letter*, monthly.

Railway Age, monthly, and Outlook and Review section, annual.

Standard & Poor's *Industry Surveys, Railroads.*

AIR TRANSPORT:

U.S. Civil Aeronautics Board, *Handbook of Airline Statistics*, biennial, updated by *Air Carrier Traffic Statistics*, monthly; and *Air Carrier Financial Statistics*, quarterly, *Airline Economic Report*, quarterly.

U.S. Aviation Administration, *Statistical Handbook of Aviation*, annual.

Air Transport Association of America; *Air Transport Facts and Figures*, annual; *Financial Review and Outlook* (irregular).

World Airline Record, 7th ed. Chicago: Roadcap and Associates, 1972.

Aviation Daily, *Aviation Daily's Airline Statistical Annual*. Washington, D.C.: Ziff-Davis Publishing Co.

Standard & Poor's *Industry Surveys, Air Transportation.*

MOTOR CARRIERS (freight):

ICC: *Transport Statistics in the U.S.*, Part VII, *Motor Carriers*, annual; *Revenues, Expenses, Other Income and Statistics of Class I Motor Carriers of Property*, semi-annual.

American Trucking Association, *American Trucking Trends*, annual; *Financial and Operating Statistics of Class I Motor Carriers of Property*, annual.

Continental Illinois National Bank of Chicago, *Financial Analysis of the Motor Carrier Industry*, annual.

Standard & Poor's *Industry Surveys, Motor Carriers.*

REFERENCES

BOWYER, J. W., JR., *Investment Analysis and Management*, 4th ed., Chapter 2. Homewood, Ill.: Richard D. Irwin, Inc., 1972.

DAVIS, G. M., M. T. FARRIS, and J. T. HOLDEN, JR., *Management of Transportation Carriers*. New York: Praeger Press, 1975.

DAUGHEN, J. R., and PETER BINZEN, *The Wreck of the Penn Central*. Boston: Little, Brown & Co., 1971.

FAIR, M. L., and JOHN GUANDOLO, *Transportation Regulation*, 7th ed. Dubuque, Iowa: Wm. C. Brown Company, 1972.

———, and W. WILLIAMS, JR., *Economics of Transportation and Logistics*, Dallas, Texas: Business Publications, Inc., 1975.

FRUHAN, W. E., *The Fight for Competitive Advantage: A Study of the United States Domestic Trunk Air Carriers*. Boston, Mass.: Graduate School of Business, Harvard University, 1972.

GRAHAM, BENJAMIN, D. L. DODD, and SIDNEY COTTLE, *Security Analysis*, 4th ed., Chapter 19. New York: McGraw-Hill, Inc., 1962.

GUTHMANN, H. G., *Analysis of Financial Statements*, 4th ed., Chapters 11, 12. Englewood Cliffs, N.J.: Prentice-Hall, Inc., 1953.

————, and H. E. DOUGALL, *Corporate Financial Policy*, 4th ed., Chapter 17. Englewood Cliffs, N.J.: Prentice-Hall, Inc., 1962.

JORDAN, W. A., *Airline Regulation in America: Effect and Imperfections*. Baltimore: Johns Hopkins Press, 1970.

KANE, R. M., and A. D. VOSE, *Air Transportation*, 4th ed. Dubuque, Iowa: Kendall-Hunt Co., 1974.

KENNEDY, R. D., and S. Y. McMULLIN, *Financial Statements*, 6th ed., Chapters 22, 23. Homewood, Ill.: Richard D. Irwin, Inc., 1973.

KNEAFSEY, J. T., *Transportation Economic Analysis*. Lexington, Mass.: Lexington Books, 1975.

LEVINE, S. N., *Financial Analyst's Handbook*, Vol. II, Chapters 5 and 25. Homewood, Ill.: Dow Jones-Irwin, Inc., 1975.

LOCHLIN, D. P., *Economics of Transportation*, 7th ed. Homewood, Ill.: Richard D. Irwin, Inc., 1972.

Motor Carrier Financing. Washington, D.C.: Economic Research Committee of the Regular Common Carrier Conference, 1976.

NORTON, H. S., *Modern Transportation Economics*, 3rd ed. Columbus, Ohio: Charles E. Merrill Publishing Co., 1971.

SAMPSON, R. J., and M. T. FARRIS, *Domestic Transportation: Practice, Theory and Policy*, 3rd ed. New York: Houghton-Mifflin Company, 1975.

WYCKOFF, D. D., *Railroad Management*. Lexington, Mass.: Lexington Books, 1976.

Securities of Banks and Savings & Loan Associations

SCOPE: Chapter 11 was devoted to investment companies, and real estate trusts were discussed in Chapter 12. Chapters 29 and 30 are devoted to the securities issued by other financial institutions. In Chapter 29, the discussion includes commercial banks and bank holding companies, and savings and loan associations and parent companies. Chapter 30 includes (stock) life insurance companies, and property and liability insurance companies.

The order of discussion in Chapter 29 is commercial banks: (1) banks and banking functions, (2) analysis of statements, (3) bank stock ratio analysis, (4) bank holding companies, (5) bank stock values, prices and yields, (6) investment outlook; savings and loan associations: (7) characteristics and investment appeal, (8) financial analysis, (9) investment record and outlook, and (10) special sources of information.

COMMERCIAL BANKS

Banks and Banking Functions

Classification of banks Banks may be classified as (1) *national* or *state*, depending on the source of charter; (2) *commercial* or *savings*, depending on the nature of operations; (3) *member* or *nonmember*, depending on membership in the Federal Reserve System; (4) *insured* or *noninsured*, depending on participation in Federal deposit insurance; and (5) *stock* or *mutual*, depending on the nature of ownership.

National commercial banks are chartered by the Federal government and are subject to uniform regulation and supervision by the Comptroller of the Currency, as well as by the Federal Reserve authorities and the Federal Deposit Insurance Corporation. State commercial banks are chartered under state banking acts and are supervised by state authority and by the Federal Reserve and the FDIC, depending on membership in these systems.

Commercial banks do a general banking business in accepting demand and time deposits, making a variety of loans and investments, performing trust functions, and offering a number of services to customers. Mutual savings banks accept time deposits and invest in selected bonds and mortgages, but do not make personal or commercial loans. They have no capital

**TABLE 29-1   Deposits and Net Worth of Commercial Banks,
December 31, 1976 (dollars in billions)**

	Number of Banks	Total Deposits	Net Worth
Federal Reserve Membership			
National (all members F.R.)	4,735	$469.4	$41.3
State			
Members F.R.	1,023	149.5	13.2
Nonmembers F.R.	8,914	219.4	18.4
Total	14,672	$838.3	$72.9
Extent of FDIC Coverage			
National (all insured)	4,735	$469.4	$41.3
State			
Members F.R. (insured)	1,023	149.5	13.2
Nonmembers (insured)	8,639	206.1	17.6
Nonmembers (uninsured)	275	13.3	.8
Total	14,672	$838.3	$72.9

Sources: Federal Reserve Bulletin, Annual Report of the Federal Deposit Insurance Corporation.

stock outstanding. They are chartered under special state legislation, but are subject to Federal Reserve and FDIC supervision if they are members of these systems. (See Chapter 5.)

Membership in the Federal Reserve System comprises all of the national banks, and the state banks that have elected to join the system, together with a few mutual savings banks.

Most banks belong to the Federal Deposit Insurance Corporation, and their depositors enjoy the protection of mutual insurance.

Investor interest is, of course, centered in the commercial banks. The smaller of these have a local following, but it is to the stocks of the larger banks and bank holding companies whose shares are traded in the exchange or over-the-counter markets that the following discussion pertains.

As of December 31, 1976, the 14,672 commercial banks in the United States had outstanding deposits totalling $838 billion and a combined net worth of $73 billion. Table 29-1 shows the relative importance of the various categories.

Banking functions   The traditional functions of the commercial bank have been to make short-term loans to business, to accept deposits (in new funds or as created by loans) and thus provide checking and safekeeping services, and to provide miscellaneous services such as collection of items and trust functions. In more recent years, commercial banks have become "department stores of finance" through the development of a wide variety of personal, real estate, and business loans, trust and investment services, and facilities such as safe-deposit vaults. They have also become the most important owners of government securities. And through the use of the holding company, services have been extended to a wide variety of fields. (See p. 591.) The banking functions *per se* are regulated by Federal and state authorities with respect to liquidity and solvency (through regulation and supervision of loans and investments and through reserve requirements) and protection against unwarranted duplication and competition. In addition, the credit-granting powers of the banks are influenced by law, regulation, and moral suasion as the credit structure (in the opinion of the Federal Reserve) requires expansion or contraction.

The essential character and the growth of bank services and the imposition of a mass of regulation indicate that, as a whole, bank stocks should constitute a safe and stable medium of investment. Until recent years the bank failure rate has been very low, but in 1973–1976, 31 banks with deposits totalling $3.8 billion failed and had to be rescued by the Federal Deposit Insurance Corporation. About 380 others, including some large and prominent institutions, were designated as "problem banks" by the FDIC, largely because of failed real estate loans. Bank stocks were hard hit by these developments and by the general stock market decline in 1973–1974.

Numerous factors revealed by analysis of bank financial statements must be considered by the would-be investor. Their interpretation also requires a knowledge of the size, character, economic stability, and growth of the community served, the types of industries in the bank's clientele, the degree of regulation imposed, the connections of the management, and the impact of Federal Reserve policy. The investor should prefer a growing bank in a growing and stable community, not dependent on any one industry or small group of borrowers, with deposits diversified both as to size and type, and with a management alert to the possibilities of new services and sources of revenue—whether by the bank itself or by its parent company—and conscious of the need for conservative asset policies, especially in times of financial stress such as the 1970s.

Analysis of Statements

Types of information   One disadvantage of many bank stocks is the lack of adequate financial information. Banks must publish "statements of condition" (condensed balance sheets) four times a year. Banks differ widely with respect to the publication of more detailed balance sheet information, and income statements are entirely a matter of discretion save for those whose shares are listed on organized securities exchanges. Policies governing the valuation of assets also differ considerably, although most banks lean toward conservatism. Book value and actual value of assets may differ substantially.

Fortunately, the larger institutions and holding companies now make available more detailed statement information, especially concerning income and expenses. And because of the highly liquid character of most bank assets, book values represent liquidating value much more closely than in the case of business corporations.

Another advantage is the availability of adequate industry data. The reports of the Comptroller of the Currency, the state bank authorities, the Federal Reserve, and the Federal Deposit Insurance Corporation contain combined statistics that are useful in judging the trends and conditions in banking as a whole and in comparing an individual bank with other banks in the industry. And a number of investment services and investment banking houses now issue comparative studies of considerable value.

Income statements The operating revenues and expenses of insured commercial banks for three years in the 1965–1976 period, are given in Table 29-2, together with the relationship of each item to total operating earnings. This group comprised 98% of the 14,672 commercial banks in the country as of the end of 1976.

These data reveal the chief sources of revenue and the chief expense items of commercial banks as a whole. The proportions vary among individual banks, depending on their size, location, and types of business emphasized. In 1976, income from loans provided 64% of operating earnings as a result of the great increase in loans in expansion of the 1960s and 1970s. Income

TABLE 29-2 Earnings, Expenses, and Dividends of Insured Commercial Banks, 1965–1976 (in millions of dollars)

	1965		1970		1976	
	Amt.	*%*	*Amt.*	*%*	*Amt.*	*%*
Operating income						
Income on loans	$11,205	66.6%	$23,975	69.0%	$51,645	64.0%
Interest on U.S. Gov. obligations	2,225	13.2	3,078	8.9	5,976	7.4
Interest and dividends, other investments	1,285	7.6	3,459	10.0	15,412	19.1
Service charges on deposit accounts	843	5.0	1,178	3.4	1,635	2.0
Other service charges, commissions, and fees	304	1.8	843	2.4	2,183	2.7
Trust department revenue	690	4.1	1,132	3.3	1,795	2.2
Other operating revenue	265	1.7	1,049	3.0	2,018	2.6
Total	$16,817	100.0%	$34,714	100.0%	$80,664	100.0%
Operating expense						
Salaries, wages, and benefits	4,288	25.5	7,717	22.2	14,752	18.3
Interest on deposits	5,071	30.1	10,484	30.2	35,004	43.4
Other interest and investment costs	190	1.1	569	1.6	4,223	5.2
Premises expense, net	732	4.4	1,255	3.6	4,486	5.6
Other operating expenses	2,205	13.1	7,563	21.9	12,285	15.2
Total	$12,486	74.2%	$27,588	79.5%	$70,750	87.7%
Net current operating earnings	$ 4,331	25.8%	$ 7,126	20.5%	$ 9,914	12.3
Recoveries and profits	209	1.2 ⎫				
Losses and charge-offs	(267)	(1.6) ⎬	(116)	(.3) ⎫	340	0.4
Net additions to valuation reserves	(730)	(4.3) ⎭		⎬		
Profits before income taxes	$ 3,543	21.1%	$ 7,010	20.2%	$10,254	12.7
Income taxes	1,029	6.1	2,173	6.3	2,411	3.0
Net income after taxes	$ 2,514	15.0%	$ 4,837	13.9%	$ 7,843	9.7%
Dividends	$ 1,202		$ 2,033		$ 3,036	

Source: Compiled from Annual Reports of the Federal Deposit Insurance Corporation.

from securities grew in both absolute and relative terms as a result of the high yields available. Trust department and service income is important, but not predominant, as a source of revenues.

Salaries, wages, and benefits require about 18% of total revenues and constitute about 21% of total operating expenses. Interest on time and savings deposits has grown to about 43% of revenues and about 50% of operating expenses, reflecting the rise in interest rates paid. Interest paid on debentures and other debt, expenses of operating the bank premises, and a host of minor items comprise the other expenses.

The net operating earnings are now only about 12% of operating revenues, so that an operating ratio of 88% is produced. The net operating earnings, which indicate the real earning power, are subject to further adjustments arising out of profits (or losses) on securities transactions and on recoveries (or losses and charge-offs) on loans. In addition, many banks charge earnings with substantial amounts for bad debts and securities losses, prior to actual liquidation experience with these assets. Variations in the handling of losses, recoveries, and reserves among banks makes comparison of their net profit before taxes somewhat difficult. Analysts recommend that in comparing banks the net operating earnings figure be emphasized.

Income taxes absorb about 3% of operating revenues, leaving a net profit which now constitutes less than 10% of revenues. This is a much lower net income margin than the 15% which prevailed in the latter 1960s and early 1970s, and has put pressure on banks' per-share earnings. Where no net income is reported, an approximation may be obtained by finding the difference between the total surplus and undivided profits in the balance sheet at two different intervals and adding back the dividends paid in the interim. An adjustment may also be necessary to allow for any surplus derived from sale of stock above par value during the period.

The larger banks of investment interest ordinarily distribute only a modest fraction of their profits as dividends, so that yields on bank stocks are low. The steady "ploughing back" of earnings is necessary if net worth is to keep pace with the expansion of deposits. The appeal of the stock in a sound and growing bank lies in the relative regularity of dividends plus the appreciation in book and possible appreciation in market value that follows the growth in net worth and earnings.

The statements of bank holding companies present somewhat different categories and relationships because of their many nonbank activities.

Balance sheets   The bank balance sheet reflects the character of the bank's activities. The chief liability items are deposits. The chief asset items are cash, loans, and investments. The data in Table 29-3 show the combined (and condensed) balance sheets of all insured commercial banks as of year-end 1965 and 1976. Significant changes took place during this period both in the amount and the relative importance of balance sheet items.

Cash, or the bank's *primary reserve*, consists of cash on hand, balances with other banks, cash items in process of collection, and legal reserves, which, in the case of members of the Federal Reserve System, consist of the required

TABLE 29-3 Assets and Liabilities of Insured Commercial Banks—as of December 31, 1965 and 1976 (in millions of dollars)

Item	1965	1976
Assets		
Cash and due from banks	$ 61,341	$ 129,578
U.S. Govt. and agency obligations	68,324	136,729
State and municipal securities	38,781	104,374
Other securities	5,315	6,336
Loans and discounts	245,299	578,712
Less: valuation reserve	4,221	18,642
Net loans and discounts	$241,078	$ 560,070
Bank premises, furniture, and fixtures	5,525	19,448
Other assets	5,530	47,485
Total assets	$425,894	$1,004,020
Liabilities and Capital		
Deposits		
Time and savings	$193,197	$ 492,719
Demand	184,203	332,283
Total deposits	$377,400	$ 825,002
Other liabilities	14,632	101,850
Capital stock	10,203	16,210
Surplus	16,263	28,791
Undivided profits and reserves	7,396	27,069
Capital notes and debentures	—	5,098
Total liabilities and capital accounts	$425,894	$1,004,020

Sources: Annual Reports of the Federal Deposit Insurance Corporation, *Federal Reserve Bulletin.*

reserve balances held at the Federal Reserve Banks plus vault cash.[1] Primary reserves are maintained against cash withdrawals as a protection to depositors and for maintenance of general liquidity. Total cash of all insured commercial banks comprised 16% of total assets in 1965 and 13% in 1976.

Investments Investments and loans are called the "earning assets" of the bank, as they produce the bulk of the income for the bank. United States Government and agency obligations, the most liquid of the earning assets, comprised 17% of total earning assets in 1965 and 12% in 1976. They reached their peak in 1946; in the postwar period, they declined in relative importance as a result of the substantial growth of commercial loans. Government obligations are not without price risk; the value of those that are marketable fluctuates with changing interest rates. Many banks minimize this risk by emphasizing short-term Treasury bills and certificates, or Treasury notes and bonds nearing maturity. Securities other than Federal

[1]As of January 1, 1977, member banks' required reserves against net demand deposits ranged from 7% (on deposits of up to $2 million) to 16 1/4% (on deposits of over $400 million, reserve banks). Against time deposits, requirements were 3% on savings, and from 1% (4 years and more maturity) to 6% (30–179 days, or over $5 million).

issues consist of the state, municipal, and corporate bonds approved for bank investment. Banks hold permanently no stock except stock in the Federal Reserve Banks (in the case of member banks) and in affiliates.

Loans and discounts   Loans and discounts represent the advances of the bank to its clients and include commercial, industrial, and agricultural loans, loans to brokers and others secured by securities, real estate mortgages, personal and consumer loans, loans to banks, commercial paper, and bankers' acceptances. Loans are usually shown net after reserve for losses. The proportion of total assets held in the form of loans, and the types of advances made, are major determinants of bank operating earnings. Reflecting the great demand for loans in the latter 1960s and early 1970s, this asset rose to 57% of total commercial bank assets at the end of 1976 from 46% in 1960. Banks that desire liquidity and, hence, concentrate on investments rather than loans, produce lower earning power but may enjoy greater safety.

To assure liquidity, the bank's second line of defense consists of its *secondary reserve* of short-term Government securities, banker's acceptances, and commercial paper. These earning assets yield relatively low returns. Hence, a high proportion of primary and secondary reserves produce lower revenues, although greater safety is achieved. For all insured commercial banks, secondary reserves were about 20% of total assets at the end of 1976.

Fixed assets   Fixed assets are relatively small. Their importance varies considerably from bank to bank, depending on the type of premises and equipment and the method of valuation for balance sheet purposes.

Other assets   Other assets include: (1) *customers' liability on acceptances*, representing claims against customers for whom the bank has accepted drafts and bills under letters of credit; this item is offset by a corresponding liability representing the obligation of the bank to honor such acceptances that are still outstanding; (2) *income accrued but not collected*, representing the accrued interest on customers' loans and on securities that will be collected at a later date; similarly, on the liabilities side of the balance sheet, a figure appears representing interest collected in advance but not yet earned; and (3) *prepaid expenses* and a variety of minor miscellaneous items.

Deposits   Deposits represent the main liabilities of the bank. They are subdivided into (1) *time* and *savings deposits*, which are not subject to check, and which bear interest; and (2) *demand deposits* due to individuals, business concerns, governments, and other banks. The relative proportion of the two main types affects the operations of the bank in several ways—the interest expense, the required reserves, and the type of investments held. Because time deposits have a slower turnover, lower reserves are held for their payment, and when they form a large portion of total deposits, the bank is justified in holding more long-term investments, such as bonds and mortgages. Where demand deposits predominate, especially amounts due to other banks, the bank must maintain higher reserves and more liquid earning assets. See Chapter 21.

The other liabilities of the bank are of minor importance and include borrowings from other banks, accrued expenses, taxes, and any reserves that represent liabilities rather than valuation and surplus reserves.[2]

The *net worth* section of the balance sheet (often designated as "capital" or "capital funds") ordinarily contains four items: (1) capital stock; (2) surplus, representing permanently held accumulated earnings transferred from undivided profits and any premiums received from the sale of stock above par value; (3) undivided profits, or "free surplus," into which current profits are credited and from which dividends are paid (national banks are required to have surplus equal to 20% of their capital stock before they may declare dividends—surplus which is ordinarily obtained by the sale of stock at a premium over par value, or built up by transfers from undivided profits); and (4) reserves, which include general, contingency, security valuation, and loan loss reserves (over and above the bad debts reserve that is allowed for income tax purposes).

A fifth category of items in the "capital funds" section consists of notes and debentures. Beginning in 1963, a number of larger banks sold notes or debentures to increase their loanable funds and provide greater support to their deposits. Although these obligations represent debt, they are subordinate to deposits in their claims on assets, and so provide additional leverage in the capital structure.

Bank Stock Ratio Analysis

The investor in bank stock should be satisfied that the bank shows a satisfactory position with respect to: (1) liquidity, (2) solvency or capital adequacy, and (3) earning power. Liquidity is the bank's ability to meet deposit obligations at short notice. Solvency measures its ultimate ability, possibly after a period of liquidation of assets, to meet its deposits. Earning power is of primary importance to the investor seeking income, price appreciation, or both. These three concepts are closely interrelated. A bank with sufficient primary and secondary reserves to meet its deposits if they were all withdrawn at once would be both liquid and solvent, but would produce little or no net earnings. A bank seeking maximum earnings would maintain only those reserves required by law and minimum daily needs, and would emphasize high-rate loans subject to greater losses or, in the absence of a demand for loans, medium- and long-term bonds subject to price variations. Such a bank would not be highly liquid; it might be solvent, given sufficient time to transfer its assets into cash. Its earnings would be high, if only for a temporary period. The problem of bank management is to steer a middle course so as to maintain liquidity adequate to satisfy the chief obligation of

---

[2]The term *reserve* has several meanings in banking. First, there are the *legal reserves* of cash or deposits that must be maintained to satisfy the law; these are assets. Second, as we have seen, groups of assets are classified as primary or secondary reserves with respect to their purpose of providing adequate liquidity. Third, bank balance sheets often contain reserves similar to those found on business corporation statements: *valuation reserves*, such as reserves for depreciation or bad debts, *liability reserves*, such as reserves for taxes or dividends, and reserves that are, in fact, merely segregations of surplus.

safety to depositors and, at the same time, provide an adequate return on the investment of the stockholders.

Tests of liquidity The basic test of liquidity is the reserve ratio, or ratio of primary reserves to deposits. For all insured banks at the end of 1976 this ratio stood at 15.7%. It tends to be higher for the banks in large cities holding deposits of other banks that are required by law to maintain higher legal reserves and whose deposits are primarily demand. Banks whose deposits are predominantly time and savings accounts feel safe with a lower reserve ratio. Banks whose assets other than cash are highly liquid also require smaller cash balances. This suggests an extension of the reserve ratio in the relationship between cash plus U.S. Government securities to deposits. This figure stood at 32% for all insured commercial banks at the end of 1976.

Another measure of liquidity is found in the ratio of (net) loans to deposits. This shows the extent to which loanable funds are invested in earning assets bearing the highest risk. For all insured commercial banks the ratio stood at 68% at the end of 1976.

Tests of solvency The traditional test of solvency is the ratio of "capital funds" (capital stock, surplus, undivided profits, surplus reserves, and debentures) to deposits. Tradition has set this ratio at 10%, but in recent years only the larger and more conservative banks have preserved this relationship. For all insured commercial banks at the end of 1976, the ratio was 9.3%. The net worth provides the cushion of protection to the bank's creditors. It also indicates the degree of leverage by which a modest rate of earnings on total resources is magnified into a respectable return on the owners' investment.

Whether the capital funds-to-deposits ratio is satisfactory can be learned only by examining other relationships. Where the bank is highly liquid and its loans and investments are well selected and managed, the ratio can safely be much lower than the average. Rapid growth of deposits and a relatively larger increase in loans than in high-grade investments have caused a number of banks in the late 1960s and early 1970s to offer new stock and notes in order to improve the ratio. The size of this relationship also has an important influence on dividend policy. Transfers from undivided profits to surplus permanently impound funds which might otherwise be available for cash dividends. The investor should determine whether an attractive rate of earnings and of dividends is at the expense of solvency as indicated by an unsatisfactory net worth position.

Other measures of capital adequacy include the ratio of (1) capital funds to *assets at risk* (total assets less cash and U.S. Government securities), (2) capital funds to *deposits at risk* (deposits less cash and Governments), and (3) capital funds to *loans*. These measure the exposure of deposits to risk of decline in value of the earning assets in general, and loans in particular. Ratios for 1960, 1965, 1970, and 1976 are shown in Table 29-4.

The declines in these ratios reflect the increase in bank activity without a similar increase in capital. This has been one of the reasons for the issuance of subordinated notes and debentures in recent years.

TABLE 29-4 Capital Adequacy Ratios, Insured Commercial Banks

	(1)	(2)	(3)
1960	13.7%	17.7%	18.4%
1965	11.7	14.1	14.9
1970	10.0	12.6	13.6
1976	9.5	10.7	13.4

Source: Annual Reports of the Federal Deposit Insurance Corporation.

Tests of earning power   The earnings record and prospects of a bank depend on all of the influences that govern the investment of its funds and the operation of its departments. Nevertheless, there are some useful specific clues.

The ratio of loans to investments, and the types of loans and of investments within these categories, have a marked influence on earnings. In general, investments are less remunerative than loans, and short-term loans and investments less lucrative than long term.

Of course, banks differ considerably in the character of their earning assets. The investor must be satisfied that quality has not been sacrificed for earning power in the selection of the earning assets.

Special attention should be paid to the trend in the growth of deposits and of loans as indicators of management. The bank's earning power depends in large measure on its ability to obtain and hold deposits, and to invest these deposits in earning assets that produce a satisfactory income. The banks that show better-than-average earnings are those that are growing at a better-than-average rate, that emphasize loans rather than investments, and that have a lower-than-average ratio of capital funds to deposits. (See below).

Where sufficient detail is available, the bank's income statement may be analyzed in the same manner as that of the business concern, except, of course, that different standards are used. The operating ratio is the relationship of operating expenses to operating earnings. For banks as a whole, it is about 88%. A low operating ratio indicates management efficiency and the ability to withstand declines in revenues without making too heavy inroads into net operating earnings. A high operating ratio must be offset by larger revenue per dollar of investment.

Certain individual expense items, notably salaries and wages and interest paid on deposits, have a marked effect on the operating ratio and on the net operating earnings. The former constitutes about 18% and the latter 43% of total revenues, and 21% and 50%, respectively, of operating expenses, for all insured commercial banks in 1976. The latter reflects the composition of deposits between demand and time. When both of these costs are rising (as during 1962–1975, when there was a wave of increases in interest paid on savings accounts), profit margins tend to narrow.

The net operating earnings (before taxes) show the result of banking operations proper, prior to any special gains or losses on loans and investments. As a percentage of operating revenues, net operating earnings before income taxes and securities gains or losses were 12.7% for all insured commercial banks in 1976. In 1960 the figure was 32%. The decline reflects the very substantial increase in operating costs and interest paid. A very large increase in the volume of loans was required to maintain earning power.

But the overall earning power of the institution is better indicated by the relation between pretax net earnings and capital funds plus deposits. For 1976 the rate for all insured commercial banks was only 1.5%. To earn a good return on its capital funds, a bank relies on the leverage provided by a substantial ratio of deposits to net worth. Banks with a capital funds-to-deposits ratio of more than 9 are likely to earn an inadequate rate on net worth. Banks with less than this ratio would, with the same net earnings, produce a very substantial return on the owners' investment but would be undercapitalized.

The adjustments to net operating earnings, representing (1) gains and losses on securities, and recoveries and charge-offs on loans, and (2) the additions to or reductions of valuation reserves, deserve close scrutiny. The size of these items depends somewhat on the original book value placed on earning assets. In addition, their amount varies considerably from year to year; they were especially large in 1973–1976. For these reasons the basic earning power of the bank is measured by the reported earnings before rather than after these adjustments.

The percentage of operating revenues carried down to net income after taxes, coupled with the turnover of capital funds, produces the rate of return on the book value of the owners' investment, which for all insured commercial banks was only 11.4% in 1976. This has fallen considerably in the postwar period, having been 36 and 24% in 1945 and 1950, respectively.

Golembe Associates calculated the average ratio at 20.7% for the period 1972–1975, for "high performance banks," in contrast to the 12.2% for all banks.[3] Most of the difference is attributable to lower expenses. The key characteristics that distinguish these banks from others are:

1. Maximization of revenues
   (a) High loan income attained by appropriate pricing and the avoidance of nonaccruing loans, rather than through high volume.
   (b) Maximization of income from tax-exempt securities.
   (c) Maintenance of sufficient flexibility in asset structure as to take advantage of changes in interest rates.
2. Expense control
   (a) Low investment in fixed assets and thus lower occupancy expenses.
   (b) Careful control of overhead and discretionary costs such as other operating expense.
   (c) Minimization of loan losses through proper credit analysis and knowledge of customers.
   (d) Control of personnel expense through the efficient use of fewer employees rather than low salaries.
3. Consistently good management
   (a) Large comparative advantages in the management of smaller controllable factors.

[3]Golembe Associates, Inc., Washington, D.C. Data and other information used by permission.

(b) Smaller comparative—but large absolute—advantages in management of larger, less controllable factors.

To the shareholder, earnings per share, and their trend and stability, is the crucial figure. For short-run analysis, per-share results are calculated from net operating earnings after taxes. For longer-run comparisons, the net after profits or losses on securities sales is valid. In common with industrial companies, some banks show earnings per share giving effect to the dilution that would result from the conversion of convertible notes and debentures.

Where, even in good years, a relatively low rate is earned on net worth, and only a fraction of net profits, say, 40 to 50%, is declared in dividends, the resulting in-pocket return to bank stockholders is bound to be modest.

Bank Holding Companies

A company that owns or controls 25% or more of the voting shares of one or more banks, or otherwise controls their boards of directors, must register with the Board of Governors of the Federal Reserve System under the Bank Holding Company Act of 1956 as amended in 1970. The Board exercises broad regulatory control.

Legislation enacted in December 1970 placed one-bank holding companies under the regulation of the Federal Reserve Board, but holding companies are prohibited from controlling any large subsidiaries unrelated to banking unless they were acquired before June 30, 1968.

A number of bank holding companies have been formed in recent years. At the beginning of 1976, there were 1,821 bank holding companies (including one-bank companies) with 3,674 affiliated banks and 18,382 branches operating in all 50 states and the District of Columbia. The affiliated banks held $528 billion, or 67% of the commercial banking deposits in the United States.[4] The usual procedure has been for a bank to be reincorporated as a holding company, at which time it exchanges shares for those of the bank or banks to be controlled.

The holding company format has a number of financing advantages, including the issuance of commercial paper and longer-term notes and subordinated debentures. Perhaps the chief factor of interest to investors is a holding company's ability to engage in a number of approved activities that differ from and yet are "closely related to banking," namely, mortgage banking and loan servicing, investment and financial counselling, personal property and computer leasing, data processing service, title insurance, and credit insurance (for subsidiaries). Another appeal of the holding company is that it may be able to acquire a number of smaller banks and thus benefit from an expansion program.

The holding company provides many services for its bank affiliates which, while separately incorporated and enjoying legal autonomy, receive the benefit of examinations, operating and reporting advice, investment advice,

[4]Association of Bank Holding Companies, *Bank Holding Companies Today*. New York, 1976.

aid in recruiting and training personnel, consultation on loan policy, and tax guidance, from their parent.

Certain differences between bank stock and stock of bank holding companies are of interest. A number of the latter are listed on organized exchanges and enjoy better marketability. In 1976 market prices were about the same in relation to earnings, but dividend yields were generally lower than for bank stocks proper.

The general approach to the analysis of bank holding company stock is similar to that of operating bank stock, except that consolidated statements are used when available. (The SEC requires parent company statements only.) The important advantage of diversification lends a stability to the earnings of a bank holding company that many unit banks cannot enjoy. However, as nonbanking services become more important, the consolidated statements become increasingly difficult to compare with the statements of operating banks and with those of other holding company groups performing a different variety of functions.

Bank Stock Values, Prices, and Yields

The market value of bank stock is determined by the earnings and dividend record and prospects of the institution and the industry, by asset values underlying each share, by the general course of the stock market as a whole, and by the valuation placed on bank earnings in terms of the price-earnings ratio. Except in periods of generally low stock prices, bank stock has traditionally sold at 1 1/4 to 2 times book value (net worth divided by number of shares outstanding). The rationale is that book values are notoriously conservative and that the bank's assets are so liquid that book value is much more accurate a measure of realizable value than in the case of business corporations. In early 1973 the stocks of the large New York banks and bank holding companies sold as high as 2 times book value, but after the big decline on the market, at a little over 1 times at the end of 1974. The figure at the end of 1976 was about 1.3 times.

Bank stocks have lost much of their former premier status. Standard & Poor's series of New York banks and holding companies showed the following per share values.[5] Prices have been volatile, and the price-earning ratio now resembles that of industrial concerns.

	1970	1973	1976
Earnings	$4.02	$4.80	$5.86
Market price range	37–49	56–75	46–57
P/E ratio (range)	9.5–12.6	11.6–15.5	8.3–10.2
Dividends	$1.76	$1.96	$1.95
Dividend yield (range)	3.6–4.7%	2.6–3.5%	3.9–7.7%
Book value	$30.50	$36.77	$40.00 (est.)

[5]Standard & Poor's *Industry Surveys: Banking and Other Financial Services.*

Because banks generally retain a considerable portion of their earnings as a means of increasing their capital funds base, dividend yields tend to be modest. A bank does well to earn 13% on its net worth, and if its stock sells at 1.5 times book value, and if one-half of its earnings are declared in dividends, the resultant yield is 4.3%. However, a modest dividend yield is compensated for by regularity of dividends and appreciation possibilities. Several large metropolitan banks have had unbroken dividend records for over 100 years.

Investment Outlook

In the late 1960s and early 1970s, the banking industry embarked on an aggressive expansion program. The holding company device was the route that many banks followed into such disparate activities as aircraft and tanker leasing, data processing, real estate trusts, mortgage insurance, farm management, and Eurodollar financing. Through the practice of "liability management," banks leveraged their capital bases by floating new debt securities to support additional loans. In the process, their debt-to-equity ratios became strained.

At their 1973 peaks, prices of many bank stocks had doubled and many were selling at historically high price-earnings multiples. When bank stock prices and earnings failed to reflect the newly placed emphasis on growth, the industry became the object of a searching reappraisal, especially after the sharp recession of 1974–1975. Investors joined bank regulators and depositors in expressing concern about bank liquidity, capital adequacy, the quality of outstanding loans, and the large charge-offs in connection with real estate investment trust (REIT) loans and other troubled borrowers. The publicized failure in October 1974 of the Franklin National Bank, New York, and the government-sponsored reorganization of the U.S. National Bank (San Diego) were other sources of worry. The W.T. Grant Company entered bankruptcy owing banks $612 million. New York City's fiscal crisis created additional fears about bank holdings of that city's obligations. Some doubts arose concerning the eventual repayment of loans made to foreign borrowers, especially in some of the Third World countries.

The years 1975 and 1976 were a period of deemphasized growth as banks paid maximum attention to liquidity. Their identified problems were large. A good deal of the troubled real estate loans had to be written off. Others were in the process of being worked out either through a swapping of assets or renegotiation of terms. Banks have built up their reserves for possible losses by amounts considerably greater than actual charge-offs. Reflecting the improved situation, operating earnings for most banks in the final quarter of 1976 were 20 to 40% above those of the same period in 1975, and the year as a whole showed increased earnings of from 2 to 15% for the 10 largest holding companies. Bank stock indexes increased substantially more than those of the market as a whole.

The investor should not expect any unusual stability of price, any extraordinary yield, or any spectacular appreciation. Earnings on bank stocks as a group are largely determined by general economic conditions, especially the demand for business loans, the level of money rates, and the rates paid on deposits. The performance of individual banks reflects the degree of leverage employed, the liquidity, the types of loans and investments made, the ability to control expenses, and the variety of services rendered. Market prices reflect differences in asset values, earnings, and dividends. Bank stocks are attractive to investors who are content with modest but regular dividend returns and who are interested in the long-run appreciation possibilities derived from operation at high leverage. They must deal with the increasing volatility of share values.

Bank debentures Notes and debentures, many of them convertible, have become an important source of financing in recent years, especially for bank holding companies. In early 1977, over $5 billion were outstanding. These are subordinate to deposits with respect to claim on assets. Their purposes have been to provide junior capital to support an increased volume of loans, to avoid the sale of stock at relatively low price-earnings ratios, and to benefit from the lower cost of debt capital. In October 1977, the yields and prices of bank debentures showed a wide range, depending on the value of the conversion privilege. "Straight" long-term bonds brought 8.5% to 8.9% yield.

Within the bank group there is a considerable range of quality and of appeal. While bank shares and debentures are recognized, in general, as conservative equities and bonds their selection demands the same careful discrimination and judgment that are required of any other securities.

SAVINGS AND LOAN ASSOCIATIONS

Characteristics and Investment Appeal

The characteristics of savings and loan associations as thrift institutions are described in Chapter 5, and their basic functions and investment policies are indicated in Chapter 22. With this information as a background, this section is concerned with the investment attributes of the stock of associations that have "permanent" capital stock outstanding, and with holding companies. As of 1976, there were 732 of these associations, chartered in 21 states, holding $86.7 billion or 22% of total industry assets.

Investment appeal The shares of many larger associations are traded on local over-the-counter markets. But the main investment interest lies in the holding companies that control one or more large associations. Shares of a number of these are traded on the organized exchanges. California companies dominate the group.

The great growth of the industry was indicated in Chapter 5. The appeal of shares of the "permanent stock" companies and of holding companies rises and falls with the changing flow of savings, the ability to compete for savings with banks and with other thrift institutions, the outlook for construction—especially residential—the level of mortgage interest rates and their relation to other capital market yields, the influence of regulation, and the success of intra-industry competition. Location, economic conditions, growth of the territory served, and successful expansion in number of branches, are key factors in the appeal of individual companies. The successful concerns have developed a loan volume whose yields will adequately cover interest costs and operating expenses and produce an attractive return on equity.

Financial Analysis

Space does not permit a detailed discussion of the features of this complex industry, and the investor is advised to consult special sources for the details of analysis. The following discussion is confined to basic factors.

Liquidity and solvency   The consolidated balance sheet of United Financial Corporation of California, a holding company that controls Citizens Savings & Loan Association with its 74 offices, reveals certain important relationships.[6] Others have been indicated in Chapters 5 and 20.

TABLE 29-5   Condensed Consolidated Balance Sheet, United Financial Corporation of California and Subsidiaries, 1976 (in thousands of dollars)

	Amount	Per Cent
Assets		
Cash items	$ 18,900	0.9%
Government and other securities (at cost)	101,001	5.0
Loans (net)	1,784,996	88.8
Real estate held for investment and sale (net)	25,529	1.3
Stock of Federal Home Loan Bank	13,633	0.7
Office premises, etc. (net)	22,581	1.1
Other assets	43,325	2.2
Total assets	$2,009,965	100.0%
Liabilities and Stockholders' Equity		
Savings accounts	$1,677,208	83.4%
Borrowings from Federal Home Loan Bank	155,922	7.8
Other liabilities	43,254	2.2
Total liabilities	$1,876,384	93.4%
Common stock and additional capital	25,110	1.2%
Retained earnings	111,127	5.5
Reaquired stock	(2,656)	−0.1
Total stockholders' equity	133,581	6.6%
Total liabilities and equity	$2,009,965	100.0%

[6]The combined balance sheet of all savings and loan associations, mutual and stock, is found in Chapter 5.

Key balance sheet ratios include:

Liquidity:
    Cash and Governments/deposits or total assets
    Liquid and other legal investments/deposits or total assets.
Solvency:
    Mortgage loans/total assets
    Real estate owned (after foreclosure) plus loans to facilitate (on transfer of
        foreclosed property)/total mortgages
    Borrowings (mainly from FHLB)/deposits
    Net worth/deposits and borrowings, or total assets
    Net worth/average assets ("equity multiplier")

Analysis of earnings   The consolidated earnings statement of United
Financial Corporation of California and subsidiaries is shown in Table 29-6.

TABLE 29-6   Consolidated Statement of Operations, United
Financial Corporation of California and Subsidiaries, 1976
(in thousands of dollars)

	Amount	Per Cent
Income		
Interest on real estate loans	$133,776,000	82.6%
Interest on consumer loans	3,849,000	2.4
Loan origination and other fees	11,402,000	7.0
Income on investments	9,312,000	5.7
Income from sale of property held for investment	2,914,000	2.0
Other income	723,000	0.3
Total income	$161,976,000	100.0%
Expense		
Interest on savings accounts	$ 98,044,000	60.5%
Interest on borrowings	12,846,000	7.9
Provision for losses	1,300,000	0.8
General and administrative	27,769,000	17.1
	$139,959,000	86.4%
Earnings before income taxes	22,017,000	13.6%
Income taxes	7,879,000	4.9
Net earnings	$ 14,138,000	8 7%

A number of important relationships for the industry have been indicated in
Chapters 5 and 21. Key income statement ratios include:

Operations:
    Total revenue/(average) assets (asset utilization)
    Mortgage loan interest/revenues
    Operating expenses/revenues
    Interest expense/revenues
    Gains or losses/revenues
    Net income/revenues

Return on investment:
>   Net income before (and after) taxes/(average) assets
>   Net income/(average) net worth

The return on net worth is, of course, a crucial figure. It is interesting to note the several components that are involved, each of which deserves separate study. They include certain of the ratios shown above. The following relationships produce the 8% return in net worth for the industry as a whole for the year 1975, in contrast to over 12% in 1973–1974.[7] The figure rose to more than 11% in 1976.

Asset Utilization		Net Income Margin		Return on Assets		Equity Multiplier		Return on Net Worth
8.20%	×	7.86%	=	0.64%	×	17.6	=	11.3%

Investment Record and Outlook

Savings and loan stocks, reflecting the influences mentioned earlier, have had a volatile record of earnings and market price. The latter is a function of both changing earnings and a changing price-earnings multiplier. The earnings per share of Standard & Poor's index of savings and loan holding company stocks rose slightly from 1974 to 1975, but increased very substantially in 1976 from increased loan volume at high yields. But the multiplier, which had been as high as 27 in 1968, fell from 7 in 1974 to 4.75 in 1975 when the housing outlook was dismal. This sent the market price per share from as high as $37 1/2 in 1973 to as low as $9 toward the end of 1974. In 1976, increases in both earnings and multiplier sent the price to $22 at the end of the year,[8] and the average market price of nine leading holding companies rose over 70%, in contrast to a 35% rise in the Standard & Poor's index.

Dividends on savings and loan stocks are miniscule. A substantial portion of earnings must be retained in the form of loss reserves. Although part of the net worth, these cannot be declared as dividends. In 1976 the average yield was only 2.5%.

Future growth and profitability of savings and loan associations are dependent on several variables. Most important is the association's continued ability to attract, retain, and invest savings productively. In the late 1960s and early 1970s, asset expansion was slowed by increased bank competition, restrictive monetary policies, and particularly by the flow of savings out of financial institutions. This process, known as disintermediation, occurs when savers, attracted by higher interest rates elsewhere, withdraw their funds. In both 1975 and 1976, savings flowed back (reintermediation), raising assets to new highs. In 1976, the net savings gain was a record $34.3 billion, an increase of 17% over 1975. The key factor in an analysis of a

[7] U.S. League of Savings Associations, *Savings and Loan Fact Book,* 1977, p. 93.
[8] Standard & Poor's *Industry Surveys, Banking and Other Financial Services.*

savings and loan stock is the ability to predict whether savings funds can continue to be employed profitably in an expanding portfolio.

The problems of watching the shifting forces of savings flows, housing construction, mortgage yields, and costs of savings, are difficult for the average individual investor. Institutions are better equipped to analyze savings and loan stocks.

Special Sources of Information

COMMERCIAL BANKS:

Periodicals, including *Federal Reserve Bulletin* and monthly bank bulletins mentioned above; bank activities, legislation, stock quotations in daily *American Banker; Banking* (the official magazine of the American Bankers Association); *Bankers Monthly; Burroughs Clearing House* (Burroughs Corporation, monthly); *Trusts and Estates* (monthly); *The Trust Bulletin* (monthly).

Annual reports of the U.S. Comptroller of the Currency (U.S. Treasury Department), the Federal Deposit Insurance Corporation, and state banking departments. Also the Corporation's *Bank Operating Statistics*, annually.

Federal Reserve System annual reports and *Assets and Liabilities of All Banks in the United States* (monthly), *Member Bank Call Report*, and *Federal Reserve Chart Book on Financial and Business Statistics* (monthly, with annual Historical Chart Book).

Moody's Manual of Investments, Bank and Finance, and current supplements.

Brochures on bank stocks issued periodically by investment houses, such as *Bank Stock Quarterly*, M. A. Shapiro & Co., New York.

Special investment services such as Standard & Poor's *Industry Surveys, Banking and Other Financial Services*.

SAVINGS AND LOAN ASSOCIATIONS:

Savings and Loan News (monthly).

Annual reports, *Source Book* (annually), and *Journal* (monthly), published by the Federal Home Loan Bank Board.

Annual reports of the Federal Savings and Loan Insurance Corporation.

Annual reports of the state building and loan commissioners.

Savings and Loan Fact Book, published annually by the United States League of Savings Associations.

Reports of investment services such as Standard & Poor's. (See above.)

Brochures issued by brokerage and investment banking firms.

REFERENCES

ASSOCIATION OF REGISTERED BANK HOLDING COMPANIES, *The Registered Bank Holding Company*, rev. ed. Washington, D.C., 1973.

———, *Bank Holding Companies Today*. Washington, D.C., 1975.

Bowyer, J. W., Jr., *Investment Analysis and Management*, 4th ed., Chapter 15. Homewood, Ill.: Richard D. Irwin, Inc., 1972.

Comparative Analysis of Major Banks and Bank Holding Companies. New York: Keefe, Bruyette & Woods, Inc., 1972.

Edwards, F. R., *Concentration and Competition in Commercial Banking: A Statistical Study*. Boston: Federal Reserve Bank of Boston, 1964.

Ernst and Ernst, *Financial Reporting Trends: Banking*. Cleveland, Ohio, 1975.

Garcia, F. L., *How to Analyze a Bank Statement*, 5th ed. Boston: Bankers Publishing Company, 1974.

Keefe Bank Stock Manual. New York: Keefe, Bruyette & Woods, Inc., annually.

Kennedy, R. D., and S. Y. McMullen, *Financial Statements*, 6th ed., Chapters 26, 27. Homewood, Ill.: Richard D. Irwin, Inc., 1973.

Levine, S. N., ed., *Financial Analyst's Handbook*, Vol. II, Chapter 7. Homewood, Ill.: Dow Jones-Irwin, Inc., 1975.

Prochnow, H. V., ed., *The One-Bank Holding Company*. Chicago: Rand McNally & Company, 1969.

Robinson, R. I., *The Management of Bank Funds*, 2nd ed. New York: McGraw-Hill, Inc., 1962.

Smith, K. V., and D. K. Eiteman, *Essentials of Investing*, Chapter 14. Homewood, Ill.: Richard D. Irwin, Inc., 1974.

Van Horne, J. C., and R. C. Helwig, *The Valuation of Small Bank Stocks*. East Lansing, Mich.: Graduate School of Business Administration, Michigan State University, 1966.

See also References, Chapters 5, 21.

Stocks of
Insurance Companies

SCOPE: This chapter discusses the stocks issued by stock insurance companies. The order of discussion is: (1) scope of the insurance industry. (2) property-liability companies, (3) life insurance stocks, (4) the market for insurance stocks, and (5) special sources of information.

Scope of the Industry

The insurance business consists of three main categories—life, property and liability, and health and accident. The division of these three types among companies is becoming less and less clear-cut as a result of mergers and acquisitions to form multiline companies, and because the health business not done by such organizations as Blue Cross and Blue Shield is almost entirely written by either life or property-liability companies.[1]

In addition, a number of company groups have been formed that involve parent and holding companies and subsidiaries offering life and property-casualty insurance and a variety of other services such as real estate and mortgage management, variable annuities, mutual funds, computer services, title insurance, and others. The consolidated statements of these groups, therefore, include a mixture of activities. The holding company structure provides greater diversification of services, income, and financial flexibility through the use of senior securities.

Life insurance companies write life insurance, annuity, and health contracts, and some have acquired affiliates in the property insurance field or are members of a group including property and liability companies. Of the 1773 life insurance companies in the United States at the beginning of 1977, about 8% were mutual companies, owned by their policyholders, and 92% were stock companies. Mutual companies accounted for slightly over one-half of total life insurance in force and about two-thirds of total assets.

---

[1]Of the $27.8 billion in health insurance benefits paid in 1974, $13.6 billion were provided by insurance companies. The balance was paid by Blue Cross, Blue Shield, and independent plans. See 1975–1976 *Source Book of Health Insurance* (New York: Health Insurance Institute).

In the property-liability insurance field, stock companies write about 71% of the premiums and own 74% of total assets. However, many are owned by life insurance, general holding, and conglomerate companies. Where several companies are controlled by a leading insurance corporation, the members of the "group" or "fleet" may each specialize in a particular type of fire or casualty business.

Data on the life insurance industry have already been presented in Chapters 4 and 22. Table 30-1 shows the relative importance of the two major categories of *stock* companies in 1975.

TABLE 30-1 Comparison of Stock Insurance Companies, 1975 (dollars in billions)

	Life	Property-Liability
Number of stock companies	1,647	909
Total assets	$ 104	$ 70
Premiums written	$ 36	$ 36
Insurance in force	$1,140	—

Sources: American Council of Life Insurance, *Life Insurance Fact Book 1976.* (New York: The Council, 1976) ; *Best's Aggregates and Averages: Property-Liability*, 37th ed. (Oldwick, N.J.: A. M. Best Company, Inc., 1976).

Property-Liability Companies

Types of risks covered Fire and casualty companies are now described as property-liability companies in recognition that various types of protection are often combined now in individual policies or written by the same companies.[2] The relative importance of the various types, in terms of net premiums written by stock companies, is indicated by the data in Table 30-2.

Functions and characteristics The principal business is that of writing contracts under which fire and other risks are insured; this underwriting activity may or may not contribute anything to the net profits. In addition, the company invests funds representing capital, surplus, and premiums collected in advance on policies that run from one to five years. It expects to net a modest return on these investments, and may achieve a capital gain on its common stock holdings. The income and dividend position of the stockholder is thus affected by the company's ability to earn a sufficient premium income to cover the outlays associated with underwriting—commissions, administrative expenses, and losses—and to produce a respectable net return on investments. The solvency position of the stockholder is determined by the value and liquidity of the assets—chiefly the investment portfolio—and the relation of the capital funds to liabilities (reserves).

[2]For information on the structure and regulation of the property-liability industry see *Institutional Investor Study Report of the Securities and Exchange Commission*, Chapter VI. 92nd Congress, 1st Session, House Document No. 92–64, Washington: U.S. Government Printing Office, 1971.

TABLE 30-2   Net Premiums, Stock Property-Liability Companies, 1975 (in millions of dollars)

	Amount	Per Cent
Auto liability	$ 8,223	23.1%
Auto physical damage	4,678	13.1
Workmen's compensation	4,634	13.0
Homeowners' multiperil	3,650	10.2
Fire and allied lines	2,949	8.3
Commercial multiperil	2,741	7.7
Accident and health	1,469	4.1
Miscellaneous liability	3,336	9.4
Marine	1,886	5.3
Fidelity and surety	758	2.1
All other	1,283	3.7
Total	$35,607	100.0%

Source: Best's Averages & Aggregates: Property-Liability, 37th ed. (Oldwick, N.J.: A. M. Best Company, 1976).

The profitable operation of underwriting is affected by the control of expenses and the premiums charged for and the losses charged to underwriting income. The property insurance business has a marked cyclical variation. Premium income rises with business prosperity, population, and the general price level. Losses are affected not only by ordinary and disaster burnings, hurricanes, and other hazards, but also by the increased moral risk during depression periods. In addition, during periods of rising prices, the costs of restoring insured property rise, and hence a squeeze is placed on income, collected as much as five years in advance. Premiums are established on the basis of the previous experience of the more efficient companies and are calculated for the majority of fire companies by the Board of Underwriters, a cooperative organization.[3]

The liability lines do not show the same degree of cyclical influence. The rates and loss trends of automobile liability, workmen's compensation, surety, and accident and health lines are affected by general economic conditions and special factors bearing on each segment of the business.

The results of the investment activity of the business are determined by the portfolio and the variations in market value of the securities held. Although there is considerably less technical leverage than in the case of the commercial bank, the net gain from investing can be magnified considerably, depending on the relative importance of owners' investment to liabilities.

---

[3]Fire losses in the United States, as reported by the National Board of Fire Underwriters, have run as follows:

Aggregate Fire Losses (in millions of dollars)

1950	$ 648	1971	$2,316
1955	885	1972	2,304
1960	1,107	1973	2,639
1965	1,456	1974	3,190
1970	2,264	1975	3,560

Sources: The Spectator; Standard & Poor's Industry Surveys, Insurance.

Property and liability insurance companies are examined and regulated by state authorities with the aim of assuring solvency and the soundness and adequacy of policy forms. Regulation of investment permits a substantial selection of common stocks. The result is that the company may obtain a higher, or more likely today, a lower current return on its portfolio than may the commercial bank, but it may also enjoy market price appreciation. It is, consequently, likely to show greater growth, and also, greater variations in liquidating value.

Investment policy Property-liability companies have considerable freedom of choice above the minimum of cash or high-grade bonds required. Although regulations vary from state to state, in general, funds equal to minimum required capital must be invested in U.S. Government bonds and/or approved mortgages; funds equal to the unearned premium and the loss reserves must be invested in cash, government, and/or approved corporate bond issues. The remaining funds may be invested in both bonds *and stocks*, as long as the issuers are solvent and have maintained adequate interest and dividend records. Common stock and surplus may be invested 100% in equities if reserves are fully backed by high-grade investments, if the "underwriting exposure" (as measured by the rate of net premiums written in relation to stockholders' equity) is low, and if the equity is large in relation to reserves.

Within the legal limits, the investment portfolios differ considerably. Since liquidity is of prime importance, funds equal to policyholders' claims (reserves) are held in the form of cash and bonds. But the stockholders' equity may be represented in one company by bonds alone, in another company by common stocks. The former would enjoy greater stability of income and less variation in market value; the latter, if the stocks were properly diversified, would (under ideal conditions) enjoy greater possible appreciation in market value, at the risk of stock market fluctuations. The investor in insurance company stocks should insist that companies with below-average capital funds in relation to insurance risks show substantial conservatism in their investment portfolios.

The distribution of the investments of all stock property-liability companies in 1975 is indicated in Table 30-4. Individual companies differ from the group as a whole. For example, common stocks may represent from 20 to 70% of a portfolio.

Insurance companies are required to file annual balance sheet and income statements with state insurance departments. These are available to the public; together with the annual report to stockholders, which includes a list of security investments, they provide adequate financial information. The use of uniform accounting practices makes for easier comparison of different companies than in the case of industrial concerns. One must now use consolidated statements in the analysis of most of the larger concerns, which have a number of subsidiaries in their "fleet." Group data on the industry are available in such services as *Best's* annual volumes, and in insurance trade journals and special studies by dealers specializing in insurance stocks.

Income statement   The income statement includes two or three sections or exhibits: underwriting, investment, and sometimes, surplus. Table 30-3 shows the aggregates for 904 *stock* property-liability companies in the United States for 1975, when underwriting losses were very substantial. The loss-plus-expense ratio was expected to decline somewhat in 1976, but remain above 100%.

TABLE 30-3   Combined Income Statement of Stock
Property-Liability Companies, 1975
(Condensed) (in millions of dollars)

Underwriting Account	
Premiums written	$35,643.8
Increase in unearned premium reserve	1,050.1
Premiums earned	$34,593.7
Losses and adj. expenses incurred	27,197.9
Expenses incurred	10,276.0
Underwriting loss	($2,880.2)
Investment Account	
Investment income	$ 3,347.2
Investment expenses	204.4
Net investment income	$ 3,142.8
Profit on sale of investments	127.5
Net investment profit	$ 3,270.3
Unrealized appreciation in book value of investments	3,298.7
Investment gain	$ 6,569.0

Source: Best's Aggregates & Averages: Property-Liability, 37th ed. (Oldwick, N.J.: A. M. Best Company, 1976).

Premiums written is the amount of premiums received on policies issued during the year less return and reinsurance premiums. *Premiums earned* is the result of deducting the increase in the unearned premium reserve from premiums written. *Underwriting profit* is derived by deducting losses and underwriting expenses—mainly acquisition costs and commissions—incurred during the year. It represents the portion of net premiums written that is applicable to the proportion of premium term that expired during the year. Since the expenses of a rising volume of business must be met immediately, and the larger premium volume is fully earned only in the future, a paradoxical situation is presented in which low underwriting profits or even losses may be reported in periods of expanding volume, and high underwriting profits in a period of declining premiums written. After heavy losses in 1963–1965, 1966–1967 showed modest underwriting profits. The years 1968–1969 again showed an unhappy underwriting experience. Not only did an exceptionally large number of catastrophies occur, but rates on such large lines as automobile and home coverage insurance were inadequate. Some improvement showed in late 1970, but again, heavy storm losses and increasing accident claims provided a setback to earnings, and the industry as a whole did little better than break even. Fortunately, the industry's expense ratio was reduced, and much improvement was evident in 1971–1972 as a result of higher rates and lower losses. But in 1973–1975 high costs again produced substantial underwriting losses. The year 1976 showed some improvement.

In 1969 pressure from professional accounting associations that insurance companies should apply "generally accepted accounting principles," led a number of companies to change their reports to stockholders. "Acquisition costs" are now amortized against unearned premiums over the life of the policies, so that current underwriting profit is ordinarily increased, as are income taxes.[4]

The *net investment income* consists of the receipts from securities and other assets less investment expenses consisting of real estate repairs, expenses, and depreciation, and expenses of administration of the portfolio. To this figure is added actual gain (or loss) from the sale, redemption, or maturity of investments, to produce the *net investment profit* for the year. The *investment gain* includes unrealized gains (or losses) on investments.

Book appreciation in securities is reported as additional investment income on official statements, but is credited directly to contingency reserves or to surplus in many of the companies' reports to stockholders. Where shown as income (or loss), the change in portfolio value introduces an element that makes reported investment results unstable and to a certain extent unreliable.

Net operating earnings is another useful figure (not shown in Table 30-3). It is the total of net underwriting profit and net investment income.

The surplus exhibit, included in official statements but sometimes omitted from annual reports, shows the net change in surplus arising from underwriting and investment profits less income taxes, dividends, and any appropriations to special reserves.

Balance sheet   Table 30-4 shows the combined balance sheet of the 909 *stock* companies in the United States at the end of 1975. The assets of a property and liability insurance company include cash, securities (U.S. Government, municipal, and corporate bonds, and preferred and common stocks), mortgages, collateral loans, real estate, agents' balances (premiums in course of collection), and miscellaneous items. The proportions of the various items, notably cash and different kinds of securities, depend on the state regulations governing investments, the types of insurance written, and the investment policies of the company. Because their policies are written for one year only, and because their premium volume is three times as large as that of a fire company in relation to stockholders' equity, making the risk exposure high, the casualty companies and multiple-line companies with a large casualty business must follow a much more conservative investment policy. This shows up in the smaller percentage of common stock in their investment portfolios.

General indications of major investment policies of stock companies in the aggregate, 1965–1975, have been: increasing interest in tax-free munici-

---

[4]An adjustment for taxes is used by some analysts, namely, a deduction of the capital gains rate on unrealized appreciation of portfolio value.

TABLE 30-4 Combined Balance Sheet of Stock Property-Liability Companies, December 31, 1975 (in millions of dollars)

	Amount	Per Cent of Total
Admitted Assets		
Cash	$ 1,251.9	1.8%
U.S. Govt. and agency bonds	5,488.4	7.9
Municipal (including revenue) bonds	23,521.6	33.7
Corporate bonds	8,448.9	12.2
Common stocks	16,455.3	23.6
Preferred stocks	2,474.1	3.5
Mortgages	151.6	.2
Real estate	869.0	1.3
Premium balances	6,080.1	8.7
Other assets	4,974.6	7.1
Total admitted assets	$69,715.5	100.0%
Liabilities		
Unearned premiums	$15,944.7	22.9%
Losses and adjustment expenses	29,292.1	42.0
Accrued commissions, taxes, etc.	974.7	1.4
Federal income taxes	171.6	0.2
Funds held under reinsurance treaties	1,071.2	1.5
Other liabilities	3,816.0	5.5
Voluntary reserves	1,361.2	2.0
Capital	2,234.0	3.2
Surplus	14,850.0	21.3
Total liabilities	$69,715.5	100.0%

Source: Best's Aggregates & Averages: Property-Liability, 37th ed. (Oldwick, N.J.: A. M. Best Company, 1976).

pal bonds (now about one third of assets); an increase in holdings of corporate bonds (to 12% of assets); and a decline in the percentage of common stocks to total assets (from 39 to 24%) as their prices and yields declined and as those of other securities increased. Equities have lost much of their value as an inflation hedge against the rising costs of repair and replacement involved in claims.

As indicated previously, individual property-liability insurance companies differ considerably with respect to the character of their portfolios. In general, the companies have maintained adequate liquidity through their holdings of cash and marketable securities. The need for marketability to meet sudden large losses explains the small interest in real estate and mortgage loans. Bonds are carried on the officially reported balance sheet at their amortized value, and stocks and nonamortizable bonds at the market value. The "convention value" of the portfolio differs somewhat, therefore, from the actual market value at the year-end. In the report to stockholders, all securities may be carried at market values as of the date of the balance sheet.

The total assets of the company appear on the published statement as *total admitted assets*, to include only those in accord with state law. The actual assets of a company may exceed its admissible assets by a small percentage.

The chief debts of the property-liability insurance company consist of reserves. The reserve for unearned premiums represents the unearned portion of the full premium collected, computed *pro rata* for the unexpired term of all policies outstanding. It is the amount that would have to be returned to the policyholders if all policies were cancelled or terminated.

Other liabilities are often designated as *reserves*. Those providing for unpaid losses and claims and incurred expenses are unique to the insurance business. Voluntary reserves are the part of the net worth earmarked for contingencies.

The total net worth, consisting of capital, surplus, and any voluntary reserves, is designated in the insurance business as *policyholders' surplus*.

Statement analysis   In selecting shares in property-liability insurance companies, the investor should be satisfied that the company is large and growing and that, either directly or through subsidiaries, it does a diversified business in a variety of fire and casualty lines. He then turns to an analysis of its statements to determine its safety, performance, and earning power in relation to the market price and yield available.

MEASURES OF SAFETY   While the ability to meet claims and losses is most important to the policyholder, it is also important to the stockholder seeking stability of asset values and earnings. The first measure of safety is the composition of the assets. A very conservative portfolio brings in lower investment income, but through careful selection of risks this may be offset by a favorable loss record.

A substantial portion of the stockholders' equity can safely be invested in common stocks, provided the company is not operating at too high a degree of leverage, as measured by the relation of the net worth to debt (reserves) or to total assets. Normally, total net worth (not including equity in the unearned premium reserve) should exceed 25% of total assets, and the more conservative companies show a ratio of much more. In a company that is very conservatively financed with respect to both type of investments and type of capital structure, a ratio of common stock assets to total assets of one fourth and a ratio of net worth to total assets of one quarter combine to produce a ratio of common stock assets to net worth of 100%. For the whole group of companies, this ratio stood at 90% at the end of 1975. Another more specific test relates *investment risk* and *underwriting risk*. The former is measured by the ratio of cash items and bonds owned to reserves, together with the ratio of common stocks owned to capital and surplus. The latter is measured by the ratio of net premiums written to capital and surplus. The higher the underwriting exposure, the greater the emphasis on conservative investments.

MEASURES OF OPERATIONS AND PROFITABILITY   Performance with respect to underwriting activities is measured by examining four ratios over a period of years: (1) The *loss ratio*, or ratio of losses and loss-adjustment expenses incurred to net premiums *earned*, indicates the company's ability to select risks. (2) The *expense ratio*, or ratio of underwriting expenses (advertising, commissions, and other expenses associated with acquiring new business) to premiums *written*, indicates efficiency in writing new business. If the ratio is high, owing to an unusually careful investigation of risks, it should be offset by a low loss ratio. If it is low, the loss ratio is likely to be high. Expenses may also be related to premiums earned to indicate their effect on the reported statutory underwriting results. (3) The *loss-plus-expense ratio* combines the previous two ratios. Where this is 100%, the company is just breaking even on its underwriting activities before "adding back" a portion of the unearned premium reserve. But even if this is the case, the company has had the use of funds representing premiums paid in advance, and hence its underwriting activities have contributed to earnings through the medium of investment income. (4) The *underwriting profit margin* is the ratio of underwriting profits or loss to premiums earned and indicates the extent to which underwriting activities are contributing directly to earnings.

Table 30-5 shows the underwriting experience of the property-liability industry, 1965–1976. Net underwriting losses reached their peak in 1965. A decreasing loss ratio, accompanied by a somewhat lower expense ratio, produced modest profits in 1966–1967. Losses increased in 1968–1969 due to the factors explained previously, but 1970–1972 showed some improvement. Large losses followed in 1973–1975 however. The year 1976 showed some improvement, and profits were expected in 1977.

TABLE 30-5   Loss Experience of Property-Liability Companies, 1965–1976

	1965	1968	1970	1972	1974	1975	1976
Losses to premiums earned	69.2%	68.8%	69.7%	66.0%	75.3%	78.8%	75.0%
Expenses to premiums written	32.7	31.2	29.6	29.4	29.7	28.7	27.3
Loss-plus-expense ratio	101.9	100.0	109.3	95.4	105.0	107.5	102.3
Underwriting profit (loss) margin	(3.1)	(1.1)	(.7)	3.5	(5.6)	(8.4)	*a*

*a*Not available.

Sources: Bests' Averages & Aggregates: Property-Liability, 37th ed. (Oldwick, N.J.: A. M. Best Company, 1976); Standard & Poor's *Industry Surveys, Insurance.*

Individual companies show a considerable range of profitability depending on the types of business written and on management competence. The investor should carefully check the types of business written by a company or group, their relative importance, their loss record, and any indications of change. For instance, in 1975 the combined loss-expense ratio was the highest, and the underwriting profit the lowest, on homeowners' multiperil and on automobile liability; the ratio was the lowest and the underwriting profit the highest on fire, marine, burglary, and theft.

The returns from the *investment* activity of the company are shown by the ratio of net investment income to the value of the investment portfolio, without considering realized or unrealized securities appreciation.[5] For all

[5]In the financial statements, bonds are carried at their amortized values and stocks at market value.

fire and casualty companies as a group, the rate has varied between 4 and 5% in the early 1970s, and was 5.3% in 1975. This is a modest return and indicates general conservativeness in investment policy. It also reflects the low yields on common stocks. In 1975, realized and unrealized gains in portfolio value produced an additional 5.3% on average portfolio value. Although such gains cannot be relied on, they add a special appeal to fire and casualty stocks and in some years help to offset bad underwriting results.

Net investment income can be computed on a per-share basis for comparative purposes. It may also be used as the basis for showing the dividend payout ratio.

MEASURES OF ASSET VALUE   Asset value per share is especially significant in the case of insurance stocks because it approximates the realizable value at the reporting date; this is because the company is required to report its holdings of stock at market value close to the year-end, and because the book or amortized value of bonds is not too different from their market value. On published statements to stockholders, both bonds and stocks owned may be carried at market value as of December 31 instead of at "convention value." In either case, net asset value per share in insurance companies' statements is much closer to reality than in those of business corporations.

The net asset value or book value per share is calculated by dividing capital stock, surplus, and surplus reserves by the number of shares outstanding. The amount is affected by the method by which the portfolio is valued on the balance sheet.

Stock values, prices, dividends, and yields   The market value of the stock of a property-liability insurance company is affected by (1) its liquidating value; (2) its earnings record and prospects, in both amount and stability; (3) its dividend policy; and (4) the condition of the stock market as a whole. In early 1977, the majority of the stocks were selling between 1 and 2 times equity value, although earlier, in periods of generally depressed stock markets, most of them had sold at substantial discounts. They were yielding very low returns on market price—in many cases below 2%—so that their chief appeal had to lie in possible price appreciation. Such low yields reflected the modest percentage of investment income distributed, and the generally high level of stock prices.

When the investor buys the stock of an insurance company below liquidating value, he is purchasing a portion of a securities portfolio at a discount. But since the company is not going to liquidate, the market value is influenced more by earnings and dividends. A low market price in relation to asset value does not suggest a bargain unless profitable underwriting is in prospect for the company.

Because of mergers and acquisitions and the growth of multiline and holding company groups, few "straight" property-liability companies remain. The analytical task becomes difficult where consolidated statements combine different types of insurance and, in some cases, a variety of other services. The investor must often rely primarily on final results: per-share earnings and dividends, price-earnings ratios, dividend yield, and price performance.

He cannot appraise the separate activities unless the company chooses to publish separate information on these lines. Fortunately, a number of companies do so.

Outlook for property-liability companies   The property-liability insurance industry is beset with many problems. Long-range profitability is dependent on finding solutions to many unresolved questions, among the principal of which are:

The compelling need to improve underwriting profitability. In 1974–1975, the industry (including multiple-line) suffered a loss of over $6 billion in underwriting activities, principally in automobile, malpractice, and product liability, and workmen's compensation coverage. Through sharply increased rates and more selective scrutiny of new business, underwriting results for most of the industry began to improve in 1976.

Inflation has exerted a devastating influence on settlement costs. The property-liability insurance company must set the price of its product before all costs can be determined. As a result, higher prices often result in higher settlement costs. Some claims filed with insurance companies have been rising much faster than the insurance premiums covering such bills. The high inflation of the past few years has sent damage claims soaring, and the underwriting results of many companies have been undermined in the process.

The industry faces a problem of capital adequacy. As we have seen, property liability risk exposure is a function of the volume of premiums written and the firm's common stock holdings in relation to net worth. The industry's capital base is not substantial enough to support the current volume of business. Estimates ranging from $20 to $35 billion of additional capital will be needed by 1985 to support an increase of premiums to $140 billion. Unless the industry can demonstrate a continuing ability to improve its overall profitability, investors will not favor it, although in individual years, such as 1976, its fortunes may improve.

Life Insurance Stocks

Nature of earnings   In computing the premiums to be charged for life insurance policies, three basic assumptions are involved: (1) mortality experience at different ages, based on conservative mortality tables; (2) a rate of earnings on that portion of the premium that represents the addition to the policy reserve and is invested, mainly in securities and mortgages; and (3) a percentage of the premium designed to cover operating expenses— the "office load." Thus, profits are derived from (1) the ratio of actual mortality experience to that assumed in the premium calculation, (2) the interest earned in excess of the amount assumed in the premium calculation, and (3) any savings resulting from operations conducted at a lesser expense than was allowed for in the premiums collected. (*Growth* in profits is a function of these factors and of the volume and types of policies written.) The first of these has been very favorable over the past two or three decades, with the trend toward lower infant mortality and greater adult longevity. By holding the assumed interest rates on new policies to 3 to 3 1/2% the companies have been able to enjoy, in recent years, an increasing net investment income derived from an increasing actual rate of interest earned, and have shared the returns with policyholders or stockholders. And the introduction of cost-saving devices and operations has kept the ratio of total expenses to operating income remarkably steady.

Investment characteristics   In the postwar period the life insurance industry has had a very substantial growth as revealed by Table 30-6. Many reasons explain this growth and its likely continuation: general growth of the economy, general increase in population, increase in young population and young families, increase in the percentage of personal income spent on insurance, decline in net premium cost (after participating dividends), introduction of new forms of policies such as the family-plan package, aggressive marketing, and increase in number of companies from 473 at the end of 1945 to 1,773 at the end of 1976. The last figure reflects the ease of entrance into the business and the possibilities of large profits to the shareholders of new stock companies.

TABLE 30-6   Growth of Life Insurance Industry, 1955–1976
(in billions of dollars)

	1955	1960	1965	1970	1976
Gross National Product	$399.3	$ 506.0	$ 688.1	$ 982.4	$1,691.6
Life insurance in force	372.3	586.4	900.5	1,402.1	2,530.8
Life insurance purchases	48.4	74.4	142.2	193.1	319.7[a]
Premium receipts	12.5	17.4	24.6	36.8	66.8
Investment income	2.8	4.3	6.8	10.1	18.8
Total assets	90.4	119.6	158.9	207.3	321.6
Disposable personal income per family	$5,100	$ 6,000	$ 7,700	$10,100	$15,200
Life insurance per family	6,900	10,200	14,600	21,800	30,100

[a]1975.

Sources: American Council of Life Insurance, *Life Insurance Fact Book* (New York: The Council, 1976); U.S. Department of Commerce, Bureau of the Census, *Statistical Abstract of the United States,* 1976.

The growth of the industry in terms of volume of business and assets has been accompanied by a steady growth in earnings. Even the threat of inflation, which makes each dollar of contracts less valuable, has encouraged increases in coverage as an offsetting factor.

Life insurance is not only a rapidly growing industry, but has also been outstandingly stable, as measured by the resistance to cyclical forces of new premiums written, insurance in force, and total income. Except for 1932 and 1933, life insurance in force has increased yearly since 1900.

The investment practices of life insurance companies and their regulation have been discussed in Chapter 22. While in the long run the overall rate of earnings on investments varies with the conditions of the capital market (in addition to shifts in investment policy), a considerable lag exists between falling or rising money rates and investment earnings, because the investments are mainly long term and held to maturity. Thus, only *new* additions to the portfolio are acquired at higher or lower yields. In the meantime any spread between the assumed rate written into premium calculation and the actual rate earned tends to be perpetuated.

Other factors favoring the industry from the investment standpoint include lack of labor problems, inventory problems, and no threat of overcapacity. In addition, it has enjoyed special income tax treatment. In 1959 a new Federal tax law was passed. The taxable portion of investment income (not required to maintain policy reserves) is determined on an individual company basis; it involves the application to reserves of an interest rate representing the average earning rate of each company in the current and four prior years. Taxable income also includes one-half of underwriting profits; the remaining half is taxable only to the extent distributed to stockholders. Federal taxes amount to about 25% of net operating profits. Net long-term capital gains are taxable at the regular corporate rate.

We are concerned here with the analysis and evaluation of the shares of stock life insurance companies, which comprise 90% of the firms but which account for about half of the life insurance in force in the United States and about 35% of industry assets.

Income statement The income statement of a stock company differs substantially from that of an industrial corporation. Table 30-7 shows a condensed (and somewhat rearranged) statement of a hypothetical company.

Some of the income statement items need an explanation. *Supplementary contracts* are agreements by which the company retains the cash sum payable under a policy and makes payments in accordance with the settlement options chosen. Net investment income is the return from securities, mortgages, and other portfolio investments, less investment expenses and taxes. Net gain after income taxes is not really a true profit figure, since it stems in part from assumptions as to mortality, interest rates, and expense loading. A gain is reported only when mortality is less, expenses less, and interest earnings greater than assumed in computing premiums. But even modest savings in these respects, compounded through the years by reinvestment, can add materially to stockholders' earnings. The "gain" does, however, indicate protection against adverse results that differ from these assumptions, and may be used to help calculate the per-share results.

In the statement in Table 30-7, premium income from life, annuity, and health insurance policies represented 77% of total income, and net investment income 23%. In 1975 the latter (before income taxes) was 6.7% on mean invested assets for all life insurance companies. For our hypothetical company, the figure was about the same. Such a high rate is very profitable because of the much lower assumed rates in most insurance and annuity policies at which reserves must be compounded.

In our hypothetical company and in the industry, operating costs consume about 16 1/2% of income. Use of data-processing equipment and strict cost control has helped, but the costs of selling, issuing, and administering new contracts are higher than those of maintaining old business, so that growth of insurance in force has imposed a penalty. Ratios vary, of course,

**TABLE 30-7   Condensed Income Statement, Stock Life
Insurance Company**

Income		
Premiums and deferred benefit contributions	$74,000,000	
Income from supplementary contracts	3,000,000	
Net investment income	23,000,000	$100,000,000
Distribution of income		
Death, accident, and health benefits	37,000,000	
Annuities and matured endowments	7,000,000	
Surrender benefits	4,500,000	
Payments on supplementary contracts	3,000,000	
Miscellaneous insurance deductions	2,000,000	
Increase in policy and special reserves	24,500,000	78,000,000
Operating costs		
Commissions to agents	7,000,000	
General expenses	7,000,000	
Taxes other than on income	2,500,000	
	$16,500,000	
Dividends to policyholders	2,000,000	18,500,000
Net operating gain before income taxes		$ 3,500,000
Income taxes		1,500,000
Net gain after income taxes		$ 2,000,000
Surplus to policyholders		
Surplus, January 1	29,000,000	
Net after income taxes	2,000,000	
Net gain from sale and maturity of investments	500,000	
Increase in market value of assets	2,500,000	$34,000,000
Less:		
Dividends to stockholders	800,000	
Increase in security valuation reserve	1,200,000	2,000,000
Surplus, December 31		$32,000,000

from company to company, reflecting the types of coverage sold and the relationship of new to insurance in force.

Balance sheet   The assets of the insurance company show that it invests funds representing reserves and other policyholders' claims in bonds and mortgages, with some funds allocated to stocks, real estate, and policy loans. (See Chapter 22.) The main liability is policy reserves, or the amounts which (with interest), together with future premiums, will pay policy claims as they mature. Additional policyholders' funds consist chiefly of proceeds of policies left with the company. The security valuation reserve provides for possible future fluctuations in security holdings. Contingency reserves are established against changes in investment income and mortality. The unassigned surplus constitutes a large general reserve for unforeseen developments and for stabilizing dividends. A hypothetical condensed statement is shown in Table 30-8.

The substantial leverage represented by policy reserves and other customers' claims in relation to net worth (the last three items on the liability

TABLE 30-8   Life Insurance Company Balance Sheet

Assets	
U.S. Govt. and agency bonds	$ 11,000,000
Foreign and municipal bonds	15,500,000
Corporate bonds	175,000,000
Mortgages	180,000,000
Stocks	37,500,000
Loans to policyholders	40,000,000
Real estate	15,000,000
Cash and other assets	26,000,000
Total assets	$500,000,000

Liabilities	
Policy reserves	$400,000,000
Claims in process of payment	10,000,000
Policy dividend accumulations, deposits, and future payments	21,500,000
Taxes payable	4,000,000
Reserve for security fluctuations	9,500,000
Other liabilities	9,500,000
Contingency reserves	9,000,000
Capital stock (1,000,000 shares, $5 par)	4,500,000
Unassigned surplus	32,000,000
Total liabilities	$500,000,000

side) is evident in Table 30-8. Such obligations totalled $10.000 for every $1.00 of stockholders' equity. The book value per share was $45.50.

Analysis and valuation   The analysis of a stock life insurance company is a complicated procedure, and the investor should rely on the information provided by brokerage and investment banking houses that have made a specialty of insurance stocks. The main points to be checked include:

General factors:

Growth in admitted assets, as reported to the state insurance departments and published in annual reports. The value of total real assets may actually be understated. (See below.)

Growth in capital funds, or total net worth, both as reported and as adjusted. (See below.) Capital funds in relation to reserve liabilities should also be checked against industry data and competitive companies.

Growth in insurance in force, premium income, and total income.

Composition of insurance in force, as indicated by the percentages of whole-life, endowment, term, group, and industrial insurance. The first type is usually the most profitable.

Amount of business other than life insurance, especially health and accident insurance, which has been profitable or has potential profitability.

Scope of the company's activities—whether it is a holding or parent company with subsidiaries or divisions in various lines of insurance and finance, or specializes in traditional life insurance and annuities.

More specific factors:

Size and trend of the net rate earned on portfolio. This is a function of the composition of the portfolio and its growth in periods of high or low interest rates. A high rate (say, 6 1/2% or more) is a great advantage to a company that has written policies based on assumed rates for reserve compounding of 3 to 4%.

Trend in the operating cost ratio. Insurance companies have offset rising labor costs by introducing computer techniques and have held the operating cost ratio to about 17%.

Annual growth rate in net gain from operations, after taxes. This reflects growth, mortality experience, portfolio earnings, and cost control.

Amount and trend of earnings per share.

Amount and trend of *book value* (stockholder's equity) per share.

Market price as a percentage of book value per share. As revealed by the data in Table 30-9, market price is often lower. In the stronger companies, market price over 1 1/2 times book value reflects growth and the high rate earned on total equity.

Market price to earnings per share. This is the traditional price-earnings ratio, now only about 10.

Dividends as a percentage of earnings per share. The payout by life insurance companies is typically low.

Dividend yield is also typically low, although now it is considerably higher than in the early 1970s.

Table 30-9 reveals the market prices, in relation to both book values and earnings, and the low dividend payout ratio which produces a low yield for the typical life insurance company stock.

TABLE 30-9 Price[a] and Earnings Relationships of Large Life Insurance Companies, 1976

	Range	*Average*
Market price to book value per share	60–150%	105%
Market price to adjusted earnings per share	7–14	9
Dividends as a percentage of net earnings	6–55%	33%
Dividend yield (at high price)	0.6–4.9	3.6%

[a]High price for this year.

Source: Standard & Poor's *Industry Surveys, Insurance.*

Market price performance   In the late 1960s, life insurance stock indexes dropped more than the general market, reaching a 10-year low in October 1970. After modest recovery, the index fell 50% in 1973–1974. Since then a small recovery sent the aggregate price-earnings ratio to a typical 9 times earnings in mid 1977. Dividend yields have remained low, reflecting the policy of plowing back most of the net investment income and any capital gains. They average (mid 1977) around 3.6%, within a range of 0.6 to 4.9%. Shares of soundly operated life and multiline companies provide an excellent medium for long-term appreciation, but only when purchased at prices commensurate with underlying values and earnings.

The Market for Insurance Stocks

A few insurance stocks are listed. Those of most of the larger companies enjoy an active over-the-counter market, and their price quotations are found in the financial sections of the metropolitan dailies and in the financial journals and services.

Stocks of insurance companies are, in general, conservative investments offering regular but modest dividends, diversification through a portfolio of selected securities, and the opportunity for long-term appreciation. The growth prospects derive from the ploughing back of any underwriting profits, capital gains, and part of the investment income. This results in growth in value per share, except under adverse general market conditions. But, as in the case of any securities, the results to the investor depend also on timing and selection—timing with respect to the course of the market as a whole and the outlook for the industry, and selection of those companies showing the most favorable record and prospects.

Special Sources of Information

Periodicals: *Eastern Underwriter* (weekly) and *National Underwriter* (weekly).

Alfred M. Best & Co. *Insurance Reports* (annually), *Life-Health, Property-Liability; Aggregates and Averages: Property-Liability* (annually); and *Insurance Guide with Key Ratings.*

Insurance Facts (annually), published by Insurance Information Institute, New York.

Life Insurance Fact Book (annually), published by the American Council of Life Insurance, New York.

Moody's Manual of Investments, Bank and Finance (annually and current).

Standard & Poor's *Industry Surveys, Insurance.*

Brochures and studies issued by investment dealers.

REFERENCES

American Council of Life Insurance, *Life Insurance Fact Book*. New York: The Council, annually.

American Mutual Insurance Alliance, et al., *Property and Casualty Insurance Companies: Their Role as Financial Intermediaries*, a monograph prepared for the Commission on Money and Credit. Englewood Cliffs, N.J.: Prentice-Hall, Inc., 1962.

American Research Council, Inc., *Life Insurance: Annual Industry Study and Investment Forecast*. Larchmont, N.Y.: The Council, annually.

Best's Insurance Reports, Property-Liability. Morristown, N.J.: A. M. Best & Co., Inc., annually.

Best's Insurance Reports, Life-Health. Morristown, N.J.: A. M. Best & Co., Inc., annually.

BRIMMER, A. F., *Life Insurance Companies in the Capital Market.* East Lansing, Mich.: Bureau of Business and Economic Research, Graduate School of Business Administration, Michigan State University, 1962.

GREEN, MARK R., *Risk and Insurance*, 3rd ed. Cincinnati: South-Western Publishing Co., 1973.

GUTHMANN, H. G., *Analysis of Financial Statements*, 4th ed., Chapter 18. Englewood Cliffs, N.J.: Prentice-Hall, Inc., 1953.

HUEBNER, S. S., and KENNETH BLACK, JR., *Life Insurance*, 8th ed. New York: Appleton-Century-Crofts, 1970.

————, KENNETH BLACK, JR., and R. S. CLINE, *Property and Liability Insurance*, 2nd ed. Englewood Cliffs, N.J.: Prentice-Hall, Inc., 1976.

Institutional Investor Study Report of the Securities and Exchange Commission, Chapter VI and Summary Volume No. 1, Chapters 2, 5. 92nd Congress, 1st Session, House Report No. 92–64. Washington, D.C.: U.S. Government Printing Office, 1972.

Life Insurance Association of America, *Life Insurance Companies as Financial Institutions*, a monograph prepared for the Commission on Money and Credit. Englewood Cliffs, N.J.: Prentice-Hall, Inc., 1962.

MEHR, R. I., *Life Insurance: Theory and Practice*, 4th ed. Austin, Texas: Business Publications, Inc., 1970.

McKIBBIN, D. L., *Comparative Analysis of Stock Life Insurance Companies.* Midland, Texas: D. L. McKibbin Investment Advisory Service, 1975.

Index